WITNESS
TO THE
FAITH

Church History for Young Catholics

Second Edition

Seton Press
Front Royal, VA

Nihil Obstat: Very Reverend William P. Saunders
Censor Deputatus

+ Michael F. Burbidge
Bishop of Arlington
September 18, 2020

The *Nihil Obstat* and *Imprimatur* are official declarations that a book or pamphlet is free of doctrinal or moral error. No implication is contained therein that those who have granted the *Nihil Obstat* or *Imprimatur* agree with the contents, opinions, or statements expressed.

© 2020 Seton Press
All rights reserved.
Printed in the United States of America

Front cover image: *Christ Giving the Keys to St. Peter*, Jean-Auguste-Dominique Ingres

Seton Press
1350 Progress Drive
Front Royal, VA 22630
Phone: (540) 636-9990

ISBN: 978-1-60704-174-0

For more information, visit us on the web at www.setonpress.com.
Contact us by e-mail at info@setonpress.com.

DEDICATED TO THE SACRED HEART OF JESUS

TABLE OF CONTENTS

Introduction 1

Chapter 1: The Early Church 2

Chapter 2: The Romans Persecute the Church 18

Chapter 3: The Church Triumphs over the Roman Empire 34

Chapter 4: The Church Overcomes Heresy and Paganism 48

Chapter 5: The Church Begins to Build a Catholic Society – Christendom 62

Chapter 6: The Church Begins Converting the Barbarian Tribes 78

Chapter 7: The Church Continues Converting Europe and Faces Its Greatest Adversary 104

Chapter 8: The Creation of the Holy Roman Empire 118

Chapter 9: The Great Schism 134

Chapter 10: The Gospel Goes North and East 146

Chapter 11: The Papacy under Attack – The Church at the End of the First Millenium 160

Chapter 12: New Fountains of Holiness Cleanse the Church 180

Chapter 13: The Reconquista, Part I (722-1109) 198

Chapter 14: The Crusades 206

Chapter 15: The Age of Pope Innocent III – The Glory of Christendom, Part I 222

Chapter 16: Medieval Society – The Glory of Christendom, Part II 242

Chapter 17: The Western Schism 262

Chapter 18: The Reconquista, Part II (1109-1492) 280

Chapter 19: The Church and the Renaissance 292

Chapter 20: The Beginning of the Protestant Revolt 312

v

Chapter 21: John Calvin Spreads the Protestant Revolt.. **330**

Chapter 22: England Is Lost to the Church **336**

Chapter 23: The Catholic Reformation **348**

Chapter 24: The Great Saints of the Catholic Reformation **360**

Chapter 25: The Church in the New World (1492-1789) **380**

Chapter 26: The Church in England and Northern Europe in the 16th and 17th Centuries **394**

Chapter 27: The Fate of France (1600-1700) **412**

Chapter 28: The Church in the Age of the "Enlightenment" (1700-1774) **430**

Chapter 29: The Church during the French Revolution **444**

Chapter 30: The Church during the Age of Napoleon **456**

Chapter 31: The Church in the United States in the 18th and 19th Centuries **470**

Chapter 32: The Church in the Nineteenth Century (1815-1878) **490**

Chapter 33: The Church Faces Modernism and World War I (1878-1919) **514**

Chapter 34: The Church Faces Nazism and Communism (1917-1958)....................................... **528**

Chapter 35: The Church in the Modern Era (1958-2020) **548**

Chapter 36: The Church in America in the Twentieth Century **566**

List of Popes.. **583**

Image Attributions.. **587**

Index **597**

INTRODUCTION

We have called this book *Witness to the Faith*. A true witness is a person whose life and faith are so completely one that when the challenge comes to stand up and testify for his faith, he does so, disregarding all risks, accepting all consequences. In this book, you will become a witness to the two great faiths of history: faith in God and faith in Man. These are mankind's two oldest faiths. The Catholic is blessed, for he has knowledge of the true Faith.

It is a duty of every Catholic to try to learn the history of the Catholic Church. It is through the knowledge of the history of the Catholic Church that you can be a witness for the Faith. Most of us will never be called upon to sacrifice his or her life for the Faith. However, many of us will have the opportunity to defend the Faith by bearing witness to the truths of the Faith. Many of those truths are part of the history of the Church. The enemies of the Church attack her on all sides. They attack her doctrine, her saints, and her history. As Catholics, we must witness to her doctrine, so we study the *Catechism*. Sometimes, we may need to defend those Catholics who have gone before us, so we study the lives of the saints. Finally, we may need to defend the reputation of the Church itself, so we study the history of the Church.

The history of the Catholic Church cannot be told in five hundred pages. The great Catholic historian, Warren Carroll, wrote a six-volume history of Christendom that is more than four thousand pages. In *Witness to the Faith*, there are many great saints whose names are not mentioned. There are many tremendous men and women whose stories are told only briefly. If this book succeeds in arousing your interest in the Church and these great Catholic men and women, we hope that your interest will be expanded by other books to fill in the details that are presented here only in summary.

In this history of the Catholic Church, we will lead you through sunny fields and dark forests. We will visit soaring cathedrals and extraordinary monasteries. We will walk through narrow gorges through which dark things slither into the shadows. We will meet men and women who devoted their lives to defending the Church, and other men and women who dedicated their lives to destroying it. In our journey, we will meet also those remarkable men and women who have earned the highest honor, the name of Saint. If we have led you correctly, at the end of the journey you will make out three crosses, from two of which hang thieves. This is the meaning of the journey.

Chapter 1
The Early Church

Abraham
Father of God's Chosen People. God promised that Abraham's descendants would become a great nation, and that all the nations of the Earth would be blessed through him.

Covenant
A special promise that binds people together. By God's covenant with Israel, they became His Chosen People, and He became their God.

Israel
The name of Isaac's son, Abraham's grandson; also the name of the nation that descended from him.

The Jewish People Await the Messiah

Immediately after Adam and Eve sinned and fell from grace, God promised them that He would send a Redeemer. The entire Old Testament of the Bible is the story of the Jewish people, God's Chosen People. It is the story of their search and preparation for the coming of the Redeemer, or *Messiah*—that is, Savior. The Old Testament prophets foretold the coming of the Messiah and explained the signs by which the Messiah might be identified. During His lifetime, Jesus Christ fulfilled all the prophecies. **He is the Messiah.**

Abraham is the "father of the Hebrew people." Abraham was the father of Isaac, who was the father of Jacob. After making a **covenant** with Jacob, Our Lord changed Jacob's name to **Israel**. Israel had twelve sons, who became the twelve tribes of Israel, the Hebrew people. Ultimately, the Hebrews, or Jews, settled in **Palestine**, the region between the Jordan River and the Mediterranean Sea. Geographically, Palestine is a desirable region because it is a *trading crossroads*. As a result, powerful nations since the dawn of civilization have sought to control it. The Assyrians, Chaldeans, Egyptians, Persians, Greeks, and Romans have all fought to rule Palestine.

The Jews, who considered Palestine their homeland, often fought, usually unsuccessfully, to defend this strip of land. The Assyrians and

2 *Chapter 1: The Early Church*

Christ Giving the Keys to St. Peter, Perugino

164 B.C. – 64 A.D.

164 B.C.
The Greeks dominate Palestine and try to impose their customs, but the Jews resist. In time, led by the Machabee brothers, the Jews win their independence.

39 B.C.
The Romans conquer the Holy Land.

33 A.D.
Death, Resurrection and Ascension of Our Lord Jesus Christ; the Church is born, and the message of Christianity spreads. Some try to stop it, including a young Pharisee named Saul, but after a vision of Christ on the road to Damascus, he begins preaching the Gospel himself.

42-44 A.D.
Herod Agrippa, to please his Jewish subjects, persecutes the followers of Christ; James is killed, and Peter escapes the same fate only by an angel's intervention. After only two years, however, Agrippa dies as well.

50 A.D.
The first council of the Church meets at Jerusalem to determine whether Gentile converts must conform to Jewish customs. After the Apostles listen and discuss the matter, Peter proclaims the verdict: such observance will not be required.

64 A.D.
Emperor Nero's persecution of Christians begins.

the Chaldeans eventually took the Jews into captivity. In 538 B.C., Cyrus, the king of Persia released them. He allowed them to return to Palestine and rebuild their Temple, which had been destroyed.

The Jews later fell under the dominion of the Greeks. In 164 B.C., the Greeks tried to impose their pagan religious customs on the Jews. However, the Jews refused to comply with these pagan rituals and instead rebelled. Under the leadership of the Machabee brothers, the Jews won their independence from the Greeks. The Machabees ruled Judea until the Romans conquered it in 39 B.C.

By the first century A.D., Rome was the greatest empire in the world. Rome ruled with a firm hand, but whenever possible a benevolent one. The Romans always believed that their subjects would be less likely to revolt if they had some

Witness to the Faith

input into their own local government and affairs. Thus, the Romans allowed the Jews to have the **Sanhedrin**, which was the Jewish supreme court of justice. The Sanhedrin was composed of a **high priest**, who was in charge, and seventy members chosen from among the priests and scribes.

In addition to the Sanhedrin, two significant religious factions also played an important role in early first-century Palestine. The first group was the **Pharisees**. The Pharisees were religious zealots. They insisted that the Jews strictly observe the Mosaic Law, even in the smallest details, including ritual washing and the consumption of food. They were also extreme nationalists. They hated the Romans. They felt that only the Jews should rule Judea.

The second religious group was the **Sadducees**. They were the exact opposite of the Pharisees. They tended to not take their religion too seriously. In addition, because they generally represented the wealthier part of Jewish society, they tried to work with the Romans to protect their prosperity. They usually supported the Romans at the expense of Judea. They tried to dampen any nationalist sentiments. They stressed personal concerns over national interests. Among the Jewish community, they had a reputation for being schemers seeking to enhance themselves personally and financially.

Palestine
The region that became the Israelites' homeland.

Sanhedrin
The Jewish supreme court of justice.

Pharisees
A group of religious authorities who insisted on strict observance of the Mosaic Law, and hated the Romans who occupied the Holy Land.

Sadducees
A group of religious leaders who were less zealous for the Law and tried to compromise with the Romans.

Christ's Message

During His public ministry, Jesus Christ, the Founder of the Catholic Church, never traveled beyond the Holy Land. He began His ministry preaching first to the people of His native Galilee. Then, He expanded his message to the people of Judea, and ultimately to the people of Palestine. During His life, Our Lord chose Twelve Apostles to continue to spread His message after His death. Initially, the Apostles continued preaching in Palestine to the Jews. However, when the Jews refused to accept the message of Christianity, the Apostles began evangelizing the Gentiles.

Christ preached a message of penance and forgiveness of sins. He instituted the seven sacraments and explained their necessity for salvation, and He established a Church that would continue to teach, convert, and bring people to salvation until the end of time.

However, Christ's message was not the Messianic message that the Jews were expecting or seeking. Christ made it plain that His Kingdom "was not of this world." The Jews were looking for a worldly leader who would free them from the Romans and restore the greatness that Israel had known under King David. Christ's message of penance, forgiveness, and eternal salvation was not what they wanted to hear. Because His message differed so greatly from what they expected, they rejected it and Him.

While many Jews were simply disappointed in Our Lord's message, the Jewish leaders found it intolerable. The Pharisees hated Jesus because he pointed out their hypocrisy. They insisted that others follow the Jewish Law, while they flaunted it. The Sadducees saw Christ as an agitator and revolutionary who would arouse the wrath of the Romans. Thus, both groups sought Our Lord's condemnation by the Sanhedrin. The Sanhedrin condemned Christ and turned Him over to the Romans for execution because the Jews lacked the authority to execute anyone.

Pontius Pilate, the Roman governor of Judea, initially showed little interest in what he perceived as a local Jewish matter. He began to realize the extent of the problem only when the scribes and Pharisees incited a mob to the edge of violence. As governor, he could not afford a riot: better to sentence one man to death than deal with a rioting city. Thus, this weak man condemned an innocent man to death.

The Growth of the Early Church

Christianity succeeded initially because Jesus Christ rose from the dead. Our Lord had promised to rise, and He did. Only God could raise Himself from the dead. St. Paul writes that if Christ had not risen from the dead, then Paul's teaching and the entirety of the Catholic Faith would be in vain (1 Cor. 15:13). The Resurrection is the culmination of Our Lord's life on Earth. It is the greatest of His miracles and the central pillar of Catholicism. This miracle confirmed the Apostles' belief in Him.

Our Lord had also promised that, once He was gone, He would send another Paraclete, the Spirit of Truth, to be with them forever (John 14:16-17). At Pentecost, when the Holy Spirit descended upon the Apostles, He fundamentally changed them. They had been cowering in the Upper Room, afraid to venture forth. Once they had been imbued with the Holy Spirit, they became fearless champions of Catholicism, ready to lay down their lives—and most of them would die as martyrs.

Led by St. Peter, the Apostles left the Upper Room and went out to face the crowds gathered for the Jewish celebration of Pentecost. Peter spoke to the crowd about Our Lord and His message of penance and forgiveness. People of many nations heard his words in their own language. His words moved them to embrace Catholicism and ask to be baptized. That day, three

The Resurrection

Witness to the Faith   5

Pentecost, Resout

Sts. Peter and John Healing the Lame Man, Nicolas Poussin

thousand men, and countless women and children, became Catholics. Henceforth, Pentecost would be celebrated as the birthday of the Church.

Following Pentecost, the Apostles began preaching and working miracles. One of the most remarkable miracles involved St. Peter, who along with St. John, had gone to the Temple in Jerusalem to pray. A man, who had been lame since birth, lay at the Temple gate begging for alms. As Peter and John walked passed, he asked them for money. Peter stopped, turned to the beggar, and told him that, though he possessed neither gold nor silver, he would give what he had. Peter told the beggar to arise and walk, in the Name of Jesus Christ of Nazareth. Cured, the beggar leapt for joy! He went with Peter and John into the Temple praising God.

News that Peter had cured the lame beggar spread throughout Jerusalem. Over the next few days, thousands more converted to Catholicism. People began carrying their sick into the streets, hoping that Peter's shadow might fall over them and cure them.

St. Stephen, the First Martyr

The members of the early Church had a great sense of community and mutual devotion. To care for one another, they created a common fund into which they placed their wealth, and from which everyone drew as needed to provide for their daily living expenses. However, even a society of the most holy people is also a society of human beings, and often people feel mistreated. Thus, some Greek Jews, who were members of the Christian community, complained to the Church leaders that they were not receiving their fair share from the common fund. To address this issue, the Apostles appointed seven deacons to care for the material welfare of the members of the early Church. This freed the Apostles from dealing so heavily with material matters and provided them with more time to focus on the spiritual challenges of the early Church.

Among the seven deacons that the Apostles chose was a Greek Jew named Stephen, who was known for his learning and holiness. In fulfilling his vocation, Stephen began working miracles among the people. He also preached and debated the Jewish leaders in the synagogue. His opponents were no match for his intelligence and eloquence. They claimed that he blasphemed against God and the Law. They dragged him before the Sanhedrin, where, despite his wonderful defense, the Sanhedrin condemned him to death. They dragged him out of the city and stoned him to death. As he died, Stephen forgave his murderers. The witnesses laid their cloaks at the feet of a young man named Saul. Thus, Stephen became the Catholic Church's first martyr. He would not be the last.

Martyrdom of St. Stephen, Carracci

The Early Church Grows Despite Persecution

Stephen's death began a period of serious religious persecution of Christians. The Apostles remained in and around Jerusalem until about 50 A.D., when the Council of Jerusalem met. However, the faithful, fearing persecution, scattered throughout Judea, Syria, and Samaria. Among those who went to Samaria was the deacon **Philip**, who had been instructed to travel there by an angel.

During his journey to Samaria, Philip encountered a man sitting in his chariot reading Isaiah the prophet. Philip discovered that the man was an Ethiopian and the treasurer for the queen of Ethiopia. Philip asked the Ethiopian if he understood what he was reading. The Ethiopian replied, "How can I unless someone explains it to me?" He asked Philip to explain Isaiah to him, which Philip did. The Ethiopian then asked Philip to accompany him on his travels.

As they traveled, Philip continued to explain Isaiah's words and how they came to be manifest in Jesus Christ. When the two men came to some water, the Ethiopian asked if anything would hinder him from being baptized. Philip told him that if he believed, he could be baptized. The Ethiopian replied that he believed that Jesus Christ was the Son of God. Philip then baptized him. The Holy Spirit suddenly took Philip away, and the Ethiopian did not see him again, but continued on his journey rejoicing.

Philip
One of the first deacons; preached the Gospel in Samaria and baptized an Ethiopian eunuch whom he met on the road.

Witness to the Faith

Simon Magus

A convert in Samaria who tried to buy the power of the Holy Spirit from the Apostles.

Simony

The sin of buying or selling spiritual things, as Simon Magus attempted to do.

Herod Agrippa

Grandson of Herod the Great; persecuted Christians, including St. James, whom he had killed. His persecution was halted when he died in 44 A.D.

Cornelius

A devout, God-fearing Roman centurion; the first Gentile to be baptized by St. Peter.

In Samaria, Philip made so many converts that Peter and John traveled there to administer the Sacrament of Confirmation. One of the converts was a man named **Simon Magus**. Simon saw the great changes that overcame converts when they received the Holy Spirit in Confirmation. Not understanding the nature of supernatural grace, Simon asked Peter to buy his "power." Peter harshly rebuked Simon for thinking that the power to bestow grace could be purchased. It is from this incident that the sin of **simony**, the buying or selling of spiritual things, had its origin.

In 42 A.D., **Herod Agrippa**, the grandson of King Herod the Great, the murderer of the Holy Innocents, became king of Judea. To win the favor of his Jewish subjects, Herod began persecuting Christians in Judea. The most prominent martyr of this time was James the Elder, whom Herod had "killed with a sword" (that is, beheaded) around 44 A.D. (Acts 12:2). Thus, James became the first of the Apostles to be martyred. Herod also arrested St. Peter. However, an angel miraculously freed Peter from prison before his execution. Agrippa died in 44 A.D., and his successor, Agrippa II, temporarily halted the persecution.

Peter Brings the Gentiles into the Church

In the early Church, the converts, who were all former Jews, continued to follow many of the practices of the Mosaic Law. In a sense, the early Catholic Church resembled a Christian synagogue, with membership limited to converted Jews. However, Our Lord had told His Apostles to go forth and convert all nations, not just Judea. He intended that both Jews and Gentiles be Catholics. Peter opened the Church to the Gentiles when he converted **Cornelius** and his family.

Cornelius was a centurion in the Roman army. Although he was not a Jew, he was a generous, devout, and God-fearing man. One afternoon, an angel appeared to him and told him that his prayers and good works had found favor with God. The angel instructed him to send a messenger to the city of Joppa and ask for Peter, who was staying at the house of the tanner. Cornelius sent three messengers to find St. Peter.

The following day, St. Peter also had a vision. He saw a great linen sheet coming down from Heaven to Earth. On the sheet were all the Earth's animals, reptiles, and birds. A voice told Peter to "kill and eat." However, Peter refused, because he had never eaten anything "profane and unclean." The voice told him that he should not call unclean what God had made clean. This happened three times before the vision ended. Peter was puzzled and wondered what the vision meant.

As Peter pondered the vision, the Holy Spirit told him that Cornelius' three servants were at the house looking for him and that he should go and accompany them "because I have sent them" (Acts 10:20). Peter went and asked the men the purpose of their visit. They gave him their master's message, and Peter invited them to stay the night. The following day, they all left for Caesarea to see Cornelius.

8   *Chapter 1: The Early Church*

When Peter arrived at the home of Cornelius, he found Cornelius, his family, and friends waiting for him. Cornelius explained his vision to Peter, and Peter told the centurion that it was God's Will that Gentiles be received into the Church. As Peter was speaking, the Holy Spirit came upon Cornelius and his family and friends. Peter called for water and baptized them. He remained with the family for a few days.

The Conversion of St. Paul

The man who would become the "Apostle to the Gentiles," and one of the greatest saints in history, was born in Tarsus (in modern-day Turkey) to Jewish parents who named him Saul, though history would know him as St. Paul. When he was a young man, Saul traveled to Jerusalem to study the Jewish Law. A tentmaker by trade, during his mission activities, he made tents to support himself. However, Saul had greater ambitions than to make tents; he desired to become an expert in Mosaic Law.

According to tradition, Saul was a smallish man with less than robust health. However, Saul possessed three qualities that made him indomitable. First, he had tremendous energy. Second, he had marvelous intelligence. Third, and most important, he had an unflagging commitment to his goal. In other words, he simply refused to give up, no matter what. As time would show, the only way to stop St. Paul was to kill him.

The Angel Appearing to the Centurion Cornelius, Jacob Backer

The Conversion of St. Paul, Murillo

Witness to the Faith 9

Ananias
A Christian at Damascus. After Saul (St. Paul) was blinded on the road to Damascus, Ananias laid his hands on him and prayed for him, restoring his sight.

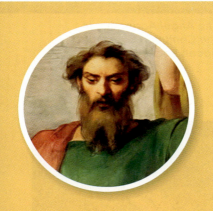

From Saul to Paul

Scholars agree that there is no reason to believe that his name was changed from *Saul* to *Paul* upon his conversion. Saul is the Semitic version, and Paul is the Greco-Roman version. The use of a double name is historically confirmed. *Simply for the sake of clarity*, we are referring to the saint as *Saul* before his Baptism, and as *Paul* after his Baptism.

Initially, Saul turned his strength toward destroying Christianity. Saul had been present at, and overseen, St. Stephen's martyrdom. He had heard Stephen defend himself. In all likelihood, Saul was the only one present who completely comprehended Stephen's ideas. However, awareness only made Saul more determined to kill Stephen. Saul was a loyal Pharisee committed to protecting Judaism. Stephen represented an existential threat to Judaism. It is not surprising that Saul came to hate Stephen and Christianity, nor that he sought to destroy it.

When the Christians fled from Jerusalem after Stephen's martyrdom, Saul decided to pursue them. In 33 A.D., he obtained a commission to travel to Damascus to hunt down and arrest any Christians he found there and return them to Jerusalem. On the road to Damascus, he had a fateful, life-changing encounter. As he rode along, a brilliant light knocked him from his horse. As he lay on the ground, Our Lord appeared to Saul. Our Lord's reproach, "Saul, Saul, why are you persecuting Me?" (Acts 9:4), effected the greatest change ever to occur in a human being. Saul asked who was speaking to him. Our Lord replied that He was Jesus. He told Saul to arise and go into Damascus, where he would receive additional instructions. When Saul rose from the ground, he realized that he was blind.

His companions led Saul into Damascus, where he remained for the next three days. Living in Damascus at the time was a Christian disciple named **Ananias**, whom Our Lord told to go see Saul. Ananias went to the house where Saul was staying and told him that the Lord had sent him. Ananias laid his hands on Saul, immediately restoring his sight, and Saul was filled with the Holy Spirit. Saul then asked Ananias to baptize him. All of the strength, energy, and determination with which Saul had persecuted the Church and its members, Paul now turned to nurturing, cultivating, and expanding that Church.

For a time, as he sought to regain his strength, Paul preached in the synagogue in Damascus. But he soon journeyed to Arabia. There, in the solitude of the desert, Our Lord prepared Paul for his life's work. Paul returned to Damascus, but remained only a short time. After learning that the Jews conspired to kill him, he fled the city. Three years after his conversion, Paul traveled to Jerusalem, where the Apostle Barnabas introduced him to the Christians there. Understandably, based on his history, the Christians in Jerusalem distrusted Paul. When he returned to Tarsus, he preached in Syria and Cilicia.

During Herod Agrippa's persecution, many Christians had fled to Antioch, where they had successfully evangelized and converted a large number of Gentiles. The community in Antioch became so large that the Church's leadership in Jerusalem sent Barnabas to Antioch to assist in the conversion. Before long, Barnabas began to feel overwhelmed by the task. Sometime around 42 or 43 A.D., he asked Paul to come to Antioch to help convert the Gentiles there. The pagans in Antioch were the first ones to call Christ's followers "Christians," to distinguish them from the Jews.

Chapter 1: The Early Church

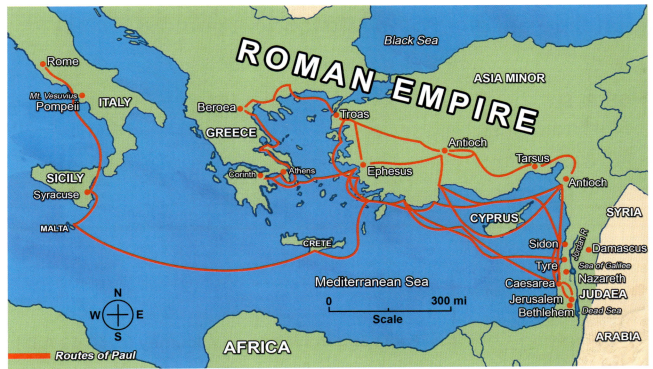

St. Paul's Missionary Journeys

Paul's First Missionary Journey (c. 45-49 A.D.)

Herod Agrippa's death ended his persecution of the Church, which experienced a time of peace. With Antioch as their base, Paul and Barnabas launched their first missionary journey, which lasted from 45 to 49 A.D. Departing Antioch, they first preached on the island of Cyprus. Next, they traveled to Asia Minor (modern-day Turkey). They continued on to Iconium and then Lystra. There, Paul was stoned, dragged out of town, and left for dead, but he quickly recovered, and they continued their journey.

After visiting numerous cities in Asia Minor, Paul returned to Antioch, where he decided to change his focus from converting his fellow Jews to converting Gentiles. During his travels, the Jews had constantly opposed his efforts and caused him trouble. When Paul publicly announced his new plan of action, "the Gentiles were delighted" (Acts 13:1-48).

The large increase of Gentiles into the Church concerned some of the Jewish Christians from Jerusalem who believed that the new converts should adhere to Jewish Law and customs. However, Paul and Barnabas argued that the new converts did not need to follow the Mosaic Law. Because the argument was causing dissension, the two sides decided to go to Jerusalem and ask the Apostles to resolve the issue.

Around 50 A.D., the first council of the Church met at Jerusalem to decide whether new converts should conform to Jewish laws and customs. The Apostles, led by Peter, James the Younger, and John,

Saint Paul

Witness to the Faith   11

Timeline of Saint Paul's Missionary Journeys

45 A.D

45-49 A.D.
From Antioch, Paul and Barnabas set out for Cyprus, and from there to Iconium, Lystra, and other cities in Asia Minor.

50-52 A.D.
Paul goes with Silas to Lystra, where they meet Timothy. They proceed to Troas and are joined by Luke, then they go on to the cities of Macedonia.

54 A.D.
Paul revisits Ephesus, where the silversmiths, led by Demetrius, stir up a riot.

Timothy
A Christian from Lystra, who became a companion of Paul.

Luke
One of the four evangelists and author of the Acts of the Apostles; friend and companion of Paul.

Saint Timothy

listened to the ideas of both sides. After much debate, Peter arose and rendered the council's decision. New converts would not be required to follow Jewish laws and dietary customs. Following the council, Paul and Barnabas returned to Antioch, where they continued to teach and preach.

Paul's Second Missionary Journey (c. 50-52 A.D.)

In the summer of 50 A.D., Paul left Antioch to undertake a second missionary journey. It would last about three years. Although Paul planned to take Barnabas with him, the two had a disagreement, and Barnabas chose to go to Cyprus. In place of Barnabas, Paul chose Silas as his traveling companion.

Paul began his second missionary campaign by revisiting many of the places he had called upon during his first expedition. At Lystra, he met a disciple named **Timothy**, whom fellow Christians recommended to Paul. Accepting their recommendation, Paul chose Timothy to accompany him. Paul had planned to travel to Asia Minor, but the Holy Spirit directed him to change course and enter Europe.

When Paul arrived in Troas (on Turkey's western coast), he met **Luke**, who was to become his biographer, constant companion, and the author of the third *Gospel* plus the **Acts of the Apostles**. Paul had a vision instructing him to travel to Macedonia, so Paul's group sailed from Troas. Paul and his companions landed in Macedonia and traveled to Philippi, Macedonia's main city. Paul preached in Philippi until local unscrupulous businessmen caused a riot and attacked Paul and Luke. Law enforcement officers scourged and imprisoned Paul. The following day, when the city's judges learned that Paul, a Roman citizen, had been scourged, they became very frightened, because Roman law forbade the beating of Roman citizens. They begged Paul's indulgence. They released him and his companions, but asked that they leave the city.

Paul and his friends next traveled to Thessalonica, where they made a large number of converts. However, the Jews in the city became jealous and once again incited a riot. Paul and his companions were

Chapter 1: The Early Church

57 A.D.
Paul returns to Macedonia, where he writes his Second Letter to the Corinthians. He visits several other cities before arriving in 58 A.D. at Jerusalem, where he is arrested.

60 A.D.
Paul travels in custody to Rome, where he is kept in a form of "house arrest" and is able to preach, remaining there for two years.

64 A.D.
Christianity becomes illegal in the Roman Empire, and Paul is beheaded.

64 A.D.

forced to flee the city to Berea. The Jews in Berea were more open-minded and listened to Paul who, once again, made many converts. However, when the Jews of Thessalonica learned of Paul's success in Berea, they traveled there to cause trouble. Paul fled from Berea to the coast. He then sailed to Athens, the heart of the Greek world.

In Athens, Paul delivered a famous speech to the Greek **Areopagus**, the city's great council. The learned men of Athens listened skeptically as Paul spoke: "You Athenians, I see that in every respect you are very religious. For as I walked around looking carefully at your shrines, I even discovered an altar inscribed, 'To an Unknown God.' What therefore you unknowingly worship, I proclaim to you" (Acts 17:22-23). Paul went on to explain that God does not live in a building made by humans, but rather He gives life to everyone and everything. Paul also told the Athenians that they needed to repent of their sins, because one day God would judge everyone. Finally, Paul spoke about Our Lord's Resurrection (Acts 17:24-31). When the Athenians heard about the Resurrection, most scoffed; however, a few were willing to hear more. Sadly, only a few became Christians.

In the autumn of 51 A.D., Paul left Athens and traveled to Corinth. Paul reunited with his companions, and the group founded a small community of believers. In Corinth, Paul stayed with **Aquila** and **Priscilla**, a Jewish couple who, like Paul, were tentmakers. While living with them, Paul wrote his two letters to the Thessalonians. Every Sabbath, Paul would go to the synagogue, where he successfully converted Jews and Greeks. Once again, Paul's success angered the Jews, who seized him and dragged him before the proconsul, Gallio. As a Roman official, Gallio had no interest in listening to Jews complain about religious matters. Thus, he refused to hear their complaints.

Sometime in the spring of 52, Paul sailed from Corinth with Aquila and Priscilla. Paul next traveled to Ephesus, where he stayed for a short time. On his way back to Antioch, he stopped in Jerusalem to fulfill a vow he had made.

Saint Luke

> **Areopagus**
> The great council of Athens. Paul preached among them when he came to the city.

> **Aquila and Priscilla**
> A Jewish couple, and fellow tentmakers, with whom Paul stayed in Corinth. When he went to Ephesus, they went with him.

Witness to the Faith 13

Paul's Third Missionary Journey (c. 53-58 A.D.)

First Letter to the Corinthians
Written from Ephesus around 54-57 A.D.

After a brief visit to Antioch, Paul began his third missionary campaign. His goal this time was to revisit Christian communities to strengthen their faith. Thus, he did not seek to make new converts so much as to revitalize and provide additional instruction to those converts he had already made.

In early 54 A.D., Paul arrived in Ephesus, where he spent nearly three years. During this time, he wrote his **First Letter to the Corinthians**. Ephesus presented unique problems for Paul. At the time, it was one of the wealthiest cities in the world. It was also one of the most pagan. Both its wealth and its paganism were the result of the presence of the temple of Diana, one of the wonders of the ancient world. Worshipers from all over the world traveled to Ephesus to pray at the temple. The silversmiths in Ephesus had become incredibly wealthy selling idols of Diana and souvenirs of Diana and the temple. As more Ephesians and people in Asia Minor became Christians, the silversmiths lost business. Eventually, a silversmith named Demetrius called a meeting of the smiths and other workers who earned income from pagan-related activities. He convinced his fellow workers that Paul not only threatened their livelihoods but also the worship of Diana. He incited the workers to riot. Soon the riot spread throughout the city, and some of Paul's traveling companions were injured. When the rioting finally abated, Paul left the city.

Second Letter to the Corinthians
Written from Macedonia about 57 A.D.

In early 57, Paul revisited Europe. He returned to Macedonia, where he wrote his **Second Letter to the Corinthians**. He followed up on his epistle with an actual visit to Corinth, where he personally judged the effects of his letter. While in Corinth, he wrote his incredibly important and majestic **Letter to the Romans**. Paul wrote this letter as he was preparing to leave for Jerusalem with money he had collected for the poor Christians in that city. From Jerusalem, he planned to travel to Rome, where he hoped to generate support for a missionary project in Spain. The Letter to the Romans served as his introduction to the Christian community in Rome and the groundwork for his request for their aid to support his mission to Spain.

Letter to the Romans
An especially long and important letter of Paul, written from Corinth about 57 A.D.

Paul Is Arrested

Paul returned to Jerusalem, concluding his third mission journey, around the time of Pentecost in 58 A.D. He met with St. James, the bishop of Jerusalem, as well as the other Church leaders, and related his accomplishments in converting the Gentiles. Paul had not been in Jerusalem a week before a mob of Jews incited a riot, seized him, dragged him from the Temple, and tried to beat him to death. When the Roman commander of the city learned of the riot, he rushed to the scene and stopped the mob from killing Paul. Before

St. Paul Preaches in Athens, Raphael

Chapter 1: The Early Church

the Romans took him to prison, Paul spoke to the Jews of Jerusalem and related his conversion story. Paul then told the soldiers that he was a Roman citizen.

To determine why the Jews were trying to kill a Roman citizen, the Roman centurion in charge took Paul before the Sanhedrin. Paul, who knew Jewish Law very well, confounded the Sanhedrin. Not knowing how to deal with Paul, the members of the Sanhedrin decided to murder him. When the murder plot became known, the Romans transferred Paul to Caesarea, where Antonius Felix was Roman governor.

Felix put Paul on trial, but failed to render a verdict. To placate the Jews, Felix imprisoned Paul. Felix kept Paul imprisoned for two years, hoping that Paul or his friends would bribe him to release Paul. In 60 A.D., Porcius Festus succeeded Felix as procurator of Judea. Almost immediately, the Jewish leaders asked Festus to turn Paul over to them. However, Paul refused to acknowledge the Sanhedrin's authority over him and demanded that Festus send him to Rome, where the emperor (Nero) would try him. Festus agreed.

Paul Finishes His Course

The Romans decided that Paul should sail to Italy, so they placed him on a boat with Luke. They set sail for his trial before the emperor. However, en route, the ship encountered a violent storm. After several days, the ship ran aground on the island of Malta, where Paul and the ship's company spent the winter. Eventually, the ship arrived in Rome, where Paul was placed under a form of "house arrest."

Because Paul was not confined, he preached the Gospel in the capital of the Roman Empire. The Jews in Jerusalem did not pursue their case against him, so for two years he preached the Gospel. In 64 A.D., a new persecution broke out under the Emperor Nero. Paul had already foreseen the end of his life. In a letter to his "beloved son" Timothy, he wrote: "The time of my dissolution is at hand, I have fought the good fight, I have finished my course, I have kept the faith" (2 Tim. 4:6-7). Because he was a Roman citizen, he was not crucified; he was beheaded. He was buried on the Ostian Way.

After his death, Paul's disciples erected a simple memorial to his memory. Later, the Emperor Constantine built a basilica on the spot of this memorial. The current basilica, **St. Paul Outside the Walls**, is one of four **major basilicas**. Beneath this incredibly beautiful church, the small tentmaker, whose boundless energy earned him the title "Apostle to the Gentiles," lies in quiet repose. He finished the course, he kept the faith, he earned his reward.

St. Paul Is Arrested

> **Saint Paul Outside the Walls**
> The basilica that stands over the site of St. Paul's martyrdom and houses his remains.

Witness to the Faith 15

St. Paul Outside the Walls

The Work of the Other Apostles

Because the Sanhedrin could not murder Paul, they chose to seek revenge on St. James. Unlike the other Apostles, James the Younger had remained in Jerusalem, where he had become bishop and was extremely well-liked by the Jewish population. Despite James' popularity, the High Priest Ananias summoned him before the Sanhedrin, which sentenced him to death.

The other Apostles followed Our Lord's final earthly command to "Go, therefore, and make disciples of all nations" (Mt. 28:19). At the Crucifixion, Our Lord gave the care of His Blessed Mother to St. John. John probably remained in and near Jerusalem until the Assumption of the Blessed Mother, sometime around the time of the Council of Jerusalem. Ultimately, John became bishop of Ephesus. **He was the only Apostle not to be martyred.** Although John was thrown into a cauldron of boiling oil, God miraculously saved him. During the persecution of Domitian, the Romans banished him to the island of Patmos, where he wrote the **Book of the Apocalypse** (or the **Book of Revelation**, as it is also known). St. John also wrote the fourth Gospel as well as three *Letters*. The last Apostle to die, John died in Ephesus around 100 A.D.

St. Matthew initially preached to the Jews and wrote his Gospel for them in their language. He then traveled to Persia and Parthia (modern-day Iran), where he preached to the Gentiles. Tradition holds that Matthew was martyred in Ethiopia.

St. Thomas is known as the "Apostle of India" because, according to tradition, he traveled to India around 50 A.D. This tradition is

Book of Revelation
The last book of the Bible, also called the Book of the Apocalypse; written by St. John on the island of Patmos, where he was banished near the end of his life.

16 *Chapter 1: The Early Church*

supported by the existence of a group in India known as the **St. Thomas Christians**. Thomas evangelized the Indian people for about two decades before suffering martyrdom around 72 A.D. His relics were buried in Edessa (southeast Turkey).

St. Jude, the brother of James the Younger, wrote a *Letter* to the Jewish converts in Palestine. St. Thomas sent Jude to the king of Edessa. According to tradition, Jude was martyred in Beirut, which was in the Roman province of Syria, around 65 A.D.

St. Mark the Evangelist accompanied Paul on his first missionary campaign with Barnabas in 44 A.D. However, Mark returned to Jerusalem in the middle of the journey. Later, Paul questioned whether Mark was reliable, which led to the disagreement with Barnabas and their decision not to work together on Paul's second missionary journey. However, Paul and Mark reconciled and, when Paul was imprisoned in Rome, Mark became one of his most trusted companions (Col 4:10). Mark also became a close associate of St. Peter, who related the events that Mark recorded in his Gospel, which he wrote between 60 and 70 A.D. Tradition holds that Mark founded the Church in Alexandria, Egypt, and became its first bishop. He was also martyred in that city.

St. Luke wrote the third *Gospel* as well as the **Acts of the Apostles**. He remained St. Paul's constant friend and companion until Paul's death. After Paul's martyrdom, Luke's history becomes unclear. He likely cut the Acts of the Apostles short because of Nero's persecutions. The earliest traditions indicate that Luke returned to Greece to write his Gospel and died in Boeotia.

Of the other Apostles, even less is known. Philip preached in Samaria and was martyred in Hierapolis (Turkey) during the reign of Domitian. Andrew preached in Scythia (modern eastern Europe) as well as along the Black Sea. He may have traveled as far east as Kiev. Tradition holds that he was martyred on an X-shaped cross in the Greek city of Patras. Of St. Simon, two traditions exist. One holds that after preaching in Egypt, Simon joined Jude and was martyred along with him in Beirut. Another tradition holds that Simon returned to Jerusalem and replaced St. James as bishop of Jerusalem after the Sanhedrin martyred James. Of St. Bartholomew, traditions teach that he preached in India and then Armenia, where he was martyred.

In the next chapter, we shall learn more about St. Peter, the first pope.

St. John Miraculously Escapes Martyrdom

St. Thomas Christians
A group of Indian Christians, held traditionally to be descended from converts made by St. Thomas the Apostle when he traveled to India.

Oral Exercises

1. Why was the early Church successful?
2. Who was St. Philip?
3. What did he do?
4. What is simony?
5. Briefly explain how the Gentiles were received into the Church.
6. Where was the first Church council held?
7. What dispute was settled at that council?
8. Briefly describe St. Paul's activities in Athens.
9. Describe the conditions in Ephesus when Paul arrived.
10. Which Apostle was not martyred?

Witness to the Faith

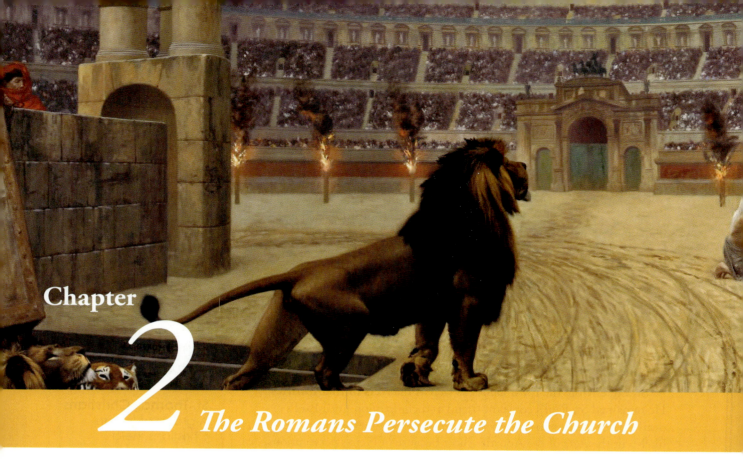

Chapter 2
The Romans Persecute the Church

The "Threat" of Christianity

The resentment the Jews felt toward the early Christians paled in contrast to the vicious, almost relentless hatred of the Roman Empire. The Roman persecutions began in 64 A.D. under Emperor Nero and lasted off and on for almost 250 years. The intensity of the persecutions depended on the emperor's feelings toward Christianity. Under some emperors, the persecution was widespread and inhumanly vicious. Under others, the persecutions tended to be more local. Their extent and degree of brutality depended on the power and opinion of the provincial governor or local official. During some periods, the Church actually thrived.

One might wonder why this great empire, perhaps the mightiest that the world has ever known, feared the power of Jesus Christ and hated his followers. The answer is found in the words of our Savior, "My Kingdom is not of this world." For Christians, this world is not the final destination or goal. During the Mass, the priest asks Our Lord to "strengthen in faith and love your *pilgrim Church on earth*." Christians are pilgrims on a journey home, not settlers. While Christians must render unto Caesar those things that are Caesar's, Christians belong first and foremost to God, and they must not give to Caesar the things that are God's. The Kingdom of God is the Catholic Church.

Lawful Authority
The authority of a legitimate government, which Christians must respect and obey as long as it does not interfere with the citizen's right to do those things necessary to save his soul.

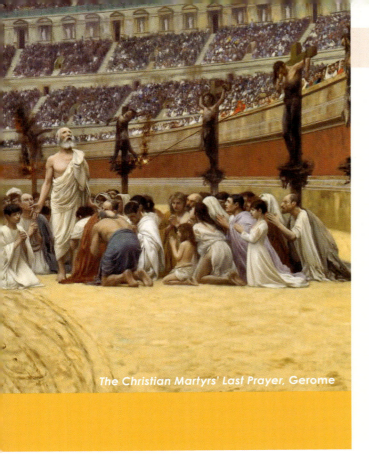
The Christian Martyrs' Last Prayer, Gerome

64 A.D. – 311 A.D.

64 A.D.
A fire destroys much of the city of Rome. Nero uses the Christians as a scapegoat. A massive persecution quickly develops.

70 A.D.
A Roman army devastates Jerusalem and destroys the Temple.

98 A.D.
Trajan becomes emperor. Christianity remains illegal, but persecution is not especially active.

161 A.D.
Marcus Aurelius becomes emperor, and a more active attack on Christians resumes.

211-222 A.D.
Many emperors succeed each other in a short time, resulting in little consistency during these years.

235-260 A.D.
Under Maximinus Thrax, Decius, and Valerian, efforts to wipe out Christianity are brutal until Gallienus becomes emperor and halts the persecution.

260-284 A.D.
Christians are mostly left alone, primarily because emperors have short reigns and spend much of that time fighting external enemies.

303 A.D.
Diocletian declares a "termination" of Christianity, mandating that Christian sacred books and places of worship be destroyed.

305 A.D.
Galerius assumes the title Augustus and the rank of senior emperor. Under him, persecution is especially vicious.

311 A.D.
Galerius dies, and his successor reigns for only two years.

However, the Romans were not interested in any life after death. They placed all their trust in this life. They sought happiness in worldly power, possessions, and pleasures. They depended on the State, in the person of the emperor, to obtain for them the fullest measure of all these things. They recognized no authority above the State, and no power above the emperor. The Roman government insisted that the State was divine, and the emperor was to be worshiped as a god.

The Church taught its members to obey the State as long as its laws did not oppose the Law of God. Roman society as a whole might conform to the idea that the State could do no wrong, but for Christians that was impossible. Christians needed to respect the **lawful authority** of the State and obey its laws

Witness to the Faith 19

The Crucifixion of Saint Peter, Caravaggio

as long as those laws did not interfere with the right of the individual citizen to do what was necessary to save his soul. Consequently, **Romans could not see how Christians could be good citizens**. They regarded the profession of Christianity as treason and a threat to the empire. Romans claimed to be broad-minded and tolerant of all religions, *but only as long as those religions did not interfere with loyalty to the State*. They mocked the claim that Christianity was the only true religion and that all others were false.

The Martyrdom of St. Peter

At first, the Romans did not understand that the Christians in Rome were not simply another group of Jews. However, by 64 A.D., differences between the two groups had become distinct enough for the Romans to realize that the Christians were a different religious group. The growing Christian population in Rome presented an opportunity to Rome's Jewish community. The Jews resented the Christians, and the Romans hated the Jews. The Jews took the opportunity to transfer some of the Romans' resentment toward them onto the Christians. The first-century Roman senator and historian Tacitus writes in his histories that as a result of this general animosity, Christians were quickly blamed for various shocking crimes, generating widespread prejudice against them.

Nero

On July 18, 64 A.D., some storehouses in Rome near the Circus Maximus caught fire. The fire quickly spread, and over the next ten days destroyed much of the city. The buildings that burned were older buildings, which Emperor Nero had been anxious to replace with newer structures. As a result, most Romans began quietly gossiping that perhaps Nero had purposely set the fires. In order to allay suspicion, Nero accused the Christians of starting the fires. Many of them lived in this poorer section of Rome, and they were already victims of prejudice. He had several Christians arrested for arson. However, these arrests did not prove sufficient to quiet the rumors. Nero ordered additional arrests. He placed Christians into the arena to provide the populace with bloody entertainment and a distraction. Nero branded Christians as public enemies and accused them of various crimes against the State. From Nero's attempts to make Christians a scapegoat for his crime of arson, a full-fledged religious persecution quickly developed.

The Roman persecution of the Church is undeniable. Both secular and Christian historians of the time (for example, Tacitus) have documented the details of Nero's persecution, as well as the persecutions that followed over the next two and a half centuries.

Chapter 2: The Romans Persecute the Church

While only God knows the number of martyrs, the Church believes that almost every pope who reigned during the first three centuries died a martyr. The first twenty-five popes almost certainly died as martyrs, beginning with the first pope, St. Peter.

The Romans martyred St. Peter on Vatican Hill, probably around the year 67 A.D., during Nero's persecution. In all likelihood, they had no idea of his position in the Church. Later emperors would try to force Church leaders to *apostatize*—that is, deny their Faith. Had they known of Peter's role as the visible head of the Church, they would have likely gone to extreme means to coerce him to deny Our Lord. However, Peter had already denied Our Lord three times. No force on Earth could have made him deny Christ a fourth time. According to tradition, Peter asked to be crucified upside down because he felt unworthy to die in the same manner as Our Lord. St. Peter's Basilica stands on the spot of his death on Vatican Hill. Every year, millions of people visit the tomb of the simple Galilean fisherman whom Christ made the first pope, the visible head of His Church, and the Bishop of Rome.

The Church Grows Despite Persecutions

Amid the virulent persecution, Linus (67-76) succeeded Peter as Bishop of Rome and head of the Church. Cletus (76-88) followed him. Cletus was succeeded by Clement I (88-97). During Clement's reign, he wrote a letter to the Church in Corinth. **This letter is one of the most important documents of the early Church because it demonstrates that Clement was acknowledged by the universal Church as the final authority on Church matters.** Even though the Apostle John still lived, the Church in Corinth, *in Greece*, accepted the authority of Clement. Despite later arguments that the pope was *only* the Bishop of Rome, all true Christians of the first century realized that the successor of Peter was the visible head of the universal Church, the Vicar of Christ. In the letter, Clement told the Church in Corinth that the laity could not appoint or remove priests and bishops, a very significant Church teaching.

Nero's death in 69 A.D. ended his persecution of the Christians. Vespasian (69-79) and then his son Titus (79-81) succeeded Nero. There were no widespread persecutions during their reigns. However, Vespasian's reign saw the fulfillment of Christ's prophecy in Mark 13:1-2 that the Temple in Jerusalem would be destroyed and that not one stone would be left upon another.

In 66 A.D., the Jews in Jerusalem rebelled against their Roman overlords. A Roman army under Vespasian besieged the city. When Vespasian was called to Rome to become emperor, Titus continued the siege. Finally, the Jews were unable to defend the city.

When the Roman army marched into Jerusalem in 70 A.D., it massacred the people, demolished the Temple, and destroyed the city.

THE FIRST FOUR POPES

**Peter
(33-67)**

**Linus
(67-76)**

**Cletus
(76-88)**

**Clement I
(88-97)**

Witness to the Faith

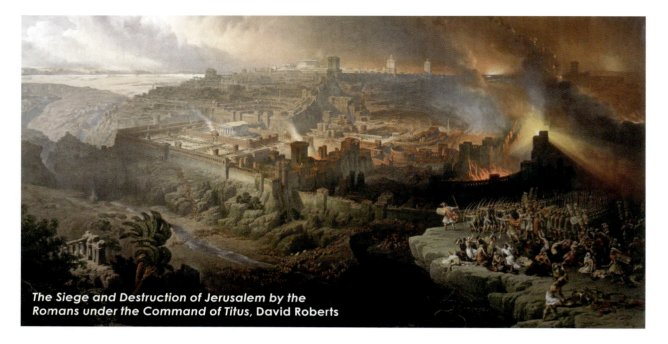

The Siege and Destruction of Jerusalem by the Romans under the Command of Titus, David Roberts

The destruction of Jerusalem caused the Jewish Christians to realize that the old religion had truly ended. However, the Jewish religion had served its purpose. It had taught men and women about the One True God and prepared them for the coming of the Messiah. Now its work was finished.

Following the death of Titus, his brother Domitian (81-96) became emperor. He reissued Nero's edicts against the Christians. Domitian ordered St. John brought to Rome, where soldiers tried to kill him in a cauldron of boiling oil.

Domitian had come to power through the strength of the Roman military. However, he was not popular with the Roman senate, and in 96 A.D., his political opponents murdered him. Following Domitian's assassination, the Roman senate named Marcus Nerva (96-98) the emperor. Nerva killed Pope Clement for refusing to offer sacrifices to the Roman gods. In 97, Pope Evaristus (97-105) succeeded Clement and guided the infant Church for eight years. St. John the Apostle, who still lived, did not attempt to supersede the authority of any pope. Despite the persecutions, the Catholic Faith spread rapidly.

The Emperor Trajan (98-117) succeeded Marcus Nerva. Trajan took a more neutral position toward Christianity than his predecessor had. He would not actively pursue individual Christians, but those who were charged with being Christians would be punished. The most well-known martyr to die during Trajan's persecution was St. Ignatius of Antioch. St. Ignatius served as the bishop of Antioch for nearly fifty years. An extremely learned theologian, he wrote seven epistles explaining the catholicity, infallibility, and holiness of the Church, and the dignity of the Holy See at Rome. He gives an outline of almost the whole of Catholic doctrine. At the time the Romans arrested him in

Saint Ignatius of Antioch

107 A.D., St. Ignatius was a very elderly man. On his journey to Rome for his execution, he worried that the Catholics in Rome would plead with the Romans to try to save him because of his advanced years. However, he desired to shed his blood for Christ. In the Roman Colosseum, the holy bishop obtained his wish. He was killed by lions.

Hadrian (117-138) succeeded Trajan. Like Trajan, he had no strong animosity against Christians and continued Trajan's policy. The empire would not actively seek to discover Christians, but anyone arrested and convicted of being a Christian would be punished. Hadrian also sought to protect Christians by informing his proconsul in Asia Minor that Christians could not be killed just to appease angry mobs.

Following the death of Hadrian, Antoninus Pius (138-161) became emperor. During his reign, Rome experienced a time of great peace and prosperity. For the most part, he continued the policies of Hadrian toward the Christians. However, the one notable saint to suffer martyrdom during his reign was St. Polycarp, the bishop of Smyrna. For almost thirty years, Polycarp had been the Apostle John's close companion. He was probably the last living man who had known one of the Apostles. In 155, at a particularly violent public festival, a mob suddenly began calling for Polycarp's arrest. The mob seized the 86-year-old bishop and dragged him before the Roman proconsul. The Roman official, having no desire to sentence an old man to death, urged Polycarp to take an oath to Caesar and renounce his Catholic Faith. When Polycarp refused, the proconsul condemned him to be burned at the stake. As his executioners began to fasten his hands to the stake with spikes, Polycarp begged them merely to tie him. The frail old bishop declared that God would give him strength to stay still in the inferno. The fire burned, and true to his word, St. Polycarp remained unmoving. To end his suffering, one of the soldiers stabbed him with a sword.

For over sixty years, the Church had experienced a time of relative peace. However, that period ended when Marcus Aurelius (161-180) became emperor. From a secular viewpoint, Marcus Aurelius was one of the better Roman emperors, as well as one of the most intelligent. He was the last emperor to rule during the **Pax Romana**, the Roman Empire's golden age of peace and prosperity. Although teachers trained him from a young age to rule, Marcus might have preferred to be a philosopher rather than an emperor. In fact, historians often refer to him as the "philosopher on the throne." His book, *Meditations*, is considered a classic of philosophy and has been praised by philosophers and writers since its publication. In *Meditations*, Marcus explained the

Saint Polycarp of Smyrna

Witness to the Faith 23

Saint Pothinus

Saint Blandina

Stoic philosophy, which he embraced because of its love of learning and appreciation of intellectual culture. *Meditations* is filled with many wise and outstanding thoughts that show that Marcus was generally open-minded and interested in learning about the world. Yet, because Christianity admired suffering and humility, he held it in complete disdain. He also saw Christianity as a growing challenge to Stoicism and the State religion. Therefore, he was determined to stop it. He ordered members of the nobility who became Christians banished. Others who converted were threatened with death.

Many Roman citizens shared the feelings that Marcus Aurelius had toward Christians. A mob of "average" Romans had attacked St. Polycarp. In 177, a similar incident occurred in Lyons. During a raucous public event, a large mob of Romans began demanding the arrest and persecutions of Christians in that town. To keep the peace, the authorities sought out and arrested many Christians. The town officials tortured the captives. Many remained resolute and refused to deny their Faith, and they were martyred. Others not only denied their Faith but also confessed to a variety of other crimes that they had not committed. In so doing, they perpetuated the Roman belief that Christians were not good citizens, but criminals.

Because some Christians had admitted to being guilty of both Christianity and other crimes, the local authorities decided to try all the Christians in the vicinity as enemies of the State. The bishop of Lyons, St. Pothinus, one of St. Polycarp's disciples, was dragged before the Roman magistrates. Despite being brutally tortured, the 90-year-old bishop refused to deny Our Lord. After two days of brutal mistreatment, St. Pothinus died in prison. However, his valiant stand encouraged his flock. Many Catholics who had apostatized returned to the Faith. Among the last to die during this persecution was a 15-year-old Christian slave girl named Blandina. Despite terrible tortures, she, like St. Pothinus, held steadfast to her faith.

Since the vast majority of converts, including most of the popes, came from the poor and slave classes of Roman society, they formed the majority of those who suffered martyrdom during this time. A few members of the nobility also gave their lives for Christ. One of the most well-known of these was a noble Roman lady named Cecilia, whose martyrdom may have taken place during the reign of Marcus Aurelius. Because it was illegal to be a Christian, Cecilia kept her conversion a secret from everyone, including her own family. When her parents

24 *Chapter 2: The Romans Persecute the Church*

The Basilica of St. Cecilia

arranged a marriage for her to a young Roman noble named Valerian, she told him her secret. He asked to learn more about Catholicism, so she took him to the pope, and Valerian became a Catholic. Later, the Roman authorities discovered that Cecilia was a Christian and condemned her to be suffocated by steam in her bathroom. However, God miraculously saved her. The Romans then beheaded her. St. Cecilia is the patroness of music and is usually shown holding, or playing, a musical instrument.

During the reign of Emperor Commodus (180-192), the persecution abated, especially after he married a Christian woman named Marcia. However, since local governors continued to enforce Trajan's decree, several people suffered martyrdom during Commodus' reign, including Pope Eleutherius (175-189).

At the beginning of his reign, Emperor Septimius Severus (193-211) possessed no particular animosity toward Christians. However, as the number of Christians increased, he began to fear for the safety and prosperity of the empire. In his mind, the success of the State religion and the success of the State were entirely intertwined. Christians, at best, ignored the State religion and at worst, believed that it was false. If a growing segment of the population turned away from the State religion, Severus believed that the Roman gods would turn away from the Roman Empire. If the gods refused to bless the empire, the empire would fall. Consequently, anyone who failed to support the official religion was not only an immoral "atheist,"

Marble Bas-Relief of Saint Cecilia

Witness to the Faith 25

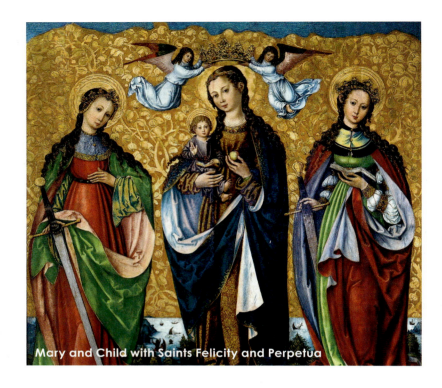
Mary and Child with Saints Felicity and Perpetua

whom Severus might tolerate, but a treacherous and undesirable enemy of the empire, which he certainly could not tolerate! As emperor, his first duty was to protect the empire against all enemies, both internally and externally. Thus, he began to attack the empire's perceived enemies, the Christians.

Based on his attacks on the Church, Severus seems to have had a better understanding of the Catholic Faith than his predecessors. His goal was apparently to try to force Christianity to simply "die out." Thus, to prevent the spread of Christianity, he banned all conversions and prohibited Baptism. He made it a crime to become a Christian or to attempt to convert anyone else. Severus also made a special effort to hunt down new Christians. That is why the majority of martyrs during his reign were either new converts or catechists.

The persecutions were worst in Egypt and North Africa, which was part of the Roman Empire. St. Felicity, St. Perpetua, and their companions were martyred in Carthage, in North Africa. St. Perpetua was a young wife and mother. During her imprisonment, Perpetua wrote an account of her persecution from the time of her arrest until nearly the moment of her martyrdom.

The other notable martyr of this period was St. Irenaeus of Lyons, who had become the second bishop of Lyons after the martyrdom of St. Polycarp. The date of his death is not certain, although the Church has traditionally placed it at the beginning of the third century during the reign of Servus. St. Gregory of Tours, the sixth-century historian, declared that Irenaeus had died as a martyr.

Saint Irenaeus of Lyons

From 211 until 222, a number of emperors led Rome, including Caracalla, who was seen as cruel and tyrannical toward everyone. Historians consider him one of the most evil men to govern Rome. Most of his oppression was directed at his political enemies, not Christians specifically. Persecutions seemed to have lessened during the reign of Alexander Severus (222-235). This may be a result of a greater acceptance of Christianity by the Roman people, or it may be that no historical documents exist from the period attesting to the persecutions.

In 235, Maximinus Thrax (235-238) came to the throne after assassinating Alexander Severus and having the Roman army proclaim

26 *Chapter 2: The Romans Persecute the Church*

him emperor. Maximinus attacked the Church in a very soldierly fashion. He knew nothing of Christianity's beliefs, but he understood a command structure. Therefore, he determined that killing the leaders of the Church, like killing an army's generals, would cause the Church to fall into disarray. As a result, he ordered that Catholic bishops be killed or exiled. Maximinus ordered Pope Pontian (230-235) to be exiled to the island of Sardinia. Pontian resigned as pope so that a new pope might be elected and continue to lead the Church. Maximinus executed Pontian's successor, Pope Anterus (235-236). In 238, the army revolted against Maximinus and assassinated him.

Most emperors had followed Trajan's passive policy of leaving Christians alone, as long as no one charged them of a crime and they didn't cause trouble. However, Emperor Decius (249-251) began an active, systematic campaign of persecution with the goal of eradicating Christianity. He began by establishing a commission in every city to investigate the populace to determine who might be a Christian. Each person called before the commission had to prove that he was not a Christian by sacrificing to the Roman gods. However, Decius' aim was not the mass execution of tens of thousands of Roman Christians. Killing so many people would have financially crippled the empire. His goal, like that of the emperors before him, was to *very strongly* persuade Christians to practice the Roman religion, which would make them "good, righteous" Roman citizens. Decius' methods of "persuasion"—death threats and torture—were so effective that many Christians, especially the wealthier members of society, did apostatize and become pagans. However, most stayed true to the Faith and died horrible deaths. Among the prominent martyrs of this persecution were Pope Fabian (236-250), who was martyred in Rome, and St. Denis, the bishop of Paris, who was beheaded in that city.

After the persecution ended, many apostates wished to be received back into the Church. The decision to allow them to return caused a great controversy. Novatian, a Roman priest, declared that apostasy was an unforgivable sin. However, Pope St. Cornelius (251-253) condemned this teaching. The Church received the apostates back, although, because they had committed a serious sin, they received serious penances, which some did for the rest of their lives.

After a brief respite, Emperor Valerian (253-260) resumed the persecutions in 257. Realizing that trying to cause individual Christians to deny their Faith did not work, he aimed his efforts at Church leaders. In 257, Valerian issued an edict against Catholic bishops and priests, demanding that they either deny the Faith or face exile. He declared that all Church organizations were illegal, and he banned Christians from conducting burial services.

Saint Denis

Witness to the Faith

St Lawrence before Valerian, Fra Angelico

Gallienus

The following year, Valerian issued an edict that simply ordered the execution of Church leaders. Valerian's numerous victims included Pope St. Stephen (254-257), Pope Sixtus II (257-258), the deacon St. Lawrence, and St. Cyprian of Carthage. The Romans arrested Pope Sixtus II and seven of his deacons during Mass. They beheaded Pope Sixtus and six of his deacons, but they did not immediately execute Lawrence, the seventh deacon. The Romans had learned that Lawrence controlled the Church's treasury. They hoped to force Lawrence to reveal the location of the money so that they might steal it.

When the Romans demanded that Lawrence give them the Church's treasures, he asked for three days to collect them. On the third day, he presented the Romans with a large crowd of poor beggars, sick people, and hungry children, all of whom he declared to be the "treasures" of the Church. Infuriated, the Roman magistrates ordered that Lawrence be tortured to death. Soldiers threw him on an iron grating and burned him to death. Tradition says that in the midst of his terrible suffering, Lawrence joked to his tormentors, "I am roasted enough on this side; turn me over."

Valerian had enacted his edicts while fighting the Persians in Asia Minor. In 260, the Persians defeated him in battle. They captured him and his entire army. They made him a slave. When Valerian's son Gallienus (260-268) became emperor in 260, he ended the persecution.

For the next twenty-four years, the Church enjoyed a period of peace, mainly because the men who became emperors ruled for only short periods. For much of this time, the emperors fought the Germanic tribes that threatened Roman's western border and the Persians who threatened the eastern border. The external enemies were a greater concern than the Christians.

Diocletian's Persecution of the Church

In 284, Diocletian, a soldier who had worked his way up through the ranks, became emperor. Diocletian would rule from 284 until 305. He would subject the Church to its greatest persecution.

After the death of the previous emperor, the army declared Diocletian the emperor. Diocletian was a clever politician and resolved to reform the government and restore Rome's former glory. Almost immediately, Diocletian realized that one man could no longer efficiently govern the empire, especially as foreign invaders threatened Rome's eastern and western borders. Therefore, around 286, he named Maximian, a former associate and army general, as co-emperor with the title *Augustus*. Under the new political system, Maximian would rule the western Roman empire, and Diocletian would rule the eastern Roman empire.

Maximian chose to govern the western Empire from Milan. Henceforth, Milan, not Rome, would be the capital of the Western empire. Meanwhile, Diocletian moved his seat of government to Nicomedia in Asia Minor.

In 293, Diocletian further divided Roman rule when he appointed two *Caesars*, basically junior emperors, to act as assistants to himself and Maximian. One Caesar was his son-in-law Galerius, who acted as his assistant in the East. Galerius established his headquarters at Sirmium (in modern-day Serbia), where he governed the Balkan Peninsula and the Danubian provinces. The other Caesar, Constantius Chlorus, aided Maximian in the West. Constantius Chlorus made Trier (in modern-day Germany) his seat of power and ruled Gaul and Britain.

Diocletian's reorganization of the empire proved tremendously successful. With others to help govern the empire, he turned his attention to Rome's external threats. By spring 299, nearly all potential invaders had been defeated, and Rome's borders were secure. For most of Diocletian's reign, the empire experienced a time of peace and prosperity in which everyone, including Christians, shared. Yet, for the Christians, it was not to last.

The main instigator of the new persecution was not Diocletian, who had no special objection to Christianity, but Galerius, who hated Christians and was determined to eliminate them. The initial persecution began in the last years of the third century. Galerius, like the other three Roman rulers, was a military commander. He came to believe that he could improve discipline and patriotism in the army if he required all his soldiers to participate in pagan worship services. Most Christian soldiers refused to sacrifice to the Roman gods and were punished, though they were usually not killed. Of those who were, the most famous is St. Sebastian, a tribune of the Praetorian Guard, who was initially shot with arrows, but survived. Later he was clubbed to death.

By 302, Galerius' hatred of Christians had grown. He continued to encourage Diocletian to promulgate a general edict against them which would allow for a far-reaching persecution of all Christians, not merely Christian soldiers. Over the course of the next several months, the two emperors argued. Diocletian felt that removing Christians from the government and the army would appease the gods, but Galerius insisted that only the execution of every Christian would pacify them. Finally, they consulted the so-called "oracle" of Apollo, which supposedly agreed with Galerius.

February 23, 303, was dedicated to Terminus, the Roman god of boundaries. On that day, Diocletian promulgated an edict ordering a universal persecution of Christians. In order to *terminate* Christianity, Diocletian also ordered the destruction of all Christian sacred books and places of worship. The edict required that all Christians publicly renounce their Faith. Those nobles who failed to comply lost certain rights, such as the right to be heard in court. For the common people, non-compliance meant slavery. Although Diocletian sought to create apostates by non-violent pressure, Galerius continued to push for more violent methods, including burning Christians to death.

When two fires erupted in the imperial palace in Nicomedia, Galerius blamed the Christians. This may have been when the

Diocletian

Maximian

Galerius

Constantius Chlorus

Witness to the Faith 29

Map of Roman Empire during the Reign of Diocletian

20,000 Martyrs of Nicomedia

Cathedral of Nicomedia, with 20,000 Christians inside, was burned to the ground by Roman soldiers. The exact date of the destruction and martyrdoms is not known, although historians place it around 303. Christians were also blamed for rebellions in Syria and Armenia. As a result of these events, and certainly pressure from Galerius, Diocletian issued a second edict in the summer of 303.

The second edict ordered Roman authorities to imprison all Catholic clergy. The clergy were so numerous that the prisons began to overflow. Real criminals were released to make room for priests and bishops. The failure of this edict caused Diocletian to issue a third. Under this edict, Christians were given the option of sacrificing to the gods or being tortured. Some Christians did apostatize, but most did not. The failure of this edict caused Diocletian to promulgate a fourth edict in early 304. Any Christian who refused to sacrifice publicly to the gods would be executed.

Although he would not see it to its conclusion, the persecution that began during Diocletian's reign was perhaps the bloodiest in Church history. The prisons were filled with Christians who were martyred. In addition, the Roman authorities hunted down Christians. In public places throughout the empire, the government erected idols of the Roman gods. Everyone was required to offer sacrifices to these pagan statues. Only God knows the number of Christians who died violently for refusing. Among the most notable martyrs of this time, the Church counts Tarsicius, Cosmas and Damian, Felix, Lucy, Catherine, and Margaret.

In 305, under pressure from Galerius, Diocletian and Maximian abdicated. Galerius assumed the title of Augustus and became the senior emperor. He remained in the East. Galerius appointed his nephew Maximinus Daia, who shared his view of Christianity, to act as Caesar. Daia would govern Egypt and Syria. In the West, the situation was far more complicated. In his attempt to take power, Galerius had failed to appoint Constantine, the son of Constantius Chlorus, and Maxentius, the son of Maximian, to the imperial thrones. Both men had been in the line of succession. Following the abdication of their fathers, both men seized power in the West.

Maxentius

In 306, Galerius issued an edict aimed at destroying the Catholic Church. Under the edict, the head of every family was to report to the Roman authorities and either sacrifice to the gods or face execution. The number of dead bodies mounted. The Romans, in an attempt to create terror, refused to allow Christians to be buried and left the bodies to rot in the streets. Soon the prisons overflowed with Christians. Every day, hundreds of Christians arrived in the mines of Cilicia, Palestine, and Cyprus, where the Romans worked them to death.

In 311, Galerius fell sick with a mortal illness. Though he had tried to eradicate the Church, he had failed. Finally, in his last days, perhaps he realized that the Christian God was the true God. He issued a decree in which he granted Christians the right to exercise their religion as long as they did not disturb the peace. He also asked Christians to pray for him. Galerius died six days after issuing the edict.

Following Galerius' death, Maximinus Daia succeeded him as emperor in the East, where the persecutions continued despite Galerius' edict. Daia realized that all religions relied on the quality of their priests for success. Therefore, Daia followed a two-pronged strategy. First, he would weaken the Catholic Church by killing its priests and bishops. Among the leaders martyred at this time were St. Peter, the bishop of Alexandria, and St. Lucian of Antioch, a leading theologian. Second, Daia decided to strengthen the Roman religion by improving the quality of pagan priests and installing a provincial high priest to oversee them. Daia also began spreading lies about the life of Christ, which he required to be taught in the Roman schools.

In the spring of 313, Daia was defeated in battle, and later killed himself. His persecution came

Constantine

Witness to the Faith

to an end. Meanwhile, in the West, Constantine, the son of Constantius Chlorus, had come to power in 306. Chlorus had never liked persecuting the Christians. His son would become the great protector of the Catholic Faith and would ultimately make it the official religion of the empire.

The Catacombs

Pagans tended to cremate their dead. The Jews, however, buried their dead, a custom that the early Church followed. The Jews of Rome built the first **catacombs** as tombs; later, Christians buried their dead in catacombs as well. The word "catacomb" probably derives from the Latin phrase *ad catacumbas*, meaning "near the lowlands"—referring to the location of many of the early catacombs near the city of Rome. Although the word "catacomb" means an underground tomb, when people speak of "the catacombs," they usually mean the catacombs underneath the city of Rome.

The Roman catacombs, the burial site for the early Christians, as well as a place of refuge from persecution, are long, narrow underground intersecting passages. The walls have hollowed out shelves, into which the bodies of the deceased were placed. Christians would then cover these niches with a slab of marble or a piece of masonry, thus entombing the body. Some of the tunnels led into small rooms or large crypts, where priests could say Mass during a time of persecution. Otherwise, the catacombs **served as tombs, not as churches**. Some catacombs are quite elaborate and consist of as many as five floors or galleries connected by staircases, as in a very large house. The top catacomb was usually built about 20 feet below the surface. The lowest could be built as deep as 80 feet.

During the barbarian invasions of the seventh and eighth centuries, the popes removed the relics of the saints buried in the catacombs and placed them in the churches of Rome. For centuries thereafter, the catacombs fell into disuse. Only during the Renaissance did the Church again begin to show an interest in the historical value of the catacombs. Today, tourists can visit selected parts of the catacombs.

The catacombs are a treasury of art, history, and apologetics. Of the approximately forty catacombs in Rome, the oldest and most famous is the catacomb of St. Callixtus, named after the deacon Callixtus. This catacomb is especially interesting because it contains the tombs of more than fifty martyrs and sixteen popes, probably all of whom were martyred.

The inscriptions in the catacombs not only identify the deceased but also, along with the art in the catacombs, provide direct evidence of the beliefs of the early Church. Based on findings in the catacombs, the Church knows that the early Christians believed in the same truths that the Catholic Church teaches today. Early Christians believed that Jesus Christ was divine, the Second Person of the Trinity. They believed in the divine institution of the papacy. They believed in the Real Presence in the Eucharist. They believed in Purgatory. They recognized Mary's special role as the Mother of God. Early Christians also realized the power and value of the intercession of the saints, and the value and necessity of praying for the dead.

Catacombs
Long, narrow, intersecting passages underground, where early Christians buried their dead. Some included small rooms or large crypts, where Mass could be said during the persecutions.

Burial of St. Cecilia, Madrazo

Chapter 2: The Romans Persecute the Church

Paintings and drawings of Our Lord in the catacombs typically portray Him as the Good Shepherd carrying the lost sheep on His shoulders. Other frequently depicted scenes include the story of Noah and the Ark, Daniel in the Lion's Den, Jonah and the whale, and Our Lord's raising of Lazarus. Since many of those buried in the catacombs were martyrs, it is not surprising that the early Christians should cover the walls with images depicting times of tribulation and pointing to the Resurrection.

A tradition that the Church kept from the catacombs is the "altar stone." The early Church said Mass on altars under which martyrs' bodies lay. From this practice comes the custom of having stones on our altars in which the Church places the relics of the saints. In the Byzantine Rites of the Catholic Church, the tradition is kept alive through the use of the "Antimension." The Antimension is one of the most important furnishings of the altar. It is a rectangular piece of cloth made of either linen or silk. It is typically decorated with representations of the descent of Christ from the Cross, or the four Evangelists, and contains inscriptions related to the Passion. A small relic of a martyr is sewn into it.

The Catacomb of St. Callixtus

A New Era

By 313, the Catholic Church had not only survived the worst that the Roman Empire could do, but had actually thrived. The fourth century would be a time of great evangelization for the Church, as a Roman emperor would actively support the Faith, rather than trying to destroy it. The Church was about to embark upon a new era.

Fresco of the Good Shepherd Found in the Catacombs

Oral Exercises

1. How did St. Peter die?
2. Why did Marcus Aurelius hate Christianity?
3. Describe the martyrdom of St. Cecilia.
4. What is an apostate? How did the early Church deal with apostates who wanted to return to the Faith?
5. Who was St. Lawrence? How did he die?
6. Name five emperors who persecuted the Church.
7. How is Our Lord represented in the catacombs?
8. What is the origin of the altar stone?
9. What does the altar stone contain?

Witness to the Faith 33

Chapter 3
The Church Triumphs over the Roman Empire

The Decline of the Roman Empire

By the time of Our Lord's birth, Rome had reached the zenith of its glory. It had magnificent art, excellent roads, a well-run government, thriving commerce, and the world's finest army. It even had a police force and a fire department. A person could walk on Roman roads from one end of the empire to the other, almost without fear of injury or assault. And the Roman Empire was large. Rome had conquered all the nations that bordered the Mediterranean Sea, from Asia Minor in the East to Spain in the West. Under the first emperor, Augustus (27 B.C.-14 A.D.), the Roman Empire began its golden age of peace and prosperity, known as the **Pax Romana**. It lasted 200 years.

Despite its outward splendor, at the heart of the Roman Empire lay a deep corruption. The corruption became apparent in 37 A.D. when the Emperor Caligula came to the throne. Members of the army and Roman senate assassinated Caligula, a personally evil and corrupt man, in 41 A.D. Other evil men such as Nero followed Caligula. Moreover, many of the emperors, so corrupted by the power that they wielded, had themselves proclaimed gods by the senate. The Roman people were willing to worship the emperor as long as he provided them with "bread and circuses"—that is, food and entertainment. The most popular sports were chariot racing and gladiatorial combats, often fought to the death.

Pax Romana
The Roman Empire's golden age of peace and prosperity, which lasted 200 years.

Baptism of Constantine, Gianfrancesco Penni

312 A.D. – 350 A.D.

312 A.D.
Constantine and Maxentius battle at the Milvian Bridge. Constantine is victorious.

313 A.D.
Constantine promulgates the Edict of Milan, which officially makes Christianity legal in the Roman Empire.

314 A.D.
Civil war breaks out between Constantine and Licinius, the emperor in the East.

324 A.D.
Constantine defeats Licinius.

325 A.D.
Licinius is executed after attempting to overthrow Constantine. Constantine is now the sole ruler of the empire.

337 A.D.
Constantine dies, leaving the empire to his three sons.

350 A.D.
After years of civil war, Constantine's son Constantius becomes sole emperor.

The corruption was not limited to the emperor and the nobility. It ran throughout Roman society. At the heart of Rome's corruption lay its pagan religion. When Rome had conquered Greece, it had absorbed the Greek religion and its pantheon of Greek "gods." However, the Greek gods were themselves immoral and provided examples of a perverted lifestyle. Many Romans had begun to grow tired of their own immoral religion and were looking for something that would give their lives meaning. As a result, some Romans started investigating Eastern mysticism, strange cults, and the teachings of the Stoics. Others simply ignored religion altogether and began living wicked lives devoted to the pleasures of the flesh. However, nothing provided the spiritual satisfaction that the Romans sought.

History shows that any time a large percentage of a society chooses to deny God

Witness to the Faith

Pentecost

or live immoral lives, that society is doomed. The family, the most basic building block of society, begins to crumble and eventually fails. In pagan Rome, this is precisely what happened. The Romans had few lifelong marriages. Married couples failed to embrace the virtue of purity. In aristocratic families, children were educated by slaves rather than by their parents. Of course, the very concept of slavery, so prevalent in the ancient world, was itself corrupting, as it encouraged the notion that some humans were inferior to others. Moreover, many of the Roman fine arts, such as literature, encouraged vice rather than virtue.

By the middle of the first century, many Romans thirsted for a religion that would give their lives meaning and purpose. They desperately sought a religion that would provide a real moral code with examples of high moral character. Catholicism filled that void and quenched that thirst.

Christ Comes to Rome

Historians have posited several theories for the date and the manner in which Christianity came to Rome. The most logical explanation is that Romans who had converted while in Jerusalem brought Catholicism to Rome upon their return home. The Acts of the Apostles mentions that during Peter's sermon at Pentecost, "travelers from Rome" were present (Acts 2:10). Another theory is that Peter himself visited Rome around 41 A.D. He may have remained in the city until 48 A.D., when an imperial edict banished all Jews from Rome. A third, less likely theory is that Roman soldiers themselves, stationed

36 *Chapter 3: The Church Triumphs over the Roman Empire*

in Caesarea, might also have spread news about the new religion when they returned to Rome. However, this seems more like gossiping about a strange new sect than actually sharing knowledge of the Faith. What is certain is that when St. Paul wrote to the Romans between 56 and 58 A.D., the Church in Rome was already well-established.

Unlike the Church in Jerusalem, the Church in Rome consisted mostly of Gentiles. However, there were a few Jews. In 61 A.D., St. Paul reached the city and began preaching to the Romans. St. Peter arrived in Rome two or three years later. Because of the efforts of these two great saints, by 64 A.D., the date of Nero's fire, Tacitus recounts that there was "an immense multitude of Christians" in Rome.

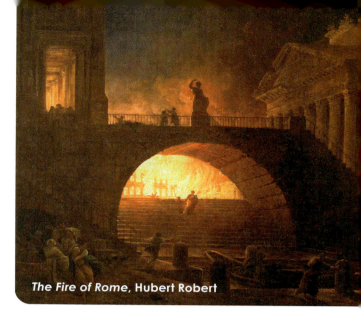

The Fire of Rome, Hubert Robert

The Life and Beliefs of the Early Christians

In the 1500s, during the Protestant Revolt, various Protestants claimed that the Catholic Church had invented certain beliefs, like the Real Presence and papal primacy, as late as the twelfth century. However, the historical record shows that the first Christians held these beliefs. They are as old as the Church.

The best source of information on the early Church comes from the early Church Fathers, or the **Apostolic Fathers**. These authors wrote at the end of the first century and the beginning of the second century. Some of these writers personally knew the Apostles and had been taught by them (e.g., St. Polycarp was taught by St. John). Others were the disciples of men taught by the Apostles (e.g., St. Irenaeus was a disciple of St. Polycarp). The Church has consistently relied on the accuracy and reliability of these writings as one of the most essential sources of Church doctrine.

The writings of the Apostolic Fathers provide a valuable insight into life in the early Catholic Church. The Church prohibited early Christians from attending the theater, because many of the performances were an occasion of sin. Christians also could not attend the public games, many of which involved men fighting to the death. Christians were prohibited from marrying non-Christians. Also, the Church strictly commanded Christians to avoid idol worship, which was so common in Roman society and ultimately caused many to suffer martyrdom. However, the Church also reminded Christians that, as Roman citizens, they needed to "render unto Caesar…." Therefore, Christians needed to behave lawfully. They had to pay taxes and serve in the army. They were encouraged to pray for their government and its leaders.

> **Apostolic Fathers**
> Early Christian writers and teachers, often taught by the Apostles (e.g., St. Polycarp was taught by St. John) or by those who knew them (e.g., St. Irenaeus was a disciple of St. Polycarp).

Antique Roman Coins

Witness to the Faith

Baptism, Masaccio

Catechumens
Converts preparing for Baptism; the term means "hearers."

In many ways, Christians represented the highest qualities and ideals of the Roman citizen. They showed charity and hospitality to others. They also practiced virtues which the pagans did not practice, such as justice and chastity. Unlike other Romans, Christians acknowledged the inherent worth of every human being, including women and slaves. They taught their own children and instilled in them a love between parent and child. Many Christians undoubtedly inspired their pagan neighbors to live better lives. However, because they removed themselves from much of public life, including the games, the theater, and the religious celebrations, Christians aroused the suspicions of others.

The early Church modeled its religious rites and ceremonies on the Jewish synagogue. Christians read the Scriptures and received Holy Communion. The faithful received under both species: the Sacred Host and the Precious Blood. The words the priest uses to consecrate the bread and wine into the Body and Blood of Jesus Christ are the same today as they were almost 2,000 years ago.

Until the end of the first century, the Eucharistic service was held in the evening in connection with a dinner known as the *Agape* feast, or Love feast. Later, it became the custom to have the Eucharistic service in the morning. From the very beginning, priests offered daily Mass.

Deacons took the Blessed Sacrament to those unable to attend Mass because of age or illness. The first Catholics were permitted to keep the Blessed Sacrament in their homes and carry it with them on journeys. The early Church made Sunday the day for religious celebration rather than Saturday, the Jewish Sabbath. The Church made this decision partly to honor Christ's Resurrection, which occurred on (Easter) Sunday, and partly to show Jewish converts and Roman pagans that Jewish Law did not bind Catholics.

Jesus taught, "No one can enter the kingdom of God without being born of water and Spirit" (John 3:5). This means that a person needs to be baptized before he or she can become a Christian. Baptism is the first Sacrament of Initiation. In the early Church, converts were baptized as soon as they declared that they believed Jesus Christ was the Son of God. Later, the Church required a period of training that lasted for two or three years. During this preparatory period, the converts were called **catechumens**, which means "hearers." The catechumens spent their time praying and learning about the Faith. The Church allowed them to participate at the Mass, but only up to the Offertory.

Chapter 3: The Church Triumphs over the Roman Empire

Once the catechumens were ready to be baptized, they went into the baptismal font, where the bishop immersed them in the water three times. Afterward, the bishop immediately confirmed them, a custom the Eastern Rite Churches still follow. The early Church baptized converts when it was convenient. Later, Holy Saturday and the Saturday before Pentecost became the appointed days for baptizing catechumens, who had to wait for these days.

From its inception, the Church has taught the necessity of infant Baptism. Both Origen and St. Augustine, two early Church Fathers, declared that the Apostles began the tradition of baptizing babies.

Any Christian who committed a serious sin was required to dress in coarse, uncomfortable clothes and take his place with the catechumens for a period of penance. After the sinner had served his penance, the bishop publicly absolved him.

St. Augustine

Creation of the Church Hierarchy

After Our Lord Jesus Christ instituted the Holy Eucharist at the Last Supper, He turned to His Apostles and said to them, "Do this in memory of me" (Luke 20:19). After His Resurrection, Jesus gave the Apostles the power to forgive sins (John 20:23). Our Lord made all the Apostles bishops and invested them with the fullness of the power of Holy Orders: the power to administer all the sacraments and to consecrate other bishops and priests like themselves (Matthew 28:18-20). The Apostles realized that they had this power and authority, and used it numerous times. We know from Scripture that the Apostles communicated the fullness of this power to a number of disciples—for example, Paul, Barnabas, Timothy, Titus, and Matthias—in order to ensure Apostolic succession (Acts 13:3, 14:22, 1:24-26, and Titus 1:5). The evidence is overwhelming that Jesus Christ did not come to Earth simply to start a religion, but also to establish a Church, which would last until the end of time. The pope and the bishops, the successors of the Apostles, would lead that Church.

***Christ Giving the Keys to St. Peter*, Peter Paul Rubens**

Witness to the Faith

Primacy
Superior rank. The "primacy of Peter" refers to the leadership of the Bishop of Rome over all the other bishops.

Primacy of Honor
A special dignity and respect; by itself, it would make Peter only the "first among equals."

Primacy of Jurisdiction
The power and authority that made Peter, and makes his successors, the visible head of the Church.

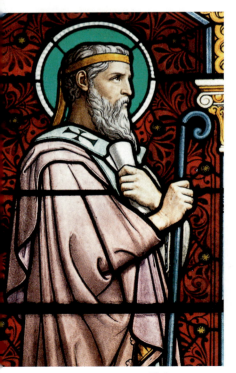

St. Irenaeus

The Primacy of Rome

One of the most difficult doctrines for non-Catholic Christians to accept is the authority of the pope over the Church. In examining the **primacy** (that is, the superiority of the Bishop of Rome over all other bishops), a distinction must be made between **primacy of honor** and **primacy of jurisdiction**. Had Our Lord granted Peter *only* "primacy of honor" over the other Apostles, He would merely have given St. Peter a special dignity and respect because of his position as perhaps the eldest or most knowledgeable Apostle. Peter would only be the "first among equals." However, *primacy of jurisdiction* gave Peter power and supreme authority over the other Apostles as the visible head of the Church.

While Our Lord certainly conveyed primacy of honor upon Peter, He also clearly meant to convey primacy of jurisdiction. Our Lord's words on this point could not be stronger. After Peter declared that Jesus was the Messiah, the Son of God, Our Lord stated that God the Father had revealed this to Peter. Christ went on to declare: "You are Peter, and upon this rock I will build my church, and the gates of the netherworld shall not prevail against it. I will give you the keys to the kingdom of heaven. Whatever you bind on earth shall be bound in heaven; and whatever you loose on earth shall be loosed in heaven" (Mt. 16:18-19). Finally, before Our Lord returned to Heaven, he appeared to the Apostles at the Sea of Tiberias and again confirmed Peter as the visible head of the Church. Because Peter had denied Him three times, Our Lord asked Peter three times to "feed My lambs," "tend My sheep," and "feed My sheep" (John 21:15-17). Our Lord was clearly speaking to Peter individually, not to the Apostles in general. Peter was the rock. Peter received the keys and the power. Any later interpretation which tries to claim that Christ meant to give the primacy of jurisdiction to all the Apostles is clearly a misinterpretation.

Almost from the very beginning of Church history, the Church in Rome, the See of St. Peter, has held the primary place among all the Christian churches, even the older sees of Jerusalem and Antioch. The Catholic Church has consistently taught that "of all the letters of Paul, that to the Christians at Rome has long held pride of place" (*New American Bible*, Rev. ed., Introduction to Romans, USCCB, 2011). Not only is the **Letter to the Romans** Paul's longest letter, but also it sets forth his thoughts on the Church's most important truths in the most systematic manner. That he sent this crucial letter to the Church in Rome, rather than another larger, better established church, indicates his understanding of the importance of Rome.

As previously noted, during the late first century, Pope St. Clement wrote to the Church in Corinth to settle a dispute. The Corinthians did not object to his intervention, but rather they welcomed it. In fact, they appreciated his effort to help them so much that, seventy years later, they continued to read his letter at their gatherings.

Additionally, many of the Apostolic Fathers, including St. Ignatius of Antioch and St. Irenaeus, acknowledged the Bishop of Rome as the visible head of the Church. Several bishops of the early Church traveled to Rome to seek official condemnation for heresies that had broken out in their dioceses. Interestingly, even people promoting false teachings sought out the Bishop of Rome in hopes that he would declare that their ideas were not heretical. They understood that if the pope declared that their beliefs were orthodox, then they were approved.

Early Defenders of the Faith: The Apologists

In order to justify the persecutions, some of the emperors and lesser Roman officials had made false charges against Christians. For example, they claimed that Christians were not good citizens, because they failed to follow the State pagan religion. Others claimed that Christians were engaging in various immoral acts. Other Romans attacked Christianity as being ridiculous, and its followers as foolish, uneducated people. During the beginning of the second century, the Church began to defend itself against these attacks. Great writers from both the East and the West began systematically to explain the Faith and to refute these charges. These writers are known as the **Apologists**.

St. Justin Martyr

The first, and to many the greatest, of the Christian apologists was St. Justin the martyr. He was born in Palestine, about 100. His parents were Greek pagans. A naturally inquisitive person, he spent years studying various pagan religions and philosophies. However, none of these satisfied him. According to Justin's own account, it was not until he met an old Christian man who told him about the Catholic Faith that he realized that, at last, he had found the truth. He began studying Christianity. During the reign of Antoninus Pius (138-161), Justin journeyed to Rome, where he founded a school of Christian philosophy. In Rome, he debated with various pagan philosophers. Eventually, his enemies denounced him to the authorities as a Christian. He was martyred in the year 165.

Although Justin may have written many defenses of the Faith, few have survived the centuries. His most famous surviving work is his *Dialogue with Trypho*. In this work, he relates his own conversion experience and answers point-by-point objections to the Catholic Faith. Justin also wrote two "Apologies" addressed to Emperors Antoninus Pius and Marcus Aurelius and the Senate and People of Rome. He refutes the charges that Christians are atheists and enemies of the State because they do not follow the Roman religion.

St. Irenaeus

One of the first great apologists in the West was St. Irenaeus, the bishop of Lyons. Recall that St. Polycarp, who had been the companion of St. John the Evangelist, had trained St. Irenaeus. Unlike St. Justin, who defended the Faith against the pagans, Irenaeus sought to explain Catholicism to his fellow Christians, as erroneous teachings had begun to appear which were creating confusion. Some Christian theologians, who had been studying some of the Eastern religions, began trying to

> **Apologists**
> Defenders of the Faith; writers who explain Christianity and refute misconceptions about it.

> ***Dialogue with Trypho***
> The most famous surviving work of St. Justin Martyr, the first great apologist. In it, he describes his conversion and answers point-by-point objections to the Faith.

St. Justin Martyr

Witness to the Faith 41

explain Christian beliefs in terms of these religions rather than the Bible and Divine Revelation. To correct these mistakes, St. Irenaeus wrote a work called *Against the Heresies*. Another of his writings, *The Proof of the Apostolic Teaching*, is the oldest catechism that exists. In it, St. Irenaeus clearly and simply explains the basic truths of the Catholic Faith.

Origen

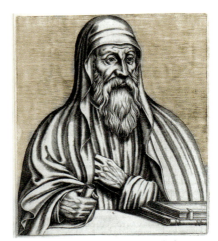

Origen

Of all the early apologists, no one produced more material than Origen, arguably the greatest intellect of the early Church, as well as one of the most important Church Fathers. He is known as the Father of Christian Theology. Origen was born in Alexandria, Egypt, about the year 184. When he was 18, he began attending the famous Catechetical School of Alexandria, where Clement of Alexandria, another Church Father, taught. Origen was tremendously brilliant, and became head of the school in a few years. Yet his success in Alexandria was cut short when he came into conflict with the bishop of the city, and was consequently dismissed from the school for disobedience. He traveled to Caesarea, where he founded another school, which became extremely successful. Because of the amount, quality, and comprehensive nature of his writings, most Christians came to regard Origen as the leading authority on theological matters. During the persecutions of Emperor Decius, Origen suffered greatly but refused to apostatize. After two years of imprisonment, the Romans released him. He died at Tyre in 254, his health and body ruined by the tortures he had sustained.

Origen wrote over 2,000 works covering a wide range of religious topics, including theology, apologetics, the spiritual life, and Holy Scripture. His most important work is the *Hexapla* (six-fold Bible), in which he provided six different translations of the Old Testament in parallel, side-by-side columns. This made it easy for students to study the Old Testament and compare the various translations. St. Jerome used the *Hexapla* in his work on Scriptural translation. Origen also wrote a book in which he defended the Faith against the charge of the pagan philosopher Celsus that Christianity was "irrational."

In 553, the Second Council of Constantinople condemned some of Origen's writings because they contained certain heretical notions. Among his errors, Origen could not understand how an all-merciful God could condemn anyone to eternal damnation.

Tertullian

Tertullian

Tertullian was born in Carthage sometime between 150 and 160. He became a Christian in his mid-thirties. Trained as a lawyer, he possessed an extraordinary vocabulary. Tertullian was the first major apologist to write in Latin as opposed to Greek. Thus, he is considered the Father of Latin Theology.

Among his most famous and important works is his *Apologeticus*. In this treatise, he proved the innocence of Christians and the bias of Trajan's laws. Furthermore, he demanded that Christians be treated the

42 *Chapter 3: The Church Triumphs over the Roman Empire*

same as other religions in the Roman Empire. Tertullian also attacked heretics. In 200, he wrote his *Prescription against Heretics*. This is a general refutation of all doctrinal errors. He also defended Apostolic succession and the primacy of the pope.

Sadly, over time, Tertullian himself began to spread false ideas. For example, he wrote that all amusements were sinful. Because he was concerned that Christians might fall into sin if they interacted with pagans, Tertullian declared that Christians should not be tradesmen, teachers, soldiers, or government officials. Even worse, he ultimately wrote that the Church could not absolve Christians who fell into mortal sin. By the time of his death, many of his views had become heretical.

St. Cyprian of Carthage

The last great apologist of this period was St. Cyprian (c. 200-258), the bishop of Carthage. Cyprian was born in Carthage to very wealthy parents, who ensured that he received the finest education. As a young man, he became a teacher of rhetoric and philosophy. Like St. Justin, Cyprian found that pagan philosophers did not satisfy his hunger for truth. He finally began studying Tertullian. Probably at the age of 46, he converted to Catholicism.

Following his conversion, Cyprian began donating his money to the poor and to promote the mission of the Catholic Church to spread the Faith. He began to study for the priesthood and was ordained. When the bishop of Carthage died in 248, the priests of Carthage elected Cyprian as the new bishop.

Cyprian wrote several famous works, most of which deal with pastoral matters rather than deep theological questions. His treatise *On the Unity of the Catholic Church* deals with the primacy of the Church of Rome. He also addressed the issue of accepting lapsed Catholics back into the Church in his treatise *On the Fallen*. In another work, he wrote about the Lord's Prayer.

The Church's Protector: The Emperor Constantine

In 305, Galerius forced Diocletian and Maximian to abdicate. By 306, Constantine (the son of Constantius Chlorus) and Maxentius (the son of Maximian) had become the rulers in the West. Constantine ruled Britain, Gaul, and Spain. Maxentius ruled Italy and Northern Africa. However, the two co-emperors did not really like each other. For several years, the two men had an uneasy friendship, and in 311 Maxentius declared war on Constantine.

With about a quarter of his army, Constantine quickly crossed the Alps into Italy to fight Maxentius. He defeated Maxentius' army in two battles in the spring of 312. However, Maxentius controlled Rome. With a good supply of food, he burned the bridges to the city and prepared for a long siege, hoping that he could outlast Constantine. However, the people of Rome had turned against Maxentius. By October, he realized that he

St. Cyprian of Carthage

***The Labarum (Constantine Receives the Standard with the Monogram of Christ as the Imperial Sign)**, Peter Paul Rubens*

Witness to the Faith

The Battle of the Milvian Bridge,
Giulio Romano

Edict of Milan
The decree that made Christianity legal in the Roman Empire, issued by Constantine in 313 A.D.

Arch of Constantine

would not survive the siege. With no other choice, in late October, Maxentius led his troops out of the city to do battle with Constantine.

Meanwhile, according to the Christian historian Eusebius, who served as Constantine's biographer, the night before the battle, Constantine saw a cross in the sky surrounded by the words "*in hoc signo vinces*" (that is, "in this sign you will conquer"). Constantine had the Roman eagles that his legions carried replaced with crosses. He also had his soldiers paint the *chi rho* symbol on their shields.

The following day, October 29, 312, the two armies met at the Battle of the Milvian Bridge, a bridge that crosses the Tiber River just north of Rome. Despite being outnumbered, Constantine won a decisive battle. Maxentius perished in the Tiber along with thousands of his soldiers. Victorious, Constantine entered Rome.

The senate erected a triumphal arch commemorating Constantine's victory. Constantine had the arch, which still stands today among the ruins of the city, engraved with the words "*instinctu divinitatis*" (that is, "by the inspiration of divinity"). There is also evidence that Constantine erected a magnificent statue, more than 40 feet high, the *Colossus of Constantine*, in which he held a Christian symbol. While symbols are important, actions mean more. Constantine quickly showed that he meant to do more for Christians than build statues.

The Edict of Milan

After the death of Galerius in May 311, his nephew Maximian Daia had become emperor in the East. Daia had shared power with Licinius. However, the two men disliked each other. Licinius allied himself with Constantine in preparation for war with Daia.

In February 313, Constantine and Licinius met in Milan to strengthen their alliance. During their meeting, they promulgated the vitally important **Edict of Milan**, which established principles of religious tolerance for both Christians and pagans. However, it is clear from the actual wording of the Edict that Constantine's main goal was to protect Christians. In fact, they are the only ones specifically mentioned in the Edict. **The Edict of Milan officially declared that Christianity was legal in the Roman Empire.**

After issuing the Edict of Milan, Constantine began a long history of bestowing benefits on the Church. He announced a law requiring that Church property which had been taken without just compensation be returned. He allowed the Church to receive gifts and bequests. He outlawed crucifixion as a form of punishment. He also built a number of magnificent churches, including the first basilicas over the tombs of St. Peter and St. Paul.

Sole Ruler of the Empire

In August 313, Daia killed himself, ending the Roman civil war. Constantine and Licinius divided the empire between themselves. Constantine took the West, and Licinius took the East. Unfortunately, the two men did not get along, despite the fact that Licinius was married to Constantine's sister.

In 314, a new civil war erupted as Licinius and Constantine fought each other. Constantine won a small victory, and the two declared a truce. Although Eusebius blames this war on Licinius' persecution of Christians, that seems unlikely, since Licinius did not begin persecuting Christians until 319. Rather, the war was politically motivated, with both men bearing some responsibility. For about the next ten years, the two men preserved a cautiously friendly relationship. In 319, Licinius did begin persecuting Christians, because he saw them as supporting Constantine over him. His persecution seemed to be limited to those Christians he saw as supporters of Constantine.

Licinius

***Triumphant Entry of Constantine into Rome**, Peter Paul Rubens*

Witness to the Faith   45

In 324, Constantine attacked Licinius. According to Eusebius, Constantine did so because Licinius was about to initiate more severe measures against the Christians. The attack ended those plans. In the summer and fall of 324, Constantine defeated Licinius in two critical battles. Initially, Constantine spared Licinius because his sister, Licinius' wife, pleaded for her husband's life. However, Constantine later ordered Licinius executed for treason when he attempted to overthrow Constantine. In 325, Constantine became the sole emperor of the Roman Empire. Finally, the man who sat on the imperial throne was not an enemy of the Church, but her friend and protector. The Church had triumphed.

Later Years of Constantine's Reign

After consolidating his power, Constantine decided that he should rule his empire from a city located in the middle of it. Thus, he founded a city which he named after himself, **Constantinople** (modern-day Istanbul). Moving the capital of the empire from Rome or Milan to the East had many unforeseeable consequences—some positive, others negative.

Constantinople
The city that Constantine founded and named for himself, designating it as his capital because it was closer to the center of the empire.

One positive aspect was the preservation of ancient Roman culture. When the barbarians invaded the Western empire and sacked Rome in the late fifth century, they destroyed much of Roman culture. Because the seat of the empire had moved to Constantinople, part of this culture was preserved. For the Church, the most positive feature of the capital's move was the freedom that the Church gained. Without the close supervision of the empire, the Church had much more freedom than it would have otherwise. This allowed the Church to grow and flourish without too much State interference. On the other hand, in the East, the Church became more and more a part of the imperial structure and less independent. It fell away from the influence of the pope. This was the greatest negative aspect of the move. In time, the Church in the East would break totally from the West. That break remains unhealed.

After a reign of almost thirty-one years, Constantine died on May 22, 337. Although many historians consider him history's first "Christian" emperor, and in some ways he tried to govern as

The Founding of Constantinople,
Peter Paul Rubens

The Death of Constantine the Great, Peter Paul Rubens

a Christian, he was not baptized until he was on his deathbed. Following his death, his three sons divided his empire. But they could not govern together, and they fought for control. Finally, after several years of civil war, in 350 his son Constantius (350-361) became sole emperor.

During his reign, Constantius worked to eliminate paganism. He made sacrificing to pagan gods an act punishable by death. He ordered pagan temples destroyed or used for other purposes. However, he allowed pagans to teach in the schools, where they promoted pagan ideas at the expense of Christianity.

Oral Exercises

1. Relate some of the ideas as to how and when Christianity was introduced in Rome.
2. Who were the Apostolic Fathers?
3. Why did the early Church make Sunday the day for religious celebration?
4. Distinguish between primacy of honor and primacy of jurisdiction.
5. What evidence do we have that the pope is the visible head of the Church? (Give three examples.)
6. What is an apologist?
7. St. Irenaeus was bishop of what city?
8. What was the *Hexapla*?
9. What serious theological error did Tertullian finally make?
10. What was the Edict of Milan?

Witness to the Faith 47

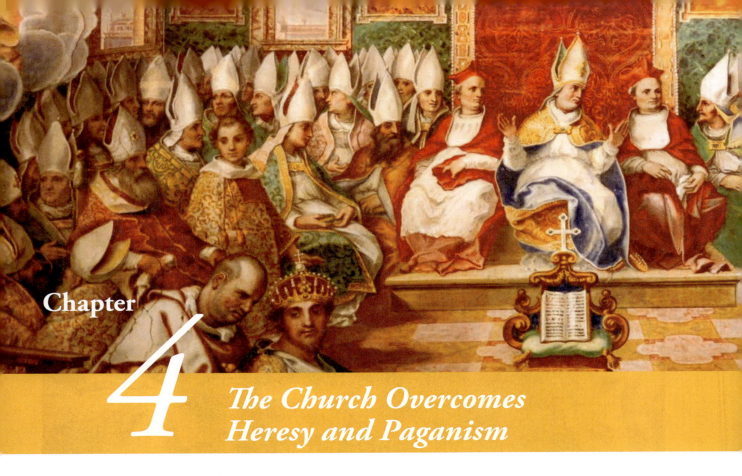

Chapter 4
The Church Overcomes Heresy and Paganism

Reasons for the Success of Christianity

By the third decade of the fourth century, not only had Christianity spread throughout the Roman Empire but also the emperor himself was a Christian. Yet, from a purely secular viewpoint, it seems that Christianity should not have increased at all. After all, unlike other religions of the time, Christianity did not promise its adherents power, wealth, fame, or any worldly pleasure. In fact, it asked just the opposite. Christ asked His followers to deny themselves and take up their cross (Mt. 16:24). Christ demanded self-sacrifice. Moreover, Christians during the first three centuries were likely to be tortured and killed for their Faith. Why then did so many people become Christian?

The most obvious reason for the success of Christianity is that Jesus Christ, the Second Person of the Holy Trinity and the Son of God, founded the Catholic Church. Christ would not have founded a Church only to see it fail. When Christ commissioned the Apostles to "make disciples of all nations," He promised that He would be with the Church "until the end of the age"—that is, until the end of time (Mt. 28:19-20).

The second reason the Faith succeeded and spread is the passion of its early missionaries and the holiness of its first members. The early missionaries, led by St. Paul, the Apostles, and the first bishops, dedicated their lives to spreading the Faith and making new converts.

Saints Peter and Paul

48 *Chapter 4: The Church Overcomes Heresy and Paganism*

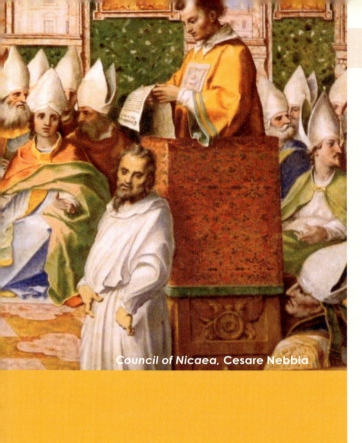
Council of Nicaea, Cesare Nebbia

Most of the missionaries and early Church leaders died as martyrs. Their deaths gave witness to the truth of the Faith they preached. Surely, only someone who deeply believed would sacrifice his or her life for that belief.

Moreover, most early Christians led praiseworthy lives. In an era when pagans cared little for their neighbors, Christians followed the Golden Rule, seeking to practice justice and charity. Even the pagans noted the difference in the Christian lifestyle. Such examples brought others to the Faith.

The unique nature of Christianity also caused it to spread. As previously noted, paganism at this time was in decline. Pagans were looking for something to satisfy their own spiritual emptiness. People realized that the Roman gods and religion did not provide any real moral

318 A.D. – 381 A.D.

318 A.D.
Arius begins to preach his heresy.

325 A.D.
The Council of Nicaea meets, composing a creed to make clear the divinity of Christ.

335-336 A.D.
Athanasius is exiled for the first time. Arius triumphantly enters Constantinople, but dies suddenly.

350 A.D.
Constantius becomes emperor and begins working in favor of Arianism.

355 A.D.
Constantius intimidates an assembly of bishops into condemning Athanasius and approving the Arian creed. When Pope Liberius rejects the decrees of this "council," the emperor banishes the pope and attempts to arrest Athanasius, who escapes, hiding in the desert for six years.

361-363 A.D.
Julian the Apostate, the last pagan emperor, tries to restore paganism to the empire, without much success.

380 A.D.
Emperor Theodosius issues the Edict of Thessalonica, making Nicene Christianity the official religion of the Roman Empire.

381 A.D.
Theodosius calls the Council of Constantinople, which reaffirms the condemnation of Arianism and adds a supplement to the creed to clarify an issue pertaining to the Holy Spirit.

Witness to the Faith 49

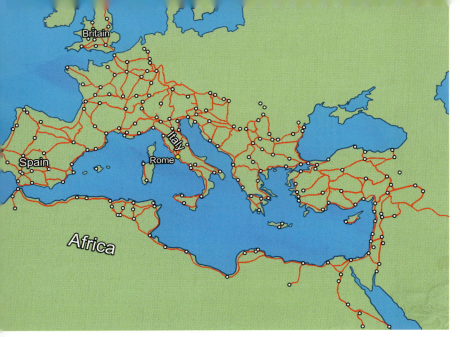

Map of Roman Roads in 125 A.D.

code. The gods were inherently immoral. Some Romans turned to Stoicism with its strict code of conduct, but that did not answer most people's needs. Catholicism offered the highest moral code and ideals. Other people began investigating Eastern mystical cults and older Roman pagan sects. However, these again did not satisfy their longings. Catholicism promised redemption and everlasting life. It met the new awakening religious consciousness of the Roman pagans as no other religion did.

The fourth cause for the success of the Faith was its *universal* appeal. Unlike other religions, Christianity appealed to rich and poor, to master and slave, to ruler and subject, and to men and women. Christianity taught that all people were equal in the sight of God. In this way, it called for an entirely new social order based on the Golden Rule. The notion of treating others with dignity and charity was a new idea. Of course, this notion of universal equality appealed strongly to the poorer elements of Roman society, which is why the vast majority of converts during the first centuries were from the slave and lower classes. Moreover, Christianity fundamentally changed the way women were treated.

Christianity also spread rapidly because of the Roman Empire and the **Pax Romana**. Rome was an extremely efficient and well-organized empire. In order to facilitate trade and travel, Rome had constructed excellent roads to every major section of its empire. Thus, missionaries could easily reach distant places. In addition, because Rome was at peace, missionaries could travel safely without fear of invading armies. Rome also had a very efficient police force, so there was little crime. Furthermore, almost everyone spoke Latin, so everywhere the missionaries went in the empire, people understood them. The *Pax Romana* provided one of the few times in history when such large-scale conversions could have occurred.

The sixth reason the Faith succeeded and spread was the Church's own internal structure. The Catholic Church, then as now, is one of the best-organized institutions in history. The visible head of the Church is the pope, the successor of Peter and the Bishop of Rome. All the other bishops refer matters of faith and morals to him, and they acknowledge that his decisions in these matters are final. The great Christian centers of the early Church, like Antioch, Ephesus, and Carthage, were closely linked with Rome, the center of Catholic religious life. Despite the Church's vast size, each community was organized into a diocese led by a bishop. The bishop had a group of priests and deacons to assist him.

50   Chapter 4: The Church Overcomes Heresy and Paganism

Reasons Christianity Should Not Have Succeeded

Despite the reasons for Christianity's success, it surely would have failed, had Our Lord not founded it. The Roman Empire, with its structure, power, and armed legions, was a force that *no purely human institution* could withstand. The *Pax Romana* existed because *Rome had destroyed all of its enemies*. Rome had almost unlimited power and resources to turn against its opponents. If Christianity had simply been another pagan religion, it would have been destroyed almost immediately. For almost three hundred years, becoming a Christian exposed a person to torture and death. Such a commitment required a degree of heroism that seems impossible to imagine. Despite the fact that untold thousands suffered and died at the hands of the Romans, more and more people continued to convert. The only plausible explanation is grace and the Holy Spirit. Only a Church founded by God Himself in the Person of Jesus Christ could have survived this dreadful onslaught.

A second reason that Christianity should not have succeeded was its position on equality. The Church argued that both slave and master were equal in the sight of God. While this attitude helped the Church with the lower classes, it hurt the Church among the nobility.

Christianity also should not have succeeded because the Romans viewed it as being intolerant of other religions. Christianity proclaimed that it was the one and only true religion, at a time when pagans worshiped a variety of gods in a variety of religions and sects. Christianity wanted to abolish paganism and replace pantheism with monotheism. The Romans hated Christians for their intolerance and "atheism."

The perceived intolerance of Christians also extended to their refusal to worship the emperor. This created an obstacle that was both religious and political. The Church taught that only God was divine and entitled to worship—not pagan gods, nor the emperor of Rome. Therefore, Christians could not worship the emperor without committing a mortal sin. As a result, the Romans considered Christians to be not only atheists and heretics but also enemies of the State who were guilty of treason.

A fifth reason that the Faith should not have spread is that the Romans had crucified Christ, its Founder. The

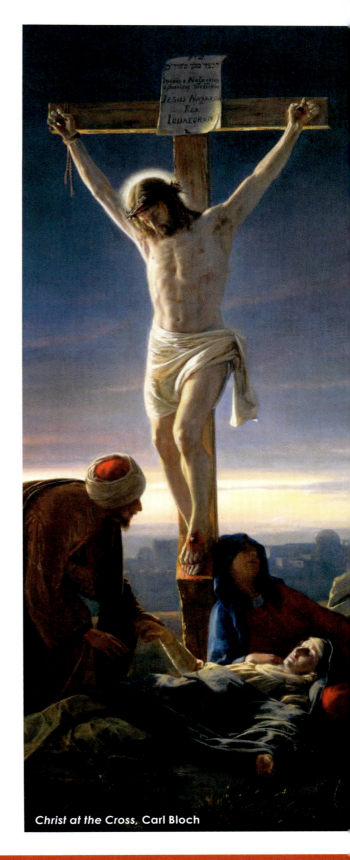

Christ at the Cross, Carl Bloch

Witness to the Faith 51

The Burial of St. Lawrence

manner and circumstances of Our Lord's death created a twofold obstacle to the spread of the Faith, especially among the nobility. The Romans crucified only slaves and dangerous criminals. Christ had been charged and found guilty of rebelling against Roman rule. It was almost impossible for a Roman aristocrat to join a religion that had been founded by someone like that.

The final impediment to the spread of the Faith—then, as it is now—was the number of lies that enemies of the Church spread about Catholicism. As noted, the apologists tried to answer these attacks; however, they had only limited success. Moreover, because Christians were being persecuted, they had to meet in secret, often at night. This created an opportunity for the Church's enemies to fabricate wild charges, claiming that all manner of immoral activities were taking place during the Christians' "secret" rituals.

The Church Explains Her Fundamental Doctrines

In the Church's earliest days, she needed to explain her doctrines in the simplest terms, because most of her members were not well educated. Most converts were slaves or from the lower classes of society. Even most of the Apostles, like St. Peter and St. Andrew, were not well-educated men. However, the Church still taught the basics of the Faith. The Church taught that Jesus Christ, the Second Person of the Blessed Trinity, had become Man and had suffered and died to redeem men and women and restore the blessings they had lost because of Original Sin. The Church taught that Christ, while on Earth, had established a Church, the Catholic Church, which would last until the end of time, and that the gates of Hell would not prevail against it. Christ had promised that the Holy Spirit would dwell in that Church to ensure that it would remain free from error and to guide the Church to achieve a complete understanding of Our Lord's teachings.

Even during the Roman persecutions, the early Church Fathers wrote about the Faith and began to explain Catholic doctrine, both to pagans and to their fellow Christians. The Church has always encouraged its theologians to seek a deeper understanding of the Faith and its doctrines. When the persecutions ended, more theologians began thinking about the Faith. The Church taught then, as now, that the truth has nothing to fear from analysis and discussion. In fact, the Church encourages it. The Church has always believed that the better people know and understand their Faith, the more they can influence those around them, defend the Faith, and make new converts.

However, the Church also has always taught that she herself is the final authority on matters of faith and morals. While debate and inquiry are good, when a theologian begins teaching error, the Church *must* correct that error. Sometimes theologians listen; sometimes they

52 Chapter 4: The Church Overcomes Heresy and Paganism

do not and cause great damage. One of the first theologians to cause great damage was a man named Arius.

The Arian Heresy

Two of the most fundamental teachings of the Catholic Church are the Holy Trinity and the Incarnation. The Holy Trinity is the belief that there is one God in three divine Persons: Father, Son, and Holy Spirit. The Incarnation is the belief that Jesus Christ, the Second Person of the Holy Trinity, became Man but also retained His divine nature.

In 318, a Libyan priest named Arius began to preach an erroneous doctrine about Christ. Arius denied that Jesus was God in the same way that the Father was God. Arius claimed that Jesus was not eternal or of the same substance as God the Father. In fact, Arius said that Christ was only a human being. At this point, the Church had not *officially* defined this teaching. Arius was very intelligent, educated, and eloquent. At times, he used his gifts to conceal the true meaning of his words. His idea fascinated many Christians, and many lapsed into heresy with him. Although his bishop condemned him and excommunicated him and his followers, his heresy quickly spread. Soon there were Arians all over the world.

Arius

The Council of Nicaea

In a very few years, the Arian heresy had become a serious problem, which threatened the salvation of untold numbers of Christians. In 325, Emperor Constantine felt that the situation had become so dangerous that he had to intervene. To settle the dispute, he suggested that the Church hold a general council. With the consent of Pope Sylvester, Constantine summoned all the bishops of the Church together at Nicaea in Asia Minor. Because of his advanced age, Pope Sylvester could not attend. Therefore, Bishop Hosius of Cordova, Spain, presided over the council as the pope's representative. Initially, 250 bishops attended the council. However, before the council held its last session, this number had grown to 318.

Pope Sylvester

Emperor Constantine at the Council in Nicaea

Witness to the Faith 53

General Council
A council in which the bishops of the Catholic Church from throughout the world meet to discuss or define matters of Church doctrine.

National Council
A council including only the bishops of a particular country.

Nicene Creed
The creed, formulated at Nicaea, which we recite at Mass. It states clearly that Jesus is "begotten, not made, consubstantial with the Father."

Arianism
One of the early heresies, started by a Libyan priest named Arius, who taught that Jesus was only a human being, not divine.

Saint Athanasius

The Council of Nicaea was a **general council**—that is, a council in which the bishops of the Catholic Church from throughout the world meet to discuss or define matters of Church doctrine. It differs from a **national council**, which includes only the bishops of a particular country, such as the United States. The Council of Nicaea had been called to address the question of the nature of Christ that had been caused by the Arian heresy. The council clearly defined the nature of Our Lord Jesus Christ and His relation to the Father. It created the profession of faith known as the **Nicene Creed**, which we recite at Mass. According to the Nicene Creed, Jesus Christ is "the Only Begotten Son of God, born of the Father before all ages." He is "God from God, Light from Light, true God from true God, begotten, not made, consubstantial with the Father...." In other words, Jesus Christ is God, made of the same substance as the Father. He is fully God, not merely a human creature.

After the council, Constantine exiled Arius and many of his followers. Unfortunately, despite the clear decrees of the council, Arius continued to spread his heretical teachings. Moreover, because the seeds he had planted ran deep, it was difficult for the Church to root out this heresy and eliminate it, even after his death. Thus, the Arian heresy plagued the Church for decades.

Although the Church taught the truth, it needed the help of the State to control the spread of these errors. Unfortunately, some of the emperors who succeeded Constantine actually believed that it was politically advantageous to promote **Arianism**. Other emperors worked to support the true Faith and sent the Arians into exile. However, it is difficult to suppress an idea. Even in exile, the Arians, many of whom genuinely believed that what they taught was true, continued to spread their heretical notions. Many of the barbarian tribes were converted by Arians and accepted an Arian version of Christianity. In fact, an Arian bishop baptized Constantine on his deathbed.

St. Athanasius

Despite his earlier efforts to defeat it, Emperor Constantine deserves much of the blame for the later success of Arianism. He permitted Arius to return to Alexandria from exile. However, so often when the Church faces a great peril, Our Lord calls forth a champion, who, often alone, stands in the breach between the Church and her enemies. In this moment, that man was St. Athanasius, the new bishop of Alexandria. The story of the battle against the Arian heresy now becomes that of St. Athanasius—embattled, exiled, often unaided, but never defeated.

Constantine had ordered Arius into exile, but Arius deceived him into thinking that he was no longer a heretic. Thus, Constantine ordered Athanasius to restore Arius to his former position in the Church. While Arius might have fooled the emperor, he did not fool St. Athanasius. Athanasius absolutely refused to allow Arius to re-enter Alexandria. Because he refused an imperial order, in 335 Constantine ordered

Athanasius Sent into Exile, by Otto Bitschnau

THE SONS OF CONSTANTINE

Constantine II

Constans

Constantius

Athanasius exiled to Trier. The next year, after stopping briefly in Alexandria, Arius was triumphantly escorted into Constantinople. However, he died suddenly. The people saw his sudden death as God's justice for his heresy.

By this time, Athanasius had become the most well-known person in the Christian world and the implacable enemy of the Arian heresy. Because the Arians had been unable to break his will or convince him that they were correct, they sought to destroy his character by spreading the most wild lies about him. Among their charges, they accused him of murdering Bishop Arsenius and cutting off his dead hand to perform magic rituals. They said he tried to stop ships carrying food from sailing from Alexandria to Constantinople. He easily answered these charges at a synod that Constantine convened at Tyre. Bishop Arsenius appeared there, alive—with both his hands.

Following Constantine's death in 337, Athanasius returned to Alexandria, where his parishioners enthusiastically welcomed him home. However, the Arians continued to oppose him. They forcibly, and unlawfully, installed an Arian as bishop. At this point, the new emperor, Constans, intervened. Realizing that this was an ecclesiastical matter, he urged the pope to seek a resolution. In 340, Pope Julius I (337-352) wrote to the Arians in Alexandria, urging them to allow Athanasius to take his rightful see. When they refused, Pope Julius convened a council in Rome later that year. The fifty bishops in attendance unanimously acquitted Athanasius of all the charges against him and declared that he was the rightful bishop of Alexandria.

In 343, Pope Julius called for a larger Church council, which met in Serdica (present-day Sofia, Bulgaria). Perhaps as many as 300

Witness to the Faith

The Persecution of Athanasius, by Otto Bitschnau

Pope Liberius

bishops from both the East and the West attended. Once again, Bishop Hosius of Cordoba presided. The Council of Serdica upheld the decision of the Council of Rome and reiterated the teachings of the Council of Nicaea. It seemed like this should have been the final word on the matter. However, the Arians refused to accept the council's decrees.

The Council of Milan

As previously noted, upon Constantine's death, his three sons divided his empire, each ruling a different part. However, like most co-emperors, the brothers did not work well together and fought one another for sole control. Two of the three sons, Constantine II and Constans, were orthodox Catholics. However, the third son, Constantius, was an Arian.

Following the Council of Serdica, under pressure from his brothers, Constantius allowed Athanasius to return to Alexandria and serve as bishop. However, he made it clear that he was doing this as a "favor" to his brothers, not because of anything that the Church councils had decreed. Nevertheless, for almost the next decade, Athanasius governed the Church in Alexandria more or less peacefully.

In 350, Constantius became sole ruler of the empire. Soon he began working in support of Arianism and against Athanasius. In 353, Constantius called a council in Arles, where the members, fearing for their lives, voted to condemn Athanasius. However, the new pope, Liberius (352-366), refused to accept the council's decrees. Liberius demanded that another council be held to investigate the situation.

In 355, Constantius convoked a council at Milan with the explicit purpose of condemning Athanasius and affirming Arianism. When the three hundred bishops in attendance protested that the emperor had no right to call a council or present them with a formulation of faith or a charge of condemnation against a fellow bishop, Constantius became furious. He declared that his will was canon law. He threatened that any bishop who refused to accept the Arian creed and the condemnation of Athanasius would be exiled or killed. Lest anyone question his sincerity, his drawn sword removed all doubts. In the face of almost certain death, only a handful of those present refused the emperor's demands. The rest agreed.

Constantius Persecutes Athanasius

Feeling that he had won a great victory, Constantius took his decrees and presented them to the pope. However, Pope Liberius knew that the

---

56   *Chapter 4: The Church Overcomes Heresy and Paganism*

bishops had only agreed to approve the decrees under duress at sword point. He would not accept them. Constantius threatened the pope with exile if he continued to refuse. After giving the pope three days to decide, the emperor banished Liberius to Berea in Thrace. Additional attempted bribes and threats also had no impact on Liberius.

Constantius next ordered the arrest of St. Athanasius. Some sources indicate that he sent as many as five thousand soldiers to arrest the holy bishop. While Athanasius said Mass in his cathedral, the soldiers surrounded it. However, as they entered the cathedral to arrest him, he escaped. With the help of Egyptian monks, Athanasius hid in the desert and avoided capture for the next six years. During this time, he remained the rightful bishop of Alexandria and wrote a number of works, including a history of Arianism. Meanwhile, Constantius unlawfully declared an Arian to be the bishop of Alexandria.

Julian the Apostate

In November 361, Constantius died. A man named Julian, who would be known in history as Julian the Apostate, succeeded him. Although Julian had been raised a Catholic, his tutor had been a pagan who exerted a great influence over the young man. When Julian became emperor, he proclaimed that he was a pagan. Moreover, he was determined to restore paganism to the Roman Empire. He decreed that paganism was once again the official religion of the Roman Empire, and he offered government jobs and benefits to any Christian who denied the Catholic Faith. He even tried to force people to sacrifice to pagan gods. However, paganism was well and truly dead. Only a few people became pagan, mostly for personal gain.

In 362, Julian declared war on the Persians, who had been attacking the eastern part of the empire. Julian made Antioch his headquarters for the campaign against the Persians. While in Antioch, Julian decided that he would try to invalidate Christ's prophecy in Matthew 24, which Titus had fulfilled when he had destroyed the Temple in 70 A.D. To that end, Julian began to rebuild the Temple of Jerusalem. However, the attempt was a complete failure. Globes of fire continually burst from the Earth near the construction site, making construction impossible.

During the Battle of Samarra in 363, the Persians killed Julian. Tradition records that his last words were, "Galilean, thou hast conquered." While likely not really spoken by him, they do form a fitting epitaph for a man who foolishly tried to destroy the Church and refute the prophecies of Our Lord.

At the start of his reign, Julian had allowed orthodox bishops, whom Constantius had exiled, to return to their dioceses. He allowed this, not to help the Church, but because he believed that if the orthodox bishops and the Arian bishops were fighting each other, it would help spread paganism. However, Athanasius urged all Christians to work together in the face of Julian's persecution. His call for unity foiled Julian's plan and angered him. Therefore, Julian exiled him.

Coin Depicting Julian the Apostate

Jovian

Coin Depicting Valens

Coin Depicting Valentinian

Following Julian's death, the Roman army quickly elected Jovian, their commander, as emperor. Jovian immediately restored Christianity to its former status and abolished paganism. The few pagans recanted and returned to the Christian fold. Jovian asked Athanasius to come to Antioch to teach him more about the Faith. However, Jovian ruled for less than a year, before he died under rather mysterious circumstances.

The Last Years of St. Athanasius

Following the death of Jovian, Valentinian (364-375), an orthodox Catholic, became emperor. He appointed his brother Valens (364-375) to be his co-emperor in the East, while he ruled the West. Valens, unlike Valentinian, did everything possible to restore Arianism in his domain. He persecuted orthodox Catholics and issued a decree ordering orthodox bishops, whom Jovian had allowed to return, including Athanasius, back into exile. However, the people of Alexandria rose up in defense of the saint, and Valens, fearing a popular uprising, allowed Athanasius to remain.

Athanasius spent the remaining six years of his life in the midst of his flock. He dedicated his final years to repairing the damage that had occurred during his various exiles and the unlawful imposition of Arian bishops. He returned to his writing and preaching undisturbed. On May 2, 373, St. Athanasius, who had fought the good fight and kept the Faith in the face of all adversity, died quietly in his own home.

The Three Cappadocians

Following the death of Athanasius, a new generation of champions stepped forward to defend the Faith. These were St. Basil of Caesarea, his brother St. Gregory of Nyssa, and their friend St. Gregory of Nazianzus. Because all three were from Cappadocia (Asia Minor), they are known as the Three Cappadocians.

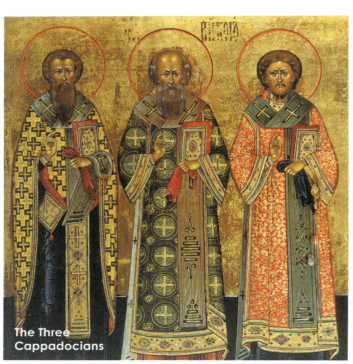

The Three Cappadocians

St. Basil (329-379) was born in Caesarea in 329. As a young man, he attended school in Athens along with his friend St. Gregory of Nazianzus and, interestingly enough, Julian the Apostate. Around 356, he made a pilgrimage to Palestine and Syria, where he lived with the monks of those regions. Upon returning home, he founded a small religious community. Over the next years, he became more drawn to the religious life. He became a deacon, and in 364 was ordained a priest. Six years later, he became the archbishop of Caesarea.

Once Basil became archbishop, Emperor Valens attempted to bribe and coerce him to compromise with the Arians. However, Basil refused. It became apparent that the only

Chapter 4: The Church Overcomes Heresy and Paganism

way to stop Basil from promoting the Catholic Faith and refuting Arianism would be to kill him—something the emperor was unwilling to do. Basil outlived Valens by one year, never having compromised.

Basil's main theological writings defend the Church against Arianism. He also wrote a famous treatise on the Holy Spirit and an account of creation. Many of his homilies still exist as well.

Unlike his friend Basil, St. Gregory of Nazianzus (330-390) seemed unsuited for the role of a bishop and missionary, yet that is exactly what he became. More suited for the life of a monk, he lived for a time with St. Basil at his religious community. However, before long, Gregory had to abandon his quiet lifestyle to help the elderly bishop of Nazianzus run his diocese. In 361, he was ordained a priest. Nine years later, when the bishop of Caesarea died, the priests of the diocese elected Gregory to replace him.

In 378, Valens died. Theodosius, a strongly orthodox Catholic, became emperor. St. Basil and other Church leaders knew that they needed a strong voice to cleanse Constantinople of its Arian influence. Basil recommended his good friend Gregory Nazianzus, who in 379 became bishop of Constantinople. When Gregory arrived, most of the city adhered to Arianism. However, after only a few years, his sermons began to turn the tide, and more than half the city returned to the true Faith.

Gregory of Nyssa (335-395) did not receive the more expensive education that his brother Basil did. However, he did receive a good education from his mother, who homeschooled him. With this background, he became a great philosopher and teacher of rhetoric. It seems that Gregory married, but after the death of his wife, he became a priest. In 372, the priests of Nyssa elected him bishop. Among his works, Gregory of Nyssa wrote a long defense of the Faith against the Arian heresy. He also wrote a catechism explaining the basic teachings of the Catholic Faith.

The Mass of St. Basil, Subleyras

The Council of Constantinople

The Arian heresy lasted so long mainly because of the support of various emperors. The death of Valens in 378 really spelled the end of Arianism, especially when Theodosius (379-395) succeeded him as emperor in the East. Gratian, an orthodox Catholic emperor, already ruled in the West. The second ecumenical council of Constantinople began to write "the end" to the Arian heresy.

Emperor Theodosius

Witness to the Faith 59

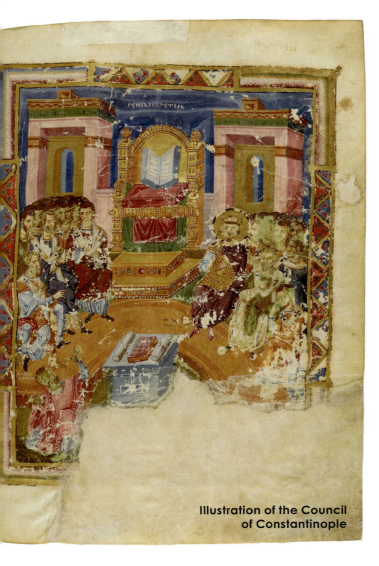

Illustration of the Council of Constantinople

The preaching of St. Gregory of Nazianzus, with its great influence in Constantinople, was another factor in the decline of Arianism. After arriving in Constantinople, Gregory of Nazianzus began preaching a series of sermons clearly setting forth the Church's position on the Holy Trinity and the Incarnation. In addition to causing massive conversions, these sermons also defined critical points of dogma.

In 381, Theodosius convened a council at Constantinople, which 150 bishops from the Eastern empire attended. St. Gregory of Nazianzus presided over the council. In order to end the Arian heresy, the council declared directly that it completely agreed with the Council of Nicaea and accepted the Nicene Creed. Moreover, it created a creed to supplement the Nicene Creed in matters pertaining to the Holy Spirit. However, the words the council fathers used to describe the manner in which the Holy Spirit proceeds from the Father and the Son lacked precision. The Catholics of the West used the words "who proceeds from the Father *and* the Son," in the creed. Those in the East preferred to use the phrase, "who proceeds from the Father *through* the Son." Correctly understood, both statements are orthodox. Nevertheless, these initial differences caused a dispute over the word *Filioque* (Latin, meaning "and the Son"). Although Arianism would continue to infect the barbarian tribes, the Council of Constantinople marked the beginning of the end of Arianism in the Roman Empire.

The End of Paganism

As Arianism finally disappeared in the East, so too did paganism die out in the West. The Edict of Milan had granted toleration of Christianity, but also to other sects, including paganism. A few members of the Roman aristocracy and high government officials remained pagans, but even Julian had been unable to revive it in any meaningful form. In 375, Gratian (375-383) became emperor. With the help of St. Ambrose (340-397), the bishop of Milan, Gratian actively began working to

Gratian

Magnus Maximus

Valentinian II

60 *Chapter 4: The Church Overcomes Heresy and Paganism*

sever the link between paganism and the government that had existed for hundreds of years. For example, he removed the pagan statue of Victory from the Roman senate, over the objection of the senators. He also abolished all the privileges of the pagan priesthood. In 383, supporters of his rival, Magnus Maximus (384-388), assassinated Gratian.

St. Ambrose negotiated a compromise that allowed Valentinian II, Gratian's brother, to rule Italy, while Maximus governed Gaul, Spain, and Britain.

Emperor Theodosius was the man who finally declared that Nicene Christianity (that is, orthodox Catholicism) was the official religion of the Roman Empire. He made this declaration on February 27, 380, in the **Edict of Thessalonica**. The next year, he issued a decree that forbade any Christian from becoming a pagan and that made various pagan acts illegal. In 390, Theodosius declared the Catholic Faith to be the faith of the Roman Empire, in both the East and the West. The next year, he issued another decree, fining anyone who entered a pagan temple. The following year, he forbade the worship of the pagan gods in private homes.

In 423, Emperor Theodosius II declared that there were almost no pagans left in his domain. "Galilean, Thou has conquered."

St. Ambrose Absolving Theodosius, Pierre Subleyras

Oral Exercises

1. List six causes for the spread of the Catholic Faith.
2. List six reasons why the Faith might not have succeeded.
3. What was the Arian heresy?
4. What did the Council of Nicaea proclaim?
5. Who called the Council of Milan, and why?
6. Name the Three Cappadocians.
7. What emperor issued the decrees that finally brought an end to paganism?

Edict of Thessalonica
The decree that made Nicene Christianity (that is, orthodox Catholicism) the official religion of the Roman Empire; issued by Emperor Theodosius in 380.

Witness to the Faith

Chapter 5
The Church Begins to Build a Catholic Society – Christendom

Christendom

At the beginning of the fourth century, the Edict of Milan granted the Church protection from persecution. As the fourth century progressed, the Church received greater protection and support from the empire. No longer fearing for its existence, the Church began to establish and build a truly Catholic society: **Christendom**. During the fourth century, the Holy Spirit blessed the Church with some of her greatest saints: St. John Chrysostom, St. Ambrose, St. Jerome, and St. Augustine. These men, and others like them, would lay the foundation for a Christian society that would last for over 1,000 years.

St. John Chrysostom

St. John Chrysostom

St. John Chrysostom was born in Antioch around 349 to a wealthy and noble family. Although his family's connections guaranteed him a successful life in the secular world, he chose instead to dedicate himself to the religious life. He began studying for the priesthood under the bishop of Antioch. In 381, he was ordained a deacon and then a priest. Shortly after becoming a priest, he wrote a famous treatise *On the Priesthood*. Over the next decade, St. John preached the beautiful homilies that earned him the nickname *Chrysostom* (Latin, meaning "Golden Mouthed") because of his great eloquence.

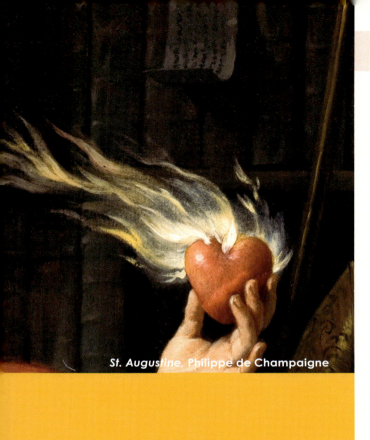
St. Augustine, Philippe de Champaigne

335 A.D. – 430 A.D.

335 A.D.
St. Athanasius, exiled at Trier, introduces monasticism into the West.

356 A.D.
Death of St. Anthony, considered the father of early monasticism.

361 A.D.
St. Martin founds the first monastery in Gaul at Liguge, one of the oldest monasteries ever founded.

374 A.D.
Ambrose becomes bishop of Milan.

382-405 A.D.
St. Jerome creates a Latin translation of the Bible known as the Vulgate.

387 A.D.
Augustine is baptized on Easter Sunday.

403 A.D.
At the "Synod of the Oak," the enemies of St. John Chrysostom, egged on by Empress Eudoxia, level false charges against him and exile him from his diocese; but soon after, an earthquake frightens the empress into allowing him back for a time. Pope Innocent I later declares the acts of this "synod" to be invalid.

428-432 A.D.
Nestorius claims that Our Lady should not be called "Mother of God," because she gave birth only to the human nature of Jesus, a distinct person from God the Son. His views are opposed by St. Cyril of Alexandria and condemned by Pope Celestine, the Council of Ephesus, and Pope Sixtus III.

430 A.D.
St. Augustine dies at Hippo, while Genseric's Vandals are besieging it.

In 397, the patriarch of Constantinople died. St. John was chosen to replace him. The common people of Constantinople loved his beautiful sermons. However, when St. John began to reform the conduct of the clergy and preach against the immorality and the lavish excesses of the imperial court, he faced opposition. Sometime around 402, matters came to a head when St. John preached a sermon on the worldliness of the imperial court. The homily offended Empress Eudoxia, who felt—probably rightly—that John meant the sermon for her.

Eudoxia, who for the most part seems to have supported orthodoxy over Arianism, was unwilling to accept St. John's loving correction. Instead, the empress recruited Theophilus, the bishop of Alexandria and St. John's enemy, in an attempt to remove St. John from his position as patriarch. In 403, Theophilus

Witness to the Faith 63

called the "Synod of the Oak" in Chalcedon. John's enemies leveled a number of false charges against him. Based on these false charges, Eudoxia removed St. John from his position and exiled him. However, Eudoxia's minions had not taken the saint very far before an earthquake shook the city. Fearing that the earthquake represented God's wrath, she begged John to return to Constantinople and continue as patriarch.

Empress Eudoxia's fear of the Lord did not last long. Two months later, she erected a silver statue of herself on the cathedral grounds. John Chrystostom publicly scolded the empress. He noted that the placement of a secular statue on sacred ground was inappropriate and amounted to sacrilege. Once again, Eudoxia failed to take St, John's correction repentantly, and she ordered him removed from his clerical position and sent into exile.

In 405, St. John Chrysostom wrote to Pope Innocent I (401-417), asking for his help with the empress. In response to St. John's plea, Pope Innocent declared the acts of the Synod of the Oak to be invalid. He also reprimanded Theophilus for mistreating St. John. Finally, Innocent demanded that Eudoxia allow John to return from exile. However, Eudoxia refused to comply with the pope's command. John remained in exile for the rest of his life.

> **Supreme Authority in the Church**
>
> That the patriarch of Constantinople, St. John Chrysostom, would ask the pope for assistance bears witness that John recognized the pope as the supreme authority in the Church.

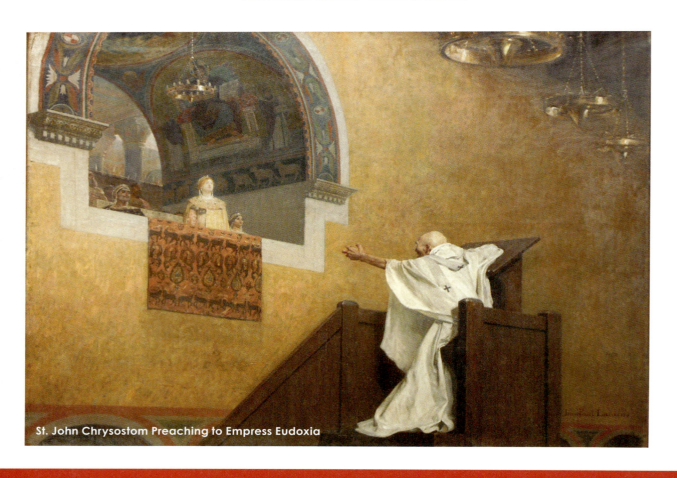

St. John Chrysostom Preaching to Empress Eudoxia

Chapter 5: The Church Begins to Build a Catholic Society – Christendom

In fact, because St. John wrote letters to the Church in Constantinople from exile, his enemies, fearing that he still had influence in the city, decided to remove him *even farther* from the city. The emperor banished him to what is today Georgia, in eastern Europe. However, the nearly 60-year-old saint never reached the site of his new exile. He died on the journey on September 14, 407.

St. Ambrose

While St. John Chrysostom was fighting imperial power and excesses in the East, St. Ambrose, the great bishop of Milan, was fighting for the rights of the Church in the West. St. Ambrose was born at Trier to Christian parents around 340. His father was the governor of the province of Gaul, a massive territory encompassing present-day France, Spain, and Britain. His mother was a member of the Roman nobility.

After his father's death, Ambrose went to Rome, where he studied law and rhetoric. With his legal background, he then joined the imperial government. In 372, Ambrose was appointed governor of northern Italy. His headquarters were in Milan. Over the next two years, he governed his territory well, and all the people under his authority recognized his excellent leadership qualities.

In 374, the bishop of Milan, who was an Arian, died. His death caused a nasty fight to break out between the Catholics and the Arians over who would succeed him as bishop. In order to restore peace, Ambrose went to Milan's cathedral, where the election for the new bishop was to occur. When he finished his appeal for harmony, someone in the crowd called out, "Let Ambrose be our bishop!" Immediately, the entire crowd began calling for Ambrose to be bishop.

Ambrose protested that he was only a catechumen; he had not yet been baptized. He pointed out that his background was in the law; he had not studied theology. He had not trained or prepared to be a priest, much less a bishop. Nevertheless, the people of Milan insisted that they wanted him, and unanimously voted to make him bishop.

Ambrose actually was a good choice for both Arians and Catholics. Although the people of Milan knew Ambrose was an orthodox Catholic, the Arians knew he governed with justice and charity. For that reason, they trusted that he would be a fair bishop.

Unable to overcome the will of the people, and undoubtedly God's Will, Ambrose consented. Within eight

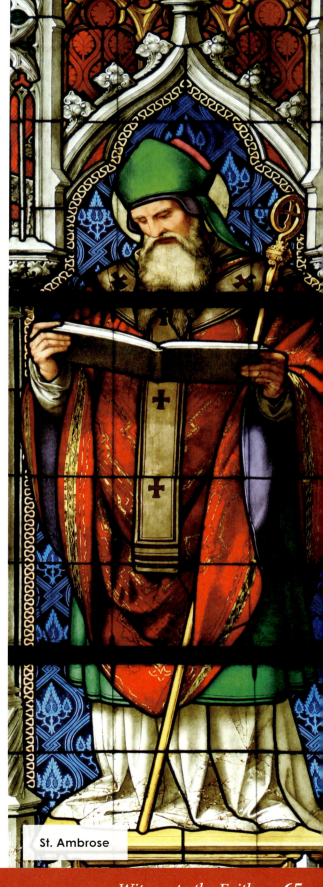

St. Ambrose

Witness to the Faith

St. Ambrose and Emperor Theodosius, Peter Paul Rubens

Christendom
The reign of Christ among men, embodied in a Christian society, such as took shape in Europe in the second half of the first millennium and lasted a thousand years.

days, he received all the necessary sacraments. He was baptized, ordained a priest, and consecrated as bishop.

Ambrose realized that he had not received the training necessary to be the leader of a great Catholic diocese like Milan. Therefore, he devoted himself to studying the Bible and the Church Fathers. He studied, not to become a great Biblical scholar, but that he might be a better pastor to his flock. He desired to be able to understand the Faith so that he could communicate it. His efforts paid off, and he became a great preacher and teacher, although throughout his tenure as bishop of Milan, his natural ability to lead remained his strongest asset.

As noted in the previous chapter, St. Ambrose worked closely with Emperor Gratian to overthrow paganism in the Western empire. Once he had accomplished that, Ambrose began the work of creating a Christian society and government to replace the pagan one. For more than a thousand years, the governments of Western Europe would actively support and promote the Catholic Faith. Catholicism would unite Europe. This united Catholic Europe was known as **Christendom** (the reign of Christ among men, embodied in a Christian society). In Christendom, the State would manage secular affairs such as collecting taxes, building roads and bridges, and waging war. However, all members of Christendom, even kings and emperors, had to answer to the Church in matters of faith and morals.

In 390, a rebellion broke out at Thessalonica. Rioters murdered the governor and several other leading citizens. Emperor Theodosius was justifiably furious at the murder of his governor and other subjects. However, he acted rashly. He had the people of Thessalonica rounded up in the city arena, where imperial soldiers massacred seven thousand unarmed people. St. Ambrose immediately sent a letter to the emperor commanding that he make a public penance, under pain of excommunication. Theodosius submitted to St. Ambrose.

Ambrose's actions in this incident revealed a strength that few people possess. Ambrose had no protection from Theodosius, who, although basically a good Catholic, could have either exiled or killed Ambrose. Clearly, in the heat of the moment, Theodosius was capable of impulsive actions. Ambrose's writings also reveal this strength of character. The hymns Ambrose wrote made a strong impression on St. Augustine. St. Ambrose is credited with inspiring Augustine to become Catholic. Although not especially known for his writing, Ambrose did pen some short spiritual articles. His most important work is "Duties of Sacred Ministers," in which he explains the rules for the priestly life.

St. Ambrose died in Milan on April 4, 397. He was buried in Milan, in the church named in his honor. Every year, hundreds of thousands of visitors honor the great saint who stood up to an emperor.

St. Jerome

While St. Ambrose may not have received the education necessary to become a priest, such was not the case for his contemporary, St. Jerome. Of all the Church Fathers in the West, none was better educated than St. Jerome. He knew Latin, Greek, and Hebrew, and he had a working knowledge of Chaldaic and Aramaic.

St. Jerome was born to wealthy Christian parents in Dalmatia sometime between 340 and 347. (Historians are uncertain of the exact date.) Because his parents wished him to receive the finest education, they sent him to Rome when he was about 12. There, he studied philosophy and learned Latin. He remained in Rome until he was about 20.

Leaving Rome, Jerome traveled with friends to Gaul, Syria, and then to Asia Minor, finally settling in Antioch. During this period, Jerome began studying theology in addition to his study of secular subjects. In 373, Jerome had a vision in which God directed him to set aside his secular education and concentrate on his religious studies. Seeking peace and time for contemplation, he moved to the desert and lived in a monastery near Antioch. He learned Hebrew and began translating the Hebrew Bible into Greek.

Although Jerome seems to have preferred to remain a monk, God was calling him to the priesthood. Sometime around 378, after Jerome returned to Antioch, the bishop of Antioch ordained him a priest. He then left for Constantinople, where for the next several years he studied Scripture under St. Gregory Nazianzus.

By 382, Jerome's holiness and knowledge had gained the attention of Pope Damasus I (366-384). Damasus was greatly concerned about ensuring the accuracy of the Bible in terms of both its content and its translation. In 382, he called the Council of Rome, which determined the official list of the books of the Bible. That same year, Pope Damasus commissioned Jerome to translate the Bible into Latin, a task that would consume the next twenty-three years of Jerome's life.

Jerome's knowledge of Hebrew provided him with an excellent understanding of the Hebrew Scriptures. Also, since he spoke Greek and Latin, he could decide which of the Greek and Latin translations were best. Because he was writing in Latin, the "vulgar" (common) language at the time, his version of the Bible became known as the **Vulgate** (from the Latin *editio vulgate*, meaning "common version"). Since the sixth century, the *Vulgate* has been the official Latin text of the Bible.

In addition to its religious impact, the Vulgate had a major impact on the development of the Latin language. St. Jerome had a unique writing style. It was so simple and clear that everyone could read it. As a result, everyone who could read Latin read the Vulgate. Thus, it influenced daily speaking and writing.

According to tradition, in the summer of 388, Jerome returned to Bethlehem in the Holy Land and moved into the cave where Our Lord

> **Vulgate**
> The Latin translation of the Bible produced by St. Jerome, called the "Vulgate" because Latin was the common (or "vulgar") language.

St. Jerome, Memling

Portrayal of St. Jerome

Artists often portray Jerome outside a cave or working inside one because of the belief that Jerome spent his last years in a cave in Bethlehem.

Witness to the Faith   67

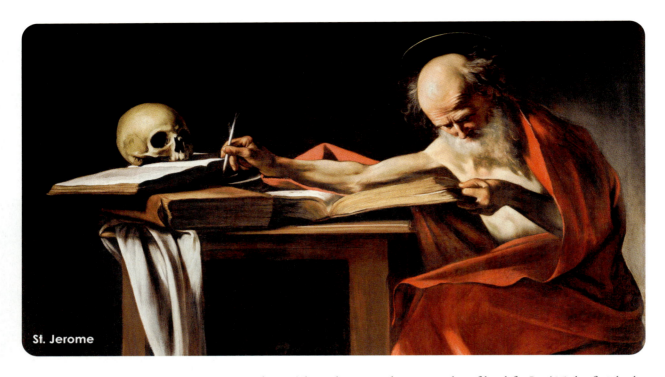

St. Jerome

St. Augustine and St. Monica, Ary Scheffer

was born. There, he spent the remainder of his life. In 405, he finished the Vulgate. For the remaining fifteen years of his life, Jerome wrote commentaries on the Vulgate, explaining why he made the choices he did in the translation. He died on September 30, 420.

St. Augustine

Of all the Fathers of the Church, none seemed less likely to achieve that distinction than Aurelius Augustinus, better known as St. Augustine. Augustine was born on November 13, 354, in northern Africa (present-day Algeria) to Roman parents. His mother Monica was a devout Christian, but his father was a pagan, and would not allow his wife to baptize Augustine or their other two children. However, she did instruct him in the Faith. In fact, all her life, Monica prayed for her son and his conversion. She would remain the most important person in his life until her death.

When Augustine was 11, his parents sent him to a local school, where he learned about Latin literature but also about paganism. When he was 17, he went to Carthage, where he studied rhetoric and continued studying the Latin classics. Augustine's time in Carthage created in him a great love of learning that lasted his entire life. On the other hand, during this time, he strayed from the moral way of life that St. Monica had taught him.

Chapter 5: The Church Begins to Build a Catholic Society – Christendom

Following the completion of his studies, Augustine taught rhetoric in Carthage and Rome. In 384, he obtained the prestigious position of professor of rhetoric at the imperial court in Milan. There, Augustine met the second most important person in his life, St. Ambrose.

Until then, religion had not played a major part in Augustine's life. Mainly, he had studied secular philosophy and literature. However, his mother's prayers and urgings began to stir his soul. In Milan, he began attending Mass, where he heard the sermons of St. Ambrose. Perhaps, in the beginning, he went to see Ambrose just to judge his rhetorical style as a fellow rhetorician. However, these homilies so impressed Augustine that he continued to attend Mass. Soon the two men became close friends. In fact, Augustine, in his autobiography *Confessions*, writes that Ambrose received him as a father.

Augustine's relationship with Ambrose caused him to begin a serious study of Catholicism. Augustine abandoned his worldly lifestyle and began living as a good Catholic. In August 386, he had a conversion experience. As he recounts in his *Confessions*, he heard a voice calling out to him to "take up and read." He believed he was meant to read his Bible, which lay close by. He opened the Bible and read a passage from the *Letter to the Romans* where St. Paul explains how Christ offers salvation. On Easter Sunday in 387, St. Ambrose baptized Augustine. The Church had gained one of its greatest champions.

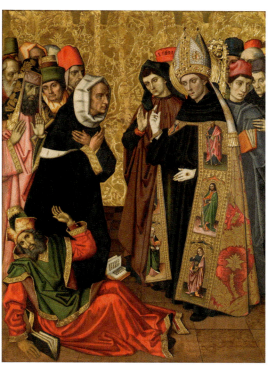

***St. Augustine Disputing with the Heretics**, Pablo Vergos*

In 388, Augustine and Monica prepared to return home to North Africa. However, Monica died in Ostia as they prepared to depart. When she realized that she was about to die, she spoke one last time to her beloved Augustine. "Son … I do not know what there is now left for me to do or why I am still here, all my hopes in this world being now fulfilled."

With both his parents deceased (his father had died earlier, soon after converting to the Catholic Faith), Augustine returned to the family estate, which he converted into a monastery. In 391, Valerius, the bishop of Hippo, ordained him a priest. Four years later, he was named coadjutor (assistant) bishop of Hippo to aid Bishop Valerius. In 396, upon the death of Valerius, he became bishop of Hippo. For the next thirty-four years, Augustine was the leading person not only in the African Church but also in all of Christendom.

Augustine achieved his high level of distinction through his exceptional writings, most of which still exist. Among his many sermons and other works, Augustine wrote two extraordinary books. The first of these was his autobiography, called *Confessions*, which he wrote in 397. In *Confessions*, Augustine relates his life story from his childhood onward. He details how God's grace led him from a sinful life to a holy one. It is one of the greatest spiritual books ever written.

Augustine's second extraordinary book, *The City of God*, is even more magnificent than the first. He wrote it at one of the most critical

Manuscript of Augustine's *City of God* (from the 1400s)

Witness to the Faith 69

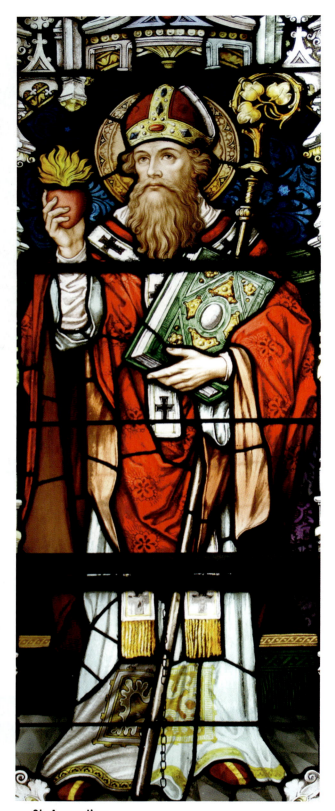

St. Augustine

moments in history—the years after the sack of "eternal Rome" by the barbarians under Alaric the Goth. Many Romans saw the sack of Rome as a punishment for abandoning Rome's pagan religion. They accused Christians of causing the decline of Rome. To answer the charges of these Romans and to comfort Christians who also suffered when Rome was sacked, Augustine wrote *The City of God*.

In his book, Augustine shows how the "City of God," which is the body of all the faithful, is in conflict with the "Earthly City" (or the "City of the Devil"), and how this conflict will last until the end of the world. St. Augustine asserts that the City of God will ultimately triumph. The Church, the City of God, will bring not only spiritual salvation and eternal happiness to men and women but also earthly joy. However, only eternal punishment awaits those in the City of the Devil. Christians need to remember that they should focus on the City of God, not this world where they are only pilgrims passing through. Jesus Christ is the ultimate goal of all human history.

Augustine faced a number of serious heresies during his tenure as bishop. Among the most insidious was the Pelagian heresy, which had been started by Pelagius, a British monk. Pelagius denied the existence of Original Sin and the need for infant Baptism. To combat the Pelagian heresy, St. Augustine wrote fifteen essays explaining the fall of Adam and Eve, the necessity of Baptism, and the nature of divine grace. His essays against Pelagius earned him the title "Doctor of Grace."

In 418, the Council of Carthage condemned Pelagianism and excommunicated Pelagius. Pope Zosimus confirmed the council's decision. Banished from the Western empire by Emperor Honorius, Pelagius appears to have found shelter with Nestorius, the patriarch of Constantinople. In 431, the Council of Ephesus condemned them both.

Virtually until the moment of his death, Augustine worked tirelessly to defend the Faith and instruct his flock. This great Doctor of the Church died on August 18, 430, while Genseric and his Vandal army were besieging Hippo. They burned the entire city but miraculously left the cathedral and St. Augustine's library untouched.

Chapter 5: The Church Begins to Build a Catholic Society – Christendom

The Council of Ephesus

On Christmas Day in 428, the brash new patriarch of Constantinople, Nestorius, preached a sermon in which he said that no human being could be the Mother of God. Immediately, turmoil erupted in the church. Among his listeners was a lawyer, who spoke out against Nestorius and defended Our Blessed Lady. Nestorius went on to deliver a series of sermons in which he developed his theme. He taught that there are *two distinct persons* in Jesus Christ, not *two natures in one person* as the Church teaches. Nestorius said that Christ's humanity was only "a garment," which God puts on. Mary conceived and bore that fleshly garment. Nestorius said that Mary could be called the "Mother of Christ," but not the "Mother of God."

St. Cyril, the patriarch of Alexandria, led those opposed to Nestorius. In 429, he entered the fray on behalf of Our Lady and orthodoxy. He wrote a letter to his monks and gave a homily on Easter Sunday in which he clearly declared that Mary should be called the Mother of God. Additionally, Cyril sent a report to Pope Celestine (422-432), detailing the history of the controversy. Nestorius also sent the pope letters explaining his position.

Nestorius

In August 430, Pope Celestine called a meeting in Rome of several learned theologians to review the material sent by both men. After a careful review, Celestine declared Nestorius' views on the Blessed Mother to be heretical. He demanded that Nestorius immediately recant his teachings, upon pain of excommunication. The pope praised the work of St. Cyril and appointed him his representative in the East to carry out his instructions.

Nestorius refused to change his views. At this point, Cyril, Nestorius, and Emperor Theodosius II felt that only an ecumenical council could resolve the dispute. Pope Celestine approved the decision to convoke a council in May 431.

On June 22, 431, St. Cyril convened the Council of Ephesus in the pope's name. As an indication of the intent of the council, the more than two hundred bishops in attendance met in the Cathedral of Mary, a cathedral dedicated to Mary as "Mother of God." The council quickly condemned the teachings of Nestorius, who refused even to attend the council. The council also removed Nestorius as patriarch of Constantinople and banished him to Egypt, where he died in 451. Pope Celestine died before the council's final session. However, his successor, Sixtus III (432-440), confirmed the Council of Ephesus' acts and decrees.

The council also banished Nestorius' followers. They scattered into Armenia, Persia, and India, where they formed the Assyrian Church of the East.

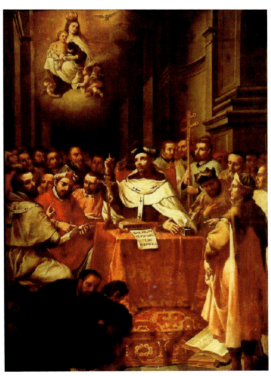
St. Cyril of Alexandria at the Council of Ephesus, Francisco Osorio

Witness to the Faith 71

Madonna and Child, Franz Ittenbach

Monasticism
A way of life dedicated wholly to the Lord, in silence and contemplation, under religious vows.

The Beginning of Monasticism

Throughout the history of the Catholic Church, men and women have sought quiet solitude, where, without the distractions of the world, they could enter into a deeper communication with Our Lord. For example, St. Paul spent years in the Arabian Desert in preparation for his missionary journeys. St. Jerome spent the last decades of his life in a cave writing the Vulgate and its commentaries.

As the Church grew during the third century, more and more holy men and women felt called to a deeper religious life than was possible while living within the boundaries of civilization. These men, like St. Paul, wanted nothing more than to dedicate their lives completely to prayer and sacrifice. Thus, they gave away their possessions and departed from their worldly lives to live in the desert, where they dedicated their lives to prayer and mortification. Although **monasticism** would have its greatest success in the West, it began in the East, in Egypt, where two great saints led the way. These men were St. Paul of Thebes and St. Anthony of Egypt—the first hermits.

St. Paul of Thebes (c. 226 - c. 341) is considered the first Catholic hermit. Much of what is known about him comes from a biography that St. Jerome wrote around 375. According to Jerome, Paul was born in Thebes, Egypt, around 226. He fled to the Egyptian desert during the time that Decius was persecuting Christians. For almost one hundred years, Paul lived a solitary life of prayer and penance in a cave.

Unlike with the case of St. Paul of Thebes, much more is known about St. Anthony of Egypt (also called St. Anthony Abbot and St. Anthony of the Desert). His fame resulted from St. Athanasius' biography of him, which became so popular and widely read that it led to the spread of monasticism in both the East and the West. The Church considers St. Anthony of Egypt to be the father of early monasticism.

Anthony was born in 251 in Coma, Egypt, to Christian parents. Wishing to keep him free from bad influences, they homeschooled him. When Anthony was not yet 20, his parents died, and he inherited a great estate. However, he felt a religious calling. So he sold his land and, after providing for his sister, gave his money to the poor. The 21-year-old Anthony retired to the desert and the life of a hermit. He dedicated his life to prayer and Scripture study.

For twenty years, he lived in complete isolation on the east bank of the Nile River. Eventually, though he did not seek fame, people learned of his holiness. They came to him, asking for his prayers and spiritual guidance.

Chapter 5: The Church Begins to Build a Catholic Society – Christendom

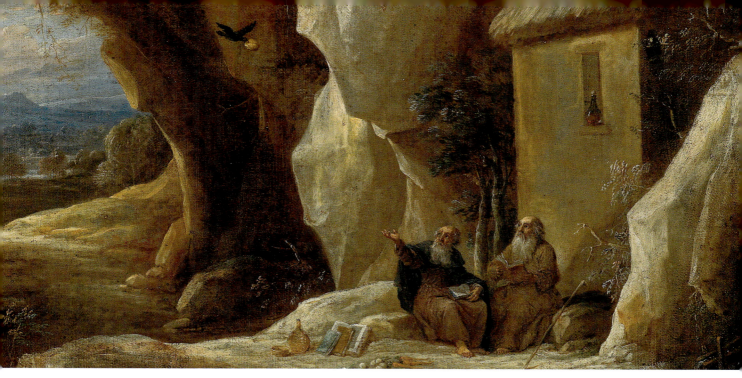

The Saints Anthony and Paul in the Desert, **David Teniers**

When Anthony was 55 years old, he founded his first monastery. Although the monks lived alone, they would gather at certain times to pray and say Mass. Over the years, he founded a number of such monasteries. Shortly before he died in 356, Anthony made a final tour of his monastic communities.

St. Athanasius introduced Eastern monasticism to the West in 335 during his first exile at Trier. While in Rome, he described monasticism to the Christians in that city. His account inflamed those Catholics with a great desire to follow a monastic lifestyle. St. Jerome and St. Ambrose also strongly supported monasticism in the West.

St. Martin of Tours

Another of the great supporters of Western monasticism was St. Martin of Tours, who played a leading role in spreading monasticism in the province of Gaul. Martin was born in 316 (although some histories give his birth year as 336) to pagan parents in Pannonia (present-day Hungary). Although his parents were pagan, Martin was drawn to Catholicism and at the age of 10 became a catechumen. When he was 15 or 16, he followed his father's example and joined the Roman army. Eventually, he came to be stationed in Gaul.

One day, while serving in Amiens, Martin met a barely dressed beggar at the city gates. The beggar

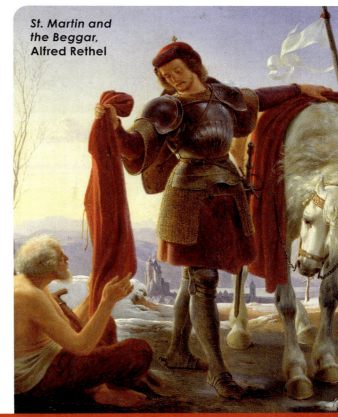

St. Martin and the Beggar, **Alfred Rethel**

Witness to the Faith   73

St. Peter

was dying from hunger and freezing in the winter cold. Moved to pity by the poor man, Martin drew his sword and cut his tunic in two. He placed half around the unfortunate man's shoulders. The next night, Our Lord appeared to Martin in a dream. Christ, surrounded by angels, wore Martin's half cloak. Our Lord said, "Martin, still a catechumen, wrapped Me in this garment."

In 339, Martin was baptized. Discerning that he had a religious calling, he resigned from the army. He journeyed to Tours, where he began studying under St. Hilary of Poitiers (Tours). Sometime around 361, St. Martin founded the first monastery in Gaul, about 5 miles from Tours, at Liguge. Although the French revolutionaries destroyed the original monastery, it is one of the oldest monasteries ever founded.

In 371, the people of Tours elected Martin as bishop by popular acclaim. One tradition holds that Martin, who wished to remain a monk and not become bishop, hid in a barn full of geese, but the honking of the geese revealed his position. Despite his initial reluctance, Martin proved to be an excellent, holy, and active bishop. He created a system of parishes to make running his diocese more efficient, and he visited each parish at least once a year. Martin also founded the monastery of Marmoutier, just outside of Tours.

Development of Church Governance during the Fourth and Fifth Centuries

Although the Church never changes its fundamental doctrines, over the centuries it has changed the way in which it governs itself. For example, during the first decades of the Church, the clergy of Rome elected the pope. During the Middle Ages, the College of Cardinals did so. Also during the Middle Ages, the Church decreed that only cardinals could become pope. However, that requirement no longer exists. Thus, the Church modifies its governance to meet the needs of the times.

The Papacy

Since the days of St. Peter, the pope had been the rock upon which heretics and opponents of the Church had crashed and scattered. During the religious disagreements of the fourth and fifth centuries,

74   *Chapter 5: The Church Begins to Build a Catholic Society – Christendom*

the popes remained the great defenders and protectors of the Catholic Faith. The emperors called most of the Church councils during this period, not because they possessed ecclesiastical authority, but because they had a greater ability to inform the bishops of the world that a council was to occur. They had a better organization at their disposal than the Church did. However, the pope always presided at the council, usually through his representative. Moreover, the pope's representative had to convoke the council in the pope's name. Finally, no decrees of a council were binding unless the pope ratified them.

For example, Pope Sylvester I ratified the decisions of the First Council of Nicaea. His successor, Julius I, supported St. Athanasius and, through his emissaries, presided over the Council of Serdica. The Council of Serdica expressly declared, "Rome is the See of Peter, to which all the bishops of every province must refer." Pope Liberius refused to accept the Council of Arles' decrees, because they had been obtained through coercion. At the beginning of the fifth century, Pope Zosimus ratified the decrees of the Council of Carthage, which declared Pelagius a heretic. Finally, in 431, St. Cyril convened the Council of Ephesus on behalf of Pope Celestine, but his successor, Pope Sixtus III, confirmed the council's acts and decrees.

The Bishops and Priests

From the time Our Lord Jesus Christ named Peter the first pope, popes have always had the right, and have publicly exercised the right, to appoint bishops. In the first centuries of the Church, when communication was difficult, the pope *allowed* the clergy and the people of a diocese to elect their bishops. Prior to the Council of Nicaea in 325, laymen could propose candidates for bishop, whom the clergy would vote upon. Laymen themselves also voted to elect their bishop. However, the Church never intended this procedure to be the normal method of choosing bishops. Starting with the Council of Nicaea, the Church began to take the power to elect bishops out of the hands of the laity. By the end of the fourth century, the election of a new bishop was in the hands of the diocesan clergy. Acting in concert with neighboring bishops and the archbishop, they elected a new bishop.

St. Athanasius

Witness to the Faith

St. Augustine Ordained a Bishop

Metropolitan
A bishop in charge of a larger area or a main city; in the modern Western world, he would typically be called an archbishop.

In every political division of the empire, there was one bishop, called the **metropolitan**, whom the Church considered superior to the others. He was in charge of the main city in the province. In addition, he supervised several other dioceses. Today, this person is known as an *archbishop*, and the term "metropolitan" is almost never used. As of August 2018, there were 35 archbishops in the United States.

In the Eastern empire, a **patriarch** had authority over a number of metropolitans. There were patriarchs in Alexandria, Antioch, Constantinople, and Jerusalem. In the Western empire, the only patriarch was the pope.

As previously noted, during the early Church, the Apostles appointed bishops to succeed them and to aid them as the Church grew. As new Catholic communities were established, a bishop was appointed, or elected, to serve the needs of the people. In the Church's first centuries, most communities were small. The bishop was responsible for the city and its nearby outskirts. Because the communities were small, the bishop could manage much of the religious duties on his own.

However, as the Church grew, especially after the Edict of Milan, bishops, like the Apostles, needed to appoint deacons to assist them in the daily operation of the Church. Like St. Lawrence, deacons helped the poor, brought Holy Communion to the sick and imprisoned, and helped the bishop at Mass. As the Church continued to expand, especially into rural areas, bishops ordained priests who could say Mass and hear Confessions. Initially, priests did not have an assigned parish. They lived with the bishop, who sent them to the places where they were needed.

In the beginning of its history, the Church permitted married men to be priests. In fact, the Bible clearly indicates that St. Peter was, or at least had been, married (Mt. 8:14-15, Mk. 1:29-31, Lk. 4:38-41). However, once a priest was ordained, the Church did not allow him to marry. In the early days of the Church, many men had voluntarily chosen not to marry and have children, in order to dedicate their lives exclusively to God and the Church. Because these men did not have family responsibilities, bishops tended to choose them to become priests rather than married men, who did have families and other responsibilities. Over time, the Church made this the rule. By the end of the third century, several dioceses in the West allowed only unmarried men to become priests.

The Winds of Change

By the latter days of the fifth century, great changes were about to take place in the civilized world. The final chapter was being written in the history of the Roman Empire. Like a great tidal wave, the barbarian invasion was gathering strength in the North. Soon it would blast south, changing the face of the Earth. The power of the Caesars would not be able to withstand it. However, Our Savior built His Church on a rock, not on the shifting sands of human empires. "The rain fell, the floods came, and the winds blew and buffeted the house. But it did not collapse; it had been set solidly on rock" (Mt. 7:25).

Oral Exercises

1. St. John Chrysostom was patriarch of what city?
2. What do we call St. Jerome's translation of the Bible?
3. Where was St. Augustine born?
4. Who baptized St. Augustine?
5. Where did St. Augustine serve as bishop?
6. What did St. Augustine call his autobiography?
7. What was the great crisis that caused Augustine to write *The City of God*?
8. Who were the first two hermits?
9. What is a metropolitan? What is a patriarch?
10. How many patriarchs were there in the West?

St. Lawrence

Witness to the Faith

Chapter 6
The Church Begins Converting the Barbarian Tribes

Goths
A Germanic tribe, one of the barbarian tribes that sought better living conditions in the Roman Empire.

Ostrogoths
The Eastern Goths.

Visigoths
The Western Goths.

The Barbarian Invasions

From about 500 B.C. until 117 A.D., the Roman Empire had grown from a small city-state around Rome to encompass most of what is now Western Europe. It stretched from Spain in the West, to Britain in the North, to Egypt and Babylon in the Southeast and East. As it grew, it absorbed other nations and peoples into its empire—the Jews, for example. Most of the land it added was gained through armed conquest. Also, the Roman Empire spent much of its resources defending its borders from invaders, such as the Persian Empire in the East. In the West, the empire defended itself against various foreign tribes, or "barbarians."

As the Roman Empire expanded north and west, it encountered a number of tribes who lived in the northern part of Europe. As Rome weakened, these tribes immigrated into the empire, usually seeking a better climate and better farmland, which they found in the warmer south of the Roman Empire. Among the tribes seeking better living conditions was a Germanic tribe known as the **Goths**.

The Visigoths

Initially, tribes like the Goths sought to enter the empire legally and settle in the more remote provinces as colonists. Also, over time, the Romans hired foreign tribes as mercenaries to defend the empire's

Chapter 6: The Church Begins Converting the Barbarian Tribes

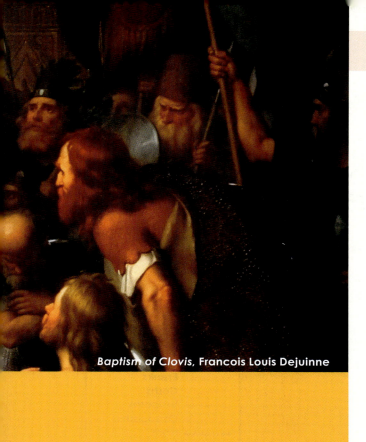
Baptism of Clovis, Francois Louis Dejuinne

410 A.D. – 597 A.D.

410 A.D.
In response to a Roman massacre, the Visigoths under Alaric sack Rome; Augustine writes *The City of God*.

434 A.D.
St. Patrick begins his sixty-year apostolate in Ireland.

451-453 A.D.
After the Battle of Troyes forces Attila the Hun to retreat from Gaul, he turns to Italy. He continues sacking and looting there, but turns away from Rome after meeting with Pope St. Leo the Great. Attila dies in 453.

476 A.D.
The Ostrogoths under Odoacer take over the Roman Empire; the last Roman emperor, 16-year-old Romulus Augustulus, is forced to abdicate.

496 A.D.
Clovis, king of the Franks, is baptized on Christmas Day.

523-530 A.D.
St. Benedict founds his monastery at Monte Cassino and writes his Rule.

527 A.D.
Justinian ascends the throne of the Byzantine Empire.

537-555 A.D.
Byzantine Empress Theodora arranges for Vigilius to become pope, hoping that he will then teach the Monophysite heresy. Once he becomes pope, however, Vigilius teaches Catholic doctrine, and suffers much for this for the rest of his life.

590 A.D.
Gregory I becomes pope.

597 A.D.
St. Augustine of Canterbury arrives in England.

borders. In essence, they hired foreigners to keep out foreigners. This arrangement might have worked had it not been for the Huns, a nomadic tribe from Asia. According to most sources, the Huns burst into eastern Europe astride their shaggy ponies sometime around 370. Like most invaders of the time, the Huns were interested in horses, cattle, and, to a lesser extent, land. Unfortunately, for the Eastern Goths, or **Ostrogoths**, they occupied the land the Huns wanted. The Ostrogoths fled. The Huns continued their westward advance. Running before them, the Western Goths, or **Visigoths**, sought the protection of Valens, the emperor of the East. In 376, Valens allowed the Visigoths into the empire. The barbarian invasions had begun.

By the early fourth century, the Church had sent missionaries to the Goths and made many converts. Ulfilas

Witness to the Faith 79

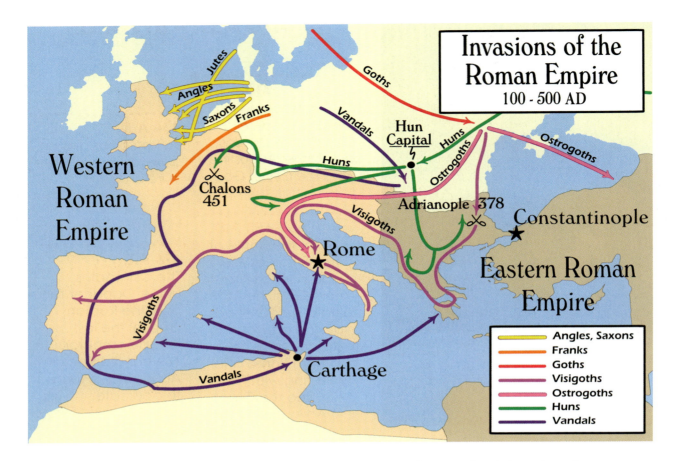

(311-383), whom the Goths had captured and then adopted as one of their own, preached the Gospel to them and ultimately became their bishop. He even translated the Bible into the Gothic language. Unfortunately, Valens told the Visigoths that he would allow them into the empire only if they became Arians. Apparently, Ulfilas had been orthodox; however, he believed Valens that the Arian heresy was not a heresy at all, but merely a disagreement over translations. Consequently, the Visigoths carried the Arian heresy with them in all their migrations.

The Visigoths, who until 376 lived in Dacia (present-day Romania), moved farther south into the empire. Valens had allowed them into the empire because he thought he could use them as soldiers. However, the Romans mistreated the Visigoths and broke the promises they had made to them. As a result, the Goths broke into open warfare against the empire. In 378, the Visigoths defeated Valens at the Battle of Adrianople, where he was killed. Valens' successor, Theodosius I, made peace with the Visigoths. That peace remained in effect until Theodosius died in 395.

For the next thirteen years, Rome and the Visigoths kept an uneasy peace. That peace ended in 408 when Roman legions massacred the families of thousands of Visigoth soldiers. In response, Alaric, the king of the Visigoths, decided to attack Rome. In 410, Alaric invaded Italy and sacked the city of Rome, prompting St. Augustine to pen *The City of God*.

Ulfilas Explains the Gospels to the Goths

Chapter 6: The Church Begins Converting the Barbarian Tribes

Alaric died shortly after looting the city, and his brother-in-law Athaulf became the new king.

Prior to his death, Alaric had been leading the Visigoths down the Italian peninsula. Athaulf stopped this march and turned his people north and west into southern Gaul. In 413, he captured Narbonne and Toulouse and began to establish a Visigoth kingdom. His people had a strong foothold in Gaul by his death in 415, when a rival assassinated Athaulf. At the time of his assassination, Athaulf had established the Visigoths so firmly in southern Gaul that Emperor Honorius gave them title to the Gallic lands in exchange for military assistance.

By the end of the fifth century, the Visigoths had captured most of southern Gaul as well as most of the Iberian Peninsula (Spain). By 500, the Visigoths' kingdom encompassed most of present-day France and Spain. As the Visigoths expanded, they spread Arianism.

Meanwhile, other barbarian tribes also began moving into the Roman Empire as it began to fall. A tribe called the Franks migrated from what is modern Germany and settled in Gaul around the area that one day would become Paris, France. The Burgundians settled in the Rhone River Valley. During their conquest of the Iberian Peninsula in 429, the Visigoths drove the Vandals out of Iberia and into North Africa. The Vandals laid waste to all the Roman provinces in North Africa. Because of their contact with the Visigoths, both the Burgundians and the Vandals became Arians.

Once they had seized control, the Vandals began persecuting the Church in North Africa. The persecution stemmed mainly from the Vandals' fanatical Arianism. The Vandal kings Genseric and Huneric seized the Church's property and gave it to the Arian clergy. They exiled and even killed Catholic priests and bishops.

Missionaries Are Sent to Convert Ireland

The effort to convert the barbarian peoples of Ireland to Catholicism began in the early fifth century. In 429, Pope Celestine I sent St. Germaine of Auxerre and St. Lupus of Troyes to Britain to fight the heresy that the British monk Pelagius had begun. After returning home to Gaul, they sent messages to Celestine, informing him of their progress in Britain. They also apparently discussed the situation in Ireland. It seems likely that while in Britain, members of the Catholic communities in Ireland visited Britain, spoke with the two papal representatives, and asked for assistance. St. Germaine and St. Lupus passed this request on to the pope, along with their recommendation to provide the requested help. In 431, Pope Celestine consecrated the deacon Palladius, who had accompanied Germaine and Lupus to Britain, and sent him to Ireland as its first bishop.

Although Irish history of this era is murky, it appears that Palladius left southern Britain and landed on the Irish coast near present-day

The Sack of Rome, Evariste-Vital Luminais

St. Lupus of Troyes

St. Germaine

Witness to the Faith

Dublin. He began working to convert the Irish people, all of whom were pagans and mostly unreceptive to his message. However, he did make some converts and build a few Catholic churches. In general, he did not accomplish very much, mainly because he died in 434. The man who would become the "Apostle of Ireland" and make Ireland a Catholic nation for the next 1600 years was named Patrick.

St. Patrick: The Apostle of Ireland

Few men have had the impact on the life of a nation that St. Patrick has had on Ireland. St. Patrick was born in Kilpatrick, Scotland, about 399, to a family of Roman nobility. Because the Roman Empire was unable to defend Britain, Irish pirates would raid Britain for slaves and other plunder. In one of these raids, pirates captured 16-year-old Patrick and took him to Ireland, where they sold him as a slave to an Irish chieftain. He worked tending his master's flocks on the Irish hillsides. In his autobiography, *Confession*, Patrick writes that during his captivity, while tending the flocks, he prayed many times during the day. On the hillsides, a remarkable change occurred in the young slave's soul. He underwent an extraordinary conversion experience.

The time Patrick spent as a slave in Ireland actually prepared him to become a missionary. First, he learned to speak Gaelic, the Irish language. Second, he learned about Irish customs and Ireland's pagan religions. Third, and most importantly, he came to love the Irish people so greatly that he dedicated his life to them.

Six years passed in prayer and study. Then Patrick escaped. According to *Confession*, one night as he slept, he heard an angelic voice whisper that he should return home. He made the perilous 200-mile journey westward to a place on the coast where he had never been before. There, a ship lay ready to sail. Patrick asked the captain to take him on board. At first, the captain refused, but then changed his mind and took Patrick as his passenger. After three days' sailing, the ship landed in Scotland. For twenty-eight days, the group wandered in the wilderness. Finally, Patrick returned home.

The next years of Patrick's life remain obscure. Certainly, a few years passed during which he contemplated his vocation. It seems very likely that Patrick met St. Germaine when he visited Britain in 429 and was ordained a deacon by him. Patrick also asked Germaine to send him to Ireland as a missionary. Germaine told him that first he needed education and training, and, for that purpose, sent Patrick to Auxerre.

Chapter 6: The Church Begins Converting the Barbarian Tribes

Over the next several months, history once again loses sight of St. Patrick's movements. He likely visited southern Gaul, Italy, Rome, and Lerins abbey in the Mediterranean. At Lerins, he saw something of monastic life and met the monks who were starting to become well-known for their learning and piety.

Eventually, Patrick arrived in Auxerre, where, for the next several years, he learned more about the Faith and to speak and read Latin. In 434, Patrick, now ordained, along with other priests, was on his way to Ireland when he learned that Bishop Palladius had died. Patrick, with Pope Sixtus III's approval, was immediately consecrated Ireland's new bishop. He resumed his journey to Ireland, arriving later that year.

St. Patrick's first converts were the people of eastern Ulster, where he had lived as a slave. He made his way to Tara, where the high-king Laoghaire had his main fortress. Although Laoghaire remained a pagan, he allowed Patrick to preach freely in his realm. Over the next fifteen years, Patrick preached over virtually every inch of the northern part of Ireland. He baptized thousands and ordained a local clergy.

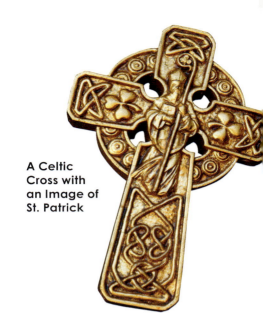

A Celtic Cross with an Image of St. Patrick

For some reason, the Irish seemed to breathe in Christianity unlike almost any other people. Historians have noted how quickly, thoroughly, and peacefully the Irish embraced Catholicism. The local pagan religious leaders, the Druids, opposed the spread of the Catholic Faith but were helpless to stop it. St. Patrick refers more than once in his *Confession* to the amazing success of his missionary endeavors. He mentions the ordination of clergy three times. For the most part, they must have been native Irishmen. Before St. Patrick died, he consecrated some of these men as bishops.

In 439, three bishops arrived in southern Ireland from Gaul to succeed Palladius. They communicated periodically with Patrick in the North. In 457, they met with him to create the initial rules governing the Irish church. One of these principles decreed, "If any grave questions arise in this island, they shall be referred to the Apostolic See" (Canons of St. Patrick, Canon XX, c. 5, quoted in *Studies in Church History*, vol. 1, 2nd ed., by Rev. R. Parsons [New York and Cincinnati: Fr. Pustet & Co., 1906], p. 304).

In 444, St. Patrick established the spiritual capital of Ireland at Armagh. He likely chose this site because of its proximity to the ancient capital of the Ulster kings. Armagh has remained the ecclesiastical capital of Ireland ever since. Today, an Anglican cathedral stands upon the spot where

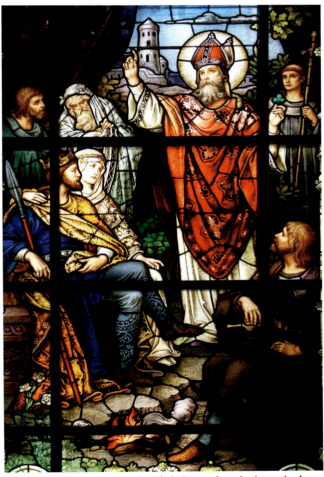

St. Patrick Preaches to Laoghaire

Witness to the Faith

St. Patrick's Catholic Cathedral in Armagh

Patrick built his stone church. Construction of the Catholic cathedral began during the latter half of the 1800s. The present Catholic cathedral replaced the medieval cathedral that the Church of Ireland had seized during the Protestant Revolt. Armagh is the only city in the world that is home to two cathedrals with the same name: St. Patrick.

St. Patrick died on March 17, 493. During his sixty-year apostolate, he organized whatever Christianity already existed and converted a large portion of pagan Ireland. When he died, the Catholic Faith was the religion of the country. Soon, St. Patrick became the hero of the Irish race. The Irish, and those of Irish descent, cherish him with a love and devotion like no other. March 17, his feast day, is celebrated as a national holiday in virtually any nation with a significant Irish population.

Attila the Hun and Pope St. Leo the Great

Since the Huns burst upon the world's stage, they had seemed more like a force of nature, like a hurricane or a flood, than a tribe of people. Other people fled before them. In 395, they attacked the Eastern Roman Empire. They very nearly conquered the Persian Empire before being defeated.

In 434, Attila became ruler of the Huns. Attila seems to have had no other ambition than to conquer everything he could. After his defeat in Persia, in 441 he attacked the Eastern Roman Empire. Although successful in many battles, he could not conquer Constantinople with its massively thick walls. Turning his attention from the East, in 451 Attila led the Huns into the Western Empire.

After crossing the Rhine River, the Huns stormed into northeastern France. They sacked a number of cities, including the great city of Amiens. They were soon intent on taking and looting Paris. Knowing that they could not withstand the Huns, the people of Paris prepared to flee. However, a saintly woman named Genevieve assured the Parisians that if they trusted in God and did penance, Christ would protect their city. He did. Attila bypassed Paris and continued south to Orleans.

Battle of Troyes
The battle in which the Roman general Aetius defeated Attila the Hun and stopped his advance into Gaul.

***Attila the Hun**, Eugene Delacroix*

Meanwhile, St. Anianus, the bishop of Orleans, had enlisted the help of the Roman General Flavius Aetius. Facing a massive Hun army, Aetius allied himself with the local barbarian tribes, including the Franks, the Burgundians, and the Visigoths. Aetius and his army managed to reach Orleans before Attila. Facing this large army, Attila retreated northeast away from Orleans toward Troyes. Aetius finally caught Attila near Troyes. On June 20, 451, the two armies fought the Battle of the Catalaunian Plains, also known as the **Battle of Troyes**.

84 Chapter 6: The Church Begins Converting the Barbarian Tribes

Aetius and his army won a small but significant victory in this battle. Attila was forced to retreat from Gaul. However, the Huns were only defeated, not destroyed. Attila turned his attention to Italy.

The year 452 found Attila plundering Italy. As he had done with Gaul, he sacked and looted numerous cities. Eventually, Attila arrived at the River Po, just outside the city of Rome. As word of the Huns' approach reached him, Pope St. Leo the Great (440-461) decided to stop Attila before he attacked Rome. Pope St. Leo went out to meet Attila in the Po River valley. The pope convinced Attila to spare the city. Attila retreated from Italy, leaving Rome in peace. He died in March 453, having ruled for less than twenty years but inflicting a hundred years of damage on the world.

Only a few years later, the Vandals under King Genseric did sack Rome. In 455, when Genseric sailed into Italy, Leo went out to meet him. Although the pope could not prevent the attack, through his intercession, he minimized the damage. The Vandals did not burn Rome, and they spared the Basilicas of St. Peter, St. Paul, and St. John Lateran, where people sought refuge.

The Conversion of the Franks

Converting the barbarian tribes proved challenging for several reasons. First, unlike the Romans of the first centuries, the barbarians had little or no education. Some had no written language. For example, Bishop Ulfilas, who had translated the Bible for the Visigoths, first had to create a Gothic alphabet. In addition, almost every tribe was Arian

Pope St. Leo the Great

The Meeting of Leo the Great and Attila, Raphael

Witness to the Faith 85

Clovis and Clotilde, Antoine-Jean Gros

because of their interaction with the Visigoths. The one exception was the Franks. They were committed pagans.

In 485, the Franks entered Roman Gaul. They occupied the territory that is present-day Belgium, Holland, northeastern France, and the Rhineland in northwest Germany. The Franks' neighbors in the south and west were the Arian Visigoths. In the east, their neighbors were the Arian Burgundians.

In 493, Clovis, the great warrior king of the Franks, married a 17-year-old Burgundian princess named Clotilde. Though Clotilde's parents were Arians, she was an orthodox Catholic. From the beginning of their marriage, Clotilde urged Clovis to become a Catholic. To that end, she constantly prayed for him. When their first child was born, she obtained his permission to baptize the baby. However, when the child died shortly after his Baptism, Clovis blamed the Christian God for the child's death. It seemed that this death had hardened his heart and driven Clovis deeper into paganism. But Clotilde was also a warrior. She refused to give up her fight for her husband's soul. She baptized their second son, who lived.

During their marriage, Clotilde had told Clovis that one day, if during a battle, he saw himself facing defeat, he should call upon Jesus Christ to save him. Such a day came. Clovis found himself facing defeat at the hands of his enemies. Remembering Clotilde's words, he called upon our Savior for aid. Immediately, the tide of the battle turned. The Frankish forces were victorious. Clovis returned to tell Clotilde that he was ready to learn about the Catholic Faith.

Clotilde summoned St. Remi, the holy bishop of Reims, to teach her husband. Although Clovis was a man of war, his heart was open to the Faith. It is said that when the agonies of Our Lord's Passion and Crucifixion were first described to Clovis, a righteous anger overtook him. He grabbed his weapons and cried out, "If only I had been there with my Franks!" St. Remi baptized Clovis along with three thousand

Clovis Leading the Franks to Victory in the Battle of Tolbiac, Ary Scheffer

86   *Chapter 6: The Church Begins Converting the Barbarian Tribes*

of his nobles and warriors on Christmas Day in 496. Catholicism had won a major victory in Gaul.

Gradually, the entire Frankish nation converted to Christianity. Like their great leader, Clovis, they were always ready to defend the Church of Our Lord against her enemies. The Franks refused to allow Arianism in Gaul. Later, the Franks conquered the whole of northern Gaul as far south as the river Loire. They called their kingdom "Francia." Paris was its capital. Since she was the first of the barbarian tribes to convert to the Faith, France has been called the "Eldest Daughter of the Church."

Theodoric and the Ostrogoths

Since Attila's departure from Italy, the Western Roman Empire had been in disarray and fighting for its very survival against the barbarian tribes. In 476, Odoacer, the king of the Ostrogoths, forced the 16-year-old Roman emperor, Romulus Augustulus, to abdicate. The Roman Empire, at least in the West, had ended. Because the last Roman emperor was only 16 years old, Odoacer took mercy on him and exiled him. Odoacer then declared himself the ruler of Italy.

St. Remi

Odoacer next sought to consolidate his power. He opened negotiations with Zeno, the Eastern Roman emperor. Zeno eventually agreed to recognize Odoacer as ruler of Italy. However, Zeno did not trust Odoacer, and looked for an opportunity to overthrow him. He found that opportunity in another Visigoth king named Theodoric, who also bore no love for Odoacer.

In 488, Zeno authorized Theodoric to overthrow Odoacer. For the next several years, the two men fought a series of battles, but neither could win a decisive victory over the other. Finally, in 493, Theodoric and Odoacer agreed to a peace treaty in which they would rule Italy together. At the banquet celebrating their agreement, Theodoric and his men murdered Odoacer and his men. Theodoric was now the king of Italy. Although Theodoric was tolerant in his religious policies, he was, like all Gothic kings, an Arian. When he became ruler of Italy and expanded his empire, Arianism was the religion he spread.

Despite his treacherous seizure of power, once enthroned, Theodoric proved to be a talented ruler. He wisely sought to create a society in which Goths and Romans could live together peacefully. Despite his Arianism, he sought to maintain a friendly

Romulus Augustulus Resigns the Roman Crown to Odoacer

Witness to the Faith 87

Statue of Theodoric

relationship with Pope Gelasius I (492-496) and Pope Anastasius II (496-498).

However, while historians would one day call Theodoric "the Great," they should never call him "the virtuous." When Justin, the new Eastern emperor and an orthodox Catholic, decided to cleanse his empire of heresy, which included Arianism, Theodoric believed that Justin somehow meant to attack him. Moreover, Theodoric believed that the pope had somehow conspired with Justin. To resolve the situation, Theodoric called Pope John I (523-526) before him. He demanded that Pope John travel to Constantinople and convince Emperor Justin to retract the anti-Arian legislation. John, a rather frail man, objected. When Theodoric threatened the Catholics in his domain, John agreed.

Upon arriving in Constantinople, Emperor Justin treated Pope John "as if he were Peter himself." Justin even requested that John crown him a second time. At John's request, Justin agreed to remove the anti-Arian legislation.

Despite Pope John's diplomatic success, Theodoric was furious with him. For some reason, he believed that John had conspired with Justin. (It seems unclear about what they conspired.) Once the pope returned, Theodoric threw him into prison. Already weak, John died in prison in 526. Theodoric died later that year, but not before working to elect John's successor, Pope Felix III (526-530). Theodoric had been an Arian and a cruel ruler, but other than Clovis, probably the best king the barbarians had produced.

Justinian

With the death of Theodoric, what once was the Western Roman Empire fell into near anarchy. The Gothic kings were degenerates, the Frankish kings after Clovis were murderers, and the Vandals were weak. Yet one man did rise above the rest to give the world hope: Justinian, the Eastern emperor. Justinian was an orthodox Catholic. Upon the death of his uncle in 527, Justinian became emperor. His reign would last almost forty years. He made such an impact that historians would call this era the "Age of Justinian."

Justinian was married to a woman who wielded a great deal of power as empress—an unusual situation for the time. Her name was Theodora.

Although a Christian, she was influenced by the **Monophysite heresy**, which taught that Christ had only one nature. Both she and this heresy would have a lasting effect on Church history. Justinian and Theodora would dedicate their lives to defeating the barbarians and restoring the Western Roman Empire to its former glory. In 535, an army from the Eastern Roman Empire, or *Byzantine* Empire, landed in Sicily commanded by the finest general of the age, Flavius Belisarius. His goal was to recapture Italy from the barbarians.

Vigilius: The Steps to the Papal Throne

A man then stepped onto the world's stage who was rare in the history of the Church. At a moment when the Church was in danger as great as it has ever been, a man came to the papal throne who himself was far from great. He was perhaps the last man whom one would have chosen to wear the Fisherman's Ring at this critical time. His name was Vigilius. If he were alive today, he would probably work as a lobbyist making back-room deals.

By the time Felix III became pope, papal elections had become very political. Candidates sought the office for its temporal value, not for its spiritual importance. Felix III realized that his own election had been "disordered." Therefore, Felix decided to appoint his successor while he lived.

It should be noted that nothing prohibits a pope from appointing his successor. The pope is the visible head of the Church during his lifetime. He has the right and authority to appoint his successor if he wishes.

Felix chose Boniface, a Roman with a Germanic heritage. This seemed like a great choice. It should have pleased both the Romans and the Germanic tribes. Despite this, as soon as Felix died, most of the priests of Rome went to the Lateran Basilica and elected a man named Dioscorus pope instead. Because this "election" clearly violated Pope Felix's instructions, it was invalid. The few priests loyal to Felix consecrated Boniface as pope. The Church was spared a terrible schism when Dioscorus died less than a month later. Everyone then recognized Boniface II (530-532) as pope.

The following year, Boniface held a synod in which he declared that he would use the "appointment method" to choose his successor. He chose Vigilius. Apparently, those who knew Vigilius realized that he was a very bad choice. In fact, he was so unsuitable, Boniface was forced to call another synod in which he repudiated the previous one and announced that Vigilius was not the new pope and had to step down.

In 532, Boniface died, and the papacy remained vacant for more than two months, during which time various candidates bribed and schemed to obtain votes. Finally, a humble parish priest, who

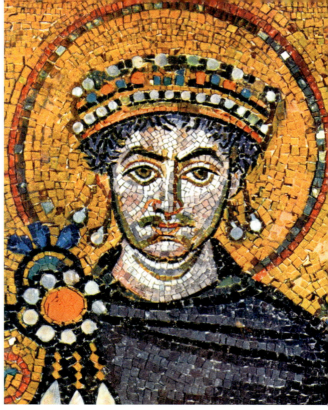

Emperor Justinian

Pope Felix III

Witness to the Faith

Pope Agapetus

apparently had bribed no one, was elected. He changed his named from Mercurius to John, becoming **the first man to take a new name upon election to the papacy**. Pope John II ruled for three years.

Upon his death, the bitter factions in the Church seemed to realize the damage that they were causing. In May 535, they unanimously elected Agapetus. Meanwhile, with the Byzantine army poised to invade Italy, the Visigoth king begged Agapetus to go to Constantinople and ask Justinian not to invade. Among those in the papal retinue was Vigilius.

In Constantinople, Agapetus deposed the Monophysite patriarch of Constantinople and replaced him with an orthodox patriarch. Although Theodora undoubtedly pressured her husband, Justinian supported the pope. On April 22, less than a year after he had become pope and a few days before a synod he had called to address the Monophysite heresy was to meet, Pope Agapetus died. He was 46 years old—young even by the standards of those times. Was he murdered? No one will ever know. However, the next events make one wonder.

Before Vigilius left Constantinople for Rome, he secretly met with Theodora. The two made a pact. When the Byzantine army conquered Rome, Theodora would make Vigilius the pope and give him 700 pounds of gold. In exchange, he would declare the Monophysite heresy to be the truth.

> **Did Justinian know about Theodora's scheming?**
>
> Although it seems impossible, there is evidence that Justinian was unaware of Theodora's scheming in this incident.

Meanwhile, on June 8, 536, a priest named Silverius was consecrated pope. Later that month, Belisarius landed in southern Italy and began marching to Rome. In December, he entered Rome. Belisarius informed Pope Silverius that Empress Theodora had ordered him to go to Constantinople to restore the Monophysite patriarch whom Agapetus had replaced. When Silverius absolutely refused, Theodora ordered Belisarius to depose him. In March 538, Silverius was sent into exile. Eight days later, under pressure from Belisarius, the clergy of Rome elected Vigilius as pope.

Pope Vigilius

At the time of Vigilius' election, Pope Silverius still lived. Thus, Vigilius was an antipope as well as complicit in the removal of the true pope. Vigilius also ensured that the pope never returned to Rome and died in exile. Thus, Vigilius was also indirectly guilty of murder. Yet, upon the death of Silverius, this man became pope.

In Constantinople, Theodora waited for Pope Vigilius (537-555) to fulfill his end of the bargain: restore the Monophysite patriarch and declare that the Monophysite heresy was the truth. She had paid 700 pounds of gold for a pope; she wanted her money's worth. Yet Vigilius remained silent. Finally, Theodora demanded an answer. In 538, he responded. Vigilius wrote that he had formerly spoken foolishly and wrongly, but that he would never restore a heretic to his former position.

Over the next years, despite his previous actions and promises, Vigilius supported and defended Catholic orthodoxy. In 544, in an

Pope Silverius

90 *Chapter 6: The Church Begins Converting the Barbarian Tribes*

attempt to reconcile the Monophysites with orthodox teaching, Justinian issued a decree condemning the writings of three dead theologians, the so-called "Three Chapters." This was Justinian's effort to resolve the religious conflict that was disrupting his empire, and also probably to please Theodora. The four Eastern patriarchs agreed to the decree; however, they insisted that Pope Vigilius also ratify it. However, Vigilius saw a trap.

In 451, the Council of Chalcedon had met and specifically condemned the Monophysite heresy. The Council had issued the *Chalcedonian Definition*, which states that Jesus is "perfect both in deity and in humanness; this selfsame one is also actually God and actually man." The council fathers had left no room for further discussion. Moreover, Pope St. Leo the Great had sent a letter to the council, known as the *Tome of Leo*, in which he had clearly declared that Our Lord had two natures, thus refuting the Monophysite heresy. In the face of the *Tome of Leo* and the *Chalcedonian Definition*, Vigilius realized that any attempt to compromise with the Monophysites would open a door that the Church had already closed. Moreover, he knew the heart of Theodora, and he did not trust her. He refused to ratify Justinian's decree.

Vigilius on the Cross

In its history, the Holy Spirit has blessed the Catholic Church with a large number of heroic popes. Many have been declared saints because they suffered martyrdom. Yet, of all the popes, none underwent such a change of heart and soul as did Vigilius.

Justinian saw the refusal to ratify his decree as an affront to his power. On November 22, 545, as Pope Vigilius was saying Mass, Justinian had him arrested. He was taken to Constantinople in January 547. There, facing Justinian and Theodora, the man who offered to sell the papacy for 700 pounds of gold stood in the Shoes of the Fisherman and declared that he feared nothing! Whatever they did to him would serve as just punishment for his sins. Moreover, he declared that while they could hold him personally captive, they could never hold the papacy captive.

Over the next years, Justinian kept him confined in a local palace. At one point, Vigilius managed to escape and, in February 552, issued a letter denouncing Justinian's treatment of him. In response, Justinian exiled the pope to a remote island and gave him only bread and water.

The Council of Constantinople

In May 553, Justinian called the Second Council of Constantinople. Only 166 bishops, most from the East, attended. Pope Vigilius refused to attend because so few Western bishops were present and because

Empress Theodora

Pope Vigilius

Witness to the Faith

Icon
The best-known Byzantine art form, done in a two-dimensional, stylized way, intended to be more symbolic than realistic.

Justinian refused to allow him complete freedom. The Council of Constantinople condemned the Three Chapters, but it also affirmed the teachings of the Council of Chalcedon. It still remained for the pope to ratify the council's acts.

Once again, Pope Vigilius faced a serious issue. Justinian had promised that he would not take the Byzantine Empire into schism, but even the discussion was a veiled threat. The possibility also existed that an antipope might be installed in his place, causing further damage to the Church. After careful reflection, Vigilius decided that the decrees of the Council of Constantinople were not heretical. Faced with no good choices, he ratified the council.

After ten years in exile and imprisonment, Justinian released Vigilius and sent him back to Rome. However, he never made it back. Vigilius died from painful kidney stones on June 7, 555, in Sicily.

The story of Pope Vigilius is not well-known, even by most Catholics. Yet he was a man who brought honor to the papacy in the finest Apostolic tradition. Though he may have started out like Judas, he ended up like Peter.

The Glories of the Age of Justinian

Although Justinian never completely revived the Western Empire, he did recapture Italy, North Africa, and part of Spain. His victories also created a great deal of prestige for the Byzantine Empire. For the next 650 years, Constantinople would be the greatest and most magnificent city in the world.

Part of Constantinople's glory lay in the great artistic achievements of the Byzantine Empire. The most well-known Byzantine art form is the **icon**. Unlike Western art, which tended to be more realistic and representational, icons, almost all of which are religious, tended to be more abstract and two-dimensional.

The greatest artistic achievement of Justinian and the Byzantine Empire was the construction of the **Church of Hagia Sophia**, or Holy Wisdom. The largest church in the world until the construction of St. Peter's Basilica in Rome, it was dedicated on December 25, 562. It remained the symbol of the Byzantine Empire for the next 900 years.

In addition to military victories and artistic triumphs, Justinian was also concerned about ruling his empire well. In 529, shortly after becoming emperor, he published the famous *Justinian Code*, a sweeping legislative reform. The Justinian Code attempted to merge Christian principles

Mosaic Icon of Virgin and Child in Hagia Sophia

92 *Chapter 6: The Church Begins Converting the Barbarian Tribes*

Hagia Sophia

with Roman law. For the first time, a legal code sought to create public morality based on Christianity. Social welfare would also be based on Christian social principles.

Justinian died in November 565, after one of the longest and most successful reigns in the history of the world.

St. Benedict and Western Monasticism

As the barbarian invasions raged around Western Europe like a hurricane, one man stood in the eye of that storm. He would change the face of Europe more than almost anyone in the history of the world. His name was Benedict.

St. Benedict was born about 480 in Nursia, Italy. His parents, who were nobles, sent him to Rome, where he studied rhetoric. However, in Rome he encountered vice rather than virtue. At the age of 20, he fled the city to live alone in a cave in the mountains of Subiaco, about 40 miles outside of Rome. He did not intend to become a well-known hermit, but simply to live alone in prayer. During the next three years, word of his holiness spread, and others joined him. He established twelve small monasteries, each housing twelve monks.

Sometime between 523 and 530, St. Benedict moved his monastery to Monte Cassino, in the mountains halfway between Rome and Naples. There is evidence to suggest that Benedict intended the Monte Cassino monastery to be a model upon which other monasteries would be

Church of Hagia Sophia
The great church at Constantinople, the largest in the world until St. Peter's Basilica, dedicated on Christmas Day in 562.

St. Benedict, El Greco

Witness to the Faith 93

St. Benedict, Hans Memling

founded. Evidence also suggests that, sometime around 523, Pope Hormisdas (514-523) asked Benedict to write a rule for monks living in a community governed by an abbot. For the past 1500 years, the Benedictines have used the Rule of St. Benedict to manage their lives.

St. Benedict's Rule can be summed up in the Benedictine's Latin motto, *ora et labora* (meaning "pray and work"). Thus, the first goal of the rule is to make the individual monks holy. However, because the monk attains holiness by living in a community, the rule contains regulations, based on Christian charity, which enable the individual monks to live together happily, peacefully, and harmoniously. Because the monks are living in a close community, like a family, the rule stresses the virtues of charity, patience, and obedience—the virtues that brothers and sisters in a family need to get along with one another. Monks need to love one another, be patient with one another, and obey the abbot. In his rule, St. Benedict gives the abbot absolute authority over all the monks. The monks work to become perfect, as their Heavenly Father is perfect. The tools they use are work and prayer.

The reason Benedict's Rule became so successful was that, unlike earlier rules, it created a moderate path which balanced the needs of the individual monk with those of the community. The individual monk could succeed in an orderly community that supported his religious vocation. Moreover, the Benedictine community could thrive as an institution.

Scriptorium
The room in a monastery where monks wrote and copied books.

Although a vow of poverty barred the monks from owning worldly possessions, it did not stop the monks from trying to better the world outside their monastery. Each monastery worked hard to help the people who lived around them. Monasteries were like small factories, making candles, bread, wine, and other items that they sold in the local marketplace. This stimulated the local economy. The monks taught farmers about agriculture so that they could raise more crops. The monks opened schools, and the monasteries became centers of learning. These monastic schools became great medieval universities.

Sample of the Book of Kells

Perhaps the most important work that the monks did occurred in the **scriptorium**. In this room, certain monks wrote down the history of the times and copied ancient manuscripts and other important books, preserving them for future generations. Historians still visit Monte Cassino to conduct research in its archives. Monks also copied manuscripts of the Bible and *illuminated* them—that is, decorated the pages

Interior of Monte Cassino, Italy

Exterior of Monte Cassino

with beautiful designs. The most famous illuminated manuscript in the world, the *Book of Kells*, contains the four Gospels of the New Testament. Irish monks probably copied it around the ninth century.

As the fame of the Monte Cassino monastery spread, men began coming to Monte Cassino looking to live under the Rule of St. Benedict. Thus began the Benedictine Order, which played such a crucial part in the history of Europe and the Church. Italian noblemen as well as barbarian converts joined St. Benedict's order. From Monte Cassino, he sent them out as teachers and missionaries into all of Europe. Wherever the Benedictines journeyed, they established new monasteries, which became centers of culture and sanctity. By the middle of the seventh century, Benedictine monks had nearly restored the European civilization that the barbarians had practically destroyed.

St. Benedict died in 547 at Monte Cassino. He left behind an institution that has served the Church faithfully. Because his rule has served as the model for every future monastic rule, St. Benedict is considered the founder of Western monasticism.

Front and Back of a Benedictine Medal

Witness to the Faith

Saint Finian and His Pupils

Irish Monasticism

By the time of St. Benedict's death, monasticism was growing rapidly throughout western Europe. Yet, no people embraced monasticism more enthusiastically than did the Irish. In some mysterious way, the monastic life irresistibly appealed to some quality in the Irish temperament.

From his autobiography, *Confession*, it is clear that St. Patrick had the highest regard for the monastic life. As bishop, he accepted the professions of many men and women to the religious life. Patrick had an especially high regard for women who became nuns, because so often they did so despite the protestations of their families. He greatly admired their courage.

By the middle of the fifth century, the barbarian invasions had made communication between Ireland and the European continent practically nonexistent. In fact, when the three bishops in southern Ireland died, no one was sent to replace them. Ireland could communicate a bit with western Britain until about 475 when the barbarians overran Britain, cutting off all communications with the outside world. Yet, as historian Warren Carroll has so beautifully written, "Sunset for the Christian Roman empire in the West was sunrise for Christian Ireland" (W. Carroll, *The Building of Christendom* [Front Royal, Va.: Christendom Press, 1987], p. 124).

The Irish, even as barbarians, had always admired and appreciated learning. The pagan priests, the Druids, were literate, knew about law and medicine, and served as advisors to the Irish kings and chieftains. Catholic priests and monks also needed to be well educated. By the beginning of the seventh century, the monastery schools had melded that which was true in the old Celtic knowledge, such as law and medicine, with the truth of the Catholic Faith. Irish priests and monks came to be well educated. Filled with missionary zeal, they went forward. First, they re-evangelized Britain, which had been almost entirely lost to paganism. Then they set out to re-evangelize the continent. Eventually, the Irish would re-evangelize all of Western Europe.

While the history of Irish monasticism would fill volumes and include numerous Irish saints, three names stand apart from the rest: St. Finian, St. Columba, and St. Columban. St. Finian is generally considered to be the founder of Irish monasticism. St. Columba founded the most monasteries. St. Columban began the process of bringing monasticism to the Franks and Lombards.

The precise details of the life St. Finian of Clonard (470-549) are somewhat murky. Born in Ireland in 470, he apparently had a vocation at an early age. He traveled to Tours, where he studied for a time at

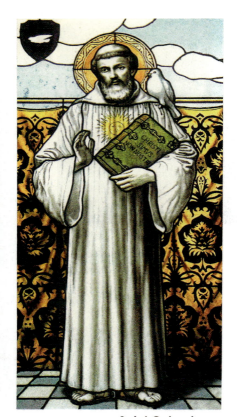
Saint Columban

Chapter 6: The Church Begins Converting the Barbarian Tribes

the monastery started by St. Martin of Tours. Later, he journeyed to Wales, in Britain, where he studied under St. Cadoc, the leader of British monasticism. Following his studies with St. Cadoc, he returned to Ireland. Sometime between 530 and 540, he founded his famous monastery at Clonard, about 30 miles from Dublin. The Clonard monastery would become the motherhouse of Irish monasticism. Men from all over Ireland flocked to Clonard to study at his abbey school and join his monastery. Some of St. Finian's students came to be known as the "Twelve Apostles of Ireland." They all became renowned abbots and founders of monasteries. Before the end of the sixth century, monasteries dotted the face of Ireland.

Numbered among the "Twelve Apostles of Ireland" is St. Columba (521-597), whom most historians consider the greatest Irish missionary of this period. St. Columba, the "Apostle of Scotland," was born in Donegal in 521, and he was educated at Clonard. Upon leaving that abbey, he founded several monasteries in Ireland. In 563, he traveled to Scotland with twelve companions. He hoped to convert the Picts, the tribe that lived in Scotland. One of the Scottish chieftains gave Columba the little island of Iona off Scotland's western coast. There, he founded the monastery of Iona, which for centuries was one of the most famous in Europe. During the remainder of his life, St. Columba founded more monasteries and preached to the Picts. When he died in 579, he had won northern Scotland to the Faith.

St. Columban (543-615) was born in Meath, Ireland, in 543. He initially served as a monk in Cluaninis monastery, but then moved to the Bangor Abbey in Ulster, where Saint Comgall was the abbot. Sometime around 545, Columban received permission from Abbot Comgall to evangelize the Franks. Thus, he set sail for the kingdom of the Franks, along with twelve fellow monks, including St. Gall, the future "Apostle of Switzerland." The party landed in Brittany in 585.

They traveled into the land of the Burgundians, and the king there greeted them warmly. They established a monastery that

Saint Columba

Witness to the Faith 97

Basilica of St. Peter in Luxeuil-les-Bains, France

Emperor Tiberius

attracted a number of monks. In 590, Columban built the monastery of Luxeuil-les-Bains. From Luxeuil, missionaries ventured into Switzerland, Germany, and even northern Italy to convert the Lombards, a barbarian tribe. These monasteries followed the rule that Columban had written and reflect his Irish heritage. Despite his rule being stricter than that of St. Benedict, its severity attracted barbarian converts, who themselves led harsh lives. As a result, many entered Columban's monasteries.

Toward the end of his life, St. Columban preached to the barbarian tribes in present-day Germany and Switzerland. In 612, he arrived in Milan, where he met the Lombard rulers, King Agilulf and Queen Theodelinda, who received him kindly. Agilulf gave Columban a piece of land called Bobbio, about 60 miles south of Milan. In 614, Columban built the world-famous Bobbio Abbey. He died at Bobbio on November 21, 615.

Pope St. Gregory the Great

Following the death of Pope Vigilius, Pelagius I (556-561) became pope. Pelagius had been a friend and confidant to Vigilius and had suffered imprisonment on his behalf. To support peace and unity in the Church, Pelagius called upon the faithful to support the Council of Constantinople.

Of the next two popes, John III (561-574) and Benedict I (575-579), little is known. During John's pontificate, Justinian died, and in 565 his ineffectual nephew, Emperor Justin II, succeeded him. In 574, Justin went insane, and was replaced by General Tiberius. Tiberius was proclaimed emperor in 578, about a week before Justin died.

Following the death of Benedict I, Pelagius II (579-590) became pope. Faced with the threat of a barbarian attack on Rome, Pelagius sent his best man to Constantinople to seek aid. That man's name was Gregory. He was the greatest man of the age, and would be one of the greatest men ever to wear the Fisherman's Ring and one of only a few popes known as "the Great."

Gregory was born in 540 to an ancient Roman aristocratic family. Because his family was wealthy and of the aristocracy, they ensured that he had an excellent education. He studied grammar, rhetoric, and literature. He also studied the law so that he could have a career in the government. Upon completion of his education, he entered the imperial service. In 573, when Gregory was in his early thirties, Emperor Justin II made him prefect of the city of Rome, essentially the mayor. However, Gregory had a calling to the religious life. In 574, following the death of his father, Gregory renounced his secular career, gave away his fortune, and became a monk.

For the next four years, Gregory lived as a monk. However, in 578, needing a reliable assistant, Pope Benedict I ordained him a deacon. Following Justin's death, the Byzantine Empire had lost interest in Italy. As a result, the Lombards had overrun Italy, ravaged the countryside, and besieged Rome. Rome's only hope was that the Byzantine Empire would send an army to drive out the Lombards. In 579, the new pope, Pelagius II, sent Gregory to Constantinople to try to convince Emperor Tiberius to provide that army.

Although Gregory probably made his case very well, the Byzantines were engaged in a deadly battle with their ancient nemesis, the Persians. They would lend no aid to Rome. In 585, Gregory returned to Rome and his monastery, where he soon became abbot.

According to tradition, during this period, as Gregory walked in the markets of Rome, he noticed some fair-haired, light-skinned youths. Their appearance set them apart from the dark-haired, darker-complexioned Romans. When Gregory asked who these young people were, his companion said that they were Angles, the tribe who inhabited Britain. Gregory corrected his companion: "No, they are not Angles, they are angels." This event inspired Gregory to evangelize the British Isles.

Gregory requested permission from Pope Pelagius to travel to Britain with some of his monks to begin converting the people of Britain. Pelagius agreed. However, Gregory's group had barely left Rome before Pelagius was forced to call them back in the face of unhappy Romans, who refused to let Gregory leave. Over the next years, Gregory served as Pelagius' close advisor.

Pope St. Gregory the Great

Witness to the Faith

Fresco of Theolinda, Queen of the Lombards

Gregorian Chant
A form of plainchant developed by Pope St. Gregory the Great, usually sung without instrumental accompaniment.

In 589, plague and other natural disasters ravaged Italy. In 590, the plague claimed Pope Pelagius. The clergy and the people of Rome chose his successor. By acclamation, they unanimously chose Gregory. On September 3, 590, Gregory I (590-604) was consecrated pope. The Barque of Peter has never had a finer captain.

In 590, the Church faced many dangers. The two most immediate were the Lombards and the plague. Gregory asked the people of Rome to pray, do penance, and beg God to end the plague and the disasters. For a time, they did end.

The Lombards, perhaps the most vicious barbarian tribe besides the Huns, continually threatened Rome. All Gregory could do, not having an army, was to pay them off. Gregory paid tribute to the Lombards so often that he called himself the "paymaster of the Lombards."

The money for these payoffs came from the "Patrimony of St. Peter." This was land that had been donated to the Catholic Church in Italy, Sicily, Corsica, Sardinia, and other more distant places. Gregory decided to repair the damage the barbarians had done to the Patrimony and to administer these lands fairly and efficiently. This was exactly the kind of work for which Gregory had trained as a young man and performed as prefect of Rome. As a result, Gregory proved very successful in managing the estates in the Patrimony of St. Peter. It must have been a surprise to his tenants that the pope was a skilled financial manager!

More importantly, Gregory was the pope, and as such he was responsible for the soul of every person on Earth during his reign, and that included the Lombards. While he kept them pacified with tribute, he also sought to convert them to Catholicism. He finally succeeded in converting Agilulf, the Lombard king, who was baptized in 603. Like Clotilde with Clovis, Agilulf's queen, Theolinda, had brought her husband into the Church. The Lombard rulers helped St. Columban found the abbey at Bobbio and erected a basilica dedicated to St. John the Baptist at Monza, near Milan. On its altar, Agilulf placed his iron crown, upon which his name was engraved along with the title "King of all Italy." Supposedly, its inner circle was made from one of the nails used to crucify Our Lord. Later, Charlemagne and Napoleon would be crowned with this crown.

When the Visigoths became powerful in Spain, Gregory worked to convert them to the true Faith. Before he died, he would see this goal bear fruit. Spain would become the great defender of the Church. He abolished paganism on the islands of Corsica and Sardinia. He defended the papacy against John the Faster, the patriarch of Constantinople, who appointed himself the "Universal Patriarch" of the Church. Gregory showed true Christian humility by referring to himself as the "Servant of the Servants of God," a title which nearly all future popes continued to use. Gregory is also credited with developing a form of music named for him, called **Gregorian Chant**. Gregorian Chant is a form of *plainchant*, essentially the simplest form of music. It is sung, usually without instrumental accompaniment.

Pope St. Gregory had never been a healthy person. As he grew older, his health declined. During his last years, he governed the Church from his sick bed. He died on March 12, 604.

The Conversion of Britain

Pope Gregory served as pope for only thirteen and a half years. However, his pontificate seemed longer because he accomplished so much. His greatest accomplishment may well have been the conversion of the British Isles.

Recall, that while he was still a monk, Gregory had encountered the fair-haired Angles in the Roman marketplace. He had organized a missionary expedition to go to Britain to evangelize them. However, Pope Pelagius had called him back almost immediately. Gregory never lost the desire to evangelize Britain. Once he became pope, he implemented this plan.

Map of the Anglo-Saxon Kingdoms

Because of the later barbarian invasions, the history of the early Church in Britain remains shadowy. Evidence suggests that Christians were present in Britain by around 180. As Britain was part of the Roman Empire, there is reason to believe that British Christians suffered martyrdom during the persecution of Emperor Diocletian around the beginning of the fourth century. The Jutes, Angles, and Saxons, who invaded Britain beginning in the middle of the fifth century, overwhelmed the few British Christians, destroyed the early Church records, and drove the Christians out of their homelands into Wales in the west of Britain.

Between them, the Saxons and the Angles founded seven kingdoms in Britain. In the south, they created Kent and Sussex. In the east, they formed Essex and East Anglia. In the west, they established Wessex. In the north, they founded the kingdom of Northumbria. The kingdom of Mercia (the Midlands) was located in the center of the island. In all seven *Anglo-Saxon* kingdoms, the people were pagans. Thus, when Gregory saw the "bright faces" of the Angle youths, he said that they should be saved from the prince of darkness.

Pope Gregory entrusted the task of evangelizing Britain to forty monks from his own monastery, under the direction of a Benedictine monk named Augustine—known today as St. Augustine of Canterbury

St. Augustine of Canterbury

Witness to the Faith 101

King Ethelbert of Kent

(not to be confused with St. Augustine of Hippo, the son of St. Monica). These missionaries left Rome in the autumn of 596. In 597, Augustine and his companions landed on the English coast and began their missionary work.

The leader of the Anglo-Saxons was King Ethelbert of Kent. He had married the Frankish princess Bertha, a Catholic. Bertha persuaded Ethelbert to meet Augustine. Ethelbert received Augustine and his monks with hospitality and listened to them speak about Catholicism. Although Ethelbert told them that he would not immediately become Catholic, he gave them permission to preach throughout his kingdom and provided them with a place to live in Canterbury, the capital of his kingdom.

On Christmas 597, after he had been consecrated the bishop of Canterbury, Augustine and his monks baptized about ten thousand people, but not Ethelbert. Ethelbert finally became a Catholic sometime in the next four years.

Following King Ethelbert's conversion, great success crowned St. Augustine of Canterbury's missionary labors. Knowing that the king's conversion would stimulate conversions in Britain, Augustine sent a letter to Pope Gregory asking for more priests. In 601, Pope Gregory appointed Augustine the "Bishop of the English." The pope sent him the pallium as a mark of his supremacy over the churches of England. Augustine established his see at Canterbury. Soon after Ethelbert's Baptism, the king of Essex followed his example. The capital of Essex was London, and its first bishop was Melletius. By the time St. Augustine of Canterbury died in 605, the Catholic Faith had grown deep roots in Britain.

Interior of the Canterbury Cathedral

Light in the Darkness

Secular historians refer to the time between the fall of the Roman Empire in 476 and the coronation of Charlemagne in 800 as the "Dark Ages." Certainly, the fall of Rome and the barbarian invasions were a dark time for Europe. However, the Church was the light that drove away the darkness. There were saints who shone especially bright: Patrick, Benedict, and Augustine of Canterbury. The Holy Spirit blessed the Church with some of its greatest popes, Leo and Gregory; and one of its most surprising, Vigilius. As Our Lord said, "I am the light of the world. Whoever follows me will never walk in darkness, but will have the light of life" (John 8:12).

Oral Exercises

1. Who forced the Gothic tribes to become Arians?
2. Why did the Vandals persecute the Church?
3. Who stopped the Huns from attacking Rome?
4. Why is France called the "Eldest Daughter of the Church"?
5. What three virtues does the Rule of St. Benedict stress?
6. Where is the spiritual capital of Ireland?
7. Who was St. Finian?
8. What was the name of the monastery that St. Columban founded?
9. Who was the first English king to convert to Catholicism?
10. Where did St. Augustine of Canterbury establish the see for the primary English bishop?

Witness to the Faith

Chapter 7
The Church Continues Converting Europe and Faces Its Greatest Adversary

St. Paulinus of York

St. Felix of Burgundy

Introduction

During the seventh century, the Catholic Church experienced some of its greatest triumphs. The Faith continued to grow in Ireland and Britain. The Gospel came to the German peoples, who embraced it. In France, the descendants of Clovis and Clotilde grew in their love for Christ and His Church. It seemed that all of Europe was turning ever more toward the Catholic Faith. However, in the desert of Arabia, one of the greatest threats that Christianity has ever known was about to sweep forth.

The Church Grows in Britain

At the time of Augustine of Canterbury's death, only Kent and Essex had entered the Church, but missionaries in Britain continued to spread the Faith. Sometime between 625 and 633, Paulinus of York converted King Edwin of Northumbria to Catholicism. Pope Gregory had sent Paulinus to Britain around 604, in answer to St. Augustine's request for more priests after the Baptism of King Ethelbert. In addition to converting King Edwin, Paulinus converted many of the king's subjects. Following the death of Edwin in 633, Paulinus returned to Kent. He was subsequently made bishop of Rochester and archbishop of York. St. Paulinus died in 644.

The conversion of King Sigebert of East Anglia seems primarily due to the efforts of St. Felix of Burgundy. As with much of Britain's early history,

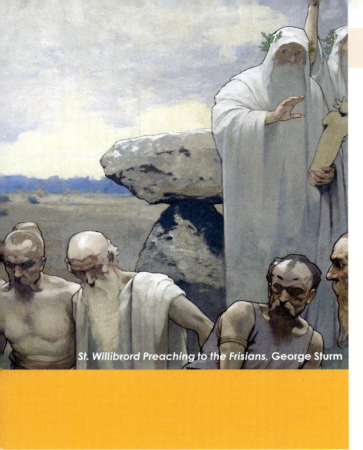
St. Willibrord Preaching to the Frisians, George Sturm

622 A.D. – 722 A.D.

622 A.D.
Mohammed and his followers are driven out of Mecca and flee to Medina, a journey known as the "hegira" (flight).

630 A.D.
Mohammed rides into Mecca at the head of an army, beginning Islam's conquest of the Arabic world.

637 A.D.
The Muslims capture Jerusalem.

664 A.D.
The Synod of Whitby resolves the date of Easter among the British and Irish.

690-739 A.D.
St. Willibrord brings the Gospel to Frisia (Germany and the Netherlands).

711-714 A.D.
A Muslim army under Tariq overruns Spain.

722 A.D.
At the Battle of Covadonga, Pelayo and his men successfully resist the Muslims' attempt to wipe out the last tiny piece of Catholic Spain.

records are scarce and unclear. Apparently, Sigebert was baptized while in France, where he obtained the services of St. Felix, whom Pope Honorius I named bishop of East Anglia. Felix traveled from Burgundy, where he had served as a monk at one of St. Columban's monasteries. He arrived in East Anglia around 630. For the next seventeen years, Felix evangelized the people of East Anglia. By the time he died in 647, he seems to have converted that kingdom.

While most of Britain was becoming Catholic, the ruler of Mercia, King Penda, resolved to remain a pagan. Penda became king around 626. Over the next years, he consolidated his power by defeating some enemies and allying with others. In 633, Penda felt strong enough to challenge Edwin of Northumbria, the strongest king in Britain. In October 633, Penda defeated and killed Edwin at the Battle of Hatfield Chase. Edwin's death forced Paulinus to

Witness to the Faith 105

King Oswald

flee Northumbria. Penda subsequently defeated the East Angles in battle, killing their king, Egric, as well as former King Sigebert, who had retired to a monastery. Egric had hoped that Sigebert's presence at the battle would boost his troops' morale. For a time, paganism became triumphant, as Penda ravaged the two conquered kingdoms.

Finally, in 654, King Edwin's nephew, Oswald, defeated Penda in battle and reconquered Northumbria. Oswald immediately requested missionaries from St. Columba's abbey of Iona. These monks built a monastery on the island of Lindisfarne, which became the headquarters for their missionary activities.

Meanwhile, Penda's baptized son, Peada, who had married Oswald's daughter, became king of Mercia. When he returned to Mercia, Peada brought along four priests to begin evangelizing his pagan kingdom. One of these men, an Irish priest named Diuma, became the first bishop of Mercia in 655.

The Synod of Whitby

By the middle of the seventh century, the situation in Britain had quieted to the point where Church leaders could discuss theological matters. Prior to this time, the Church had simply sought to evangelize and exist in the face of the barbarians and pagans like Penda. The issue that caused the consternation involved the question of the date of Easter.

Unlike other holy days, such as Christmas, Easter does not fall on a fixed date every year. A dispute erupted between the Irish, who followed the tradition established by St. Patrick and St. Columba, and those Catholics with a Roman background, who followed the tradition of Augustine of Canterbury. The Romans celebrated Easter a week later than the Irish did. Of course, disorder, disagreements, and disharmony resulted.

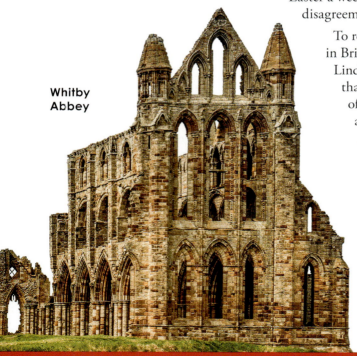

Whitby Abbey

To resolve the Easter issue, in 664 Church leaders in Britain convened a synod at Whitby. Monks from Lindisfarne represented the Irish position. They argued that their Easter practices were based on the traditions of St. Columba. The Romans, based in Canterbury, argued that Rome, the center of the universal Church, must control such questions. They agreed with the Irish that St. Columba was a good and holy saint, but they felt that in this instance he had made a mistake, which they now needed to correct. When the two sides failed to reach an agreement, King Oswald, the leading British king, decided the issue by declaring that at least Northumbria would follow the tradition of the popes.

The Hierarchy in Britain

In 665, when Pope Vitalian (657-672) learned of the way that King Oswald had dealt with the Easter controversy, he was very pleased. He encouraged Oswald to continue working to bring Catholicism to all parts of Britain. To assist Oswald, in 668 Vitalian sent a group of Benedictine monks to Britain, led by St. Theodore of Tarsus, a 66-year-old Greek monk whom Vitalian had named archbishop of Canterbury.

When Archbishop Theodore arrived in Britain the following year, he completely reorganized the English hierarchy. He created several new sees and appointed excellent leaders to them. For example, he installed Wilfrid, a monk from Lindisfarne, as the archbishop of York—the second most important ecclesiastical position in England. Wilfrid had been the principle proponent of the "Roman" position on Easter at the Whitby Synod.

During Theodore's twenty-two years as archbishop (668-690), he dedicated himself to educating his flock. He quickly established a monastery school at Canterbury, which taught literature, astronomy, mathematics, Latin, and Greek. St. Aldhelm, the future bishop of Malmesbury in Wessex, was educated at Canterbury. Among the Benedictine monks who accompanied St. Theodore from Rome was Benedict Biscop. In 685, Benedict founded the monasteries of Wearmouth and Jarrow. Benedictine monk St. Bede (673-735), who is considered the "Father of English History" because of his famous *Ecclesiastical History of the English People*, spent almost his entire life at Jarrow, first as a student and then as its most famous teacher and author. It is from these English monastic schools that the leaders of the Carolingian renaissance of the late eighth century would come. With the help of scholars like Alcuin of York, Charlemagne would usher in a new era of learning, causing even secular historians to agree that the "Dark Ages" had indeed ended.

St. Theodore of Tarsus

The Church in German Lands

The Irish Monks

Probably because Ireland is a small island, the Irish had an almost insatiable desire to explore what lay beyond their shores. This desire, coupled with their missionary zeal, drove them to nearly every corner of the known world—and some unknown corners. For example, St. Brendan of Clonfert (484-577), one of the "Twelve Apostles of Ireland," is known as "The Navigator," because of a remarkable voyage he made which may have reached Iceland, or even, some claim, North America.

Although the exact location of Brendan's voyage remains a mystery, others of the Twelve Apostles of Ireland traveled to the European continent, where they built monasteries and evangelized the barbarian tribes. Recall that St. Columban had established the monastery of Luxeuil in France. Luxeuil became the center for the reconversion of Europe.

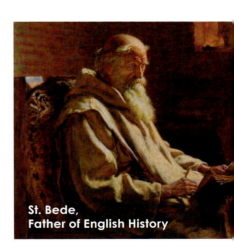

St. Bede, Father of English History

Witness to the Faith 107

St. Rupert Baptizes the Bavarian Duke Theodo II, Francis de Neve

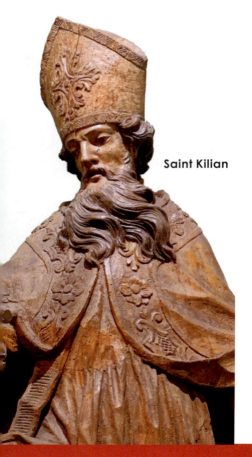

Saint Kilian

The Rhine River provides one of the main waterways through northern Europe. Because it was always easier and faster for people of this period to travel by water than by land, people settled along rivers. Several barbarian tribes had made their homes along the Rhine River or its tributaries and in its nearby forests. Among these tribes were the Bavarians, the Alemanni, and the Thuringians.

One of the first missionaries to the Bavarians was St. Emmeram, who established the Church of Ratisbon (present-day Regensburg) and preached to their leader, Duke Theodo II (625-714). St. Emmeram's work was cut short by his martyrdom in 652. The man most responsible for the Bavarians' conversion was St. Rupert of Worms, the founder of the city of Salzburg, Austria. Rupert preached to the Bavarians and baptized Duke Theodo sometime in the early part of the eighth century. In May 716, Pope Gregory II (715-731) sent Bishop Martinian to create a Church hierarchy in Bavaria. Additional missionaries followed. With Duke Theodo's assistance and protection, Saint Erhard of Regensburg founded a number of monasteries. During a pilgrimage to Rome, Frankish monk St. Corbinian met Gregory II. Gregory made him a bishop and sent him to evangelize Bavaria. In 724, Corbinian arrived in Bavaria. He built a Benedictine monastery and school in Freising. He died in 730 and is buried in Freising Cathedral. Many of the towns in Bavaria, still a strongly Catholic area of Germany, developed from and around the monasteries and churches that Irish monks had started with the help of Duke Theodo.

The Germanic tribes known as the Alemanni lived in the area around the Upper Rhine River. Clovis had conquered them in 496 and made their land part of his kingdom. However, he had not ruled them very strictly, so they remained somewhat independent and pagan. Late in his life, St. Columban left Luxeuil to preach to various barbarian tribes, including the Alemanni. Columban and several companions sailed up the Rhine and established a monastery at Bregenz. When Columban continued to Italy to evangelize the Lombards, he left St. Gall behind to continue the work among the Alemanni. For more than thirty years, Gall evangelized the Alemanni. He also trained other monks, who went forth spreading the Faith. A strikingly beautiful monastery, named in his honor, was built on the spot where he had lived as a hermit. Today the Abbey of Saint Gall possesses one of the finest libraries in the world, with books dating from the ninth century. For his work in converting the Alemanni, St. Gall is rightly called "The Apostle of Switzerland."

Around 686, Pope Conon (686-687) consecrated Irish monk St. Kilian as bishop to a Germanic pagan tribe, the Thuringians, who lived in central Germany. Kilian converted Duke Gosbert of Franconia and founded the Church of Wurzburg. According to tradition, Kilian had told Gosbert that his marriage to his brother's widow, Geilana, was invalid. One day in 689, while Gosbert was away, Geilana, who had not converted, had Kilian and two of his companions murdered. Despite this setback, the Catholic Faith thrived in Franconia, and future popes sent more missionaries to the Germans.

St. Willibrord

When Theodore became archbishop of Canterbury, he reorganized the English hierarchy. Part of Theodore's reorganization involved making St. Wilfrid the archbishop of York in the kingdom of Northumbria. Over the years, Wilfrid and the king of Northumbria had a series of disagreements that led to the king expelling Wilfrid from Northumbria in 677. Because Theodore may have also played a role in Wilfrid's expulsion, Wilfrid chose to go to Rome to ask Pope Agatho (678-681) to resolve the matter.

Depending on the historical source, Wilfrid either intentionally sailed to Frisia (northwest Netherlands) or had his ship blown off course and landed accidentally in Frisia. Either way, once Wilfrid arrived in Frisia, Aldgisl, the Frisian ruler, received him with great honor and friendship. Wilfrid spent several months wintering in the Frisian capital of Utrecht, preaching the Gospel before continuing to Rome. In October 679, Pope Agatho held a synod, which restored Wilfrid to his diocese.

St. Willibrord Preaches the Gospel

When Wilfrid returned to England, he spoke about Frisia and the evangelization opportunity there to the monks in his monastery at Rippon. With the approval of Pope Sergius I (687-701), in 690 twelve English monks, led by St. Willibrord, left for the continent. Their goal was to preach to the Frisians in present-day Germany and the Netherlands. Upon their arrival, Willibrord placed himself and his monks under the protection of the Frankish leader Pepin, who had conquered southern Frisia in 689. Willibrord established his initial base in Antwerp.

In 695, Willibrord was in Rome, where Pope Sergius consecrated him as bishop of the Frisians. Upon his return, he established his see at Utrecht, where he built a cathedral and began recruiting a native clergy. In 698, he built the monastery of Echternach (in present-day Luxembourg) on land that had been donated to him. He began to preach the Gospel in Thuringia, where Catholic Duke Heden II warmly received him. Until his death in November 739, Willibrord preached, founded monastic communities, and established schools throughout Frisia. He succeeded in eliminating all traces of paganism. In fact, Willibrord was so successful in planting the seeds of the Catholic Faith that the area in which he preached has, with a few exceptions, remained Catholic to the present day.

Basilica in Echternach

Witness to the Faith   **109**

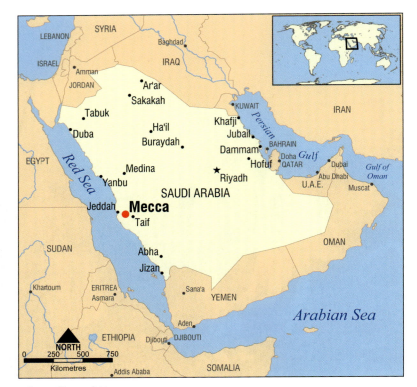

Location of Mecca

Sand Dunes of the Rub al Khali Desert in Saudi Arabia

The Rise of Islam

Since the first century, Arabia had resisted conversion by the Church and assimilation into the Roman Empire. This is due in part to geography. Nearly the entire country is desert. Some geographers estimate that only 1 percent of the country can be used for agriculture. It is a harsh, hot, barren place.

In the seventh century, in the Arabian town of Mecca (in present-day Saudi Arabia), there was a famous shrine called the "Kaaba." The Kaaba served as the headquarters for a strange religion that mixed aspects of Judaism with idolatry. The Kaaba was a small, cube-shaped building, inside of which was a spring. To the followers of the Kaaba religion, the spring held a special significance. They believed that the Angel Gabriel had miraculously created the spring to quench the thirst of Hagar and her son Ishmael, who had become lost and were dying of thirst in the desert. In addition to the spring, the Kaaba also contained 360 idols, one for each of the Arabian tribes.

In 571, a son was born in Mecca to the family who cared for the Kaaba. They named him Mohammed. He would change the world.

Mohammed's parents died when he was 6 years old, and his grandfather and uncle raised him. He began to earn a living as a camel driver and a shepherd. In his thirties, he also began spending time in a cave, where he claimed to receive revelations from God given to him by the Angel Gabriel. About 613, Mohammed, who had come to believe that God was calling him to overthrow the idols and restore true worship to God, began preaching his doctrines in public.

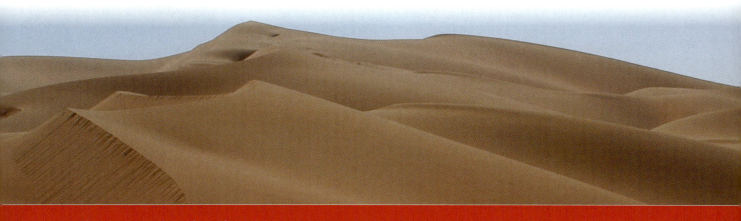

110 *Chapter 7: The Church Continues Converting Europe and Faces Its Greatest Adversary*

At first, Mohammed had few followers, mainly because he called for the destruction of the accepted religion. In particular, because he declared that the idols in the Kaaba had to be destroyed, many people hated him and his new teaching. Nevertheless, his magnetic personality drew followers, and his movement grew.

However, on July 16, 622, Mecca's rulers forced Mohammed and about seventy of his followers to flee Mecca for Medina, 250 miles away. The flight from Mecca to Medina is known as the "hegira" (flight) and marks the beginning of the Muslim era. In Medina, Mohammed's power grew, as did the number of his followers. In 630, he returned to Mecca at the head of an army, seized the city, and destroyed all the statues in and around the Kaaba. All his enemies accepted his new religion. Over the next two years, he consolidated his power by conquering the rest of Arabia. By the time he died in 632, he had won all of Arabia to his new religion. While there had been a significant number of Christians in Arabia before Mohammed, by 650 there were almost none.

> **Islam**
> The religion founded by Mohammed, summed up in the creed, "There is no god but Allah, and Mohammed is his messenger."

The Tenets of Islam

Of all major world religions, **Islam**, the religion founded by Mohammed, is by some measures the simplest. The Muslim creed (called the *shahada*) in its most common form is utterly stark and simple: "There is no god but Allah, and Mohammed is his messenger." Reciting this creed with the right understanding and belief makes one a **Muslim**.

> **Muslim**
> One who adheres to Islam.

The *shahada* is the first of the *Five Pillars of Islam*. The others are prayer, almsgiving, fasting, and pilgrimage. Muslims observe certain hours for prayer, five times a day. They are required to give alms, fast every day during the month of Ramadan, and abstain from wine, pork, and gambling. Every Muslim who is able must make at least one pilgrimage during his lifetime to Mecca, which Muslims consider to be a holy city.

There are two major sources of doctrine in Islam: the **Quran** (Islam's "holy book") and the **Hadith** (a collection of sayings and actions ascribed primarily to Mohammed). Islamic religious law, or *sharia* law, is largely based on the Hadith and the interpretations of Islamic scholars. The Quran is composed of the so-called "revelations" that Mohammed claimed were

Witness to the Faith 111

given to him by God through the Archangel Gabriel. These "revelations" were originally handed on as oral tradition, and later written down and collected into a single book about two decades after Mohammed's death.

The Quran emphasizes concrete descriptions of the life to come, including the physical pleasures of Paradise. According to the Hadith, on the Day of Judgment all men must try to cross a narrow, dangerous bridge over the fires of Hell, to Paradise. The righteous are swept across quickly, others cross with injuries, but the wicked fall down into Hell.

Quran
Islam's "holy book," detailing the so-called "revelations" that Mohammed claimed were given to him by God through the Archangel Gabriel.

The moral teachings of the Quran are based on the false doctrine of **fatalism**, which negates human freedom. All worship is reduced to acts of formalism. Moreover, the Quran and Hadith both teach that God made men superior to women. Thus, Muslim countries tend to greatly limit the rights and freedom of women. Although this is beginning to change in some modern Muslim countries, in many cases women are still treated as little better than slaves.

A fully Islamic society is a *theocracy* uniting religious and civil authority. Violations of religious law, such as apostasy, are punished by the State. Those who apostatize, or leave Islam, are traditionally judged to be deserving of death.

Mohammed the Man

Since his death, historians, both Christian and non-Christian have evaluated Mohammed. The central issue revolves around the sincerity of his beliefs. Was he genuine in his belief system or unscrupulous, using Islam as a way to promote a personal agenda to enrich himself? In the end, only God can read a man's heart. However, history reveals a number of interesting facts that set Mohammed apart from other religious leaders, especially those who began major religions—for example, Christianity, Hinduism, and Buddhism. Mohammed actually led troops in battle and engaged in personal combat. He ordered the assassination of several political enemies. Also, Mohammed had fourteen wives.

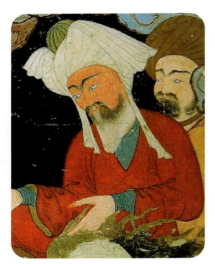

Abu Bekr

The Spread of Islam

As Mohammed proclaimed his new religion in the East, almost no one in the West knew anything about it. Little is known about the popes of this period either. Boniface IV (608-615) became pope following the death of Boniface III, who had ruled less than a year. Boniface IV did consult with Mellitus, the first bishop of London, on matters relating to the Church in Britain. Adeodatus I was pope from October 615 to his death in 618. Following his death, the papacy remained vacant for one year before the pontificate of Boniface V (619-625). Boniface also seems to have had a special desire to spread the Faith in England. Following his death, Honorius I, who sent St. Felix to East Anglia, became pope.

As the Church was converting Britain and the Germanic tribes, the armies of Islam swept out of Arabia like "the red whirlwind of the desert"

112 *Chapter 7: The Church Continues Converting Europe and Faces Its Greatest Adversary*

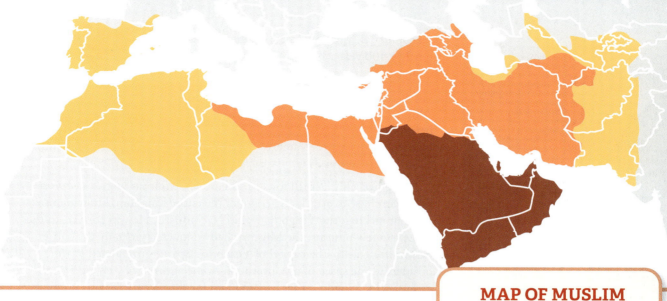

MAP OF MUSLIM CONQUESTS

● **Under Mohammed, 622-632**
● **Conquests of 632-661**
● **Conquests of 661-750**

(G.K. Chesterton, *The Everlasting Man* [London: Hodder & Stoughton, 1925], p. 147). By the end of 632, Abu Bekr, the new Muslim leader, prepared to launch attacks to spread Islam. To the people who prepared to fight them, attacks from desert raiders were nothing new. However, this time the raiders did not intend to steal horses and depart. They planned to conquer and stay.

In 636, the Islamic army won the Battle of the Yarmuk River, one of the most decisive battles in world history. They defeated the Byzantine forces under Emperor Heraclius, who had organized a massive army. The Islamic wave was about to crash into Christendom.

The defeat at the Yarmuk River caused Syria to fall into Muslim hands. Muslim armies pressed on, conquering Persia and Turkestan, and pushed into India. In 637, they captured Jerusalem. Still attacking, the Muslims subjugated Tripoli, Algeria, and Morocco in North Africa. Only fifty years after the death of Mohammed, they had extended their conquests as far as the Atlantic Ocean. Amazingly, despite fighting on two fronts, the Muslims won nearly every battle. Everywhere they went, they persecuted non-Muslims.

The Muslim conquests in these first decades are unprecedented. At the time of his death, almost no one outside of Arabia had heard of Mohammed or Islam. Yet, in a short span of time, the Muslims had conquered the ancient kingdom of Persia, as well as Egypt, and had reduced the power of the Byzantine Empire to almost nothing. Moreover, *all of these conquests have endured!* With only one or two exceptions,

Fariz, January Suchodolski

Witness to the Faith

Roderic, King of the Visigoths

no country that has become Muslim has ever been won back from it, in nearly 1,400 years. Yet there is one prominent exception: Spain!

After conquering North Africa, the Muslims crossed the Strait of Gibraltar, the narrow strip of water that separates Europe from Africa. Although the Visigoths tried to defend their kingdom, they were betrayed. Led by a Muslim named Tariq, with the help of the traitor Count Julian, they defeated King Roderic at the pivotal Battle of the Guadalete River in 711.

Tariq had only a small force, and Gothic Spain was large, but he was bold. He chose to attack and conquer the entire kingdom, knowing that without its king, the Visigoths would be confused. He was correct. In the space of a few months, the Muslims had conquered virtually the entire peninsula. Toledo, the capital of Visigothic Spain, surrendered to the invaders in the space of one afternoon in the autumn of 711. By 714, the great Gothic kingdom that had endured for three centuries was no more.

It had taken the Muslims three years to conquer the entire Iberian Peninsula. This was a task that Hannibal could not accomplish, and it would be beyond the powers of Napoleon. The Roman legions, the finest soldiers in the world in their day, had taken the greater part of a century to conquer the land. Now, only a small remnant of the Gothic kingdom remained, huddled in a cave in the north of Spain. Yet, from that cave would be launched the greatest comeback in the history of the world.

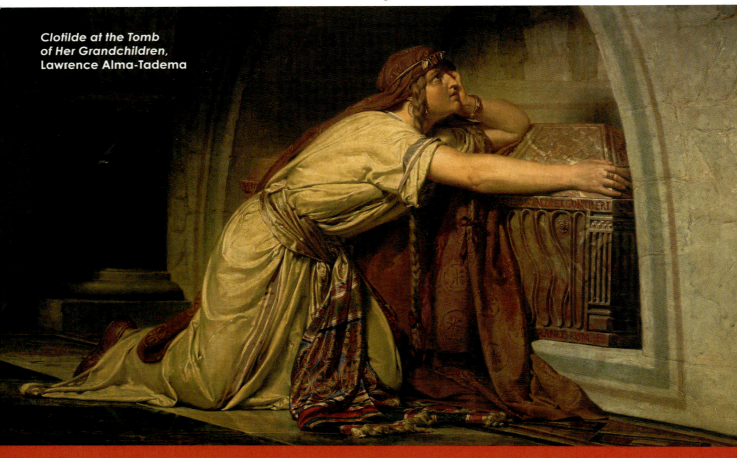

Clotilde at the Tomb of Her Grandchildren, Lawrence Alma-Tadema

The Church in France

Following the death of Clovis, the kingdom of the Franks experienced some bad times. Clovis had converted to Catholicism, but when he died in 511, he divided his kingdom among his four sons, who did not obey the Faith and some of whom were even murderers. One can only imagine the suffering of Queen Clotilde, who lived until 545 and had to endure her children murdering her grandchildren and living immoral lives. Nevertheless, despite the personal immorality of some of its kings, the Church in France continued to thrive.

Clovis was the first king in a line of Frankish rulers known as the **Merovingian Dynasty**, which lasted until 752. Before the Merovingian period, the clergy and people of a city selected their bishop. During the Merovingian Dynasty, the Frankish kings began recommending candidates for bishop. Since the king wielded so much power, his choice really meant that the electors had no alternative but to elect his candidate as bishop.

Although a king should have chosen a bishop based on his orthodoxy and obedience to the Holy Father, that was rarely a consideration during this period. While the bishop did lead his flock spiritually, he also possessed a great deal of temporal power and influence. Nearly all bishops were wealthy landowners. Kings, princes, wealthy citizens, and others who wanted to support the Church donated land to the Church. The bishop owned this land. The bishop could use the land to establish a monastery or build a church or a cathedral. It could be used to generate wealth from crops. The wealth of a citizen was measured in terms of the land they owned. In later days, landowners would raise and support armies from their lands. Thus, kings often wanted men in the position of bishop who supported them and their policies, not necessarily holy men working on behalf of the Church.

As a result, abuses crept into the choosing and election of bishops. However, good kings realized

Tomb Sculpture of Clovis in the Basilica of Saint-Denis

Merovingian Dynasty
The line of Frankish rulers descended from Clovis; it lasted until 752.

Map of the Four Merovingian Kingdoms Ruled by the Sons of Clovis after His Death: Austrasia, Neustria, Burgundy, and Aquitaine

Witness to the Faith 115

King Pelayo

that having good and holy bishops would benefit the kingdom. These men would work to make the lives of the people better, both spiritually and physically. Generally, the Merovingian kings tried to select virtuous candidates to serve as bishops. In addition, Church synods worked to limit the greed of dishonest clergy. The bishop controlled the Church funds, from which he paid his priests, built and maintained diocesan churches, and provided for the needs of the poor.

Since the time of the Apostles, the Church has always been concerned about providing for the basic needs of all human beings, as Our Lord taught in the seven corporal works of mercy. Over time, as more money became available, the Church did more. During this period, the priests and bishops were able to feed, clothe, and shelter the poor. Eventually, a hospital or hospice was built in every episcopal city to care for the poor.

In addition to the corporal works, the bishop sought to act as protector to the weak, the defenseless, and orphans. He protected the weak so that local rulers could not charge them with crimes without informing him. He appointed a trained priest to defend them in civil matters. In addition to visiting prisoners and making sure that they had food, he often worked with the courts to lessen their sentences.

Although it would not be until 1435 that the Church officially condemned slavery, bishops in Merovingian France worked to better the lives of slaves in their diocese. First, the bishop would excommunicate any master who killed his slave without court authorization. Second, the bishops decreed that marriages involving slaves were lawful and valid. This had an important moral component regarding chastity as well as recognizing the sanctity of marriage. Finally, the bishops decreed that a slave who had been baptized could not be sold to non-Christians.

As the Faith spread from the cities into the rural districts, the bishops needed to create "rural parishes." The priests charged with running these parishes were known as "priests of the people." Wealthy families also created parishes on their own estates. The parish church served as a private oratory for the family.

The Salvation of Spain

The seventh century saw the Church grow in England, Ireland, France, Germany, and the Netherlands. On the other hand, it also saw the birth of its greatest adversary: Islam. By 722, the Muslims had reduced the Gothic kingdom of Spain to a tiny speck of land, perhaps no more than twenty square miles, where a handful of Catholic warriors huddled. According to a ninth-century source, the Muslims sent a bishop to seek the surrender of these pitiful warriors. The bishop asked their "king," Pelayo, to surrender. Pelayo thanked the bishop but declined. Pelayo replied, "Our hope is in Christ; this little mountain will be the salvation of Spain and of the Goths; the mercy of Christ will free us from that multitude [the Muslims]."

As King Pelayo hunkered down in his cave, he prepared to wage the longest war in the history of the world. By May 722, the Spaniards who huddled in that cave knew nothing of the outside world. Had Islam overrun all of Christendom? They did not know. All they knew was their tiny realm. The Muslims, though, had grown tired of Pelayo and his "kingdom," and decided to wipe him out.

After the invaders offered terms of surrender, which Pelayo declined, the battle ensued. Accustomed to fighting on flat ground, the Muslims were no match for the Spaniards, who rained boulders down upon them, in their mountain fastness. Deciding it was not worth killing "thirty barbarians on a rock," the Muslims retreated. The Spanish had won the Battle of Covadonga. The Battle of Covadonga was the first battle in the 770-year war to reconquer Spain from the Muslims.

King Pelayo in Covadonga,
Luis de Madrazo

Oral Exercises

1. What is Lindisfarne?
2. What did the Synod at Whitby decide?
3. Where did St. Gall establish his monastery?
4. Who was sent to convert the Thuringians?
5. Who converted the Frisians and founded monastic communities throughout Frisia?
6. Who founded Islam?
7. What false doctrine is the basis for the moral teachings of the Quran?
8. What was the "hegira"?
9. What is the significance of the Battle of the Guadalete River?
10. What were some of the things the bishops of this period did to help slaves?

Witness to the Faith

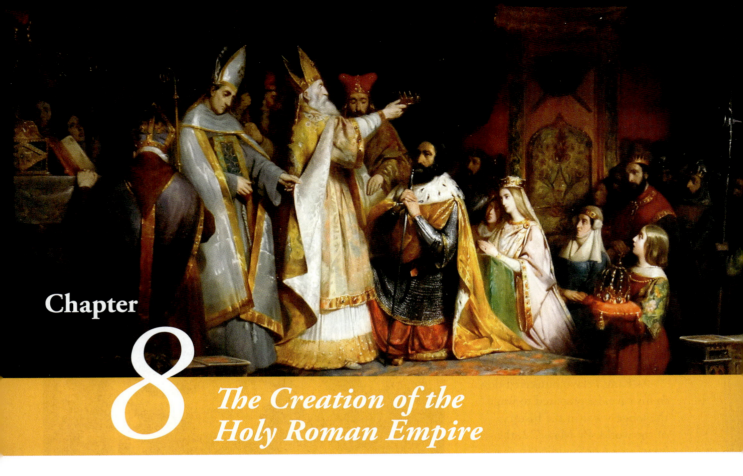

Chapter 8
The Creation of the Holy Roman Empire

Introduction

In the beginning of the eighth century, Europe was struggling through chaos. The various tribes were developing into the European nations, but no culture in the West had risen significantly above barbarism since the fall of Rome. The continent was a patchwork of Christianity and various forms of paganism. In addition, the Muslim armies had swept through Spain, and now turned to attack France. Although the century's beginning was turbulent, by its end, the Holy Roman Empire would arise, leading Western civilization into a new era.

St. Boniface, Apostle of Germany

In 718, a zealous young English monk named Winfrid (675-754) journeyed to Rome, where he met Pope Gregory II and offered him his services as a missionary. Gregory, who had already sent numerous missionaries into Bavaria and the Rhine River regions, accepted the young man's offer. He renamed his new missionary "**Boniface**" ("he who does good") and sent him into the Rhineland.

The following year, Boniface crossed the Rhine River at Mainz and traveled into Thuringia to continue the work that St. Kilian had started. He also worked in Bavaria. In 721, Boniface traveled into Hesse, a completely pagan area in central Germany, becoming the first missionary

St. Boniface
Brought the Faith to the Germanic tribes; eventually became archbishop of all Germany; was martyred trying to evangelize the Frisians in the Netherlands.

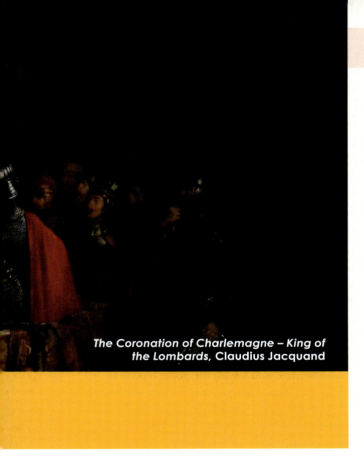
The Coronation of Charlemagne – King of the Lombards, Claudius Jacquand

719 A.D. – 814 A.D.

719 A.D.
Boniface begins his missionary labors in Germany.

732 A.D.
Charles Martel defeats the Muslim army at the Battle of Tours.

751 A.D.
On Christmas Day, Pope Stephen III crowns Pepin king.

754 A.D.
St. Boniface is martyred in the Netherlands and buried in his abbey at Fulda.

774 A.D.
In response to Pope Adrian I's call for help, Charlemagne defeats the Lombards, who are again attacking Rome, and annexes their lands into his empire.

778-812 A.D.
Charlemagne's wars with the Muslims gradually drive them out of France and help to push them back in Spain.

781-796 A.D.
Alcuin works as the director of Charlemagne's palace school, teaching, writing, and improving the educational system of the realm.

785 A.D.
After many attacks and rebellions, the Saxons finally surrender, and their leader, Widukind, receives Baptism.

800 A.D.
Pope Leo III crowns Charlemagne as Holy Roman Emperor.

814 A.D.
Charlemagne's death leaves the empire to his only living offspring, Louis.

---

to preach to the people there. Everywhere he went, he made numerous conversions.

Like all the missionaries of this time, Boniface brought people to the Faith *peacefully*, without force. The missionaries had no armies to support them. They carried no weapons. Boniface converted pagans by first asking them to explain their beliefs to him. Then he would gently and kindly point out flaws and inconsistencies in their beliefs. Finally, he contrasted what they believed with a general explanation of the Catholic Faith. Like his fellow missionaries, Boniface relied on the grace of the Holy Spirit, rather than intellectually brilliant theological arguments.

In 722, Boniface reported on his success to Pope Gregory, who called him back to Rome. On November 30, 722, the pope rewarded his efforts by consecrating Boniface as the bishop for all of Germany

Witness to the Faith

Fulda
Site of an abbey founded by St. Boniface, which houses his remains.

Pope Gregory III
Reigned 731-741; made Boniface archbishop and papal legate to Germany.

Pope Zachary
Reigned 741-752; acknowledged Pepin as king of the Franks, thereby helping to start the Carolingian Dynasty.

Archbishop of Mainz
Ranked as metropolitan over all of Germany, a position first held by St. Boniface.

east of the Rhine River. Essentially, Boniface was bishop for all of Hesse and Thuringia—a massive diocese. The following year, the new bishop returned to Hesse to win more souls to Christ.

In Hesse, Boniface literally dealt paganism a fatal blow. Under the advice of some Hessian Christians, he personally chopped down the sacred "Thunder Oak" tree at Geismar. This huge old oak, which had stood for hundreds of years, was dedicated to the Norse "god" Thor. The pagans had venerated this tree for countless years. The local Christians told Boniface that chopping it down would show the pagans how powerless their "gods" really were. When Thor failed to prevent Boniface from chopping down his sacred oak, thousands of Germans realized that Christ was the true God.

To help with the conversion of his massive mission territory, Boniface called on his British countrymen. They came in great numbers. Many became abbots and bishops in Germany. Soon native clergy joined with the English clergy. Boniface and his subordinates founded beautiful convents for women, as well as magnificent abbeys and monasteries for men—most notably, the Benedictine abbey at **Fulda**, which became a great shrine and cathedral.

Meanwhile, Boniface remained in contact with the pope, reporting on his successes and seeking advice on sacramental preparation and other regulatory matters. In 732, Boniface again traveled to Rome and met with **Pope Gregory III** (731-741). Gregory, impressed with the incredible accomplishments of Boniface, named him archbishop of all Germany. Boniface received the authority to consecrate bishops as well as organize and create dioceses throughout Germany. From 732 on, Boniface devoted all his time and energy to reforming and organizing the hierarchy in Germany as well as improving the spiritual lives of the clergy. In 737, he made a third trip to Rome, where Pope Gregory made him papal legate to Germany.

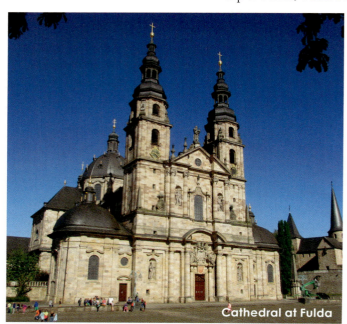
Cathedral at Fulda

After returning from Rome, Boniface created four dioceses in Bavaria: Passau, Salzburg, Regensburg, and Freising. He appointed bishops to administer each diocese. Boniface also decided to rehabilitate the ancient Frankish sees of Reims, Sens, and Rouen. He modeled this hierarchy on the one that had proven so successful in Germany. Boniface and his followers also wrote disciplinary rules to improve the clergy. In 745, **Pope Zachary** (741-752) appointed Boniface as the **archbishop of Mainz**. Mainz became the metropolitan see of all Germany, just as Canterbury was in England.

In February 742, Boniface had written to Pope Zachary, asking for permission to hold a German-Frankish synod. The new Frankish king, Carloman, desired a synod to address issues of morality and discipline among the

Chapter 8: The Creation of the Holy Roman Empire

clergy. In his letter, Boniface noted that it had been more than eighty years since the Franks had held a synod, and many abuses had arisen. The Franks held a series of synods over the next several years. All the bishops and abbots in the Frankish kingdom attended the final synod, which was held in 747. At this synod, these prelates agreed to "maintain the Catholic faith and unity and our subjection to the Roman Church as long as we live" ("Boniface to Archbishop Cuthbert of Canterbury Reporting the Establishment of Frankish Synods and the Obstacles to His Work (747)" in *The Correspondence of St. Boniface*, Internet Medieval Sourcebook [New York: Fordham Univ. Center for Medieval Studies, 2000], no. 35).

In 754, Archbishop Boniface was nearly 80 years old. Yet the same missionary zeal that had inflamed the young English monk named Winfrid still burned in his heart. Determined to convert the Frisians, Boniface took a small group with him to Frisia. Although he made a number of converts, on June 5 a mob of pagan Frisians attacked his party at Dokkum in the Netherlands. As he held the Gospel before him, the Frisians slashed through the book, martyring the holy bishop. The body of St. Boniface, along with the slashed Gospel book, was returned to the monastery of Fulda, where he is buried. The slashed book can still be seen today—one of the more moving Catholic relics. Because of the nature of his death, St. Boniface is often depicted dressed in his bishop's robes and holding a sword upon which a book is impaled.

The Victory over the Muslims

The Muslims had rolled across Iberia and conquered the Visigoths in a matter of months. The Visigoths had not fought a war in over a hundred years, so perhaps they were not the strongest opponent to face the Muslims. Once Gothic Spain fell to the Muslims, the next logical target was Frankish Gaul. The Franks were still, at heart, a barbarian people. In their veins flowed the blood of Clovis and Clotilde, warriors to the end. The words of Clovis were at last going to be fulfilled: "If only I had been there with my Franks!"

Beginning in 723, the work of St. Boniface was greatly aided by the protection he received from Frankish leader **Charles Martel**, and then from his sons Carloman and Pepin. Boniface went so far as to write that without their protection, he could not govern his people, maintain discipline over his priests, or stop the practice of paganism in Germany. The assistance that Charles Martel gave to the Church was invaluable, but his greatest accomplishment occurred on the battlefield, where he saved Europe from Muslim conquest.

In 719, the Muslims crossed the Pyrenees from Spain into southern France. They swept north, taking possession of three cities in southern France before slowing outside of Toulouse. In 721, a Christian army defeated them at the Battle of Toulouse. The Muslims were slowed but not completely defeated.

> **Charles Martel**
> Frankish military leader and "Mayor of the Palace"; ruled France, though without the title of king; defeated the Muslims at the Battle of Tours.

Charles Martel

Witness to the Faith 121

Battle of Tours,
Charles de Steuben

Battle of Tours
A crucial battle between the Muslims and the Franks that halted Muslim expansion into Europe.

Carloman
Son of Charles Martel; inherited Germany. After slaughtering the Alemanni, Carloman repented and, on the advice of Boniface and the pope, entered a monastery.

Pepin
Son of Charles Martel; inherited France and, on his brother's abdication, all the lands of the Franks.

Mayor of the Palace
The man who held the real power in France after Clovis' descendants became figureheads. The last "Mayor of the Palace" was Pepin, who became the first Carolingian king.

In 725, another round of battles began. The Muslims took Carcassonne in the south, then sacked Autun in the middle of France. By 732, they had destroyed the shrine of St. Hilary in Poitiers. The shrine of St. Martin of Tours, the richest shrine in all of France, lay just 50 miles to the north. In October, they decided to attack Tours. Yet Tours is about halfway from the southern border of France. This was no mere raid. The Muslims would have taken Tours, then Orleans, and then Paris, and soon all of Europe would have been theirs. France was the only great power in Europe at the time. Only the Franks could stop them. The words of Clovis were about to be fulfilled. This time, Charles Martel would be there with his Franks!

On October 10, 732, at Poitiers, just outside Tours, in perhaps history's most decisive and critical battle, Charles Martel defeated the Muslim army. Contrary to Frankish custom, he placed his heavy cavalry on the defensive. It was a bitterly cold October day in France, but the Muslims were dressed for the warm Spanish summer. The Frankish warriors, wrapped in their wolf skins, stood before the Muslims like a wall of ice. The Muslim light cavalry, which was very fast, hurled itself repeatedly against this wall, but they could not break through the Frankish lines. Finally, the Franks counterattacked. When night fell, the Muslim commander was dead on the battlefield, and his troops had fled. After one hundred years of almost constant victories, the Muslim invaders had suffered their greatest, most crushing defeat at the hands of the Franks. Two generations later, Charles' successors would completely expel the Muslims from France.

The importance of the **Battle of Tours** cannot be overstated. Had Charles Martel lost, France could have become a Muslim country. Moreover, as their every action demonstrated, the Muslim army would not have stopped at France. They would have attacked Germany, Italy, and the rest of Europe, as they would try to do years later. Since the Muslims had no sea power, Britain and Ireland might have been safe, but they would have been completely isolated. Because of Martel's fierce opposition, which ended Muslim advances and set the stage for centuries of war thereafter, Islam moved no farther into Europe.

Charles Martel died on October 22, 741. He was buried at the Abbey Church (later, Basilica) of Saint-Denis in Paris. Wisely, he had divided his kingdom among his adult sons a year earlier. **Carloman** received Germany, and **Pepin** received France.

Although neither Pepin nor Carloman was a saint, the Church has never had two more loyal supporters. In fact, both men tended to place the welfare of the Church before their personal interests and even that of their nations. To them, what was good for the Church was good for their nation.

Chapter 8: The Creation of the Holy Roman Empire

Carloman had been educated at St. Willibrord's Abbey of Echternach, whereas Pepin had received his education at the Abbey Church of Saint-Denis. Both men knew St. Boniface well, and Carloman, who ruled Germany, worked especially closely with him. In fact, Carloman and Pepin asked Boniface to call the first German synod shortly after their father died.

The Carolingian Dynasty

In 737, Carloman, who had been waging war against the Alemanni, treacherously massacred them during what should have been a peaceful meeting. Although this action was brutal and inexcusable, it was fairly typical of the barbarian culture from which Carloman had come. But Carloman was also a Christian, and, unlike so many of his predecessors, he repented of his sin. Like Theodosius before St. Ambrose, Carloman placed his soul in the hands of St. Boniface. Boniface absolved him. But, for his penance, Carloman was instructed to go to Rome to see the pope, who made him a Benedictine monk. Carloman spent the last seven years of his life in the monastery of Monte Cassino. In all of world history, few rulers have willingly given up their thrones. Perhaps St. Boniface had quoted St. Mark's Gospel to Carloman: "For what shall it profit a man, if he gain the whole world, and suffer the loss of his soul?" (Mark 8:36)

Before he left, Carloman named Pepin his successor in Germany. Thus, Pepin came to rule all the Franks, and he would be the one in his family to begin the royal dynasty.

Charles Martel, although he had ruled the Franks, was not the Frankish king. He was the "**Mayor of the Palace**." For several decades, the Merovingian kings, the descendants of Clovis, had held the title of "king" but had not exercised any real power. The current Merovingian king was Childeric III, who became king in 743. Although history is filled with examples of "kings" who had no power (as is the case with the current monarchy in England), for Pepin the situation was unacceptable. So he sent a messenger to Pope Zachary, asking him a simple question: should the king be the person who wielded royal power? Pope Zachary affirmed that the man who wielded the royal power should be the king. Thus, the Holy Father acknowledged Pepin as king of the Franks.

St. Boniface traveled to France where, on Christmas Day, 751, he crowned Pepin in Soissons. The next year, Pepin regained much of southern France from the Muslims. In the meantime, the Lombards had taken Ravenna and were preparing to march on Rome. In 754, **Pope Stephen III**

Confusion of the Number of Popes Called Stephen

There has been confusion regarding the numbering of popes named Stephen since March 752, when Pope Stephen III was elected. Earlier in the same month, another pope had been elected who took the name Stephen II, but he died three days later, before he could be consecrated. For this reason, he is not listed as a pope in the *Annuario Pontificio*, the official Directory of the Holy See, which lists all the popes. Some historians refer to him as "pope-elect Stephen."

For the purposes of this history, the authors have followed the example of noted Catholic historian Dr. Warren Carroll in numbering the popes named Stephen. Dr. Carroll points out that, under canon law at the time, once a man was elected and consented to his election, he was pope; he need not be consecrated. Pope Paul VI changed that law in 1975, which explains why the *Annuario Pontificio* does not list "pope-elect Stephen." However, during their pontificates, all the popes named Stephen were known according to the older numbering. So, for the purposes of this history, it is practical to use that numbering when referring to those popes.

Witness to the Faith 123

Pope Stephen III
Reigned 752-757; crowned Pepin king. Pepin defended him from the Lombards and gave him towns reconquered from them, thus making the pope a temporal as well as a spiritual leader.

Carolingian Dynasty
The line of kings descended from Charles Martel, beginning with Pepin.

The Donation of Pepin
The land and towns that Pepin took back from the Lombards and gave to Pope Stephen III.

Abbot Fulrad Giving Pepin's Written Guarantee to the Pope

Stephen IV
Reigned 768-772; was the validly elected successor to Pope St. Paul I, following the thirteen-month reign of the antipope installed by Duke Toto of Nepi.

(752-757) traveled to Paris where, in a lavish ceremony, he crowned Pepin in the Abbey Church of Saint-Denis, as well as bestowing on him the honorary title "Patrician of the Romans." It was the first time that a pope had crowned a secular ruler. Thus, Pepin became the first king of the **Carolingian Dynasty**—named in honor of his father, Charles.

While in Paris, Pope Stephen asked Pepin for his aid against the Lombards. Although Pepin had no economic or political reason to do so, he crossed the Alps several times during the remainder of his life to defend the pope because he believed it was his duty as a Catholic monarch. Pepin promised that he would aid the pope against the Lombards. Then he sent messengers to Aistulf, the Lombard king, requesting that "out of respect for the Apostles Peter and Paul," he not attack Rome. When Aistulf refused his request, Pepin crossed the Alps, defeated Aistulf, and besieged his armies at the Lombard capital, Pavia. The defeated Lombard king promised to make full restitution for the damage the Lombards had done, but broke his promise. Once again, the pope called for help, and Pepin responded. He crossed the Alps again and once more defeated the obstinate Aistulf. Pepin then gave Pope Stephen III twenty-two towns that he had reconquered from the Lombards: "**the Donation of Pepin**." Thus, the pope became a temporal as well as a spiritual leader.

Pope Stephen III died in April 757. His brother and successor, Pope St. Paul I (757-767), was a prudent and holy man. During his ten-year pontificate, he maintained a close relationship with King Pepin.

Pope Paul I made a good and trusted priest named Christopher the papal chancellor. Upon Pope St. Paul I's death, Christopher took charge of the preparations for the election of Paul's successor. A faction of Roman nobles, led by Duke Toto of Nepi, had gathered an army in Rome. Toto promised Christopher that he would not try to exert any pressure on the election of the new pope, but this oath proved worthless. At the head of an armed band, he forced his way into the Lateran Palace where the election was taking place and proceeded to proclaim one of his brothers, a layman named Constantine, pope.

Duke Toto compelled Bishop Theodore, whom he captured in the Lateran Palace, to pass Constantine through all the clerical orders in a single day. On July 5, Constantine was declared "pope," taking the name Constantine II. This antipope governed the Church for thirteen months. During that time, he wrote several times to Pepin. King Pepin, who apparently knew that Constantine was not the true pope, did not reply.

Meanwhile, Christopher had fled from Toto and his army but had not surrendered. Desperate, Christopher sought help from Desiderius, the new Lombard king. In July 768, the Lombards, always happy to attack Rome, defeated Toto and his followers. Christopher imprisoned antipope Constantine. On August 1, Christopher held a valid election, and a Sicilian priest was chosen as pope. He took the name **Stephen IV** (768-772). In April 769, Stephen convoked a council at the Lateran Palace which also acknowledged him as the true pope. The election of

124 *Chapter 8: The Creation of the Holy Roman Empire*

Pope Adrian I (772-795) proceeded smoothly following Stephen's death in 772.

Charlemagne

Since before the time of Pope Gregory I, the Lombards had always been a danger to the Church. Although some Lombard kings would help the Church, others would threaten her. When Desiderius had helped Christopher defeat Toto and Constantine, he had likely not done so because of his burning zeal to support the true pope, but rather because he had a material interest in mind. That interest became clear when he tried to annex the land that Pepin had given the pope. Once again, the pope called upon the king of the Franks, the great protector of the Church.

By this time, the Franks had a new king, but one with the same noble spirit as Pepin. Pepin had died in 768, and his two sons, Charles and Carloman, had succeeded him. In December 771, when Carloman died, Charles became sole ruler. History has bestowed the title "the Great" on few persons—some deservedly, others not. In the case of Charles the Great, or **Charlemagne** (742-814), history chose wisely.

More than any other person, Charlemagne was responsible for the creation of **Christendom** (the reign of Christ among men, embodied in a Christian society). Like his father, he was dedicated to the protection and promotion of the Catholic Church. He also loved learning and was devoted to the spread of learning and education. He dedicated his life to defending Christendom from the infidel without (the Muslims) and the heretic within. This was to be the mission of the **Holy Roman Emperor**—to be the sword and shield of Christendom.

Charlemagne knew St. Boniface. He had been an 11-year-old prince when Pope Stephen had crowned his father. He had been raised in a strongly Catholic family. Even as king, he attended daily Mass. When Pope Adrian called on Charlemagne for help against the Lombards, he answered.

After some unsuccessful negotiations with the Lombards, Charlemagne crossed the Alps into Italy in the summer of 773. In the face of the mighty Frankish military, the Lombard army melted away, offering little resistance. Only their capital, Pavia, held out. In June 774, Pavia fell after a long siege. Charlemagne captured the treacherous Desiderius, who died in prison. Charlemagne took the Iron Crown of the Lombards for his own and annexed their lands into his empire.

While his army besieged Pavia, Charlemagne showed the depth of his commitment to the Church and his own faith. He traveled to Rome, where he arrived on Holy Saturday, 774. Acting as a pilgrim, he walked from the outskirts of the city to St. Peter's Basilica. When he arrived at St. Peter's, he ascended its steps on his knees. On Easter Sunday, he

Charlemagne, Meissonier

Pope Adrian I
Successor to Stephen IV; reigned 772-795; was a friend and advisor to Charlemagne.

Charlemagne
Son of Pepin; extended his realm across much of Europe, and thus came to be called "Holy Roman Emperor."

Holy Roman Emperor
Title held by Charlemagne and his descendants.

Witness to the Faith

The Destruction of Irminsul by Charlemagne, Heinrich Leutemann

attended Mass at the Basilica of St. Mary Major. Three days later, at a meeting with Pope Adrian, he ratified the Donation of Pepin, and even enlarged it. After Pavia fell, the pope regained possession of several towns that the Lombards had taken from him.

Charlemagne and the Saxons

Although Charlemagne was a great ruler, he was also human, and like his uncle Carloman, he committed a great sin. As Charlemagne celebrated Easter, the Saxons, who lived just outside his realm, raided his kingdom and plundered the church in Fritzlar that St. Boniface had built. Upon hearing the news, Charlemagne immediately marched north into Saxony to punish the raiders. This was not the first time that he had fought against the Saxons. In 772, he had led an attack when they raided the Netherlands. Unlike most pagan tribes, the Saxons who had remained in northern Germany (not to be confused with their Anglo-Saxon cousins in Britain), viciously hated both Christianity and the Franks because they had become Christians. In fact, Saxony was the citadel of paganism.

Moreover, unlike most pagans, the Saxons practiced ritual human sacrifice and cannibalism. This accounts for the missionaries' lack of notable success among them. In fact, the Saxons killed many missionaries. Charlemagne was determined to conquer Saxony and bring peace to his empire. He also resolved to destroy Saxon paganism, though it seems that he did not intend to *force the Saxons* to become Christians. He had not forced other pagan tribes under his power to convert. He believed that once paganism was obliterated, missionaries, using the peaceful methods of St. Boniface, would bring them into the true Faith.

Paderborn Cathedral

In 775, Charlemagne successfully relaunched his campaign against the Saxons. Charlemagne's forces gained possession of two key Saxon fortresses. They also destroyed the "Irminsul," a colossal tree that the Saxons regarded as the pillar upon which the whole world rested. The defeated Saxons pledged fidelity to Charlemagne. They also accepted Baptism. However, although no one forced them to be baptized, the Saxons apparently were baptized only to appease Charlemagne. In 777, during a great national assembly held at Paderborn, which made Saxony part of Charlemagne's kingdom, an even larger number of Saxons were baptized.

Charlemagne then divided Saxony between the dioceses of Mainz, Cologne, and Wurzburg. The Abbey of Fulda became the center for the conversion mission to the Saxons. **Abbot St. Sturm**, the beloved disciple of St. Boniface, personally preached Catholicism to the Saxons. Sturm and his monks built churches on the site of pagan temples and shrines. However, the peace was uneasy and, before long, the Saxons broke their promise to Charlemagne. They rose against the Franks, indiscriminately massacring Frankish priests and soldiers. They destroyed many of the churches that Sturm had built. In 779, Charlemagne returned to Saxony to restore peace.

Once again, the peace lasted only a few years. In the autumn of 782, the Saxons revolted, defeated a Frankish army, and destroyed several churches. Charlemagne, frustrated and furious with the deceitful Saxons, took reprisals that were appalling and excessive. In the only serious stain on his illustrious life, he ordered the execution of 4,500 Saxon prisoners at Verden. Although no one knows what he may have said privately in the confessional, Charlemagne never publicly acknowledged the wrongfulness of this act or sought pardon for it. In 785, after a campaign of three years, the Saxons finally surrendered. Widukind, their leader, received Baptism. Charlemagne then issued a decree imposing the death penalty on anyone who damaged a church or killed a member of the clergy.

With the reasonably sincere conversion of Widukind, Saxony finally had peace. At last, the Church had a realistic chance to make conversions. Several new dioceses were founded. When the Imperial Assembly, known as a "**Diet**," met in **Aachen** (**Aix-la-Chapelle** in France) in 797, it put the final touches to these civil and ecclesiastical transformations. The work of organizing Saxony helped create what would become medieval Germany, in which the Saxons played a critical role.

Charlemagne and the Muslims

The covenant between the Holy Roman Emperor and the Church was that the Holy Roman Emperor would defend the Church from the infidel without and the heretic within. Charlemagne took this covenant very seriously. He was, after all, the grandson of Charles Martel. Thus, he waged war to drive the Muslims out of France, and he also fought them in Spain.

In 778, Charlemagne crossed the Pyrenees at the head of an immense army. At Saragossa, Spain, the Muslim army defeated him. As his army retreated back across the mountains, the Muslims attacked

Charlemagne Receives the Submission of Widukind at Paderborn, Ary Scheffer

Abbot St. Sturm
Disciple of St. Boniface; preached the Faith to the Saxons.

Diet
The imperial assembly of the Holy Roman Empire.

Aachen (Aix-la-Chapelle)
A city in Germany; became Charlemagne's capital. Among other things, it was the location of his palace school, part of his effort to revive literacy and culture.

Witness to the Faith **127**

William of Toulouse

the army's rear guard, dropping boulders to separate it from the main body of the army. They completely crushed the Frankish rear guard in the narrow mountain pass of Roncesvalles. Many French soldiers perished, including the gallant knight Sir Roland, immortalized by the epic French poem *The Song of Roland*.

Following this defeat, Charlemagne fortified the Aquitaine, a province in southern France, to protect the frontiers of France from the Muslims. He entrusted this bulwark to Duke William of Toulouse. In 793, the Muslims invaded the Aquitaine with as many as 100,000 soldiers. Duke William engaged and defeated this army, forcing their retreat. In 801, William commanded a Frankish force that freed Barcelona from the Muslims. During the next decade, the Franks liberated a number of Spanish cities, including Pamplona and Tarragona. In 812, the Franks and Muslims declared a truce. Duke William had retired to the abbey of Gellone, which he had founded.

Roland at Roncevaux, Gustave Doré

Papal States
Included Ravenna, parts of Tuscany and Lombardy, and other Italian cities. Given to the pope by Charlemagne, this territory remained under papal rule until the nineteenth century.

The Papal States

In 781, Charlemagne was again in Rome. He gave the pope additional lands, including Ravenna, parts of Tuscany and Lombardy, and several other cities in Italy. Thus, the **Papal States** were constituted in the shape in which they existed until the nineteenth century.

Chapter 8: The Creation of the Holy Roman Empire

The Birth of the Holy Roman Empire

By 798, Charlemagne was unquestionably the greatest Christian ruler in the world and regarded by all as the defender of Western Europe. He had conquered all of France and Germany. The Slavic people in the East of his empire paid him homage. His reach even extended into England, where he had sent ambassadors. More and more, the people of Europe began to think of him not as a mere king, but as an emperor.

On Christmas Day, 795, Pope Adrian died. He had been a close friend and adviser to Charlemagne, who surely grieved at his passing. The next day, **Leo III** (795-816) was unanimously elected pope. Unlike many of the previous popes, Leo was not a member of the nobility. Whether from greed, ambition, or prejudice, some relatives and supporters of former Pope Adrian conspired to murder Pope Leo. On April 25, 799, as he led a public procession through the streets of Rome, these treacherous conspirators attacked the Holy Father, severely wounding him. Leo barely escaped, sustaining wounds so life-threatening that many considered his survival a miracle.

Pope Leo III

When Charlemagne learned of the attack, he provided an escort for Leo out of Rome to Paderborn, where the Frankish court was at that time. To ensure the pope's safety, Charlemagne sent his son Pepin. At Paderborn, Pope Leo was received with the greatest respect. Once he had recovered, Charlemagne had him escorted back to Rome by a bodyguard of Frankish nobles and bishops. Leo arrived in Rome on November 29, 799, amid great rejoicing.

The following year, Charlemagne appointed a commission of ten men, six bishops and four noblemen, to try the pope's attackers. The commission spent a few days examining the accusations that Leo's enemies made against him; however, the pope's assailants had no excuse for attacking him. After finding the conspirators guilty of a number of heinous crimes, the commission sent them to France, where Charlemagne would decide their final punishment.

> **Leo III**
> Reigned 795-816; barely survived an attempted murder in 799, and was protected by Charlemagne, whom he later crowned as Holy Roman Emperor.

In November 800, Charlemagne departed for Rome to meet with Leo. On December 23, a special assembly of archbishops, bishops, priests, and leading laymen met in St. Peter's Basilica before Charlemagne and Pope Leo. They called upon Charlemagne to accept the title of emperor. Since he was, in fact, the emperor of what had been the old Western Roman Empire, he should have the title. Charlemagne consented, and the **Holy Roman Empire** was born.

In later years, some secular historians would jest that Charlemagne's empire was not holy, nor Roman, nor an empire; but this is simply false on its face. Charlemagne ruled over what had been the Roman Empire. All the imperial seats of government in the West, such as Rome and Ravenna, were united in his kingdom. Charlemagne pledged to protect the Church and not oppress it. His realm would be holy,

> **Holy Roman Empire**
> Included practically all of Western Europe, united into an empire under Charlemagne.

Witness to the Faith

Leonine Triclinium – Mosaic of St Peter, Pope Leo III, and Charlemagne

because the Church was holy and would make his subjects holy. Finally, Charlemagne and his successors ruled over a number of kingdoms, including France, Germany, and Hungary. When a political entity includes several kingdoms, it is called an empire—in this case, the Holy Roman Empire.

Two days later, on Christmas Day in the year 800, Charlemagne came to St. Peter's Basilica. As he knelt before the high altar, Pope Leo III placed a jeweled crown upon his head. The people shouted their approval. All of Western Europe recognized Charlemagne as emperor.

Charlemagne's coronation made him the defender of Christendom and the pope's associate in the task of governing Christendom. The emperor oversaw temporal issues, such as defending Christendom from the Muslims. The pope oversaw spiritual matters, such as appointing bishops and promulgating regulations for the clergy. This new concept of shared authority is embodied in the Lateran mosaics, in which Pope Leo and Emperor Charlemagne are shown kneeling before St. Peter. Peter gives Leo the pallium, the sign of the spiritual authority. To Charlemagne, he gives the banner, the sign of temporal power.

The Church and the Holy Roman Empire

The *ideal* of the Holy Roman Empire, as envisioned by Charlemagne and Pope Leo III, was a Christian society such as St. Augustine describes in *The City of God* (Charlemagne's favorite book). Of course, like all human institutions, this empire did not always function perfectly. It worked best when the emperor was

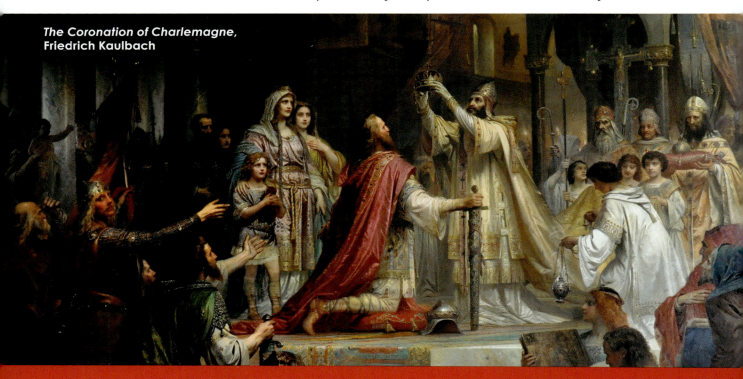

The Coronation of Charlemagne, Friedrich Kaulbach

130 Chapter 8: The Creation of the Holy Roman Empire

a man like Charlemagne, who had great strength, courage, and virtue, and the pope was a man of great holiness and wisdom. The basic problem was that both pope and emperor were men with human frailties. The pope was a spiritual leader, the visible head of the Church, but he was also a temporal ruler. The emperor was a temporal ruler, but bishops in his realm wielded a great amount of secular power as large landowners. While emperor and pope should have worked together, and generally tried to do so, they also were often in conflict with each other.

Although many of the emperors, especially those of the Hapsburg Dynasty, would be great defenders and loyal supporters of the Church, some emperors tried to control the Church. Some attempted to exert more influence over the election of the Supreme Pontiff than was appropriate. Others meddled in affairs over which they lacked authority.

On the other hand, sometimes the pope forgot that his main responsibility was to act as the Vicar of Christ on Earth. Some popes showed more concern for their temporal power than for the souls of the faithful. In later centuries, as the papacy became wealthier and more powerful, certain popes began to be more concerned about their own worldly pleasures and neglected important spiritual matters.

Charlemagne himself strayed beyond the lawful bounds of his authority over the clergy even before becoming emperor. Although well intentioned, he involved himself in the spiritual affairs of the Church. For example, he sought to control Church property. As bishops were, in fact, secular leaders, he often treated them as government officials under his jurisdiction. Concerned about the sacredness of the Mass, he issued rules about ecclesiastical chant and the sacred liturgy. Seeing some clerics not living exemplary lives, he reminded them of their obligations to lead by example. He issued a regulation strictly forbidding clerics to carry weapons. Many of these decrees, such as priests not carrying swords, certainly fell under his authority. Other decrees he made were less clear-cut. At a time when bishops exercised such great secular power, it was often difficult to separate their religious role from their secular one. Thus, Church and State clashed.

Aachen Cathedral

Charlemagne Supports the Arts and Education

The fields of literature and the arts are two areas in which the so-called "Dark Ages" were in fact dark. When Charlemagne became king

Witness to the Faith 131

Charlemagne Receives Manuscripts from Alcuin, Jules Laure

Alcuin
An Anglo-Saxon Benedictine monk who became the director of Charlemagne's palace school. He was a leading figure of the Carolingian Renaissance and an advisor to the emperor.

Carolingian Renaissance
The revival of learning and culture that took place under Charlemagne.

of the Franks, illiteracy was practically universal, and artistic development was almost nonexistent in Western Europe. Thankfully, the Benedictine monks preserved much of the great ancient Greek and Latin literature in their scriptorium. Benedictines had done their best to start monastic schools in Italy and wherever else they traveled. The Irish monks had spread their knowledge to Britain, which, by the seventh century, had produced some great minds. However, the barbarian invasions had greatly hindered the spread of knowledge, especially among the Germans and the Franks. Charlemagne was determined to change that.

While traveling in Italy, Charlemagne had been impressed by the education of the clergy there. He realized that his own native clergy, as well as his lay people, would benefit from such an education. Thus, he asked several of the monks in Italy to work with him in Aachen, where he had established his palace school. They would also assist in the creation and oversight of many other episcopal and monastic schools throughout his kingdom.

While in Italy in early 781, Charlemagne met **Alcuin**, an Anglo-Saxon Benedictine. Impressed with his great learning, Charlemagne asked Alcuin to become the head of the palace school, where he would educate Charlemagne's four sons as well as the sons of the Frankish nobles. More importantly, Alcuin would oversee the entire educational system in the Frankish kingdom. These included the monastic schools, which every abbey was required to maintain for the boys of the kingdom, as well as the seminaries for priests and missionaries.

The choice of Alcuin for the position of director of the palace school was indeed inspired. He was perhaps the leading scholar of the time. Born in York in 735, he studied under Archbishop Egbert, one of St. Bede's best students, at York's cathedral school. There, Alcuin benefited from the mix of Irish and Latin learning that made Ireland's monks the most learned men in Christendom. Following his graduation, Alcuin became a teacher, eventually rising to become the director of the school and library associated with the cathedral of York.

Although he loved his native Britain, Alcuin realized that Charlemagne was offering him the opportunity of a lifetime, and so accepted the offer. More than almost any other person, Alcuin was responsible for the **Carolingian Renaissance**, the preservation of ancient literature and the advancement of new learning. Alcuin himself wrote works on grammar, composition, literature, and theology.

Yet Alcuin was more than a teacher. He was also one of Charlemagne's closest advisers. For example, Alcuin strongly urged Charlemagne to help Pope Leo III after Leo was attacked. He also advised the emperor not to force pagans to be baptized.

Alcuin directed the palace school for fifteen years. He also worked with Charlemagne to improve the schools throughout his kingdom, as well as establish new schools. Under his direction, three types of schools emerged: the village schools directed by local parish priests, the schools of church music intended to prepare men for the priesthood, and the monastic and cathedral schools, which were similar to the school at York where Alcuin had been director. From these latter two kinds of schools came an army of bishops, abbots, priests, and missionaries whose life's work was to advance the cause of learning. In 796, Alcuin retired to a monastery, but he continued to be Charlemagne's adviser until his death in 804.

The Death of Charlemagne

Under Frankish tradition, the king divided his kingdom among his sons. In 806, Charlemagne allocated to each their share. However, in 810, his son Pepin, only 33 at the time, died, as did his daughter. The next year, his eldest son Charles also died. One can only imagine the grief he felt at the death of three children in two years. Nevertheless, the deaths of his two sons meant that the empire would not have to be divided.

Charlemagne assembled his nobles, the clergy, and the people at Aachen and solemnly proclaimed that his son Louis was to succeed him. Unfortunately, he was the least capable of Charlemagne's children. Charlemagne died on January 28, 814. One of the most influential figures in history, he had helped create the modern world. More than that, he had showed that *Christendom* was a real possibility, not merely a utopian dream. The Holy Roman Empire would last for nearly 1,000 years. Ironically, another French ruler would destroy it.

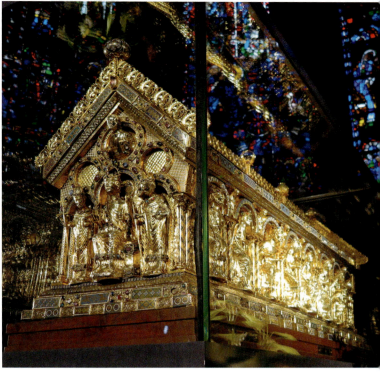

Casket of Charlemagne in Aachen

Oral Exercises

1. Which pope named Boniface the metropolitan of Germany?
2. What is the significance of the Battle of Tours?
3. Where is St. Boniface buried?
4. Who reformed the Church in France?
5. What is the Donation of Pepin?
6. Why was the election of Constantine as pope invalid?
7. Who crowned Charlemagne?
8. Who was Alcuin of York?

Christendom
The reign of Christ among men, embodied in a Christian society, such as took shape in Europe in the second half of the first millennium and lasted a thousand years.

Witness to the Faith

Chapter 9: The Great Schism

Introduction

The terrible tragedy known as the **Great Schism**, or the **Great Eastern Schism**, occurred in 1054 when the Eastern (or Greek) Orthodox Churches broke away from the Catholic Church and the pope. Until then, these Eastern Churches had been in communion with Rome and the Catholic Church. The refusal of these Churches to continue submitting to the authority of the pope or to remain in communion with the Catholic Church is called a **schism**. This schism still exists today.

The reasons for the Great Schism are both varied and complex. It did not occur because of one specific disagreement between a pope and an Eastern patriarch. Such momentous events do not occur without decades of issues involving theology and individual personalities. Perhaps, had there been a serious heresy, a Church council could have addressed it and resolved it. Yet, at first, there was no insurmountable doctrinal issue. Over time, the problems of faith became wrapped in the personalities of the people involved. In the end, doctrine became an excuse and a provocation. More than anything, it was pride that caused the fall. Over the centuries, as the parties were unable to resolve their differences, small problems became large ones. Although the two great schismatics, **Photius** and **Michael Cerularius**, deserve much blame, the seeds of the Great Schism were planted long before them, and continued long after they were gone.

Great Schism (Great Eastern Schism)
The split between Eastern and Western Christianity in which the Eastern Orthodox Churches broke away from the Catholic Church.

Schism
The refusal to continue submitting to the authority of the pope or to remain in communion with the Catholic Church.

Hagia Sophia

726 A.D. – 1054 A.D.

726 A.D.
Emperor Leo issues an iconoclastic decree, ordering the destruction of all images in the churches in his empire.

754 A.D.
Leo's son, Constantine V, launches a campaign of iconoclasm.

767 A.D.
Constantine's envoys hear the term *Filioque* for the first time, beginning a controversy that will escalate over the coming centuries.

787 A.D.
The Second Council of Nicaea condemns iconoclasm, and defines the veneration of honor due to sacred images.

858 A.D.
Emperor Michael III and his uncle Bardas exile St. Ignatius and appoint Photius in his place.

867 A.D.
Photius endeavors to create division between East and West. Pope Nicholas dies in November.

869 A.D.
The Fourth Council of Constantinople reinstates St. Ignatius as patriarch.

877-886 A.D.
Upon Ignatius' death, Photius manages to become patriarch again, and fosters division. He is eventually banished.

1052-1053 A.D.
Patriarch Michael Cerularius challenges certain Latin Rite customs, prompting the pope to send Cardinal Humbert with a letter to Constantinople.

1054 A.D.
The cardinal and patriarch excommunicate each other, marking the split between the East and the West.

The Seeds of a Schism: Iconoclasm

Strictly speaking, the Catholic Church experienced schisms since the time of the Apostles. In St. John's Third Epistle, John writes of a Christian named **Diotrephes** who refused to accept his teaching (3 John 1:9-10). Heresies, such as Arianism, produced serious schisms. Interestingly, for some reason, most schisms originated in the East, perhaps because these Catholics lived farther from the pope. The Great Schism also began in the East.

Throughout the history of the Catholic Church, Christians have venerated images. Depictions of the Blessed Mother, the saints, and Our Lord, especially as the Good Shepherd, are found throughout the catacombs. Such veneration continues in Catholic churches around the world today. The people represented by the statues and

Witness to the Faith 135

Catholic Armies Carry Sacred Images into Battle

Leo III, the Isaurian
Byzantine emperor from 717 to 741; first to officially oppose the veneration of images.

Holy Shroud
The burial cloth of Christ, on which His image is imprinted.

Iconoclasm
False teaching that sacred images are forbidden by God and therefore must be rejected or destroyed.

St. John Damascene
A leading opponent of iconoclasm in the East; wrote treatises explaining and defending the veneration of images.

pictures that Catholics venerate really exist. Catholics understand that they are venerating the *person*, not the statue or icon. The artistic representation simply draws the viewer's attention to the actual person and allows the faithful to focus on that saint.

Over time, as the Faith became more accepted, symbols were drawn or placed on shields and uniforms. Recall Emperor Constantine drawing the Cross on the shields of his soldiers. Soon armies began carrying sacred images into battle. However, in the East, the practice of venerating images met with resistance. Judaism and Islam both regarded the depicting of the human form, especially in a religious context, as idolatrous. Even some Catholics regarded the veneration of images as inappropriate, generally because they misunderstood the Church's teachings. Finally, there probably were abuses in the veneration of images, again by those who misunderstood what the Church taught.

In 726, a volcanic eruption in the Aegean Sea caused the Byzantine emperor, **Leo III, the Isaurian** (717-741), to believe that he and his people had done something to displease God. Less than ten years earlier, Leo had bravely—and perhaps miraculously—defeated a massive Muslim attack on Constantinople, so he was perhaps more open to seeing the hand of God in natural disasters than were others. Leo concluded that the reason for God's displeasure was widespread idolatry in his empire.

While abuses in devotions involving images existed in the Byzantine Empire, most devotions were simply part of the typical fervent Catholic piety that Christians practiced since the days of the catacombs. The majority of abuses resulted from either misunderstandings of the Church's teachings or a deliberate departure from those teachings. Of course, some images, such as the **Holy Shroud** at Edessa, were deserving of the highest veneration.

Iconoclasm is the false teaching that sacred images are forbidden by God and therefore must be rejected or destroyed. In 726, Leo issued an iconoclastic decree, ordering the destruction of all images in the churches in his empire. He also ordered the destruction of a famous statue of Christ, which stood on the front gate of the imperial palace. The order and the destruction of the statue of Jesus caused an insurrection, which Leo quickly and violently suppressed. In 727, in Greece, Leo bloodily suppressed another major revolt against his edict. The Greeks even proclaimed a man named Cosmas, whose fleet was promptly destroyed, as the new emperor. In Italy, the people and most imperial officials considered the law to be foolish and irreverent, and hardly anyone even paid attention to it.

Chapter 9: The Great Schism

Meanwhile, as the people fought Leo's decrees with swords and ships, Church leaders fought Leo with theology and philosophy. In the East, **St. John Damascene** led the opposition to Leo's iconoclasm. St. John wrote three treatises on images. He enlarged the scope of the controversy and cleverly connected it with the part that ceremonies and sacramentals play in the work of human sanctification.

In the West, **Pope St. Gregory II** (715-731) led the attack. In the autumn of 727, Gregory held a synod in Rome to discuss the issues raised by Leo's iconoclasm. The synod completely defended the proper veneration of images. Following the synod, the pope sent a letter to Leo, perfectly setting forth the Church's teachings on images and rejecting Leo's false accusations: "You say: 'We worship stones and walls and boards.' But it is not so, O Emperor; but they serve us for remembrance and encouragement, lifting our slow spirits upwards, by those whose names the pictures bear and whose representations they are." Pope Gregory also condemned Leo: "It would have been better for you to have been a heretic than a destroyer of images."

To strengthen his position, in 730 Emperor Leo ordered **St. Germanus**, the 90-year-old patriarch of Constantinople, to countersign his iconoclastic edict. When Germanus refused, Leo appointed a man named Anastasius to replace him. Anastasius agreed to a decree prohibiting all representations of Christ, the Blessed Mother, saints, or angels in churches and elsewhere. Pope Gregory, who had earlier written to congratulate Germanus for his strength of character, refused to acknowledge Anastasius as patriarch.

Pope Gregory II died in February 731. His successor, **Gregory III** (731-741), continued to defend the use of images as aids in Christian worship. Upon his election, he immediately called a synod in Rome, which ninety-three bishops attended. The synod excommunicated anyone who professed iconoclasm. The following year, Leo replied to the synod by sending a fleet to Italy to "correct" the pope. But the ships never arrived, as a storm wrecked the fleet in the Adriatic Sea.

In another effort to control the pope, Leo attempted to place all the churches in his empire, including those in Italy, under the ecclesiastical authority of the patriarch of Constantinople. From that point forward, the Byzantine emperors and the popes would rarely work together on any significant issues. Leo III, who had done so much to defend the Byzantine Empire from the Muslims, had planted the seeds that would lead to the final, formal break of the Greek Orthodox Church from Rome in 1054.

Iconoclasm Spreads

The destruction of his fleet and the opposition of the people reduced the zeal with which Leo implemented iconoclasm. Perhaps Pope Gregory II's letter had touched his heart somewhat as well. Leo decided that, while he would continue to pursue the same policies, he would not resort to violence or persecutions.

Pope St. Gregory II
Reigned 715-731; responded to Emperor Leo's iconoclasm with a synod and a letter explaining the Church's teachings.

St. Germanus
Patriarch of Constantinople, whom Leo removed for his refusal to countersign the iconoclastic edict.

St. John Damascene

Gregory III
Reigned 731-741; called a synod at Rome which excommunicated anyone who professed iconoclasm.

Witness to the Faith   **137**

Gold Coin Depicting Irene and Her Son, Constantine IV

Constantine V
Byzantine emperor; called a synod at Hieria which decreed that images were idolatrous, and then persecuted those who continued to honor them.

Tarasius – Patriarch of Constantinople

In June 741, Leo died, and his son **Constantine V** became emperor. Constantine was very much like his father. An excellent military leader, he managed to repulse the Arab Muslims and recapture some of his lost empire. However, he also shared his father's views on iconoclasm. In fact, Constantine seems to have written a series of theological essays on the subject, arguing that the veneration of images is blasphemous. In February 754, after removing any bishops who opposed his position from the hierarchy, Constantine convoked a synod at Hieria, just outside of Constantinople. The bishops all declared that "painting living creatures blasphemed the fundamental doctrine of our salvation." They denounced anyone who depicted the saints in paintings or other forms.

Although over three hundred bishops attended the synod of Hieria, neither the pope nor his representative attended it. Thus, it was not a valid council. Its decrees lacked authority.

Unfortunately, Constantine saw the synod as a mandate to enforce his iconoclastic policies. In the churches throughout the Byzantine Empire, sacred images were destroyed. Constantine demanded that landscape paintings, paintings of animals, or paintings of huge golden crosses on deep blue fields replace the sacred images. Although the Eastern bishops had agreed with Emperor Constantine's theological views, the monks in their monasteries held fast. Their resistance made Constantine furious. He launched a bitter persecution in which many monks suffered martyrdom, torture, or exile. As so often happens when the truth is lost, Constantine continually moved further away from sound doctrine, eventually even decreeing that praying to the saints was heresy.

Meanwhile, Church leaders persevered in teaching the truth. In 767, a council was held in Jerusalem, where the patriarchs of Antioch, Jerusalem, and Alexandria were represented. The council condemned iconoclasm. Pope Stephen IV called a council in 769 in Rome, which also condemned iconoclasm.

When Constantine V died in 775, his son Leo IV became emperor. Leo supported iconoclasm but ruled for only five years before he died. In 780, his 5-year-old son Constantine VI became emperor. Because of Constantine's age, his mother Irene ruled as regent. Irene did not support iconoclasm, and she decided to restore the veneration of images. Ultimately, she convoked two synods to abolish iconoclasm.

In 784, Irene named her secretary, Tarasius, as patriarch of Constantinople. Tarasius supported the veneration of images and desired to improve relations with the pope. Irene also managed to win a number of bishops to her side, through either flattery or intimidation. She requested that Pope Adrian I grant permission to convoke an ecumenical council to refute the errors of the synod of Hieria.

Irene convened the council at Constantinople in 786. Unfortunately, Leo III and his successors had filled not only the Church hierarchy in the

138   *Chapter 9: The Great Schism*

East but also the Byzantine army with supporters of iconoclasm. Some of these soldiers rioted, forcing the council to stop meeting. Irene disbanded the unruly troops and transferred the conference to Nicaea.

In 787, Irene convoked the **Second Council of Nicaea**, the seventh general council of the Church. Two papal legates attended as the pope's representatives. The council condemned iconoclasm as heretical. The council also precisely defined the veneration that is due to images: they receive a *veneration* of honor, *not* the *adoration* that is due to God alone.

Although Emperor Constantine VI signed the council's documents, it seems that he supported iconoclasm. In 790, Constantine reached adulthood and began trying to rule as emperor in his own right, but he was largely incompetent in every regard as a ruler. In April 797, Irene overthrew her son, killing him in the process. She proclaimed herself empress. Irene was deposed five years later.

The Gap between East and West Widens

When Pope Leo III crowned Charlemagne in 800, the Byzantines saw it as a direct insult to their culture and their politics. The Byzantines felt that they, not the uncivilized Frankish king, were the true inheritors of the Roman Empire. They wondered where the great Frankish culture was. Where was the Frankish Constantinople? Where was the Frankish *Hagia Sophia* (the patriarchal cathedral in Constantinople)? To the Byzantines, it appeared that the pope had fallen into the hands of the barbarians. The coronation of Charlemagne was celebrated as a great occasion in the West, but it was seen as a great calamity in the East. It widened the political gap between the East and the West and further sowed the seeds of distrust.

> **Second Council of Nicaea**
> In 787, condemned iconoclasm as heretical, and precisely defined the veneration due to images, as opposed to the adoration due to God alone.

Coronation of Charlemagne, Raphael

Witness to the Faith 139

Filioque Controversy
A dispute between Greek and Latin theologians about whether the Holy Spirit proceeds from the Father and the Son or only from the Father.

Photius
A cunning, deceitful nobleman, made patriarch of Constantinople by Emperor Michael III; resisted or undermined the pope's authority in various ways throughout his reign.

St. Ignatius
Patriarch of Constantinople, ousted by Michael in favor of Photius, but defended the truth and was eventually reinstated by the Fourth Council of Constantinople.

The *Filioque* Controversy

In an atmosphere of distrust, almost any small flame can set the world ablaze. Thus, the matter known as the "*Filioque* Controversy," which, at another time, theologians with open hearts and minds might have dealt with calmly and rationally, burst during this period into another conflict between the Church in the West and in the East. *Filioque* (Latin, meaning "and the Son") is found in the Nicene Creed that we say at Mass. The sentence in the Creed refers to the Holy Spirit and reads, in part, "who proceeds from the Father and the Son." Both the Greek and the Latin Fathers of the fourth century clearly taught that the Holy Spirit proceeds from the Father and the Son. Yet this phrase was not included when the Nicene Creed was written in 325, simply because the dogma of the "double procession" was not an issue at that time.

Over the next centuries, the word "filioque" became more common in theological treatises. The Spanish added it to the Creed in the fifth or sixth century to clarify difficulties they were having with the Arians. By the eighth century, it was generally accepted as the correct theological interpretation of the relationship of the three Persons of the Trinity. Yet the use of "filioque" in the West caused controversy when envoys of Byzantine Emperor Constantine V attended a synod held at Gentilly (France) in 767.

Matters continued to heat up when, in the early ninth century, Greek monks heard the word in the Creed from Latin Benedictine monks of Bethlehem. The Greeks accused the Latins of heresy. The Latin monks appealed their case to the pope and the emperor. This situation finally came to a boil under **Photius**, the patriarch of Constantinople.

Photius versus St. Ignatius

Since the first century, when Pope Clement I wrote to the Church in Corinth, the patriarchs of Constantinople had always recognized the pope's authority over them. However, at various times, for political or religious reasons, they had ignored the pope. The popes had not governed the Eastern Church as closely as they had the West, mainly because of the distances involved. Nevertheless, during the entire iconoclast controversy, Byzantine Church leaders and secular leaders (for example, Empress Irene) had appealed to the pope for leadership and decisions.

In 847, Empress Theodora, acting as regent, appointed **St. Ignatius** as patriarch of Constantinople. Ignatius was a monk and a strong opponent of the iconoclasts. As such, he had the strong backing of the monks, who had always supported the orthodox position. Ignatius was also a prince, which might have caused him to act rather independently when he should have contacted the pope.

140   *Chapter 9: The Great Schism*

In 856, Michael III turned 17 and began to rule as emperor. Unfortunately, he fell under the influence of his uncle, Bardas, a truly evil man who corrupted the morals of his young nephew. Ignatius admonished Bardas and, in January 858, publicly refused him Holy Communion. Ignatius paid dearly for this courageous act. In November, Bardas and Michael charged Ignatius with treason and exiled him.

During Ignatius' exile, Bardas and Michael strongly pressured him to resign as patriarch. At this point, the facts become murky. Ignatius may or may not have resigned. But, if he did, it was likely at sword point; Bardas had murdered others. Thus, even if Ignatius did agree, it was probably not a valid resignation, as no agreement made under duress is legally binding. In any case, a synod of bishops met in Constantinople to nominate a new patriarch. The man whom Bardas and Michael wanted was a nobleman named Photius.

On the surface, Photius seemed like the best man to be the next patriarch of Constantinople. First, from a literary, theological, and scientific perspective, he was probably the most learned man of his time. Second, he opposed iconoclasm. He was the nephew of the great Patriarch Tarasius, whom Empress Irene had appointed. Thus, he appealed to the orthodox party, as well as to Michael and Bardas. However, as time would show, he was also worldly, cunning, ambitious, and deceitful. Although he was a layman, the synod at Constantinople nominated Photius. They quickly ran him through all the Holy Orders and consecrated him patriarch of Constantinople on Christmas Day in 858. A bishop from Sicily, who was an opponent of St. Ignatius, consecrated him.

In February 859, the supporters of St. Ignatius met in a synod. They demanded that Photius resign and Ignatius be reinstated, regardless of any "resignation" or agreement he may have made. Photius refused. He held his own synod, which not only upheld his election but even declared that Ignatius had never been legally elected in the first place! Bardas and Michael also began persecuting Ignatius' followers. Despite support from the Byzantine hierarchy, who always seemed to follow the emperor's commands, Photius had little support among the people.

About a year and a half after his elevation to the see of Constantinople, Photius sent a letter to **Pope St. Nicholas I** (858-867). The letter cleverly distorted the facts of his election and consecration, and delicately and craftily referred to Ignatius' arrest and removal from office. However, in Pope St. Nicholas, Photius had a worthy adversary. The pope fired back a letter asking Photius and Emperor Michael exactly how Ignatius had left his office and why the pope had not been notified sooner. He also mentioned that Photius had risen from layman to patriarch in a remarkably short period.

St. Ignatius – Patriarch of Constantinople

Pope St. Nicholas I
Reigned 858-867; confronted the problems caused by Photius and defended Ignatius as the rightful patriarch.

Witness to the Faith   **141**

Pope St. Nicholas I

Basil the Macedonian
Became emperor through schemes and tricks; initially imprisoned Photius, then supported him again. Eventually, Photius conspired against him.

Determined to learn the facts for himself, Pope Nicholas sent two bishops to Constantinople to investigate the affair. Photius either completely tricked the two bishops or, more likely, simply bribed them with horses, money, and rich clothing. They confirmed him in his see. In May 861, a council was quickly convoked, consisting of 318 bishops, who, under orders from Emperor Michael, declared Photius to be the lawful patriarch.

Ignatius refused to accept the decision of the synod, which everyone knew was based on false testimony, bribes, and coercion. Even Photius and Emperor Michael realized that the synod would not withstand papal scrutiny. To bolster their case, they tortured Ignatius, but they had never dealt with a man who was a bishop, a prince, and a saint. He simply would not yield. Finally, one of his tormentors seized his hand and traced his signature on a document of resignation. Then they released him. Upon his release, Ignatius wrote a long, detailed letter to Pope Nicholas, appealing for his help and judgment.

In early 862, Ignatius' letter reached Nicholas along with other reports. Almost immediately, Pope Nicholas wrote to the other three Eastern patriarchs, declaring that Ignatius had been illegally deposed from his see by Photius, who must be removed as patriarch of Constantinople. In 863, Pope Nicholas convened a synod in Rome, at which he declared that Ignatius was the rightful patriarch of Constantinople, and that Photius was not a lawful bishop. The pope also notified Photius that he would be excommunicated if he did not accept Ignatius as patriarch. In addition, all clergy ordained by Photius were suspended from their priestly functions.

In 865, Emperor Michael sent a letter to Pope Nicholas threatening to attack Rome if he did not reverse his judgment and acknowledge Photius as patriarch. Nicholas responded by explaining Church law but also, amazingly, offering to hear the case between Photius and Ignatius personally in Rome. Michael ignored the offer.

Meanwhile, control of the Byzantine Empire was about to fall into the hands of one of history's most sinister figures. Since the end of Theodora's regency, the real ruler of the Byzantine Empire had not been Emperor Michael, but Bardas. Over the years, a man named **Basil the Macedonian** had become friendly with Michael and gained his confidence. He slowly turned Michael against Bardas. In April 867, Basil murdered Bardas as Michael watched. A month later, Michael made Basil co-emperor.

The situation became more intensified when the Bulgarians decided to join the Church as Roman Catholics. In 867, Photius sent letters to the three Eastern patriarchs and the Bulgarians. He sought to create division and strengthen his position against Pope Nicholas by stressing the theological, canonical, and liturgical differences between the Greeks and the Romans. In August, Photius also called the patriarchs of the Eastern Church to a synod at Constantinople. This synod

Chapter 9: The Great Schism

claimed to "depose" Pope Nicholas for interfering with the Church of Constantinople.

In September, Basil assassinated Michael, becoming sole emperor. The following day, he confined Photius in a monastery and reinstated Ignatius as patriarch. Likely, he simply wanted the devious Photius out of the way. Moreover, having just murdered the previous emperor, he needed the support of the people, who loved Ignatius. Certainly, Basil, a murderer and blasphemer, did not act in the best interests of the Church or out of respect for Pope Nicholas.

Pope Nicholas died on November 13, 867. His successor, **Adrian II** (867-872), was elected the next day. Emperor Basil entered into friendly relations with Pope Adrian. In October 869, the Fourth Council of Constantinople was held. Called by Basil and Pope Adrian, it was attended by more than one hundred bishops and three papal legates. The council officially reinstated Ignatius and returned Photius to the lay state. It also reaffirmed the teaching of the Second Council of Nicaea regarding the proper veneration of holy images. It seemed that the council had written "The End" to the Photius matter. As time would show, however, those were words Photius refused to read.

The Return of Photius

When St. Ignatius died in 877, Photius somehow regained the favor of the malevolent Emperor Basil, who appointed him again as patriarch of Constantinople. The new pope, **John VIII** (872-882), was in a rather weak position. Without Ignatius or someone like him to oppose Photius, he had few options. Moreover, his life was actually at risk from a Muslim invasion of Italy (discussed in Chapter 11). In the summer of 879, desiring unity with the Byzantines, Pope John sent a letter to the emperor and the Byzantine clergy, stating that he was willing to recognize Photius as patriarch of Constantinople on certain conditions. Photius had to apologize publicly for his past behavior; restore Bulgaria, which had followed him into schism, to the Roman Catholic Church; and make no laymen bishops. Lastly, the pope asked that Photius work with the supporters of Ignatius to bring peace to the Eastern Church.

Photius, in his pride, refused. Apparently, he found any sort of apology unacceptable. In November 879, he convoked a council at Constantinople. Prior to the council, he *rewrote* John's letters to him! During the council (over which Photius himself presided), through various dishonest means, he had the papal legates annul the decrees of the Council of Constantinople of 869-870.

When his legates returned to Rome in the summer of 880 with the documents of the council, Pope John should have been furious. However, he wrote again to Photius, asking him to humble himself and follow his initial requests. Photius again ignored the pope. Finally, in 881, with no other options, Pope John VIII excommunicated Photius.

Coin of Basil the Macedonian

Adrian II
Pope from 867 to 872; called the Fourth Council of Constantinople, which officially reinstated Ignatius as patriarch and returned Photius to the lay state.

John VIII
Pope from 872 to 882; tried to reason and negotiate with Photius, but without success, and finally had to excommunicate him.

Pope John VIII

Witness to the Faith

Michael Cerularius
Patriarch of Constantinople; declared Pope Leo IX unorthodox for following certain Latin Rite practices, and eventually claimed to "excommunicate" him.

Pope St. Leo IX
Reigned 1049-1055; pope during the time of Michael Cerularius; sent a letter and legates to deal with the patriarch's challenges, but died before the matter could be resolved.

Emperor Leo VI

However, Photius still had Emperor Basil's support, and therefore he refused to relinquish his office. In his conflict with John, Photius adopted new tactics. Instead of directly attacking the pope's authority, and the differences in customs and traditions between the Byzantine and Roman Churches, he focused his attention on the *filioque* question. Photius maintained that it was the belief of the Greek Church that the Holy Spirit proceeds from the Father only.

Meanwhile, Photius also began to play a more dangerous political game in which he hoped to emerge not only as patriarch but also as emperor. In 879, the death of Basil's son, probably the only person Basil ever truly loved, drove him somewhat insane. In the following years, Photius engaged in conspiracies to depose Basil, and was likely involved in Basil's assassination in August 886.

The new emperor, Leo VI, had Photius and another conspirator arrested and tried for treason. Photius, always the cleverest man in the empire, escaped the death penalty, but Leo removed him as patriarch and banished him to a monastery in Armenia. Photius died in 891 or 892. The Greek Orthodox Church still maintains that he was not guilty of the charges that Pope John VIII brought against him.

Michael Cerularius Makes the Final Break

The next 150 years were a period of relative harmony between the pope and the Greek Church. However, that changed in 1043, when **Michael Cerularius** became patriarch. Like many of the patriarchs before him, Cerularius seems to have been more concerned with politics than religion. In fact, he became a monk only as an alternative to death or exile because of a failed attempt to overthrow the government. Throughout his life, he retained his lust for power. Since Photius, no man was less suited for the religious life and the office of patriarch than Cerularius. In fact, it seems that his only goals as patriarch were to take the Byzantine Empire out of the Catholic Church and make himself emperor.

In the history of the Church, there have been few popes as holy or as capable as **Pope St. Leo IX** (1049-1055). Under other circumstances, perhaps Leo could have dealt with Cerularius and avoided the schism. However, when Cerularius began his conflict with Rome, Pope Leo IX was a prisoner of the Normans.

In late 1052, Cerularius outlawed certain Latin Rite customs in the Byzantine Empire, a direct challenge to the pope. The next year, a Byzantine bishop sent a letter, probably dictated by Cerularius, to the Latin bishops decrying certain Latin customs, especially the use of unleavened bread for the Holy Eucharist. The letter declared that the pope was no longer orthodox for following these customs. In response, Leo prepared a letter explaining papal primacy to Cerularius. The letter also contained a firm warning not to call the pope a heretic. Leo's most trusted advisor, Cardinal Humbert, carried the letter to Constantinople.

Meanwhile, Pope Leo had fallen into his last illness. The Normans, showing some compassion, allowed him to return to Rome. On April 19, 1054, after hearing Mass and receiving the Blessed Sacrament at St. Peter's, he died.

As Pope Leo lay dying, Cardinal Humbert and his party arrived in Constantinople, where Emperor Constantine IX received them graciously. However, Humbert did not meet with Cerularius for several weeks, which infuriated the proud patriarch. From the moment of his arrival, it became clear that Leo's choice of Humbert was tragically flawed. Although a good and holy man, Humbert was rash, headstrong, and excessively zealous at a time that called for prudence and diplomacy. Perhaps Cerularius never intended to negotiate. In any case, the determined cardinal and the arrogant patriarch could not agree on anything.

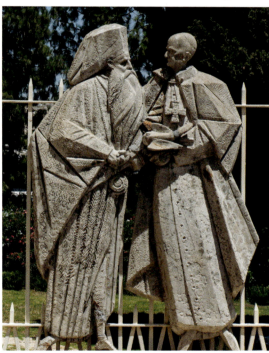

Statue of Pope Paul VI and Patriarch Athenagoras I

The situation grew more complicated when news of Pope Leo's death reached Constantinople, probably in mid- to late June 1054. With Leo dead, his legates had no authority. Strictly speaking, Cerularius no longer had to obey them. He almost certainly knew that they had no authority until a new pope made them his legates, or new legates were sent.

On July 16, 1054, Cardinal Humbert and his party solemnly processed into the Church of Hagia Sophia. Although he had no authority to do so, Humbert slammed a notice excommunicating Patriarch Michael Cerularius on the church's high altar. The emperor tried to bring the parties together, but Humbert and Cerularius refused to meet. Cerularius responded by burning the notice and claiming to "excommunicate" the pope. This was the final break, the Great Schism, between the Greek Church and the Catholic Church.

Although attempts have been made, there has been no reunion as of 2020. In 1966, Pope Paul VI and the patriarch of Constantinople revoked the joint excommunications of 1054. Since then, both Pope John Paul II and Pope Benedict XVI have met with different patriarchs to discuss reconciliation. In 2016, Pope Francis met with the patriarch of the Russian Orthodox Church, the first pope to do so since the Great Schism began (although both Pope John Paul II and Pope Benedict XVI had tried).

Oral Exercises

1. What is the heresy called iconoclasm?
2. What evils resulted from iconoclasm?
3. What is a schism?
4. How did the Greek Schism come about?
5. Who was Michael Cerularius?

Witness to the Faith

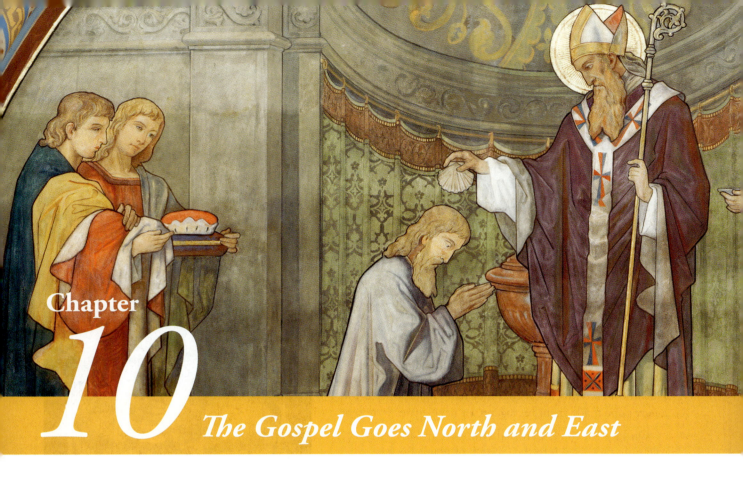

Chapter 10
The Gospel Goes North and East

Scandinavia
A large portion of northern Europe; includes Denmark, Norway, Sweden, and Finland.

Scandinavia: Present-Day Denmark, Norway, Sweden, and Finland

Introduction

During the ninth and tenth centuries, even as Western Europe fought for its very existence against Muslim invasions and Viking raids, the Church never forgot its mission: to go forth and make disciples of all nations. The Church sent missionaries north into Scandinavia, where they risked their lives to convert the ruthless Vikings. Other missionaries worked to evangelize the Poles and Hungarians, two peoples in whom the Faith became so deeply entrenched that virtually no human force could uproot it. Missionaries would also venture into the mysterious land known as Russia, a territory of brutally murderous pagans. Yet, even in Russia, saints would emerge.

St. Ansgar: The Apostle of Scandinavia

Ultimately, as St. Boniface and other missionaries so beautifully showed, conversion of the pagans relied on the grace of the Holy Spirit, not force or clever intellectual arguments. Yet some pagans held more intensely to their beliefs than others. For example, St. Paul struggled to convert the people of Ephesus, because their religious beliefs were entwined with their financial dealings. The Ephesian silversmiths forced Paul out of town as much because he was ruining their business as because he was working to convert the

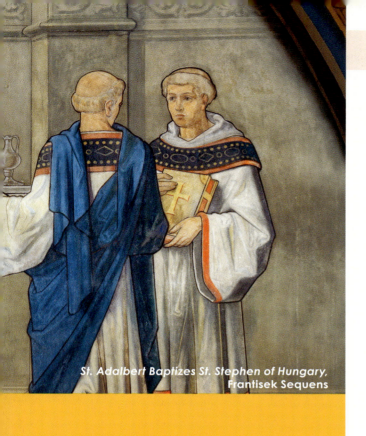

St. Adalbert Baptizes St. Stephen of Hungary, Frantisek Sequens

826 A.D. – 1000 A.D.

826-865 A.D.
St. Ansgar works to evangelize Scandinavia.

862 A.D.
Duke Rastislav of Moravia asks for Slavonic-speaking missionaries; Cyril and Methodius are sent, and work with great success.

864 A.D.
King Boris of Bulgaria is baptized and works to convert his country.

966 A.D.
Duke Mieszko is baptized; Poland accepts the Faith.

987 A.D.
Vladimir receives Baptism, marking the beginning of Russia's conversion.

995-1000 A.D.
Olaf, as king of Norway, reshapes it into a Christian nation.

996 A.D.
St. Adalbert baptizes the Hungarian prince who will become King St. Stephen.

1000 A.D.
St. Adalbert is martyred in Prussia.

people. Attempts to convert the Vikings presented much the same problem.

Once Charlemagne had conquered, pacified, and helped convert the Saxons, he opened the lands farther north to missionaries. However, the people in those lands, known as **Scandinavia** (present-day Denmark, Norway, Sweden, and Finland), strongly resisted being converted and joining the other nations of Western Europe in Christendom. Much of the reason had to do with geography.

Scandinavia, located so far north, is cold, making it a difficult region to farm, and nearly all of it is coastline. Thus, the people of Scandinavia turned to the sea for their survival. While some people chose to become fishermen, many found that money could be made more easily by robbing their neighbors to the south.

Witness to the Faith 147

Norsemen (or Vikings)
Scandinavian raiders who made their living by pillaging towns and cities along the coasts and rivers of Europe.

St. Ansgar
The "Apostle to Scandinavia"; spent his life spreading the Gospel in Sweden and Denmark.

Pope Gregory IV
Reigned 827-844; named Ansgar as the archbishop of Hamburg and papal legate to Scandinavia, essentially the spiritual head of the whole region.

In time, the **Norsemen** (or **Vikings**) became the scourge of Europe. They frequently pillaged the coasts of England, France, and the Netherlands. Sailing up Europe's rivers, they plundered churches and monasteries. No city or village on a river was safe from the Vikings in their light longboats, and most great cities were on rivers. *Truly accepting Christianity meant an end to this profitable enterprise. Thus, the Vikings did not want to convert!* However, missionaries understand the challenge and the danger of converting such people. **St. Ansgar**, who would be known as the "Apostle to Scandinavia," accepted both.

Ansgar was born to noble Frankish parents. When his mother died, he was sent to Corbie Abbey. Benedictine monks raised him, so it was no surprise when he joined that order as a young man. In 822, Louis the Pious, the son of Charlemagne, provided the funds to establish a monastery in Saxony. Ansgar was sent with other missionaries to found the abbey of Corvey in Westphalia (northern Germany).

In 813, King Harald of Denmark, who was in the middle of a civil war, visited Louis and asked him for help. With the aid of Louis, Harald regained his throne. Because of his relationship with Louis, King Harald, his wife, and about four hundred members of his court were baptized in 826. Harald also agreed to allow missionaries to preach the Gospel in his kingdom. Ansgar was chosen to go, but had barely arrived when he had to leave because Harald fell from power.

The following year, the Swedish king asked for missionaries again, and Ansgar answered the call. He preached in the Swedish lands for many years before returning to the imperial court in 831. Late that year, he was named archbishop of Hamburg. As archbishop, he had the authority to send missionaries into Scandinavia and to consecrate bishops for that region. Later, Ansgar went to Rome, where **Pope Gregory IV** (827-844) named him papal legate for Scandinavia.

In 845, the Vikings sacked Hamburg, destroying all the church's treasures and books. Despite this terrible catastrophe, Ansgar never lost hope. He continued preaching to the Danes. In 848, he returned to Sweden, where he spent two years renewing the Faith in that kingdom. Viking raids continued to hamper his efforts, but Ansgar, undismayed, continued his missionary work. St. Ansgar died in Bremen in 865.

At the time of Ansgar's death, Christianity was barely taking root in Scandinavia. Despite a lifetime of service to the Danes and Swedes, he had made very little progress. The Vikings remained

Saint Ansgar

Chapter 10: The Gospel Goes North and East

a constantly murderous threat to the rest of Europe. Nevertheless, Ansgar had planted the seeds. His successors eventually reaped the benefit of his labors. A century later, the Church created three bishoprics in Danish territory. The missionaries continued working slowly but patiently, and gradually succeeded. Denmark was considered a converted kingdom by around the end of the tenth century.

The Conversion of Norway

Unlike in most kingdoms, the conversion of Norway was due not primarily to a saint, a monk, or a bishop, but rather to one of the most interesting rulers in the history of Scandinavia. His name was **Olaf Tryggvason**. Before his conversion, he had been a Viking adventurer.

Olaf's life demonstrates the harshness of the Viking culture. Enemies murdered Olaf's father before Olaf was even born. His pregnant mother fled into hiding to give birth to her son. In time, his mother and the man who was protecting them were killed because they were too old to be sold as slaves. Olaf, young and strong, was sold into slavery. At 18, he was fighting as a Viking raider. In 991, in command of a company of Vikings, he won a battle in Britain. Three years later, he unsuccessfully attacked London. At that point, the bishop of Winchester baptized Olaf, who promised never again to attack England.

During this period, many Vikings were baptized and made such promises, and their promises almost always proved worthless. However, Olaf's conversion was genuine; he really meant what he promised.

In 995, Olaf, generally considered the Vikings' finest leader, left Britain and landed in Norway. A Norse bishop, who had been raised as a Catholic in Britain, accompanied him. The people of Norway immediately proclaimed Olaf king. Over the next five years, Olaf worked to evangelize the people there. Many of them accepted the Faith gratefully. Some refused, whereupon Olaf, who still may have had some barbarian habits, forced them to be baptized.

Olaf also invited missionaries from Germany and England to evangelize his people. The missionaries established schools throughout his kingdom. Olaf changed the laws of his nation to bring them in line with the Catholic Faith.

Olaf also worked to convert the people of Iceland and Greenland. In 999, he convinced Leif Ericsson to be baptized. Leif returned to Greenland in 1000, but there is no evidence that he tried to evangelize the people there. Nevertheless, the Faith did still spread to Greenland. Fifty years later, there were ten thousand Christians there, and the island received its first bishop.

In 1000, while Olaf was sailing home from Pomerania, several of his enemies ambushed him in the western Baltic Sea. Despite his best efforts, they overwhelmed him. Olaf died at the Battle of Svolder. In five years, he had managed to convert Norway.

> **Olaf Tryggvason**
> A Viking leader who converted to Christianity and, upon becoming king of Norway, proceeded to make it a Christian country.

Evidence of the Beginning of Olaf's Conversion

Some evidence suggests that a hermit had introduced Olaf to Christianity during a raid he conducted on the Scilly Isles, off the southwest coast of Britain. This conversion would have been the final step in a years-long process.

Olaf Tryggvason

Witness to the Faith 149

Saints Cyril and Methodius

Saints Cyril and Methodius: The Apostles to the Slavs

At about the same time that St. Ansgar was trying to convert the Nordic people in Scandinavia, two brothers from Greece were evangelizing the Slavic people of Central Europe. The Slavs had originally lived in the eastern portion of Europe. However, like so many people from that part of the continent, they had been driven away by the persistent attacks of the Huns. So they migrated west and dispersed throughout eastern and central Europe (that is, the areas which today include the Czech Republic, Slovakia, Poland, Hungary, and Serbia).

Between the seventh and ninth centuries, three groups of Slavic tribes emerged. The Southern branch included the Serbs, Slovenes, and Croatians. They lived in present-day Serbia, Croatia, and Greece. The Eastern branch, also known as the Northern Branch, included the Radimichs and Ulichs. These Slavs lived in what is now Russia. The Western branch counted the Slovaks, Czechs, and Moravians among their numbers. They lived mostly in present-day Poland. In the west, their lands bordered Saxony and Bavaria, which after 800 were part of the Holy Roman Empire. In the middle of these Slavic tribes resided a tribe called the Avars. Little is known about them except that they were nomads and pagans, and they wanted to rule the Slavs.

To protect themselves from the Avars, the Western Slavs placed themselves under the protection of the Frankish kings and accepted Frankish rule. The Franks, desiring to convert the Slavs, sent missionaries to preach the Faith to them. However, the Slavs did not like or understand the German missionaries because they did not speak Slavonic, the Slavic language.

In 846, Rastislav became the duke of Moravia, essentially the ruler of the Western Slavs. Over the years, he enhanced his power, and he sought independence from the Holy Roman Empire. He defended and gradually expanded Moravia, always seeking to make it more independent. As part of his plan for independence, he wished to rid himself of the German missionaries, who he felt supported the Holy Roman Empire. In 862, he petitioned Byzantine Emperor Michael to send him missionaries. Duke Rastislav specifically requested missionaries who could speak Slavonic. Michael sent Saints **Cyril** (826-869) and **Methodius** (815-885), who were brothers.

Amazingly, during the height of the Photian schism, Emperor Michael sent probably the two most qualified men in his empire. Because Cyril and Methodius were from Thessalonica, Greece, which had a large Slavic population, they both spoke the difficult Slavonic language perfectly, and they possessed a thorough understanding of Slavic customs. They were of noble birth and well educated, but rather than choosing lofty careers in business or the government, they entered the monastic life. One may imagine that the brothers also relished the opportunity to be away from the intrigues of Emperor Michael and the wicked Basil.

Since Cyril and Methodius used the Slavonic language in their preaching and celebrated the liturgy in Slavonic, the people of Moravia enthusiastically received the brothers. However, saying Mass in Slavonic, a barbarian language, caused a major controversy, especially among the German missionaries who had returned to Moravia in 864 as part of an arrangement between Duke Rastislav and King Louis the German. The German missionaries declared that Mass should be said in Latin. Another quarrel involved certain German bishops who felt that Moravia fell within their jurisdiction. They likewise directed that only Latin be used at Mass.

In 867, the brothers left Moravia for Croatia, where they continued to preach and say Mass in Slavonic. Later that year, they traveled to Venice, where they defended this practice before a group of bishops, priests, and monks who had objected to it. When Pope Nicholas heard of the great work that the brothers were doing, he invited them to Rome.

Although Nicholas died before they arrived, in 868 the brothers arrived in Rome, where they presented their case to Pope Adrian II. Adrian found nothing wrong with saying the Mass in Slavonic. In fact, he went so far as to place the brothers' Slavic liturgical books on the altar of St. Mary Major, and he had the Slavonic liturgy celebrated in the four Roman basilicas. He then appointed Methodius as archbishop and papal legate to the Slavic nations.

Note on Cyril's Name

"Cyril" was actually named Constantine. He did not take the name Cyril until a few months before his death.

Cyril
One of two brothers who brought the Gospel to the Slavs, using the Slavonic language and even creating an alphabet for it.

Methodius
Cyril's brother; became archbishop of the Slavic lands and suffered much from those who opposed him and his Slavonic liturgy.

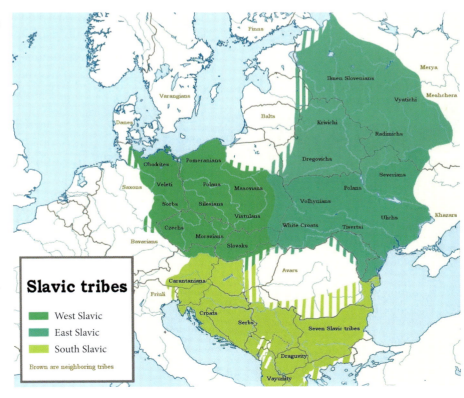

Map of Slavic Tribes in the Seventh to Ninth Centuries

Witness to the Faith   151

Saints Cyril and Methodius with Rastislav, Anselm Wisiak

Near the end of 868, as the brothers prepared to return to Moravia, Cyril (Constantine) fell seriously ill. He became a fully professed Basilian monk, and it was at this time that he took the name Cyril. He died in Rome on February 14, 869. Thus, Methodius returned alone, only to find that Moravia had fallen under the control of the Germans. Duke Rastislav had been betrayed by his nephew Svatopluk, who had turned Rastislav over to King Louis the German. Rastislav was imprisoned, and he died in prison in 870.

Meanwhile, Methodius had his own problems with the German bishops, who apparently had decided to ignore the pope's appointment of him as archbishop of the Slavic lands. In 870, the German bishops of Passau, Salzburg, and Freising convoked a Bavarian council in which they placed St. Methodius on trial. During the trial, Bishop Hermanrich of Passau accused Methodius, exclaiming, "You are teaching in our territory!" Methodius calmly replied, "I would have avoided it, had I known that it was yours, but it belongs to St. Peter." Amazingly, the bishops deposed Methodius and imprisoned him in a monastery! He remained there for almost two and a half years until Pope John VIII ordered his release.

Following his release, Methodius was restored by the pope to his position as archbishop, and he was allowed to continue to preach in Slavonic. However, Pope John forbade him from using the Slavonic liturgy. At this juncture, Methodius, though always obedient to the Holy Father, apparently believed that Pope John did not understand the conditions in Moravia. He decided that, rather than lose the converts he had made, he would not follow Pope John's instructions until he could personally explain the situation to him.

In 872, Pope John summoned Methodius to Rome to answer charges made by his enemies that he was still using the Slavonic liturgy. Once Pope John heard the complete account from Methodius in person, he agreed to allow Methodius to say the Mass in Slavonic. The pope only required that during Mass, before the Gospel was read in Slavonic, it be first read in Latin.

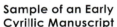

Sample of an Early Cyrillic Manuscript

Despite his continued papal support, Methodius' opponents, notably the German bishops and certain clergy, continued to harass him. Their harassment became so bad that, the following year, Pope John had to reprimand them. St. Methodius died in 885.

The value of the labors of Saints Cyril and Methodius is almost incalculable. To honor them, in 1980 Pope John II declared them the patron saints of

152   *Chapter 10: The Gospel Goes North and East*

Europe, along with St. Benedict. In addition to the souls they saved, they also immeasurably changed the culture of the Slavic peoples. In order to translate the Bible as well as write books for the Mass, Cyril created a new alphabet—later named the *Cyrillic* alphabet in his honor—a version of which is still used today in certain Eastern European nations, including Russia.

The Southern Slavs Accept the Faith

The Croatians were the first Slavonic nation to convert completely to Catholicism. Although records are unclear, it seems that both Byzantine and Benedictine missionaries preached the Gospel to them during the early part of the seventh century. The missionaries followed the example of St. Boniface, and as a result, most conversions were peaceful and genuine. By the beginning of the ninth century, they were completely Catholic.

Map of Croatia

During the ninth century, Croatian rulers built churches and monasteries. In 879, Croatian Duke Branimir wrote a letter to Pope John VIII, promising loyalty and obedience. Pope John replied to the duke, saying that he had celebrated a Mass in which he prayed for Branimir and his people.

In 1076, a representative of Pope Gregory VII crowned Demetrius Zvonimir as king of Croatia. Zvonimir promised to support the Church in Croatia. He also donated the Benedictine monastery of Saint Gregory in Vrana to the pope.

In 745, another Southern Slavic tribe, the Slovenes, made an alliance with the Bavarians to protect themselves from the Avars. The Slovenes had settled on the border of the diocese of Salzburg, and they had received the knowledge of the Catholic Faith from its bishops.

The conversion of the Serbs began around 632, during the reign of Byzantine Emperor Heraclius (610-642). The Serbs, seeking protection from their enemies, appealed to Heraclius for assistance. Heraclius appears to have granted their request on the condition that they be baptized. Apparently, at least some of the Serbian leaders were baptized.

Demetrius Zvonimire

Over time, the Faith grew among the Serbs. By 870, most of the Serbs had become Catholic, and it was considered a converted kingdom. In fact, they sent a delegation to Emperor Basil asking for missionaries to baptize those Serbs who remained unbaptized. In 871, the first bishopric in Serbia was founded at Ras.

The Bulgarians Join the Church

The main actor in the conversion of Bulgaria was their great **King Boris**, who had been baptized in 864. As was the practice of the time, he ordered that all his subjects also receive Baptism. Two years later, he sent an embassy to Rome asking Pope St. Nicholas I to send him a bishop and some priests. He also had some questions for the pope about the obligations that the Catholic Faith imposed upon his people. The pope responded to his questions and sent along two bishops.

> **King Boris**
> King of Bulgaria; received Baptism in 864 and instilled the Faith in his country.

Witness to the Faith 153

King Boris of Bulgaria

Under Boris, the Faith continued to spread with the establishment of schools and monasteries. Books were translated into Slavonic under his patronage. With the conversion of his country well underway, Boris did something few kings have ever done. In 889, he abdicated his throne and entered a monastery. His oldest son, Vladimir, succeeded him. However, when Vladimir began to move the country back to paganism, Boris came roaring out of his monastery like an old lion from his lair. He replaced Vladimir with his younger son, who kept Bulgaria on the true path. Then Boris returned to his monastery, where he spent the last fourteen years of his life in prayer. He died in 907.

It appeared that Bulgaria had become permanently Catholic, but it was not to be. The revolt of Photius, which broke out a few years later, plunged this young Catholic kingdom into schism. When the Greek Church broke away, Bulgaria went with them. The old lion was gone.

The Conversion of the Poles

Of all the magnificent Catholic peoples of the world, perhaps none has been so badly treated by their neighbors as the Poles. Throughout their history, their nation has been conquered and divided. At various times, Poland has actually vanished from the map of Europe. Yet despite the terrible suffering that they have endured over centuries, no people have held more strongly to the Faith than the Poles. In the more than one thousand years since their conversion, the Poles have given the Church great saints, great leaders, and even a pope called "the Great"—an accomplishment few other nations can boast.

During the period when the history of Poland began (about 960), the Germans, ruled by Emperor Otto the Great (983-1002), were the most powerful nation in Europe. In 962, **Duke Mieszko** (962-992), the Polish leader of Poznan, became ruler of Poland. In an effort to maintain peace with the Germans, Mieszko acknowledged Emperor Otto as his overlord.

In 965, Duke Mieszko married **Dubravka**, a Catholic Bohemian princess. Dubravka was the sister of the king of Bohemia, and she had received a splendid Catholic education at the royal court. When she came to Poland, she brought a Flemish priest named Jordan with her from Bohemia. Princess Dubravka and Father Jordan would be the ones mostly responsible for the spread of the Faith in Poland during those early years. The year after marrying Dubravka, Mieszko became Catholic, along with most of the Polish people who had not already converted—almost certainly due to Dubravka's influence.

In 968, **Pope John XIII** (956-972) made Father Jordan the first bishop of Poland, with his see at Poznan. From the beginning, the pope intended that the Church in Poland be independent of the German hierarchy. In 972, German leaders, unhappy at Poland's political and religious independence, attacked Poland but were defeated.

In March 973, Otto the Great called together all the rulers under his domain. He acknowledged the independence of Poland. However, in

Duke Mieszko
Ruled Poland 962-992; became Catholic in 966, along with most of the Polish people who had not already converted.

Dubravka
Duke Mieszko's Bohemian Catholic wife. Along with a priest named Jordan, she introduced the Faith at the Polish court.

Pope John XIII
Reigned 956-972; made Fr. Jordan the first bishop of Poland, with his see at Poznan, thus creating the Polish hierarchy independent of that of Germany.

order to confirm Mieszko's continued allegiance, he asked that the duke send his 7-year-old son, **Boleslaw**, to the imperial court for his education. Mieszko and Dubravka must have wept at the separation from their child, but they also realized that he would receive a better education at the imperial court than in Poznan. Mieszko sent a lock of their son's hair to the pope, placing him under papal protection. Meanwhile, from Germany and Bohemia, numerous missionaries entered Poland to baptize the people. Monks came from all over Western Europe and began to build convents and monasteries.

Shortly before his death in 992, Duke Mieszko "donated" Poland to the pope. He thus placed Poland under the pope's special protection and created the extraordinary relationship between Poland and the Holy See that still exists even today. Perhaps the duke hoped that one day Poland would give something more unique to the papacy than merely land.

Duke Mieszko's son Boleslaw, known as "Boleslaw the Brave," succeeded him as ruler of Poland. He ruled as duke from 992 to 1000, when he was crowned the first king of Poland. During his reign, the Catholic Faith continued its rapid spread. Like his father, he worked for Polish independence and defended Poland against her enemies.

At the beginning of Boleslaw's reign, Poland, though largely independent, remained under the overall dominion of the German Emperor Otto III. In 997, **St. Adalbert**, the former bishop of Prague, was martyred by the pagans of Prussia, to whom he had gone as a missionary. Boleslaw purchased the saint's body from the Prussians and placed it in a tomb in the Church of the Blessed Virgin Mary at Gniezno, Poland. This act greatly pleased Otto III. St. Adalbert had been Otto's confessor when Otto had become the Holy Roman Emperor. Adalbert had deepened and strengthened Otto's faith.

In the spring of 1000, Otto made a pilgrimage to Gniezno to pray at St. Adalbert's shrine. With papal permission, while he was in Poland, Otto established four new Polish dioceses under a metropolitan bishop at

Map of Europe, Highlighting Poland

Boleslaw
Son of Mieszko and Dubravka, known as "Boleslaw the Brave"; crowned Poland's first king in 1000.

St. Adalbert
Bishop of Prague in Bohemia, then missionary in Hungary; baptized the future King St. Stephen; went on to be confessor to the young Emperor Otto III, and died a martyr in Prussia.

Witness to the Faith   **155**

St. Stanislaus
Bishop of Krakow; tried unsuccessfully to bring King Boleslaw II to repentance; finally excommunicated the king, who then killed him.

Boleslaw the Brave

Gniezno. This placed these dioceses outside of German control. He also crowned Boleslaw, which granted Poland full political independence.

The last great pagan uprising in Poland occurred during the reign of King Casimir I (1039-1058). Casimir successfully suppressed the pagans. From then on, Poland was a thoroughly Catholic country.

Casimir's son, Boleslaw II (1058-1081) began his reign as a model Catholic king, supporting the Church and reform. But in 1079 he turned against the Church. **St. Stanislaus**, the bishop of Krakow, unsuccessfully tried to make him see the error of his ways. The saintly bishop finally excommunicated him. Enraged, Boleslaw came to the cathedral, where he found the holy bishop praying at the altar. Boleslaw drew his sword and slew him. When the people learned of this despicable act, they revolted against the king, who fled for his life. He sought refuge in a monastery, where he died a short time later.

Hungary Becomes Catholic

The conversion of the Hungarian people is due to the work of two remarkable men—one of them a king, and the other a bishop and martyr. The king was St. Stephen, the patron saint and great hero of Hungary. The bishop and martyr was St. Adalbert.

The conversion of Hungary began when the great Hungarian military leader Geza converted to Christianity. His wife was an Eastern Rite Catholic, and Geza encouraged missionaries from Germany to evangelize in Hungary. One of the men sent was **St. Adalbert**.

Adalbert had become bishop of Prague in Bohemia in 982. Though he was a good man, it was not until he heard his predecessor on his deathbed decry his lack of commitment to the Faith that Adalbert became a truly holy man. Over the next ten years, Adalbert had a contentious relationship with Duke Boleslav of Bohemia. At one point, probably in 990, when the duke committed a war crime and refused to listen to Adalbert, the bishop resigned and began a pilgrimage to the Holy Land. Adalbert returned toward the end of 992, only after Boleslav promised to respect his authority.

Three years later, members of Prague's nobility murdered a woman whom Adalbert was sheltering in Prague's cathedral. He excommunicated the murderers, but Boleslav and the leaders of Bohemia ignored him. Adalbert then left Prague, never to return.

St. Adalbert next journeyed to Hungary, arriving around 996, and he baptized Geza's son Stephen. Then Adalbert left Hungary and became

Chapter 10: The Gospel Goes North and East

the confessor to the young Emperor Otto III. After receiving papal permission and conferring with Boleslaw the Brave, Adalbert ventured into the lands of the pagan Prussians, where he was martyred in 997.

In that same year, Stephen became king of Hungary. After suppressing a pagan uprising, **King St. Stephen** (997-1038), who ruled Hungary for the next forty years, donated his kingdom to the pope, much as Duke Mieszko had donated Poland a few years before. In return, Pope Sylvester II and Emperor Otto III gave Stephen a royal crown and permission to establish dioceses and consecrate bishops in Hungary. Stephen established the first diocese in Hungary at Esztergom.

The Church in Hungary continued to grow and flourish during Stephen's reign. Toward the end of his reign, Stephen appointed St. Gerard, a Venetian monk, as bishop of southeastern Hungary. St. Gerard recognized that there was a lack of native Hungarian clergy. So he launched a successful campaign to create a native clergy by educating Hungarian boys in cathedral schools and selecting the most promising for ordination.

Toward the end of his life, King Stephen planned to abdicate and retire to a monastery. He intended to hand the kingdom over to his son, Emeric, who had shown every sign of being a good king and a true son of the Church. This plan was shattered when, shortly after Stephen publicly announced his plan, Emeric was wounded in a hunting accident and died in 1031. Future events suggest that the Hungarian nobility may have murdered him.

Stephen mourned for a very long time over the death of his son. With no living children, Stephen struggled to find someone among his relatives capable of competently ruling Hungary and preserving Catholicism. He did not trust his cousin, Duke Vazul, whom he suspected of following pagan customs. Vazul later took part in a plot to murder Stephen, but the assassination attempt failed, and Stephen had Vazul executed. Although Stephen knew the Hungarians would resent a foreign ruler, he finally designated his nephew, who was not Hungarian but Venetian, as his heir. King St. Stephen died on August 15, 1038, at Szekesfehervar, where he was buried.

As Stephen had anticipated, the Hungarians did not like their new king, Peter Orseolo, also known as Peter the Venetian. Civil war and pagan uprisings characterized his reign. His successor, King Andrew I, came to power in 1046 in the midst of these wars. He had Peter executed. Andrew ruled until 1060, during which time Hungary continued to deal with paganism and internal conflicts. Andrew died in battle in 1060.

In December 1060, Andrew's brother Bela became king of Hungary. Although he ruled less than three years, he managed to end the civil wars and begin the work of defeating the pagans. Unbelievably, Bela died as a result of an accident when his heavy wooden throne collapsed as he was sitting on it.

The Murder of St. Stanislaus

> **King St. Stephen**
> Ruled Hungary from 997 to 1038; did much to bring about the conversion of his country.

Witness to the Faith

The Baptism of St. Stephen, Gyula Benczur

Solomon, King Andrew I's oldest son, then became king of Hungary. To avoid another civil war, Bela's three sons acknowledged Solomon as king. This peace lasted until around 1072, when war again erupted between Solomon and Bela's sons. Following several defeats, in 1081 Solomon abdicated the throne in favor of Bela's son Ladislas. King Ladislas reigned until his death in 1095. The last traces of paganism finally disappeared from the kingdom during his reign.

The Conversion of Russia

During their incursions and explorations, the Vikings had established trading posts along Russia's larger rivers. Over time, these trading posts became towns. In time, the Vikings from northern Europe married the Slavic peoples of the East. This intermarriage created the early Russian people. Over the centuries, the Russians built a country.

The country they built was thoroughly pagan, virtually untouched by Christianity, due mainly to its distance from the rest of Europe. Moreover, Russian paganism was not only deep and abiding; it was also cruel. The Russians practiced a form of paganism that included ritual human sacrifice. Like the Saxons and the Prussians, the Russians were more likely to kill a missionary than listen to him.

In 945, **Olga**, the wife of a Russian Viking chieftain, became ruler of the Grand Duchy of Kiev (Russia) when her husband was killed in battle. While visiting Constantinople in 957, Olga was drawn to Catholicism and was baptized. However, she could not convert her son, who died a pagan. When her son died, his three sons succeeded him.

Vladimir, one of Olga's three grandsons, became the sole ruler of Russia when he had his brother assassinated in 977. (The other brother had died in battle the previous year.) Vladimir was completely and staunchly pagan.

In 987, Vladimir married **Anna**, the sister of the Greek Emperor Basil II. In order to marry her, he had to be baptized, so he was baptized on the day of his marriage. The baptism and marriage were clearly part of a military and political deal that Vladimir had made. In exchange for marriage to Anna, Vladimir agreed to provide Basil with several thousand Viking warriors. Basil, facing a serious rebellion, had little option but to agree. During the next two years, Vladimir defeated Basil's enemies, fulfilling his part of the bargain.

Chapter 10: The Gospel Goes North and East

There is nothing to suggest that Vladimir's conversion was sincere. However, the history of the Church is the story of the Holy Spirit working in the minds and hearts of men and women. The channels of grace are hidden, but the effects can be spectacular.

Once Vladimir was baptized, the intensely focused nature of his character, which had been aimed at increasing his power, was now focused on discovering what a follower of Christ would do, and doing it. Unfortunately, he did force Baptism on many of his subjects. But he also did much good. He began reading the Bible. He built Catholic schools in Russia. He destroyed the pagan shrines and built Catholic churches in their place. He became a saint.

Much of the help that Vladimir received in his conversion mission came from Constantinople, which was still in communion with Rome. Vladimir was also in contact with the Holy Father. In 990, **Pope John XV** (985-996) sent bishops to Russia to establish dioceses. Other important meetings between King Vladimir and the Church occurred in 994 and 1000. Until his death in 1015, Vladimir continued close relations with the papacy and the other Catholic kingdoms of Europe. In fact, his three daughters became the queens of France, Poland, and Sweden, respectively. By the time of his death, nearly his entire kingdom had become Catholic.

Throughout his reign, Vladimir always acknowledged the authority of the Holy Father. Moreover, he consistently accepted the teachings of the Catholic Church. In time, the Greek Orthodox Church and then the Russian Orthodox Church would try to assert that Vladimir had supported them or some earlier version of them. However, the historical record simply does not support that contention.

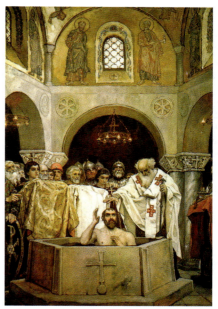

The Baptism of Vladimir, Viktor Vasnetsov

Olga
A Russian queen who was baptized in 957. She was the first Russian ruler to accept Christianity, but was unable to pass on her new Faith to her son or her people.

Vladimir
Olga's grandson; converted upon marrying a Byzantine princess named Anna, and proceeded to make Russia a Christian nation.

Anna
Vladimir's wife, sister of the Byzantine emperor Basil II; Vladimir's conversion seems to have been initially in order to obtain the marriage.

Pope John XV
Reigned 985-996; aided the growth of the Church in Russia, sending bishops there to establish dioceses.

Oral Exercises

1. Briefly describe St. Ansgar's labors among the Scandinavians.
2. How did Olaf help in the conversion of Greenland?
3. Who were Saints Cyril and Methodius?
4. How did the Church in Poland become independent of Germany?
5. Who was Saint Stanislaus of Krakow?
6. Describe the work of King Boris in the conversion of Bulgaria.
7. How was Hungary converted?
8. What is the name of the saint who baptized the future King Stephen of Hungary and was Holy Roman Emperor Otto III's confessor?
9. Through whose influence did Russia embrace the Faith?

Witness to the Faith

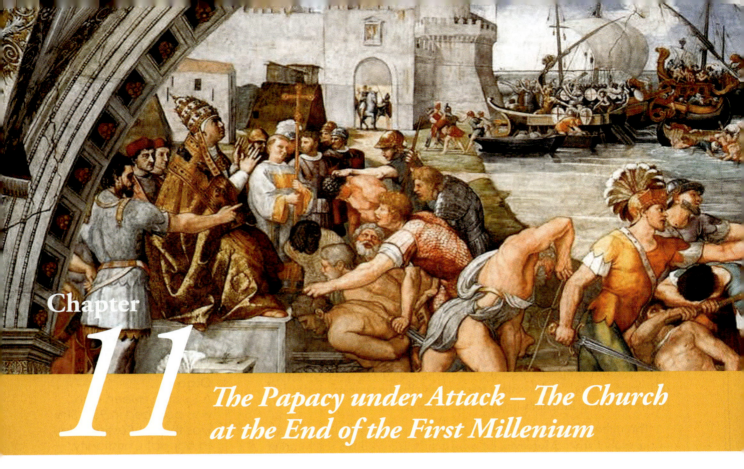

Chapter 11
The Papacy under Attack – The Church at the End of the First Millenium

Map of Italy

Saracens
Muslims from North Africa, who raided the coast of Italy and southern France during the seventh, eighth, and ninth centuries.

Introduction

If there was a period of "dark ages" for Christendom, it occurred in the forty-three years between 867 and 910. G.K. Chesterton summarized these terrible years in his immortal lines from *The Ballad of the White Horse*:

And there was death on the Emperor
And night upon the Pope....

Death fell heavily on the emperor between 867 and 910. Seven Holy Roman Emperors died, and a rival blinded an eighth. Night fell on the papacy, as at least four of the fifteen popes who reigned during this time were *certainly* murdered. Half of the others *may have been* murdered, although no definite evidence exists. From the north, the Vikings in their longships pillaged and ravaged Northern Europe. From the south, the Muslims attacked Italy. Not since the time of the Roman persecution had the Church, especially the pope, been under such attack. Yet, a thousand years earlier, Our Lord had promised that "the gates of hell shall not prevail against" the Church.

The Muslims Attack Italy

The key to conquering Italy from the south lay in the conquest of Sicily, the island on the "toe" of the boot of Italy. Realizing this, the **Saracens**, Muslims from North Africa, had begun raiding Sicily as early

160　Chapter 11: The Papacy under Attack – The Church at the End of the First Millenium

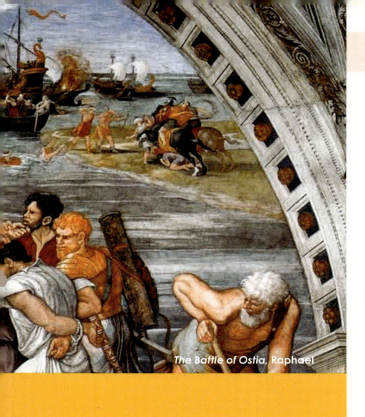
The Battle of Ostia, Raphael

843 A.D. – 1046 A.D.

843 A.D.
The signing of the Treaty of Verdun.

849 A.D.
The Saracens mount an assault on Italy, but are repulsed at the Battle of Ostia.

852 A.D.
The Leonine walls, erected in response to the Saracens' sack of Rome in 846, are completed by Lothair.

882 A.D.
Pope John VIII is murdered on December 16.

897 A.D.
The "Trial of the Corpse" causes a 30-year conflict around Formosus.

904-911 A.D.
Sergius III becomes pope. He declares Formosus' ordinations invalid and helps Theophylact in his rise to power over Rome.

928-935 A.D.
After having Pope John X thrown in prison and killed, Duchess Marozia of the Theophylact family manipulates the papacy until her own imprisonment and mysterious death.

962-965 A.D.
Pope John XII crowns Otto I emperor of the Holy Roman Empire; the pope turns against the emperor, and the emperor attempts to appoint a new pope.

1002 A.D.
Otto III dies without an heir. The crown goes to Henry, duke of Bavaria.

1046 A.D.
The Council of Sutri. Emperor Henry III helps resolve a conflict about who should be pope, and obtains the power to nominate popes and invest bishops.

as 652. The Sicilians had repulsed their attacks, but the Saracens had attacked relentlessly for the next 175 years.

In June 827, the Muslims landed a force in Sicily strong enough to conquer the island. In September 831, they captured Sicily's capital, Palermo. From their base at Palermo, they launched an invasion of the Italian mainland. Over the next decade, they ravaged the coast of Italy, as well as southern France. In 841, they captured the city of Bari in southeastern Italy.

In 843, the Holy Roman Empire was permanently divided into three parts by Charlemagne's three grandsons. The eldest brother, Lothair, retained the title of Holy Roman Emperor. All three brothers pledged to be loyal to one another. Yet none possessed the power, or the wisdom, of Charlemagne. In the dark days to come, Christendom would need a Charlemagne.

Witness to the Faith

Lothair

Battle of Ostia
A battle between the Saracens and a coalition of papal and Italian forces, who defeated an attempted invasion.

Louis the Pious

On August 26, 846, the Saracens sacked Rome. They attacked St. Peter's Basilica as well as the Basilica of St. Paul Outside the Walls. After returning to their ships with as much booty as they could carry, they sailed away, but a storm sank nearly the entire fleet as it approached their base in Sicily.

Prior to the sack of Rome, Lothair and his brothers had shown little interest in defending the Church or even listening to the pope. But Lothair was the grandson of Charlemagne. He knew the history of the Battle of Tours. The sack of St. Peter's and St. Paul's Basilicas was something he could not abide! He pledged to provide soldiers to man a new defensive wall, which he would build for Rome. His brothers soon joined in the pledge. Working with Pope St. Leo IV (847-855), the brothers completed the "Leonine Wall" (named in Pope Leo IV's honor) around the city in 852.

Meanwhile, in 849, at the naval **Battle of Ostia**, beautifully immortalized in Raphael's fresco, a coalition of papal and Italian forces completely defeated another attempted Saracen invasion. Before the battle, Pope Leo, who observed the conflict, blessed the Catholic fleet. The victory at Ostia not only increased Christian morale but also ensured that a Muslim force would never again threaten Rome.

The Rise of Feudalism

The empire that Charlemagne had created did not survive long after his death. Although the Holy Roman Empire lasted until the early nineteenth century, that was, *strictly speaking*, not Charlemagne's empire. Ruling an empire as vast and complex as Charlemagne's required a person of unique abilities. Few people possess those skills. Only a great leader could have kept his empire together, and his successors were not great.

When Charlemagne died in 814, his son, known as "Louis the Pious," became emperor. As his nickname suggests, Louis was a good and holy man, but the empire needed a man called "Louis the Wise and Decisive." Louis was neither. Under his rule, the empire began to disintegrate. Although he tried to avoid it, civil war broke out as his sons rebelled. In 833, Pope Gregory IV spent five days trying to mediate an end to the civil war. Louis died in June 840, while still at war with his sons.

A year later, his eldest son, Lothair, declared war on his other two sons, Charles the Bald and Louis the German. They fought a terrible battle at Fontenoy, but neither side won a decisive victory. In 843, the brothers met at Verdun and signed the treaty that divided the empire. Lothair received the title "Holy Roman Emperor" and would rule the Netherlands, Switzerland, and Italy. Charles the Bald would rule France.

162 *Chapter 11: The Papacy under Attack – The Church at the End of the First Millenium*

Charles the Bald **Louis the German**

Louis the German would rule Germany. The Treaty of Verdun also helped concretize what is known as feudalism. **Feudalism** (or the **feudal system**) was the social and political structure of medieval Europe, characterized by a hierarchical system of protection in which commoners banded together under regional rulers, who in turn recognized the king as their lord.

Even before Charlemagne died, the threat of Viking attacks filled the hearts of Europeans with terror. The Vikings attacked every city and settlement they could reach in their shallow-draft long boats. Moreover, they attacked suddenly, without warning, sailing out of the mist, looting, burning, and then sailing away. Almost no place was safe.

As Charlemagne's empire had fractured, there was no strong central power to deal with these raiders. The Viking raids caused the people to realize that the king was not strong enough to keep the peace internally or to deal with external aggression. They had to defend themselves. Thus, the common people (the farmers, blacksmiths, etc.) organized themselves around tough men with military experience who could defend them. These men were often **knights**. They built sturdy fortresses, which over time became castles. In times of danger, the people took refuge in these fortresses.

To protect themselves further, local landowners banded together under a regional ruler—often a duke, a count (or an earl), or a baron. These regional rulers could call together all the local landowners in times of danger, such as a Viking raid or a Muslim attack. In other words, the regional ruler could raise an army. In return for his protection, the regional ruler required that he own all the land, the only real source of wealth during the Middle Ages. His **vassals**, those who promised him allegiance, could use the land so long as they furnished the ruler the promised military service when he called upon them. Over time, the local rulers (that is, the wealthy landowners) became the nobility and the **aristocracy**. In many places, the nobility became more powerful than the king.

Theoretically, the nobles recognized the king as their lord. The king reigned at the top of the pyramid that formed European society. The nobles were the vassals of the king. They promised to provide him with troops during a foreign war. In fact, there was a special ceremony in which a noble (a duke or a count) swore allegiance to the king, kneeling before

---

Feudalism (or Feudal System)
The social and political structure of medieval Europe, characterized by a hierarchical system of protection in which commoners banded together under regional rulers, who in turn recognized the king as their lord.

Serfs
Peasants who were bound to the land they worked.

Knights
Tough military men who could defend the people against enemies like Vikings.

Vassal
One who owes allegiance to another. In the feudal system, the common people were vassals to their local rulers, and these rulers were vassals to the king.

Aristocracy
The nobility, the highest class of society.

Witness to the Faith

Manor
The land belonging to a nobleman, on which his vassals lived and worked.

Act of Investiture
The ceremony in which a noble swore allegiance to the king, and the king conferred the noble's manor on him.

Medieval King Investing a Bishop with the Symbols of Office

Crosier
The staff representing a bishop's authority over the Church in his diocese.

him and swearing an oath of fealty. The noble placed his hands within the hands of the king, who gave him a twig or a piece of dirt as a sign that he was conferring the noble's land, the manor, upon him. By this **Act of Investiture**, the noble became the king's vassal. He had all the duties of the vassals under him. Most importantly, he provided the king with men and money to run the kingdom or wage war.

Although feudalism had many positive aspects, there were problems with it as well. As nobles became more powerful, they began to try to exert more influence over the Church. Moreover, as the emperor became weaker, he was unable to respond to calls from the pope for protection. The Saracens would threaten not only the pope but also those who had sworn to protect him.

The Church under Feudalism

By the beginning of the ninth century, feudalism was not only a good system for Europe but also probably a necessity. The Roman Empire had maintained order through its strong military and its police force. It had also defeated nearly all its enemies. Without any such powerful structure, Europe in the Middle Ages faced two existential threats: the Vikings and the Muslims. The Vikings were basically thieves. They robbed a city and left. The Muslims were the greater threat. Their goals were conquest and conversion. Once they conquered a place, they could be driven out only by force. With no strong national army or police force, people in the Middle Ages had to defend themselves against these two threats. Feudalism was the best way. However, feudalism also caused problems for the Church, almost from the beginning.

The problems of the Church with feudalism fell into three categories: land, money, and military. In an era when land meant wealth, the issue of land ownership was critical to the very existence of the feudal system. Kings claimed the right to invest their vassals, the various noble rulers under them. As bishops were among the greatest landowners in Christendom, kings wanted to make them their vassals as well by investing them with their power. They wanted to be the ones to give the bishop his staff, the **crosier**, the symbol of his authority over the Church in his diocese. They also expected the bishops to swear fealty to the king, just as a duke or a baron would. But the bishop could not answer to the king in spiritual matters; in fact, in such matters, the king was subject to the bishop. Yet there was no denying that the bishop, as a major landowner, did play a secular role. In time, the kings' determination to invest bishops would lead to the "**Investiture Controversy**."

Kings also expected their vassals, both secular and ecclesiastical, to pay money to support the kingdom. This caused another problem, as wealthy, unworthy men often purchased a bishopric. Kings exercised a great deal of influence in choosing bishops, and they sometimes chose the man who could pay more for the office rather than someone who was holy and devout. Wealthy families, whose sons would not inherit the family land, saw the Church as a way to advance their careers. During the Middle Ages, many such men rose to prominent positions in the Church and did great damage.

Finally, regional leaders were usually expected to lead their troops in battle. The Feudal Age saw a number of bishops lead troops in battle against fellow Christians. The most famous case involved Pope Julius II (1503-1513), who led troops against the French. Such action gave scandal then and remains a source of scandal today.

The Decline of the Holy Roman Empire

The Treaty of Verdun placed Italy under the dominion of Lothair. The Sack of Rome had caused Lothair and his brothers to set aside their differences. For the remainder of Lothair's life, the brothers tended to work together and ceased their civil warfare. When Lothair died in 855, he divided his kingdom between his two sons, and Louis II became ruler of Italy.

Investiture Controversy
The conflict that arose because kings wanted to invest bishops, thus making the bishop subject to the king in the same way as any vassal.

Pope St. Leo IV died in 855 as well. Louis II tried to interfere in the election of the new pope, but the clergy and people of Rome forced him to accept the election of Benedict III (855-858). Following Benedict's short reign, the incomparable Pope St. Nicholas I succeeded him. Pope Nicholas exerted the authority of the Holy See over Louis when he tried to replace his first wife and marry another woman. Nicholas told Louis that the Church would not allow such an act. Despite this, Louis generally acted in the best interests of the Church. For example, he resolutely fought the Muslims in Italy. In recognition of his support, Pope Adrian II crowned Louis as emperor in 872.

In 872, Pope Adrian died, and Pope John VIII (872-882) succeeded him. John would be the last great pope for almost two generations.

When John accepted the Fisherman's Ring, enemies beset him on all sides. In response, the following year he engaged in one of the most remarkable correspondences in the history of the Church. In 873, Pope John received a letter from Alfonso III, the young king of Spain. Alfonso informed him that, while Spain was in the process of driving out the Muslims, he had begun building a magnificent cathedral at **Santiago de Compostela** to bury the bones of the Apostle St. James ("Santiago" in Spanish). He asked the pope for his blessing. John responded by giving his blessing and writing that he prayed that Spain would soon be freed from the Muslims. Then he asked for cavalry horses to fight the Muslims in Italy. In the pope's hour of need, Spain's monarch,

Santiago de Compostela Cathedral

Witness to the Faith 165

Pope John VIII

Pope Martin II

Pope Adrian III

Pope Stephen VI

Pope Formosus

as he or she would so often do, answered the papal plea. Alfonso sent cavalry horses to Pope John.

In 875, Louis II died. In the hopes of ending the civil wars between the Frankish rulers (which had resumed a few years after Lothair's death), Pope John crowned Charles the Bald as the Holy Roman Emperor on December 25, 875. Pope John believed that Charles would be a better emperor than his brother Louis the German. He also hoped that Charles would defend Rome and the papacy against the Saracens, who continued to pillage southern Italy and threaten Rome. The coronation of Charles had no effect. The civil wars continued. Even after Louis the German died the following year, the fighting continued under his son, Louis of Saxony.

By May 877, Pope John had become desperate as the Muslims neared Rome. He wrote to Charles, begging him for aid. Although Charles was a valiant ruler and devoted to the Holy See, as king of western France, he commanded only a small army. Still, he was the grandson of Charlemagne. He decided to march to Italy to aid the pope. He had barely crossed the Alps when he learned that Carloman of Bavaria was attacking France. Charles prepared to return home, but fell ill and died in 877 while crossing the Alps again.

The downward spiral of the Holy Roman Empire now began in earnest, as weak men became emperors. Without a strong emperor, noblemen seized more power. Without a protector, the pope's life was often imperiled.

Following the death of Charles, his eldest son, Louis II, became king in October 877. A weak and sickly man, he ruled for only two years. During his reign, in the winter of 878, Duke Lambert of Spoleto sacked Rome and imprisoned Pope John VIII. After a month of pillaging the Eternal City, Lambert withdrew his troops.

In February 881, in an attempt to find someone who would defend the papacy, Pope John crowned Charles III, known as "the Fat," a great-grandson of Charlemagne, as Holy Roman Emperor. As emperor, Charles the Fat was ineffective at best and cowardly at worst. Internal factions and external enemies tore at the empire. In 885, a fleet of 700 Viking ships attacked Paris. Rather than defending the city, Charles offered the Vikings a bribe and did not fight them. The French finally grew tired of the cowardly and slothful Charles. They deposed him at the Diet of Tribur in 887, replacing him with Berengar, a grandson of Louis the Pious. Charles died the next year.

Meanwhile, on December 16, 882, one of the most horrific events in the history of the Catholic Church occurred. On that date, Pope John VIII was murdered, almost certainly by a priest, possibly by one of John's relatives. Night had fallen on the papacy. It would last nearly thirty years.

The murder of Pope John VIII widened the gulf between the various clerical factions in Rome. Nevertheless, they managed to elect Pope Martin II (882-884), who had support from John's supporters as well as his enemies. But Martin reigned for only two years before his death. His

166 Chapter 11: The Papacy under Attack – The Church at the End of the First Millenium

successor, Pope Adrian III (884-885), reigned a little more than a year. He was deeply involved in the intrigues of Roman secular and religious politics. Some evidence suggests that his enemies murdered him as he journeyed to meet with Charles the Fat.

In September 885, Stephen VI (885-891) became pope. Although the pope cannot teach error when defining dogma, he can make poor decisions. Stephen's pontificate was filled with poor decisions. For example, following the death of St. Methodius, Stephen banned the Slavonic liturgy in Moravia. This emboldened the German bishops to expel most of the native Slavic clergy that Cyril and Methodius had trained, bringing Moravia under German influence.

Stephen next faced the issue of choosing a Holy Roman Emperor. No good candidates presented themselves. One of the two strongest candidates was the Italian Duke Guy of Spoleto, the brother of Lambert—infamous for sacking Rome and imprisoning Pope John VIII. The other contender was a German, Duke Arnulf of Carinthia. Stephen hesitated to support either man. Although the pope probably would have preferred Arnulf, simply because distance made him less likely to interfere with the papacy, Guy of Spoleto put more pressure on the pontiff. Pope Stephen VI reluctantly crowned him emperor in February 891.

Less than eight months later, Stephen died. His successor, **Pope Formosus** (891-896), remains one of the most controversial popes in the history of the Church. Formosus had been a leading candidate for the papacy since the election of John VIII. In 876, Pope John VIII had excommunicated Formosus. However, John's successor, Pope Martin II, had absolved him. The five years of Formosus' reign were a time of massive upheaval in the Holy Roman Empire.

After Pope Stephen's death, the Spoleto family pressured Pope Formosus to crown Guy's son, Lambert, as co-emperor, which he did in April 892. Determined to control the papacy, the Spoleto family increasingly made demands and threats on the pope. In desperation, Formosus appealed to Arnulf in Germany for help. In early 894, Arnulf crossed into Italy, liberating most of the northern part. As thanks, Formosus crowned Arnulf king in Rome. In the spring, Arnulf returned to Germany.

In December 894, Guy died. If either Formosus or Arnulf thought that Guy's death would cause the Spoleto family to give up, they were sadly mistaken. At Guy's death, his widow, the ruthless Ageltrude, and her son Lambert took up the battle against Arnulf and Formosus. They raised an army against Arnulf and placed an antipope on the papal throne after imprisoning Formosus. In February 896, Arnulf took Rome. However, as he marched south to fight Lambert, he suffered a paralyzing stroke, which destroyed all his hopes, together with those of Pope Formosus. At the advanced age of 80, Formosus died of grief in 896. What followed was the greatest desecration to occur in the history of the Church until the Protestant Revolt.

> **Pope Formosus**
> Reigned 891-896; was harassed throughout his pontificate by the Spoleto family, who eventually imprisoned him and set up an antipope, and even "judged" and desecrated his corpse.

Arnulf of Carinthia

Witness to the Faith 167

Pope Stephen VII

Pope Romanus

Pope Theodore II

The Trial of Pope Formosus

In early 897, Duchess Ageltrude and Lambert II, now calling himself emperor, seized Rome. Ageltrude ordered the decayed body of Pope Formosus removed from its tomb in St. Peter's Basilica, where it had lain for nine months. Clothed in the papal vestments, including the hair shirt that the pope had worn in life, the corpse was put on "trial"—the so-called "Synod of the Corpse." Newly elected Pope Stephen VII (896-897), a tool of the Spoleto family, pronounced the corpse guilty. Formosus was deposed, and his acts were declared null and void. His papal robes and hair shirt were stripped from the body. Finally, his body was handed over to the mob, who cast it into the Tiber River. For the next thirty years, a heated battle raged around Pope Formosus. The conflict focused mainly on the validity of the ordinations he had made.

Pope Stephen VII soon suffered his own trials. In the summer of 897, he was arrested and thrown into a dungeon, where he was strangled for reasons unknown.

Pope Romanus succeeded Stephen VII, but he reigned for only four months. Theodore II succeeded Romanus, but he reigned for only twenty days. Nevertheless, during those three weeks he courageously tried to repair the outrages inflicted on Pope Formosus. Pope Theodore obtained the body and solemnly buried it again in St. Peter's Basilica. He also proclaimed the validity of the former pope's ordinations. Theodore was clearly a good and brave man. One wonders if he died a natural death, given the times in which he lived.

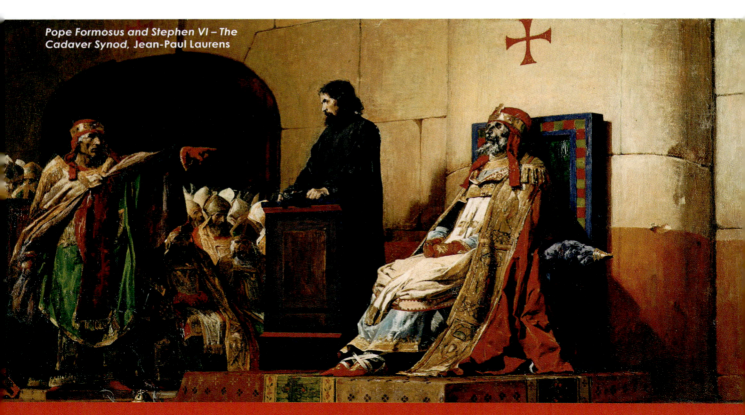

Pope Formosus and Stephen VI – The Cadaver Synod, Jean-Paul Laurens

The next pope, John IX (898-900), also rehabilitated Formosus and convoked three councils to that effect. Pope John IX entirely repudiated the "Synod of the Corpse," completely annulling all its actions. He also condemned all of the synod's participants. However, he pardoned all of them except six, because they claimed to have acted under pressure from Duchess Ageltrude.

The next two popes, Benedict IV (900-903) and Leo V (903-904), were only passing figures. After them, the man who had been antipope during the reigns of Theodore and John IX was validly elected, taking the name Sergius III. He promptly opposed his predecessors' policy and reopened the trial of Formosus.

In the history of the Church, the majority of popes have been good and holy men, a striking number have been saints, and many have died as martyrs. In the case of Pope Vigilius, an evil man became good. However, evil men have also walked in the Shoes of the Fisherman. Sergius III ranks among the worst men ever to reign as pope.

Pope Sergius III (904-911) had participated in the "Synod of the Corpse." In fact, he was one of the six men whom Pope John IX had not pardoned, largely because Sergius had set himself up as antipope in opposition to Pope John. In January 904, Sergius arrived in Rome at the head of an army supplied by allies of the Spoleto family, and was soon proclaimed pope. But Pope Leo V still lived, imprisoned by his enemies. The only way for Sergius to ensure his election was to have Pope Leo V killed, which he almost certainly did. He also decided that those clerics whom Formosus had consecrated needed to be ordained again. During Sergius' reign, the infamous Theophylact family began its rise to power.

The Theophylact Family and the Papacy

With the breakdown of the Holy Roman Empire, aristocratic families, such as the Spoleto family, had seized power. Among the most powerful Italian families in the tenth century was the **Theophylact** family, a Spoleto ally. The head of the family, Theophylact, was count of Tusculum, a town near Rome. With the help of the Spoleto family, he helped Sergius III become pope. In appreciation, Sergius granted him various titles and, with the help of Rome's nobility, essentially made him ruler of the city of Rome. Unfortunately, Theophylact had so much power in Rome that he could almost choose the pope.

In 911, Sergius died. Almost nothing is known of the two popes who succeeded him other than their names (Anastasius III and Lando) and that Theophylact approved of them. In March 914, the Holy Spirit once again placed the right man on the papal throne. Although he was the candidate of the Theophylact family, Pope John X (914-928) demonstrated courage, determination, and independence. Eventually, the last trait would get him killed.

At the time of John's election, the Saracens had a large army based just outside of Monte Cassino and were threatening to capture the

Pope John IX

Pope Benedict IV

Pope Leo V

Pope Sergius III

> **Theophylact**
> Count of Tusculum, head of a powerful Italian family which eventually came to control Rome and the papacy.

The Exterior of the Lateran Basilica and Palace

Above: The Interior of the Lateran Basilica
Below: The Apse of the Lateran Basilica

monastery. Pope John X succeeded in forming a powerful alliance, consisting of the feudal rulers of central and southern Italy and the Byzantine emperor. The pope himself led the Christian armies into battle. They surrounded the Saracens in their fortress at Garigliano and completely defeated them in 915.

In December, John crowned Berengar, who was the king of Italy and a member of the alliance against the Saracens, as the Holy Roman Emperor. John's motives remain unclear. The coronation may have been a *quid pro quo* (Latin, meaning "something for something") for Berengar's aid against the Saracens, or perhaps John genuinely believed that Berengar would make a good emperor. Although not a particularly holy man, Berengar was a competent military leader and seemed like a good counterbalance to the Theophylact family.

In 924, Berengar was assassinated, leaving Pope John X without a protector. The following year, Duchess Marozia, the new head of the Theophylact family, married Marquis Guido, the powerful duke of Tuscany (also known as Guy of Tuscany). The two began plotting against John, who they felt was growing too independent. In 926, John attempted to appoint Hugh, the duke of Provence, as Berengar's successor, naming him the king of Italy.

In spring 928, fearing that the creation of a new emperor might diminish her influence in Rome, Marozia and her husband, Guy of Tuscany, incited a revolt. Their soldiers invaded the Lateran Palace, where they seized and murdered the pope's brother, Peter. They threw John himself into prison, and they smothered him to death.

Marozia now controlled the papacy. Mercifully, the men to whom she gave it ended up ruling briefly and ineffectually.

Chapter 11: The Papacy under Attack – The Church at the End of the First Millenium

Pope Leo VI ruled for only seven months. Of him, Warren Carroll writes: he "is not even so much as a shadow in history; he is a wisp" (W. Carroll, *The Building of Christendom*, p. 406). Pope Stephen VIII ruled for two years, from 929 to 931, but almost nothing else is known about him. In 931, Marozia may have killed Stephen to create a vacancy that would allow her own son to become pope. In 931, her son, who was about 25 years old, became Pope John XI (931-935). In these moments of crisis, as Marozia exercised a stranglehold on the papacy, no great leader stepped into the breach to stop her.

Marozia's ambition knew no bounds. Not satisfied with controlling the papacy, she sought to become empress. Thus, after the death of her husband, Guy of Tuscany, she decided to marry Hugh, duke of Provence, the former candidate for emperor. However, because Hugh was her brother-in-law, she needed a special dispensation from the pope before she could marry him. Pope John XI obligingly provided it. The path to the imperial crown seemed clear. Pope John would certainly crown his mother and stepfather. However, while Marozia was diabolically clever, Hugh was not.

Hugh of Italy

Marozia had another son, named Alberic, whom Hugh foolishly insulted on the day he married Marozia. Alberic raised a small army and besieged his mother and her new husband, forcing Hugh to flee. Alberic captured Marozia and put her in prison, where she met with a mysterious death. Alberic also confined his brother, Pope John XI, for the remainder of his life. Although it seems that Pope John XI died a natural death, he was only about 30 when he died.

Following Marozia's imprisonment, Alberic became the ruler of Rome. Popes Leo VII (936-939), Stephen IX (939-942), Martin III (942-946), and Agapetus II (946-955) served at his pleasure. Unlike his mother, Alberic seems to have given more freedom to the pope. Although he refused to allow the pope any secular authority, he tended to leave him alone ecclesiastically. For example, Pope Agapetus intervened in a dispute involving the see of Reims. He ordered synods to be held at Ingelheim, Trier, and Rome. He helped create monasteries and convents in France and Germany. He also demanded that leaders who had seized monasteries return them to the Church.

Despite the way he came to power, Alberic did do some good. For example, he re-established order in Rome. After meeting Abbot St. Odo of Cluny in 936, Alberic came to respect the right of monks and priests to elect their own abbots and bishops. He also worked with Odo to rebuild monasteries that the Saracens had destroyed. These monasteries were reformed under the model of St. Odo's monastery in Cluny.

Marozia

Unfortunately, his contacts with St. Odo had not caused a full conversion in Alberic's heart. In 954, as he lay on his deathbed, he obtained an oath from his nobles that, upon the death of Pope Agapetus, they would make Alberic's son, Octavian, pope. Pope Agapetus II died the following year, and Octavian became both the ruler of Rome and the pope. He took the name John XII (955-964). He was only 18 years old.

Witness to the Faith **171**

Henry the Fowler
Duke of Saxony, then ruler of all Germany; father of Otto the Great, who became the Holy Roman Emperor.

Pope John XII was one of the most immoral men ever to serve as pope. Although he never contradicted Church doctrine, he did cause the Church great scandal, both then and now. The pope's scandalous private life caused him to lose support in Rome. He was forced to call for help from the last great German king, Otto I (also known as Otto the Great).

The Church and the German Kings

Otto the Great

Since the overthrow of Charles the Fat, the Holy Roman Empire had fragmented into several different parts. The rulers of these parts constantly fought one another for control. In 912, **Henry the Fowler** became duke of Saxony. Over the next twenty-four years, Henry either defeated his enemies in battle or made them his vassals. When he died in 936, Henry was the ruler of Germany. In fact, he ruled more territory than anyone had since Charlemagne. When Henry died, he named his eldest son, Otto, as his successor.

In some ways, Otto was perfectly qualified to be Holy Roman Emperor. He was a devout Catholic who attended daily Mass and said the Divine Office every day. Although he was only 24, he was conscientious and thoughtful. He was also a remarkably good judge of character. He chose men based on ability, not noble birth. But he was barely literate.

Whether Otto always intended to become Holy Roman Emperor, or whether that decision came to him later, he certainly wished to rehabilitate Charlemagne's empire and increase the prestige of Germany. As a first step, Otto had himself crowned at Aachen by the archbishop of Cologne. Next, he sent soldiers to defend his kingdom against the Vikings in the North and the Slavs in the East. In 939, he put down a rebellion of ambitious German dukes, including his own younger brother, Henry. His victory over the Hungarians permanently ended their invasions.

In 951, Otto crossed the Alps, determined to restore order in Italy. In Pavia, he met and married St. Adelaide, a royal princess with whom he would have two children. Otto managed to bring the northern part of Italy under his dominion, but Rome remained under the control of Alberic. By 955, most of Western Europe had come to view Otto as their temporal leader, much as they had Charlemagne more than a century and a half earlier. Thus, it was no surprise when Pope John XII, having lost the support of both the people and the aristocracy of Rome and facing the threat of the ever-dangerous King Berengar, appealed to Otto for help.

Otto responded, crossing into Italy at the head of a massive army. Defeating Berengar at Pavia, Otto drove him from Italy. In gratitude for his services, Pope John XII crowned Otto as emperor on February 2, 962, in St. Peter's Basilica. The Holy Roman Empire had been restored.

Otto the Great, Holy Roman Emperor

Following his coronation, Otto donated about three-fourths of the kingdom of Italy to the pope. He also swore to protect these temporal possessions. For his part, Pope John XII unwisely swore an oath of fidelity to the emperor. Moreover, he promised that his successors would also swear such an oath before the ceremony of their ordination. Pope John also renewed the imperial rights over Rome and papal elections that Pope St. Leo III had granted to Charlemagne.

No sooner had Otto returned to Germany than Pope John decided that he did not like or trust Otto. The pope broke his oath and gave his support to Adalbert, the son of Berengar. At this point, Otto, who otherwise was a good man and an excellent ruler, lost his patience with the duplicitous pope. In late 963, Otto marched on Rome to battle the opposing faction and completely routed it.

Because of the defeat, John XII fled the city with Adalbert. In November, Otto held a pseudo-council of bishops in Rome that declared Pope John XII unworthy of his high office and deposed him. They elected a layman named Leo as pope. Otto had the new candidate ordained a deacon and a priest on the same day. He took the name Leo VIII.

However, the Church has always taught that no one on Earth, not even an emperor, can sit in judgment of the pope, no matter how unworthy he is. Pope John XII quite rightly rejected the judgment of the "council" and the election of Leo VIII. Unless he resigned, Pope John XII would be the only legitimate pope as long as he lived.

Almost the moment Otto left Rome, the people of the city revolted in support of Pope John. In February, with the people's support, John XII re-entered Rome. However, in May 964, despite being only about 28 years old, John seems to have suffered a massive stroke and died.

The Romans, still upset at Otto, continued their resistance by electing a new pope, Benedict V (May 964), without the emperor's input. Otto was furious. He returned once again to Rome, which he besieged. In the face of the imperial army, the people retreated. Otto attempted to once again impose his choice of Leo VIII on the papacy. Benedict V, a good and holy man, resigned to avoid further damage to the Church, and apparently accepted (at least implicitly) Leo as pope, making Pope Leo VIII (964-965) the legitimate pope rather than an antipope. Otto took Benedict to Germany, where he was treated with great respect. Benedict died in 965 and was buried in the cathedral in Hamburg. Leo VIII reigned as pope for about eight months.

This entire incident provided a forewarning of the future. If a man as normally good and just as Otto could let his pride override his judgment, what would happen when lesser men

> ### Note on the Title of Otto I
> Because the emperor was a German king, he was also known by the title "Holy Roman Emperor of the German Nation."

The Throne of Charlemagne Where Otto I Was Crowned King of Germany, Aachen Cathedral

Witness to the Faith 173

became emperor? Indeed, history shows that future emperors would seek to control the pope, not defend him. Rather than protecting the Church and Italy, they would more often oppress them.

After Leo VIII's death, Otto and the Roman electors agreed on John Crescenti, the bishop of Narni in central Italy, for the next pope. John was related to the Theophylact family. Perhaps Otto hoped this move would win some of his political opponents to his side, but it seems that he was never destined to have peace during his life.

Pope John XIII (965-972) tried to rein in the power of the turbulent Roman nobles. However, with Otto back in Germany, the Roman nobles, led by the treacherous Adalbert, once again revolted. In December 965, they arrested the pope and imprisoned him in Castel Sant'Angelo, a fortress on the banks of the Tiber. Once again, Otto was forced to return to Rome to suppress the rebellion. Upon his return, he restored the pope to the Holy See. This time, Otto remained in Rome for six years, essentially ruling his empire from Rome. On Christmas Day in 967, he had his 13-year-old son, Otto II, crowned co-emperor by Pope John XIII. In August 972, the imperial family returned home to Germany.

In 973, Otto celebrated Easter with all the great kings and nobles in his empire. He dealt with certain quarrels among his vassals. He granted others certain benefits, including recognizing the independence of Poland. Seven-year-old Boleslaw the Brave came to live at the imperial court. It was the culmination of Otto's magnificent life and career. Six weeks later, on May 7, 973, Otto died. He had accomplished what every good leader desires: he left his country better than he had found it.

Adalbert

Castel Sant'Angelo

174 *Chapter 11: The Papacy under Attack – The Church at the End of the First Millenium*

Otto II

Upon his father's death, Otto II became Holy Roman Emperor. He was just 18 years old. Meanwhile, Pope John XIII had died on September 6, 972, and, unlike most popes, was buried in the Basilica of Saint Paul Outside the Walls. The papal electors chose Benedict VI (973-974) to succeed John. He was elected in the fall of 972. However, because of the agreement that the Holy Roman Emperor must approve the selection, Benedict was not consecrated until January 973.

Following the death of Otto I, the Roman nobility, who viewed him as an oppressor, saw an opportunity to free themselves. Once again, they revolted. In 974, Crescentius the Elder (one of the leading Roman nobles) and Cardinal Franco Ferrucci had Pope Benedict murdered. In his place, they installed Cardinal Franco. Antipope Franco took the name Boniface VII.

As his father had done before him, Emperor Otto II (973-983) put down the revolt and expelled the conspirators. Antipope Boniface fled to Constantinople. Before running away, he stole as much gold as he could from the Vatican treasury. It seemed that Rome had seen the last of the treacherous Boniface, but future events would prove otherwise.

With the consent of Otto II, in October 974 the papal electors chose the bishop of Sutri, who took the name Benedict VII (974-983). His pontificate proved difficult because of the opposition of those who felt he was merely Otto's puppet. Otto often had to provide troops to protect him. Nevertheless, Benedict displayed great zeal for the reform of the Church. He worked strongly to oppose simony, which had become a very serious issue during the Feudal Age. In fact, in March 981 he even convoked a synod in Rome that prohibited simony.

Pope Benedict died in July 983. Otto II returned to Rome in September. His candidate for pope was the bishop of Pavia, who eventually became Pope John XIV (983-984). Suddenly, tragedy struck. Although he was only 28, Otto contracted malaria and died in December. The archbishop of Mainz crowned Otto's 3-year-old son, Otto III, king of Germany in Aachen on Christmas Day in 983. Because Otto III was only a child, his mother, the Byzantine Princess Theophano, reigned as his regent.

Otto III

The death of Otto II and the succession of a child to his throne caused rebellion against the emperor in Germany and against the pope in Italy. During Otto's youth, Theophano and then his grandmother, the Empress Adelaide, served as regents. While they did their best, they were not the warrior kings needed in this iron age of feudalism. Eventually, the German Diet recognized Otto's right to rule, but war erupted throughout the empire. In 994, at the age of 16, Otto became emperor.

Otto II, Holy Roman Emperor

Theophano, Holy Roman Empress

Witness to the Faith

Otto III

St. Henry II

Meanwhile, no longer fearing the emperor, and with the support of the always-fractious Roman nobles, antipope Boniface VII returned from Constantinople. Boniface and his thugs arrested Pope John XIV and imprisoned him in Castel Sant'Angelo, where they murdered him. Finally, on July 20, 985, Boniface, the murderer of two popes, died by the sword himself when he was murdered.

In 996, Otto III conceived the plan of organizing a Catholic empire, with Rome as its capital. He traveled to Italy, where he claimed the imperial crown as well as that of king of Italy. Otto restrained the Roman nobility and appointed to the papacy the imperial chaplain, a priest named Bruno, his cousin and a grandson of Otto the Great. Upon his elevation to the Holy See, Bruno took the name Gregory V (996-999), becoming the first German pope. Gregory crowned Otto III emperor in May 996 in St. Peter's Basilica. While in Rome, Otto met St. Adalbert, who served as his confessor for almost a year. St. Adalbert instilled a great love and appreciation of monastic life in Otto.

In December 996, Otto left Italy to return home to Germany. He had barely left Rome before the Italian nobles, under the leadership of Crescentius II, once again rebelled. They drove Pope Gregory out of Rome and proclaimed the archbishop of Piacenza as John XVI. Upon receipt of the news, Otto III returned to Italy, deposed the antipope, and executed the rebels. However, neither Gregory nor Otto would long enjoy their victory.

Within a year, Gregory died. To succeed him, Otto III strongly supported his long-time tutor, the French scholar Gerbert of Aurillac, who was elected and took the name Sylvester II (999-1003). The choice of the name "Sylvester" was clearly intended to link this pope with the first Pope Sylvester, who had acted as spiritual director to the first Christian emperor, Constantine. The hope was that Otto III and Sylvester II would become the feudal equivalent of Constantine and Sylvester I. But it was not to be.

In January 1002, while again on his way to deal with an uprising in Rome, the 21-year-old Otto suddenly died. Again, it seems that malaria was the cause.

Otto had never married, so he had no children, which meant he had no heirs. There was no obvious successor to his throne. Once again, the future of the empire, as well as the safety of the pope, was very much in doubt.

St. Henry II

Following Otto III's death, a number of German nobles claimed the German throne. One of the stronger claimants was Henry, the duke of Bavaria, who was one of Otto III's

176 Chapter 11: The Papacy under Attack – The Church at the End of the First Millenium

cousins and a great-grandson of Henry the Fowler. After several months of warfare, Henry defeated his rivals, and in July 1002 was crowned king of Germany.

Although Henry may not have been a perfect ruler, he remains one of the few monarchs to be canonized and the only German sovereign so blessed. His commitment to the Catholic Faith and his desire to protect and defend the Church is unquestioned. Moreover, he led a genuinely holy personal life deserving of veneration.

Henry had received his early education at the monastery of Hildesheim. Later, St. Wolfgang, the bishop of Ratisbon, served as Henry's teacher. A solid Catholic, Henry II was thoroughly familiar with the needs of the Church. As king of Germany, then as king of Italy, and finally as Holy Roman Emperor, he committed to give the Church his full protection. He stated that he would become involved in the affairs of Italy only as a protector and for the greater good of the Church. Moreover, he had the deepest commitment to monastic reform in his empire. In 1014, following his coronation, he placed his crown, scepter, and orb on the altar of the monastery at Cluny.

St. Wolfgang

The year after Henry became king of Germany, Pope Sylvester II died. Because Henry was engaged in a series of wars against the Poles, he paid little attention to the papal elections. As a result, after the death of Pope Sylvester II, the Roman nobles once again gained control. They influenced the elections of Popes John XVII (1003), John XVIII (1003-1009), and Sergius IV (1009-1012). None of these popes made any significant contributions to the Church, although some evidence suggests that in 1009, following the destruction of the Church of the Holy Sepulcher in Jerusalem by the Muslims, Pope Sergius issued a call that they be driven from the Holy Land.

Following the death of Sergius, the two strongest noble families in Rome each nominated a candidate, supported by an army. The Crescenti family nominated Gregory, while the Theophylact family nominated Benedict, grandson of Alberic and great-grandson of Marozia. Neither candidate possessed particularly good credentials. The dispute was resolved in 1012 when Henry became involved in the papal election. He supported Benedict, who was elected and became Benedict VIII (1012-1024). The election of Benedict launched an era of peace and harmony between the pope and the German emperor.

Pope Benedict VIII

Despite his rather unusual election, Pope Benedict proved to be a good pope. He encouraged the Italians to drive the Muslims from Sardinia. He called upon Henry II to protect Italy from the Byzantine Empire. He also enforced clerical celibacy and condemned simony. For his part, Henry promised to support the pope's secular and ecclesiastical directives. On February 14, 1014, Pope Benedict crowned Henry II as Holy Roman Emperor. Following the coronation, the two men

Benedict VIII's Lineage

Benedict's grandfather was Alberic, and his great-grandmother was Marozia.

Witness to the Faith

Conrad II

promulgated a decree proclaiming that all future papal elections must be conducted according to the sacred canons. Over the next ten years, both pope and emperor worked to reform the monasteries, following the pattern established at Cluny (discussed in the next chapter), as well as reform the clergy.

Pope Benedict VIII died in April 1024. Henry died three months later. Once again, because Henry had no children, there was no clear heir to the German throne.

In 1147, Pope Eugene canonized St. Henry II. Pope Innocent III canonized his wife, the Empress Cunigunde, in 1200. Catholics in Germany and Switzerland especially revere both Henry and Cunigunde.

Conrad II

Following Henry's death, Conrad II was chosen to succeed him. Conrad received the support of Henry's widow, Empress Cunigunde, as well as St. Odilo of Cluny, the leading reformer in the Church. Both of these future saints believed that Conrad would continue to support the Church and the reform of the monasteries. For the most part, during his fifteen-year reign, Conrad did not disappoint them.

Henry III

In 1039, Conrad died and was succeeded as emperor by his son Henry III. Although only 22, Henry III had been groomed to rule from an early age. More importantly, he was devoted to the Church and its reform.

Meanwhile, following Pope Benedict IX's death in 1024, John XIX (1024-1032) had become pope. John continued to work to restore the dignity of the papacy and the reform of the monasteries. However, when John died in 1032, the Theophylact family arranged through a combination of threats and bribery to have John's 20-year-old nephew elected pope. He took the name Benedict IX (1032-1048). Once again, a remarkably unworthy man sat on the Throne of St. Peter. Warren Carroll writes that with the election of Benedict, "the Papacy became an object of needed reform rather than a source of it" (W. Carroll, *The Building of Christendom*, p. 460). During Benedict's reign, both Conrad and Henry nevertheless still worked to reform the Church.

In 1044, the people of Rome drove Benedict from the city, probably because of his scandalous lifestyle. In May 1045, he resigned in favor of John Gratian, who took the name Gregory VI (1045-1046). With the resignation of Benedict, everyone, including Emperor Henry, recognized Gregory VI as the true pope. But then Benedict changed his mind and decided that he still wanted to be pope.

As the secular leader of Christendom, Henry attempted to resolve the matter. Henry and Gregory called a council at Sutri,

Henry III

178   Chapter 11: The Papacy under Attack – The Church at the End of the First Millenium

just outside of Rome, in December 1046. At the Council of Sutri, Pope Gregory voluntarily resigned. Although some secular historians claim that he was deposed, this is not correct. No secular authority can depose the pope, as Emperor Henry clearly understood.

Emperor Henry then nominated the bishop of Bamberg to be the new pope, and the clergy of Rome elected him as Pope Clement II (1046-1047). On Christmas Day in 1046, the new pope crowned Henry as Holy Roman Emperor. Henry then asked for the power to nominate popes and invest bishops. Having just endured the pontificate of Benedict IX and the machinations of the Theophylact family, he acted with the best of intentions. However, this request, which was granted, would cause the Church unimaginable sadness in the years to come.

During the remainder of his reign, Henry would nominate three more Germans who would be elected pope. Two served for only a short period: Damasus II (1047-48) and Victor II (1055-1057). In 1049, Henry, certainly an excellent judge of character, nominated Bishop Bruno of Toul. In February, he was consecrated pope, and took the name Leo IX (1049-1054). He would be one of the greatest popes of the Middle Ages and a saint. Leo's election signaled the end of the "night upon the Pope." A new day was dawning for the Church.

The Imperial Crown of the Holy Roman Empire

Oral Exercises

1. What was feudalism?
2. How did feudalism affect the Church?
3. Who crowned Guy of Spoleto as emperor?
4. Who was the first person to be called the "Holy Roman Emperor of the German Nation"?
5. Who was the first German pope?
6. Who is the only German king to be canonized?
7. Why do you think Henry II was friendlier to the Church than many of the other German emperors of this period?

Pope Leo IX

Witness to the Faith   179

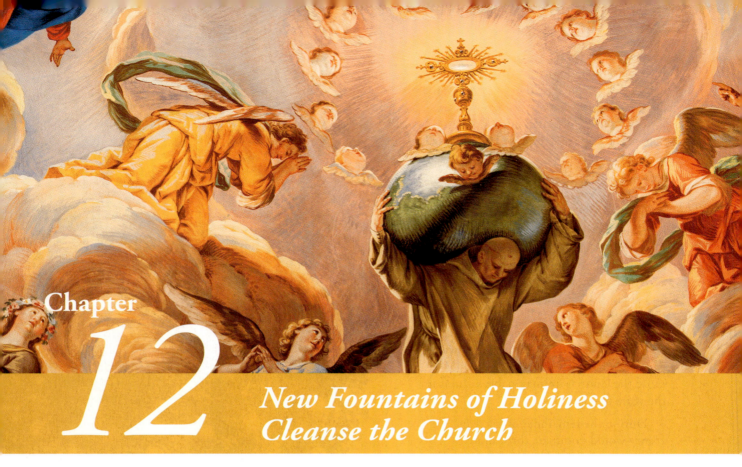

Chapter 12

New Fountains of Holiness Cleanse the Church

Abbey of Cluny
A French abbey that was directly under papal supervision, which helped it retain its religious spirit; spread monastic reform throughout Christendom.

Introduction

As the tenth century dawned, darkness had enveloped the Church. The papacy was under the control of cold and ruthless men. It seemed that the Church and Christendom were on the very brink of destruction. Yet Our Lord had made a promise to St. Peter, and God keeps His promises.

The Monastic Reform of Cluny

The monasteries did not escape the darkness that fell over the Church in the ninth and tenth centuries. Under the feudal system, their abbots were often the vassals of kings and emperors. The monks began leading worldly lives, as the initial strict discipline was relaxed.

However, the monasteries never entirely lost the old spirit of holiness and discipline. Scattered throughout Christendom, monks and abbots worked for discipline and prayed for the return of this spirit. Many monasteries still adhered to the ideals of St. Benedict and faithfully observed his rule. Yet, in this time of darkness, the monasteries clearly needed reform. In France, at the dawn of the tenth century, a light began to gleam in the darkness.

In 910, Duke William of Aquitaine, along with Abbot Berno of Baume, had founded the **Abbey of Cluny** in Burgundy, France. Berno had served as abbot of Baume, which strictly followed the Rule of St.

St. Bruno and the Glory of the Eucharist, Granada

910 A.D. – 1170 A.D.

910 A.D.
Duke William of Aquitaine and Abbot Berno of Baume found the Abbey of Cluny.

1059 A.D.
Pope Nicholas II holds a synod that establishes the rules on how popes are to be elected (i.e., the pope must be chosen by the College of Cardinals). He also establishes an alliance with the Normans.

1066 A.D.
At the Battle of Hastings, William the Conqueror becomes king of England.

1075 A.D.
Gregory holds a synod in Rome condemning simony, clerical marriage, and lay investiture. Later that year, Henry IV openly disobeys the decree, marking the beginning of a long and intense conflict.

1084 A.D.
Henry IV attacks Pope Gregory in Rome. Robert Guiscard and the Normans drive Henry back, but in the process do much damage in Rome. The consequent anger and frustration of the Roman people forces Gregory to leave the city.

1106 A.D.
Pope Paschal II makes an agreement with Henry I of England to resolve the Investiture Controversy in that country.

1113 A.D.
St. Bernard enters the Citeaux monastery, along with thirty of his family and friends, sparking the first real growth of the Cistercian Order.

1122 A.D.
Legates of Pope Calixtus II meet with Henry V at the Concordat of Worms, which resolves the Investiture Controversy in Germany.

1170 A.D.
Thomas Becket is martyred in the Canterbury cathedral.

Benedict. Cluny did as well. Unlike most monasteries, Cluny never fell under the control of a secular authority. The abbot was not a vassal to any secular ruler. Cluny remained directly under papal supervision. In a sense, it was outside the feudal system. As a result, Cluny never departed from its initial monastic discipline. In fact, Cluny was independent not only of secular power but also of any unworthy bishops who might try to control it.

Because of its unique freedom, Cluny not only maintained its original strict discipline, but even strengthened its internal organization. The reform that began with the monks at Cluny spread to the Church as a whole. The monks and abbots became a powerful aid to the papacy. The monks of Cluny, and those who followed their example over the next two hundred years, would complete the building of Christendom.

Witness to the Faith

St. Dunstan

Movements do not simply exist as natural forces. Men and women acting with God change history for the better. The success of the Cluniac reform was due to the saintly men who were drawn to the abbey and became monks. The abbots of Cluny were especially holy men. From its founding in 910 until 1156, eight men served as abbot, including such luminaries as St. Berno, St. Odo, St. Odilo, and St. Hugh. In fact, all but one are saints. Because these abbots were exceptional men, they served as counselors and confessors to popes, kings, and emperors. They changed both the secular and the religious realms. In their extensive travels, they reformed monasteries throughout Christendom using the Cluniac model.

St. Dunstan: England's Reform

Meanwhile, as reform of the monasteries on the continent struggled, it went rather smoothly in England. St. Dunstan, the future archbishop of Canterbury, deserves most of the credit for monastic reform in England. Born about 910, Dunstan became a priest and a monk in 943 at Glastonbury Abbey. Within a few years, the other monks elected him abbot, and he instituted the Rule of St. Benedict. Glastonbury would become the center of English monasticism and reform.

Dunstan became bishop of London in 958, and archbishop of Canterbury in 960. During this time, he served not only as advisor to the king but almost as prime minister, actually governing the kingdom. As advisor to the king, Dunstan helped establish about forty monasteries in England. He also worked to enforce clerical celibacy and abolish simony. In 972, a synod was held to promote monastic reform.

In 978, King Edward was assassinated by his stepbrother. No longer favored at court, Dunstan "retired" to Canterbury. However, his retirement involved prayer, daily Mass, preaching, and various other activities, which kept him busy almost the entire day. He died in 988. For the next several hundred years, Dunstan remained the most popular English saint. He still remains one of the most popular.

The Popes Work to Reform the Church

Feudalism, almost by its very nature, created abuses in the Church. The two most serious problems the Church faced during the tenth and eleventh centuries were simony and the failure of clerics to live celibate lives. These issues caused serious scandal. Church reformers realized that both of these issues needed to be resolved, and that they grew from the same seed: unworthy men in Church positions.

Although it is important that priests be intelligent, it is even more important that they be holy. Colleges and universities can produce great scholars, but only the Church produces saints. As St. Peter Damian, the great reformer of this time, wrote, "what makes a bishop is a good life, and an unceasing effort to acquire the virtues of his state…." He went on to say that bishops, especially the Bishop of Rome, needed to live

Chapter 12: New Fountains of Holiness Cleanse the Church

exemplary lives with high morals and strict discipline. Peter Damian, like all good Church leaders, realized that when unworthy men purchased a clerical position (which is the sin of simony), they injured the Church. Moreover, these unworthy men often did not lead holy lives. They were not prepared for the priestly vocation. For example, they were not willing to practice clerical celibacy. Thus, the two issues often went hand in hand. The popes believed that if they could curb simony, they could more easily enforce celibacy.

As bishop of Bamberg, Pope Clement II had been a reformer. As pope, he continued to reform the Church. In 1047, he called a council at Rome that strongly condemned simony—to the point of excommunication.

Pope St. Leo IX had already earned a reputation as a strong supporter of the Cluniac reform when he was the bishop of Toul. In fact, on his way to Rome to accept the papacy, he had met with Abbot Hugh of Cluny. In 1049, Pope Leo also held a synod in Rome which condemned simony and insisted on clerical celibacy. Unlike most popes, Leo spent most of his pontificate traveling throughout Europe, holding synods to promote his reforms and settling disputes among his bishops. Realizing that simony was as much a secular as a religious problem, Leo also worked with secular leaders such as Emperor Henry III, King Henry I of France, and King St. Edward the Confessor of England.

Pope Leo IX's successor, Victor II, held a council in Florence in June 1055 that condemned simony and clerical marriages.

Pope St. Leo IX

St. Peter Damian

At this moment, a remarkable saint emerged to combat simony and the moral laxity that had infected the clergy. Born in 1007, Peter Damian showed signs of piety and brilliance at an early age. He excelled in school, and by the age of 25 had become a teacher at the University of Parma. Finding that the secular world did not satisfy him, he became a monk in 1035. He also instructed his fellow monks and soon became well known for his preaching. As a preacher and teacher, he traveled to various monasteries instructing other monks. His travels enabled him to see the problems and scandals that affected the monasteries.

In 1047, Peter attended the synod in Rome that condemned simony. He also attended the Florence synod in 1055. In 1057, Pope Stephen X appointed Peter as bishop of Ostia. It was at this time that Peter wrote to his fellow bishops explaining the nature of a good bishop. Throughout his life, Peter Damian worked to reform the clergy and abolish simony. In one particularly notable incident, at the end of 1059, the pope sent him to Milan, because that diocese had fallen into serious trouble. Simony ran rampant. Clerics openly "married" their girlfriends. Peter confronted the sinners in the cathedral of Milan, and only after receiving their public repentance and the promise of future good behavior did he absolve them.

St. Peter Damian

Witness to the Faith

College of Cardinals

The priests (now usually bishops) who elect the pope. "Cardinal" initially meant a priest associated with a cathedral; over time, the title became more prestigious.

Historical Note on the term "Cardinal"

Historically, the word "cardinal" (from the Latin *cardo*, meaning "hinge") was initially applied to priests associated with cathedrals. These priests acted like intermediaries between the parish priests and the bishop. They were like "hinges" connecting the parish churches with the cathedral. Over time, the title came to imply a level of respect. The Roman cardinals participated in the papal elections and helped govern the Church. Thus, by 1059, it made sense that those men most involved in running the Church would elect its visible head on Earth.

Peter Damian died in 1072. In 1828, Pope Leo XII declared him a Doctor of the Church.

Emperor Henry IV

In October 1056, with Pope Victor II at his bedside, Henry III died. He asked the pope to serve as guardian to his 6-year-old son, Henry IV. Victor probably would have made an excellent guardian and teacher to young Henry, but no one will ever know. Victor died suddenly nine months later.

Not really expecting young Henry or his regent mother to submit a papal candidate, five days later the clergy of Rome elected Cardinal Frederick of Lorraine as pope. He took the name Stephen X (1057-1058). During his brief, eight-month reign, he supported Leo IX's reforms and consecrated Peter Damian as bishop of Ostia.

In December, Church leaders met in Siena and elected the bishop of Florence, a leading reformer, to be the new pope. He chose the name Nicholas II (1059-1061). Although he reigned for only a short time, Pope Nicholas II is responsible for establishing the Church's current norms on how popes are elected. In April 1059, Pope Nicholas held a synod with more than 100 bishops. They determined that in the future the **College of Cardinals** would elect the pope. The right of the Holy Roman Emperor to approve the choice was essentially eliminated.

Nicholas next sought protectors against the seemingly always-riotous Roman nobles. Henry IV was still a child, and the German kings were always far from Rome. The pope needed help from people in Italy. Hildebrand, the pope's most trusted advisor, had an answer: the Normans.

Becoming the allies of the Normans seemed both risky and unwise, mainly because, for hundreds of years, they had pillaged Italy. Since the time of Gregory the Great, the Church had paid them to keep the peace. In addition, under Robert Guiscard, they had captured and imprisoned Pope Leo IX. Yet they were well ensconced in Italy and were not leaving. In fact, the allied forces of the Eastern Empire, the Holy Roman Empire, and the papacy had failed to expel the Normans from Italy. Moreover, in some respects, it was logical for them to be allies with the pope. First, since the Great Schism of 1054, the Normans were the enemies of the Byzantine Empire. Second, they had been the unyielding foes of the Muslims for hundreds of years. Third, they were Catholic.

In June 1059, Pope Nicholas made an agreement with the Normans. He reconciled Robert Guiscard to the Church, and the Normans paid homage to the Holy See. In a sense, Pope Nicholas became their feudal lord. He recognized their authority over various parts of southern Italy, including Sicily, which the Muslims had controlled for more than 250 years. In return, the Normans swore that they would be faithful vassals and defend him.

In 1061, Robert Guiscard and his younger brother Roger, with the encouragement of the pope, invaded Sicily. In June 1063, Roger

184 *Chapter 12: New Fountains of Holiness Cleanse the Church*

defeated about 50,000 Muslims at the Battle of Cerami. Although Sicily would not fall to the Normans until 1091, after Cerami, the conquest of Sicily was only a matter of time.

At the end of July 1061, Pope Nicholas II suddenly died. He was in his 60s, elderly for the times. In his brief pontificate, he had accomplished two great achievements: the stable election of popes and the alliance with the Normans. The alliance with the Normans and their invasion of Sicily would set the stage for one of history's greatest movements: the Crusades.

After the death of Pope Nicholas II, certain German bishops and fractious Roman nobles elected the bishop of Parma, and he took the name Honorius II. However, this election was clearly not in conformity with the new rules that Pope Nicholas II had established, and therefore was not valid. Meanwhile, the College of Cardinals elected Bishop Anselm of Lucca, who took the name Alexander II (1061-1073). The cardinals did not consult with Emperor Henry.

Following the election of the antipope Honorius II, the bishops who supported him, in an effort to legitimize his election, had 11-year-old Henry IV invest him. Based on future events, it seems that this act so affected young Henry that he really came to believe that he alone had the authority to invest the pope—or remove him! Henry's situation worsened when his holy mother, who had acted as regent, was no longer able to tolerate the imperial court and entered a convent. Power-hungry German nobles surrounded the boy emperor.

Roger I of Sicily at the Battle of Cerami in 1063, Prosper Lafaya

Over the next years, various councils excommunicated the antipope Honorius and declared for Pope Alexander II. The most notable event of Alexander's pontificate occurred in 1066, when William, the duke of Normandy, invaded England. King Edward the Confessor of England had died in early 1066 without an heir and had named Harold Godwinsson as his successor. However, Duke William also had a strong claim to the throne. He sent representatives to Pope Alexander, seeking his support. They pointed out that the Church in Normandy was thriving, whereas the archbishop of Canterbury had obtained his position through simony. Moreover, despite the pope's condemnation, this archbishop had held his position for thirteen years because Harold Godwinsson and his father had supported him.

Given the option of Duke William, who promised to support Church reform in England, and Harold Godwinsson, who supported simony, Pope Alexander had an easy choice. He proclaimed William the rightful king of England and ordered him to reform the Church there. (In fairness, Pope Alexander should have at least given Harold a hearing, which apparently he never did.) On October 14, 1066, at the **Battle of Hastings**, William defeated Harold and conquered England.

Meanwhile, following some disruptions in the Byzantine Empire, Robert Guiscard drove the last remaining Byzantines from Italy. He had been working to drive them out for several years. In 1071, their final stronghold fell.

> **Battle of Hastings**
> The battle in which Duke William of Normandy defeated Harold Godwinsson and became king of England.

Witness to the Faith 185

The Election of Pope St. Gregory VII

In May 1073, Pope Alexander II died after reigning for more than twelve years. The day after his death, the people of Rome acclaimed Cardinal Hildebrand as pope. In order to comply with the decree established under Pope Nicholas II, the College of Cardinals unanimously confirmed him. To honor his friend and teacher, Pope Gregory VI (1045-1046), Hildebrand chose the name Gregory VII.

Extremely intelligent, insightful, and holy, a man who was truly worthy to walk in the Shoes of the Fisherman now sat upon the papal throne. The Church has been blessed with many great popes, but few, if any, have been greater than Pope St. Gregory VII (1073-1085). More than almost any person during his lifetime, he advanced the cause of reform in the Church and the renewal of the power and prestige of the papacy. More than any other person, he created what became the era of High Medieval Christendom. Every pope in the Middle Ages since Gregory VII viewed him as indispensable.

Maria del Priorato (formerly the Monastery of St. Mary of the Aventine)

The future Pope Gregory VII was born in southern Tuscany in 1020. He was educated at the Roman monastery of St. Mary of the Aventine, which was under the jurisdiction of the abbot of Cluny. When he finished his studies in Rome, he went to Cluny, where he spent several years in prayer and study under Abbot St. Odilo. When Pope Gregory VI came to Rome in 1045, he chose Hildebrand to form a guard to protect the city, especially the pilgrimage sites. It would be the beginning of their lifelong friendship. Hildebrand became Pope Gregory VI's personal secretary, which allowed him to see firsthand the problems that beset the Church in general and the papacy in particular. When Pope Gregory VI resigned in December 1046, Hildebrand accompanied him into exile in Germany.

In 1048, Hildebrand led a group of priests who convinced Henry III to nominate Bishop Bruno to the papacy. On his way to Rome, the future Pope Leo IX stopped at Cluny and asked Hildebrand to accompany him to Rome. Perhaps acting on Hildebrand's advice, Leo entered Rome as a pilgrim. He did not put on the papal vestments until after the people and the clergy had legally elected him.

Like Pope Gregory VI before him, Pope Leo IX realized that Hildebrand was a very special man. Pope Leo ordained Hildebrand as a deacon and made him a cardinal. From that moment forward, Hildebrand became one of the most important, leading figures in the Church. He not only advised the pope but also led special missions on the pope's behalf, such as the mission to the Normans. The four popes who succeeded Leo IX all relied on Hildebrand for advice and support. Perhaps he played a role in the decree issued under Pope Nicholas II establishing the norms for papal elections.

In 1058, as Pope Stephen X lay on his deathbed, he performed a remarkable act. He ordered the Roman clergy, on pain of excommunication, not to elect his successor until Cardinal Hildebrand returned from a papal mission in Germany. Whether Pope Stephen expected them to elect Hildebrand as pope, no one can say, but Pope Stephen certainly believed that Hildebrand's presence at the election was vital.

Cardinal Hildebrand had been a leading candidate for the papacy since the death of Leo IX. At the funeral of Pope Alexander II, it seems that voices in the crowd began calling out, "Let Hildebrand be pope." Thus, Hildebrand became one of only a handful of men to be "acclaimed" pope.

The Pontificate of Gregory VII

When Gregory VII became pope, Christendom was nearing its zenith. Virtually all of Europe was Catholic. There was almost no heresy and no slavery. Although men and women still sinned, they at least acknowledged that morality existed. Nevertheless, the Church still faced three serious problems: simony, clerical marriage, and lay investiture. Gregory believed that lay investiture, such as what Henry IV had attempted with the antipope Honorius II, was at the root of the problem of simony and the other abuses in the Church.

Pope Gregory VII always believed that when Christ had made Peter the pope and entrusted the Church to him, He had not intended to exclude kings and emperors from being under the pope's authority. The pope's authority is not temporal like that of a king or emperor, but the pope has the moral authority to *judge* kings and emperors, just as any priest has the authority to judge a sinner. Christ had given the Apostles the power to either forgive sins or retain them. Priests could require public or private penance. In the case of an unrepentant public sinner, the priest could even excommunicate him. When a king or emperor was excommunicated, his subjects no longer had to obey him.

Thus, while Gregory always tried to work with the secular authorities (for example, he had the idea to reconcile with the Normans), he insisted that the spiritual take precedent over the secular. He had no desire to encroach on the legitimate power of the State. But he insisted that the State not intrude on the legitimate authority of the Church. He

Pope Gregory VII

Witness to the Faith   187

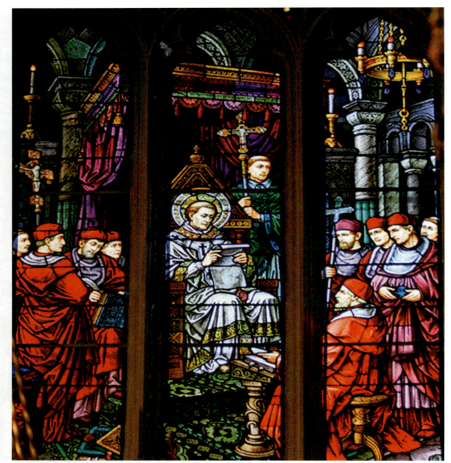

Pope Gregory VII
Proscribing Lay Investiture

intended to abolish the abuses and scandals that resulted from secular interference. Always a man of action, Pope Gregory quickly launched an attack on lay investiture.

In 1075, Pope Gregory called a council in Rome to address the issue of lay investiture. He demanded that several bishops from Germany, where the practice was especially prevalent, attend. The council explicitly condemned simony, clerical marriage, and lay investiture. In fact, from the council, Gregory issued a decree excommunicating any ruler who conferred an investiture, and he declared that any bishop or abbot who had received such an investiture was no longer a bishop or abbot. For two hundred years, feudalism had done great damage to the Church. Pope Gregory VII was about to end that damage.

Pope Gregory's Conflict with Emperor Henry IV

Pope Gregory's decree against lay investiture affected Emperor Henry IV more than any other ruler. Lay investiture had become common in Germany. Furthermore, German bishops and abbots ranked among the wealthiest nobles. They had long been under the control of the emperor, who used them to keep his other vassals, especially rebellious barons, under control. Thus, Henry saw the decree, not as an attempt to reform the Church, but as a threat to his throne.

Henry was only 22 years old when Gregory became pope in May 1073. Henry had grown up at an imperial court filled with dissension and corruption of all kinds. In March 1065, the immature 14-year-old had begun ruling Germany in his own right. Corrupted by the scheming barons around him, and lacking a positive parental or religious influence, he had ascended to the throne as a strong king but perhaps not as a good man.

During the early years of Gregory's pontificate, he and the young emperor had a good relationship. Henry pledged his loyalty to the pope and apologized for his past behavior. He promised to work on abolishing simony, which, he admitted, ran rampant through Germany. Gregory later wrote to some Saxon nobles, who were rebelling against Henry, that they should cease their revolt.

Once Henry had defeated the rebellious Saxons, he changed his conduct toward Gregory. Knowing that he could rely on the German clergy, many of whom deeply opposed clerical celibacy, Henry acted. In the autumn of 1075, in direct violation of Pope Gregory's decree, he invested three bishops in Italy. In Germany, he made one of his favorites the bishop of Bamberg, and he installed his candidate as bishop of Cologne despite the protests of the clergy and people of that city.

Gregory appealed to Henry IV to listen to reason. On December 8, 1075, Pope Gregory sent Henry the last letter he would ever address to him. It began, "Gregory, servant of the servants of God, to King Henry, health and apostolic benediction if he yields to the Apostolic See that obedience which is due from a Christian king." While the letter overflowed with kindness, written from a father to a disobedient child, it scolded Henry for consorting with men who had been excommunicated and for appointing them to official positions.

Pope Gregory also sent ambassadors to meet with Henry. They told Henry that if he did not change his policies and reform his life, Gregory might excommunicate him, which also meant that the pope would no longer recognize him as emperor. Henry refused to heed Gregory's warnings. Instead, in January 1076, he convoked an emergency meeting of the German Diet (the Congress) at Worms, which most of the German bishops attended. In a fit of rage, Henry claimed to "depose" the pope. He ordered, with threats, that the dozens of bishops and abbots in attendance sign a decree denying that Gregory was pope. Perhaps facing instant martyrdom, all present signed.

Henry sent his decree of "deposition" to Gregory, who was holding a synod in Rome. It began with the insulting statement: "Henry, king, not by usurpation, but by the holy will of God, to Hildebrand, now no longer the pope, but a false monk … Condemned by all our bishops and by us, vacate the place which you have usurped." When Henry's representative, Roland of Parma, began reading this extraordinary document to the pope at the synod, the loyal soldiers and nobles present were so furious that they tried to kill Roland. Gregory saved Roland's life by interposing his own body between him and them.

The following day, with the unanimous support of the Roman synod, Gregory excommunicated Henry IV, and he released Henry's subjects from their oath of allegiance to him. Also excommunicated were any bishops who had signed the decree at Worms attempting to depose him as pope, unless they had acted under duress.

Henry's excommunication immediately began to cause him serious problems. Many bishops and priests, as well as secular leaders

Emperor Henry IV

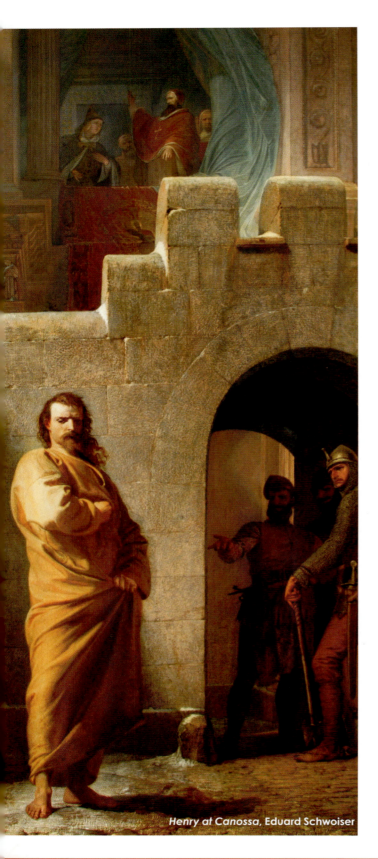
Henry at Canossa, Eduard Schwoiser

who supported reform, abandoned the imperial cause. In October 1076, a Diet met in Tribur, attended by a large number of bishops and secular leaders. They ordered Henry to make peace with Pope Gregory or be removed as emperor. The Diet determined that it would meet again in Augsburg in February to address the question of Henry's fitness to be emperor. Pope Gregory would preside over the Augsburg Diet. In the meantime, Henry was forbidden to exercise his royal authority.

Henry knew that he would lose his throne if Pope Gregory arrived to judge him publicly. Henry's only hope was that the pope would forgive him, remove the sentence of excommunication, and renew his support for him as emperor. Whether Henry was motivated solely by political considerations or whether the prayers of Pope Gregory had touched his heart—Henry was still a young man of only 25 years, not a hardened sinner—what he did next showed remarkable courage.

In the dead of winter, with his wife and young son, Henry secretly crossed the Alps amid great hardships, often crawling through the snow on his hands and knees. Finally, the small party arrived at the castle of Canossa. Pope Gregory, who had heard that Henry was raising an army, had taken refuge in the impregnable castle of Canossa.

On January 25, the emperor appeared before the ramparts of the castle and asked for absolution. The pope refused. He declared that he would give his decision at Augsburg.

Henry took off his shoes and dressed as a penitent. For three days, he knelt barefoot in the snow outside the gates of the castle, begging Gregory to forgive him. On the evening of the third day, Pope Gregory agreed to hear the emperor's confession on the condition that Henry abide by Gregory's decision regarding his right to rule and that the papal legates be given safe conduct in Germany. Henry agreed. The following day, Pope Gregory heard Henry's confession.

The Last Days of Pope Gregory

To regain possession of his throne, Henry IV had to await the decree of his reconciliation, which was to be issued in the presence of a large assembly in Germany by the pope himself. However, his opponents did not wait for the assembly. They met at the Diet of Forchheim, where they deposed him and elected Rudolf of Swabia as his successor. Civil war broke out in Germany in April 1077 and lasted until 1080 without any clear victor. For three years, two men claimed to be king of Germany.

Meanwhile, Henry had broken his promises to Gregory. The pope remained patient until Henry demanded that Gregory recognize him as emperor or see an antipope installed in his place. In March 1080, at a synod in Rome, the pope then issued a double sentence of excommunication and deposition. Gregory also recognized Rudolf as Germany's new ruler. Henry retaliated in June by setting up Bishop Guibert of Ravenna, whom Gregory had excommunicated two years earlier, as an antipope under the name Clement III.

The events that followed favored Henry. Rudolf fell at the Battle of Merseburg. In spring 1081, Henry set out for Italy. After a series of battles and sieges, in March 1084 he gained possession of Rome. Henry had himself crowned emperor in the Lateran Basilica by the antipope Clement III.

Meanwhile, as Henry was about to take Rome, Gregory took refuge in Castel Sant'Angelo. Henry was besieging the castle and was about to capture Gregory when Robert Guiscard came to his rescue at the head of a powerful Norman army. Robert, the finest general of the time, forced the Germans to retreat.

However, when the Normans assaulted a city, they were impossible to control. Over the course of three terrible days, the Normans pillaged the city and set it on fire. The flames burned an entire section of Rome to the ground. The Roman people blamed the pope. Gregory VII was no longer safe in a city whose people were frustrated by his many troubles. When the Normans withdrew, he went with them. He spent the last months of his life at Monte Cassino and then Salerno, where he died in 1085. The epitaph on Gregory's tomb in Salerno Cathedral reads, "I have loved justice and hated iniquity, therefore I die in exile." Pope Paul V canonized him in 1606.

Investiture Controversy Ends in Germany

Following Gregory's death, Victor III became pope but ruled for only a few years. In 1088, Pope Urban II (1088-1099), another great pope, came to the Throne of St. Peter. Although Urban is most well known for calling the First Crusade (discussed in an upcoming chapter), he continued the work of Pope Gregory VII in fighting against lay investiture in Germany. Following his election, Pope Urban excommunicated Henry IV and the antipope Clement III.

After his defeat by the Normans, Henry returned to Germany, where he attempted to quash those opposing him. But Germany had fallen into a civil war that would last the rest of his life. In 1099, a

Rudolf of Swabia

Robert Guiscard

Witness to the Faith 191

Emperor Henry V

new pope, Paschal II (1099-1118) was elected. In 1102, he convened a council, which again solemnly excommunicated Henry. Moreover, the pope told Henry's son, Henry V, that, as long as he restored the Church in Germany, it would be no sin to overthrow his father. With the pope's blessing, Henry V rebelled against his father in December 1104. In March 1106, Henry IV died, and Henry V became king of Germany.

Henry V seemed to be an obedient son of the Church until he became king. Once he had defeated his opponents and had become Germany's undisputed ruler in 1109, he changed. Like his father, he continued to invest bishops. Henry journeyed to Italy, seemingly to be crowned, but really to impose his views on Pope Paschal II. When Paschal refused to agree to Henry's demands, Henry took him prisoner and carried him away to Germany, holding him there for two months.

The controversy was finally settled during the reign of Pope Calixtus II (1119-1124). In September 1122, papal legates met with Henry V at Worms, where they made an agreement: the **Concordat of Worms**. In this agreement, both parties made important concessions. **The spiritual authority of bishops would be separated from their temporal authority.** Since a bishop possessed both an episcopal see and a fiefdom, the parties agreed to confer upon him two investitures. The canons of the cathedral would elect the bishop, whose religious investiture with the staff and the ring would be conferred by a prelate appointed by the pope. The emperor would confer the feudal investiture with the scepter and the sword. The Investiture Controversy in Germany had finally been resolved.

The Investiture Controversy in England

Because the feudal system also existed in England, so did the Investiture Controversy. The leader of the fight in England was the great archbishop of Canterbury, **St. Anselm**. As in Germany, English abbots and bishops were large landowners. The king wanted to invest them, but Anselm objected. His stand for the Faith caused him to be exiled twice, first by William Rufus and then by Henry I, both sons of William the Conqueror. Finally, in 1106, Pope Paschal II made an agreement with Henry I, similar to the Concordat of Worms, which allowed Anselm to return to England. Under the agreement, bishops should be freely elected and then invested with their religious authority, and after that ceremony, they should pay homage to the king.

St. Thomas Becket

For the next fifty-five years, the relationship between the king of England and the Catholic Church remained good. Trouble began again under Henry II, one of the most ambitious and ruthless men ever to rule a nation, who became king of England in 1154. He was determined to exercise the control over the Church that his grandfather Henry I had.

In 1161, when the archbishop of Canterbury died, Henry saw an opportunity to gain control over the Church in England. He had his close friend and chancellor of England, Thomas Becket, named as the

Concordat of Worms
The agreement that resolved the Investiture Controversy, separating the bishop's religious authority from his feudal status.

St. Anselm
Archbishop of Canterbury; exiled twice for objecting to the king's desire to invest bishops.

192 *Chapter 12: New Fountains of Holiness Cleanse the Church*

new archbishop. Henry was certain that Thomas would support him in whatever he did. Henry was wrong.

As in the case of Pope Vigilius so many centuries earlier, something changed in the soul of Thomas Becket. Once Thomas had been consecrated as archbishop, he renounced his worldly ways. He gave away his possessions and embraced a life of rigid austerity. Rather than supporting Henry, he became his greatest opponent and a fearless defender of the Church.

Soon an issue arose in which Henry demanded that clerics charged with certain crimes be handed over to the secular courts for trial. He argued that ecclesiastical tribunals were not strict enough in these matters; therefore, it was imperative for the civil power to intervene. Thomas argued that only ecclesiastical courts could try cases involving Church matters.

When Thomas refused to agree to Henry's demands, Henry placed him on trial. Thomas forbade the English bishops to take any part in his trial and appealed to Rome. Meanwhile, Henry's court found him guilty of treason and condemned him. In 1164, Becket fled England and sought refuge in France.

Enraged, Henry swore revenge on Thomas Becket. He expelled all of Becket's relatives from England and confiscated the lands of Pontigny Abbey, because the abbot had given Becket sanctuary. In response, Thomas excommunicated all the king's supporters, both secular and religious.

Meanwhile, Thomas sought the support of Pope Alexander III (1159-1181). The pope supported Thomas but sought a resolution to the situation. Thomas also had a friend in King Louis VII of France, Henry II's main rival. Eventually, Pope Alexander III and King Louise VII convinced Thomas to meet with Henry. In July 1170, they met and made peace. Henry seemed to yield and agreed to let Thomas return to England.

Unfortunately, peace between Thomas and Henry did not last long. In June 1170, the archbishop of York, assisted by the bishops of London, Salisbury, Rochester, and Durham, had crowned Henry's son Prince Henry. This not only violated the archbishop of Canterbury's privilege of coronation; it was also an act of disobedience. In February 1170, the pope had explicitly prohibited any bishop besides Thomas Becket from crowning Prince Henry. When Thomas Becket complained to Pope Alexander III, the pope excommunicated the archbishop of York along with the bishops of London, Salisbury, and Rochester, and he suspended the bishop of Durham.

A few weeks later, word of the excommunications reached King Henry. He burst into a violent rage and exclaimed, "Will no one rid me of this meddlesome priest?" Four knights who were present heard the king's words. They immediately rode to

King Henry II of England

St. Thomas Becket

Witness to the Faith **193**

St. Bruno

Canterbury, where they murdered Thomas Becket in his cathedral. Pope Alexander III demanded public reparation for the crime, and Henry did public penance for his role in the murder. For the remainder of his life, nineteen years, the murder of Thomas Becket haunted Henry, as his wife and children turned against him. He would watch as year after year, hundreds of thousands of his citizens made pilgrimages to Canterbury to venerate one of England's greatest saints. Pope Alexander III canonized Thomas Becket in 1174.

New Monastic Orders

The reforms of the eleventh century caused a blossoming of vocations in the Church. The twelfth century witnessed a revival in monastic life and the establishment of several new monastic orders. Among the most outstanding monks of the twelfth century were St. Bruno, St. Bernard, St. Robert, and St. Norbert.

St. Bruno

St. Bruno founded the **Carthusian Order**. Bruno was born in Cologne around 1030. Little is known of his youth, but he was probably taught at the cathedral school at Reims. Upon finishing his education, he became a teacher at the school, where one of his pupils was the future Pope Urban II. In 1055, he returned to Cologne, where he became a priest. The following year, he went back to Reims, where the bishop put him in charge of all the diocesan schools.

For many years, Bruno had secretly desired to lead a quiet life in some remote location, away from the scandals that affected the city. So he went to Molesme, where he lived under the direction of St. Robert, the future founder of the Cistercian Order. In June 1084, with six companions, he settled in a wild and desolate valley called La Chartreuse (*Carthusium* in Latin), located a few miles from Grenoble, France. There, the small band built a monastery. They divided their time between prayer, manual labor, and the reading and copying of manuscripts. In the opening years of the thirteenth century, the Carthusians added an affiliated order for women. St. Bruno died on October 6, 1101. At the time of the French Revolution in the late 1700s, which suppressed the Carthusians, the order had 170 monasteries and thirty convents.

St. Robert of Molesme

Another great monastic revival began at Citeaux. The founder of the new monastic order there, the **Cistercians**, was St. Robert of Molesme. (The name "Cistercian" derives from the French *Cistercien*, which comes from *Cistercium*, the Latin name of Citeaux.) Robert was born in France about 1029. He entered a Benedictine monastery at the age of 15. He eventually became abbot, and he set out to reform his community. When the monks refused to reform, he withdrew to Molesme. In 1075, Robert and about twenty other monks established **Molesme Abbey** in Burgundy. Over time, Robert's reputation for

---

Carthusian Order
Founded in a remote French valley by St. Bruno in 1084, devoted to prayer and manual labor.

Cistercians
Order founded by St. Robert of Molesme and vitalized by St. Bernard; austere in its monastic rigor, the order grew quickly across Europe.

Chapter 12: New Fountains of Holiness Cleanse the Church

sanctity attracted more and more followers, including St. Bruno. People sent their children to the abbey to be educated. Other non-monastic activities began to control the monks' daily life.

Over time, the monks became lax in their lifestyle. Rich people donated to the monastery. As the order became wealthier, the abbey began attracting the wrong kind of men. They challenged Robert's enforcement of St. Benedict's Rule. In 1098, Robert and a group of his more dedicated monks left Molesme, planning never to return. They founded **Citeaux Abbey** in a deep forest.

The following year, the monks of Molesme asked Robert to return and promised to follow the Rule of St. Benedict. He agreed, and the monks kept their promise.

Neither St. Robert nor his two successors intended to found a new order. However, the arrival of an extraordinary novice signaled a remarkable transformation in the monastic movement. That novice was named Bernard.

St. Bernard of Clairvaux

Although St. Robert founded the Cistercians, it was St. Bernard of Clairvaux who transformed them into one of the greatest orders the Church has ever known. He would lead the coming of the "White Monks."

Bernard was born in 1090, the son of French nobles. From an early age, he proved to be an excellent student, who had an intense love for the Blessed Mother. In 1112, three years after the death of his mother, who had greatly influenced him, Bernard entered the monastery at Citeaux. Amazingly, he possessed such a strong character and engaging personality that he persuaded thirty of his friends and family to enter Citeaux with him!

The Citeaux Abbey grew quickly. Three years later, Bernard and twelve other monks were sent to establish a new monastery, which Bernard named *Claire Vallee*, or Clairvaux, on June 25, 1115. As the abbot of Clairvaux Abbey, Bernard strictly enforced the Rule of St. Benedict. Despite its austerity, Clairvaux attracted many monks and grew rapidly. Much of its growth was due to St. Bernard's reputation for holiness. Before long, the monks outgrew Clairvaux and had to found new abbeys. By this point, Bernard, who was not yet 30 years old, had become a prominent figure in the Church.

In 1128, Bernard was one of the leading participants at the Council of Troyes, which dealt with certain regulatory matters of the Church in France. By 1130, he was counseling the pope and the emperor. Although Bernard wanted to remain a simple monk, for the remainder of his life, he would act as advisor, counselor, theologian, and diplomat for kings, emperors, and popes.

Meanwhile, Bernard sent bands of Cistercians into nearly every country in Europe. In 1145, one of Bernard's monks became Pope

Molesme Abbey
Established in 1075 by St. Robert. The monks gradually became lax, prompting Robert to leave and found Citeaux Abbey, but later they asked him back and faithfully followed their rule.

Citeaux Abbey
Gave the Cistercian Order its name. After St. Bernard entered at Citeaux, it became the seedbed of a rapidly blossoming order.

St. Robert of Molesme

Witness to the Faith 195

St. Bernard of Clairvaux

Eugene III. Later that year, Pope Eugene commissioned Bernard to preach the Second Crusade. When this crusade failed to accomplish as much as had been hoped, Bernard felt personally responsible.

Bernard died on August 20, 1153. During his life, he had helped to found more than 160 monasteries across Europe. He had introduced a monastic ideal beyond what St. Benedict had imagined. Yet, despite its severity, thousands of men flocked to it, willing to accept its rigor.

In 1174, Alexander III canonized Bernard. In 1830, Pope Pius VIII named him a Doctor of the Church. He is often called the "Mellifluous Doctor" because of his eloquence.

St. Norbert

St. Norbert was born in 1082 in Xanten, Germany. As a young deacon, he served as chaplain to German Emperor Henry V. Norbert lived at the imperial court, where he behaved more like a young nobleman than a deacon. One day in 1115, as he was out riding, lightning narrowly missed striking him but caused his horse to throw him. The near-death experience caused Norbert to undergo a conversion experience. He renounced his place at court, gave away his possessions, and was ordained to the priesthood.

Clairvaux Abbey

Chapter 12: New Fountains of Holiness Cleanse the Church

Norbert attempted to reform the secular clergy of Germany and France, who were living much like he had been living at court before he had become a priest. However, he soon discovered that the task exceeded his abilities. Ultimately, he met with Pope Gelasius II, who gave him permission to become an itinerant preacher. He likely visited Citeaux and Clairvaux and learned about the Cistercians there.

In October 1119, Pope Calixtus II asked Norbert to start a religious order. The following year, Norbert founded the **Canons Regular of Premontre**, named for the forest valley in which it was established. St. Norbert's new religious community was composed of monks who did the work of parish priests, particularly in country districts, while living under a strict rule as monks. They combined the active life with the contemplative life, fulfilling the duties of both monks and parish priests. Pope Honorius II approved the new community in 1126. The new order spread rapidly, not only in France but also in other countries. Less than thirty years after its founding, the order had one hundred abbeys. A century later, the order had one thousand monasteries and five hundred convents. These monks are known as the **Norbertines**.

The Eleventh Century

The beginning of the tenth century had been a difficult time for the Church. Yet, by the end of the century, much had changed. As a new century began, Christendom was united in a singular purpose never seen before or since: the Crusades!

St. Norbert of Xanten

Oral Exercises

1. Name three saints who were abbots of Cluny.
2. What two major problems in the Church did the great reformer St. Peter Damian combat throughout his life?
3. What is the name of the pope who is responsible for establishing the Church's current norms on how popes are elected?
4. What did Pope Gregory VII believe was the greatest evil facing the Church?
5. Describe the actions of Emperor Henry at Canossa.
6. Why was Pope Gregory VII forced to flee Rome?
7. Henry II named Thomas Becket as the archbishop of Canterbury so that Henry could gain control over the Church in England. Did Henry's plan work? Why or why not?
8. Who founded the Order of the Carthusians?
9. Who founded the Cistercian Order?

Canons Regular of Premontre
Order founded by St. Norbert, composed of monks doing the work of parish priests while living under a monastic rule, combining active and contemplative life.

Norbertines
Another name for the Canons Regular of Premontre; also the religious order for women that St. Norbert founded.

Witness to the Faith

Chapter 13
The Reconquista, Part I (722-1109)

Introduction

On May 28, 722, the Spanish won the Battle of Covadonga. It was the first victory in the 770-year war known as the *Reconquista* (Spanish, meaning "Reconquest"). Over the next eight centuries, there would be truces and lulls, but never lasting peace. When the Muslims were finally driven from Spain in the late 1400s, Spain emerged as the strongest nation on Earth for almost a century and a half, and became the great defender of the Catholic Church.

The Kingdom of Asturias

In 722, Pelayo and his men knew almost nothing of the world outside their tiny **kingdom of Asturias**. Perhaps they were the last Catholics on Earth! Yet they remained faithful Catholics. Spanish tradition holds that before the Battle of Covadonga, they prayed for the intervention of the Blessed Mother. Pelayo ruled Asturias until 737, expanding his little kingdom during his reign.

In 739, Alfonso the Catholic, Pelayo's son-in-law, became king of Asturias. He led an ambitious raid almost 150 miles into Muslim territory. Knowing that he could not hold the land he captured, he returned to his kingdom, but he brought with him every man, woman, and child who wished to leave the Muslim-controlled area. So many

---

Reconquista
The 770-year war in which the Catholic Spanish gradually took back Spain from the Muslims.

Kingdom of Asturias
The tiny kingdom that Pelayo and his men held at the beginning of the Reconquista, and expanded during his reign.

Statue of El Cid in Burgos, Spain

722 A.D. – 1091 A.D.

722 A.D.
The Spanish win the Battle of Covadonga, marking the beginning of the Reconquista.

739 A.D.
Alfonso the Catholic introduces the practice of raids to rescue Christians, and creates the Desert of the Duero.

829 A.D.
Construction begins on the shrine of Santiago de Compostela.

878 A.D.
Alfonso the Great ambushes and defeats the Muslims at Polvoraria, who ask for a truce. The truce lasts three years.

924 A.D.
The kingdom of Asturias gives way to the kingdom of Leon, under Alfonso's son Fruela.

939 A.D.
At the Battle of Simancas, a massive Muslim army of light cavalry under the caliph of Cordoba is defeated by a force of heavy cavalry under Ramiro II of Leon.

981-1002 A.D.
Almanzor ravages Catholic Spain.

1055 A.D.
The Spanish resume the Reconquista under King Ferdinand I.

1085 A.D.
The Spanish take Toledo, which becomes a base for assaults on cities further south.

1086-1091 A.D.
The Almoravids take control of most of the southern half of Spain. But they do not conquer Toledo or, thanks to El Cid, the port city of Valencia.

people accompanied Alfonso that the land was actually depopulated. This created the so-called Desert of the Duero, a buffer zone between the Christians and Muslims. For the next five hundred years, raids to rescue Christians were an integral part of the Reconquista. Alfonso expanded Asturias by reconquering Galicia and Leon.

When Alfonso died in 757, his son, Pelayo's grandson, became king. Fruela I exemplified most rulers of Spain for the next thousand years. Despite fighting to reconquer his kingdom, he never forgot that Spain was a Catholic nation. As a result, Fruela helped restore and establish a number of monasteries, most notably in Oviedo, where he is buried.

By the late eighth century, communication between Catholic Spain and the pope became more accessible

Witness to the Faith   199

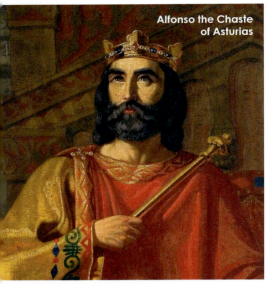

Alfonso the Chaste of Asturias

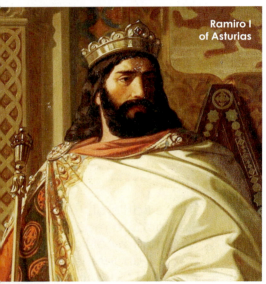

Ramiro I of Asturias

Alfonso the Great

than ever before. In 786, Pope Adrian I wrote to the bishops of Spain, condemning a heresy which had arisen there.

In 791, Alfonso the Chaste, so-called because he never married, became king of Asturias. It was a time when Spain needed a great king. In Alfonso, they had one. In 794, a mighty Muslim army captured Alfonso's capital, Oviedo. Like Pelayo before him, Alfonso fled into Spain's mountains to avoid capture. During the next year, the Muslims wreaked havoc on Alfonso's kingdom. By spring 796, the Muslims, believing that they had destroyed the kingdom of Asturias, withdrew their forces and headed south.

Many factors lead to victory in war. Having good soldiers willing to fight is one. Persistence, the determination not to surrender, is another. Alfonso was blessed with both. Following the Muslim withdrawal, he rallied his men. In 798, he led them on a daring raid to Muslim-controlled Lisbon on the Atlantic coast. He sent some of the plunder from the raid to Charlemagne, who he hoped would join him in the Reconquista. In fact, Charlemagne did launch attacks into Spain that resulted in the capture of Pamplona.

For a time, Alfonso had a truce with the Muslims. He returned to Oviedo, where he rebuilt the church that his father had established but that the Muslims had destroyed. He rededicated the church in 812.

During the reign of Alfonso, the bones of St. James the Apostle were found in a field in northwestern Spain. According to tradition, a hermit discovered the bones because angels were singing and stars were gathering over the meadow in which the Apostle's bones lay. Alfonso built a church there and, in 829, construction began on a monastery dedicated to St. James, "Saint Iago" (*Santiago* in Spanish). St. James would become the patron saint of the Reconquista. The monastery, **Santiago de Compostela** ("Saint James of the Field of the Stars") became, and remains, the greatest shrine in Spain and one of the greatest shrines in the world.

Toward the end of Alfonso's reign, the Muslims sent three massive armies against him, but he beat them back. Alfonso died in 843, having dedicated his life to God, the Church, and Spain. He had ruled for fifty-two years, one of the longest reigns in European history.

Alfonso's successor, Ramiro I, accomplished a feat virtually unknown in European history. He defeated the Vikings. In 844, the Vikings attacked Corunna, a port city in Asturias, and began to loot and pillage the town and the surrounding countryside. Ramiro attacked, defeated them, and burned their fleet. His victory was so devastating that the Vikings did not bother Christian Spain for the remainder of the century.

A Light in the Darkness

As darkness fell upon Christendom during the latter decades of the ninth century, the light shone brightly in the Spain of Alfonso III (also known as Alfonso the Great). Like his predecessors, Alfonso was dedicated to promoting the Church and driving the Muslims from Spain.

During his reign, Alfonso sent emissaries to Pope John VIII. They informed the pope that the Church in Spain continued to grow. They apprised him of the construction of a cathedral at Santiago de Compostela and asked for his blessing. Pope John then made the unusual request of a unit of cavalry, which Alfonso sent him. During Alfonso's reign, God blessed Spain with three saintly bishops who had a major impact on the growth of the Church: St. Frolian, the bishop of Leon; St. Attilanus, the bishop of Zamora; and St. Gennadius, the bishop of Astorga.

In 878, the Muslims gathered a large army from all of Muslim-occupied Spain. They hoped to defeat Alfonso in a decisive campaign and regain all their lost territory. The vast Muslim force rode north, but Alfonso ambushed them at **Polvoraria**, inflicting massive losses on them. As a result of the Catholic victory, the Muslims, for the first time in the long war, asked for a three-year truce. At the end of the truce, the Reconquista resumed.

Santiago de Compostela
The great shrine of St. James in northwestern Spain, built to house his bones.

Polvoraria
Site of Alfonso III's ambush of a large Muslim army riding north against him; he inflicted such great losses that the Muslims asked for a truce.

St. James the Apostle, Bartolomé Esteban Murillo

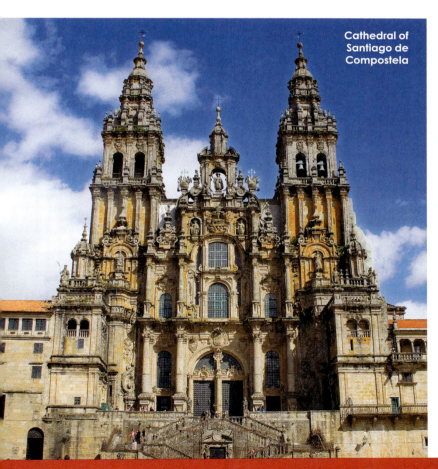

Cathedral of Santiago de Compostela

Witness to the Faith

Kingdom of Leon
Expanded Spanish Christian kingdom that replaced Asturias after the time of Alfonso III.

For the remainder of his reign, Alfonso continued to expand his kingdom. When he died in 910, after a forty-four-year reign, he divided his kingdom among his sons. His eldest son, Garcia, became king of Leon; Ordono became king of Galicia; and Fruela became king of Asturias. Although this action probably prevented a civil war between the sons, it may have hurt Spain's ability to wage war, since a single large kingdom is stronger than three small ones. Thankfully, when Garcia died without an heir, his kingdom passed to Ordono. When Ordono died, his kingdom passed to Fruela. Thus, the kingdom of Asturias gave way to the **Kingdom of Leon**.

The Kingdom of Leon

In 931, the wife of Alfonso IV, the king of Leon, died. He was so overwhelmed at the loss of his beloved wife that he abdicated the throne and entered a monastery. His brother, Ramiro II, became king of Leon.

As king, Ramiro faced the greatest challenge to confront Spain since the days of Pelayo. The Emirate of Cordoba, which occupied the southern two-thirds of the Iberian Peninsula, was one of the richest and most powerful nations in the world. In 939, the caliph of Cordoba gathered the largest Muslim army ever formed in Spain by declaring a "holy war" against Christian Spain. In the spring, the caliph led his army of 100,000 men north to conquer the Christian nation. Ramiro, at the head of his army of 30,000, rode out to give battle on hard, sunbaked Spanish plains near the town of Simancas.

Ramiro II, Rufino Casado

The **Battle of Simancas** favored the Muslims. They outnumbered the Christians more than 3 to 1. The battle was fought on an open plain where the Muslim cavalry, considered among the finest in the world, could maneuver easily. The Spanish could not launch a surprise attack, as they had done at Polvoraria. In almost three hundred years, the Muslims had never lost a battle under these conditions. But times change. Against the Muslim light cavalry, Ramiro covered his knights and their horses in heavy iron mail, thus turning them into a kind of tenth-century tank.

As Warren Carroll recounts in his book *The Building of Christendom* (pp. 411-412), the battle began on August 5, 939, and the superiority of Ramiro's heavy cavalry quickly became apparent as several charges devastated the Muslims. On the second day of the battle, Ramiro's men almost captured the caliph himself, who fled the battlefield and returned to Cordoba. The Battle of Simancas was one of the most decisive and critical of the Reconquista.

Battle of Simancas
A critical battle in which the heavy Spanish cavalry defeated a much larger army of Muslim light cavalry.

Throughout the remainder of his reign, Ramiro continued to expand the kingdom of Leon. An excellent general, he won several battles, which expanded his realm south into the Emirate of Cordoba. He also expanded his kingdom by marrying a princess of Navarre. When he died in 951, the kingdom of Leon had been greatly enlarged.

Ramiro's reign also saw the establishment of the famous monastery of Montserrat near Barcelona. Monastic reform occurred in Spain as it had in the rest of Christendom. In 951, two bishops from Spain traveled to Rome to ask Pope Agapitus for the "Cluny privilege," meaning they would be directly under papal authority. He happily granted their request.

In 981, one of the greatest generals in world history took the field against Catholic Spain. His name was **Almanzor**, which means "the Victorious." In 984, he reconquered all the land south of the Duero River. The following year, he sacked and burned Barcelona. He then marched west and destroyed Coimbra in present-day Portugal. In 988, Almanzor destroyed the city of Leon, the capital of Christian Spain. In each city, he made a special effort to destroy the churches and monasteries. Over the next years, Almanzor continued to recapture land and destroy churches and monasteries. Finally, on August 11, 997, he stood before the great cathedral shrine of Santiago de Compostela. He sacked the town and destroyed the cathedral. He took the shrine's great bells to Cordoba as spoils of war.

Bust of Almanzor

For the next five years, Almanzor continued to win victories as well as destroy towns and churches. Finally, in 1002, the 63-year-old Muslim general died. For more than twenty years, he had been the scourge of Catholic Spain. No one could defeat him in battle. With his death, Spain now had a chance to rebuild.

Despite his amazing victories, Almanzor possessed the weakness of many great generals. He could not win the peace. He failed to repopulate, with Muslims, the lands he captured. He tended to defeat his enemies, loot and destroy, and move on. Thus, his victories were never consolidated. Although Almanzor had severely damaged Catholic Spain, the damage was not long lasting. Santiago de Compostela would be rebuilt.

Almanzor
The most effective Muslim general of the Reconquista.

The Kingdom of Leon and Castile

The first fifty years of the new millennium were not a good time for Spanish Catholics. In Spain, the caliphate of Cordoba ended in 1031. However, the Spanish failed to take advantage of the confusion among the Muslims as they fought one another for control. The Christians were too busy fighting among themselves to drive out the real enemy. King Ferdinand I did become ruler of a united Leon and Castile, but it was not until 1055 that he continued the Reconquista.

Witness to the Faith   203

During the last decade of his life, Ferdinand launched several campaigns to recapture large parts of Spain. He raided south to Seville and east to Valencia, and he captured Coimbra in Portugal. On Christmas Day in 1065, he was carried in a litter to Mass at St. Isidore's Cathedral. He laid his crown upon the altar, offering his kingdom to God, from whom he had received it. He died the next day. Ferdinand divided his kingdom among his three sons, but by 1072, it had been reunited under King Alfonso VI.

From the start of his reign, Alfonso proved to be a great supporter of the reforms of Cluny. He personally gave generously to Cluny and encouraged the Spanish nobility to follow his example. He also placed three of the largest Spanish monasteries directly under Cluny's authority. On the other hand, Alfonso fell into the sin that so many other kings of this time committed: simony. He apparently sold the position of abbot for the monastery at Sahagun to Robert of Cluny, an unworthy man. Pope St. Gregory VII would not stand for such an action. He excommunicated Robert of Cluny. At the council of Burgos in 1080, the Spanish bishops gave their full support to the pope. In 1083, a holy Cluniac monk named Bernard, appointed by Pope Gregory, became abbot of Sahagun. The monastery of Sahagun was placed under the direct guidance and protection of the pope.

Early in Alfonso's reign, he continued to expand his kingdom and win back the lands held by the Muslims. In 1085, he captured the city of Toledo and the area that would eventually become Madrid. The capture of Toledo ranks as one of the most important strategic events in the entire Reconquista. From Toledo, the Spanish could launch assaults on the southern cities of Seville, Cordoba, and Grenada.

The Almoravid Invasion

The fall of Toledo was perhaps the greatest catastrophe to befall the Muslim kingdom in Spain since the war began more than 360 years earlier. The Spanish Muslims issued a call for help to the Almoravid Muslims of North Africa—

Ruins of the Monastery of Sahagun

a fierce, determined group of fighters. In July 1086, the **Almoravids** crossed the Strait of Gibraltar into Spain.

Wasting no time, the Almoravid army marched north and, in October, defeated Alfonso at the Battle of Sagrajas. Alfonso, seriously wounded in the battle, retreated to Toledo. In April 1087, he sent word throughout Spain and into France, calling for what amounted to a crusade. Raymond of Toulouse, who would later lead the First Crusade, came to Spain to fight the Muslims.

In December 1086, just two months after the defeat at Sagrajas, Bernard of Sahagun was named primate of Spain. The ceremony for his installation as primate was held in the new cathedral of Toledo, previously a Muslim mosque. The symbolism could not have been more important. The Catholics of Spain might lose battles, but they would continue to fight the war. They would persist; and, in persistence, they would find victory.

In June 1090, the Almoravids launched an assault on Toledo. However, located on high cliffs, the city was virtually impregnable. Alfonso and his army, along with help from King Sancho Ramirez of Aragon, threw back the invaders.

By September 1091, the Almoravid invaders controlled most of the southern half of Spain. Both sides realized that the most strategic city was the port of Valencia, located about halfway down Spain's eastern coast. Rodrigo Diaz de Vivar, known as **El Cid**, Spain's greatest national hero, defended Valencia.

Over the next years, the war went badly for the Christians. Alfonso was defeated at the Battle of Jaen. King Sancho Ramirez died in battle. Lisbon fell to the Muslims, who killed many of its defenders. Only El Cid stood victorious. In December 1094, an Almoravid army of 150,000 men attacked Valencia.

Vastly outnumbered, El Cid did the one thing the Muslims did not expect. He attacked! The **Battle of Cuarte** was one of the most decisive battles in the history of the Reconquista. El Cid defeated the superior Almoravid army. He ruled Valencia until his death in 1099, when his wife began to rule the city. Valencia eventually fell to the Muslims in 1102, but only after Alfonso had burned the city.

By 1102, the Muslims faced a greater threat than Alfonso VI. A united Christendom had launched the greatest effort in its history. Its goal was to retake the Holy Land from the Muslims.

Almoravids
A force of North African Muslims who invaded Spain in the late eleventh century.

El Cid
Nickname of Rodrigo Diaz de Vivar, Spain's greatest national hero; led the defense of Valencia, an important port city, and ruled it until his death.

Battle of Cuarte
Battle in which El Cid defeated the Muslims' attempt to take Valencia.

Oral Exercises

1. What is the name of the 770-year war to recapture Spain from the Muslims?
2. Who is the patron saint of the effort to reconquer Spain?
3. What is the name of Spain's greatest shrine?
4. Who were the North African Muslims who invaded Spain in the eleventh century?
5. Who is Spain's greatest national hero?

Witness to the Faith   205

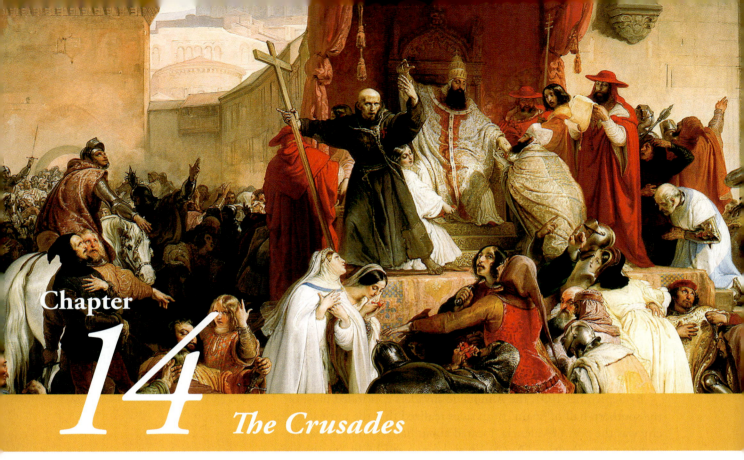

Chapter 14
The Crusades

Introduction

Since Mohammed had founded Islam, Muslims had converted by the sword. From Arabia, Islam had swept across North Africa, crossed into Spain, and attempted to conquer Europe, only to be stopped by Charles Martel at the Battle of Tours. The Muslims had also attacked the Byzantine Empire, which had lost ground to them over the centuries. The intent of the Muslims was clear: conquer Europe and convert it to Islam. Thus, Islam presented an existential threat to Christendom.

With the exception of a few places, such as Spain and Sicily, prior to the late eleventh century, Christendom had been fighting a mostly defensive action against Muslim aggression. Numerous popes had called for more offensive measures, but because of various internal struggles between popes and emperors and between emperors and barons, no truly united effort had materialized. Now, finally, the heroic pontificate of Pope Gregory VII had begun to unify Christendom. It would take a few more years, but under Pope Urban II, Christendom would finally launch the long-awaited offensive: the Crusades.

What Were the Crusades?

The **Crusades** were expeditions undertaken by Western Europe in the eleventh, twelfth, and thirteenth centuries to deliver the Holy Land,

The Crusades
Military expeditions by Western Europe in the eleventh, twelfth, and thirteenth centuries to deliver the Holy Land, especially Jerusalem, from the Muslims.

206 *Chapter 14: The Crusades*

Pope Urban II Calls the First Crusade, Francesco Hayez

1095 A.D. – 1291 A.D.

1095 A.D.
Pope Urban II calls for a crusade. Knights throughout Christendom respond and "take up the Cross."

1099 A.D.
The crusading army takes Jerusalem in July and establishes the "Latin Kingdom of Jerusalem."

1147-1148 A.D.
The Second Crusade sets out in response to renewed Muslim aggression, but it is almost a complete failure.

1187 A.D.
Saladin takes back practically everything the crusaders conquered in their first expedition, including Jerusalem.

1190-1192 A.D.
The Third Crusade is led by Richard the Lionheart, who signs a treaty with Saladin: the Muslims keep Jerusalem, but Christians may visit the Holy Land.

1202-1204 A.D.
The knights of the Fourth Crusade sack the nearby town of Zara, then invade Constantinople.

1217-1221 A.D.
The Fifth Crusade attempts to conquer Egypt before marching on Jerusalem, and proves a disaster.

1228-1229 A.D.
Emperor Frederick II sets out on the Sixth Crusade and makes a deal with the Muslims.

1248-1270 A.D.
King St. Louis IX leads the two last crusades.

1291 A.D.
The Muslims retake Tripoli and Acre.

---

especially Jerusalem, from the Muslims. During these expeditions, several nations of Europe banded together into one vast army. Historians have called the Crusades "the external wars of Christendom."

Reasons for the Crusades

Europe fought the Crusades for two fundamental reasons that everyone involved understood. The first reason was religious. For the Catholic people of Europe, it was upsetting that the Holy Land—the very ground where the Son of God had walked, lived, taught, died, and rose from the dead—was under the control of people who rejected that Jesus Christ was the Son of God and who attacked Christianity. Also, Europeans, then as now, made pilgrimages to the Holy Land to visit the holy sites and shrines where Our Lord had lived and died. Over time, the Muslims had made it increasingly

Witness to the Faith   207

difficult for pilgrims to visit these holy sites. By the latter decades of the eleventh century, it had become very dangerous to visit the Holy Land.

The second reason for the Crusades was military. It allowed Europe to take the fight to the enemy and open what amounted to a "second front" in the ongoing battle for survival. By the latter part of the eleventh century, the Muslims had begun another assault on the Byzantine Empire, Christendom's eastern front. The Christian nations of the West had to act if they were to save themselves. In fact, by the closing decade of the eleventh century, two critical events compelled Catholic Europe to launch the Crusades. (These events are discussed in the next section.)

Finally, by the end of the eleventh century, many people in the Holy Land, perhaps even the majority of the population, were still Christian. The Christians had at least as much right, if not more, to the land than the Muslims did, but they were being oppressed by the Muslims. Although this was not a major reason for the Crusades, it is certainly a justification for them.

Pope Urban II

The first event that compelled launching the Crusades was the destruction of the Church of the Holy Sepulcher in Jerusalem. Because it contains the tomb of Our Lord, Christians considered it one of the most holy sites in the world. Since at least the fourth century, it had been a major pilgrimage site. In 1009, the Muslim leader Al-Hakim ordered the complete destruction of this church. The attack on the Church of the Holy Sepulcher was part of a general campaign against places of Christian worship in Egypt and the Holy Land. The Muslims razed the Church of the Holy Sepulcher to the ground, then destroyed its foundations. Catholic Europe was deeply shocked and saddened. Al-Hakim had thrown a stone into the pond, setting off a chain reaction of waves that would ripple for centuries.

The second catastrophe to strike Christendom in the eleventh century was the capture of Jerusalem by the Turks. Arabian Muslims had captured Jerusalem in 637. However, they considered it to be a holy city. So, for the most part, they treated it with reverence and did not destroy its holy places (the incident in 1009 by Al-Hakim being one notable exception). Moreover, they tended to be somewhat reasonable in allowing Christian pilgrims to visit Jerusalem and the Holy Land. The Arabs generally permitted Christians to worship at shrines without much interference. This all changed in 1073 when the Turks, who had become Muslims, captured Jerusalem. Unlike the Arabs, they persecuted Christian pilgrims to the extent that visiting the Holy Land became extremely dangerous.

During his pontificate, Pope Gregory VII had desperately wanted to launch a crusade to free the Holy Land from the Turks, but his constant conflict with Emperor Henry had made it impossible. However, in 1088, the College of Cardinals elected a former monk of Cluny as pope. Young

Pope Urban II

Church of the Holy Sepulcher
A church in Jerusalem containing the tomb of Our Lord.

208 Chapter 14: The Crusades

(only 46), vigorous, and determined, Pope Urban II (1088-1099) would accomplish what none of his predecessors had been able to do: he would launch the First Crusade!

Pope Urban realized that only a united Christendom, which meant the Eastern Empire as well, could stand against the Muslim threat. Therefore, on assuming the papacy, Urban contacted Byzantine Emperor Alexius Comnenus with four remarkable messages. First, he removed the excommunication against the emperor. Second, he promised Alexius that the Normans would not attack him. Third, he promised to do everything he could to send military support for the Byzantine war against the Muslims. Finally, he asked if there was a way to end the Great Schism and reconcile the Eastern Church with the Western Church.

In 1095, Urban convoked a council at Clermont to discuss reform of the French clergy. On the final day of the council, Pope Urban determined that the moment had come to launch the Crusades. Before a vast crowd, he described the sufferings of the pilgrims to the Holy Land. He described Jerusalem, which Christ "consecrated by suffering, redeemed by His death, [and] has glorified by burial." He said that Jerusalem, which is "now held captive by His enemies … desires to be liberated." He exhorted those present to make a vow to go on a "holy pilgrimage" to liberate Jerusalem and the Holy Land. They should wear the Sign of the Cross on their forehead or breast while on the pilgrimage. When they returned, they should wear the Sign of the Cross on their back between their shoulders (W. Carroll, *The Building of Christendom*, p. 521).

Council of Clermont

The pope's eloquence filled the hearts of his listeners. The cry went up from the lips of all those present, "God wills it! God wills it!" The recruits adopted a cross of red cloth as their insignia. Within an hour, every strip of red cloth in Clermont had been sewn into a cross (ibid., p. 530). (This accounts for the name "crusade": it is derived from the French word *croisade*, meaning "marked with the cross.")

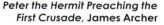

> **Peter the Hermit**
> A preacher who promoted the First Crusade after his own experience of persecution from the Turks while traveling in the Holy Land.

For the next year, Pope Urban II traveled throughout France preaching the crusade. Priests and monks followed his example. They preached in France, the Low Countries (the territory that today includes Belgium, the Netherlands, and Luxembourg), and Italy. One especially effective preacher was Peter the Hermit, who had traveled to the Holy Land and had personally suffered persecution from the Turks. Peter preached in France and Germany, arousing the people to join the Crusades.

The Crusades united Christendom as never before. Europeans saw the movement as an opportunity to devote themselves and their possessions to the cause of Christ.

Peter the Hermit Preaching the First Crusade, James Archer

Witness to the Faith

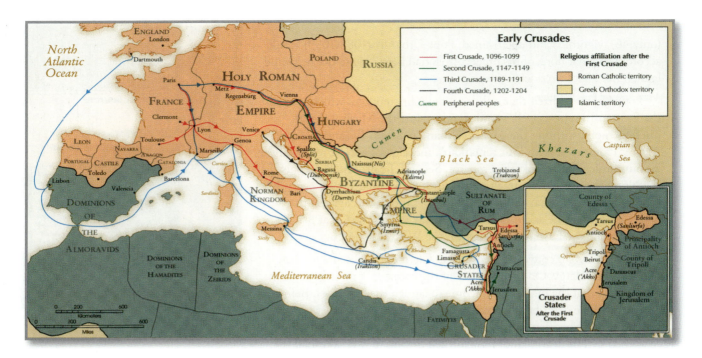

Thousands of men sold their possessions to buy armor and weapons to participate in the struggle that would free the Holy Land. To them, Bethlehem, Nazareth, and Jerusalem meant the Person of Jesus Christ. These were the places where Our Lord had walked and lived. They had more right to these sacred places than those who did not believe He was the Son of God. Moreover, they keenly felt that the Holy Land had been taken from the Christians by brute force. As many as 100,000 men answered the call to join the First Crusade.

The First Crusade

Under normal circumstances, the Holy Roman Emperor would lead such a monumental military venture. However, in 1095, the emperor was Henry IV, the very last man Pope Urban would trust with this most important mission. In place of the emperor, some other king would be appropriate. Yet, for various reasons, none of the other European kings were suitable, many also having been excommunicated. In fact, most of the kings of Europe showed little interest in the crusade. Thus, it fell to the nobility to lead the First Crusade.

Most of the men who fought in the First Crusade were French. The declaration that Clovis had made so many years ago was sounding through the ages: "If only I had been there with my Franks!" This time, the Franks would be there. The leaders of the First Crusade were French nobles Godfrey of Bouillon and Raymond of Toulouse. Bohemond (Robert Guiscard's son) and Tancred (Bohemond's nephew) led a Norman army.

Between August and October 1096, four armies left for the Holy Land. By April 1097, all four had reached Constantinople, where their leaders met with Emperor Alexius, promising him their support. The

Godfrey of Bouillon

210 *Chapter 14: The Crusades*

following month, the crusaders besieged Nicaea, which they captured in June. At this point, they had the element of surprise. It is doubtful the Muslims imagined that such a massive force would travel so far to fight them.

On July 1, the Muslim Turks attacked the crusaders with a large force but were defeated at the Battle of Dorylaeum. The Turks retreated, burning the fields as they fled. The crusaders pushed onwards.

By late October, the crusaders finally arrived at the gates of Antioch in Syria. In early June 1098, after an eight-month siege, they took Antioch despite various attempts by the Turks to relieve the city. However, only a few days later, a large Turkish army, which had been sent to relieve Antioch, arrived. The besiegers had become the besieged!

At the end of June, Bohemond, every bit the son of the great general who was his father, led the crusaders out of Antioch and attacked. Outnumbered perhaps 5 to 1, the crusaders inflicted a devastating defeat upon the Muslims. Antioch was now firmly under the crusaders' control. The route to Jerusalem lay open before them.

By now, though, the crusading army was tired. Marching to Jerusalem through the summer heat would have proven disastrous. The leaders wisely decided to wait until November to launch their assault on the Holy City. In November, they left for Jerusalem, seizing various Muslim strongholds along the way.

On June 6, 1099, the leading element of the army made camp at Emmaus. For the first time, the crusaders could actually see Jerusalem. The Turks, who held Jerusalem, had expelled all Christians, lest they help the crusaders. The Turks had a strong force in the city, as well as plenty of food and water to withstand a siege. The crusaders did not even have siege engines. They began to build them.

Meanwhile, in early July, word came that a large army from Egypt was on its way to relieve Jerusalem. If the crusaders did not capture the city, they would be caught between the city's garrison and the powerful Egyptian army. Time was running out. They needed to conquer Jerusalem—soon.

On July 14, the siege engines were finished and pushed against the city walls. As dawn broke the following morning, the crusaders launched their desperate attack. Godfrey and Raymond led the attack. They managed to fight their way over the walls and into the city. They opened the gates, and the crusading army poured in. On Friday, July 15, 1099, the crusaders captured Jerusalem.

Siege of Antioch, Jean Colombe

Latin Kingdom of Jerusalem
The kingdom set up in the Holy Land after the capture of Jerusalem in the First Crusade, led by Godfrey of Bouillon, the "Defender of the Holy Sepulcher."

Note on the Fact of the Crusaders Returning Home

This very fact disproves the conclusion of so many secular historians that the Crusades were fought for treasure and land.

Witness to the Faith

King Louis VII of France

Emperor Conrad III

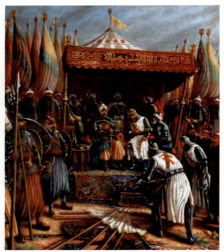

Surrender to Saladin after the Battle of Hattin

Saladin
The sultan of Egypt, an excellent general who took back the lands that the crusaders had conquered in the First Crusade, and negotiated with King Richard in the Third.

The crusaders then decided to found the Latin Kingdom of Jerusalem. They offered the crown to Godfrey of Bouillon, one of the most popular and unselfish leaders of the crusade. He accepted the title "Defender of the Holy Sepulcher," but he refused to wear a crown of gold in the city where Christ had worn a crown of thorns. Of all of the crusades, the First was the most successful.

Meanwhile, on July 29, only two weeks after the liberation of Jerusalem, and too soon for him to have received the news, Pope Urban II died. The majority of the crusaders, having fulfilled their vow, returned home. In July 1100, Godfrey suddenly died. Godfrey's brother Baldwin was crowned Defender of the Holy Sepulcher.

The Second Crusade

The First Crusade had attained all its goals. It had captured large parts of the Holy Land. Most importantly, the crusaders had liberated Jerusalem. However, as difficult as it had been to capture the Holy Land from the Muslims, it was even more difficult to hold it.

In November 1144, the Muslims besieged Edessa. They captured the city on Christmas Eve and massacred its French defenders. The fall of Edessa threatened the entire crusader kingdom in the Holy Land, from Antioch to Jerusalem. When he learned of the threat to Edessa, Pope Eugenius III called for a Second Crusade.

St. Bernard of Clairvaux preached this crusade throughout France, Germany, and Switzerland. The Second Crusade had even more support than the First Crusade. King Louis VII of France and the German Emperor Conrad III led the crusade. While fewer soldiers fought in the Second Crusade, they were better disciplined and were recruited almost entirely from the military. Despite all these advantages, the enterprise was almost a complete failure.

On the way to Jerusalem, the Turks defeated both armies in Asia Minor. After arriving in Jerusalem with what remained of their armies, Louis and Conrad besieged Damascus in 1148. Damascus was the key to the Holy Land. If the crusaders could capture it, they could cut the Muslim power base in two. However, the Muslims quickly defeated the crusaders, forcing them to retreat to Jerusalem.

The only success of the Second Crusade occurred when some Flemish, Norman, English, and Scottish crusaders who were sailing to the Holy Land stopped and helped the Portuguese capture Lisbon in 1147.

The Third Crusade

In 1174, Saladin became the Sultan (Muslim ruler) of Syria and Egypt. One of the finest generals of the age, he immediately began a campaign to retake Jerusalem from the crusaders. In 1187, at the Battle of Hattin, Saladin's Muslim army devastatingly defeated the crusader army. Most of the crusaders were either killed or captured.

By mid-September, Saladin had taken almost all the towns that the crusaders had captured during the First Crusade. On October 2, 1187, Jerusalem surrendered.

Meanwhile, on October 20, before news of the fall of Jerusalem could have reached him, Pope Urban III (1185-1187) died suddenly. His successor, Gregory VIII, reigned less than two months. His only act was to call for a Third Crusade. The first to answer the call was King Richard I of England (1189-1199). A renowned battlefield commander, he would be known to history as Richard the Lionheart. Although he would be king for eleven years, he would spend less than one year as king in England.

Following the sudden death of Urban III, the College of Cardinals elected Clement III (1187-1191), who continued to urge Europeans to unite and join the crusade. Ultimately, Emperor Frederick Barbarossa, King Philip II of France, and King Richard the Lionheart took up the Cross.

As a young man, Frederick Barbarossa had marched with Emperor Conrad on the Second Crusade. He had greatly damaged the Church as emperor, but apparently viewed the crusade as a way to make amends. Although he was now in his 60s, Frederick was still a vigorous and robust man. More importantly, he was a good general and leader. On June 10, 1190, as he was crossing a river, his horse slipped. Frederick was thrown into the river and drowned. His army was never able to recover from his death—nor was the Third Crusade.

Meanwhile, back in Europe, Henry II of England had died, making Richard the king. Although Richard and Philip II of France did not trust each other, they decided to leave together for the Holy Land. The French and the English set out for the Holy Land by way of the sea. From then on, the sea route was the one followed in all the crusades. On his way, Richard conquered the island of Cyprus. In early June, Richard arrived in Acre, which the crusaders had been besieging for almost two years. Richard took Acre in less than two months.

On August 20, Richard began marching toward Jerusalem, but stopped to rebuild the castles he captured along the way. Thus, it was not until January 1192 that he reached the outskirts of the city. At this point, it seems that Jerusalem would have fallen to an attack. Although the city was well defended, Saladin's

King Richard the Lionheart

Witness to the Faith

troops had low morale, while Richard's men had won a string of victories. Throughout history, great military commanders have often found ways to exploit their enemies' weaknesses. "Fortune favors the bold." But, for some reason, Richard chose to retreat. He never took Jerusalem.

Instead, Richard made an agreement with Saladin. On September 2, 1192, the two leaders signed a treaty by which Jerusalem would remain under Muslim control, but unarmed Christian pilgrims would be allowed to visit the city. Richard's failure to take Jerusalem would lead to the Fourth Crusade six years later.

Saladin died the following March. His death caused his kingdom to break apart. Had Richard remained in the Holy Land for a few more months, he could have conquered the city, but by then he had returned to Europe. Fortune favors the bold—and those who persevere.

The Fourth Crusade

Pope Innocent III (1198-1216) had always wished to launch a crusade to free the Holy Land. During the first year of his pontificate, he sent out preachers and issued a call for a new crusade to capture Jerusalem. The natural leader for this Fourth Crusade would have been Richard the Lionheart, but the 42-year-old king had been killed in March 1199 while besieging a castle. His brother John, who had succeeded Richard, had no interest in leading a crusade; nor did any of the other kings of Europe. Nevertheless, the First Crusade, the most successful thus far, had not been led by kings, but by knights. It seemed that knights would also lead the Fourth Crusade.

Pope Innocent III

At the outset, it appeared that the Fourth Crusade was better organized than the others. All the soldiers gathered in Venice, where the Venetians agreed to transport them by ship to the Holy Land. However, the leader of Venice, the *doge*, demanded a huge sum of money to transport the crusaders.

By March 1202, it became clear that the crusaders could not pay this outrageous sum. So the doge offered a solution. If the crusaders would conquer a city named Zara for him, he would reduce the price of their transport. The doge truthfully said that until recently Zara had been under Venice's rule. Yet Zara was a Catholic city, and had done nothing to provoke the assault. That the crusaders would even consider such a heinous and immoral act is disgusting. To actually attack Zara violated everything the Crusades stood for.

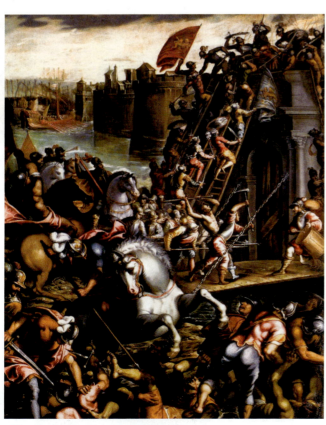

The Crusaders Conquering the City of Zara in 1202, Andrea Vicentino

214 *Chapter 14: The Crusades*

Conquest of Constantinople by the Crusaders in 1204, David Aubert

When Pope Innocent learned of the impending attack, he issued a letter threatening anyone who attacked Zara with excommunication. The doge ignored the letter. He told the crusaders that they had promised to attack Zara, and he demanded that they fulfill their promise. With only two exceptions, the crusaders' leaders attacked the city on November 24. They even plundered the churches.

Following the sack of Zara, winter storms made sailing to the Holy Land impossible until the spring of 1203. Meanwhile, the doge next suggested that the crusaders conquer Constantinople. He argued that this would end the Greek Schism and bring the Byzantine Empire into the Church. Most of the crusaders thought this was a great idea. They sailed for Constantinople in April 1203, and arrived in late June.

Of course, the Byzantines, not wanting to be conquered, resisted the so-called "crusaders" (who now were no longer worthy of that name). On April 12, 1204, Constantinople fell to the Western attackers. They then subjected the city to a hideous carnage that lasted for three

Count Baldwin of Flanders

Witness to the Faith 215

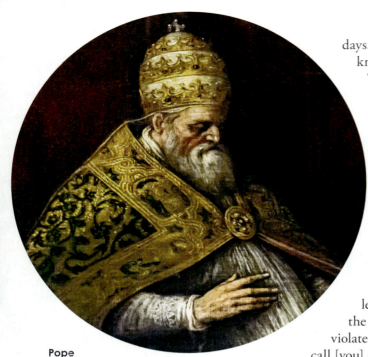

Pope Honorius III

days. In place of the Byzantine Empire, the Western knights erected a Latin Empire of Constantinople. This empire crumbled in 1261 without achieving anything for the cause of Christianity. The sack of Constantinople has had repercussions down to the present day. Likely, whatever hope remained of reconciliation between the Greek Orthodox Church and the Catholic Church was set aflame in those three terrible days in April 1204.

Pope Innocent III originally thought that the crusaders had achieved some good. However, when he learned the truth, he wrote a letter to Count Baldwin of Flanders, the leader of the men who sacked Constantinople. In the letter, Pope Innocent denounced him in some of the harshest language a pope has ever used: "You have violated the purity of your vows…. No wonder the Greeks call [you] dogs."

The Fifth Crusade

The Fourth Crusade had been a stain on the entire ideal of the Crusades. But men still believed in the crusading spirit. They still longed to free the Holy Land and Jerusalem from the Muslims. Despite the failure of the Fourth Crusade, Pope Innocent III was still determined to free the Holy Land. In November 1215, he summoned the Fourth Lateran Council, where preparations for launching a Fifth Crusade were discussed. Pope Innocent died suddenly in 1216, but his successor, Honorius III (1216-1227), continued Innocent's policies. Under his reign, a Fifth Crusade was launched.

In May 1217, a fleet carrying German and Frisian soldiers sailed to the Holy Land. In July, crusaders from central Europe, led by King Andrew II of Hungary and Leopold VI, duke of Austria, also sailed for the Holy Land. Both groups stopped to help fight the Muslims in other countries before they arrived in Acre in May 1218. They decided that before they attacked Jerusalem, they would attempt to conquer Egypt.

In July 1218, the crusaders began besieging Damietta, 2 miles from Acre. The struggle for Damietta lasted for more than a year. Finally, in November 1219, the crusaders simply wore down the Muslims and occupied the city, but then spent the next months arguing about who should control Damietta.

Finally, in July 1221, the crusaders began marching south toward Cairo. They could not have chosen a worse time for the advance. The summer heat drained them, and the Nile flooded. The Muslims, who understood the Nile floods, used them against the crusaders. In one battle, the Muslims attacked the Christians and flooded a dry canal,

Holy Roman Emperor Frederick II

216 Chapter 14: The Crusades

blocking their retreat. Running low on supplies, the knights had to turn back. As the crusaders retreated, the Muslims attacked, inflicting terrible losses on them. Those who were not killed were forced to surrender.

Under the terms of the surrender, the crusaders gave up Damietta. Everything that they had accomplished in the previous years was lost in a matter of days. The Muslims agreed to an eight-year peace treaty and released their prisoners, but Jerusalem remained in their hands. Another crusade had failed.

The Sixth Crusade

On March 18, 1227, Pope Honorius III died. The following day, Gregory IX (1227-1241) was elected pope. He immediately wrote a letter to Emperor Frederick II, reminding him of his vow to take up the Cross that he had made more than eleven years earlier. Finally, threatened with the loss of his empire, Frederick heeded the pope's call and launched the Sixth Crusade.

On June 28, 1228, Frederick, at the head of a sizable force, sailed from southern Italy for the Holy Land. He landed in Acre in September. However, because he had not sailed during the required period, the pope had excommunicated him, and many knights would not march with his army. Frederick immediately began negotiating with the Muslims controlling Jerusalem.

On February 18, 1229, Frederick signed a ten-year peace treaty with the Muslims. The Christians would receive control of Jerusalem for the next ten years. In exchange, Frederick promised not to make war on the Muslims during those ten years.

The Final Two Crusades: The Crusades of King St. Louis of France

Frederick's treaty ended in 1239. For the next few years, Christians managed to maintain control of Jerusalem. However, in August 1244, Muslim mercenaries captured Jerusalem, slaughtering the almost 6,000 Christians living there. In October, a Muslim army completely defeated what remained of the Christian forces at the Battle of Gaza. In November, the bishop of Beirut sailed to Europe to beg Christendom to launch a new crusade. Although many good men had led crusades in the past, for the first time a crusade would be led by a saint: King St. Louis IX of France.

St. Louis IX of France

Witness to the Faith **217**

At the end of 1244, Pope Innocent IV (1243-1254) called for a crusade, but only France answered the call. King St. Louis IX and two of his brothers, also rulers of domains in France, would lead the Seventh Crusade. For the next three years, Louis made preparations. Although Louis IX was unquestionably the finest monarch ever to rule France, he was not a particularly good general. His lack of military skill would be the undoing of this crusade.

In 1248, the well-funded and well-organized crusader army set sail from France. They sailed to Cyprus, where they spent the winter. Louis planned to attack Egypt, which he would use as a base to launch an assault on Jerusalem. In 1249, the crusaders landed in Egypt and marched on Cairo. In February 1250, they fought the Battle of Al Mansurah, where the Muslims inflicted heavy losses upon them. For two months, King Louis stubbornly refused to retreat, despite the loss of his supply lines. Finally, in April he was forced to make a disastrous retreat, during which he was taken prisoner at the Battle of Fariskur. Over the next month, he negotiated his release but had to pay the Muslims an enormous ransom.

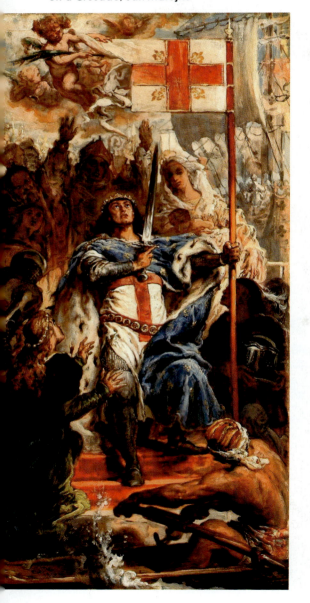

St. Louis, King of France, Goes on a Crusade, Jan Matejko

In May, Louis arrived back in Acre. Despite his massive losses, he was not discouraged. He announced that he would remain in the Holy Land for a while but released his men from their vow to remain on crusade with him. Most returned home, including his one living brother. Louis remained in the Holy Land for four more years, rebuilding the fortifications of Acre, Jaffa, Caesarea, and Sidon. Though it was his greatest desire, he was not able to conquer Jerusalem or negotiate for its return. When his mother's death required that he return to France, he still hoped that one day he would return to the Holy Land.

Even after he returned to France, Louis continued to financially support the Christian outposts in the Holy Land. Moreover, he never abandoned his dream of freeing the Holy Land from the Muslims. Meanwhile, Baybars, the general who had defeated Louis at Al Mansurah, had continued to win victories in the Holy Land. By 1265, Baybars, now the Sultan of Egypt, had attacked Galilee, destroyed the cathedral of Nazareth, and captured Caesarea. In March 1268, he took Jaffa and killed most of the Christians there. In May, Antioch suffered the same fate.

Clearly, Baybars had the will and the means to recapture all the territory the Christians had won in the Holy Land since the First Crusade unless Christendom intervened. The crusading spirit, so alive in 1095, had begun to wither and die. Nevertheless, in May 1269, King St. Louis, now sick and elderly, announced that his crusade would embark in a year.

218   *Chapter 14: The Crusades*

The Eighth Crusade, led by Louis and two of his three sons, would be the last.

Louis and his sons set sail on July 1, 1270, and landed at Carthage. He planned to seize Tunis and make this city the base of his operations against Egypt. This plan, not particularly good to begin with, never came to fruition. An outbreak of plague swept through the army. Louis became sick and died on August 25. The crusade, which had scarcely begun, abruptly ended.

Without the aid of the West, the Christian cities in the Holy Land had no chance to survive. In 1291, the Muslims captured Tripoli and Acre, the last Christian outposts. The Holy Land was once more under Muslim control. It would remain so until the twentieth century, when the State of Israel would come into existence, and Jerusalem would become part of a Jewish nation.

Assessing the Crusades

If the goal of the Crusades was to recapture the Holy Land, especially Jerusalem, from the Muslims, then all but the First Crusade failed. The Crusades also failed to reunite the Eastern Church with Rome. In fact, the Fourth Crusade made that goal less likely.

On the other hand, the Crusades also sought to open a second front against the Muslims and stop their advance on Europe and the Byzantine Empire. In that regard, they succeeded. The Muslims had to defend the Holy Land and focus their efforts on its recapture. From a military point of view, the Crusades succeeded in keeping the Turks from attacking Europe.

The crusaders accomplished a great deal of good in other ways as well. Since they were fighting in a spiritual cause, the ideals of the knights were uplifted and their lives ennobled. In addition, the people of the West became better acquainted with the East. Crusaders brought many of the finer parts of Greek culture back to Italy, Germany, and France. In the fourteenth century, these ideas would help lead to the Renaissance. The crusaders also introduced products from the East, like spices and silks, into Western Europe. This caused a development in commerce and banking. Explorers would soon set out to discover better, faster, and safer trade routes. As a result, in 1492, Columbus would discover America.

The Dedication, Edmund Leighton

Witness to the Faith 219

Jerusalem, Israel

The Military Orders

During the Crusades, a new kind of religious order emerged: the warrior monk. These orders consisted of fighting men who swore to fight against the Muslims, to protect pilgrims, and to care for the sick and the wounded. Their rule committed them to perform acts of bravery and heroism. Usually, the orders consisted of three classes of members: knights, serving brothers, and chaplains. Only the chaplains were priests. The three most important military orders were the Knights of St. John of Jerusalem, the Knights Templars, and the Teutonic Knights.

The Knights of St. John were also known as the Knights Hospitallers. Their name came from the hospital in Jerusalem where they were first located and where they received pilgrims and cared for the sick. In the thirteenth century, following the loss of the Holy Land, they moved their headquarters to the island of Rhodes, and then in 1530 to the island of Malta, where they became the Knights of Malta. The Knights of Malta still exist today.

Founded in 1119, the Knights Templars had a strong supporter in St. Bernard of Clairvaux, who endorsed the order at the Council of Troyes in 1128. With his blessing, they became one of the most powerful of the crusading orders. They derived the name "Knights Templars" from their original home on the Temple Mount in Jerusalem near a captured mosque. They referred to the mosque as Solomon's Temple. It was from this location that they took their official name, "Poor Knights of Christ and the Temple of Solomon," or Knights Templars.

While the Knights Templars started out as "Poor Knights," over the decades, these fine soldiers became very wealthy. In time, their wealth engendered the jealousy of King Philip IV of France, who, deeply in debt, saw their wealth as an opportunity to solve his financial problems. In 1307, he had all the Knights Templars in France arrested, and he seized their property. To justify his action, he claimed that they were engaging in sacrilegious rituals. In reality, the Knights Templars had gained possession of the burial cloth of Our Lord, the Shroud of Turin. Their ritual was merely the veneration of the Shroud. Philip, in his lust for money, murdered most of them. Under pressure from Philip, Pope Clement V disbanded the Knights Templars in 1312.

The Teutonic Knights were founded in Acre in 1192 during the Third Crusade. Germans organized this order, and its members were German. Its official name is "Order of the House of St. Mary of the Germans in Jerusalem." After the Christians were driven from the Holy Land, the Teutonic Knights moved to Europe, where they fought various campaigns. Although Adolf Hitler abolished the order, it was reinstated following World War II and still exists today.

Since they were monks, the knights of the military orders also took vows of poverty, chastity, and obedience. Since they were soldiers, they wore armor under a cloak. The Knights Hospitallers wore a black cloak with a white cross. The Knights Templars wore a white cloak with a red cross. After the majority of the crusaders returned home, the military orders became a kind of permanent army, which, because of their knowledge of the land and the enemy, proved to be a valuable asset.

Knights Hospitaller Insignia

Knights Templar Insignia

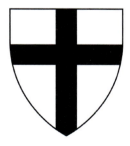

Teutonic Knights Insignia

Oral Exercises

1. Why were the Crusades undertaken?
2. What was the most important result of the First Crusade?
3. Which pope preached the First Crusade?
4. Which English king led the Third Crusade?
5. Which pope preached the Fourth Crusade?
6. Why is the Fourth Crusade not worthy of the name "crusade"?
7. Why did Louis IX's last crusade fail?
8. What were the overall results of the Crusades?
9. Why were the religious orders founded during the Crusades called military orders?
10. Name the three most important of these military orders.

Witness to the Faith 221

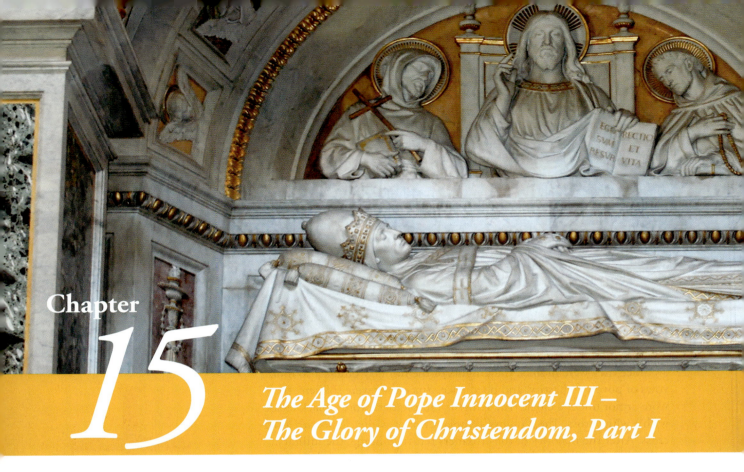

Chapter 15

The Age of Pope Innocent III – The Glory of Christendom, Part I

Introduction

Few men or women have had an era named after them. That is reserved only for those who have made such an impact that they have changed the course of history. Pope Innocent III was such a man. During his pontificate, which was part of the period known as the High Middle Ages, the papacy began to reach the pinnacle of its power and the height of its glory.

Not all of this is due to Innocent III alone. Other great popes reigned during the thirteenth century: Honorius III, Blessed Gregory X, and Gregory XI. Moreover, two of the greatest saints lived during this time: St. Francis of Assisi and St. Dominic. Their legacy lives on today. Yet they are only a few of the remarkable individuals who contributed to the glory of that century. Hundreds of thousands of such men and women are known only to God. These are the dedicated Catholics who built the great Gothic cathedrals that soar heavenward. These are the people responsible for the glory of Christendom.

The Guelphs and Ghibellines

Although the Concordat of Worms had resolved the Investiture Controversy, it had not resolved the underlying conflicts between the pope and the emperor. Since the time of Charlemagne, the pope had crowned

Louis VII and Conrad III Set Out for the Second Crusade

222 Chapter 15: The Age of Pope Innocent III – The Glory of Christendom, Part I

The Tomb of Pope Innocent III

1158 A.D. – 1273 A.D.

1158 A.D.
Frederick Barbarossa begins his quest to conquer Italy.

1176 A.D.
Frederick is defeated at the Battle of Legnano, ending his ambitions in Italy.

1184 A.D.
At the Council of Verona, Frederick and Pope Lucius III set forth the basic idea of the Inquisition.

1205 A.D.
Francis of Assisi becomes a beggar for Christ.

1208-1229 A.D.
Under Simon de Montfort, a Crusade is fought against the Albigensians in southern France.

1209-1216 A.D.
Otto of Aachen becomes emperor, but is excommunicated when he plunders Italy and the Papal States. He is defeated at the Battle of Bouvines. Frederick II is chosen as emperor.

1215 A.D.
King John signs the Magna Carta. In France, St. Dominic founds a new religious community, which is approved by Pope Honorius III in 1216 as the Order of Preachers.

1240 A.D.
Frederick II attacks the Papal States, but withdraws when confronted by Pope Gregory IX. Gregory dies, leaving the papacy vacant for nearly two years.

1245 A.D.
The Council of Lyons deposes Frederick, who dies five years later. For over twenty years afterwards, there is no emperor.

1273 A.D.
Rudolf of Hapsburg becomes the new Holy Roman Emperor.

---

the emperor. This effectively meant that the emperor received his authority and throne from the pope. It also demonstrated that the pope had spiritual authority over the emperor. Charlemagne and Emperor Otto had agreed that the emperor would approve the election of the pope. However, even after Pope Nicholas II changed this arrangement, emperors still wanted to approve papal elections. Ultimately, the emperors would have preferred an arrangement like the one that existed in the Byzantine Empire, where the State controlled the Church. Of course, no pope would ever agree to such an arrangement—the stronger the pope, the fiercer the opposition.

In May 1125, Emperor Henry V died without any heirs. Lothair II became king of the Germans. When he died in 1137, the German nobility elected Conrad, the first king of the

Witness to the Faith 223

Emperor Frederick Barbarossa

Hohenstaufen dynasty, to be king of Germany. Conrad helped lead the Second Crusade. Interestingly, Conrad never attempted to have himself crowned Holy Roman Emperor. However, his successor certainly did.

Conrad died in February 1152 and named his nephew Frederick to succeed him as king of Germany. History would know Frederick I as "Frederick Barbarossa" ("Red Beard"). Although secular historians generally consider him one of the best emperors of the Middle Ages, he was no friend to the Church. A man of great determination, perhaps he simply never expected that popes would challenge him. When they did, Frederick reacted angrily, more determined to have his way. However, he was an able administrator, a remarkable organizer, and other than Richard the Lionheart, the finest general of the time.

When Frederick Barbarossa became king of Germany, his ultimate goal was to unite the more than 1,600 individual German states into a single nation. Sadly, he came to feel that the Catholic Church stood in his way. He believed that in order to unite Germany, he had to conquer Italy and be able to choose the pope. As a result, he engaged in virtual open war against the papacy—something his great-grandfather, Emperor Henry IV, knew very well. This warfare would continue under his successors and last for over one hundred years. It would finally end with the complete destruction of the Hohenstaufen dynasty.

It is important to note that this struggle between the emperor and the pope, like so many before, **did not involve doctrine**. The emperor and his followers did not deny the Real Presence, the Holy Trinity, or other Catholic doctrines. Unlike the Investiture Controversy, which had a religious element—that is, unworthy men in priestly offices—this struggle was *political*, not religious for the most part. It involved the appropriate political power of the two parties. Popes had crowned the emperor, and the papal coronation seemed necessary before the emperor could assume his imperial title and authorities. On the other hand, the emperors had nominated many of the popes. Moreover, nearly all the popes up to the time of Urban II had waited for imperial approval before being consecrated pope.

During their conflicts, some people sided with the pope, and others with the emperor. The *Ghibellines* (the emperor's supporters) were not necessarily heretics, and the *Guelphs* (the pope's adherents) were not necessarily saints. The names "Guelph" and "Ghibelline" originated in Germany. They come from the rivalry between the Welfs

224 Chapter 15: The Age of Pope Innocent III – The Glory of Christendom, Part I

of Bavaria and the Hohenstaufens of Swabia, whose ancestral castle was located at Waiblingena. When the Welfs and Hohenstaufens began fighting for the imperial crown in Germany and Italy at the end of the twelfth century, their names were introduced into Italy. "Guelfo" and "Ghibellino" are the Italian forms of Welf and Waiblingen. No one on either side questioned the pope's authority in spiritual affairs. The issue was how much authority the pope had in temporal matters, and how much authority the emperor had in Church affairs.

Pope Adrian IV

Frederick Barbarossa Is Crowned Emperor

Frederick Barbarossa began his reign on friendly terms with the papacy. In March 1153, he signed a treaty with Pope Eugene III (1145-1153) in which he promised to defend the papacy. In return, Pope Eugene promised to crown him emperor.

In December 1154, Nicholas Breakspear, an English cardinal, was elected pope. Nicholas, who had a reputation as a reformer, took the name Adrian IV (1154-1159). The new pope agreed to meet Frederick in June 1155. They planned to discuss Frederick's coronation.

Since the time of King Pepin and Charlemagne, it had become customary for the emperor (or emperor-to-be) to hold the pope's stirrup as he dismounted his horse. Frederick refused to do so, for fear of appearing to be the pope's vassal. As a result, Adrian refused to give him the traditional kiss of peace. However, Frederick appears to have reconsidered, because the following day he did hold the pope's stirrup, and Adrian bestowed the kiss of peace upon him. Now that they were friends, on June 18, 1155, Adrian crowned Frederick as Holy Roman Emperor.

Pope Adrian and Emperor Frederick maintained an uneasy peace until 1158, when Barbarossa journeyed into northern Italy. He claimed the right to rule over all cities of Italy, including the city of Rome, because he was "King of the Romans." In August 1159, Frederick attacked the tiny town of Crema. A coalition of more powerful Italian cities banded against him. The pope told him he had forty days to stop his invasion or be excommunicated. Adrian never lived to see if Frederick complied. On September 1, Adrian died of a heart attack.

War with Frederick Barbarossa

Within a week following Adrian's death, the College of Cardinals elected Cardinal Roland Bandinelli, the papal chancellor, who took the name Alexander III (1159-1181). A small minority of three cardinals, under the influence of Frederick, set up an antipope named Victor IV. Although each man would excommunicate the other and cause a schism in the Church, the validity of Pope Alexander's election is unquestioned. Eventually, the kings of England, France, Spain, and Ireland all acknowledged his election. Only Barbarossa supported Victor, to whom he had apparently promised the papacy. Not only did his actions cause

Pope Alexander III

Witness to the Faith

a schism, but they actually led to open warfare between the papacy and the empire. Alexander III fled Rome but remained in Italy.

In 1160, Barbarossa held a synod in Pavia, in which bishops under his control and threat of violence proclaimed Victor as pope. When Alexander learned of the synod later that month, he excommunicated Frederick and released his subjects from their allegiance to him. However, Frederick, unlike Henry IV, had support in Germany. He did not need to come to Canossa. In fact, he attacked Italy.

In the spring of 1161, Frederick attacked Milan with an army numbering 100,000 men. For a year, Milan valiantly held out. However, in March 1162, the starving Milanese surrendered. Frederick, who as Holy Roman Emperor had promised to defend Italy, completely destroyed the city. The fall of Milan forced Alexander to flee Italy to France, where King Louis VII received him warmly.

In 1164, Victor IV died. However, Frederick was not to be deterred by his death. He had a new antipope elected, Guido of Crema, who took the name Pascal III. Like Victor, Pascal was Frederick's puppet. At the Diet of Wurzburg in 1165, the German princes and bishops once again declared themselves for Barbarossa's antipope.

Sens Cathedral in France, Where Pope Alexander III Took Refuge

In late November 1165, Alexander III re-entered Rome with the help of the Normans from Sicily. Despite his troubles with Frederick, Alexander was the head of the Church and responsible for every soul on Earth. In early 1166, he confirmed Thomas Becket as papal legate to England, thus giving Becket more support in his ongoing conflict with Henry II. On May 3, Alexander demanded that Henry return Becket's property to him.

Unfortunately for the popes of this time, Frederick Barbarossa was the greatest general of his age. Once again, Frederick sallied into Italy. In late July, he attacked Rome. He seized the city and, on July 30, had himself crowned emperor by the antipope in St. Peter's Basilica, while Alexander III, disguised as a pilgrim, fled. The next night, a torrential rainstorm forced the sewers to overflow, which caused an epidemic to break out in Barbarossa's army. He was compelled to leave Rome. However, he did not leave Italy. For the next several years, an alliance of sixteen cities in northern Italy battled Frederick.

The Battle of Legnano

Frederick and the Italians waged their final decisive battle on a plain outside the town of Legnano, near Milan, on May 29, 1176. Frederick, despite all his faults, was an incredibly brave man. He led a cavalry charge, during which he was unhorsed. He disappeared into a crowd of men, and word went out that he was dead. Upon hearing this, his army fell apart. The victory at Legnano ended Barbarossa's ambitions in Italy.

226 Chapter 15: The Age of Pope Innocent III – The Glory of Christendom, Part I

The Reconciliation of Pope Alexander III and Frederick Barbarossa, Francesco Salviati

Frederick then began negotiations with Pope Alexander, which resulted in the Peace of Venice in 1177. The emperor prostrated himself before the pope under the archway of St. Mark's Cathedral in Venice. He humbly pleaded for forgiveness and acknowledged Alexander as the true pope. Like his great-grandfather, he had finally come to Canossa, but, also like his great-grandfather, he would not become an obedient son of the Church. In less than a decade, Frederick would once again make trouble for a pope.

In 1179, the Third Lateran Council confirmed the Peace of Venice. To avoid the possibility of another schism, it amended the decree that Nicholas II had issued in 1059 on papal elections. In the future, **a two-thirds majority of the College of Cardinals would be required for the valid election of a pope**.

The Election of Pope Innocent III

In September 1180, King Louis VII of France died. Probably the second best king to rule France, he had protected both St. Thomas Becket and Pope Alexander. He had led the Second Crusade and governed France exceedingly well for forty-three years.

St. Mark's Basilica, Venice

Witness to the Faith 227

Tomb of Pope Alexander III

Emperor Henry VI

Less than a year later, Pope Alexander followed King Louis to his eternal reward. Alexander had had one of the longest pontificates in history and reigned during one of the most difficult times. Yet he had shown unerring wisdom and judgment in dealing with Frederick Barbarossa, Henry II, and other challenges.

Following Alexander's death, Pope Lucius III (1181-1185) succeeded him. After a short and relatively uneventful pontificate, the elderly Lucius died in 1185 and was succeeded by Urban III (1185-1187). Urban was the archbishop of Milan. Both he and his family had suffered greatly when Frederick had razed Milan. Urban was about to excommunicate Frederick once again, but died suddenly in 1187. His successor, Pope Gregory VIII (1187) reigned for less than two months but issued a call for a third crusade.

Gregory's successor, Clement III (1187-1191), also called for a crusade. Additionally, he told Frederick that he was open to peace negotiations. Now Frederick, perhaps truly repentant for all the damage that he had inflicted upon the Church, took up the Cross. Frederick was arguably the greatest battlefield commander of the time. Had he not died fording that river in Asia Minor, perhaps the Third Crusade would have ended differently.

Meanwhile, as the crusaders experienced triumph and tragedy, in March 1191, old and sickly Pope Clement died. He had reigned for more than three years—longer than most of his contemporaries expected. The Sacred College elected Pope Celestine III (1191-1198). Although he was 85 years old, he was remarkably fit and healthy. The day after he was consecrated pope, he crowned Frederick Barbarossa's son, Henry VI, as Holy Roman Emperor.

Henry VI proved rather unlike his father. In early 1195 (three years after the end of the Third Crusade), Henry declared that he would go on a new crusade to the Holy Land. In the summer, he and Pope Celestine jointly proclaimed the crusade. The army arrived in the Holy Land in September 1197. They took Acre and Beirut. However, Henry, who had stayed in Sicily to deal with imperial matters, suddenly fell sick and died. He was only 32 years old. His army returned home. His son Frederick was only 3 years old, too young to be emperor.

When Henry VI died, he had left his son under the care of Pope Celestine. However, the pope was in his 90s and died the following January. Pope Celestine had led the Church well for more than seven years. In the history of the world, few men past the age of 85 have accomplished as much as he did. Perhaps history would have given him more credit for his accomplishments had his successor not been one of the greatest popes the Church has ever known.

Following the death of Celestine, the College of Cardinals elected Lothario Conti of Rome, who took the name of Innocent III (1198-1216). Unlike the previous popes, at 37 years old, Innocent was one of the youngest men ever to wear the Fisherman's Ring. Yet he was also one of the most qualified. Incredibly intelligent, insightful, and determined, Innocent had distinguished himself as an ecclesiastical writer and as an adviser to his predecessor. Moreover, because he had avoided Church politics, he had the support of almost all the cardinals in the Sacred College. Because he had worked closely with Pope Celestine, he had a thorough knowledge of the Church's organization and government. Finally, he had a clear understanding of the relationship between the papacy and the emperor. In fact, in his first address following his consecration, he reiterated the policy set forth by Pope Gregory VII and declared that the pope is the moral judge of kings and emperors.

Young and vigorous, Innocent had a definite plan. First, he felt strongly that a new crusade should be launched. (Sadly, this Fourth Crusade did not end up going at all the way Pope Innocent had intended.) Additionally, he appointed good and holy bishops and archbishops throughout Christendom. Also, he insisted that rulers not interfere with the proper administration of the Church in their realms.

Pope Celestine III

Innocent III and Germany

As always, one of the main issues confronting the pope was the situation in Germany. When Henry VI died, his son was only a young boy. Thus, his mother Constance served as his guardian. However, when she died, Pope Innocent became guardian to young Frederick II. Although Frederick was still too young to become Holy Roman Emperor, Innocent did crown him king of Sicily.

Meanwhile in Germany, two factions, the aforementioned Welfs of Bavaria and Hohenstaufens of Swabia, contended for the throne. Following Henry VI's death, his supporters elected his brother, Philip of Swabia, king of Germany. The Welfs elected Otto of Brunswick. Otto was able to capture Aachen and have himself crowned king by the archbishop of Cologne. Both

Pope Innocent III

Witness to the Faith

The Royal Destiny of the Infant Frederick II, Pelagio Palagi

claimants appealed their case to the pope. Innocent negotiated a settlement that would have made Philip emperor, but then Philip was murdered. Otto reconciled with Innocent, who finally gave him his support. In October 1209, Innocent crowned him emperor.

However, Innocent had barely crowned Otto when the new emperor began to show that he was as bad as any Hohenstaufen was. He set out to conquer the entire Italian peninsula. By January, Otto had plundered much of Italy and the Papal States. Innocent III remonstrated with him and finally excommunicated him in November. Thereupon, in 1212, the German princes chose the pope's ward, Frederick II, as king of Germany. Otto, realizing that he was losing his throne, returned to Germany. However, most of the German leaders had turned against him for what they considered his foolish adventures in Italy. In July 1214, Philip Augustus of France, who had come to support Frederick II at the pope's invitation, finally crushed Otto at the Battle of Bouvines. By 1216, Frederick II was the undisputed head of the German Empire. Otto, the only Welf emperor, died in 1218.

Innocent III and King John of England

As Innocent was dealing with Otto and the Germans, he also had to deal with Richard the Lionheart's younger brother, King John. Following Richard's sudden death in 1199, John, Henry II's youngest son, became king. Notable for being one of history's worst rulers, John had many of Henry's worst qualities.

In 1208, Innocent placed England under an **interdict**—that is, he closed all of the churches in England. This was because King John insisted on the appointment of his own candidate as archbishop of Canterbury even though the pope had already appointed Cardinal Stephen Langton. The following year, Pope Innocent excommunicated King John, deposed him, and offered England to King Philip of France. To save his kingdom, King John submitted to the Holy Father in May 1213. He offered England to the pope as a fief, agreed to pay an annual tribute, and acknowledged himself to be the Holy Father's vassal. Two years later, in 1215, the English barons rose up against King John. At Runnymede, the barons forced him to sign the great charter of English liberty, the **Magna Carta**. Pope Honorius III ratified the Magna Carta in November 1216.

Innocent III and King Philip of France

Although Innocent worked with Philip to help resolve matters in Germany and England, Philip II, also known as Philip Augustus, was not always a faithful Catholic. Philip was the son of Louis VII and had been crowned "junior" king in November 1179 as his father entered his final illness. Philip was also quite ambitious.

Interdict
A decree withholding the sacraments from a person or territory. In the Middle Ages, a pope might punish a disobedient monarch by placing his country under an interdict.

Magna Carta
A document stating the rights of the people of England, which the English barons forced King John to sign.

One of Philip's ambitions was to rule England. For that reason, he married 18-year-old Danish princess Ingeborg on August 14, 1193. Because of the intricacies of European royal marriages, Ingeborg gave him a tenuous claim to the English throne. However, Philip immediately developed a strange aversion to her and announced that he wanted the marriage annulled. In November, a council of bishops and barons convened and annulled the marriage. Though she was young, she was determined to defend the Sacrament of Marriage. Although Philip had her locked in a convent, she appealed her case to the pope. Philip also locked the legates that Pope Celestine III had sent to investigate the case in the monastery at Clairvaux. In May 1195, Pope Celestine overruled the French council, declaring that Philip was lawfully and sacramentally married to Ingeborg and that while she lived, the Church would not recognize any other marriage of Philip's. In open defiance of the pope, Philip then married Agnes, a Bavarian countess.

Pope Innocent III continued to defend Ingeborg. He ordered Philip to take her back as his lawful wife. When Philip again refused, in January 1200 Innocent placed France under interdict. In the face of his outraged subjects, who could not attend Mass, Philip finally yielded. However, he was not sincere. He would again imprison Ingeborg. It would be thirteen years before he reigned with Ingeborg at his side.

King Philip Augustus

St. Dominic

So often throughout history, in the times of the Church's deepest need, the Holy Spirit calls upon men and women to change adversity into glory, and darkness into light. As the thirteenth century dawned, Our Lord called two men to His service. In a brief span of time starting in 1206, these two remarkable men would change the history of the Church and the world. Their names were Dominic and Francis.

St. Dominic was born Domingo de Guzman in Caleruega, Spain, in 1170. According to a story, before he was born, his mother had a dream in which a dog leapt from her womb carrying a flaming torch in its mouth. (That is why artists often portray St. Dominic with a dog holding a torch.) One day, he and the other friars in the Order of Preachers that he would establish, the Dominicans, would be known as the "Hounds of the Lord" because of their zeal in preaching the Gospel.

As a young man, Dominic received an excellent education in the schools of Palencia. In 1194, following his graduation, he became an Augustinian monk. In the spring of 1206, he began working in southern France to convert the *Cathars*, a dangerous group of heretics. Although other Catholics were preaching to them, they had not been able to reconcile the Cathars back into the Church. Dominic felt that the preachers were not able to connect with the Cathars on a personal

Saint Dominic

Witness to the Faith **231**

level. The local priests lived rather lavishly, while most of the people were poor. Dominic believed that to win the people back to the Faith, he must speak and live as one of them, even begging for his food. From that moment onward, St. Dominic devoted himself to the task of preaching to the people. In November, Pope Innocent approved this new **mendicant** (begging) order for southern France.

In 1215, Dominic gathered a few zealous priests together, and they decided to live a common life under the Rule of St. Augustine. To counter the austerity of the Cathars, they took the vow of absolute poverty. Dominic said, "Zeal must be met by zeal, humility by humility, false sanctity by real sanctity, preaching falsehood by preaching truth." From this little group grew an order whose main purpose was preaching the Gospel and educating clerics who could defend the Faith. In January 1216, Pope Honorius III approved the *Ordo Praedicatorum* (O.P.), or "Order of Preachers," more popularly known as the Dominicans. The Dominicans' distinctive garb consists of a white habit with a long black mantle.

St. Dominic believed strongly that all of his Dominicans needed to have an excellent education. He felt that unless his preachers were well educated in philosophy and theology, they could not preach successfully to the people and answer the questions people would ask about the Faith. Consequently, he sent his Dominicans to Paris to study. Once they were educated in theology and philosophy, Dominic sent them out in pairs throughout Europe. Because they were able to answer questions and intellectually defeat their opponents, they succeeded. Their intelligence, learning, and lifestyle helped defeat heresies as they appeared. In time, the Dominicans came to be regarded as the most well-educated and respected men in Christendom. Some of them, such as St. Albert the Great and St. Thomas Aquinas, numbered among the most brilliant professors at the University of Paris. When St. Dominic died in 1221, his order numbered sixty religious houses. In a mere fifteen years, he had transformed the world.

St. Francis of Assisi

Meanwhile, at virtually the same moment that Dominic decided to preach to the Cathars, Giovanni di Pietro di Bernardone, known to his friends and family as Francesco (Francis), knelt in prayer before the crucifix at the little rundown church outside of Assisi dedicated to St. Damian. As he prayed, he heard Our Lord say, "Francis, go and repair My Church, which is nearly falling down." The 22-year-old, taking these words literally, devoted his time and resources to trying to rebuild the little church. His actions aroused the displeasure of his father, a wealthy merchant. His father tried to reason with Francis, who until then had led a carefree life.

Francis had loved music and poetry, especially French music and poetry. His father, Pietro, had seen to that last part; Pietro had a great admiration for French culture, which was also why he had named his son *Francesco*. Francis had been a good young man, just not particularly religious. Thus, his behavior confused his father.

Mendicant
A word meaning "begging"; the mendicant orders are those that beg for their living, like the Franciscans and Dominicans.

Pope Honorius Approving the Dominican Order

Approval of the Franciscan Rule by Pope Innocent III, **Antonio Carnicero**

Finally, after many disputes with his father, Francis renounced his inheritance and rid himself of his fine clothes, as a sign that he was through with the world. He went around as a common beggar, collecting alms for the repair of neglected churches.

Over the next few years, Francis realized that Christ meant for him to repair the entire Church, not merely a few decaying chapels. In early 1208, Francis began a life of preaching and begging, moving from town to town. By the end of the year, he had gathered eleven disciples. He wrote out a simple rule based on the observance of strict poverty, penance, and preaching two by two. Thus began the Franciscan Order. They made up their minds to live by manual labor and by begging. They called themselves *Fratres Minores* ("Little Brothers"), formally *Ordo Fratrum Minorum* (OFM), to indicate that they belonged to the common people to whom they preached. They wore a simple gray habit of coarse wool and a pointed hood, knotted at the waist with a white cord. Since they preached more by example than by word of mouth, their influence was remarkable.

In the spring of 1209, Francis and his band of brothers went to Rome to seek the pope's recognition of their order. On April 16, 1210, Pope Innocent III approved the order and made Francis its leader. The pope sanctioned their right to preach the Gospel publicly. Francis was ordained a deacon but considered himself unworthy to become a priest.

Following the pope's approval, the Franciscan Order grew rapidly. In 1211, a young noblewoman named Clare heard Francis preaching in Assisi. Clare realized that she had a vocation. Together, Francis and Clare established the **Poor Clares**, or the Second Order of St. Francis.

Poor Clares
The women's branch of the Franciscan Order, established by St. Francis and St. Clare.

Witness to the Faith 233

St. Francis Receiving the Stigmata, Peter Paul Rubens

Albigensian Heresy
A heresy, based mainly in southern France, which taught that a good principle created the spiritual world, and an evil principle created the material world.

Later, Francis formed a Third Order for lay members who continued to live in the world with their families rather than in a religious community. This order would give pious Catholics an opportunity to live a semi-religious life and share in the spiritual advantages of the Franciscan Order. The Third Order of St. Francis is also known as the Secular Franciscan Order.

Amazingly, Francis was so determined to spread the Gospel that he attempted to convert the Muslims. In the spring of 1212, he sailed for Jerusalem. However, his ship wrecked, forcing him to return to Italy. Undaunted, he tried again the following year. This time, sickness caused him to retreat. In 1219, during the Fifth Crusade, Francis finally reached the Holy Land. In August, he arrived in Damietta as the crusaders were besieging the city. He told them that he had come to convert the Sultan of Egypt. The crusaders were aghast. Such a notion was impossible. Until the twentieth century, conversion from Islam or preaching conversion held the death penalty. The Sultan would never convert. Nevertheless, Francis strode boldly into his camp.

Amazingly, the Sultan, a nephew of Saladin's, received Francis warmly. He listened to Francis, offered him gifts, and finally escorted him back to the crusaders' battle lines. However, he did not convert. Francis left the Holy Land for Italy in the latter half of 1220.

Over the next years, the Franciscan Order grew rapidly. In 1220, Francis, who never had any desire to administer an order, turned over its management to others. He withdrew from its daily operation to devote himself more to prayer. He would go alone to Mount Alvernia to pray. On September 14, 1224, the Feast of the Exaltation of the Holy Cross, Francis saw a vision of a six-winged angel attached to a cross and shining in glory. St. Francis was filled with love and appreciation for Our Crucified Lord. When the vision passed, he discovered that his hands, feet, and side bore the wounds of the stigmata. Francis died on October 3, 1226. Less than two years later, Pope Gregory IX canonized him.

In a span of just twenty years, St. Francis of Assisi, known as the Little Poor Man, had, like his contemporary St. Dominic, completely changed the world.

The Albigensian Heresy

Some heresies are so far removed from the most fundamental doctrines of Christianity that they no longer deserve to be called Christian. Such was the case with the **Albigensian Heresy**. This heresy had its roots in Manicheanism, the heresy that St. Augustine had apparently destroyed during the fourth century. However, the heresy had not been destroyed, but had merely gone underground.

Based mainly in southern France around Toulouse, the members of this sect were known as Albigensians because the town of Albi was also a major site of their operations. The members referred to themselves as *Cathari* (the Pure), because they claimed to possess a degree of purity that others did not. Like the Manichees, the Cathari believed that there was one good principle and one evil principle. They believed that the good principle created the spiritual world, whereas the evil principle created the material world. Consequently, they rejected Christ's humanity and the goodness of marriage and childbearing. They taught that the human body, the material part of a person, must be brought under control by fasting and mortification. However, if the forces of evil proved too overwhelming for someone, then, according to the Cathari, that person should commit suicide.

The Albigensian heresy was one of the most terrible heresies to attack the Church. Catholic historian Godefroid Kurth described its spread as a "dark night which came down with the weight of lead and with the coldness of ice upon the mind and upon the heart, a chancre of death which ate at all the luminous and elevated faculties of the human soul, a deadly folly that choked the joy of living and made existence here below like a bad dream" (G. Kurth, *The Church at the Turning Points of History* [Norfolk, Va.: IHS Press, 2007; originally published in Helena, Mont.: Naegele Printing Co., 1918], p. 50). Nevertheless, this "death" cult spread across southern France. By 1165, the Cathars were so numerous and so strongly supported by many of the nobles that they preached their heresy openly. The bishops dared not move against them. The Cathari were helped by King Philip's refusal to acknowledge the seriousness of the situation, despite the warnings of Pope Innocent III.

In the early years of the thirteenth century, St. Dominic and his Dominicans did all they could to bring the Cathari peacefully back to the Faith. However, the evil of the Cathari was too deeply entrenched. The time had come to launch a crusade.

The Albigensian Crusade

With no other choice, Pope Innocent III declared in March 1208 that the war against the Cathari in southern France was a crusade. Although popes had been opposed to wars against fellow Christians, the Cathari constituted a real threat to the existence of the Church and the people of southern France. Innocent called upon King Philip to lead the crusade. However, Philip, who still refused to take the pope seriously, was engaged in a conflict with King John of England. As a result, he declined to lead the crusade. In fact, because of his determination to defend the rights of the Church, Innocent was not on good terms with any of the kings of Europe. Thus, it fell to one of history's greatest knights to lead the crusade: Simon de Montfort.

St. Dominic Blesses Simon de Montfort

Witness to the Faith

The Pope and the Inquisitor,
Jean-Paul Laurens

Simon de Montfort had been one of only two knights *not* to attack Zara and Constantinople during the infamous Fourth Crusade. Now, at the head of an army of about 200,000 men, recruited mainly from northern France, he once again answered the pope's call. For nine years, Simon led the crusader army. He died during the siege of Toulouse in June 1218. The crusade would continue until 1229, when the Albigensians were finally suppressed. The Albigensian Crusade would also lead to the creation of the Inquisition.

The Suppression of Heresy: The Inquisition

Of all the anti-Catholic propaganda spread about the Church, none has been as successful as that aimed at the Inquisition. Part of the reason is that modern people simply cannot understand that there was a time when a person's religion was literally a matter of life and death. Yet, in the Middle Ages, this was in fact the case. During that time, the only religion in Europe was Catholicism, and the Church and the State were joint powers, so heresy was regarded as a crime against society and was punished as such. The heretic in Christendom was as dangerous to public order as a terrorist is today. The Cathari had proven that. It had taken a crusade to suppress them.

Moreover, the Cathari were not unique. Anywhere heretics established themselves in sufficient numbers, they brought violence, war, and terror. It was to protect the Church and society that Pope Gregory IX established the Inquisition in 1234. The Inquisition would fight heresy but at the same time protect civil society.

Secular historians make much of the fact that people accused by the Inquisition were not allowed to face their accusers or know their names. (For Americans, who have the right to face an accuser in court, this is especially upsetting.) However, this rule was created to protect witnesses from retribution. Also, the Inquisition told the accused to make a list of all personal enemies. No testimony was used against the accused from anyone on the list.

Because they were considered the most learned men in the Church, the Dominicans became the order that most frequently administered the Inquisition. All inquisitors were well educated and had university decrees. The Dominicans could discern whether a person was a heretic or simply ignorant of the Church's teachings. They would travel around Christendom conducting hearings. Generally, a person was given a month to recant their heresy and do penance. Only if the person remained obstinate would a public trial be held. If the person was found guilty and still refused Confession and penance, they would be turned over to the secular authorities for punishment. This usually meant being burned at the stake.

The Inquisition did use torture. However, it was used less than most secular historians claim and generally without long-term effects.

Unfortunately, during the Middle Ages, torture was a common practice, as were violent and brutal forms of death. Courts routinely imposed severe forms of the death penalty, such as hanging and burning at the stake, for serious crimes like murder and treason. Heresy was considered a very serious crime. Arguably, the Church should have tried harder to temper justice with mercy. Torture is wrong, but even priests and religious do not always recognize the evils that their contemporary society takes for granted.

The Inquisition had its origins in the second half of the twelfth century. At that time, various rulers came to realize that heresies were undermining both the Church and the civil society. These rulers asked that the Church not merely condemn heresy but actually root it out. In 1184, at the Council of Verona, Pope Lucius III and Emperor Frederick Barbarossa reached an accord addressing the manner in which the Church and empire would deal with heretics. Heretics would be "sought out" (*inquisito* in Latin), then brought before an ecclesiastical court for examination. Those who failed to recant their errors would be excommunicated and turned over to the civil authorities for just punishment.

Initially, the task of seeking out heretics fell to the bishops. However, bishops have authority only in their own dioceses, and heresies rarely exist in a single diocese, but rather spread over vast areas. **Episcopal inquisitions** (that is, inquisitions run by bishops) simply lacked the authority to deal with the problem. The popes realized that they needed agents who possessed more extensive authority—that is, papal legates.

To ensure that the accused had a fair trial, the Inquisition adopted the following procedure. Prior to beginning his investigation of a town or village, the inquisitor promulgated two edicts. He addressed the "Edict of Faith" to the faithful and commanded them under pain of excommunication to identify all heretics. He addressed the "Edict of Grace" to any heretics. This edict ordered them to appear before him. The inquisitor promised to forgive them if they renounced their heresy within thirty days. If a person charged with heresy failed to admit his or her errors within the allotted time, that person became a suspect. Suspects were either closely watched in their home or jailed prior to their public trial.

Those who repented were given a suitable penance. Sometimes this involved participation in a crusade or a pilgrimage to the Holy Land. Other punishments might involve paying a fine or losing property. If the heretic remained obstinate and failed to recant, the inquisitor turned him over to the civil authorities for punishment. Although anti-Catholic propagandists claim that the Inquisition killed most of those who appeared before it, even H.C. Lea, the Protestant historian of the Inquisition, admits that less than 5 percent of those convicted of heresy died at the stake. In the 50 years from 1227 to 1277, while the Cathari were finally being eradicated from southern France, only about 5,000 heretics were executed, a small percentage of the total of those executed for serious crimes in the region. Recent research even further enhances the reputation of the Inquisition as a very fair forum for justice.

> **Episcopal Inquisitions**
> Courts run by bishops, set up to detect heretics in their dioceses.

Frederick II

Witness to the Faith 237

Frederick II Wages War on the Papacy

Pope Honorius III

In 1212, Frederick II had become king of Germany. During his youth, he had been the ward of Pope Innocent III and the student of the man who would become Pope Honorius III. It seemed that he was destined to be a great emperor and defender of the Faith. However, although most historians consider him a great emperor, he was actually a great enemy of the Church.

Frederick was well educated. He spoke six languages, including German, Latin, and Arabic. He loved literature and promoted it at his court. During his reign, the Holy Roman Empire grew to its largest extent. However, Frederick was excommunicated four times. It seems that despite his contact with two good and holy popes, Frederick was not really a Catholic.

At the time of his coronation as king of Germany, Frederick had promised his former guardian, Pope Innocent III, that he would protect the papacy and Italy as well as go on a crusade. As time would show, however, no promise of Frederick's could ever be trusted.

In July 1216, Pope Innocent III fell ill with fever. Within a few days, he was dead, at only 56 years old. Who knows what he would have accomplished had he lived another twenty or thirty years? Three days after his death, the Sacred College elected Cencio Savelli, Frederick's former teacher, as pope. He took the name Honorius III (1216-1227).

Although elderly and not as vigorous as Innocent III, Honorius was committed to the policies of his predecessor. He was most determined that a crusade be launched and led by Frederick II. Unlike Innocent III, he sought to win Frederick first through kindness.

When the Fifth Crusade left in 1217, Frederick failed to accompany it but provided Pope Honorius with various excuses. Nevertheless, in April 1220, Frederick II was elected emperor, and Pope Honorius crowned him in Rome in November. Following his coronation, he promised to leave in August on crusade. However, in August 1221, Frederick did not join the crusade. When the crusade failed, Honorius placed much of the blame on Frederick's absence.

In November, the pope threatened to excommunicate Frederick if he did not go on crusade. Over the next five years of Honorius' pontificate, Frederick provided a litany of excuses for not crusading. Honorius, perhaps too kind-hearted, never excommunicated him.

Despite his trials with Frederick and the failure of the Fifth Crusade, Honorius had one of the Church's most blessed pontificates. In 1216, he approved the Dominican Order. In 1223, he solemnly approved the second rule of the Franciscan

Pope Gregory IX

Chapter 15: The Age of Pope Innocent III – The Glory of Christendom, Part I

Order (St. Francis had rewritten the simple rule that Pope Innocent III had approved in 1209). Honorius died in March 1227. His successor would be a worthy match for Emperor Frederick II.

Following the death of Honorius, the Sacred College elected Cardinal Ugolino Conti, the great Pope Gregory IX (1227-1241). Pope Gregory was the great-nephew of Pope Innocent III and a fervent disciple of Francis of Assisi. During his pontificate, he embodied the finest virtues of both men: the strength of Innocent and the kindness of Francis. Though he constantly sought to save the soul of Emperor Frederick, he refused to allow Frederick to take advantage of his kindness.

Emperor Frederick Makes a Deal with the Muslims

Gregory IX began his pontificate by reminding Frederick of his vow to take up the Cross. Only four days after his consecration as pope, Gregory wrote to Frederick reminding him that he had promised to leave on a crusade no later than August 15, 1227 (the Feast of the Assumption). Although some of the crusaders did leave on the appointed date, Frederick failed to depart until September 8. However, even after he did sail, he claimed to fall ill and returned to Italy. On September 29, Pope Gregory excommunicated him.

In June 1228, Frederick, despite his excommunication, left for the Holy Land. In the Holy Land, he negotiated the treaty that returned Jerusalem to the Christians for ten years. Two years later, since Frederick had finally fulfilled his vow, he and Gregory reconciled, and the pope removed the excommunication. Unfortunately, their peace was short lived.

In 1236, Frederick attempted to seize control of northern Italy. Over the next three years, he fought against the people of that region. On Palm Sunday, 1239, Pope Gregory excommunicated Frederick a second time, in this case for murdering priests and trying to turn the people of Rome against the pope. Frederick, who ruled Germany with an iron fist, now sought to control Italy as well. He ordered anyone who supported the pope to be put to death.

A Relic of the True Cross

In January 1240, Frederick launched an attack on the Papal States. By February 22, he arrived outside of Rome with a large army. The vanguard of Frederick's army reached St. Peter's Basilica, where Pope Gregory, carrying a piece of the True Cross, confronted them. The pope said that he would not flee but placed his trust in Saints Peter and Paul. The vanguard and then the rest of the army fled before the elderly pope. In June, Frederick offered to negotiate a peace treaty, but Gregory no longer trusted the deceitful Frederick. In February 1241, Gregory declared a

Witness to the Faith

Council of Lyons

crusade against the emperor, who had shown that he was no longer a Christian—if he had ever been one. In August, Pope Gregory IX, who had spent the previous two years in a life-and-death struggle with Frederick, finally succumbed to old age. Frederick rejoiced.

At this critical moment, when the Sacred College needed to act quickly to elect a pope to face Frederick, the cardinals were divided and afraid. At the time, there were only fourteen cardinals in the Sacred College. Frederick held two as prisoners and refused to release them. Two feared returning to Rome. Six were willing to vote for Frederick's candidate. Four refused to vote for anyone who would not oppose Frederick. Thus, under the two-thirds requirement for a papal election, no pope could be elected.

The End of the Hohenstaufen Dynasty

One of the cardinals soon died. Then, in October, the remainder voted for a dying man. Pope Celestine IV reigned for sixteen days. Following his death, six cardinals fled Rome. For a year and a half, no conclave met. In May 1243, one of the cardinals that Frederick held prisoner died. Frederick released the other, believing he could count on this cardinal's support. The next month, the Sacred College unanimously elected Pope Innocent IV (1243-1254).

Prior to his election, Innocent IV had been friendly toward Frederick. However, as pope, he resembled his namesake, Innocent III. The new pope insisted that Frederick free the bishops and priests he held captive. He also told the emperor to renounce his claims to northern Italy. However, Frederick continued to refuse all offers of peace.

Meanwhile, the pope created five new cardinals, bringing the total to twelve. Fearing that Rome was no longer safe, he fled to Lyons, France, in December 1244. Later that month, Innocent declared that in June he would hold a council in Lyons to decide the fate of Frederick. In the meantime, Innocent once again renewed Frederick's excommunication. When the Council of Lyons met in June 1245, it took the remarkable action of deposing Frederick as emperor and king of Germany for his various crimes against the Church. The pope told the Germans to elect a new ruler.

For the last five years of his life, Frederick remained an implacable enemy of the Church, fighting her constantly. He died of a sudden illness in December 1250. Frederick's three sons all died tragic deaths. Thus, the royal family of Hohenstaufen ended.

Pope Innocent IV died in 1254. He had done his job. He had paved the way for a royal family who would support the Church. It would fall to a future pope to find a man who would defend the Church from the infidel without and the heretic within.

Pope Innocent IV

240 Chapter 15: The Age of Pope Innocent III – The Glory of Christendom, Part I

The Rise of the Hapsburg Dynasty

Following Frederick's deposition, the imperial throne remained empty for more than twenty years. During this vacancy, Pope Alexander IV (1254-1261), Pope Urban IV (1261-1264), and Pope Clement IV (1265-1268) served as pope. Following the death of Clement IV, the Sacred College became hopelessly deadlocked between French and Italian cardinals. For two years and nine months, the longest election in papal history, the cardinals were unable to reach a two-thirds consensus. Finally, they elected someone who was not a member of the Sacred College. Amazingly, they elected a saint.

In September 1271, the cardinals chose Teobaldo Visconti, who took the name Gregory X (1271-1276). This vigorous pope felt that it was time to choose a man to be the new Holy Roman Emperor, a position that had been vacant since the fall of the Hohenstaufens. With no dominant noble family in Germany, the pope was able to choose a family who would support the papacy. Pope Gregory X made one of the greatest choices in the history of the Church: he chose **Rudolf of Hapsburg** to be the new emperor. In 1273, Rudolf was elected king of Germany. For the next six hundred years, the Hapsburg family would be the sword and shield of Christendom and would give Christendom some of its greatest leaders.

Rudolf of Hapsburg

Rudolf of Hapsburg
Chosen to be Holy Roman Emperor by Pope Gregory X; first of the imperial Hapsburg dynasty, which would figure so prominently in Europe for the next six hundred years.

Oral Exercises

1. Who were the Guelphs and Ghibellines?
2. Which emperor was placed in the care of Pope Innocent III?
3. Why did Pope Innocent III place England under interdict?
4. Why did Pope Innocent III place France under interdict?
5. Why was the Albigensian heresy so terrible?
6. What was the Edict of Faith? What was the Edict of Grace?
7. Who founded the Order of Preachers?
8. If a priest has the abbreviation OFM after his name, to which order does he belong?
9. Why was Frederick II excommunicated the first time?
10. Whom did Pope Gregory X choose to be the Holy Roman Emperor after the fall of the Hohenstaufens?

Witness to the Faith 241

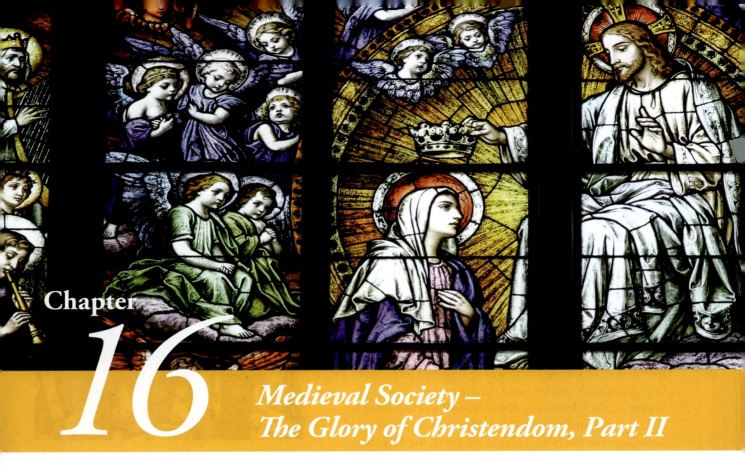

Chapter 16

Medieval Society – The Glory of Christendom, Part II

Madonna and Child, Duccio di Buoninsegna

Introduction

In many ways, the Catholic Church reached its greatest heights during the period known as the High Middle Ages, especially in the thirteenth and fourteenth centuries. Not only was it the Age of Innocent III, Dominic, Francis, and Thomas Aquinas, but it was also a time of some of the deepest devotion to the Faith that the Church has ever known. It was the age of the great cathedrals. It was the beginning of almost five hundred years of the world's greatest art: Catholic art.

While historians will never know the names of most of the men and women who built the great cathedrals or decorated them with incredible stained-glass windows, statues, and carvings, they do know the names of some of those who helped create this era of great Catholic culture. We know of Abbot Suger, who helped create the Gothic cathedral. We know Dante Alighieri, who developed the Italian language and wrote the monumental *Divine Comedy*. We know the sculptor Lorenzo Ghiberti and the painters Cimabue and Duccio.

Medieval Devotion

The Mystery Play

A society reflects the hopes, goals, and beliefs of its people. These feelings and beliefs form that society's culture—that is, their customs,

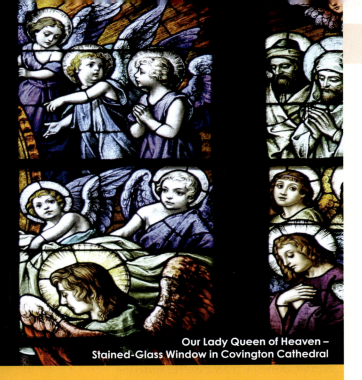

Our Lady Queen of Heaven – Stained-Glass Window in Covington Cathedral

arts, and social institutions. During the Middle Ages, a period lasting from approximately 476 (the fall of the Western Roman Empire) until 1453 (the fall of Constantinople), the Catholic Faith was the center of European culture and society. The people were working to build Christendom, the Kingdom of God on Earth. In addition to their religious and political institutions, they accomplished this through their art, literature, and architecture. However, none of this would have been possible were it not for the deep love that the people had for Our Blessed Lord and the Church He established.

The faith of medieval Christians was strong. There were few heresies during the Middle Ages. The people loved to attend Mass, and the life of a town or village revolved around the liturgical year. The clergy worked to promote the Faith in numerous ways, most obviously

1135 A.D. – 1476 A.D.

1135 A.D.
Abbot Suger begins rebuilding the Basilica of Saint-Denis, marking the beginning of Gothic architecture.

1150 A.D.
The University of Paris is founded.

1163 A.D.
Construction is begun on Notre Dame Cathedral in Paris.

1215 A.D.
The Fourth Lateran Council decrees that Catholics must go to Confession and receive Holy Communion at least once a year.

1248 A.D.
Construction is begun on the cathedral of Cologne, though never entirely completed until 1880.

1251 A.D.
Our Lady gives the Brown Scapular to St. Simon Stock.

1265-1273 A.D.
Thomas Aquinas writes his *Summa Theologica*.

1308-1311 A.D.
Duccio paints the *Maesta*.

1320 A.D.
Dante's *The Divine Comedy* is completed.

1476 A.D.
Chaucer's *The Canterbury Tales* are published.

Witness to the Faith 243

Mystery Play
A play that visually represented some element of the Faith, like the Incarnation or Crucifixion, or perhaps the life of a saint.

Guilds
Associations of artists or merchants in a particular trade. Thus, in a given city, there would be a guild of blacksmiths, a guild of weavers, etc.

through preaching and teaching. One means that was unique to the Middle Ages was the **mystery play**. These "plays" were simply visual enactments of the teachings of the Church on various topics, such as the Incarnation or Crucifixion, or a depiction of the life of a saint.

In early mystery plays, the actors, usually priests or clerics, would simply repeat Scripture, but over time the plays became more elaborate. Music was added, as was additional non-Biblical dialogue. By the thirteenth century, various **guilds** (associations of artists or merchants in a particular trade) began to stage the plays. The mystery plays started to look more like modern plays. They began to be performed in the public square rather than in the church. As they continued to develop, the mystery plays became the precursors to the plays of Shakespeare and other playwrights.

The Mass and the Sacraments

Although medieval Catholics had a deep devotion to Our Lord and His Church, they were still sinners. That was why Our Lord had instituted the Sacrament of Confession. Sadly, over time, some people had forgotten the value of frequent Confession.

In 1215, the Fourth Lateran Council issued a decree ordering Catholics to receive Holy Communion and go to Confession at least once a year. This decree shows that, even in the best of times, people need the Church's direction. The Lateran Council also decreed that *in the Roman Rite*, Catholics would receive only the Sacred Host as Communion. They would not receive under both species.

During the Middle Ages, the nature of penances began to change. First, public penances began to disappear. The Church imposed public penance only for grievous sins, such as a physical attack on a bishop. However, in a period when life was much rougher than it is today, a penance tended to reflect the harshness of the times. Although prayers were often given as penance, other penances included paying money, fasting, and making pilgrimages to holy places. In some cases, for serious sins, the penitent might be required to join a crusade. Penances also became more linked to doing good works on behalf of the Church, such as helping build the local church. As a result, the practice of granting indulgences also increased. The *Catechism of the Catholic Church* (no. 1471) defines an *indulgence* as follows:

> "An indulgence is a remission before God of the temporal punishment due to sins whose guilt has already been forgiven, which the faithful Christian who is duly disposed gains under certain prescribed conditions through the action of the Church which, as the minister of redemption, dispenses and applies with authority the treasury of the satisfactions of Christ and the saints."
>
> "An indulgence is partial or plenary according as it removes either part or all of the temporal punishment due to sin." The faithful can gain indulgences for themselves or apply them to the dead.

244 *Chapter 16: Medieval Society – The Glory of Christendom, Part II*

Simply put, an **indulgence** is a remission (reduction) of the temporal punishment due to sin, the guilt of which has already been forgiven. Therefore, to receive an indulgence, a penitent must confess his sins and be forgiven. A **partial indulgence** decreases the amount of temporal punishment that a person must undergo in Purgatory; a **plenary indulgence** removes all of it.

Unlike personal penances, such as saying a Rosary, indulgences tended to be made available to anyone in the universal Church who performed a specific act. For example, popes granted indulgences to anyone who went on a crusade. Pope Innocent III granted an indulgence to everyone who assisted in the construction of a bridge over the Rhone River. Innocent IV granted an indulgence to people who helped build Cologne Cathedral.

The Blessed Mother

Devotion to Our Blessed Mother was especially strong during the Middle Ages. In fact, some of the beautiful prayers that Catholics say today originated during this period. For example, the most popular devotion to Our Lady, *the Rosary*, developed during this time. Although no one is certain of the Rosary's exact origin, one popular Catholic tradition holds that St. Dominic received this devotion during a vision of the Blessed Mother. He used the Rosary to try to convert the Albigensians. Whether the tradition is accurate, Church historians do know that the structure of the Rosary gradually developed between the twelfth and fifteenth centuries. Catholics recited fifty Hail Marys that were connected with "Joyful" events from the lives of Jesus and Mary. This form of prayer came to be known as a *rosarium* (a "rose garden" for Mary). Over time, the Sorrowful and Glorious mysteries were added. By the sixteenth century, the Rosary that we know today with its five decades, based on the three sets of mysteries, with the Our Father preceding each, had come into existence. The Rosary remained unchanged until 2002, when Pope St. John Paul II added the Luminous mysteries.

The Middle Ages also saw the introduction of the devotional **scapular** (from the Latin word *scapula*, which means "shoulder blade"). By wearing a small scapular, Catholics could, in a way, imitate the monks. Perhaps the most popular scapular is the "Brown Scapular." According to tradition, Our Blessed Lady, in her role as Our Lady of Mount Carmel, appeared to St. Simon Stock, an English monk, in 1251. She gave him the Brown Scapular, with the promise that no one who died wearing it would suffer the pains of Hell. To date, the Church has approved eighteen different types of scapulars.

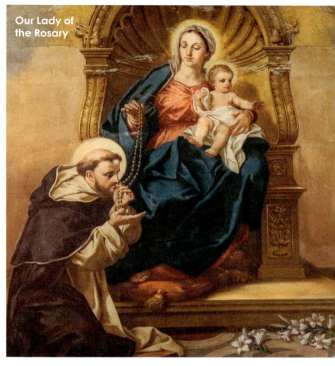

Our Lady of the Rosary

> **Scapular**
> A word meaning "shoulder blade"; refers to a kind of sacramental worn between the shoulders. The best known is the Brown Scapular, worn in honor of Our Lady of Mount Carmel.

Witness to the Faith 245

Scholasticism

> **Scholasticism**
> A method of study and teaching in medieval scholarly circles; emphasized the harmony between faith and reason.

The period known as the Middle Ages was the golden age for philosophy and theology. Led by such brilliant minds as St. Albert the Great, St. Thomas Aquinas, and St. Bonaventure, the Church developed a new philosophy: **Scholasticism**. These great thinkers knew that God is the Author of creation and that nothing in science can contradict Him, Divine Revelation, or Scripture. Scholasticism demonstrated the harmony that exists between faith and reason. It proves that Catholicism is *reasonable*. The arguments of the Scholastics are as valid today as they were more than seven hundred years ago.

In addition to a new philosophy, the Middle Ages also saw great developments in Catholic theology. Three conditions made these developments possible. The first was the rise of the universities, which became centers for theological dialogue. The second was the arrival in the universities of new teachers, especially those belonging to the Dominican and Franciscan Orders. Finally, theology blossomed with the rediscovery and analysis of Aristotle's teachings by these orders.

The Church and the Universities

Despite the contention of its critics, the Catholic Church is now, and always has been, the great leader in education at all levels. Nowhere is this more apparent than at the university level, where the Church established the great medieval universities. For example, the University of Salerno, founded in the ninth century, was the finest medical school of the Middle Ages. The University of Bologna, founded in 1088, was a great law school, teaching both civil and canon law. Today, it is considered the oldest operating university in the world. Finally, the University of Paris (also known as the Sorbonne) was founded in 1150. It was the best theological and philosophical institution in the world.

In time, the University of Paris became the most important educational institution in Christendom and gradually came under the direct authority of the pope. The popes then began to consider it the Church's official school of theology. The popes also started relying on this university's professors to analyze and judge possible heresies. St. Dominic recognized the excellence of this university and insisted that all his Dominicans attend it. In time, Dominicans (such as **St. Albert the Great** and **St. Thomas Aquinas**) and Franciscans (such as **St. Bonaventure**) became the leading professors at the University of Paris.

St. Bonaventure, also known as the "Seraphic Doctor," received his master of theology in 1257 from the University of Paris. He later became the seventh general of the Franciscan Order. Bonaventure also worked for the election of Pope Gregory X, a fellow Franciscan. Bonaventure's writings are numerous, but he always regarded philosophy as the assistant of theology. Thus, St. Augustine and Aristotle influenced his writings. In his work *The Triple Way*, which he wrote for his fellow Franciscans, he describes the three paths that lead to God: meditation, prayer, and

St. Bonaventure

> **St. Albert the Great**
> Dominican teacher and scholar; helped make Aristotle accessible to Western students; best known as the teacher of St. Thomas Aquinas.

> **St. Thomas Aquinas**
> A Dominican and one of the greatest minds of the Church; also drew much on Aristotle, and had a great influence on subsequent theology.

> **St. Bonaventure**
> A Franciscan scholar, theologian, and spiritual writer, known as the "Seraphic Doctor."

contemplation. Bonaventure died in 1274 and was canonized in 1482. In 1588, Pope Sixtus V declared him a Doctor of the Church.

St. Albert the Great was born around 1200 in Bavaria. While studying at the University of Padua, he decided to join the Dominicans, and he became a member around 1223. Throughout the remainder of his life, he wrote and taught extensively, mostly in Germany. Between 1245 and 1248, he composed a sort of scientific encyclopedia, which made all the teachings of Aristotle accessible to Western students. Pope Alexander IV officially approved his encyclopedia in 1256. Albert subsequently became a theology professor at the University of Paris. He died at Cologne on November 15, 1280. Pope Pius XI canonized him and proclaimed him a Doctor of the Church in 1932.

While at the University of Paris, St. Albert the Great taught the greatest mind that the Catholic Church has ever known: St. Thomas Aquinas. Born in 1225 in Aquino, Italy, St. Thomas first studied at the monastery school at Monte Cassino. Later, he studied at the University of Naples, where he encountered a Dominican preacher who influenced him to join the new order. Despite the protests of his family, who strongly objected to his decision, St. Thomas became a Dominican. In 1245, the order sent

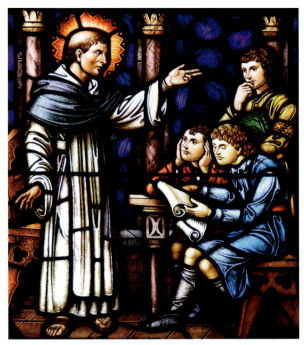

St. Albert the Great Teaching

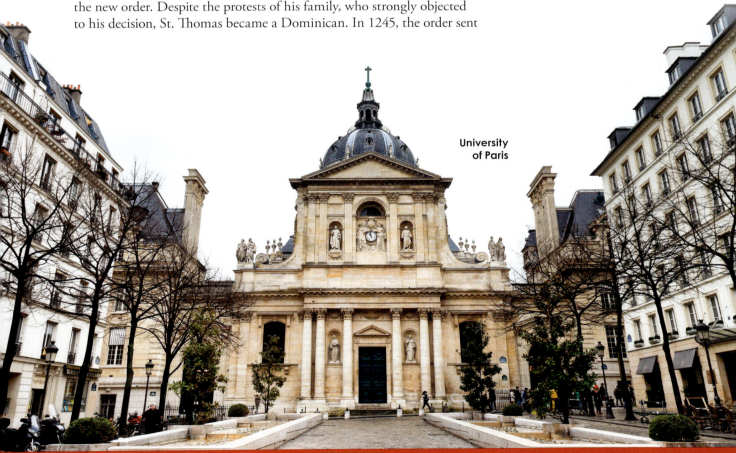

University of Paris

Witness to the Faith

him to Paris, where he studied under Albert the Great and received his doctorate. He later accompanied Albert when he returned to Cologne. In 1252, Thomas returned to Paris. In 1256, he became a professor of theology at the University of Paris.

Throughout his time teaching, Thomas wrote extensively. In 1261, Pope Urban IV called Thomas to Rome, together with the Flemish preacher William of Moerbeke. Urban asked William to translate Aristotle directly from the Greek, and he asked St. Thomas to comment on Aristotle based on the new translation.

Thomas wrote his greatest work, the *Summa Theologica*, between 1265 and 1274. A summary of both Catholic theology and philosophy, the *Summa* is probably the leading work on these subjects. It summarizes all of Western theology up to that point in time. The *Summa* covers the existence of God and His attributes. It discusses the angels, the creation and nature of man, and mankind's salvation by means of the sacraments. It deals with the divine government, virtues, vices, and laws.

In December 1273, as Thomas prayed before the crucifix, he had a mystical experience in which Our Lord appeared to him. From this moment on, Thomas would write no more, stating that all he had written seemed "like straw" to him. Thus, the *Summa* remained unfinished.

In 1274, Pope Gregory X summoned St. Thomas to the Council of Lyons, not realizing that Thomas was ill. On the way, Thomas struck his head heavily on a low-hanging branch across the road. He died on March 7, 1274. He was only 49 years old. Thomas Aquinas was canonized in 1324. Pope Leo XIII declared him the patron saint of Catholic schools and scholars. St. Thomas is called the *Angelic Doctor*, as much for the clarity and precision of his writings as for the holiness of his life.

The Church and Education

While cathedral schools, monastery schools, and universities provided a higher (or "secondary") education, the Church also operated schools that offered boys and girls an "elementary" education. Some of these were run by the local parish priest. In addition, there were the "chantry schools." These schools developed from the donations that wealthy donors made to build a chapel in a local church or a special altar in a cathedral. Also, then as now, people donated money when asking that Mass be said for the repose of the soul of a friend or family member. Such a donation, whether it was given for a chapel or in conjunction with a Mass request, was called a *chantry*. The priest who received the donation used the money to provide a free education for the poor.

As the Middle Ages dawned, most Europeans, including the kings and nobility, were illiterate. Usually only clerics could read and write. However, over time, with the development of the universities and elementary schools, more and more people were able to read and write a little. It seems safe to assume that by the time the Middle Ages ended in the middle of the fifteenth century, most people, with the exception

St. Thomas Aquinas

of the very poorest, could read and write. This fact is supported by the rapid development and spread of the printing press at that time. If the majority of the people could not read and write, there would not have been such a great demand for books to be printed.

Charitable Institutions

Since its beginning, the Catholic Church has been the world's leading charitable institution. The Apostles appointed seven deacons to assist in the care of the poor. Since then, the Church has established hospitals, homes for the aged, and orphanages around the world. Even its greatest enemies acknowledge the Church's charitable efforts.

As the Church grew and became a greater part of European society, it established hospitals, homes for the elderly and the poor, and refuges for pilgrims. All of these efforts increased during the Middle Ages. Priests and religious worked tirelessly to care for the poor and sick during the Black Plague.

The Catholic Church, especially through the Franciscan Order, also created money-lending organizations known as *montes pietatis* (Latin, meaning "mountains of mercy"). These charitable organizations lent money at either very low interest or no interest. At a time when it was difficult to obtain money, this gave people an opportunity to borrow money in cases of emergency or other needs. The first *montes pietatis* organization was founded in London in 1361.

Literature

The High Middle Ages saw the creation of some of the world's greatest literature. Two men especially are associated with this period: **Dante Alighieri** and **Geoffrey Chaucer**. Their impact on world literature rings down through the ages.

Of the two men, Dante (c. 1265-1321) is probably the more important, since he influenced Chaucer. His monumental work, *The Divine Comedy*, is generally ranked the most important work of the Middle Ages and the greatest piece of literature ever written in the Italian language. Unlike other literary works, which were written in Latin, *The Divine Comedy* was written in Italian, which made it more accessible to the average Italian. In fact, Dante is often credited with inventing the modern Italian language.

The true greatness of *The Divine Comedy* lies in Dante's depictions of the afterlife. In *The Divine Comedy*, Dante describes his journey through Hell, Purgatory, and Paradise. Yet, while he writes as a poet, the work contains the theology of the Catholic Church, as Dante allegorically describes the soul's journey to God. Thomas Aquinas might well have written *The Divine Comedy* had he been a poet. It has had a lasting impact on artists and authors since its completion in 1320.

Among those most influenced by Dante's work was Geoffrey Chaucer (c. 1343-1400), who is often considered the "Father of English Literature."

Dante Alighieri

> **Dante Alighieri**
> Great Italian poet; author of *The Divine Comedy*.

> **Geoffrey Chaucer**
> Called the "father of English literature"; author of *The Canterbury Tales*.

> **The Divine Comedy**
> Dante's masterpiece, an account of a journey through Hell, Purgatory, and Heaven, allegorically describing the soul's journey to God.

Witness to the Faith

Chaucer wrote many books. However, his masterpiece is **The Canterbury Tales**, in which a group of pilgrims traveling from London to the shrine of Thomas Becket in Canterbury relate various stories to pass the time on their journey. In the twenty-four stories that comprise *The Canterbury Tales*, Chaucer uses the tales and the descriptions of the pilgrims to render an account of England at the time. He portrays members of all the social classes, as well as members of the clergy.

Medieval Architecture

Romanesque

The eleventh century saw the advent of the style of architecture known as **Romanesque**. The main feature of Romanesque architecture was the use of round arches and very thick walls. The walls had to be thick to support the roof, which, instead of being flat and wooden, was arched and built of stone like the rest of the building. Also, so that the walls could hold their full strength, they were built without large windows. This accounts for the semidarkness usually found in Romanesque churches. The most beautiful examples of Romanesque churches are the cathedrals of Speyer, Worms, and Mainz.

Gothic

Although Romanesque churches are certainly beautiful, most viewers would describe them as "short and squat." Moreover, because they lack windows, their interiors are dark. As medieval architects began to understand construction techniques better, they developed the defining architectural form of the Middle Ages: **Gothic architecture**.

The term "Gothic" was originally created for architecture, and architecture remains the area in which its characteristics are most easily

Geoffrey Chaucer

The Canterbury Tales
Chaucer's masterpiece, about pilgrims who tell stories while traveling to St. Thomas Becket's shrine at Canterbury.

Romanesque
A style of architecture characterized by round arches and very thick walls.

Gothic Architecture
A style marked by pointed arches, thinner and higher walls, large stained-glass windows, and flying buttresses.

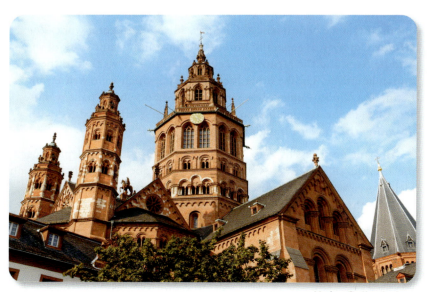

Mainz Cathedral

250 *Chapter 16: Medieval Society – The Glory of Christendom, Part II*

identified. The Gothic style was the leading form of architecture from about 1140 to 1250, the Age of the great cathedrals. In the beginning, Gothic sculpture was part of the church building. The finest Gothic sculptures were created between 1220 and 1420. Artists created the greatest Gothic paintings between 1300 and 1350 in central Italy. This style of painting flourished north of the Alps after 1400.

Three features distinguish Gothic architecture. The first is pointed arches rather than round arches. Pointed arches, which are stronger than round arches, allow for thinner and higher walls. This allowed architects to design churches with spires and walls that soar heavenward. Second, because the walls are thinner, Gothic churches have **large stained-glass windows**, which allow light to flood into the church. Finally, Gothic churches have **flying buttresses** (external supports), which help support the high walls.

Gothic architecture was born at the Basilica of Saint-Denis, a few miles north of Paris, about 1140. From St. Denis, it spread to the rest of France, and by 1400 to almost all of Europe. It dominated architecture for the next two hundred years. Today, Gothic architecture has spread throughout the world, including the United States. St. Patrick's Cathedral in New York City is perhaps the most famous example in America. The man most responsible for developing the Gothic style was not an architect; he was an abbot. His vision changed not only the face of Europe but also the face of the world.

In 1122, a monk named **Suger** became abbot of St. Denis, the royal abbey church. The Basilica of Saint-Denis was one of the most important churches in France because it contained the relics of St. Denis, the first bishop of Paris and the man who brought the Faith to Gaul. Denis and his two companions preached in the area around what is now Paris, and built a church on one of the islands in the Seine River. However, the large number of conversions angered the local pagans, who seized and beheaded St. Denis and his companions in 275. (Artists usually portray St. Denis carrying his head because, according to legend, after he was beheaded he carried his head into town.) The Christians buried the three martyrs and erected a small shrine over their graves.

Early in the seventh century, Benedictine monks refounded the church as the Abbey Church of Saint-Denis. In the ninth century, the monks built a beautiful basilica that held both the saints' relics and the tombs of almost all the Frankish kings. As the site of the tombs of the Frankish kings, the Basilica of Saint-Denis became the royal church of France. By 1122, when Suger became abbot, the old basilica had fallen into disrepair.

From what historians know of Abbot Suger, he seems to have been a most remarkable man. Born in 1081 to commoners, he rose over time to become the chief advisor to both King Louis VI and King Louis VII. When Louis VII joined the Second Crusade, Suger governed as regent of France.

Even before Suger became abbot, the Basilica of Saint-Denis had played a dual role in French society. First, it had religious significance as the shrine of St. Denis, the patron saint of France. Second, it had

> **Flying Buttresses**
> External supports reaching from the upper walls of a building to another structure below, rather than to the ground.

> **Suger**
> Abbot of the Basilica of Saint-Denis who oversaw its reconstruction; chief advisor to King Louis VI and King Louis VII.

Abbot Suger

Witness to the Faith 251

Interior of the Basilica of Saint-Denis in Paris

political importance as the chief memorial of the Carolingian dynasty. Pepin, the first Carolingian king, and Charlemagne had been consecrated kings there. Moreover, it was the burial place of the French kings. Suger wanted to make St. Denis a pilgrimage church where pilgrims would feel both religious and patriotic enthusiasm. To become the greatest pilgrimage church in France, the old basilica had to be enlarged and rebuilt. In 1135, Abbot Suger began rebuilding St. Denis, but he died before the church was finished.

Suger wrote extensively about this reconstruction of his beloved St. Denis. He writes with such detail that some art historians believe Suger designed the new Basilica of Saint-Denis, making him the "inventor" of Gothic architecture. Other historians point out that Suger had no training in architecture and that he almost certainly relied on master builders. Even if the latter historians are correct, they should credit Suger for recognizing how fresh and extraordinary the new artistic style was.

Upon entering St. Denis, the visitor is struck not only by the serenity of the basilica but also by the lightness of the interior. The lightness is of two kinds. First, colored light, which pours through the yards and yards of stained glass, fills the church. The glass is no longer just a hole in the wall, but has in fact become a translucent wall. Second, compared to the heaviness of the Romanesque style, the architectural forms of St. Denis are incredibly light and graceful.

Higher, thinner walls are not the only reason for the abundance of stained-glass window light in St. Denis. Another cause is the heavy buttresses that jut out between the chapels and contain the outward pressure of the vault (ceiling). The main weight of the construction is concentrated on them, yet they are visible only from the outside. The interior appears so wonderfully airy because visitors cannot see the heaviest parts of the structural frame.

The great cathedrals erected throughout Europe in the twelfth and thirteenth centuries are not simply magnificent architectural achievements. They are enduring reminders of the great love that the people had for God and the Church.

Notre Dame de Paris

No cathedral better reflects the Gothic style than the **Cathedral of Notre Dame of Paris**, begun in 1163. Notre Dame is located on an island in the Seine River. Pointed arches are used throughout the church, allowing for thin, high walls that are filled with windows. To hold these tall, thin walls, a new system of buttresses had to be used.

The architect of Notre Dame chose to use **flying buttresses**, exterior supporting arches that reach upward to the critical spots where the outward thrust of the ceiling is concentrated, thus countering that thrust. Flying buttresses had been used a decade earlier in some smaller Gothic churches; however, Notre Dame is the first massive cathedral in which they were used. Though originally designed for its practical applications, the flying buttress soon became artistically important. Architects began to design them in a variety of intriguing styles. Like most Gothic cathedrals, because of its sheer size, Notre Dame needs to be seen from a bit of a distance in order to be fully appreciated. The flying buttresses, the pinnacles, and the rose window with its tracery work together in a remarkable harmony that Abbot Suger surely would have appreciated.

| **Cathedral of Notre Dame of Paris** One of the best-known Gothic cathedrals.

Cathedral of Notre Dame, Paris

Witness to the Faith

Gothic Architecture Spreads

In 1269, the abbot of a monastery in the German Rhineland hired an architect from Paris to rebuild his church. The architect rebuilt the church in the Gothic style. This style had actually begun to spread even earlier; however, by the second half of the thirteenth century, it had become the dominant style in Western Europe. A number of factors contributed to the rapid spread of Gothic art. First, as the German abbot recognized, French sculptors and architects were incredibly talented. Second, France possessed a high status in Europe because it had some of the greatest centers of learning in the world (for example, the University of Paris). In the end, the most obvious reason for the international spread of Gothic art was the extraordinary beauty of the style itself. People who saw Gothic churches fell in love with them. They still do.

Germany

In Germany, the Romanesque tradition remained dominant until about the middle of the thirteenth century. However, by about 1250, the Gothic style began to have a strong impact on the Rhineland. Cologne Cathedral, begun in 1248, represents an ambitious attempt to implement the French system. Interestingly, the cathedral was not finished until 600 years later.

Archbishop Konrad von Hochstaden laid the foundation stone for Cologne Cathedral on August 15, 1248. Work continued slowly until about 1530. Then lack of money and a general lack of interest stopped the construction. Builders enclosed the cathedral with a makeshift roof. Although unfinished, the cathedral was still large and suitable for services, which the people of Cologne apparently considered satisfactory. They continued to decorate the interior over the following centuries. However, from 1560 until 1842, *work on the exterior stopped completely*.

In 1794, French revolutionary soldiers captured Cologne. They desecrated the cathedral and began using it for secular purposes. However, in 1801 it was reconsecrated as a church.

In 1842, the designs for the fourteenth-century facade were unexpectedly discovered. This discovery, coupled with the nineteenth century's enthusiasm for the Middle Ages and the Prussian government's financial backing, caused construction of the cathedral to resume. "Gothic revival" architects completed the cathedral according to the original plans. They added the two 515-foot towers and the 422-foot nave with its two side aisles, making Cologne the largest cathedral

Konrad von Hochstanden

Cologne Cathedral

254   Chapter 16: Medieval Society – The Glory of Christendom, Part II

in northern Europe. In 1880, the completion of Cologne Cathedral was celebrated as a national holiday.

While the nineteenth-century builders strictly followed the medieval plans as to the cathedral's form, they used modern building techniques. Thus, the outer appearance looks like the original Gothic church, but iron construction covers the entire building, and the roof was a modern steel construction. As a result, the cathedral is remarkably well constructed. During World War II, fourteen aerial bombs hit it. However, once its windows were blown out, the later explosions caused no serious damage.

Italy

Milan Cathedral

When the people of Milan decided to rebuild their cathedral, they invited architects not only from Italy but also from Germany and France. The various architects never agreed on the cathedral's design, so the final product was a compromise between the experts and the city leaders. Proportionately, Milan Cathedral is typically Italian, meaning that it is very wide in relation to its height. The exterior of the cathedral, with its decoration and delicate stonework, is clearly Gothic. In fact, the pinnacles and the fine tracery might be found on almost any Gothic cathedral in France. However, like so many great cathedrals, Milan Cathedral took centuries to build, and during that time, new ideas in art emerged.

Begun in 1386, Milan Cathedral was not completed until 1910. Thus, while it started during an era when the Gothic style was in fashion, before long, the Italian Renaissance style became predominant, and the Gothic became outdated. As a result, the cathedral's facade is a mix of late Gothic and early Renaissance styles. The interior contains huge stained-glass windows (68 by 28 feet). The cathedral is built from brick covered with marble. The roof of the cathedral is renowned for the forest of openwork pinnacles and spires, set upon delicate flying buttresses.

Stained-Glass Windows

More than any other art form, stained-glass windows defined the Gothic cathedral. Stained glass was an integral part of Gothic architecture from the beginning. However, the art of making colored glass is very old. Ancient Egyptian artists fashioned many intricate colored-glass objects. Architects had used colored glass in churches as early as the fourth century. This skill developed over time, and by the Romanesque period, the art of crafting stained glass was well known.

Immaculate Conception Stained-Glass Window from the Cathedral of Mdina in Malta

Witness to the Faith   **255**

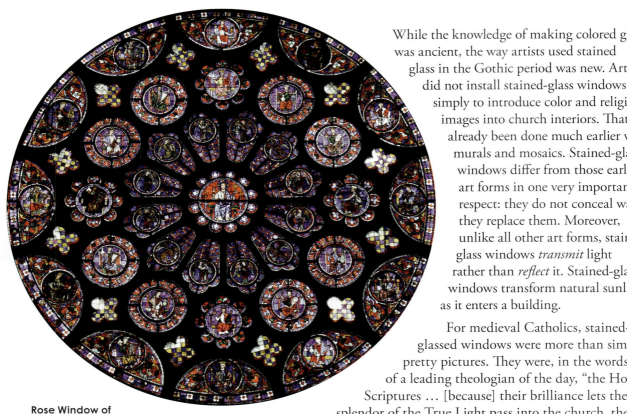

Rose Window of Chartres Cathedral

While the knowledge of making colored glass was ancient, the way artists used stained glass in the Gothic period was new. Artists did not install stained-glass windows simply to introduce color and religious images into church interiors. That had already been done much earlier with murals and mosaics. Stained-glass windows differ from those earlier art forms in one very important respect: they do not conceal walls; they replace them. Moreover, unlike all other art forms, stained-glass windows *transmit* light rather than *reflect* it. Stained-glass windows transform natural sunlight as it enters a building.

For medieval Catholics, stained-glassed windows were more than simply pretty pictures. They were, in the words of a leading theologian of the day, "the Holy Scriptures … [because] their brilliance lets the splendor of the True Light pass into the church, they enlighten those inside." Another thirteenth-century theologian wrote that stained-glass windows were "Holy Scriptures, which expel the wind and the rain, that is, all things hurtful, but transmit the light of the True Sun, that is God, into the hearts of the faithful."

Gothic Sculpture

During the Gothic period, most of the great sculpture was fashioned for the facades of the Gothic churches. **The Royal Portals** on the west facade of Chartres Cathedral, which were created between 1145 and 1155, are probably the oldest and most complete examples of early Gothic sculpture. Chartres Cathedral's western entrance is known as the "Royal Portals" because of the statue columns of the Old Testament kings and queens that flank the three doorways.

The sculptors of the Royal Portals have proclaimed the greatness of Our Lord by carving scenes from His life. Above the doorway on the right portal, the Child Jesus sits in the lap of His Blessed Mother. Immediately below this scene is the Presentation in the Temple, and below this are the Annunciation, Visitation, Nativity, and Proclamation to the Shepherds.

The left portal shows Our Lord's Ascension into Heaven on a cloud with two angels at His side. Immediately below this are angels, and below the angels are Apostles.

The central portal shows the Last Judgment. Christ is enthroned within a **mandorla** and surrounded by the symbols of the four

---

The Royal Portals
The doors on the west facade of Chartres Cathedral, flanked by statues of Old Testament kings and queens and carved with images from the life of Christ.

Mandorla
Meaning "almond"; an almond-shaped frame of light surrounding the figure of a holy person, especially Jesus or Mary, in sacred art.

The Royal Portals, Chartres Cathedral

evangelists. Below him in the lintel are the Twelve Apostles. The main difference between this Last Judgment and those of the Romanesque period is the nature of Our Lord. He seems less a figure of judgment, and more a figure of love and salvation.

Even more interesting is the central role of Our Lady on the portal. On this portal, the artist has sculpted a depiction of the teaching that Mary is mediatrix for the faithful. During the Gothic age, the role of Our Lady in salvation history was stressed much more than it had been. Her image appeared more often. Almost every Gothic cathedral in France was named "Notre Dame" ("Our Lady") in her honor. She became the ultimate symbol of womanhood. Artists replaced Romanesque sternness with Gothic gentleness in the person of the Blessed Mother.

The doorjambs of the Royal Portals are decorated with kings and queens from the Old Testament. These Old Testament figures are dressed in twelfth-century clothing, which caused most contemporary observers to believe they were images of the kings and queens of France. These early Gothic statues began to show a new realism and naturalism that was not present in Romanesque statues. This realism is most evident in the statues' faces. The statues generally possess a happy appearance rather than the mask-like severity of Romanesque statues. The statues would have appeared even more lifelike because of the paint that originally decorated them.

When the Chartres Cathedral's sculptors began to render statues with realistic human faces, they started a trend that continued into

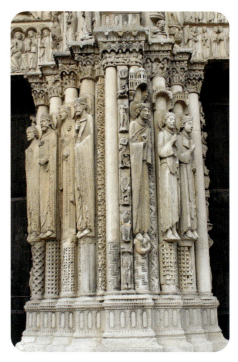

Doorjamb Statues of the Royal Portals, Chartres Cathedral

Witness to the Faith 257

modern times. Artists became concerned with portraying individuality and personality. Around 1400, artists began to depict specific people.

Lorenzo Ghiberti

Between 1330 and 1335, Andrea Pisano designed the south doors for the baptistery of San Giovanni in Florence. In 1401, the wool merchants' guild sponsored a competition to find a sculptor to design bronze doors for the baptistery's north entrance. Each contestant would submit a panel showing "The Sacrifice of Isaac" at the moment the angel grabs Abraham's arm, stopping him from killing his son. Of all the panels submitted, only those of the two finalists, **Filippo Brunelleschi** (1377-1446) and **Lorenzo Ghiberti** (1378-1455), have survived.

Brunelleschi's panel is a masterpiece of Gothic art. It shows a frantic angel lunging at the knife to halt Abraham in the instant before he kills his son. He presents the biblical story in an emotional and dramatic fashion. Yet he lost the competition!

Ghiberti's panel is also a perfectly crafted masterpiece. The smooth shimmer of the surfaces and the exquisitely precise detail caused the wool merchants to award him the prize. Unlike Brunelleschi's dramatic panel, Ghiberti's panel exudes a certain calmness and elegance. Ghiberti's angel seems not to rush to the rescue. Abraham seems to have paused briefly after drawing back his knife to strike.

Filippo Brunelleschi
Italian artist and architect, best known for designing the dome of Florence's cathedral; competed with Ghiberti to design the doors for Florence's baptistery.

Lorenzo Ghiberti
Italian artist; created the doors of the baptistery in Florence.

The Sacrifice of Isaac, Filippo Brunelleschi

The Sacrifice of Isaac, Lorenzo Ghiberti

258 *Chapter 16: Medieval Society – The Glory of Christendom, Part II*

Northern Baptistery Doors of San Giovanni in Florence, Lorenzo Ghiberti

Witness to the Faith

Painting

At the beginning of the fourteenth century, Italy produced an explosion of creative energy as spectacular and as far-reaching as the rise of the Gothic cathedrals in France. Medieval Italy had always maintained close contact with Byzantine civilization. In fact, the Byzantine style had dominated medieval Italian painting.

Cimabue

> **Cimabue**
> Italian artist, one of the first to begin experimenting with the realism and three-dimensional depth absent from Byzantine art.

One of the first Italian artists who began moving away from the Byzantine style was a Florentine painter named Cenni di Pepo, better known as **Cimabue** (c. 1240-1302). His huge altar panel, *The Madonna Enthroned with Angels and Prophets*, rivals the finest Byzantine icons. Yet, despite his reliance on the Byzantine style, especially in the faces and the gold background, viewers begin to see the realism that characterizes the Gothic style. In a sense, Cimabue took Byzantine art ideas and applied the Gothic style to them, and he created a three-dimensional depth that is missing in Byzantine art.

Duccio

While Cimabue was painting in Florence, one of the greatest Italian painters of the Middle Ages, Duccio di Buoninsegna (c. 1255-1318), was laboring in Siena. Like Cimabue, Duccio blended the stiffness of Byzantine art with the new spirituality and naturalism of the Gothic style. The greatest of all his works is the *Maesta* (*The Virgin Mary Enthroned in Majesty*), the huge altarpiece for Siena Cathedral's main altar.

Commissioned to paint the *Maesta* in 1308, Duccio and his assistants took nearly three years to complete it. (Like a good Catholic, Duccio signed the painting, "Holy Mother of God, grant peace to Siena, and life to Duccio because he has painted you thus.") The *Maesta* was a large horizontal rectangle painted on both sides, since it could be seen from all directions when installed on the main altar.

The front central panel shows the Madonna and Child enthroned in the middle of a heavenly court of saints and angels. Siena's four patron saints kneel at their feet. The Blessed Mother, whom Duccio has painted slightly larger than the other figures, sits on a large and magnificent throne of multicolored marbles. She inclines her head slightly as if listening to the prayers of the faithful.

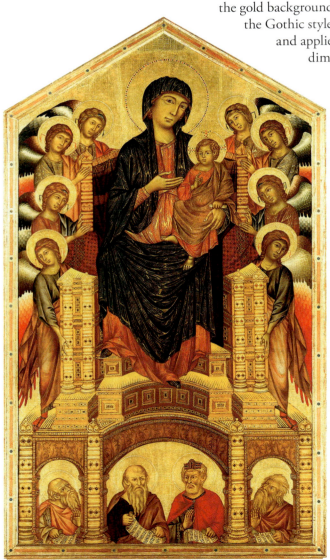

The Madonna Enthroned with Angels and Prophets, Cimabue

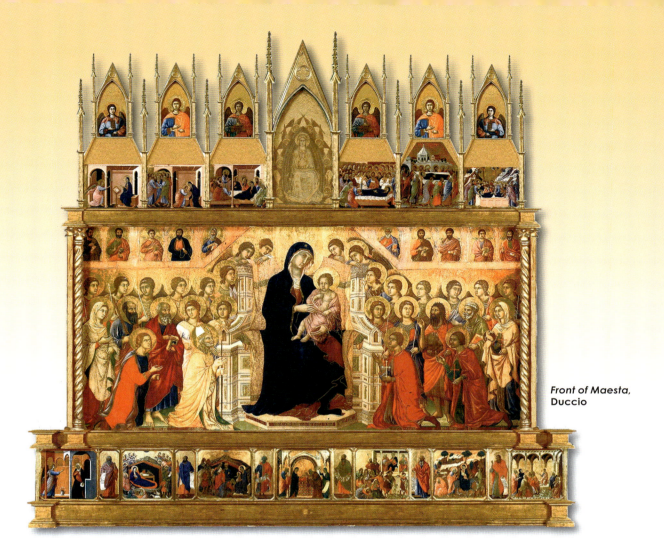

Front of Maesta, Duccio

The stiffness and the symmetry with which Duccio has arranged the groups of adoring figures show the influence of the Byzantine tradition. Yet Duccio softens the Byzantine style. For example, the characters turn to interact with one another, and they glance affectionately at one another. Also, their clothes fit naturally on their bodies. Most remarkably, the facial features of each of the thirty figures are unique and beautiful. This is especially evident in the naturalness of the curly-haired Baby Jesus. Duccio thus perfectly blends the Byzantine ideal of power and dignity with the Gothic spirit of tenderness and realism.

Oral Exercises

1. Name the three great medieval universities.
2. What was St. Thomas Aquinas' greatest work?
3. What was the main feature of Romanesque architecture?
4. What are the three main features of Gothic architecture?
5. For whom were most Gothic cathedrals in France named?
6. Who painted the *Maesta*?

Witness to the Faith

Chapter 17
The Western Schism

Location of Viterbo, Italy

Conclave
The method designated for papal elections at the Second Council of Lyons, by which cardinals remain gathered in isolation until they elect a pope.

Introduction

The nearly three-year stalemate that finally resulted in the election of Pope Gregory X demonstrated the terrible conflict between the French and Italian cardinals in the Sacred College. Despite their sacred duty, they simply could not work together. During those nearly three years, both prelates and kings addressed the Sacred College, which was meeting at Viterbo. They told the cardinals that their failure to elect a pope was causing great harm and scandal to the entire Church. Still, they did not elect a pope. In desperation, the people of Viterbo took the roof off the building in which the Sacred College was meeting, thus exposing the cardinals to the elements! Still, they did not elect a pope. Finally, a six-man commission, with three cardinals from each side, elected Pope Gregory X. However, the writing was on the wall. The French and Italian cardinals could not work together. A disaster was in the offing.

The Cardinals

In an attempt to prevent a disaster, Gregory X convoked the Second Council of Lyons in 1274. Among its other decrees, it created specific rules regarding the duties that the cardinals had in the election of the pope. The role of the cardinals had been expanding over the years as

262 *Chapter 17: The Western Schism*

St. Catherine of Siena Persuading the Pope to Return to Rome

1268 A.D. – 1414 A.D.

1268-1271 A.D.
A papal election is deadlocked for over two years, ultimately ending with the election of Pope Gregory X.

1274 A.D.
Pope Gregory X calls the Council of Lyons, which rules that after a pope's death, the cardinals must hold a "conclave" to elect a new pope.

1303 A.D.
Philip IV sends men to kidnap Pope Boniface VIII. Boniface is rescued but dies shortly after.

1305 A.D.
The "Babylonian Captivity" begins.

1347 A.D.
The Black Death sweeps across Europe, wiping out a large percent of the population.

1367-1369 A.D.
Pope Urban V takes up his seat in Rome, but returns to Avignon only two years later.

1377 A.D.
At the urging of St. Catherine of Siena, Pope Gregory XI finally returns the papacy to Rome.

1378 A.D.
After Gregory XI's death in March, his successor, Urban VI, soon has to deal with an antipope. The resulting division drags on for thirty-seven years.

1409 A.D.
The Council of Pisa attempts to resolve the schism, but instead ends up electing a second antipope.

1414 A.D.
The Council of Constance finally resolves the schism.

---

the Church had grown. For example, the pope had come to rely more often on the cardinals for advice on matters of faith and morals. He would seek their counsel on serious matters such as canonizations and the approval of religious orders. Because the cardinals were often more familiar with their own nations than the pope, he also consulted with them before deciding to create a new episcopal see or a new university. However, their single most important duty remained the election of a new pope. Thus, to motivate the cardinals to act swiftly, the Council of Lyons decreed that ten days after the pope's death, the cardinals were to gather and be sequestered from the rest of the world in "**conclave**" (from the Latin phrase *cum clave*, meaning "with a key"). The council fathers hoped to avoid another three-year papal vacancy.

Witness to the Faith 263

Gregory X

Innocent V

Adrian IV

John XXI

Nicholas III

Conclaves of Conflict

Pope Gregory X, the last of the great medieval popes, became sick during Christmas 1275. Two weeks later, he was dead. Had he done nothing more than name Rudolf of Hapsburg emperor, his pontificate would still have ranked as one of the most successful in Church history. His successors, on the other hand, would lack his wisdom and foresight. Though none would teach error, they would act imprudently in secular matters.

Following the death of Blessed Gregory X, the cardinals elected a number of popes who had short pontificates. Innocent V (1276), Adrian IV (1276), John XXI (1276-1277), and Nicholas III (1277-1280) all reigned briefly. The conclave that elected Nicholas had four Italian cardinals and three French cardinals. The conclave would have been deadlocked had one of the French cardinals not died!

Although Nicholas III reigned for less than three years, he appointed nine new cardinals, including three non-Italians. Moreover, two of the nine were Dominicans and two were Franciscans. Unlike so many others, Nicholas understood that the Church came before nationalities. Throughout his brief pontificate, he appointed Dominicans and Franciscans to high positions in the Church. Unfortunately, although he appeared strong and vigorous, Nicholas died in August 1280; he was 64 years old.

When the new conclave met, anti-Italian forces captured one of the Italian cardinals. As a result, the remaining twelve cardinals elected Cardinal Simon de Brion, who was French. He took the name Martin IV (1281-1285). Although the Italian cardinal had been imprisoned, he never objected to Martin's consecration. Thus, the election was valid. However, Martin proved to be a very poor pope.

First, whereas previous popes, dating back to Innocent III, had tried desperately to bring the Eastern Empire back into the Church, Martin excommunicated the Byzantine emperor. Martin seems to have taken this action simply to justify the desire of his sponsor, Charles of Naples, a French king, to conquer Constantinople. Second, throughout his pontificate, Martin supported Charles at the expense of other Christians. In early 1284, the people of Rome became so incensed that they rose up against Martin, forcing him to withdraw some of his support for Charles. Martin died in 1285. During his four years as pope, he deepened the wounds of the Great Eastern Schism and acted as an agent of the French crown. Though not personally a bad man, Martin IV may have inflicted more harm on the Church than any pope before or since.

The conclave that elected his successor chose Honorius IV (1285-1287), a 75-year-old Italian whom none of the cardinals expected to live long; he did not. But he did recognize the Carmelite Order in 1286.

Upon his death, the conclave of fifteen cardinals was again deadlocked. The stalemate lasted from spring until summer. During

264 *Chapter 17: The Western Schism*

Rome's summer heat, seven cardinals died. The rest fled the city without electing a pope. It was clear that politics had become more important to the cardinals than religion. However, in February they managed to elect a Franciscan cardinal. This good and holy man took the name Nicholas IV (1288-1292).

During his reign, Nicholas tried to organize a crusade. However, Martin IV had declared a crusade against Christians in Spain and Sicily on behalf of Charles of Naples, thus mortally wounding the crusading spirit. Rudolf of Hapsburg, who might have led the crusade, lay on his deathbed, and no other European king had any interest in taking up the Cross. Thus, the crusade never materialized. In 1291, Acre, the last outpost of the crusader kingdom, fell to the Muslims. The crusades were over; the Christians had lost.

Nicholas died in April 1292. The conclave that met to elect his successor consisted of only twelve cardinals. Once again, they could not elect a pope, because they all had political agendas. The cardinals argued fruitlessly for four months, during which time one of the French cardinals died. The rest fled the city. After more than two years, the cardinals finally elected the saintly hermit Peter Murrone, who took the name Celestine V (1294). Lacking any understanding of the intrigues that now infected the papacy, Pope Celestine quickly became aware that he was unfit to be pope. He resigned after five months. However, Pope Celestine V, who would later be canonized, created twelve new cardinals.

Having just experienced a two-year vacancy, none of the cardinals wanted a repeat performance. Thus, in just a few days, the cardinals elected Benedetto Caetani, a 60-year-old Italian cardinal, who chose the name Boniface VIII (1294-1303). Boniface was a man of exceptional ability and strong beliefs. Almost immediately, he came into conflict with France, which was slowly replacing Germany as Christendom's leading power.

Pope Boniface and King Philip of France

The dispute with King Philip IV of France (also known as "Philip the Fair") concerned the taxation of the clergy. However, this issue involved not only Philip but also King Edward I of England, who insisted that half of all the money collected by the Church be turned over to him in taxes. Edward proved a great annoyance; however, because he was focused on conquering Scotland, he posed less of an immediate threat. Moreover, England's bishops supported Boniface. On the other hand, Philip, the strongest king in Europe, presented an immediate threat to the Church. Also, Philip had more control over the French clergy.

Philip's fundamental problem was twofold. First, he managed his kingdom's finances poorly. Second, because he sought to expand France by conquering other nations, he fought numerous costly wars. Thus, Philip seized money from any wealthy person in his realm, especially

Martin IV

Honorius IV

Nicholas IV

Celestine V

Boniface VIII

Witness to the Faith 265

William de Nogaret
Chief adviser to Philip IV; assisted him in his plot to kidnap Pope Boniface VIII.

Sciarra Colonna
An enemy of the pope, who also took part in Philip's plot, and later crowned Louis of Bavaria as emperor.

Babylonian Captivity
The seventy-two years during which the popes lived at Avignon, rather than in their see at Rome.

Philip the Fair

the clergy. Philip eventually suppressed the Knights Templar, simply to take their money.

In 1296, Philip convoked a council in Paris to demand that the French clergy pay new taxes. As both Edward and Philip were now making serious demands on the clergy in their kingdoms, Boniface issued the papal bull (letter) *Clericis Laicos*. In it, Boniface threatened to excommunicate any ruler who tried to tax the clergy without papal permission, as well as any cleric who paid such taxes to any government. Philip, rightly believing that the bull was meant for him, responded by forbidding any money to be exported from France. Boniface explained that he did not object to the clergy paying taxes, but that it had to be done with papal permission. The French bishops later convinced Boniface to allow Philip to tax the Church in France in the event of an emergency.

Perhaps the taxation issue might have been resolved, but in 1301 Philip arrested the bishop of Pamiers, who was also a papal legate. The king seized the bishop's property and ignored his pleas for a papal hearing. In November and December, Boniface sent Philip two letters correcting him, but Philip ignored them.

Unable to come to an understanding with Philip, in November 1302 Pope Boniface VIII issued one of the most famous of all medieval bulls, *Unam Sanctam*, in which he strongly insisted on the subjection of the temporal authority to the spiritual authority. In blunt language, Boniface declared that unless Philip yielded, he would be excommunicated. Unfortunately, like so many of Boniface's statements, this one overstated his position. Boniface declared that everyone had to be subject to the pope in order to be saved. His language made it seem like he was declaring himself a temporal ruler, something that the popes had never done. He followed this letter with another in which he again threatened Philip with both spiritual and *temporal* punishment unless Philip subjected himself to Boniface.

In response, Philip began plotting against Boniface. Two men assisted Philip in this sinful conspiracy: his chief adviser, **William de Nogaret**, a thoroughly evil man, and **Sciarra Colonna**, one of the pope's greatest enemies. By early 1303, Nogaret had created a plan to kidnap the pope and bring him to France. He also began making a number of false charges against Boniface. The conspirators chose September 7 as the day they would kidnap the pope.

As morning dawned on September 7, more than 1,300 men stormed into the tiny town of Anagni. For a while, the town mounted a defense. However, in the early evening, Nogaret, Colonna, and their band of thugs broke into the pope's home. Boniface had acted imprudently through much of his papacy and made many mistakes. Now in this terrible moment facing death, he stood before them as St. Peter— a rock! Pope Boniface VIII was 70 years old and in bad health. Colonna and his henchmen verbally abused the old pope. When they

266 *Chapter 17: The Western Schism*

realized that Boniface was not wilting under their verbal abuse, and was even ready to die a martyr's death, Sciarra Colonna punched the pope in the face with his mailed fist. The pope remained in the power of these brutes for three days before the citizens of Anagni finally rescued him. Soon, four hundred Roman knights arrived and escorted Boniface to Rome. However, he died a month later from the injuries he had received.

The conclave to elect Boniface's successor met nine days after his death. Amazingly, William de Nogaret attended as King Philip's representative! The cardinals quickly chose an Italian cardinal, who took the name Benedict XI (1303-1304). Blessed Benedict XI tried to settle the dispute with Philip peacefully. Yet he knew that he had to take action against those who had attacked Boniface. However, most of Christendom was either unaware of the events in Anagni or indifferent toward them. In addition, after Martin IV and Boniface VIII, who had been unpopular, papal prestige had fallen. Pope Benedict excommunicated those who had directly assaulted Pope Boniface VIII. However, he absolved Philip from excommunication, though Philip showed no signs of repentance. Apparently, Benedict felt that his position was not strong enough to discipline Philip directly. Pope Benedict XI died after a reign of only one year, most likely murdered by Sciarra Colonna and his agents.

Colonna Strikes Pope Boniface VIII

The Beginning of the "Babylonian Captivity"

Following Pope Benedict XI's death, the Holy See remained vacant for eleven months, as once again the Sacred College was hopelessly deadlocked between the French and Italian cardinals. Finally, someone suggested a French bishop, Bertrand de Got of Bordeaux, even though he was not a cardinal. Because he was from Aquitaine, a region of France ruled by England, the cardinals felt that Bishop de Got would not be under Philip's control. In June 1305, they elected Bishop de Got, who took the name Clement V (1305-1314).

Soon the cardinals learned that they were quite wrong about Bishop de Got. Not only did Pope Clement V often do Philip's bidding, but he was also the first of a line of French popes who, for the next seventy-two years, reigned in Avignon, France, rather than in Rome. Historians have likened these seventy-two years to the ***Babylonian Captivity*** of the Jews, because the popes resided at Avignon for about as long as the Jews had remained captives in Babylon. Thankfully, with the exception of Pope Clement V and Pope Clement VI, these popes were not greatly influenced by the French kings.

Map Showing Avignon, France

Witness to the Faith 267

The End of the Knights Templar

Philip IV was a determined man, willing to kill to achieve his goals. It would have taken a pope like Innocent III or Gregory VII to stand up to him. Clement V was not the measure of these men. Though a good and kind man, Clement was weak when the papacy needed strength. From the beginning of his reign, his weakness showed.

Although most of the cardinals begged Clement to come to Rome to be crowned pope, Clement agreed to be crowned in Lyons in the presence of Philip on November 14, 1305. Moreover, Clement then decided that, rather than incurring Philip's wrath, he would remain in France. In early 1306, Pope Clement V annulled *Clericis Laicos* and *Unam Sanctam*. The following year, Philip met Clement at Poitiers. He demanded that Clement create a tribunal to try Pope Boniface VIII as a heretic, reminiscent of the horrific Synod of the Corpse that had "tried" Pope Formosus. Philip also claimed that he had evidence that the Knights Templars were engaged in various sacrilegious activities.

The Final Day of Jacques de Molay, the Last of the Knights Templar, Fleury-Francois Richard

Unfortunately, Clement assisted the avaricious king in the prosecution of the Knights Templar. Under torture, the Knights confessed to the charges brought by William de Nogaret, now the chancellor of France. In February 1311, in the presence of the papal representative, the Knights recanted their confessions. Meanwhile, Philip continued pressing Clement to suppress the Knights, remain in France, and condemn Pope Boniface VIII as a heretic. Clement then announced to the College of Cardinals that he would remain indefinitely in Avignon. In a sad moment for the papacy, Clement finally suppressed the Knights in 1311. Fifty-four of the brave Knights were burned at the stake. However, Clement postponed acting against Boniface VIII, at one point claiming he could not hold the trial because he had a nosebleed. Eventually, Philip let the matter drop.

Pope John XXII and Louis of Bavaria

Clement V and Philip the Fair both died in 1314. Once again, because of the distrust that the French and Italian cardinals held for each other, they could not choose a successor. Thus, the Holy See remained vacant for more than two years. Finally, the Sacred College elected another French cardinal, who chose to be called John XXII (1316-1334). Because he was 72 at the time of his election, the cardinals probably felt that he would die soon and they could vote again. However, he surprised them by living to be 90. Steadfast and courageous, though sometimes imprudent, Pope John was determined to defend the independence of the Church in the spirit of Gregory VII and Innocent III.

The first issue facing the new pope was choosing a new Holy Roman Emperor. Following the sudden death of Henry VII in 1313, two men claimed the throne. **Louis of Bavaria** had been elected over Frederick of Hapsburg, the Duke of Austria and the grandson of Rudolf. Pope John, aware of the Hapsburg family's support for the papacy, clearly preferred Frederick, but urged the parties to negotiate a settlement. Meanwhile, Pope John upheld the right of the papacy to settle all disputed imperial elections, and he declared that neither man should call himself emperor until he had resolved the issue.

In September 1322, Louis defeated Frederick at the Battle of Muhldorf in Austria. Louis even took Frederick prisoner. At this point, for some reason not clear to most historians, Pope John took a dislike to Louis. He demanded that Louis abandon his claim to the throne in favor of Frederick. Louis, who had been validly elected, did not seem to have done anything to displease the pope. However, John was adamant, and he reminded Louis that it was the pope's prerogative to approve or reject the imperial candidate. For two years, Louis worked on a compromise. However, Pope John would not be moved.

In early 1327, Louis entered northern Italy at the head of a large army. Before an assembly of Ghibelline lords, he declared Pope John XXII unfit to be pope. He promised to take his army to Rome. When John learned of this, he condemned Louis and excommunicated many of his followers.

Meanwhile, Louis marched on Milan, where he was crowned king of Italy in May. The following January, he arrived in Rome, where none other than Sciarra Colonna crowned him emperor. Louis put Pope John on trial and declared him deposed. A commission then created an antipope, who called himself Nicholas V. Louis, who seems to have gone a bit insane, began persecuting any member of the Roman clergy who failed to go along with him. Eventually, the Romans rebelled against him and his ministers. Milan also rebelled. Louis had no option but to return to Germany. Antipope Nicholas V, without imperial support, resigned and begged Pope John XXII for mercy. John continued to reign as pope until his death in 1334.

Following John XXII's death, the conclave quickly and unanimously elected French Cardinal Jacques Fournier as pope. He took the name Benedict XII (1334-1342). Although Louis and Benedict tried to negotiate an end to the dispute that had begun under Pope John XXII, no settlement was forthcoming. During his stay in Avignon, Benedict built the Palace of the Popes. It seemed as if he meant for the papacy to remain in Avignon for a long while. Meanwhile, in May 1337, Philip VI declared war on England's Edward III, thus beginning the Hundred Years' War.

When Benedict XII died, Pierre Roger, one of King Philip's leading councilors, was elected Pope Clement VI (1342-1352). Like his predecessor, Clement sought to negotiate a peaceful

Louis of Bavaria
Claimant to the imperial throne; when Pope John XXII opposed him, Louis initially tried to compromise, but grew rebellious. The conflict ended only with Louis' death.

The Coronation of Louis Bavaria in Rome, August von Kreling

Witness to the Faith 269

Emperor Charles IV

resolution to the war between France and England. However, both sides remained defiant. In 1346, Clement excommunicated Louis of Bavaria. Nine days later, he accepted the promises of Charles of Moravia to support the papacy and revoke all of Louis' acts. Later, the German princes elected Charles as emperor. It seemed that a civil war in Germany was inevitable, but when Louis died in October 1346, all opposition to Charles evaporated.

The Pope Returns to Rome – Briefly

People make history, but at times natural forces influence their decisions. In the fall of 1347, one of the worst natural disasters to afflict the world struck Europe: the **Black Death**. This terrible plague killed perhaps half the population. As often happens in terrible situations, people sought scapegoats: they blamed the Jews. On July 4, 1348, Pope Clement VI warned that anyone who mistreated Jews would be excommunicated.

Despite the plague's effects, European civilization continued. Among the most affected were the priests and other religious who cared for the sick. Thus, the Church was weakened, not because the people lacked faith, but because it lacked priests.

In December 1352, Pope Clement VI died. He was not a great pope, and he was often very imprudent. However, during the Black Death, at the moment of the Church's great need, he had acted with greatness. When the conclave met, the head of the Carthusian Order, a good and holy man, was considered but quickly rejected. The cardinals, now quite worldly themselves, felt that he was perhaps too good and holy. They chose the 70-year-old bishop of Clermont, who took the name Innocent VI (1352-1362).

Once a man puts on the Fisherman's Ring, the power of the Holy Spirit comes over him. Pope Innocent VI, seemingly old and feeble, proved to be neither. In June, he ordered Spanish Cardinal Albornoz to Rome to prepare it for his return. Two months later, Albornoz left on his mission. Over the next two years, he pacified and recaptured the Papal States.

The Black Death
Also called the bubonic plague; a deadly disease that ravaged Europe beginning in the mid-fourteenth century.

Palace of the Popes in Avignon, France

270 Chapter 17: The Western Schism

Meanwhile, in 1355, Charles IV was crowned Holy Roman Emperor. The protector of Italy, not its ruler, Charles would return there only once during his twenty-three-year reign. In Germany, he worked to support the Church.

For some unknown reason, Innocent VI, despite the resolve to return to Rome that had filled his heart at the beginning of his pontificate, and despite the successes of Cardinal Albornoz which would have allowed his return, never returned to Rome. Innocent died at Avignon, apparently overcome by misery and grief, feeling that he had failed as pope. While only God can judge his papacy, he had certainly failed to return to Rome.

Interestingly, the conclave of 1362 elected Hugh Roger, Pope Innocent's brother, but he refused to serve. The cardinals next elected a holy Benedictine abbot, who took the name Urban V (1362-1370). During his pontificate, Urban sought to return the papacy to Rome.

Soon after his election, Urban proclaimed a crusade against the Ottoman Turks, who had become a serious threat to Christendom. Emperor Charles IV supported it, as did several other kings. However, other than an attack on Alexandria, nothing came of this "crusade."

At the beginning of his papacy, Urban V showed little interest in returning to Rome, despite the urgings of Charles IV and the holy mystic **St. Bridget of Sweden**. In June 1365, Charles offered to personally escort Urban back to Rome, but he declined. However, he changed his mind and the next June informed the Sacred College of his decision. Finally, at the end of April 1367, Pope Urban V left Avignon and arrived in Rome that October.

However, he stayed in Rome for only two years. The people of Rome implored him to remain. St. Bridget of Sweden warned him that if he returned to France, he would die soon thereafter. Urban refused to heed their pleas and warnings. He returned to Avignon, where he died three months later. Despite his refusal to remain in Rome, the Church viewed Urban's life as one of holiness. In 1870, Pope Pius IX beatified him.

It seemed that if the pope were to return to Rome permanently, it would require a saint with the power and determination of St. Paul. In a small room in Siena, the Holy Spirit was "on the road to Damascus."

St. Catherine of Siena

So often in the Church's hour of need, the Holy Spirit calls forth saints of such energy and determination that, by His grace and the force of their personality, they change history. Saint Paul was such a person. So was **St. Catherine of Siena**.

Born in Siena on March 25, 1347, Catherine began to have visions of Our Lord when she was only 6 years old. Based on these visions, she decided to devote her life to Christ. As a teenager, she convinced her parents to allow her to become a Third Order Dominican. In her room, she led a strict form of religious life, maintaining almost constant

St. Bridget of Sweden

> **St. Bridget of Sweden**
> Mystic and visionary; urged Pope Urban V to return the papacy to Rome, which he did, but only for two years.

> **St. Catherine of Siena**
> Another visionary and messenger of Christ; persuaded Pope Gregory XI to return to Rome.

Witness to the Faith 271

silence. She united herself with God in prayer. When Catherine was 21, she experienced a "mystical marriage" with Our Lord. A few years after her mystical marriage, Christ told her that she needed to leave her cloistered life and become more active in the world.

Beginning in 1374, Catherine began to work more generally with the people and the Dominicans in Italy, preaching repentance and trust in God. She also met St. Raymond of Capua, who became her confessor, and later her biographer. In 1375, Catherine received the *stigmata*, although, at her request, it was visible only to her. At this time, she also began corresponding with the various secular rulers, most often urging them to make peace with one another.

The Pope Finally Returns to Rome

Meanwhile, following the death of Urban V, the Sacred College quickly elected Clement VI's nephew, who chose the name Gregory XI (1370-1378). Within a few days of his election, St. Catherine wrote to him telling him that it was God's Will that he return to Rome and that God would punish him most severely if he did not. However, Gregory kept dithering, due in part to the ongoing Hundred Years' War as well as trouble caused in Italy by Florence. The Italians simply did not trust the French. Gregory did not help matters when he created nine new cardinals, only one being an Italian and seven being French.

Whereas there seemed to be no way to end the Hundred Years' War, Pope Gregory did take action against the rebellious Florentines. He placed the city under interdict. In hopes of restoring peace, Catherine tried to negotiate a settlement. She went to the leaders of Florence, who explained the conditions under which they would agree to peace. Finally, Catherine, no longer content to write letters, journeyed to Avignon, where in June 1376 she spoke with Pope Gregory XI.

Initially, the well-educated pope did not want to listen to the 29-year-old woman, who spoke no French or Latin. Yet, before him stood a woman with the fiery intensity of an Old Testament prophet! At the time of his election to the papacy, Gregory had made a secret vow to return to Rome. St. Catherine told the pope that she knew about his vow. Since he had never told anyone about this, Gregory realized that Catherine was God's messenger. He agreed to return to Rome, and he finally departed Avignon in September. Wherever he stopped on his journey, he found Catherine waiting for him. She was at Marseilles when he boarded the ship for Genoa. She was in Genoa when he landed, and she accompanied him to Rome in January 1377.

Having successfully concluded her mission, Catherine returned to Siena. She continued to preach peace and the reform of the clergy. In late 1377, Pope Gregory sent Catherine to Florence to attempt to negotiate a peace treaty. However, Gregory died before a treaty could be concluded. It would be a year later before Rome and Florence signed a peace treaty.

The Mystic Marriage of Saint Catherine of Siena, Christopher Unterberger

St. Catherine of Siena Leads Pope Gregory XI Back to Rome

Origin of the Western Schism

Pope Gregory XI died on March 27, 1377. In accordance with canon law, the cardinals met ten days later, on the evening of April 7, to elect a new pope. The conclave consisted of sixteen cardinals: eleven Frenchmen, four Italians, and one Spaniard. The Spaniard was Cardinal Pedro de Luna, the man most responsible for keeping the schism alive during his lifetime. Unlike in past conclaves, the French cardinals were split. Some favored the French cardinal of Limoges; others favored the Italian archbishop of Bari, Bartolomeo Prignano.

As the conclave met, a crowd of Romans gathered around the church. They demanded that the cardinals elect a Roman or at least an Italian as pope. They were concerned that another French pope would return the papacy to Avignon as Urban V had done. As the night went on, the crowd became a mob. Finally, in the early morning of the next day, the cardinals voted unanimously to elect Archbishop Prignano, an Italian but not a Roman.

Cardinal Orsini then went outside to announce Archbishop Prignano's election to the now loud and unruly mob. However, in a time before loudspeakers, the people could not hear him above the noise they were making. Exasperated, Cardinal Orsini gave up. By late afternoon,

Witness to the Faith 273

Urban VI
First pope to reign from Rome after the Babylonian Captivity; worked for reform with more zeal than tact, and was soon confronted with the Western Schism.

Robert of Geneva
Chosen as antipope Clement VII in opposition to Urban VI; more a general than a priest, he tried to take Rome by force.

Pope Urban VI

a rumor had spread through the crowd that a pope had been elected, but no one knew who it was, or (more importantly to them) his nationality.

In the evening, Cardinal Orsini tried again to inform them, but the crowd was even louder and more worked up than before, and he still could not be heard. The mob, which had been growing increasingly agitated from waiting all day without news, finally broke into the conclave. The cardinals, fearing for their lives, said that they had elected a Roman, the aged Cardinal Tebaldeschi, whom the crowd knew very well. The frightened cardinals forcibly dressed him in the papal vestments while Tebaldeschi repeatedly cried out that he was not the pope. Finally, the crowd began to listen to Tebaldeschi. They had an Italian pope, but not him.

By April 9, news of Prignano's election had spread through the city, to the satisfaction of the Roman people. The pope-elect then met with the cardinals and asked if they had freely and canonically elected him. They confirmed in writing that they had. They asked him if he accepted election. He said that he did and would take the name of **Urban VI** (1378-1389).

On April 18, Easter Sunday, Urban was consecrated as pope. He blessed the cardinals and all the people of Rome. The next day, all sixteen cardinals who had elected Urban wrote to the six cardinals still in Avignon, informing them of the election of Urban VI.

Following Urban's election, the cardinals began seeking their accustomed favors from the new pope. However, he quickly disappointed them. Pope Urban VI was a genuine reformer, but he lacked prudence and tact. He immediately began scolding the cardinals for their worldly ways and insulting them. When St. Catherine learned of this, she wrote to Urban, urging patience and charity toward the cardinals. However, it was too late.

Highly incensed, the eleven French cardinals and Pedro de Luna met in Anagni and elected French Cardinal **Robert of Geneva** as antipope. He chose to be called Clement VII. The remaining three Italian cardinals (Cardinal Tebaldeschi had died) all abstained but recognized Clement VII as pope. When St. Catherine learned of this treacherous deed, she wrote to the Italian cardinals. She warned them that they knew Urban VI was pope, and that if they failed to acknowledge him, God would punish them.

The disloyal cardinals, all of whom Pope Urban had excommunicated, then dispatched messengers to the various European monarchs to justify their actions. Initially, only King Charles V of France, seeing the chance to have the pope in Avignon, supported the antipope. In time, however, Castile and Flanders also supported him. Scotland, always opposed to England, supported Clement because England supported Urban. Italy and the Holy Roman Empire supported Urban, as did the king of Hungary and Poland. Pope Urban VI was also supported by St. Catherine of Siena and St. Catherine of Sweden, St. Bridget's daughter.

Most theologians also supported Urban. In fact, outside of France, Clement had almost no support.

Meanwhile, St. Catherine worked to end the schism. In late November 1378, Pope Urban VI called her to Rome, where she worked tirelessly on his behalf. She became his adviser, and many times she saved him from making mistakes. She wrote letters to both secular and religious leaders throughout Europe, trying to convince them to follow the lawful pope. Such labors were more than her always fragile constitution could stand.

St. Catherine of Siena died in Rome, on April 29, 1380, at the age of 33—the same age as Our Blessed Lord. Her body remains incorrupt. Pope Pius II canonized her on June 29, 1461. On October 4, 1970, Pope Paul VI named her a Doctor of the Church.

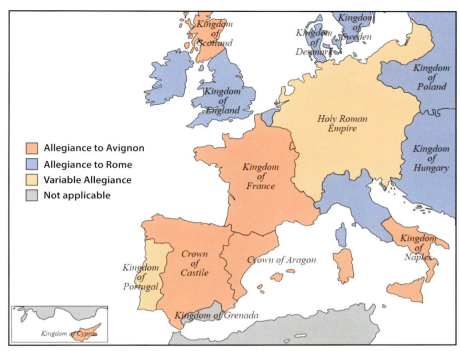

Map of Allegiances of the Western Schism

Attempts to End the Schism

It is vital to remember that in an age before radio, television, and the Internet, it was difficult, and sometimes impossible, to obtain all the facts of a case. Some of the people who supported the antipope did so with the best of intentions, but out of ignorance. Others who supported him knew that his election was invalid. Regardless, the Catholic world was divided in two.

Meanwhile, antipope Clement VII, who was a better general than a priest, decided that he could validate his claim to the papacy only if he reigned from Rome. Since the Italians supported Pope Urban VI, Clement's only option was to attack Rome. With the help of the French monarchs, Clement launched a series of attacks into Italy aimed at conquering Rome. However, these expeditions into Italy were disastrous, costing both men and money. The clergy began to complain bitterly. People were growing tired of the schism, but Clement seems never to have had any desire to end the schism other than by becoming pope. He died in Avignon on September 16, 1394.

Meanwhile, Pope Urban VI had died in October 1389. However, prior to his death, he had created an entirely new College of Cardinals who supported him. The fourteen cardinals still loyal to him elected the cardinal of Naples, Pietro Tomacelli, as pope. He chose to be called Boniface IX (1389-1404).

Antipope Clement VII

Witness to the Faith 275

Pope Gregory XII

Antipope Benedict XIII

Antipope Alexander V

As the schism dragged on, the people of Europe became increasingly dissatisfied with the perceived lack of leadership in the Church. Even those ruling in France began to see that the schism was hurting their country. Thus, when antipope Clement VII died in 1394, they urged the cardinals meeting in Avignon to wait before electing a new "pope," hoping that the two sides might reach a settlement. Despite their pleas, Pedro de Luna had himself elected *less than two weeks later*. The new antipope decided to call himself Benedict XIII. He would live another twenty-nine years, causing the Church misery every day.

With no end to the schism in sight, secular and religious leaders began proposing different plans to end the schism. One plan, developed by the University of Paris, suggested that both claimants to the papacy resign. Antipope Clement VII had refused, but his successor, antipope Benedict XIII, was a wilier sort of character. He declared himself in favor of arbitration. However, this plan failed.

Another plan suggested that a council be called to resolve the dispute. However, Pope Boniface IX rightly pointed out that no council could be convoked without his approval, and he refused to convoke one. Perhaps Boniface acted unwisely, but he was the pope. Over the next several years, antipope Benedict began to lose support in France. Various French national councils urged him to resign. He steadfastly refused, promising never to resign.

Pope Boniface IX died in October 1404. The cardinals loyal to him met and sent a letter to the French royal court. They promised not to elect a successor if antipope Benedict XIII resigned, thus allowing the French cardinals to participate in the conclave. Benedict again refused. The eight loyal cardinals then elected Pope Innocent VII (1404-1406).

However, Innocent was sickly, indecisive, and imprudent. He reigned for just over two years, accomplishing almost nothing to end the schism. The thirteen cardinals who met in the conclave of 1406 all promised beforehand that if they were elected, they would dedicate their pontificate to ending the schism. Moreover, they promised to resign as pope if that would end the schism. The Sacred College then elected Cardinal Angelo Correr. He chose the great papal name Gregory. Pope Gregory XII reigned from 1406 until 1415.

From almost the moment of his consecration, Pope Gregory XII declared that he would meet with antipope Benedict XIII anywhere he

Cathedral of Pisa

276 *Chapter 17: The Western Schism*

chose. It seemed that reconciliation was at hand, but Benedict suddenly withdrew his consent. Pope Gregory then withdrew his consent and declared that he would never resign. He also created four new cardinals, even though at the 1406 conclave he had promised not to do so. In response, several of his formerly loyal cardinals abandoned him.

In late June 1408, six cardinals who had abandoned Gregory and six who had abandoned Benedict met at Livorno in northern Italy. They suggested that a council be held in Pisa in June of the following year to depose the two papal claimants and elect a new pope. At this point, Pope Gregory XII had almost no support. He created ten new cardinals to increase the Sacred College to fifteen.

The Council of Pisa met in June 1409. The participants claimed to depose Pope Gregory XII, as well as antipope Benedict XIII. Then they elected a third claimant, Alexander V. However, it is long-established canon law that an ecumenical council **cannot be held** without papal approval. Pope Gregory XII did not call the Council of Pisa, nor did he recognize its authority. Therefore, he quite rightly did not accept its decision. Although they may have acted with the best of intentions, the cardinals at Pisa did not unite the Church; instead, they created more division. There were now three papal claimants and three colleges of cardinals. The following year, the Pisa antipope died and was succeeded by antipope John XXIII.

While the Church was struggling with the Western Schism, a far more deadly threat loomed. In England, a man named **John Wyclif** was sowing the seeds of what would one day become the Protestant Revolt.

The Heresies of John Wyclif

John Wyclif was born in Yorkshire, England, in 1324. He studied at Oxford University and was ordained to the priesthood. He later became a professor at Oxford, the center of the heretical movement. While a professor, he wrote a thousand-page book in which he declared that some souls were predestined to go to Heaven, and others to Hell. According to Wyclif, those souls destined to Heaven may indulge in all sorts of sinful action because sin cannot harm them, whereas those predestined to Hell pray in vain because God has already decided to ignore their prayers. Wyclif rejected most of the sacraments, denied the Real Presence in the Eucharist, and declared that the pope was not necessary.

In 1377, Pope Gregory XII condemned nineteen of Wyclif's ideas as heresies and ordered Oxford University to investigate his teachings. The bishop of London summoned Wyclif before a Church tribunal to answer for his heresies, but his powerful friends in the nobility protected him; Oxford University took no action.

However, in 1382, when one of his disciples began to incite rebellions against England's wealthy landowners, his supporters abandoned him. A synod under the direction of the archbishop of Canterbury convened in London and declared that Wyclif had taught a number of heretical doctrines. The archbishop ordered Oxford to fire

John Wyclif

John Wyclif
Oxford professor who taught several heresies, including the heresy that some souls were predestined to go to Heaven, and others to Hell.

Witness to the Faith

Jan Hus
Bohemian professor who promoted John Wyclif's heresies.

Council of Constance
Accepted Pope Gregory XII's resignation, deposed the two antipopes, and elected a new pope, thereby ending the Western Schism.

Wyclif, according to the decrees of the synod. Although the chancellor of the university initially refused, Oxford eventually dismissed Wyclif from his position. He was forbidden to continue teaching. Nevertheless, for the remainder of his life, he continued to publish pamphlets attacking the pope, the sacraments, and the priesthood. John Wyclif died in December 1384. However, his heresies endured in those he influenced, including a Czech professor named **Jan Hus**.

Jan Hus

The marriage of the English King Richard II to Princess Anne of Bohemia in 1382 created a close relation between those two countries. English students at the University of Prague in Bohemia introduced John Wyclif's heresies there. Among those most affected by Wyclif's ideas was Jan Hus, a professor at the University of Prague.

Jan Hus had earned his degree from the University of Prague, been ordained a priest, and then begun a career as a professor at the university. As Wyclif's heresies spread into Bohemia, Pope Gregory XII ordered his writings suppressed. Despite the papal command, Hus not only promulgated them, but even translated them so that the Bohemians could read them. Hus promoted all of John Wyclif's heresies, except his denial of the Real Presence. Eventually, all the writings of Jan Hus were condemned. In 1411, Hus was excommunicated. In late November 1414, he was arrested and imprisoned, pending a trial as a heretic. The Council of Constance would determine his guilt or innocence.

The Council of Constance: End of the Schism

The Council of Pisa had done far more harm than good. However, it demonstrated that the people of Christendom were determined to end the schism. They realized that Our Lord had made Peter—a single man, not a committee—the pope. The Chair of Peter was exactly that, a chair, not a couch. Despite the contention between the parties, everyone agreed that there could be only one pope.

Jan Hus Defends His Doctrines before the Council of Constance

As the schism dragged on with no end in sight, the Pisa antipope, John XXIII, appealed to Emperor Sigismund as the protector of the Holy See. Sigismund, who had been dealing with Jan Hus, longed to end the schism and resolve the Hus matter. He notified Pope Gregory XII and antipope Benedict XIII that he intended to call a council to meet in Constance (Switzerland) at the end of 1414.

278 *Chapter 17: The Western Schism*

Throughout November and December of 1414, the council delegates arrived. Ultimately, twenty-nine cardinals, thirty-three archbishops, and more than three hundred bishops, as well as almost every leading layman and theologian in Christendom, attended. Everyone realized how important this council would be.

Antipope John XXIII had agreed to the council because he believed that it would ratify his election as pope. However, when he arrived in Constance, he discovered that the general feeling among the delegates was that all claimants should resign. Not willing to resign, he fled Constance in disguise. The council immediately agreed to depose him because he had continued the schism by his sudden departure.

The essential fact in all of Church history and canon law is that an ecumenical council **cannot be held and is not valid** without papal approval. At this point, Pope Gregory XII, the true pope, had the least public support. One contender had fled because he thought he would not be elected. Another contender remained obstinate, fought to be pope, and, until his death in 1422, continued to call himself so. Only the true pope was willing to sacrifice. Pope Gregory XII was willing to resign, but he had one condition: his representatives must convoke the council and authorize all its future acts.

On July 4, 1415, the representatives of the true pope convoked the council, giving it legitimacy. The council then accepted Pope Gregory's resignation. Next, the council deposed antipope Benedict XIII.

On November 11, 1417, Cardinal Otto Colonna was elected pope and took the name Martin V (1417-1431). After nearly forty years, the Western Schism had finally ended.

Pope Martin V

The **Council of Constance** also dealt with Jan Hus. The council condemned thirty of his ideas as heretical. Despite this, he refused to recant his errors. He was condemned as an obstinate heretic and handed over to the secular authorities, who burned him at the stake. However, Hus had planted seeds that had deep roots. For the next two decades, his followers, the *Hussites*, fought bloody religious wars that devastated Bohemia and parts of Germany. Almost exactly one hundred years later, a German monk would take up his cause and set Europe aflame.

Oral Exercises

1. What was the root of the conflict between Pope Boniface VIII and King Philip of France?
2. Why do historians call the time spent by the popes at Avignon the Babylonian Captivity?
3. Which pope suppressed the Knights Templar?
4. To which order did St. Catherine of Siena belong?
5. Which pope did St. Catherine finally persuade to return to Rome?
6. Why was the Council of Pisa in 1409 unlawful?
7. What did Pope Gregory XII require before he would resign?
8. What was John Wyclif's heresy?
9. Why was Jan Hus burned at the stake?

Witness to the Faith

Chapter 18

The Reconquista, Part II (1109-1492)

Alfonso the Battler
King of Aragon from 1104 to 1134; outstanding general who devoted his life to the Reconquista.

Alfonso I of Aragon, Francisco Pradilla y Ortiz

Introduction

When Alfonso VI died in 1109, the Reconquista was almost exactly at its midpoint. The outcome remained in doubt. In the twenty-three years since the Almoravid Muslims had invaded Spain, Alfonso's victories had been rare. He had seen almost all the gains of his early reign lost in his last decade as king. Yet the Spanish knew that victory lay in persistence and in their Catholic Faith. For the next 390 years, they would rely on both.

Since the beginning of the Reconquista, Spanish Catholics had fought their way from their mountain aerie at Covadonga, mile by mile to the center of Spain. In 1109, Spain and Portugal were about evenly divided between Catholics and Muslims. However, the invasion of the Almoravids had turned the tide in favor of the Muslims. It would take a man like El Cid to turn that tide back.

Alfonso the Battler

During the last years of his life, Alfonso VI had fought the Almoravids, almost entirely without success. On May 29, 1108, at the end of his life, he fought them one last time and was soundly defeated. Yet he refused to surrender. Wounded and dying, Alfonso galloped back to Segovia, where he called his daughter Urraca to meet him. He gave her

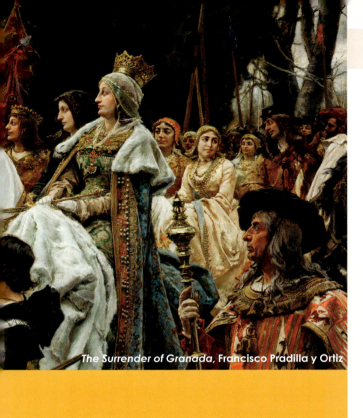
The Surrender of Granada, Francisco Pradilla y Ortiz

1126 A.D. – 1492 A.D.

1126-1127 A.D.
Alfonso the Battler leads a great raid across Andalusia, marking a revival in the Reconquista.

1164 A.D.
Pope Alexander III officially recognizes the Order of Calatrava.

1196 A.D.
Pope Celestine III reprimands the Spanish kings for forming alliances with the Muslims.

1212 A.D.
The great Spanish victory at the Battle of Las Navas de Tolosa decisively defeats the Almohads and opens southern Spain to reconquest.

1224 A.D.
King St. Ferdinand III begins a series of attacks in which he retakes a great deal of Spain.

1248 A.D.
Ferdinand captures Seville, Spain's greatest city at the time.

1251 A.D.
Portugal is completely freed from the Muslims.

1352-1369 A.D.
Spanish Catholics are again fighting among themselves, due to King Pedro of Castile's selfish quarrels.

1469 A.D.
The marriage of Princess Isabel of Castile to Prince Ferdinand of Aragon, soon to be queen and king of their respective kingdoms, unites Spain.

1482-1492 A.D.
Grenada surrenders to Ferdinand and Isabel, completing the Reconquista.

---

one last command. Upon his death, she was to marry the greatest Spanish warrior of the age: Alfonso I, the king of Aragon, who was known as **Alfonso the Battler**. The marriage would potentially unite the kingdoms of Castile and Aragon.

Alfonso the Battler, who had never married, lived for combat. During the four years he had been king of Aragon, he had dedicated his life to recapturing Spain from the Muslims. It seemed Alfonso VI had made a good choice to lead a united Spain.

Because Urraca and Alfonso were cousins, their marriage required a special dispensation. Archbishop Bernard of Toledo refused to give it. Despite this, the two married. In 1110, Pope Paschal II declared the marriage annulled.

The marriage of Alfonso and Urraca was not a loving or happy one. In

Witness to the Faith 281

Zaragoza
A city that was the Muslims' northernmost Spanish stronghold until Alfonso the Battler took it back in 1118. This was his greatest victory.

Andalusia
A region of southern Spain.

fact, it was quite the opposite. From 1109 until 1114, Alfonso spent more time fighting with Urraca than with the Muslims. However, in 1114, he again took up the cause of the Reconquista. In 1118, he won his greatest military victory when he recaptured **Zaragoza**, the northernmost Muslim-controlled city in Europe. Over the next two years, Alfonso strengthened his hold on Aragon, turning it into a formidable Spanish kingdom.

Meanwhile, the popes continued to take an interest in Spain. Pope Gelasius II blessed the campaign to capture Zaragoza as a crusade. Pope Calixtus confirmed Archbishop Bernard of Toledo as metropolitan for Spain, and he threatened to excommunicate Queen Urraca when she imprisoned the bishop of Santiago de Compostela. The mediation of Pope Calixtus helped ensure a smooth transition when Urraca died in 1126 and was succeeded by her son Alfonso VII, who became king of Castile and Leon. Pope Calixtus also worked to create a better relationship between Alfonso the Battler and Alfonso VII.

In 1126, Alfonso the Battler, now 53 years old and probably the world's finest general, led the most daring and ambitious raid in the history of the Reconquista—and perhaps in the history of the world. In response to a call from Catholics in Grenada, deep in southern Spain, he led an army of just under 20,000 men through hundreds of miles of Muslim-occupied territory. As he marched south, he urged other Christians to join his army. By the time he reached Grenada, his force had swelled to over 50,000 men. On January 7, 1127, he camped outside the walls of Grenada. However, he had no siege engines to batter down the walls. Moreover, he could not feed a force that large if they stayed encamped. For Alfonso, the choice was obvious: fight!

Over the next several months, Alfonso marched across **Andalusia** (southern Spain) fighting Muslims. When he finally retreated to Aragon in May, he took more than 10,000 Christians from Grenada with him. The message he sent was clear: Catholic

Urraca of Leon,
Carlos Mugica y Perez

282   Chapter 18: The Reconquista, Part II (1109-1492)

Spain was on the offensive. No part of Muslim-controlled Spain was safe from reconquest. The tide had turned.

As Alfonso approached the end of his life, he began to consider what to do with his kingdom. He had no children. His only brother was a monk who had spent his entire life in an abbey—certainly not the kind of man to lead a kingdom of fighters. Alfonso had dedicated his life to the Reconquista, as had no other leader before him. Perhaps it was not unexpected that he left his kingdom to the three crusading orders that had recently been formed in the Holy Land.

Alfonso continued to fight against the Muslims until the last day of his life. His final command to his troops was to continue the Reconquista, no matter how long it took. He died on September 9, 1134, and was buried in Huesca at the monastery of San Pedro, which he had built.

Spain: Land of the Crusaders

Alfonso's idea of the military orders, headquartered in the Holy Land, governing Spain was completely impractical. The Spanish nobility, although they had sworn to uphold his plan, ultimately refused. From the confusion that resulted, Count Ramon Berenguer of Barcelona came to rule Aragon and Catalonia, now united as the kingdom of Aragon.

With the launch of the crusades in 1095, Spain became a land of crusaders. In October 1147, French and Italian crusaders helped the Spanish conquer Almeria on the southern coast of Spain. Also in October, knights from the Second Crusade captured Lisbon and drove out the Muslim invaders. After the city was successfully captured, Gilbert of Hastings, an English monk who had accompanied the crusaders, was named bishop of Lisbon.

In 1158, a Cistercian monk named **Diego Velazquez**, who had been a knight before entering the monastery of Fitero, founded the **Order of Calatrava**, a Spanish military order. Diego formed the order primarily to defend the castle of Calatrava from a new invasion of North African Muslims known as the **Almohads**. Diego's abbot gave him permission to defend the castle. Then the archbishop of Toledo granted a plenary indulgence to anyone who would help defend Calatrava. Hundreds of young men flocked to help Diego. The Abbot of Fitero organized the men under the Cistercian rule, and the Order of Calatrava was born. Pope Alexander III officially recognized the order in 1164.

For the next few years, the rulers of Castile and Portugal worked together to rid Iberia of the Muslims. However, by late 1170, they had begun to fight among themselves rather than against their common enemy. Matters might have become even worse had Pope Alexander III not sent a legate to Spain in the summer of 1173 to make peace. The kings of Leon, Castile, and Aragon all agreed to work together.

Alfonso VII of Leon, Jose Maria Rodriguez de Losada

Diego Velazquez
A Cistercian monk and former knight; founder of the Order of Calatrava.

Order of Calatrava
A Spanish military order, formed primarily in defense against the Almohads.

Almohads
Muslims from North Africa who invaded Spain in the twelfth century.

Witness to the Faith

Las Navas de Tolosa, Francisco de Paula Van Halen

Alfonso Henriques
First king of Portugal, acknowledged as such in 1179 by Pope Alexander III.

Las Navas de Tolosa
Important battle in which the Spanish victory nearly destroyed the Almohads' power in Spain and opened the south of the ccountry to reconquest.

Although none of the Spanish kings wanted to acknowledge **Alfonso Henriques** as king of Portugal, in 1179 Pope Alexander resolved the matter himself. He formally acknowledged that Alfonso was the first king of Portugal. Meanwhile, the kings of Spain, to maintain the peace, all agreed on where the borders of their kingdoms would be, once the Muslims were finally expelled from their territories.

The last decades of the twelfth century proved contentious among Spain's monarchs, as once again they fought too often among themselves and not enough against the Almohads. The situation reached its lowest point when Alfonso IX of Leon and Sancho VII of Navarre actually entered into an alliance with the Muslims! When Pope Celestine learned of this incredible betrayal of the Catholic cause, he wrote to both kings in March 1196. He threatened them with excommunication if they did not abandon this alliance and make peace with all Catholic monarchs in Spain and Portugal. Although Sancho obeyed the pope's order, Alfonso did not. Celestine excommunicated him and released his subjects from their obedience to him. It would be a year before Alfonso finally obeyed the pope.

In 1212, the Spanish won one of the most decisive battles of the war. In April, Pope Innocent III wrote to the bishops of France urging them to preach a crusade in Spain to assist the Spanish, who were hard pressed by the Almohads. Thousands of knights answered the call. In the early hours of July 16, the forces of King Alfonso VIII of Castile heard Mass, went to Confession, and then strapped on their arms and armor. At **Las Navas de Tolosa** in Andalusia, the heavily outnumbered Spanish forces attacked the Almohads. After a day of fighting,

Chapter 18: The Reconquista, Part II (1109-1492)

Alfonso's army, supported by the military orders and a number of French knights, completely defeated the Muslims. In thanksgiving, Alfonso VIII sent the Muslims' battle standard to Pope Innocent III.

The Catholic victory at the Battle of Las Navas de Tolosa nearly destroyed the power of the Almohads in Spain. Southern Spain lay open to reconquest. Alfonso VIII's grandson, one of Spain's finest kings—and one of its holiest—would very nearly complete the Reconquista of Spain.

King St. Ferdinand III

In the history of the world, few monarchs have been declared saints. In Germany, Holy Roman Emperor Henry II was so blessed. In France, the great crusader King St. Louis IX was canonized a saint. Spain's great king and saint was **Ferdinand III**, the king of Castile, grandson of Alfonso VIII.

In October 1214, Alfonso VIII of Castile died. His oldest son and heir, 11-year-old Henry, died tragically in an accident three years later. Alfonso VIII's daughter, Berenguela, the queen of Leon, then became queen of Castile. However, she renounced the throne in favor of her son, Ferdinand. When his father, King Alfonso IX of Leon, died, the kingdoms of Castile and Leon were to be united under King Ferdinand. At the end of August 1217, 19-year-old Ferdinand became king of Castile. Thirteen years later, he became king of Leon.

The victory at Las Navas de Tolosa had created an incredible opportunity for the recapture of southern Spain. In 1224, the Almohad caliph died, further weakening the Muslims. Ferdinand believed that the time to strike had arrived.

Over the next decades, Ferdinand, along with James I of Aragon ("the Conqueror"), launched a series of attacks. They recaptured almost all of Andalusia. In June 1236, Ferdinand captured the great city of Cordoba, which the Muslims had held since the eighth century. He declared that the city's mosque, known as the *Mezquita*, would henceforth be a Catholic cathedral. Ferdinand also ordered that the bells from Santiago de Compostela, which Almanzor had taken two hundred years earlier and placed in Cordoba, be returned to

King St. Ferdinand III
King of Castile; strengthened the Church in his kingdom and retook all of Spain except the kingdom of Grenada.

Royal Family Relations

Berenguela's sister Blanche was the mother of King St. Louis IX.

King St. Ferdinand III

Witness to the Faith 285

Kingdom of Grenada
The remnant of Muslim rule in southern Spain for the last 246 years of the Reconquista.

Balearic Islands
An island chain off Spain's eastern coast, retaken from the Muslims by King James I of Aragon in 1235.

their home. Upon hearing of Ferdinand's victory, Pope Gregory IX sent him money to aid in his crusade.

In 1246, Ferdinand captured Jaen after a long siege. Under the terms of the Muslim surrender, they would keep Grenada, Malaga, and the area around those cities. Thus, the Muslim **Kingdom of Grenada** came into existence. It would last until 1492, when Spain's greatest queen finally conquered it.

In June 1246, the people of Seville, Spain's greatest city, rebelled against the Muslims occupying the city. Ferdinand immediately rushed to Seville. Although some of his generals urged an immediate assault, others suggested that he conquer the surrounding countryside, which he did. Meanwhile, as Seville is a port city, it was determined that Spain needed a navy to blockade it. Ferdinand began construction of the Spanish navy. One day, it would become the most powerful navy in the world.

Cathedral of Burgos

In April 1247, Pope Innocent IV granted Ferdinand permission to take one third of the tithes the Church collected in Castile to finance the capture of Seville. In the summer, Ferdinand began the siege of Seville. For over a year, the defenders held out, but they could not be reinforced, as the Spanish navy now controlled the seas around Seville. Ferdinand, on the other hand, received constant reinforcements. In October 1248, the Muslims asked for Ferdinand's terms of surrender. He told them they could leave the city with whatever they could carry. In November, the Muslims surrendered. Three days before Christmas, King Ferdinand, accompanied by his wife and children, entered Seville in a triumphal procession. He went to Seville's main mosque, which he had consecrated as a cathedral dedicated to the Blessed Mother. The capture of Seville was the most magnificent victory of the Reconquista.

Meanwhile, in 1235, King James I of Aragon had finished his conquest of the **Balearic Islands**, an island chain off Spain's eastern coast. Although historically Spanish, they had fallen to the Muslims. James' finest victory came in 1238, when he finally captured Valencia after a long campaign. James also brought Barcelona, which the French had ruled, into the kingdom of Aragon when he made a treaty with King St. Louis IX.

During Ferdinand's reign, as the Reconquista was more successful, Spain's bishops began playing a larger role in international Church issues. In 1245, at the Council of Lyons, which met to discuss excommunicating Emperor Frederick II, the Spanish bishops urged Pope Innocent IV to take strong action against the disobedient emperor. They promised the pope that they would support and defend him with their very lives if necessary. It is likely that their powerful backing encouraged Pope Innocent to depose Frederick.

In 1251, the Catholics in Portugal finally finished the liberation of their country when they recaptured Portugal's southernmost province.

By 1252, almost the entire Iberian Peninsula had been recaptured. In a bold move, King Ferdinand decided to invade North Africa to begin its recapture. Sadly, it was not to be. Although he was only in his early fifties, Ferdinand had given his life to the Reconquista in a way that no other man had since Alfonso the Battler. The spirit was willing, but the flesh was simply too weak. In May, Ferdinand died in his palace in Seville. His family buried him in the city's cathedral.

During his reign, King Ferdinand had worked to strengthen the Church in his kingdom. He had built the Cathedral of Burgos. He had supported the Benedictines, the Cistercians, and the new mendicant orders, the Dominicans and Franciscans. In fact, he had become a member of the Third Order of St. Francis. In 1671, Pope Clement X canonized San Fernando.

The Intervening Years

When Ferdinand died in 1252, only the Kingdom of Grenada remained in the hands of the Muslims. Yet it would be another 240 years before that kingdom was finally captured. In a sense, the Reconquista was on hold. However, the kingdoms of Castile and Aragon became more involved in the international affairs of Christendom and the Church.

In late 1281, civil war broke out in Castile, as King Alfonso X's son Sancho sought to depose him. In 1283, Pope Martin IV condemned the rebellion,

King Alfonso X of Castile

Witness to the Faith

King Sancho of Castile

Pedro de Luna
Cardinal who took part in the Western Schism; supported antipope Clement VII, then succeeded him as antipope Benedict XIII.

but few people in Spain paid any attention to his decree. The war finally ended when Alfonso died in April 1284 and Sancho became king. However, Sancho lived only another fifteen years before dying of tuberculosis. Sancho is claimed to have said that his death at age 36 was God's judgment upon him for breaking the Fourth Commandment.

Over the next hundred years, Spain had conflicts both internally and with the Muslims in Grenada. Yet the Church in Spain continued to grow and thrive. Additionally, more Spanish bishops were named cardinals. Pope Gregory X named Pedro Julião, the archbishop of Braga, to the Sacred College. During the pontificate of Pope Boniface VIII, Gonzalo Perez Gudiel, the archbishop of Toledo, and Pedro Ispano, the bishop of Burgos, were made cardinals. Pope John XXII and Pope Clement VI also appointed Spanish bishops to the College of Cardinals.

In 1340, the Spaniards defeated an invasion of Muslims from Morocco. Following a sermon from Archbishop Gil Albornoz of Toledo, the primate of Spain, the Spaniards received Holy Communion and launched their attack. Although outnumbered, the Catholic forces decisively defeated the new invaders. Pope Clement VI made Archbishop Albornoz a cardinal in 1350.

Meanwhile, 1350 saw the Black Death sweep across Spain as it did all of Europe. In March, Alfonso XI, the king of Castile, fell sick and died. His son, 16-year-old Pedro, became king of Castile. Pedro would cause the Reconquista to stall for the next several decades.

The Problems with King Pedro

In early 1352, King Pedro fell in love with a Castilian girl named Maria de Padilla, whom he secretly married. However, the Spanish nobility insisted that in order to maintain peace with France, he marry a French princess, Blanche of Bourbon. Despite his marriage to Maria, he married Blanche in the summer of 1353. However, he soon left her for a third woman, Juana de Castro, whom he also married. When Pope Innocent VI learned of this third wedding (apparently he did not know of the first secret one), he ordered Pedro to return to Blanche. However, Blanche fled to Toledo, where the archbishop gave her sanctuary in the cathedral. Furious, Pedro declared that Toledo was in revolt. Civil war then erupted in Castile.

288 Chapter 18: The Reconquista, Part II (1109-1492)

Until March 1369, when his enemies killed him, Pedro kept Spain embroiled in wars. Once he captured Toledo, he went to war with Aragon the following year. Despite papal excommunication, the selfish king refused to obey. Meanwhile, this terrible situation was tragically resolved when Queen Blanche died mysteriously in May 1361, and Maria de Padilla, though she was only 28, died mysteriously in July of the same year. The remainder of Pedro's life was filled with treachery and murder, including his own.

The Problems with Cardinal Pedro

On January 17, 1377, Pope Gregory XI returned to Rome, thus ending the Avignon Papacy. However, he did not live much longer. He died in March of the following year. Events then unfolded that led to the Western Schism, in which Spanish Cardinal **Pedro de Luna** played so terrible a part.

Pedro de Luna had been at the conclave that elected Pope Urban VI. He knew the election was valid but chose to ignore this fact. He and other disobedient cardinals then elected antipope Clement VII. Because de Luna was from Aragon, Clement VII sent him to Spain to attempt to influence Castile, Aragon, and Portugal to support Clement's claims. When Clement VII died, a group of mostly excommunicated cardinals elected Pedro de Luna as antipope Benedict XIII. The growth of the Church in Spain was evident, even at this tragic meeting, as four of the cardinals present were Spaniards.

The Council of Constance, which ended the schism, declared Pedro de Luna a schismatic and excommunicated him. Even the advice of St. Dominic would not move the stubborn cardinal. Like so many of his countrymen, de Luna was incredibly persistent, and his persistence caused the schism to drag on longer than it otherwise might have. After the ruling of the council, he fled to Aragon, the only kingdom that still considered him pope. In Aragon, King Alfonso V gave him sanctuary. Pedro de Luna died in Aragon in 1423.

King Pedro of Castile

Witness to the Faith

Pedro de Luna as Antipope Benedict XIII

Once More into Battle

Meanwhile, as Pedro de Luna was prolonging the schism, in Castile King Henry III was preparing to resume the Reconquista, which internal warfare had sidetracked for more than fifty years. He launched a new campaign against Grenada in 1404, but he made little progress and in 1406 signed a two-year peace treaty with the Muslims there. When the treaty expired, Henry was preparing to personally lead an expedition against Grenada, but he suddenly died.

Because Henry's son Juan was less than 2 years old, his brother Ferdinand became regent. Ferdinand, who was as committed to the reconquest as his older brother, attacked and captured a few cities in the Kingdom of Grenada. However, the final conquest of Grenada would be made by Henry's granddaughter, Queen Isabel of Castile, and her husband, King Ferdinand II of Aragon—known to history as *Los Reyes Catolicos* (the Catholic Monarchs).

The Catholic Monarchs

On October 19, 1469, 18-year-old Princess Isabel married 17-year-old Prince Ferdinand. The marriage would unite Spain. Their descendants would rule a united Spain, but unless they conquered the Kingdom of Grenada, it would not be a fully liberated Spain.

King Ferdinand II of Aragon

Queen Isabel of Castile

290   Chapter 18: The Reconquista, Part II (1109-1492)

Isabel became queen of Castile in 1474, and Ferdinand became king of Aragon five years later. From the time they came to the throne, they had a singular determination to complete the Reconquista. In 1482, they launched the final assault, a ten-year campaign known as the *Grenada War*. Throughout the war, Pope Sixtus IV supported their efforts with prayers and money set aside for a crusade.

Starting in 1482, the Catholic Monarchs launched a series of campaigns against the Kingdom of Grenada. Each year, they liberated part of the kingdom, as they slowly fought their way to the city of Grenada itself. In 1485, they freed Marbella. Two years later, they liberated Malaga. By 1490, little of the kingdom remained other than the city of Grenada itself. However, its ruler, Boabdil, despite being surrounded and cut off from any supplies from friendly Muslims, refused to surrender.

In April 1491, the Catholic army encamped outside the walls of Grenada and began to besiege the city. With no hope of reinforcements or new food supplies, the fall of the city was only a matter of time. On January 2, 1492, Grenada officially surrendered. The 770-year-long Reconquista had finally ended. Spain was free.

In 722, Pelayo had declared, "Our hope is in Christ; this little mountain will be the salvation of Spain … the mercy of Christ will free us from that multitude [the Muslims]" (*Cronica de Alfonso III*). It had taken almost eight centuries, but Pelayo was right.

The Surrender of Granada, **Vicente Barneto y Vazquez**

Oral Exercises

1. Which Spanish king captured the city of Zaragoza?
2. Where is Andalusia?
3. What important city did the knights of the Second Crusade capture?
4. Which Spanish military order did Pope Alexander III officially recognize?
5. Which Spanish king is also a saint?
6. Which Spanish king conquered Cordoba and Seville?
7. Who eventually freed Grenada?

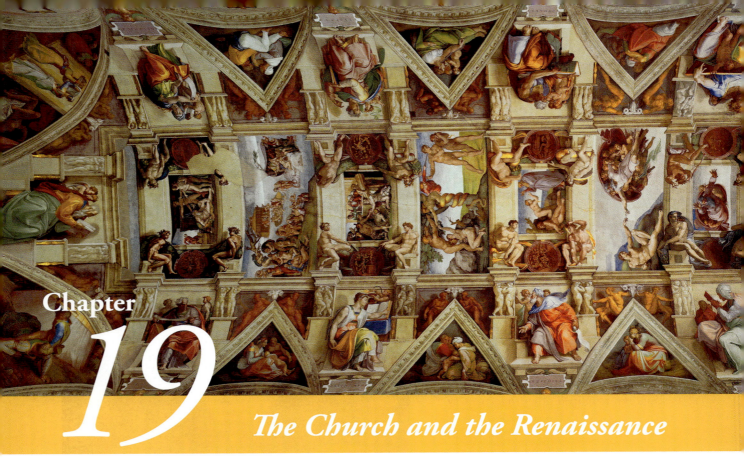

Chapter 19
The Church and the Renaissance

Renaissance
The era during the fifteenth and sixteenth centuries in which an intellectual movement aimed at reviving the classical cultures of ancient Greece and Rome dramatically influenced philosophy, art, and literature in Europe.

Introduction

The Council of Constance had once again united the Church. However, it would take time to heal the wounds and repair the damage that the Western Schism had caused. Constance had also dealt with the first major heresy in more than two hundred years. Jan Hus had chosen not to reconcile with the Church and was executed. The Hussites remained a problem, but eventually were suppressed. Christendom was again at peace. In times of peace, art and literature flourish. Such was the case during the era known as the *Renaissance* (French, meaning "Rebirth"). The **Renaissance** was the era during the fifteenth and sixteenth centuries in which an intellectual movement aimed at reviving the classical cultures of ancient Greece and Rome dramatically influenced philosophy, art, and literature in Europe. This movement began in Italy.

The Renaissance Papacy

Historians often refer to the pontificates of the nineteen popes from Martin V (1431-1447) to Pius IV (1559-1565) as the "Renaissance Papacy." For the most part, these popes supported the Renaissance. Most of them came from wealthy noble families, and they supported painting, sculpture, and architecture. Thus, during the Renaissance, the popes made major contributions to the arts and literature.

The Sistine Chapel Ceiling, Michelangelo

1415 A.D. – 1512 A.D.

1415 A.D.
The English devastatingly defeat the French in the Battle of Agincourt.

1418 A.D.
Thomas a Kempis writes *The Imitation of Christ*.

1428-1431 A.D.
Joan of Arc leads the armies of France against the English invaders, turning the tide of the Hundred Years' War and saving her homeland from English rule. She is captured after two years, and killed after a year in prison.

1431-1445 A.D.
In a crisis of the conciliar movement, the Council of Basel declares the pope deposed, and elects an antipope. The schism is short-lived, and Pope Eugene IV resolves the crisis before his death.

1450 A.D.
Johann Gutenberg's printing press begins to function.

1453 A.D.
Constantinople falls to the Ottoman Turks. Many in Europe are shocked and devastated. For a while afterwards, popes call for a crusade to free the city, but no such expedition ever comes.

1456 A.D.
A Hungarian army under John Hunyadi defeats a much larger Muslim force at Belgrade, driving the invaders back from Europe for almost a generation.

1492 A.D.
Rodrigo Borgia becomes Pope Alexander VI. His eleven-year pontificate is possibly the most scandalous.

1508-1512 A.D.
Michelangelo paints the Sistine Chapel ceiling.

However, the Renaissance presented the Church with serious challenges, some of which the Church struggled to overcome. In certain cases, this was because the Renaissance Popes were living worldly lives. However, at its core, **the Renaissance was a revival of pagan culture**. The ancient Greeks and Romans were pagans who did not believe in the One True God. In time, the Church converted them. But the philosophy, art, and literature that the leaders of the Renaissance promoted were from that pagan culture.

Many of the Renaissance leaders believed that studying the classic cultures (that is, the Greeks and Romans) would transform people into perfect humans. However, the Church has always taught that it is through the sacraments and grace that people are transformed to become holier and more pleasing to God. In many cases, people began to live more

Witness to the Faith 293

Agincourt
Battle in which King Henry V all but wiped out the French army; nearly cost the French the Hundred Years' War.

like the immoral ancient pagans about whom they were studying than the saints whom they should have been imitating.

Unfortunately, because some of the most learned individuals of the time embraced these pagan notions, their influence began to affect the Church and society. Moreover, with the advent of the printing press around 1453, their ideas spread much more easily and widely than ever before. By the later part of the fifteenth century, public morality had become seriously weakened.

At the same time, the Renaissance marked one of the greatest periods of Catholic art. In some of this art, the influence of the Greeks and Romans is evident. However, most of the religious paintings and sculptures from the Renaissance truly do glorify God, at a time when many were turning their backs on Him.

Pope Martin V

Following his election by the Council of Constance, Martin V (1417-1431) slowly returned to Rome. The schism had caused a great disruption in Italy. As a result, Martin spent several years restoring order in Italy so that he could safely enter Rome, which he finally did in September 1420. For the remainder of his papacy, in addition to dealing with the Hussites and other crises, he worked to restore the buildings and churches of Rome, which had fallen into serious disrepair. Some historians consider Martin's rebuilding efforts as part of the beginning of the artistic phase of the Renaissance.

Appearance of Sts. Catherine and Michael to Joan of Arc, Hermann Stilke

St. Joan of Arc

As the Council of Constance met in 1415, an epic battle had taken place on the fields of **Agincourt** that seemed to turn the tide of the Hundred Years' War. King Henry V's English Longbow men, the finest soldiers of the day, had virtually wiped out the French army in one afternoon. Henry V continued his conquest of France until he died suddenly at the age of 35 in 1422. However, England still possessed the finest army in the world. His successors felt confident they could finish the job. Over the next few years, they came very close to doing so.

Meanwhile, in the summer of 1425, a 13-year-old French peasant girl named Joan, living in Domremy, began to have visions of St. Michael the Archangel. Over the next three years, the messages Michael gave Joan became very specific. She was to see that Charles VII was crowned king of France, and—incredibly!—she was to lead the French soldiers in battle to defeat the English. Over the next three years, Joan heard heavenly "voices" speak to her, not only of St. Michael but also of St. Catherine of Alexandria and St. Margaret of

Antioch, virgin martyrs of the early Church. In time, their instructions became very specific. They told her to go to the nearest large town to meet a knight who would take her to Charles. In May 1428, she went.

The knight laughed at Joan and told her to go home. However, her "voices" told her to try again. She returned to the knight in January 1429. She told him about a battle that the French had just lost, something that she could not possibly have known on her own. Now, believing in Joan, this knight sent her to Charles. For her protection, she wore men's clothes, a practice she would continue for the rest of her life.

On March 9, Joan met Charles, who tried to deceive her by remaining anonymous in the crowd of nobles. However, Joan immediately recognized him. In private, she told him a secret known only to him and God. Now totally convinced by her, Charles gave her command of a French army.

Joan of Arc in Battle, Hermann Stilke

On April 27, she began her campaign to free France from the English. In the next months, she defeated the English army commanded by some of the finest generals of the time. In July, she stood beside Charles VII as he was crowned king of France in Reims. She next attempted to capture Paris. However, Charles failed to provide the necessary support. In May 1430, during a skirmish, she was captured and taken prisoner.

Joan's captors were Burgundians, Frenchmen allied with England. They sold her to the English for a king's ransom. The English put her on trial before fifty-six of the most educated men they could find in the hopes of breaking her will. However, the 19-year-old girl was their equal. Nevertheless, they burned her at the stake on May 30, 1431.

In a little over a year, Joan of Arc had accomplished the seemingly impossible. She had led the French army to victory and had seen Charles VII crowned king. Within twenty-five years of her death, the French had almost completely driven the English from France. Joan of Arc had changed the course of history. When the Hundred Years' War ended in 1453, what had seemed an inevitable English triumph in 1415 was a French victory.

Long considered a saint in France, Joan of Arc was canonized by Pope Benedict XV in 1920.

Joan of Arc's Death at the Stake, Hermann Stilke

Witness to the Faith   295

Pope Eugene IV

The Conciliar Movement

Following the death of Martin V, the conclave quickly elected Pope Eugene IV (1431-1447). A Venetian from a wealthy family, he was also the nephew of Pope Gregory XII. As pope, he faced one of the most critical issues that has ever faced the Church: Did the pope or a council ultimately govern the Church? Could a council remove the pope? These questions lie at the heart of what is called the **conciliar movement**.

The authority of a Church council had not been an issue until the Western Schism, when the notion began to take form that perhaps a Church council not called by the pope was superior to the pope and could remove him. However, nothing in the entire history of the Catholic Church, since the Council of Jerusalem in 50 AD, had provided any such authority to a council. For 1,400 years, the pope, not a committee, was the recognized head of the Church, but supporters of the conciliar movement began to attack the Church, and have continued to do so right up to the present day.

The conciliar movement was born when the Council of Basel, which Martin V called, refused to obey Pope Eugene. Martin called for the council in February 1431 to meet in Basel, Switzerland, the following month. However, less than three weeks later, Martin suddenly died. Eugene, prior to his election, had agreed to hold the council. In July 1431, Martin V's legate convened the Council of Basel. Meanwhile, Pope Eugene suffered a stroke that incapacitated him for several months. During this time, the council took several actions of which Eugene did not approve, so in December he wrote to the council and dismissed it. Amazingly, the participants of the council refused to dissolve! They wrote back, insisting *that councils were superior to the pope*, and they ordered Eugene to appear before them. Thankfully, the council and the pope worked out a solution before another serious problem erupted. In January 1433, Pope Eugene agreed to allow the council to continue and declared that it could reconvene under his authority. For the moment, the crisis had been averted—but not resolved.

In June 1435, the council began trying to restrict the pope's authority regarding the collection of money and the appointment of bishops. It seemed that the Council of Basel was determined to usurp papal authority. In October 1437, the council stated that councils were superior to popes. In January, it declared that Pope Eugene was suspended as pope. In response, Pope Eugene convoked a council in Ferrara. The Ferrara Council excommunicated all the members of the Basel Council.

The Council of Basel next went into full schism. It declared Pope Eugene deposed in June 1439. Then, in November, it elected the Duke of Savoy as the antipope Felix V. Thankfully, Felix began to lose support. The clerics at Basel, of whom there were only a handful, began to regret their decisions. In this group was a young man named Aeneas Sylvius Piccolomini, later to be Pope Pius II. In March 1445, he returned to Rome, where he made a public confession to Pope Eugene. Three weeks before dying, Pope Eugene resolved the crisis.

Following Eugene's death, the Holy Roman Emperor, Frederick III of Hapsburg, urged all his subjects to recognize Eugene's successor, Nicholas V as pope, which they did. Pope Eugene had guided the Church through one of its most turbulent times but had emerged triumphant. In fact, he had actually strengthened the papacy.

The Popes and the Fall of Constantinople

Pope Nicholas V (1447-1455) was a noted student of ancient literature, theology, philosophy, law, and medicine. His ambition was to make Rome the great center of all art and science. To this end, he founded the Vatican Library. He collected every manuscript he could buy and every translation that any scholar could make. In his day, the Vatican Library contained five thousand volumes. He also invited some of the great artists of his day, like Fra Angelico (also known as Beato Angelico), to come to Rome to decorate its churches.

Nicholas' reign also saw Constantinople fall to the Ottoman Turks in 1453. Fortunately, many of the literary classics had been brought from Constantinople to Rome before its capture. On March 29, 1453, Constantine XI, the last of the Roman emperors, perished fighting against the Muslims. The Roman Empire had finally ended.

When news of the loss of Constantinople reached Rome in July, the city fell into shock. Nicholas called for a crusade, but the age of crusades had ended. Though some rulers made a few noble gestures, nothing ever came of it.

The trauma of Constantinople's capture proved too much for Pope Nicholas. In March 1454, he fell ill. He remained bedridden until his death a year later.

The conclave to elect Nicholas V's successor was split. As they had so often done in the past, the cardinals elected an old man not expected to live long. They chose a Spaniard, Alfonso Borgia, who took the name Calixtus III (1455-1458). Calixtus came from the long line of Spaniards who had spent the past seven centuries fighting to free their homeland from the Muslims. He immediately called for a crusade to free Constantinople and sent out cardinals and bishops to preach the crusade throughout Europe.

However, this crusade was not called to free the Holy Land. The Muslims had invaded Eastern Europe and were threatening Belgrade in Hungary. In July 1456, General **John Hunyadi**, who

> **Conciliar Movement**
> A movement supporting the idea that a Church council is superior to the pope and may even remove him from office.

Pope Nicholas V, Peter Paul Rubens

Witness to the Faith 297

John Hunyadi
Commander of the Hungarian army which defeated the Turks at Belgrade in 1456.

Nepotism
The practice of favoring relatives with high positions, which was common among the popes during this time.

had been fighting the Turks for almost two decades, led the Hungarians against the Muslim forces at Belgrade. Despite being outnumbered 4 to 1, the Hungarians were victorious. The Muslims retreated and did not threaten Europe again for almost a generation.

Pope Calixtus had lived to see a great victory. However, this victory had not been followed up—a great mistake. Calixtus made another great mistake during his pontificate: he made his 25-year-old nephew, Rodrigo, a cardinal.

The practice of putting papal relatives into key positions in the Church became an ever-increasing issue during the Renaissance. This great evil that the popes used to strengthen their power was called **nepotism**. The popes made their nephews (*nepos* in Italian) cardinals. They gave their brothers leading roles in the government of the Papal States, and in general they enriched their own families. Of the thirteen popes who reigned from 1431 to 1534, all but three were related by blood to one of their predecessors or successors. Nepotism lowered people's respect for the papacy, which caused the popes to lose their influence in spiritual matters.

Pope Pius II

The conclave that convened following the death of Calixtus III elected Cardinal Aeneas Sylvius Piccolomini, who had changed greatly since his days at the schismatic Council of Basel. In fact, as Pope Pius II (1458-1464), he became one of the strongest opponents of the conciliarism heresy. In addition, Pius dedicated his entire pontificate to defending Christendom against the aggression of the Ottoman Turks. He even took the extraordinary measure of announcing that he would lead a crusade himself in hopes of shaming the powerful of Europe to join him. In June 1464, he actually took up the Cross and left Rome, intending to lead a crusade. However, though the spirit was willing, Pius was old and sickly. He died on August 14, 1464.

The Early Renaissance Popes

Pius II had ruled for six years. He had shown remarkable courage and determination. However, it had not been enough to launch his dream of a crusade. For a while, Pius would be the last pope who successfully led the Church. In the next decades, the popes would focus more on art and their own personal agendas.

Following Pius II's death, the conclave quickly elected Paul II (1464-1471). Like most of his successors, Paul accomplished little as pope.

Pope Pius II

298   *Chapter 19: The Church and the Renaissance*

Sixtus IV (1471-1484) succeeded Paul II, and he greatly damaged the papacy by his reckless nepotism. He appointed numerous relatives to positions of authority within the Church and the College of Cardinals. Sixtus was also one of the Renaissance's greatest art patrons. He invited some of Italy's greatest artists to Rome to work on its churches. In 1477, Sixtus ordered the restoration of the Sistine Chapel, to which his name has ever since been attached.

The conclave that met to elect Sixtus' successor was composed of twenty-five cardinals, making it one of the largest conclaves in decades. However, Sixtus had appointed most of the cardinals, and they were all worldly men not really suited for the priesthood. During the conclave, various armies surrounded Rome, and gangs roamed the streets. Finally, after the cardinals had made some deals among themselves, they elected Innocent VIII (1484-1492).

Although Innocent was not personally a bad man, he was sickly and weak. He lacked the physical and mental ability to lead the Church. He also practiced nepotism. His pontificate again reduced the prestige of the papacy.

The conclave to elect Innocent VIII's successor was one of the most dramatic in Church history. As so often had happened, the College of Cardinals was split. Nine cardinals favored one candidate, while another nine favored a different choice. Four cardinals remained undecided, but their votes would still not provide the required two-thirds majority. Over three ballots, the cardinals remained deadlocked. Soon the name **Rodrigo Borgia** began to be mentioned.

A Spanish cardinal, Rodrigo Borgia had been the papal chancellor for thirty-five years. However, he was considered one of the most immoral men ever to be a member of the Sacred College. His personal immorality was known throughout Christendom. Nevertheless, he was elected pope. Rodrigo Borgia took the name Alexander VI (1492-1503).

Sadly, Alexander was no Pope Vigilius. As pope, Alexander continued to live an immoral life. He appointed many of his relatives to high Church offices. His life and actions caused the Church great scandal, then and now.

Girolamo Savonarola

In response to the immorality of the Renaissance in general and of Alexander VI in particular, one man cried out in defense of Catholic morality: **Girolamo Savonarola** (1452-1498), a Dominican friar from Florence, Italy. Florence was a center of Renaissance art and thought. Its rulers, through their embrace of pagan ideas, had created a city filled with every sort of vice. These sins affected the clergy as much as the secular rulers. Savonarola, a holy man and a gifted preacher, worked to "reconvert" Florence into a city of real Catholic culture.

In late 1494, King Charles VIII of France, at the urging of one of Pope Alexander's enemies, invaded Italy and captured Florence.

Rodrigo Borgia
Became Pope Alexander VI in 1492; one of the most immoral popes.

Pope Alexander VI

Girolamo Savonarola
Dominican friar in Florence who defended Catholic morality and denounced the sins of Alexander VI. As the tone of his preaching became more violent, the pope ordered him to be silent. He disobeyed the pope, even after being excommunicated, and was condemned to death by the rulers of Florence.

Savonarola Preaching against Prodigality, Ludwig von Langenmantel

Savonarola viewed the capture of Florence as a chance to reform the city. However, Charles failed to transform the city, merely driving out its secular rulers. Charles' failure to reform Florence left Savonarola deeply disappointed. Nevertheless, a group who supported reform came to power in Florence and outlawed many of the worst vices.

By early 1495, Savonarola began to claim a gift of prophecy. Also, his sermons became increasingly violent in their tone. His criticism of Alexander reached the pope, who attempted to silence him. Savonarola complied with the order to be silent, but after four months resumed his preaching. He violently denounced the corruption in the papacy and the hierarchy in Rome. Because of his disobedience, Pope Alexander excommunicated him in May 1497. However, Savonarola continued to denounce the pope.

Pope Julius II

For all his justified denunciations, Savonarola was now acting in open disobedience to the demands of the pope. As a result, his popularity decreased. Alexander VI ordered the Florentines to surrender Savonarola or to at least prohibit him from preaching. Savonarola retorted that he would abide only by the decision of a general council. In early 1498, the rulers of Florence arrested Savonarola. They tried him and condemned him to death. In May, they burned Savonarola at the stake.

In August 1503, Pope Alexander fell ill and died. He had done immeasurable damage to the prestige of the papacy, but not to its doctrines. As noted papal historian Ludwig Pastor writes, "It is noteworthy that in matters purely concerning the Church, Alexander never did anything that justly deserves blame.... Her doctrines were maintained in all their purity" (L. Pastor, *The History of the Popes*, Vol. VI, 4th ed., trans. by F.I. Antrobus [St. Louis, Mo.: B. Herder Book Co., 1923], p. 140).

Renaissance Popes at the Beginning of the Sixteenth Century

Following the death of Alexander VI, the cardinals elected Pius III, a man who seems to have been on his deathbed at the time of his election. He reigned less than a month. He was succeeded by one of the toughest men ever to sit on the throne of St. Peter: Pope Julius II (1503-1513).

One of Pope Sixtus IV's nephews, Julius was a great statesman and a great soldier, who personally led troops in battle on at least two occasions. In his youth, he had lived an immoral life. However, perhaps seeing the damage that Alexander VI had inflicted on the Church and Christendom, Pope Julius worked to promote the welfare of the Church. Through a series of ingenious diplomatic moves, he saved the Papal States and expelled the French from Italy. In May 1512, he convoked the Fifth Lateran Council, which clearly established that the pope's authority is superior to that of any council.

In the history of the Church, no pope has helped bring about the creation of more magnificent art than Julius II. During his pontificate, he ordered the beginning of the construction of the current St. Peter's Basilica. Michelangelo painted the Sistine Chapel ceiling, generally considered the greatest artistic achievement in history. Raphael began painting the "Raphael Rooms" in the Vatican, which include such notable works as the *School of Athens*.

When Julius died in 1513, the Raphael Rooms were not finished. Julius' successor, Pope Leo X (1513-1221), had Raphael finish the

Portrait of Pope Leo X, Peter Paul Rubens

The School of Athens, Raphael

Witness to the Faith 301

Giotto di Bondone
Great artist of the Early Renaissance; pioneer of accurate detail and depth perspective in painting.

Masaccio
First great painter of the fifteenth-century Italian Renaissance; painter of realistic frescoes.

Fra Angelico
Dominican friar who painted to lift men's hearts to God. Beatified in 1982, he is the patron saint of Catholic artists.

Fresco of *The Last Judgment*, Giotto di Bondone

project. Unfortunately, Leo X was a greater patron of the arts than he was a priest. In fact, at the time of his election, Leo is reputed to have said, "God has given us the papacy; let us enjoy it." During his pontificate, the Fifth Lateran Council, which Julius II had convoked, ended its sessions. However, Leo failed to follow through with any of its reforming measures.

Pope Leo X created more than forty cardinals. While some of them were relatives, a number were excellent appointments, such as Thomas Cajetan, the leading theologian of the time and the head of the Dominican Order. Leo also insisted that the cardinals live exemplary lives. In 1514, he issued a papal bull in which he required cardinals to live chastely and piously, and to abstain not only from evil but even from the appearance of evil.

Leo X would also deal with the most serious crisis ever to confront the Church: the Protestant Revolt.

The Early Artistic Renaissance in Italy

Historians recognize two successive and distinct periods in Italy during which artists worked to revive popular interest in the arts. Art historians often refer to these periods as the Early and Late Renaissance. Giotto, Masaccio, and Fra Angelico inaugurated the Early Renaissance, which was more Catholic.

The first great artist, and the man who almost single-handedly started the Italian Renaissance, was **Giotto di Bondone** (1267-1337). Giotto served for a time as Cimabue's apprentice. However, the pupil soon outgrew the master. Giotto was the first artist to break decisively with the Gothic style, in which people appear in only two dimensions. He began to add three dimensions to painting by using *perspective*. He introduced the technique of drawing accurately from life. Giotto's great masterpiece is the series of frescoes that decorate the *Scrovegni Chapel* in Padua. After many years, Giotto completed his frescoes around 1305. This fresco cycle depicts the life of the

302 *Chapter 19: The Church and the Renaissance*

Blessed Mother and the life of Christ. Historians consider it one of the finest masterpieces of the Early Renaissance.

The second great artist of this period, and the first great painter of the fifteenth-century Italian Renaissance, was **Masaccio** (1401-1428). In Florence, Masaccio studied the works of Giotto. His frescoes introduced a realism previously unseen in figure painting. Masaccio died quite young, however, so he never realized his full potential.

The third great artist of the Early Renaissance was the Dominican friar John of Fiesole, who was called **Fra Angelico** (1395-1455) because he painted like an angel. In his paintings, Fra Angelico used bright colors, gold and blue backgrounds, and tints of rose and blue. The figures in his paintings are known for their calm expressions and astonishing beauty. As his paintings were intended to be devotional, his figures all possess a graceful dignity, whether they are part of a Crucifixion scene or an Annunciation scene. He meant his art to draw viewers into the scene and lift their minds and souls to the glory of God.

The Virgin of the Annunciation, Fra Angelico

In 1436, Fra Angelico was one of several monks who moved to the recently built monastery of San Marco in Florence. This move placed him in the city that had become the center of artistic activity. For the next ten years, he decorated the monks' cells with frescoes depicting scenes from the life of the Blessed Mother and Our Lord.

Pope John Paul II beatified Fra Angelico in 1982. He is the patron saint of Catholic artists.

The Early Renaissance in Northern Europe

The Renaissance was not limited to Italy. As artists visited Florence and Rome, they learned from what they saw, and they took this knowledge back home with them. Thus, the Renaissance spread into present-day Germany, the Netherlands, and Belgium. The four outstanding masters of the Northern Renaissance were **Jan van Eyck**, **Rogier van der Weyden**, **Hans Memling**, and **Robert Campin**. All four were active in **Flanders** (present-day Belgium). Unlike their Italian counterparts, the Flemish painters are distinguished by the exquisite detail of their paintings. Like the Italians, they mostly produced religious paintings. However, they also created a number of secular works, mainly portraits.

Robert Campin (1375-1444) is considered the first of the great Flemish and Northern European masters of the Early Renaissance, as well as one of the greatest painters of all time. His paintings depict a level of realism never seen before. Some details are so fine that they

Jan van Eyck
Flemish painter; best known for his Ghent Altarpiece, of which the highlight is *The Adoration of the Mystic Lamb.*

Rogier van der Weyden
Flemish painter; was Campin's apprentice and acquired a similar realistic style. *The Descent from the Cross* is generally considered his best.

Hans Memling
German who moved to Flanders; was Rogier van der Weyden's apprentice.

Robert Campin
Considered the first of the great Flemish and Northern European masters. Among his masterpieces is the Merode Altarpiece, which depicts the Annunciation.

Flanders
A region of northern Europe, part of present-day Belgium.

Witness to the Faith 303

Merode Altarpiece,
Robert Campin

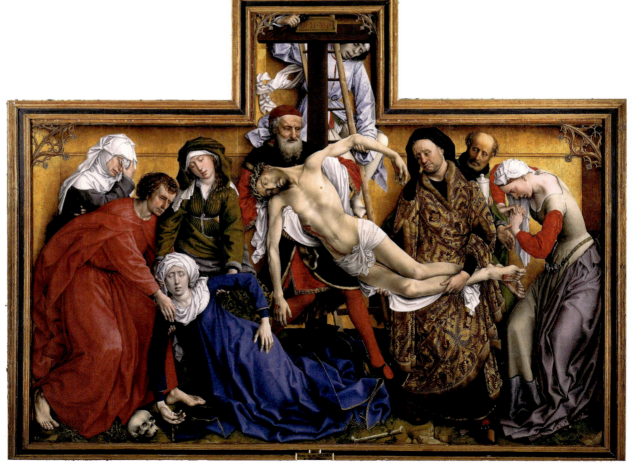

The Descent from the Cross, Rogier van der Weyden

appear to be painted with a brush no wider than a single bristle. His most astonishing masterpiece may be the *Merode Altarpiece* (1427), a *triptych* of the Annunciation. Campin depicts the moment when the Angel Gabriel, who has just entered the room, is about to tell Mary that she will be the Mother of Jesus. The right wing shows Joseph working in his carpenter's shop, drilling holes in a board. The left wing shows the donors kneeling in prayer as they look through an open door at the scene of the Annunciation in the center.

Jan van Eyck's (1390-1441) most important work is *The Adoration of the Mystic Lamb*, which forms part of the *Ghent Altarpiece*. Located in St. Bavo's Cathedral in Ghent, Belgium, *The Adoration of the Mystic Lamb* shows saints and clerics adoring Our Lord as the Lamb of God. The Lamb stands upon an altar, and from a wound in His chest, His Blood flows into a chalice.

Rogier van der Weyden (1400-1464) served as an apprentice under Robert Campin and helped paint the *Merode Altarpiece*. As a result, his work is very reminiscent of Campin's style. Like those of his master, van der Weyden's paintings have an almost photographic realism to them. Among his many paintings, *The Descent from the Cross* (c. 1435) is generally considered his finest masterpiece. *The Descent* shows Our Lord being taken down from the Cross. The figures are dressed in fifteenth-century clothing. The drama of the moment is so intense that Mary has fainted and must be supported by St. John. The profoundly human figures, especially Our Lord, Whose mangled Body is lovingly

The Adoration of the Mystic Lamb (Part of the Ghent Altarpiece), Jan van Eyck

Witness to the Faith   305

The Annunciation, Hans Memling

handled by Joseph of Arimathea, create a strong emotional effect upon the viewer.

Hans Memling (1430-1494) was born in Germany but moved to Flanders, where he worked as an apprentice to Rogier van der Weyden from 1455 to 1460. Like his fellow Flemish painters, he painted mostly religious works but also created a large number of portraits. Although Memling produced many paintings, none can be called his *definitive* masterpiece. Typical of his style is an *Annunciation* he painted between 1480 and 1489. Memling modeled his *Annunciation* on a painting by Rogier van der Weyden. However, Memling shows Mary being supported by two angels, rather than kneeling.

The High Renaissance in Italy

Three of the greatest artists in history dominated the High (or Late) Renaissance in Italy: Leonardo da Vinci, Michelangelo, and Raphael.

Historians have described **Leonardo da Vinci** (1452-1519) as a true "Renaissance Man," meaning someone who had a wide range of knowledge and talent. Leonardo was incredibly talented and excelled at almost everything he did. He was a sculptor, an architect, a painter, and an engineer. Many historians consider his painting the *Mona Lisa*

Leonardo da Vinci
One of three great artists of the High Renaissance; a brilliant painter, sculptor, architect, and engineer.

Mona Lisa, Leonardo da Vinci

The Last Supper, Leonardo da Vinci

306 *Chapter 19: The Church and the Renaissance*

(1503) among the ten greatest paintings in the world. It is probably the best-known painting in the world.

In addition to his secular paintings, Leonardo created a number of remarkable religious works. Among his finest religious paintings are *The Annunciation* (1475), two versions of *The Virgin of the Rocks* (1483 and 1495), *St. John the Baptist* (1508), and *The Virgin and Child with St. Ann* (1508). As magnificent as these paintings are, most historians consider *The Last Supper* to be his finest religious work.

Leonardo painted *The Last Supper* for the refectory of the Convent of Santa Maria delle Grazie in Milan, Italy, sometime around 1495. It remains there today. Leonardo depicts the most dramatic moment of the Last Supper, in which the Apostles react to Our Lord when He proclaims, "Behold, one of you will betray me." Because Leonardo always tried new ways to accomplish things, he painted *The Last Supper* on the wall with oil paint. Almost the minute he finished, the painting began to flake off. Despite efforts to save and restore this magnificent work, very little of Leonardo's original painting remains today.

Michelangelo Buonarroti (1475-1564) began his career as a sculptor and always considered himself primarily a sculptor. However, he also worked as a painter and an architect. Pope Julius II employed him to construct and adorn his tomb, which was never fully completed. The most impressive part of the tomb is the statue of Moses. Michelangelo sculpted Moses as a heroic, muscular figure with long flowing robes and a long flowing beard.

Pope Julius also commissioned Michelangelo to decorate the Sistine Chapel ceiling. Painted almost solely by Michelangelo between 1508 and 1512, the ceiling contains nine scenes from the Book of Genesis. Five of these scenes portray events dealing with the creation of the world and the creation of Adam and Eve. One panel shows the expulsion from Eden, and the last three show events from the life of Moses. Many art historians consider the Sistine chapel ceiling to be the supreme masterpiece in all art.

Pope Leo X later commissioned Michelangelo to finish the work on St. Peter's Basilica in Rome after the first architect, Bramante, died. Michelangelo demonstrated that he was not only a great painter and sculptor but also a remarkable architect. He crowned St. Peter's with its glorious cupola.

> **Michelangelo Buonarroti**
> Great artist of the High Renaissance; preferred sculpting, but was also a painter (notably of the Sistine Chapel) and an architect (notably of St. Peter's Basilica).

Moses, Michelangelo

Witness to the Faith

Sistine Madonna, Raphael

Raphael Sanzio
The third great artist of the High Renaissance; produced a large number of paintings despite his premature death.

Bernardine of Siena
Franciscan missionary priest and renowned preacher; traveled throughout Italy urging people to reform their lives.

St. Vincent Ferrer
Spanish Dominican priest and a traveling preacher.

Gerard Groote
Deacon from the Netherlands; led a reform movement called *Devotio Moderna*; founded the Brothers of the Common Life, Sisters of the Common Life, and Canons Regular.

Raphael Sanzio (1483-1520) is known mostly as a painter. Despite a short career, he produced an incredibly large body of work. Although Raphael created a number of extraordinary paintings, he is best known for his beautiful and tender Madonna paintings.

One of Raphael's finest Madonna paintings is his *Sistine Madonna*, which he painted for Pope Julius II in 1512. In the painting, the Blessed Mother, holding the Christ Child, stands on billowing clouds. Behind her, barely visible, scores of cherubs fill the heavenly background. On one side stands Pope St. Sixtus II, for whom the painting is named. On the other side, looking downward, stands St. Barbara, identifiable by the tower just visible over her right shoulder. At the bottom of the painting, two winged cherubim, resting on their elbows, gaze up at the scene above them.

Raphael also created a number of Biblical paintings. His best known is probably *The Transfiguration* (1520), his final painting. *The Transfiguration* actually portrays two events. In the top half of the painting, Raphael depicts the Transfiguration. In the bottom part, Raphael shows the Apostles trying to free a boy possessed by a demon (Matthew 17:14-21). They fail, but Jesus succeeds. The boy's mouth is open, showing that Jesus has cast out the demon.

Among Raphael's masterpieces are the Raphael Rooms (or *Stanze di Raffaello* in Italian), which he painted in the Vatican Palace. Most of these rooms contain depictions of historical subjects, including one that contains four paintings devoted to the life of the Emperor Constantine. Other paintings include *The Meeting of Leo the Great and Attila* and *The Battle of Ostia*. The Holy Eucharist is also featured in some paintings. *The Disputation of the Holy Sacrament*, in which both the saints in Heaven and the people on Earth adore the Sacred Host, demonstrates the triumph of Christianity over the ancient philosophies represented in the painting on the wall that is opposite this painting, *The School of Athens*. In that painting, which shows Aristotle, Plato, and other Greek philosophers debating, Raphael illustrates that truth can be discovered through reason, as St. Thomas and the scholastics had taught. The *Stanza della Segnatura* ("Room of the Signature") in which these paintings are located stands as a defense of the Blessed Sacrament. Painted in 1511, it seems Providential that Raphael created them when he did, for soon there would be many heretical sects that would deny the Real Presence.

Catholic Society during the Renaissance

Often, during times of peace and prosperity, morality declines. This occurred in the fourteenth and fifteenth centuries, both privately and publicly. People began to lead immoral lives. To justify their immorality, they refused to enforce the laws prohibiting public vices, which flourished. Yet, despite their sinfulness, the people of the Renaissance remained Catholics. Surprisingly, the Faith grew and in many places thrived. For example, the number of religious societies increased. People gave generously to the Church, even if they intended the money to promote the arts rather than help the poor. Many people fasted for their sins.

308 *Chapter 19: The Church and the Renaissance*

The Disputation of the Holy Sacrament, Raphael

Several new religious orders for women were established at this time. St. Bridget of Sweden founded the Order of the Holy Savior. St. Jane of Valois (1464-1505), the daughter of French King Louis XI, founded the Order of the Annunciation, which devoted itself to the veneration of the Blessed Mother.

The scandals and decline in morals caused a number of clerics to call for reform. Among the most prominent of these Church reformers were St. Bernardine of Siena and St. Vincent Ferrer. **Bernardine of Siena** (1380-1444) was an Italian priest and Franciscan missionary. During his lifetime, he was the most famous preacher in Italy. He traveled throughout Italy preaching against paganism and urging the people to reform their lives. **St. Vincent Ferrer** (1350-1419) was a Spanish Dominican who traveled throughout Christendom preaching penance and working miracles. Interestingly, Vincent initially supported antipope Clement VII and then antipope Benedict XIII during the Western Schism. When he finally concluded that Benedict was not the true pope, he tried to convince him to resign.

In the Netherlands, **Gerard Groote** (1340-1384) led a successful reform movement called *Devotio Moderna*, or

List of Raphael's Works of Art in This Book

Many of Raphael's paintings have been used in this book:

- *St. Paul Preaches in Athens*: p. 14
- *The Meeting of Leo the Great and Attila*: p. 85
- *Coronation of Charlemagne*: p. 139
- *The Battle of Ostia*: pp. 160-161
- *The School of Athens*: p. 301
- *Sistine Madonna*: p. 308
- *The Disputation of the Holy Sacrament*: p. 309
- *The Transfiguration*: p. 310
- *Portrait of Leo X*: p. 311

Witness to the Faith

The Transfiguration, Raphael

Thomas à Kempis
Monk of the Canons Regular; author of *The Imitation of Christ*.

The Imitation of Christ
Famous devotional book by Thomas à Kempis.

Gutenberg Inventing Printing Press, Jean-Antione Laurent

Modern Devotion. Groote was born at Deventer in the Netherlands. A bright young man, he graduated from the University of Paris in 1358. Upon his graduation, he began to lead a rather worldly life. However, he happened to meet a Carthusian monk, which caused him to undergo a sort of conversion experience. He renounced his worldly possessions, was ordained a deacon, and became, in time, a famous preacher in the Netherlands. Like St. Vincent and St. Bernardine, Gerard preached mainly against the impurity in society. During his lifetime, he founded the Brothers of the Common Life and the Sisters of the Common Life. Gerard died in 1384 from the plague, which he had contracted while caring for the sick. After his death, a third order that he had planned, the Canons Regular, was formed. Among their number they counted the famous author, Thomas à Kempis, who wrote a very special book.

Thomas à Kempis was born in 1380 and educated by the Brothers of the Common Life at Deventer. He spent his entire life as a monk in the Monastery of the Canons Regular. In 1418, Thomas wrote a little book called *The Imitation of Christ*. In this moving book, the reader catches a glimpse of the thoughts of holy men and women. Many people consider *The Imitation of Christ* to be the most beautiful book ever written. Perhaps no book, other than the Bible, has brought more comfort and inspiration to the hearts of men and women ever since.

The Bible, the Printing Press, and the Renaissance

The advent of the printing press in the mid-1450s caused a greater appreciation of the Bible than ever before in human history. It is no accident that the first book that Johann Gutenberg published was a Bible. Far from being a "forgotten book," as many of the so-called Protestant "Reformers" would claim in the sixteenth century, the Bible was widely read; it was translated into the local language (vernacular) of every Christian country in Europe.

In Italy, a complete version in the vernacular was made by Dominican Nicholas de Nardo in 1472. The first printed Bible was made in Venice in 1471. In Spain, the first printed Bible was made in Valencia in 1478 following an Old Testament version from the French and Latin. It was in the Catalonian dialect and was the work of the General of the Carthusians, Boniface Ferrer, St. Vincent Ferrer's brother. The first Bible for Catholics in Holland was printed at Delft in 1475. In Scandinavia, Hungary, Ireland, and Scotland, the Bible (or parts of it) had been translated into the vernacular prior to 1500.

In France, individual books of the Bible were translated as early as the twelfth century. The first entire translation dates from the mid-thirteenth century. Produced for King St. Louis IX, the "Bible of St. Louis" was incredibly well received by the people of France. In 1487, Jean de Rely, the confessor to King Charles VIII, published a complete French Bible.

German translations of the Bible date from the seventh and eighth centuries. By the fifteenth century, prior to the Gutenberg

Bible, a German Bible was in widespread use throughout Germany. Following the invention of the printing press, numerous Bibles in the vernacular appeared throughout Germany—at least five before 1477. Prior to the Protestant Revolt (1517), twenty popular translations of the Bible had appeared in Germany. Many complete prayer books in the vernacular were available throughout the country. There were more than one hundred editions of these prayer books.

In England, monks began translating part of the Bible into English by the early eighth century. The process continued over the centuries, as more books were translated into English. By the middle of the fourteenth century, the "English" translation of the Bible was in the Anglo-Norman dialect of the period. It seems that by the fourteenth century, a complete English version of the Bible existed. However, England was slow to print the Bible. No part of the English Bible was printed before 1525. No complete English Bible was printed before 1535, and no Bible was printed in England in the vernacular before 1538.

The Door at Wittenberg

As the year 1517 dawned, it had been almost one hundred years since the Council of Constance had ended the Western Schism. The Church had begun to heal, but scandal had plagued her. The Renaissance Popes, for the most part, had been decent men, but they had been weak and not provided strong leadership. In 1517, Raphael painted a magnificent portrait of Pope Leo X. On either side, he is bracketed by two cardinals, his nephews. Clearly, there were problems in the Church that needed to be addressed. Vincent Ferrer and Bernardine of Siena knew this.

In Wittenberg, an Augustinian monk took a hammer and nailed ninety-five statements to the door of the cathedral. His name was Martin Luther. A hammer is a tool that can be used to build or destroy. Luther used his hammer to destroy. The glory that was Christendom was coming to a close, never to be seen again.

Portrait of Leo X, **Raphael**

Oral Exercises

1. Who founded the Vatican Library?
2. What was papal nepotism?
3. Who was Girolamo Savonarola?
4. What was Giotto's masterpiece?
5. Whom did Pope John Paul II name as the patron saint of artists?
6. Who were the four outstanding masters of the Northern Renaissance?
7. What book did Thomas à Kempis write?

Witness to the Faith 311

Chapter 20

The Beginning of the Protestant Revolt

Introduction

From the beginning of Christendom, its unifying factor was the Catholic Faith. Catholicism permeated society in a way that seems unimaginable today. Every aspect of life revolved around the Church and the Faith.

During the fourteenth and fifteenth centuries, the Catholic Faith remained strong in Christendom. The appearance of the Franciscans and Dominicans and their roles as teachers in Europe's universities strengthened the Faith. However, Our Lord had established the Sacrament of Confession for a reason: people sin. During the Renaissance, most of the popes were decent men, but they lost their focus on the City of God, and began to focus *too much* on art, literature, and the politics of Italy.

By the beginning of the sixteenth century, the need for reform in the Church was clear. Many good and holy men called for reform and worked to bring it about in the Church. Such reforms have occurred throughout the Church's history. Heresies and misunderstandings have afflicted the Church since the time of the Apostles. The first council in Jerusalem met to decide the issue of the rules governing new converts when a dispute arose between St. Paul and other Church leaders. These reforms corrected errors and improved conditions in the Church *without harming its unity*. However, by the beginning of the sixteenth

> **Protestant Revolt**
> The movement, beginning in the early sixteenth century, in which many Christians left the Church to form their own groups, leaving Christendom split in many pieces.

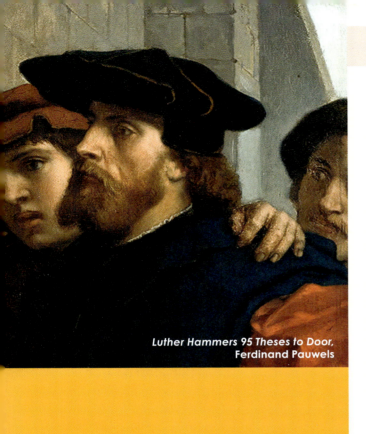

Luther Hammers 95 Theses to Door, Ferdinand Pauwels

1517 A.D. – 1555 A.D.

1517 A.D.
Luther puts forth his ninety-five theses.

1519 A.D.
Luther and John Eck debate at Leipzig.

1521 A.D.
At the Diet of Worms, Luther is asked to recant his errors, and he refuses.

1524-1525 A.D.
Mobs of peasants rise up throughout Germany and Austria in the Peasants' War.

1526 A.D.
Under the first Diet of Speyer, Luther and his followers establish their own state churches. Monasteries and churches in those places are seized.

1530 A.D.
Philipp Melanchthon presents the "Augsburg Confession," a summary of Protestant doctrines. The Schmalkaldic League is formed.

1545 A.D.
The Council of Trent opens its first session, beginning the true reformation of the Church.

1548 A.D.
Charles V issues the Augsburg Interim.

1552 A.D.
Maurice of Saxony revolts; the Augsburg Interim ends. A truce is arranged.

1555 A.D.
The Peace of Augsburg determines that the religion of each state is to be chosen by its ruler.

century, events occurred which divided Christians on an unprecedented scale.

Causes of the Protestant Revolt

The movement that began early in the sixteenth century, which historians have wrongly labeled "the Reformation," should be called the **Protestant Revolt**. It was a revolt against the Catholic Church and Catholic society. By 1520, Martin Luther, the principal architect of the revolt, clearly stated that his goal was not to reform the Catholic Church but to destroy it and replace it with a church of his own. In June 1520, Luther wrote that the Catholic Church had become a dwelling place of "dragons, evil spirits, goblins, and witches." He urged the German nobility to "assail with arms" the pope, cardinals, and bishops. These are

Witness to the Faith 313

not the words of a man calling for reform. They are the words of a man calling for an armed insurrection!

The Protestant Revolt had many causes. Some of the causes were religious, but others were social, economic, and political. Some of the problems that afflicted the Church were real. However, other reasons given for attacks on the Church were false and merely excuses.

During any other period, the Protestant Revolt likely would have failed, as had other revolts, such as the revolts of John Wyclif and Jon Hus. However, in the early sixteenth century, events in Europe created an atmosphere that allowed Martin Luther's revolt to flourish. Several factors made this revolt successful.

First, many European rulers, especially in the Holy Roman Empire, had developed a **negative attitude toward the papacy and envied the Church's wealth**. Second, the Renaissance had created an atmosphere in which **people began turning away from God and more toward man**. Corruption had spread across society and affected not only the laity but also the clergy, including the bishops, cardinals, and popes, which in turn created **scandal**, the third cause of the Revolt. Fourth, scandal caused a lack of moral authority, which in turn created a **general spirit of disobedience and rejection of authority**, especially the authority of the Church. In this atmosphere of lax morals, leaders began to act in their own interests rather than the best interests of their subjects and the Church.

Greed

By 1500, the Catholic Church was the wealthiest organization in the world. It owned churches, cathedrals, abbeys, convents, and monasteries throughout Christendom. All of this land produced income. However, the Catholic Church did not enrich itself with the money. The Church used the money for charitable purposes, operating orphanages, hospitals, schools, and colleges. The Church also used the money to maintain its churches, cathedrals, monasteries, abbeys, and shrines. For hundreds of years, the Church's wealth had aroused the greed of Europe's rulers, who coveted the Church's land and the income that it generated. These rulers welcomed a new religion which declared that these rulers could seize this land for themselves.

Paganism and Immorality

During the Middle Ages, the monks and scholars who studied the ancient Greek and Roman literature were guided by the principle that man was made for God, in His image and likeness. They focused on living their lives according to God's Law. Thus, when they studied the ancient texts, they did so through the lens of Faith. They took what was good from the ancient philosophers, but left the rest.

However, during the Renaissance, many of those who studied the ancient Greeks and Romans embraced the pagan ideas as being good and true. They focused their lives on the physical world, rather than on God

Scandal
"An attitude or behavior which leads another to do evil" (*Catechism*, no. 2284).

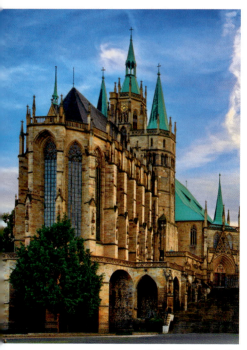

Erfurt Cathedral

and the spiritual world. In fact, they tended to abandon any interest in life after death. Their earthly lives became more interesting and important to them than their eternal lives. For many of the educated people during this time, the spirit of ancient paganism became the spirit of the Renaissance. The immoral conduct of the pagans replaced the morality of the Catholic Church. Vice replaced virtue.

Scandal

As public morality declined, even the clergy began leading immoral lives. This created terrible scandal—as it does today. The laity looks to Church leaders to lead exemplary lives. People hold bishops and the pope to a higher standard *because they are Church leaders*. While the Renaissance Popes, with the exception of Alexander VI, were not bad men, they failed to live exemplary lives. They also failed to address the scandal that Renaissance paganism had caused. Their inaction, more than their actions, led common people to become disillusioned and unhappy with the Church.

Disobedience to Authority

Finally, the Western Schism had created a terrible situation, which led even bishops and cardinals to question the ultimate authority of the pope. Those who embraced the conciliar heresy had claimed that a council could remove the pope and that councils were the final authority on matters of faith and morals. Luther's new religion would continue this heretical position. Moreover, princes who wished to oppose their king or the emperor would find justification in a religion that allowed everyone to determine the rightness of their own actions.

Martin Luther

The Solution to the Revolt: The Catholic Church

Covetousness among rulers, unhappiness among the common people, paganism among the educated, and disrespect for authority among nearly everyone were **the real causes of the Protestant Revolt**. The scandals, abuses, and laxity among the clergy that existed were not the cause. They were the excuses to destroy the one power that could oppose the greed of the mighty, provide comfort to the suffering, Christianize the pagans, and restore respect for authority. Moreover, only the Catholic Church could reform the scandals and abuses that afflicted priests, bishops, and even the pope. It was into this climate of discord, scandal, and envy that Martin Luther appeared with his message of revolt. Sadly, too many people had too many reasons to embrace it.

Who Was Martin Luther?

Martin Luther was born in Germany on November 10, 1483. He was a good student, so after completing his early education, he entered the University of Erfurt in 1501. Luther received his degree four years

Indulgence
A remission (reduction) of the temporal punishment due to sin, the guilt of which has already been forgiven.

John Tetzel
Dominican who promoted an indulgence for anyone who donated to help rebuild St. Peter's, using the indulgence as a fundraiser. The "selling" of indulgences was a common abuse during this time.

John Tetzel

later and decided on a legal career. At this point, there is no evidence that he had any sort of religious vocation. In June 1505, during a break from school, he returned to visit his family. The following month, while walking back to the university, he was caught in a thunderstorm that nearly killed him. Lightning struck so close to him that it knocked him down. In a moment of terror, he cried out in prayer and vowed that if he lived he would become a monk.

Luther carried out his vow, against the advice of his father and friends. Luther felt no joy in his vow and would later write of it with deep sadness and regret. Nevertheless, he had made up his mind, and no one could dissuade him. Two weeks after the storm, Luther joined the Augustinian Order at Erfurt. This proved to be a terrible mistake for Luther—and the world.

Intelligent and determined, Luther advanced quickly in the order. In 1506, he took his final vows. Two years later, he was sent to the University of Wittenberg to teach moral philosophy. In 1512, he became a doctor of theology. However, he was constantly unhappy with his life. Although Luther was a priest, he hated Confession and never liked to say Mass. In an October 1516 letter, he wrote that he avoided saying Mass whenever possible. Two years later, he wrote, "The word which I hated most in all the Scriptures was the word penance."

Luther's fundamental problem was that he felt he was not worthy of salvation. Luther believed that nothing he did would merit God's forgiveness or his eternal salvation. His problems *in feeling personally unworthy of salvation* increased until he finally sought peace of mind and the promise of his eternal salvation in a new religion.

Between November 1515 and September 1516, Martin Luther delivered a series of lectures that became his *Commentary on the Epistle to the Romans*. In these lectures, he declared that man is utterly incapable of anything good and is saved solely by faith. God communicates faith to the sinful soul, by which it acknowledges itself bad, puts its trust in Him, and receives justification as its reward. **The two fundamental doctrines of Lutheranism are justification by faith alone and the utter corruption of human nature as the result of Original Sin.** These doctrines created a spiritual refuge for Luther so that he no longer needed to deal with his own sense of personal unworthiness. In July 1517, Luther publicly preached a sermon in which he declared his doctrine of salvation by faith alone, stating, "Nobody who possesses this faith need doubt his salvation."

Luther's Ninety-Five Theses

The occasion of Luther's break with the Church involved indulgences. An **indulgence** is a remission (reduction) of the temporal punishment due to sin, the guilt of which has already been forgiven. Archbishop Albert of Mainz had established an indulgence for anyone who donated money to help rebuild St. Peter's Basilica. In 1516, Dominican **John Tetzel** was sent to Germany to preach the indulgence.

Luther Nailing the 95 Theses,
Julius Hubner

Although the record is not clear, it appears that Tetzel was overzealous in his preaching. He apparently went so far as to say that once the coin hits the money box, the soul jumps out of Purgatory. This regrettable practice seems to have been common in Germany at the time and is an example of area in which the Church needed reform.

In response to Tetzel's preaching, Luther wrote out ninety-five theses, mostly dealing with the doctrine and practice of indulgences. However, rather than focusing on Tetzel's inappropriate "sales pitch," Luther attacked the very idea of indulgences! He declared that God did not recognize indulgences, and that the Church had no treasury of grace from which to dispense them. On October 31, 1517, he nailed his ninety-five theses to the door of the Wittenberg palace church. Luther quickly found supporters for his cause—with the issue of indulgences being their excuse for breaking with the Church.

When Archbishop Albert learned of the ninety-five theses, he sent them to Rome in December. He asked that Luther be silenced. He also requested that anyone preaching indulgences do so in a more dignified manner. Finally, he suggested that the money used to rebuild St. Peter's be more closely accounted for.

Pope Leo X Intervenes

In response to Archbishop Albert's letter, Pope Leo X asked Luther's superior to admonish him. However, the superior supported Luther, so he took no action.

Pope Leo X

Witness to the Faith   **317**

Cardinal Thomas Cajetan and Martin Luther, Ferdinand Pauwels

Cardinal Thomas Cajetan
Headed the papal tribunal that judged Luther's teaching at Augsburg in 1518; tried to persuade Luther to retract his statements.

John Eck
Dominican theologian; debated with Luther at Leipzig.

Disputation of Leipzig
Debate between Luther and Eck, in which Luther invented the principle of private judgment.

Luther learned of the pope's intent to admonish him. Initially, he *publicly* appeared to be obedient toward Pope Leo. However, as early as May 9, 1518, Luther *privately* wrote to a former teacher that "reform of the Church was impossible" and that the Church had to be "thoroughly uprooted." This is not the letter of someone seeking to reform the Church, but rather a revolutionary seeking to destroy it. On May 30, 1518, Luther sent Pope Leo X an explanation of his theses, along with a humble letter.

Pope Leo then summoned him to Rome. Luther refused to go but offered to justify his position. At the request of Luther's strongest supporter, the Elector Frederick of Saxony, Leo allowed Luther to appear at Augsburg before a tribunal headed by the papal legate **Cardinal Thomas Cajetan**. Cardinal Cajetan almost immediately recognized the harmful nature of Luther's teachings. He asked Luther to retract his heretical statements. Cardinal Cajetan relied on St. Thomas Aquinas, whom Luther despised, to bolster his arguments. Luther declared that only an argument based solely on Scripture would convince him. Eventually, he agreed to sign a vaguely respectful statement, but refused to recant his errors.

During the night of October 20, Luther secretly left Augsburg. A month later, he issued a pamphlet calling for a general council. He was able to remain defiant because of the protection of Frederick of Saxony, who forbade Cardinal Cajetan from condemning Luther until some university had judged him.

The actions of Frederick in opposing Cardinal Cajetan typify the problems that allowed the revolt to spread. The entire history of Luther's revolt is one of tragic geography. The Holy Roman Empire at the time was a patchwork quilt of principalities, each ruled rather independently. Luther lived in a part of Saxony where he received protection. Had he lived in a different part of Saxony, its ruler, a staunch Catholic, would have turned him over to the pope for trial. Luther would have been declared a heretic, dealt with, and made no impact on history.

Luther Publicly Breaks with the Church

In December 1518, Dominican **John Eck** agreed to debate one of Luther's friends and strongest supporters at the University of Leipzig on the issues of indulgences, penance, and free will. In addition to being the foremost theologian in Germany, John Eck was also Germany's finest debater. In February 1519, Luther himself asked to join the debate, the so-called **Disputation of Leipzig**, to defend his positions. In June, Eck and Luther held their debate.

During Luther's presentation, Eck realized that Luther's doctrines were identical to those of heretics John Wyclif and Jon Hus. Eck asked Luther if he supported Jon Hus or the Council of Constance, which declared Hus a heretic. Luther upheld the teachings of Hus. Luther went on to reject all authority, both the authority of the pope and Church councils, leaving no final authority in the Church whatsoever. He referred all questions to Sacred Scripture, which he declared could be interpreted by each person according to his own judgment. Thus, he created the **principle of private judgment**, which doomed Protestantism to doctrinal anarchy.

The minutes of the Disputation of Leipzig were sent to the Universities of Paris, Louvain, and Cologne. All three condemned Luther. In June 1520, Luther retorted by issuing his pamphlet *On the Papacy at Rome*, in which

Luther and Eck Dispute in Leipzig

he declared that the "wrath of God" had come upon the pope and that Rome had become the dwelling place of dragons and evil spirits. Two months later, in his *Address to the German Nobility*, he called upon them to launch an armed assault on the Catholic Church and "wash [their] hands in [the] blood" of the pope and the cardinals.

Pope Leo X then condemned Luther's teachings on indulgences, justification by faith alone, and the denial of Church authority. The pope gave Luther sixty days to recant his teachings. However, as subsequent events would show, Luther almost never changed his mind or obeyed anyone but himself. On January 3, 1521, Pope Leo X finally excommunicated Martin Luther.

The Steps to the Throne of the Hero King

Like all of history, the Protestant Revolt occurred because of the people involved in specific times and places. Pope Leo X acted wisely and properly in nearly every decision he made regarding Luther. However, while Leo had papal authority, he lacked moral authority. There was a great deal of anti-clericalism in Germany at the time. Moreover, the lives of the Renaissance Popes had scandalized the German people. Leo, though personally a decent man, practiced nepotism. Recall Raphael's painting showing him with his two nephews whom he had made cardinals. Leo also threw lavish banquets in the Vatican. These actions resulted in his lack of *moral* authority at a time when he desperately needed it. Thus, Leo was not able to stop Martin Luther's revolt. It would fall to a teenage boy to try.

Principle of Private Judgment
Luther's teaching that every believer can interpret Scripture for himself.

Witness to the Faith 319

In 1517, as Luther nailed his theses to the door of Wittenberg's church, the king of Spain was a 17-year-old boy named *Carlos*, "Charles" in English. He was the son of Ferdinand and Isabel's daughter Juana and her husband, Philip of Hapsburg, the son of the Holy Roman Emperor. Charles had been born in Ghent, Belgium, but when his grandparents died and his mother went insane, he became king of Spain. In 1517, Spain was the strongest nation in the world, as well as the most devoutly Catholic. For the remainder of his life, Charles would need that strength. For more than thirty years, he would stand virtually alone in the breach, as the threats against the Church and Christendom threatened to destroy both.

In February 1516, King Ferdinand of Spain died and named his grandson Charles the king of Spain. In September 1517, Charles left Flanders and, after a series of adventures, arrived in Spain—a country whose language he did not speak. Over the next two years, Charles learned Spanish and won the hearts of the Spanish people, who would support him almost without question for the remainder of his life.

Meanwhile, in Germany, Emperor Maximilian, Charles' other grandfather, had fallen ill. Before he died in January 1519, Maximilian made it clear that he wished Charles to succeed him as Holy Roman Emperor. At this point, Pope Leo X, who had acted so wisely in dealing with Luther, showed why the Renaissance Popes had scandalized the Church. Rather than backing Charles, a devout Catholic, Leo ordered his legate in Germany, Cardinal Cajetan, *three months after his encounter with Luther*, to support Luther's main defender, Elector Frederick, as the new emperor. Leo clearly put the political situation in Italy above the religious needs of the Church. Thankfully, at the end of June, as Luther and Eck were debating in Leipzig, Charles was elected Emperor Charles V.

It now fell to the 19-year-old Charles to deal with Martin Luther's revolt, the greatest threat to Christendom since the Muslims. In the history of the world, perhaps no other 19-year-old has had such a great responsibility. Charles, the greatest emperor since Charlemagne, set himself to the task.

Charles V Seeks to End Luther's Revolt

In spring 1520, Charles told his Spanish subjects that he had to leave Spain to attend a German Diet the following year, where he would be crowned. He asked the Spanish for money to fight the growing danger to the Catholic Faith from Luther, as well as the ever-present threat from the Muslims. He promised to return in three years.

The Imperial Diet met at Worms on January 27, 1521. One of its first actions was to hear the papal legate read Pope Leo X's excommunication of Luther, issued January 3. The legate also publicly read many of Luther's more violent writings and urged Charles to enforce the excommunication of Luther, whom he described as a violent revolutionary. Many of those present had not been aware of the true nature of Luther's beliefs. Once they realized what he advocated, many of his supporters changed their attitudes.

Emperor Charles V

320 *Chapter 20: The Beginning of the Protestant Revolt*

In April 1521, Emperor Charles summoned Luther to the Diet of Worms. When asked to recant his errors, Luther requested 24 hours to prepare his answer. When he returned the following day, he said, "I believe neither in the pope nor in the councils…. I cannot and do not desire to recant anything."

That night, Charles V wrote his answer to Luther. The following day, he declared at the Diet: "You know that I am born of the most Christian emperors of the noble German nation, of the Catholic kings of Spain … who were all to the death true sons of the Roman Church, defenders of the Catholic Faith…. **It is certain that a single monk must err if he stands against the opinion of all Christendom. Otherwise, Christendom itself would have erred for more than a thousand years.** Therefore I am determined to set my kingdoms and dominions, my friends, my body, my blood, my life, my soul upon it [the defense of the Catholic Faith]" (K. Brandi, *The Emperor Charles V* [London: J. Cape, 1965]). Thereupon, the Diet issued the **Edict of Worms**, which declared Luther an outlaw under sentence of death and condemned his heresies.

Luther at the Diet of Worms, Anton von Werner

Charles V realized that the vocation of the emperor was to defend the Church from the infidel without and the heretic within. For almost the entirety of his adult life, he would fight Protestant revolutionaries in Germany and the Muslims in the East. Almost single-handedly, he would try to hold Catholic Europe together. Charles had looked Luther in the eye and taken the measure of the man. He knew the danger Luther represented and what Luther intended. However, Charles had promised Luther safe passage to and from the Diet of Worms. Charles kept his word, even though his Spanish soldiers wanted to arrest Luther.

Pope Leo X hailed the Edict of Worms as a great victory. He probably believed it had ended the matter of Martin Luther. However, the Edict was only worthwhile if it could be enforced. While Charles V did all he could to enforce it, Luther was still very popular with the German princes, and they protected him. Even some high-ranking Catholic clergy supported Luther. Cardinal Archbishop Albert of Mainz refused to sign or enforce the Edict in his archdiocese. In 1523, the Diet of Nuremberg decreed that the implementation of the Edict of Worms should be postponed and that a general council should re-examine Martin Luther and his doctrines. Meanwhile, Luther's revolt grew.

The Peasants' War

Luther had called for the people of Germany to "wash [their] hands in [the] blood" of the Catholic clergy. In 1524, he got his wish, as much of central Europe erupted in the **Peasants' War**. Amazingly, although Luther was the main instigator of the war, he was also its main antagonist.

Edict of Worms
The decree of the Diet of Worms that declared Luther an outlaw under sentence of death and condemned his heresies.

Peasants' War
Uprisings of angry peasants, encouraged by Anabaptist preachers, in Germany and Austria; caused great destruction until suppressed.

Witness to the Faith

The inherent problem with Luther's teaching was his doctrine of *private judgment*, or the "*priesthood of the believer*," which states that each person can interpret the Bible according to his own judgment. In essence, everyone becomes pope. Because each person is considered correct in his interpretation, all interpretations must be considered correct. The result is a constant split between believers because, according to this doctrine, *there is no single infallible authority that is free from error*—that is, the true pope. Almost immediately, Luther and his followers fell into this doctrinal trap, as people within his revolt began to desert him.

At Zwickau, in Saxony, Thomas Muntzer, a traveling preacher, and Nicholas Storch, a tailor, organized the sect known as the **Anabaptists**. These fanatics rejected infant Baptism because they believed that a person had to make a conscious decision to be baptized, something babies clearly cannot do. They violently hated the beliefs and practices not only of Catholics but also of most other Christians. Finally, they believed that they alone were the elect of God.

Muntzer and Storch went to Wittenberg, determined to conquer it for their new religion. They convinced a Catholic priest named **Andreas Carlstadt**, who had been one of Luther's early supporters and who had debated John Eck at Leipzig, to join them. Carlstadt turned into one of the revolt's most radical leaders. Under his influence, Wittenberg became one of the most revolutionary places in the empire. Mass was prohibited, the sacraments were abolished, mobs attacked priests, and statues and paintings in the churches of Wittenberg were destroyed. By December 26, 1521, Carlstadt decided to marry, apparently abandoning the Catholic Faith.

In March 1522, Luther returned to Wittenberg. He apparently supported Carlstadt in all his actions, except perhaps his marriage. Luther strongly supported the abolition of the Mass, which he saw as the basis of the Catholic Church and the greatest obstacle to his revolt. In this assessment at least, he was absolutely correct.

The violence in Wittenberg upset Elector Frederick, who, though willing to protect Luther, was not willing to see his realm in flames. Thus, Luther condemned the violence in Wittenberg. The radical Anabaptists were driven from the city, but that did not put an end to their erroneous preaching.

Driven from Saxony, Thomas Muntzer began preaching his revolutionary doctrines in southwestern Germany. In late 1524, he managed to incite the people against the clergy and the nobles. Soon armies of angry peasants staged a series of uprisings throughout Germany and Austria that caused terrible destruction and loss of life. Angry at the wealth of the Church and incited by the radicals of the new religion, the peasants plundered monasteries, convents, churches, and castles. They burned more than a thousand convents and castles to the ground. During the Peasants' War (1524-1525), perhaps as many as 300,000 peasants revolted. Because the peasants were not trained or well armed,

Anabaptists
A sect organized by Thomas Muntzer and Nicholas Storch; named for their rejection of infant Baptism.

Andreas Carlstadt
A priest who joined the Anabaptists and helped to establish their movement in Wittenberg.

they proved no match for the armed and well-trained knights of the princes of the empire. Thus, they suffered terrible casualties. More than 100,000 peasants may have died or been wounded during the war.

On May 15, 1525, Thomas Muntzer led his troops against Catholic forces at the Battle of Frankenhausen in Saxony. His troops were defeated, and he was captured. Several days later, he was executed. The Battle of Frankenhausen essentially ended the Peasants' War, as the peasants no longer had a leader.

In 1525, Martin Luther harshly condemned the peasants and their violent uprisings. He completely supported the German nobles, many of whom supported him. He had urged rebellion, but when it occurred, he abandoned his followers.

Meanwhile, Andreas Carlstadt fled Saxony for Switzerland. He served as a minister in Switzerland for the rest of his life. Carlstadt died in 1541 from the plague.

The Conclave of 1521

On December 1, 1521, Pope Leo X died. He was only 46 but had been ill for some time; however, his death was unexpected. Though he had worked diligently to oppose Luther, Leo probably never realized how much his own nepotism, lavish lifestyle, political intrigues, and failure to reform the Church had helped fuel Luther's revolt. The conclave, consisting of thirty-nine cardinals, met at the end of the month to elect Leo's successor.

The Catholic Church has always taught that the Holy Spirit is present in a special way at a papal conclave, bestowing extraordinary blessings on the cardinals to help them elect a good man to lead the Church. Sometimes His presence is more obvious than other times. In 1521, His presence was more obvious than perhaps any time since Pentecost.

St. Katharine's Church in Zwickau, Where Thomas Muntzer Preached

Battle of Frankenhausen

Witness to the Faith 323

The conclave of 1521 consisted of cardinals who were typical men of the Renaissance. They seemed more concerned with things of this world than the next. Since thirty-six of them were Italians, they appeared to care more about the political situation in Italy than reforming the Church. Only two men stood apart at the conclave: the great Dominican Cardinal Thomas Cajetan and one other, the next pope.

After eight ballots, the conclave was deadlocked. In the face of the greatest threat the Church had ever faced, a period without a pope would be incredibly devastating. At this moment, the Holy Spirit seems to have conferred a special grace upon one of the cardinals.

Cardinal Adrian of Utrecht
Became Pope Adrian VI; a good and holy man who worked for reform, but was unable to achieve much.

On January 9, 1522, Cardinal Giulio Medici, not a holy man, stood up and announced that the conclave appeared to be deadlocked; therefore, they must choose a man known for his piety. He proposed **Cardinal Adrian of Utrecht**, the teacher of Emperor Charles V. Most of the Italians did not even know Cardinal Adrian, who was in Spain acting as Charles' regent. However, they elected him. Both Charles and Adrian were amazed. Charles, still only 21 years old, believed the Holy Spirit acted in the election. He wrote to a Spanish bishop and told him that the choice of Adrian as pope was "the choice of God, [rather] than of men."

In his humility, Cardinal Adrian decided to retain his own name rather than choose a new papal name. Thus, he became the sixth pope named Adrian (1522-1523). He would be one of the last two men not to choose a new name.

Pope Adrian VI

Pope Adrian realized that the Church was in mortal danger, as much from her leaders' own inaction as from Luther and his followers. The moment he arrived in Rome, Adrian immediately began to reform the Church. On September 1, 1522, he addressed the College of Cardinals, declaring that the Church desperately needed reform. The worldly cardinals, however, found his German accent funny and failed to understand his lack of appreciation of Renaissance art, much of which he found immodest. Nevertheless, for the next year, Adrian worked to reform the Church. Sadly, he worked almost entirely alone. On September 14, 1523, the finest pope the Church had known for many years died, having failed to achieve any real reforms.

Pope Clement VII

With the election of Adrian VI, the Sacred College had chosen a good and holy man, who had nonetheless failed to accomplish anything. With the election of Cardinal Giulio Medici, they chose to take another approach. Cardinal Medici had honorably recommended the choice of Cardinal Adrian. However, at the 1523 conclave, he essentially bought the papacy through a series of promises and bribes to the other cardinals. Medici chose the name Clement VII (1523-1534).

Pope Adrian VI

Unlike the holy Pope Adrian VI, Pope Clement VII had a reputation as a clever and worldly politician who could get things done. Although he seemed at times to consider making reforms to the Church, he never did. During his pontificate, Luther's errors continued to spread. Once again, it fell to Charles V to try to stop the spread of the revolution against the Church and Christendom.

The Rise of Protestantism

By 1526, the new heretical sects had become so strong in Germany that it had become impossible to enforce the Edict of Worms. In order to maintain peace in the empire, a Diet met at Speyer in the summer of 1526, in the hopes of making peace between the Lutherans (who were led by John the Elector of Saxony and Philip of Hesse) and the Catholics. The Diet issued an order that suspended the Edict of Worms, causing terrible consequences. Emperor Charles was not present; however, he had little choice but to accept the Diet's decision.

Pope Clement VII

The Diet of Speyer's order meant that Luther and the princes who supported him could now begin establishing separate state churches in the various principalities of the Holy Roman Empire. The ruler of the realm would determine that realm's religion, which would become the state religion replacing Catholicism. Since Luther's new religion allowed princes to seize the property of the Catholic Church, many German princes joined his movement, and it spread quickly. They took churches and monasteries that the Catholic Church had owned for hundreds of years. In many of the churches they seized, Luther's followers destroyed the beautiful altars and statues. Within a short time, civil rulers in almost every principality in northern and central Germany also seized control over religious matters. They worked to abolish two sacraments: the Holy Eucharist in the Mass and Confession.

In March 1529, a second Diet met in Speyer. It attempted to slow the spread of Luther's revolt, which had grown dramatically since the first Diet of Speyer. Charles V's brother Ferdinand presided over the Diet in his brother's absence. He condemned the princes at Speyer for their attacks on the Church. He declared that Catholicism was the official religion of the empire and that they had no right to choose other religions for their realms. In response, on April 25, the Lutherans in the Diet formally protested all the actions of the Diet. This act created the name **Protestant**, which from that time forward would be applied to all those who profess to be Christian but oppose the Catholic Church.

> **Protestant**
> The name given, since the time of Luther, to those who profess to be Christian but oppose the Catholic Church (because, like the Lutherans after the Second Diet of Speyer, they are effectively "protesting").

Witness to the Faith 325

Charles V Struggles to Suppress Protestantism

As emperor, Charles V tried to halt the spread of the Protestant Revolt. However, other "Catholic" rulers who should have aided him instead attacked him. Charles spent much of his reign fighting King Francis I of France. The first war with France began in 1521 and lasted six years. The last war with Francis began in 1542, after Francis had allied himself with the Muslims against Charles!

Additionally, Charles fought almost continuously with the Muslim Turks, led by their sultan, Suleiman the Magnificent. The Muslims constantly threatened Catholic Europe and trade in the Mediterranean. The war against the Muslims was doubly hard to fight, as the Protestants in the German government often refused to give Charles the money he needed to wage the war. These Protestants saw the Muslims as a good counterweight to the Catholic power.

Forced to wage wars with France and defend Europe from the Muslims, Charles was not able to devote the time or resources necessary to fight the Protestant rebels. Moreover, Pope Clement VII rendered little aid to Charles—either politically, at times supporting King Francis, or spiritually, by failing to convoke a council to reform the Church. As a result, the Protestants in the empire consolidated their power and expanded. The various Diets simply did not slow their rebellion. Consequently, from 1524 to 1530, Protestants destroyed almost all the monasteries in Germany, and many in Switzerland.

The fact is that the problem was too deeply rooted. For too long, bishops, cardinals, and even popes had attained their offices because they were the brothers, children, or friends of those who appointed or elected them. Many of them were unworthy men. The heresy that afflicted the Church was in great part of their own making. Only good and holy men could undo it, but the men in positions of authority were often too greedy and grasping.

In February 1530, although Charles had already been emperor for eleven years, Pope Clement crowned him as Holy Roman Emperor. The coronation's delay was due in part to Charles' bitterness over Clement's support for King Francis. On June 15, Charles arrived in Augsburg, where the next Imperial Diet was to be held. He hoped that perhaps a reconciliation between the Catholics and the Protestants might be possible. He would try one last time before Christendom was torn completely and irrevocably asunder.

Emperor Charles V opened the Diet of Augsburg by declaring that he wished to end the religious disputes in Germany fairly. To achieve that result, he was willing to listen to a statement of the Protestants' beliefs and the reasons for them. Since Luther, who was still considered a criminal, could not appear before the Diet, his friend and associate **Philipp Melanchthon** presented a summary of

Philipp Melanchthon

Philipp Melanchthon
Luther's friend and associate; presented the Augsburg Confession for him at the Diet of Augsburg.

326   *Chapter 20: The Beginning of the Protestant Revolt*

the Protestants' doctrines. Historians have named this summary the *Augsburg Confession*.

Among other doctrines, the Augsburg Confession condemned private Masses, clerical celibacy, monastic vows, and compulsory Confession. It reaffirmed salvation by faith alone but did not mention Luther's doctrine of the priesthood of the believer. After six weeks, the Catholic theologians who studied it, among them John Eck, refused to accept it.

In the meantime, Charles asked the Protestants to return the Church property they had taken. They refused. Charles pointed out that stealing someone else's property is forbidden by the Bible, as well as civil and canonical laws. Nevertheless, the Protestants still refused to return the stolen Church property.

In September, Charles presented the Protestants with his response, rejecting the Augsburg Confession. He declared that Catholic theologians had examined it and, based on Sacred Scripture, had refuted it. He gave them until the following April to decide to rejoin the empire and the Catholic Church until a future Church council rendered a further decision. In the meantime, they were not to spread their message or to steal any Catholic Church property.

When the Protestants replied that they would not comply with Charles' order, he issued an imperial edict in November commanding the strict enforcement of the Edict of Worms. It directed that the authority of bishops be restored in all places and that confiscated church property be returned to its rightful owners. A month later, the Protestant princes formed the **Schmalkaldic League** as a military alliance against Charles' attempts to enforce his decrees.

Before Charles could deal with the Schmalkaldic League, his two arch-foes, the Muslims and King Francis, attacked, compelling him to make peace with the Schmalkaldic League. Charles and the League signed the Peace of Nuremberg in 1532, which declared that until the next council, or at least until the next Diet, the Protestants would be left in peace and Charles' earlier edicts would not be enforced. For more than a decade, Charles had to concentrate his time and energy on fighting Francis and the Muslims. During those years, the Protestants had time to spread their heresy.

Schmalkaldic League
The league of Protestant princes formed against Charles V.

Council of Trent

Charles V at Muhlberg

Battle of Muhlberg
Victory of Charles V over the Schmalkaldic League; gave him control of northern Germany.

Augsburg Interim
Charles V's temporary solution to the religious unrest, a kind of compromise between the Church and Protestants.

The Peace of Augsburg
The decree that formally approved state churches, determining that the religion of each state would be chosen by its ruler.

In 1544, Charles finally made peace with the treacherous King Francis and his Muslim allies. He was now able to concentrate all his efforts on the Protestant Revolt in the empire. In 1545, the Council of Trent, which Charles had been asking the pope to call, convened its first session, thus beginning the true Reformation of the Catholic Church. In 1546, the year Luther died, the emperor declared war on the Schmalkaldic League. His troops defeated the Protestants and drove their troops from southern and western Germany. In 1547, Charles won a decisive victory at the **Battle of Muhlberg**, defeating and capturing Elector John of Saxony and Philip of Hesse. The victory gave Charles control of northern Germany.

Although Charles had won several military victories and defeated the Schmalkaldic League, Germany remained volatile, as Protestantism had spread throughout the empire. Charles realized that a political and religious resolution was the only way to create a lasting peace. In May 1548, in an attempt to quell the growing religious unrest, Charles issued the **Augsburg Interim**, which created a temporary solution—though without papal approval—until the Council of Trent could finally resolve the issues confronting the Church and create peace and unity. The Augsburg Interim commanded Protestants to readopt traditional Catholic beliefs and practices. However, it allowed them room to accept Luther's teaching on salvation by faith alone. Even though Philipp Melanchthon was willing to accept the Interim for the sake of peace, most Protestants disliked it, and it ultimately failed.

The Peace of Augsburg

In 1552, Protestant leader Maurice of Saxony revolted and destroyed the fragile peace created by the Augsburg Interim. The warring parties met in the summer of 1552 and arranged a truce that would last until 1555, when a Diet would be held that would finally resolve the religious question. This Diet convened at Augsburg in February 1555.

By that time, Charles, although he was only 55 years old, was physically exhausted. For his entire life, he had defended Christendom from the infidel without and the heretic within. He had begun to abdicate the various crowns that he had worn for the past forty years. Thus, it fell to his brother Ferdinand to try to obtain a religious peace at Augsburg.

The Peace of Augsburg, which was concluded in September 1555, formally approved state churches. It explicitly recognized Lutheran states for the first time. The religion of each state was to be chosen by its ruler. The jurisdiction of bishops and the Catholic Church was suppressed throughout Protestant domains. The Protestants were permitted to retain all Church property seized before 1552. Although the pope never accepted these decrees, the Peace of Augsburg became the law of the land in Germany, and the fighting there ended. The Protestant princes had won a final victory over the emperor, whose authority in Germany was now extremely limited.

The Final Path of the Hero King

In 1556, Charles V, old before his time and racked with painful illnesses, turned over Spain and the Netherlands to his son Philip II. His brother Ferdinand succeeded him on the imperial throne. Charles then withdrew to the Spanish monastery at Yuste, where he died a holy death in 1558. Karl Brandi, Charles V's finest biographer, writes of the noble emperor: "We may search the annals of history in vain for such another scene, for such another generation of princes such as these of the Hapsburg dynasty, who were ready of their own free will to retire from the scene of their sovereignty…" (K. Brandi, *The Emperor Charles V*).

Luther's Last Years

On the other hand, Martin Luther's last years were very unhappy. The effects of his teachings upon his followers proved disastrous. Luther knew that they used his teachings to justify their evil lifestyles. They reasoned that if no good acts could save a person, then no evil acts could condemn them. Faced with the wars and immorality of which he was the cause, Luther gave in to despair. He began drinking heavily. Yet, to the end of his life, he raged against the pope. He constantly referred to the Holy Father as "the Antichrist." Martin Luther was 63 when he died in 1546.

Abdication of Charles V

Lasting Effects of the Protestant Revolt

The effects of Luther's Revolution continue to the present day. It seems unlikely that the wounds the Revolt inflicted on Christendom will ever heal. Since the seventeenth century, not one Western nation has changed its majority religion from Protestant to Catholic or vice versa, or has even come close to doing so.

Oral Exercises

1. What were the real causes of the Protestant Revolt?
2. What order did Martin Luther join?
3. What evidence do we have that Luther was not a reformer?
4. What is "the principle of private judgment"?
5. Which pope excommunicated Luther?
6. What was the Edict of Worms of 1521?
7. What was the Augsburg Confession?
8. What was the Schmalkaldic League?
9. Where did Luther nail his ninety-five theses?
10. Where did Charles V die?

Witness to the Faith

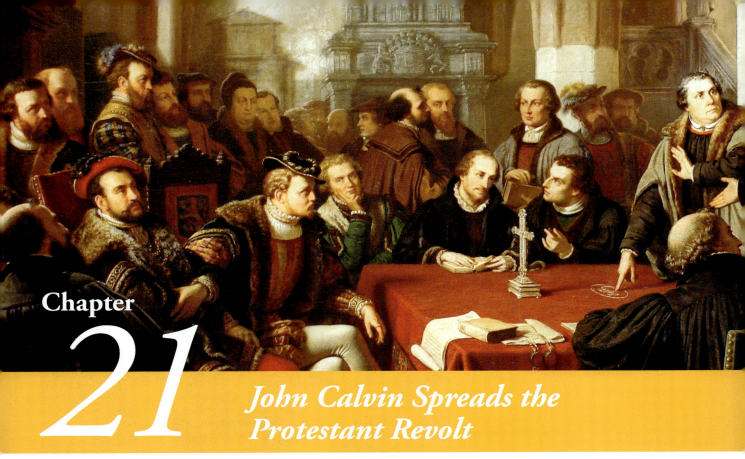

Chapter 21

John Calvin Spreads the Protestant Revolt

Ulrich Zwingli
Leader of the Protestant movement in Switzerland; denied man's free will and argued against Luther that the Eucharist is only a symbol.

Einsiedeln
Site of a famous Benedictine abbey in Switzerland.

Introduction

Although the Protestant Revolt had begun in Germany, it spread like a disease throughout the rest of Europe. In a little more than twenty years, with the exception of Spain, Portugal, and Italy, Christendom had begun to show the devastating effects of the Revolt. For the next hundred years, religious wars would tear Europe apart.

In the first decades as the Revolt spread, almost no Catholic bishop in Europe stood up for the Faith. In England and Denmark, only one bishop in each nation defended the Faith. In Germany and Switzerland, there were none. In fact, some bishops were actually revealed as Lutherans! In Italy, the bishops were not heretics, but were so involved with worldly matters, especially the politics of Italy, that they seemed unwilling to address the problem. Thus, the Revolt spread almost unhindered.

Ulrich Zwingli

From Germany, the Protestant Revolt spread to nearby Switzerland, which quickly broke into full-scale religious warfare. The man who brought the religious wars to Switzerland was named **Ulrich Zwingli**. Zwingli's education exposed him to the false notions of the Renaissance. Ordained to the priesthood around 1504, he was later stationed at **Einsiedeln**, home of the famous Benedictine abbey. Over the next

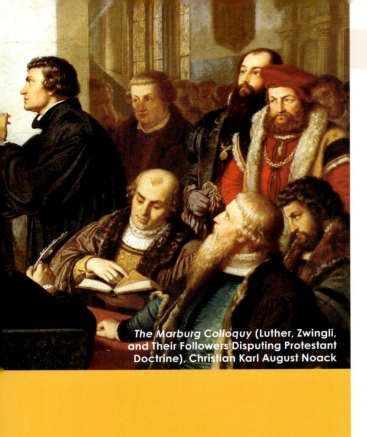

The Marburg Colloquy (Luther, Zwingli, and Their Followers Disputing Protestant Doctrine), Christian Karl August Noack

1522 A.D. – 1564 A.D.

1522 A.D.
Ulrich Zwingli begins his campaign for "reform" in Switzerland.

1529 A.D.
Luther and Zwingli have a meeting in which they are unable to agree whether the Eucharist is the Body of Christ or only a symbol, foreshadowing centuries of doctrinal splintering.

1531 A.D.
At the Battle of Kappel, a force from the Swiss Catholic *cantons* defeats a force from Zurich led by Zwingli, who is among the casualties.

1536-1538 A.D.
John Calvin writes his *Institutes of the Christian Religion*. Later that year, he and William Farel create a new way of life for Geneva. Their teachings are successful at first, but after doctrinal arguments break out, Calvin and Farel are forced to leave.

1541 A.D.
Calvin is invited back to Geneva and becomes its ruler, imposing strict laws to conform people's lives to his theology.

1553 A.D.
Calvin has Michael Servetus burned at the stake, whereupon his enemies speak out against the execution and hope it may weaken his power.

1564 A.D.
Calvin dies, having ruled Geneva practically unopposed for twenty-three years.

decade, he became well known as a scholar and preacher. In 1518, his superiors assigned him to the *Grossmunster* ("Great Church"), the principle church in Zurich.

In Zwingli, the problems created by Martin Luther's doctrine of the priesthood of the believer began to bear bitter fruit. Because of issues with his personal salvation, Luther had made justification by faith alone the central tenant of his creed. Zwingli took this teaching to its next logical step. He declared that man has no free will and is at the complete mercy of God, who accomplishes both good and evil in him.

In 1522, Zwingli began publicly calling for so-called "reforms." These included abolishing the Mass, clerical celibacy, and sacred images. He also sought to eliminate the mendicant orders, monasteries, and convents. Zwingli

Witness to the Faith 331

Baroque Interior of the Abbey of St. Gall

John Calvin
One of the most prominent of the "reformers"; he spearheaded the doctrine of predestination.

soon put his "reforms" into action when he himself married. His preaching led to numerous iconoclastic insurrections. His supporters systematically plundered the beautiful churches of Zurich and demolished statues, images, and altars. In 1525, he replaced the Mass with a service he called the "Lord's Supper." Zwingli replaced the altar with a simple table, and the Eucharist with a reading from the Bible.

Zwingli's movement spread rapidly through Switzerland. In 1528, the leaders of Zurich ordered all the gold and silver chalices and other valuables of the churches melted down. They also abolished the Mass. At Basel, Zwingli's followers seized weapons and forced that city's leaders to abolish the Mass. At St. Gall, his followers completely ransacked the magnificent abbey church. Two years later, the abbot began a restoration of St. Gall's. Today, it is considered the most important Baroque building in Switzerland.

In October 1529, Luther and Zwingli held a meeting that heralded the future of Protestantism to the present day. The two leaders agreed that man had no free will, but disagreed on the subject of the Eucharist. Luther contended that the words "This is My Body" actually meant that the Eucharist was the Body of Christ. Zwingli disagreed; he said the words were intended only to "signify" that the Eucharist was the Body of Christ. After a final angry confrontation, they left the meeting unable to come to an agreement. This meeting, held barely a decade after the beginning of the Protestant Revolt, demonstrated that the Protestant churches would be the victims of **unending subdivisions of doctrine** because they had no earthly authority on which to rely for a final decision.

Victory for the Catholic Cantons

Meanwhile, five of the Swiss *cantons* (states) remained faithful to the Catholic Church and opposed Zwingli's radical revolution. These cantons, because they were located in the Swiss Alps, had not fallen victim to Renaissance paganism. Moreover, their remote location protected their priests from the worldliness and immorality that affected so many other priests in more urban areas. To defend themselves from Zwingli and his supporters, in April 1529 they signed an alliance with King Ferdinand of Austria, Emperor Charles' brother.

Over the next few years, the Catholic and Protestant cantons maintained an uneasy peace, very nearly going to war in June 1529. Nevertheless, most Swiss wanted to avoid war. They hoped that, despite their religious differences, some compromise might be reached. However, the Catholic cantons, having seen the results of Zwingli's "reforms," were determined not to allow Zwingli and his disciples to preach in the Catholic cantons.

By May 1531, Zwingli was urging an attack on the Catholic cantons. Rather than waiting to be attacked, the Catholics struck first. On October 9, at the Battle of Kappel, the Catholics attacked a force from Zurich led by Zwingli. The decisive victory for the Catholics left several hundred Protestants dead, including Zwingli.

John Calvin

With the exception of Martin Luther, **John Calvin** did more to spread the Protestant Revolt than any of the other "reformers." Calvin was born in France in 1509. He attended the University of Paris, where he studied philosophy. Upon his graduation, he studied law at Bourges, where he came under the influence of a Lutheran professor. Sometime around 1530, having the same concerns and anxiety about his salvation as Luther, Calvin rejected the Catholic Faith and, finding consolation in Luther's doctrine of salvation through faith alone, became a heretic. His heretical views forced him to go into hiding and eventually to flee France. In 1535, he fled to Basel, Switzerland, which for years had been under the control of Zwingli's followers. The following year, he wrote down his doctrines and theology in a book entitled *The Institutes of the Christian Religion*. He would rewrite and revise this book over the course of his lifetime.

Most of Calvin's doctrines were similar to Luther's. The main difference was in Calvin's teaching on **predestination**. According to Calvin, God creates some people to go to Heaven, and other people to go to Hell, and nothing they do in their lives, good or bad, can change their destiny. This dogma of absolute predestination, which is both incredibly cruel and yet gratifying to those who think they are saved, constitutes the very essence of Calvinism. It creates in the believer the notion of "eternal security," which for Calvin and Luther was absolutely necessary, as it relieved them of personal responsibility. However, their followers realized that if nothing they did in this life made any difference, then they might as well dedicate their life to personal pleasure—because no evil act would condemn them, and no good act would save them.

Calvin believed in two "sacraments," Baptism and the Eucharist, but not in the Catholic sense. First, because of predestination, he taught that neither was necessary for salvation. Second, he denied the Real Presence. He had a "Lord's Supper" religious service that resembled Zwingli's at Zurich. Like Zwingli, Calvin was an iconoclast. He despised images, statues, paintings, and altars. He permitted only the Bible and a sermon at his services. As a result, any place where Calvinism took hold, the Calvinists painted the walls a stark white and removed all the sacred art. They destroyed hundreds of years of precious art in their fanatical desire to "reform" the churches. Even today, the Protestant churches in northern Europe are sterile, barren, joyless places.

Geneva, the Stronghold of Calvinism

For a few months in the summer of 1536, Calvin returned to France to visit his family. However, the situation there became too dangerous for him, so he decided to travel to Strasbourg on the French-German border. On the way, he stopped in Geneva, where he met **William Farel**, another French "reformer." Farel convinced Calvin to remain in Geneva and help

> ***The Institutes of the Christian Religion***
> Calvin's book, containing his doctrines and theology.

John Calvin

> **Predestination**
> Calvin's teaching that God creates some people to go to Heaven, and other people to go to Hell, and nothing they do in their lives can change their destiny.

> **William Farel**
> An associate of Calvin's, who first invited him to stay in Geneva and helped him create a new system for the city.

Witness to the Faith

Theocracy
A government that claims to be under divine leadership.

Ecclesiastical Ordinances
The religious constitution Calvin wrote for Geneva.

Michael Servetus
Protestant doctor who incurred Calvin's wrath by denying predestination; Calvin burned him at the stake.

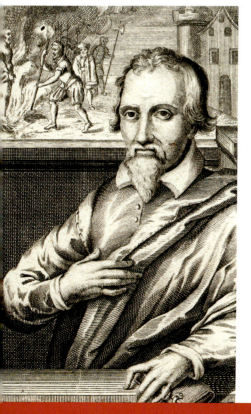

Michael Servetus

him "improve" the Church there. Calvin assumed the role of preacher and professor of theology.

In late 1536, Farel and Calvin wrote a document that essentially created a new religion in Geneva. The two men set forth the beliefs and commandments of this religion, which they presented to the Geneva town council in January 1537. The town council accepted these rules and the new religion immediately. From that point on, every citizen had to agree to Calvin's statement of faith and his laws, under pain of exile. Growing ever more despotic, Calvin then claimed the right to supervise the private lives of the citizens of Geneva. However, as would happen time and time again, a doctrinal difference split the Protestants in Geneva. Farel and Calvin fell out of favor with the town council and the people of Geneva. Following an Easter riot over the celebration of the "Lord's Supper" in 1538, the two men were forced to leave town.

Calvin went to Strasburg. For the next three years, he worked as a Protestant minister, studied theology, and rewrote his *Institutes*. Meanwhile, in Geneva, the political and religious situation had changed. The people asked him to return. In September 1541, Calvin returned to Geneva, having been promised extraordinary powers over the city if he did.

Almost immediately, Calvin began to establish a **theocracy** (a government that claims to be under divine leadership), with John Calvin as its earthly leader. To enact his vision of a perfect government, in late November he drew up the *Ecclesiastical Ordinances*, a religious constitution that reorganized the Geneva Church. The *Ecclesiastical Ordinances* created various religious officials who would supervise the city and enforce the laws he enacted. The laws Calvin created in Geneva were very harsh. Since Geneva was a theocracy, Calvin imposed the death penalty for idolatry, heresy, blasphemy, and adultery. Calvin also required that everyone attend Protestant church services. (The Mass was, of course, completely forbidden.) Music and all entertainment were forbidden. Calvin punished anyone caught dancing, gambling, or wearing fine clothes. To enforce his laws, he had spies everywhere who reported on the activities of the people of Geneva. His supporters even forced themselves into private homes in order to catechize the citizens. Over the next nine years, Calvin effectively became Geneva's dictator.

John Calvin, Dictator of Geneva

At a time when most governments had little impact on the lives of their citizens, the intense control that Calvin imposed on his subjects caused many people in Geneva to resent him. Within a few years, beginning in 1546, people began to speak against him and even to threaten his life. However, as late as 1553, his opponents did not have the political power to force him to leave. Then, in August 1553, it seems that Calvin provided his enemies with the opportunity they had been seeking. Their opening involved a Spanish doctor named **Michael Servetus**.

Michael Servetus was a well-regarded doctor and Protestant "reformer" who for years had engaged in correspondence with John Calvin. In his letters, Servetus denied predestination, which invoked Calvin's undying anger. In fact, Calvin was so incensed at Servetus that he turned him over to the Catholic authorities and used copies of his letters to prove that Servetus was a heretic. Servetus managed to escape the Catholic authorities, and then, unwisely, traveled to Geneva, where he was recognized and arrested.

After a trial, Calvin had Servetus burned at the stake. However, because Servetus was not a citizen of Geneva, all that Calvin legally could have done was exile him from Geneva or perhaps Switzerland. Executing him far exceeded any legal authority Calvin possessed. Calvin's opponents denounced the execution and hoped it would weaken him, but it did not. In fact, it had the opposite effect. Calvin wrote a book in which he argued that all heretics should be executed. More important for Calvin, the government of Geneva now more strongly supported him and his policies. By 1555, he was once again in control of the city. Until he died in May 1564, Calvin ruled Geneva without any serious opposition.

Theodore Beza

The Spread of Calvinism

During the last decade of Calvin's life, under his leadership, Geneva became a base and a haven for Protestants from all over Europe. In order to train them in his religious doctrines, he created two schools. One was basically an elementary and high school, whereas the other was a more advanced school which taught theology. This theology school would ultimately become the **University of Geneva**. To administer the theology school, Calvin employed **Theodore Beza**, another French religious revolutionary, who would ultimately succeed Calvin as head of the Church in Geneva. (Along with Calvin, Farel, and John Knox, Swiss Protestants consider Beza one of the great heroes of the "Reformation.")

From his theology school, Calvin sent out missionaries to spread his anti-Catholic, revolutionary message. During the last years of his life, he helped spread Calvinism into England and Scotland, where John Knox, the Scottish "reformer," was one of his closest disciples. However, since Calvin was a Frenchman, his main desire was the destruction of the Catholic Church in France. He devoted his greatest energy to promoting Protestantism in France by sending hundreds of missionaries there.

University of Geneva
An institute of higher learning established by Calvin to teach theology.

Theodore Beza
An important "reformer," appointed by Calvin to administer the University of Geneva.

Oral Exercises

1. Who was the leader of the Protestant forces in Zurich?
2. What was the main difference between Calvinism and Lutheranism?
3. Where did John Calvin rule as a dictator?
4. What was the name of John Calvin's book?
5. What kind of government did Calvin establish?
6. What nation did Calvin most want to make Protestant?

Witness to the Faith

Chapter 22
England Is Lost to the Church

Catherine of Aragon

Introduction

Many nations fell away from the Church because of doctrinal differences. However, England fell away because one woman was unable to have a son, and then England failed to return because that woman's daughter was unable to have a baby. Thus did the great events of history turn on the ability of two noble women to have children.

"Defender of the Faith"

In 1517, when the Protestant Revolt broke out, it seemed that England would be safe from its effects. King Henry VIII (1509-1547), a staunch Catholic who had showed himself a champion of the Church, ruled England. In fact, Henry wrote a defense of the seven sacraments which attacked Martin Luther's teaching and which Henry dedicated to Pope Leo X. In gratitude, Pope Leo, in 1521, granted Henry the title "Defender of the Faith." Some historians believe that St. Thomas More, Henry's close friend, played a role in writing this book. However, even if Henry only commissioned the work, it still shows that he was determined to stand up for the truths of the Faith. Moreover, despite all his actions against the Church in his later years, Henry VIII never accepted Luther's doctrines.

1527 A.D. – 1558 A.D.

An Allegory of the Tudor Succession: The Family of Henry VIII (Showing Henry VIII, His Children, and Philip II of Spain)

1527 A.D.
Henry VIII begins to seek an annulment of his marriage to Catherine of Aragon so that he can marry Anne Boleyn.

1529 A.D.
The papal representative, Cardinal Campeggio, opens hearings at the end of May to judge the case between Henry and Catherine, and closes them in July.

1532 A.D.
Henry forces the bishops to accept the "Submission of the Clergy," a document stating that he must approve any Church decrees or meetings of bishops in England.

1534 A.D.
The Act of Supremacy is passed, and everyone is required to take an oath in support of it or be executed.

1535 A.D.
Sts. John Fisher and Thomas More are beheaded just two weeks apart.

1538 A.D.
Monasteries are closed and property given to Henry's supporters. Cromwell openly promotes Lutheranism, but he is executed two years later.

1547-1553 A.D.
Henry VIII dies. Edward becomes king, but a regency council rules for him, since he is a child, and he receives a Protestant education. Protestantism is increasingly imposed on England until Edward's early death.

1553-1558 A.D.
Mary becomes ruler of England and sets about restoring Catholicism. She, too, has a short reign, and names Elizabeth her heir.

During the first decades of the sixteenth century, England and Spain had formed an alliance against France. To strengthen this alliance, King Henry VII of England had his oldest son and heir to the throne, Arthur, marry Catherine of Aragon, a daughter of King Ferdinand and Queen Isabel of Spain. But Arthur died when he was only 15 years old, after being married to Catherine for less than six months. To maintain the alliance, his brother Henry became engaged to Catherine a year later. However, before they could be married, they needed to obtain a special papal dispensation (which Pope Julius II granted), because Catherine had been married to Henry's brother.

King Henry VII died in April 1509, and his 17-year-old son, Henry, succeeded him as king. In June, Henry VIII married Catherine. Although Catherine and Henry loved each other, God did not bless their

Witness to the Faith   337

**Anne Boleyn
and Henry VIII**

**Cardinal
Thomas Wolsey**
Chancellor of Henry VIII;
did his utmost to obtain
an annulment of Henry's
marriage to Catherine
of Aragon.

Divorce in the 1500s

The concept of "divorce"
was unthinkable in a
Catholic society in 1527.
Thus, Henry had to have his
marriage *annulled*—that
is, declared invalid, and
therefore null and void.

Annulment
A declaration by the
Church that a marriage
was never valid, and
therefore is null and void.

marriage with many children. Their only child, Mary, was born in February 1516. By 1525, events were in place that would cause Henry to take England out of the Catholic Church.

Anne Boleyn

History is more often changed by perseverance than by brilliant strategy. Had King Richard the Lionheart persevered outside the gates of Jerusalem, the history of the Crusades might well have been different. Had the Spanish not persevered, the history of the Reconquista would have been transformed. Anne Boleyn possessed a ruthless determination and a limitless ambition that changed the course of history. She, as much as anyone, would cause the English schism. Henry VIII took England out of the Church for two reasons: one political and one personal. Anne Boleyn accounted for both. Politically, Henry believed that Anne, who was in her mid-twenties, could give him a male heir to the English throne. Personally, he allowed his strong attraction to her to lead him into sin.

By 1525, Catherine of Aragon was 40 years old, unlikely to have more children. It was becoming more and more evident that she would not give Henry a male heir who would become England's king. Henry knew that since the twelfth century, England had never had a female ruler. In fact, the last time England had been ruled by a queen, the Empress Matilda, a long civil war (1135-1154) had resulted. However, there had been excellent female rulers, most notably Queen Isabel of Spain, who had governed during Henry's life.

Thus, while concern for a male heir, which also meant the continuation of the Tudor dynasty, was a major concern for Henry, it was probably not the only reason that he acted as he did. (Within a decade of Henry's death, England would have two queens, both of whom were competent rulers.) The second reason dealt with Henry's attraction to Anne. However, Anne told Henry she was unwilling to commit adultery. She demanded that Henry marry her and *make her queen of England*. Anne seized on Henry's desire for her and for a male heir. Around 1525, she began an aggressive campaign to become queen. By 1527, Henry was determined to bring this about. However, he was legally and sacramentally married to Catherine of Aragon. On May 8, 1527, Henry called on his chancellor, **Cardinal Thomas Wolsey**, to discuss how his marriage to Catherine could be *annulled*. An **annulment** is a declaration by the Church that a marriage was never valid, and therefore is null and void.

Cardinal Thomas Wolsey embodied nearly all the problems with the Catholic Church at this time in history. Appointed archbishop of York and a cardinal, Wolsey had become chancellor of England in 1515. In 1518, Pope Leo X had made him a papal legate to England. Although personally corrupt, Wolsey was one of the finest statesmen of the time. In fact, that was the problem: he cared more for the affairs of England than those of the Church.

338   Chapter 22: England Is Lost to the Church

King Henry's Annulment

Acting more like the king's butler than a cardinal in the Catholic Church, Wolsey agreed without hesitation to Henry's wishes. Henry and Wolsey quickly put their plan into action to annul Henry's eighteen-year marriage to Catherine. In petitioning Pope Clement VII for the annulment, Henry argued that his marriage was null and void because Divine Law forbade a marriage with his deceased brother's wife. Henry's plan was to have Pope Clement annul the marriage, as well as the papal dispensation that Pope Julius II had originally granted, so that he would be free to marry Anne.

Henry and Wolsey must have thought their plan would be almost certain to succeed. Pope Clement VII, the former Cardinal Giulio Medici, had shown no signs of personal holiness or strength since becoming pope. They certainly believed he would grant the annulment. They were wrong.

When Henry personally informed Queen Catherine of his decision to annul their marriage, although she had been aware of his plan for several days, she broke down in tears. However, if Henry thought those tears demonstrated weakness on her part, he was wrong. Catherine had the support of the English people, who loved her, and the support of her nephew Charles, the Holy Roman Emperor, who also loved her. Her marriage had been her life. She would now defend it to the death.

Pope Clement was determined to delay any decision as long as possible in the (unrealistic) hope that Henry would change his mind. To that end, Clement sent—perhaps mistakenly—one of the few honest and incorruptible men in the College of Cardinals, **Lorenzo Campeggio**, to England to hold hearings on the issue of the annulment. Among his instructions, Pope Clement told Cardinal Campeggio to travel to England as slowly as possible. At this critical moment in history, having a pope like Clement was indeed tragic. As Warren Carroll has pointed out, he "seemed constitutionally incapable of making a firm stand for anything" (W. Carroll, *The Cleaving of Christendom* [Front Royal, Va.: Christendom Press, 2000], p. 121). Cardinal Campeggio eventually arrived in England in October 1528. After delaying as long as he could, he and Cardinal Wolsey began holding hearings in London at the end of May 1529.

In many ways, the trial was a total sham. The evidence of the validity of the marriage was overwhelming and conclusive. Henry's claim that his conscience compelled him to "divorce" Catherine was an outright lie, made for personal and political reasons.

In early July, Queen Catherine's formal plea that the pope personally hear her case finally arrived in Rome. Pope Clement wrote to London that he planned to judge the case himself. However, before the letters arrived in London, Cardinal Campeggio, having heard enough of King Henry's "evidence," closed the trial proceedings. He told Henry that he would not render a decision until he had conferred with Pope Clement.

The removal of the trial to Rome spelled the downfall of Wolsey, who had to acknowledge his total failure. Failing King Henry always resulted in

Lorenzo Campeggio
The good and honest cardinal who heard the case between Henry VIII and Queen Catherine.

Cardinal Thomas Wolsey

Witness to the Faith 339

Thomas Cromwell
Statesman who did much to destroy the Catholic Church in England.

Submission of the Clergy
Document stating that any Church decrees or meetings of bishops in England had to be approved by the king.

Thomas Cromwell

dire consequences. Henry forced him to resign as chancellor. In November, Henry had Wolsey arrested. When Wolsey's doctors told Henry that the former chancellor would die in prison, Henry compassionately released him. Wolsey returned to his see at York, where he had not been for fifteen years. However, Anne Boleyn was not one to forgive. In late October 1530, she demanded that Henry arrest Wolsey again. He died on the way to the Tower of London in November. Yet it seems that in his last months at York, Wolsey had undergone a conversion experience. He acknowledged that he had put the service of his king before the service of God and now was paying the just price. Hopefully, Cardinal Wolsey made a good and sincere Confession before he died. Following Wolsey's resignation, King Henry appointed Thomas More to be chancellor of England.

At this moment, one of the greatest enemies of the Church maneuvered his way onto history's stage. For seven years, **Thomas Cromwell** had been Cardinal Wolsey's assistant. The fall of Wolsey almost certainly meant the downfall of his helpers. In desperation, Cromwell arranged a meeting with King Henry VIII in November 1530. At this meeting, he presented the king with an audacious plan: *declare yourself the head of the Church in England!* Henry loved the idea. The next month, Cromwell put this plan into action.

Meanwhile, in Rome, Pope Clement VII continued his policy of delay. Although he was a weak pope, he was the Vicar of Christ. He could not and would not annul a marriage that a lawful dispensation had rendered valid and which eighteen years of marital life had consecrated. When Henry's agent, the Duke of Norfolk, pressured Pope Clement, he encountered a firmness that could not be shaken. In January 1531, Pope Clement threatened ecclesiastical penalties against all persons who attempted to refer the king's case to an English tribunal. He also warned Henry not to remarry until the pope had rendered a decision.

In June 1531, Catherine of Aragon showed that she was the true daughter of Queen Isabel and the Spanish warriors of the Reconquista. When pushed by Henry's minions to enter a convent, she replied that marriage was her vocation and that she would defend her marriage to the death. The queen steadfastly defended her rights and relied on the protection of her nephew, Emperor Charles V.

Throughout 1532, despite warnings from Charles V, Queen Catherine, and Cardinal Campeggio, Pope Clement took no action on the matter of Henry's wedding. However, Henry and Thomas Cromwell continued to plot. Driven by his hatred for the Church and an insatiable greed, Cromwell began moving to take England out of the Church.

On May 10, 1532, Henry forced the bishops to accept the **Submission of the Clergy**. Under this document, King Henry

Chapter 22: England Is Lost to the Church

had to approve any Church decrees in England or any meetings of the English bishops. Clearly, he was moving to become head of the Church in England. The next day, Thomas More resigned as chancellor of England.

Thomas Cranmer

Normally, it would have fallen to the archbishop of Canterbury, **William Warham**, as the leading Catholic churchman in England, to stand up to Henry's threats to the independence of the Church. However, history will never know whether Archbishop Warham had the courage of a St. Thomas Becket, because he died in late August. The path was now clear for Henry to appoint someone to the see of Canterbury who would support his marriage to Anne Boleyn. He chose **Thomas Cranmer**.

Thomas Cranmer had spent virtually his entire adult life as a student and then a professor at Cambridge University. Although he had been ordained a priest in 1520, he was wholly unsuited to become archbishop of Canterbury. First, he was likely a Lutheran. Second, in July 1532, despite being a priest, he secretly married the niece of a leading German Protestant! However, he opposed the pope deciding the question of Henry's marriage, which made him a perfect choice for Henry. On October 1, 1532, with the consent of Anne Boleyn, King Henry appointed Thomas Cranmer the archbishop of Canterbury.

In January 1533, Henry and Anne secretly wed. Since no annulment of his marriage to Catherine had been granted, this new "marriage" was clearly an act of bigamy. Certainly, even Henry and Anne realized that. Henry ordered Cranmer to grant him an annulment immediately!

By various schemes, Cranmer paved the way for the annulment. On May 10, 1533, he opened his tribunal. He called the noble Queen Catherine to appear, but she refused and did not even send a proxy to what she knew was merely a sham. Two weeks later, Cranmer declared Henry and Catherine's marriage null and void, claiming the pope had not had the power to grant a dispensation. Five days later, Cranmer validated the king's secret "marriage" to Anne Boleyn. On June 1, Anne Boleyn was crowned queen at Westminster amid the protests of the people, who still almost universally loved Queen Catherine. The pope declared the annulment and the so-called "marriage" of the king to Anne Boleyn null and void, and excommunicated Henry unless he repudiated his "marriage" to Anne.

In September, Anne gave birth to a baby girl, Elizabeth. She would have no more children. This would earn Henry's wrath.

The Act of Supremacy

In January 1534, Parliament passed the **Act of Supremacy**, which finalized the English schism. Besides officially recognizing the annulment of Henry's marriage to Catherine and declaring his marriage to Anne to be valid, the Act of Supremacy conferred upon King Henry VIII the title "Supreme Head of the Church of England." The Act transferred all ecclesiastical power to the king, who then delegated it to the bishops, and

> **Thomas Cranmer**
> Appointed archbishop of Canterbury by Henry VIII; supported Henry's marriage to Anne Boleyn and wrote *The Book of Common Prayer*.

Henry VIII Condemns St. John Fisher to Death for Refusing to Sign the Oath of Supremacy and Divorce

> **Act of Supremacy**
> Declared that Henry's marriage to Anne was valid and conferred on him the title of Supreme Head of the Church of England.

Oath of Supremacy
Oath that all the English people were required to swear in support of the Act of Supremacy, on pain of death for treason.

St. Thomas More
Henry's chancellor after Cardinal Wolsey; resigned when he could not continue in good conscience, and was imprisoned and then executed rather than take the Oath of Supremacy.

St. Thomas More

he would solely decide their election. The Act also denied the authority of the pope. Henry soon had Parliament pass Treason Laws that supplemented the Act of Supremacy. These laws declared that support for the pope or any opposition to Henry's marriage to Anne was treason punishable by death. The entire population was required to take an oath supporting the Act of Supremacy or else face death for treason.

Realizing that Henry would likely have them killed, the clergy and the laity raised little opposition. Royal commissioners were sent throughout the land to make people take the **Oath of Supremacy**. Catherine and the people in her personal household never took it, and she was banished from the king's court. Some of the English Franciscans refused to take the oath as well. As a result, their monasteries were seized, and they were either killed or exiled. However, out of fear, most of the population took the oath—with two notable exceptions.

St. Thomas More and St. John Fisher

Thomas More was the greatest of all the English learned men of the Renaissance. However, his learning always centered on the truths of the Catholic Faith. A close friend of King Henry's for many years, Thomas had accepted his appointment as chancellor, knowing that he faced a terrible situation. He finally resigned when the position became an impossible choice between God and king. Thomas refused to take the Oath of Supremacy, and in April 1534 Henry had him thrown into prison. Although every attempt was made to force him to take the oath, he refused. Finally, Henry had his good friend Thomas beheaded on July 6, 1535. As Thomas stood on the scaffold, he declared that he "died the king's good servant, but God's first."

In October 1504, **John Fisher** was appointed bishop of Rochester, a position he held for the rest of his life. As bishop, he tutored Henry, the Prince of Wales—the man who thirty years later would order his execution. Like Thomas More, John Fisher also bravely refused to take the Oath of Supremacy. So, the 77-year-old bishop was thrown into prison, convicted of high treason. He was beheaded on June 22, 1535.

Pope Pius XI canonized Thomas More and John Fisher in 1935. Their shared feast day is June 22.

The Last Days of Henry VIII

On January 7, 1536, Queen Catherine of Aragon died, possibly from heart cancer. Shortly before her death, she had written to her nephew Charles V, asking that he protect her daughter, Mary Tudor. Mary would be the last hope for a Catholic England. Like her mother and grandmother before her, she was steadfast in her faith.

342   Chapter 22: England Is Lost to the Church

In May 1536, Henry had Anne Boleyn beheaded for adultery and high treason. The following day, he married Jane Seymour. She died in October 1537, after having given birth to the future King Edward VI.

The opposition to the Oath of Supremacy offered by a few monasteries gave King Henry the excuse to confiscate them all. In 1538, under the direction of Thomas Cromwell, all the monasteries in England were suppressed, and their property was given to Henry's supporters. That same year, Pope Paul III finally excommunicated Henry and released his subjects from their oath of allegiance. However, by then, Henry had too strong a grasp on the English throne. No one, either inside England or outside it, had the power to enforce the excommunication.

By 1538, Cromwell also felt strong enough that he could openly begin attacking the Catholic religion and replace it with Lutheranism. He began a campaign of iconoclastic destruction, which climaxed in September with the destruction of the centuries-old shrine of St. Thomas Becket at Canterbury.

Cromwell might well have despoiled every shrine and suppressed every monastery in England if he had lived long enough. However, in 1539, he made a fatal mistake. For political reasons, he advised Henry to marry a Lutheran princess, Anne of Cleves. Anne was related to the leader of the Protestant princes of Germany. However, Henry found her unattractive—not at all like her portrait—and his bishops annulled the marriage in 1540.

Cromwell's heretical "reforms," along with his efforts to convince Henry to marry Anne of Cleves, gave Cromwell's enemies the ammunition they needed to move against him. They had him arrested and charged with heresy and treason. On July 28, 1540, Henry married Catherine Howard, and he had Cromwell beheaded on the same day. Two years later, Catherine was beheaded for adultery. The following year, Henry married his sixth wife, Catherine Parr, a Protestant, who outlived him. Henry died in 1547. At the funeral, the court orators forbade the people to weep for their monarch, saying that such a pious king must surely have gone straight to Heaven. The "pious" king had executed over seventy thousand of his subjects, roughly 3 percent of the entire population.

Jane Seymour

Anne of Cleves

Catherine Howard

Catherine Parr

Witness to the Faith

The Spread of Protestantism in England

Although Henry VIII himself had not been a Protestant, he had created an environment in England that had enabled heresy to take root and grow. Moreover, he had done little to stop men like Cromwell and Cranmer from spreading heretical teachings, as long as they arranged his domestic relationships. Thus, when he died in 1547, the Catholic Church in England was terribly weakened.

King Henry VIII had three children from his six "marriages." **Mary Tudor**, Catherine of Aragon's daughter, was a devout Catholic, whom Henry seemed to have loved enough at least not to have her beheaded. However, ever since her mother's death, Mary had lived in constant fear for her life. **Elizabeth Tudor**, Anne Boleyn's daughter, could never be regarded by Catholics as the child of a lawful marriage, because she was born while Catherine was still alive.

Henry's last child was Jane Seymour's son, Edward. Since Catherine had died before Henry's marriage to Jane, Catholics recognized Edward as the child of a lawful marriage. Following Henry's death, the young Edward was proclaimed **King Edward VI**. Because Edward was only 9 years old, a regency council, headed by the Duke of Somerset, ruled in his name. During his father's lifetime, Edward seems to have been raised as a Catholic. However, upon his father's death, Archbishop Cranmer began the work of instructing the young king in the doctrines of the new religion. Within a few years of becoming king, the young Edward VI had become thoroughly permeated with the teaching of Protestant preachers, going so far as to call the pope "the anti-Christ."

During Edward's reign, the Church in England began moving openly toward Protestantism. Clerical celibacy was abolished. In 1549, Cranmer wrote *The Book of Common Prayer*, which removed all references to sacrifice from the Mass and replaced all Catholic prayers with Lutheran alternatives. Parliament passed the **Act of Uniformity**, which required the entire Kingdom of England to use *The Book of Common Prayer*.

Despite being a rather moderate Protestant book, *The Book of Common Prayer* was unpopular. Many of the ordinary people of England remained Catholic. They did not want to be "reformed." A revolt broke out in the western part of England, where the people demanded a return to the traditional Catholic Faith. An army of mercenaries hastily recruited by the Duke of Somerset defeated the Catholics.

In the next few years, Edward became increasingly determined to impose "reform" on England. More and more, he fell under the influence of Cranmer and John Knox, the Scottish preacher who had been John Calvin's best disciple. Catholic bishops who refused to accept the new religion were arrested, imprisoned, and replaced. In 1552, Cranmer established a communion service that completely denied the Real Presence in the Eucharist, thus effectively abolishing the Mass. It seemed that Cranmer's desire for a complete "reform" of the Church in England

---

Mary Tudor
Daughter of Henry VIII and Catherine of Aragon; succeeded Edward VI, and tried to return England to the Catholic Faith during her five-year reign.

Elizabeth Tudor
Daughter of Henry VIII and Anne Boleyn; succeeded Mary; persecuted the Church for decades.

Edward VI
Son of Henry VIII and Jane Seymour; succeeded Henry VIII as king when he was only 9 years old; was raised by Protestant regents, and died at the age of 16.

Edward VI

The Book of Common Prayer
Written by Thomas Cranmer; removed all references to sacrifice from the Mass, and replaced all Catholic prayers with Lutheran alternatives.

Act of Uniformity
Required the entire Kingdom of England to use *The Book of Common Prayer*.

was within his grasp when, in February 1553, King Edward, who had been healthy until then, suddenly became seriously ill. When Edward died in July, it appeared that all of Cranmer's work would be for nothing.

Mary Tudor Seeks to Return England to the Church

The Protestants in England were so determined that a Catholic not become ruler of England that, following Edward's death, they attempted to give the throne to **Lady Jane Grey**, a relative of Edward's mother, rather than to one of his sisters, Mary or Elizabeth. Jane was known to be a devoted Protestant. However, the English people were not ready to abandon hundreds of years of tradition. After nine days of civil unrest, Jane Grey was defeated, and Mary Tudor was recognized as the rightful queen of England.

However, in nineteen years, England had moved from schism to heresy. Mary stood almost alone. She was the last best chance to return England to the Faith. But would she be enough?

When Mary came to the throne of England, she had but one goal: return England to the Catholic Faith. To that end, she began to reverse the measures that her father and brother had instituted. Anti-Catholic laws were repealed. Many of the leaders of the revolt returned to the Faith. Pope Julius III made their return easier when he decreed that laymen would be allowed to keep the Church lands that Henry VIII had given them. Mary removed Cranmer as archbishop of Canterbury, and the pope appointed **Cardinal Reginald Pole** in his place, asking him to reconcile England with the Catholic Church. Cardinal Pole removed the papal censures against England and restored it to communion with Rome.

As Mary's reign began, Protestantism was not yet deeply entrenched in England. Many English people still loved and respected the Mass, the Real Presence, and the ancient customs and traditions of the Church. Therefore, a law abolishing the so-called "reforms" that King Edward and Thomas Cranmer had made would have been appropriate and might well have proven sufficient to begin moving England back to its proper place in the Church. England had not left the Church suddenly. Mary should have proceeded cautiously. Everything was proceeding well until Mary, against the advice of Cardinal Pole and Emperor Charles V, decided to persecute the heretics.

By any reasonable standard, the trial and execution of Archbishop Thomas Cranmer was justified and probably inevitable. He had declared Henry's marriage to Mary's mother, Catherine, invalid, and he had persecuted Queen Catherine. In fact, Mary believed

Lady Jane Grey
A relative of Jane Seymour and a devoted Protestant, whom Protestants in England attempted to make queen instead of Mary.

Cardinal Reginald Pole
Archbishop of Canterbury and papal legate to England during Mary Tudor's reign.

Cardinal Reginald Pole

Witness to the Faith 345

Mary Tudor

that Cranmer had caused the premature death of her mother. He had done much to expedite the English schism and to cause England to leave the Church. Moreover, he was an unrepentant public heretic. On December 4, 1555, Pope Paul IV deposed Cranmer as archbishop of Canterbury, excommunicated him, and turned him over to the civil authorities for his just punishment. After making six successive recantations of heresy, none of them sincere, Cranmer was sentenced to death.

In addition to Cranmer, Queen Mary also had three other Protestant bishops executed. Moreover, against the advice of Cardinal Pole, she had 273 Protestants burned at the stake. In her zeal to purify England of heresy, she may have done more harm than good to her own cause.

Despite her struggle to restore the Church during her lifetime, Mary realized that unless she had an heir who would continue her policies after her death, her efforts would ultimately fail. Her sister Elizabeth, who would be queen if she did not have an heir, would almost certainly rule as a Protestant, because Catholics did not recognize her mother's "marriage" to Henry as lawful. Mary, who was 37 years old, knew that she had to marry and have a child as soon as possible.

Queen Mary made a decision, which she felt was divinely inspired. She decided to marry her cousin King Philip II of Spain. (Ferdinand and Isabel of Spain were Mary's grandparents and Philip's great-grandparents.) Philip, Charles V, and Pope Julius III all supported the marriage as a brilliant idea. Although almost all historians feel that Mary's marriage to Philip was a great mistake, one of the greatest

346   *Chapter 22: England Is Lost to the Church*

Catholic historians of the twentieth century does not agree. Dr. Warren Carroll writes: "This historian firmly believes that Queen Mary's acceptance of Philip II of Spain as her husband was the best possible decision she could have made under all the circumstances. If only she had been able to conceive a child, it would have changed the whole history of Christendom and the world, very much for the better from the Catholic standpoint" (W. Carroll, *The Cleaving of Christendom*, p. 237).

Dr. Carroll goes on to point out that it was Queen Mary's belief that "only Spanish orthodoxy … was sufficiently untainted to rid England of heresy" (ibid., W. Carroll quoting H.F.M. Prescott, *Mary Tudor*). Mary also believed that she needed the power of Spain to defend her against France, England's traditional enemy, and also against Scotland (ibid.), where John Knox was having a great influence. Most important, though, was Mary's fervent belief that she could conceive and bear a son who would succeed her on the throne of England and who, as a Catholic monarch, would keep England in the Church.

Although no one knew it at the time, this was perhaps the most important marriage in the history of the world. Consider what the future might have been like if England had remained in the Church. For example, the colonies England founded would likely have been Catholic. Sadly for the history of the world and of the Catholic Church, Mary was unable to have a child.

Queen Mary died in 1558. She was only 42. She named her half-sister Elizabeth Tudor as her successor, on the condition that Elizabeth would maintain the Catholic Faith in England. However, it was not a promise that Elizabeth would keep.

Philip II of Spain

Elizabeth I of England

Oral Exercises

1. Why did Henry VIII desire to have his marriage to Catherine of Aragon annulled?
2. Why is there no doubt that Henry VIII's marriage to Catherine of Aragon was valid?
3. Briefly describe the character of Pope Clement VII.
4. Who was Thomas Cranmer?
5. What title did the Act of Supremacy confer upon King Henry VIII?
6. Who were the two English men that famously refused to take the Oath of Supremacy?
7. Who was Cardinal Pole?
8. Why did Mary Tudor marry Philip II of Spain?
9. What were the names of Henry VIII's three children, in order of their succession to the throne of England?

Witness to the Faith

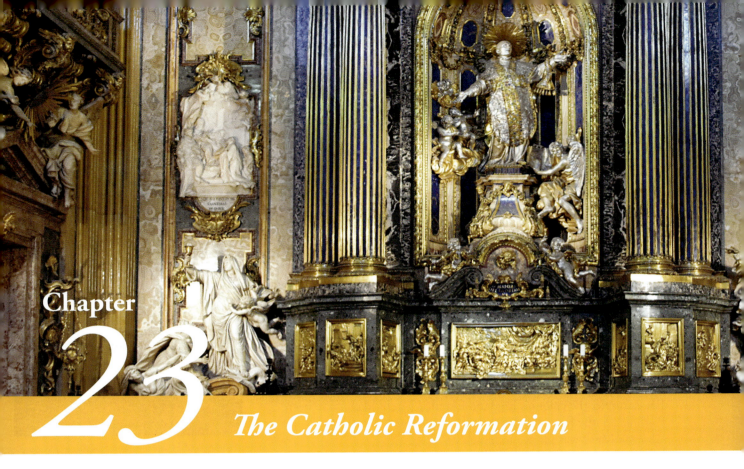

Chapter 23

The Catholic Reformation

Introduction

The pontificate of Pope Clement VII was not crowned with glory. However, there had been one shining moment in his otherwise dismal papacy. Despite all the threats and cajoling of Henry VIII, Clement, in his own way, had defended the marriage of Catherine of Aragon—and hence the Sacrament of Marriage. Although never a great or wise pope, in this one instance he had stood like a lion, albeit a cautious one.

At Clement's death, the Church still needed reform. It still faced its greatest threat. For decades, it had been led by popes who had not guided her with strength and vigor. More than ever, the Church needed a pope with the courage and determination of St. Paul. It was about to get one.

New Religious Orders Work to Reform the Church

Even before the Protestant Revolt began, devout Catholics everywhere, both priests and lay people, shocked by the corruption and scandals that plagued the Church, looked to bring about reform. This true spirit of reformation began in the monasteries and religious orders. However, it quickly spread to include the laity.

One of the most noteworthy orders founded at this time was a new branch of the Franciscan Order called the **Capuchins**, which began in Italy. In 1525, Franciscan friar **Matteo da Bascio** felt inspired to start

Capuchins
A branch of the Franciscan Order characterized by strict poverty and missionary preaching.

Matteo da Bascio
Founder of the Capuchins.

348 Chapter 23: The Catholic Reformation

The Altar of St. Ignatius of Loyola, Church of the Gesu in Rome

1521 A.D. – 1566 A.D.

1521 A.D.
In bed after being wounded in battle, Ignatius of Loyola spends time reading about Jesus Christ and the saints, and is inspired to begin a new life.

1524 A.D.
The Theatine Order begins under St. Cajetan and Peter Caraffa.

1525 A.D.
Matteo da Bascio starts the Capuchins to revive St. Francis' spirit of poverty and preaching.

1527 A.D.
Charles de Bourbon's army, unpaid and rebellious, sacks Rome.

1534 A.D.
Cardinal Thomas Cajetan dies, followed by Pope Clement VII a few weeks later. Clement's successor, Pope Paul III, will oversee significant milestones of the Catholic Reformation.

1540 A.D.
The Jesuit Order is established.

1545-1563 A.D.
The Council of Trent clarifies and defends the Church's teachings and addresses abuses that have crept into Catholic life.

1566 A.D.
Following a directive of the council, a new catechism is issued to summarize Catholic doctrine for all the faithful.

the Capuchins. He believed that the Franciscans had moved away from the strict lifestyle of the order as founded by St. Francis. In 1528, Pope Clement VII approved the Capuchins. The Capuchins practiced severe poverty. They owned no property, not even sandals. They received all their needs through begging. They devoted themselves to the spiritual welfare of the common people. Like their Franciscan brothers, they were great preachers who traveled throughout Europe and eventually the world. Despite some initial setbacks, the Capuchin Order thrived. Their incredible self-sacrifice, along with their love of God and their trust in Him, comforted and strengthened the faith of millions, who otherwise might have left the Church.

In 1524, several Catholic priests, including St. Cajetan and Peter Caraffa, founded a religious order quite unlike the

Witness to the Faith   349

Pope Clement VII

St. Cajetan
Founder of the Theatines.

Theatines
An order of priests, established to reform the clergy by living simple, holy, priestly lives.

Capuchins. (**St. Cajetan** should not be confused with **Cardinal Thomas Cajetan**.) The order was known as the **Theatines** because Caraffa was archbishop of Chieti (*Theate* in Latin). Whereas the Capuchins received all their income from begging, the Theatines prohibited begging. As a result, most Theatines were members of the nobility. The Theatines sought to reform the clergy by their holy lifestyle. They led simple lives and dressed in simple black cassocks. They hoped that through their example they would show members of the clergy how to lead a more priestly life. Pope Clement approved the Theatines in 1524.

The Need for a Council

By 1503, following the pontificate of Alexander VI, the Borgia pope, it was evident that the Church desperately needed a council to address the issues of reform. While individuals called for reforms, made reforms locally, and even started new religious orders, the Church needed universal reform. Only the pope could convoke a council that would address these problems, issue decrees, and then implement them.

Before the Protestant Revolt started, the council was needed to address the scandals and corruption that infected the Church, from parish priests to cardinals. After the Revolt began, the council became even more vital. It needed to define with care and precision the Church teachings that the Protestants were questioning. Sadly, many good Catholics became Protestants, because they did not know the true teachings of the Catholic Church. They had not been properly catechized. When Luther and Calvin sent out their missionaries, they found receptive listeners who simply did not know their Faith!

Since the death of Alexander VI, every pope worked more or less diligently to call a council. Both Emperor Maximilian and Emperor Charles V begged the popes to convoke a council. In fact, by 1540, Emperor Charles was begging the papal nuncio to have the pope open a council anywhere! Pope Julius II actually did convoke the Fifth Lateran Council, which lasted from 1512 to 1517. However, Julius was so involved with the politics of Italy and in fighting wars with France and Venice that he did little to implement the few decrees that the council promulgated. After the death of Julius, his successor, Leo X, continued the council, but Leo had no great desire to reform the Church. Thus, he failed to act on the council's decrees. Luther nailed his ninety-five theses to the church door seven months after the council had closed.

The best hope for true reform lay with Leo's successor, Pope Adrian VI. The finest pope elected in generations, he was a voice crying in the wilderness. He planned to reform the Church but found that he would have to do it alone. A man of great determination, Adrian very well might have succeeded, with the help of his former pupil Charles V, had Adrian not died after a pontificate of less than two years.

Clement VII also considered calling a general council during his pontificate. Unfortunately, several factors caused him not to call it. The first was his own personal inability to act decisively. The second was his ongoing conflict with Henry VIII. The third was his inability to find a safe place where the council could meet. England was not suitable, and France and the Holy Roman Empire were almost constantly at war. The final problem was the sack of Rome in 1527.

The Sack of Rome

In early March 1527, an imperial army arrived outside of Bologna in the Papal States. Although the army was nominally that of Emperor Charles V, it was actually composed mostly of Lutherans, and it was commanded by a mercenary named **Charles de Bourbon**, who routinely failed to pay his soldiers. In April, not having been paid, the army rebelled. Close to Rome, the mutinous army decided to march on Rome and plunder it.

On May 6, the army stormed into Rome and captured the city. Pope Clement VII barely escaped as his brave Swiss Guards gave their lives in his defense, enabling him to flee St. Peter's Basilica. Dressed in his white cassock, the pope ran for his life, pursued by a Lutheran army that had sworn to kill him. Running down the passage between St. Peter's and Castel Sant'Angelo, he barely made it to the impregnable fortress. But Castel Sant'Angelo was indeed impregnable, and it was his only refuge. Outside, the Lutherans had turned Rome into Hell on Earth.

The destruction, looting, and pillaging of Rome lasted for a week. The terrors and inhumanity inflicted on the men, women, and children were too terrible to tell. Had Attila and the Huns taken Rome, they would have done no worse. The Vatican Library and the Raphael rooms were spared, only because they became the headquarters for the army's commander.

In December, Pope Clement was finally able to leave Castel Sant'Angelo. He went to Orvieto, about 60 miles from Rome. On Palm Sunday, 1528, he told the cardinals that the Church needed reform and that the sack of Rome was "a chastisement for their sins." However, this realization had come too late to Clement. He never called a council.

The Conclave of 1534

On August 19, 1534, the College of Cardinals was greatly diminished when Cardinal Thomas Cajetan died. He had been one of the Faith's most heroic defenders. With the possible exception of Cardinal Campeggio, he was probably the finest cardinal alive.

Less than two weeks later, Pope Clement VII was also stricken with his final illness. He died on September 25.

Charles de Bourbon
The mercenary leader of the army that sacked Rome in 1527.

Was Charles V Responsible for the Sack of Rome in 1527?

Historians have blamed Charles V for the sack of Rome, almost since it occurred, because he and the pope were at war. However, the army was not under Charles' command or under any of his subordinates. Moreover, the army had rebelled. Additionally, Charles was in Spain at the time. He could not have learned of the rebellion in time to do anything to stop it, even if he had had another army in Italy, which he did not. Finally, Charles' personality and his entire life were dedicated to protecting Christendom. Sacking Rome, the heart of Christendom, is so contrary to his life that this accusation is simply not believable.

Witness to the Faith

Paul III
Pope from 1534 to 1549. Among the high points of his accomplished pontificate were calling the Council of Trent and aiding in the establishment of the Jesuits.

Pope Paul III

Society of Jesus (Jesuits)
Order founded by St. Ignatius of Loyola; established excellent schools and converted many Protestants and non-Christians.

History must regard Clement VII as one of the worst men ever to reign as pope. He showed incredibly poor judgment in almost every instance except his unwillingness to grant Henry VIII's annulment. His refusal to convoke the desperately needed ecumenical council allowed the growth and spread of Protestantism. Contemporary Catholics from Germany to England felt betrayed by Clement's lack of leadership and his desire for wealth rather than the salvation of souls.

The Sacred College met quickly to elect Clement's successor. His name was Alessandro Farnese. He had become a cardinal at the age of 20 because he was the brother of Pope Alexander VI's girlfriend. Although he had led an immoral life before his ordination, he changed his life when he was ordained a priest in 1519. Cardinal Farnese took the name **Paul III** (1534-1549). Clement VII had been one of the worst popes; Paul III would be one of the best.

Among his other achievements, Pope Paul III would be responsible for two great accomplishments. First, he would finally call the long-awaited council and begin true reform of the Church. Second, he would aid in the establishment of the **Society of Jesus**, better known as the **Jesuits**, the largest and most successful order in the history of the Catholic Church.

The Creation of the Jesuits

At certain times in history, as the Church is in crisis, Our Lord has called on special men and women, like Catherine of Siena and Joan of Arc, to change the course of history. In 1521, the Church faced perhaps its greatest crisis, and Our Lord called on one of His greatest saints.

Ignatius of Loyola was born in 1491 to a noble family in Loyola, Spain. At the age of 13, he became a page. He received the usual training of a page, which meant little formal schooling, but he did learn to read and write. As a young man, Ignatius dreamed of becoming a soldier. When he was about 17, he was knighted and began his career as a Spanish soldier.

Throughout his early life, Ignatius showed no signs of having a religious vocation. However, he was a natural leader whom men eagerly followed. He showed evidence of his leadership in May 1521, while fighting for Spain against the French at the siege of Pamplona. When the commanders of his force were killed, Ignatius took charge. As he was repelling the French, a cannonball severely wounded him, breaking his leg in several places. His company was defeated, and he was captured.

The French doctors set his broken leg, but incorrectly. He returned to Loyola to recover from his wounds, but the leg would not heal. His leg had to be broken again and reset. This procedure nearly killed him, and he was given the Last Rites. Amazingly, he recovered. However, the injured leg was now shorter than the other, which would leave him with a limp for the rest of his life. In this moment, the unyielding character and determination of Ignatius of Loyola, which would change the face of the world, was dramatically revealed. He demanded that the leg be broken

352 *Chapter 23: The Catholic Reformation*

and reset yet again! In September, his doctors performed a third operation—successfully.

As Ignatius lay in his bed for months recovering, this man, who had never been a student or a great reader, asked for some books to read. Only two were available. One of the books was about the life of Jesus Christ. The other was about the lives of the saints.

A religious vocation is a call from God. It is a call to dedicate one's life to the service of God. There are many vocations, and most have no great historical significance, although the spiritual value is inestimable. However, in moments of historical crisis, a vocation may be more, summoning a man or woman to play a role in saving the entire Church. Such was the vocation of St. Paul on the road to Damascus. Such was the vocation that came to Ignatius as he lay reading.

As he read the lives of the saints, Ignatius began to realize that many of them were remarkable heroes. St. Francis of Assisi and St. Dominic very much impressed him. In 1521, Ignatius decided to give up his career as a soldier and devote his life to the service of the Church. This was the same year that Martin Luther left the Catholic Church. It cannot be a coincidence that Ignatius was called at this exact historical moment. Although they would never meet in person, these two men would do battle through the centuries.

It took Ignatius some time to decide what form his service to the Church would take. He spent many weeks in prayer and in meditation. Then he wrote a book called the *Spiritual Exercises*. Next, he made a pilgrimage to the Holy Land, where he became interested in converting the Muslims. On his return to Spain, he decided to improve his education. He realized that if he really intended to help others, he had to become a priest. Although he was 33 years old, he resumed the study of Latin for two years. Then he entered the University of Alcala and the University of Salamanca, where he studied philosophy and theology. Next, he attended the University of Paris, where at the end of seven years he received his master's degree in 1535.

Saint Ignatius of Loyola, Peter Paul Rubens

Witness to the Faith

While he was studying in Paris, Ignatius' holy life attracted the attention of several of his fellow students, especially six devoted companions who decided to join him in his mission. On the Feast of the Assumption, 1534, all seven took a vow. They promised to practice perpetual poverty and chastity. They also promised to make a pilgrimage to the Holy Land, where they would work to convert the Muslims, or, if they could not go to the Holy Land, to place themselves at the disposal of the pope.

Three years later, the seven friends arrived at Venice, where they prepared to embark for the Holy Land. Venice was then at war with the Turks, so for an entire year they waited in vain. They then went to Vicenza to carry out the second part of their vow, and they laid the foundations of the new Society of Jesus (S.J.). Ignatius and two others journeyed on to Rome. In September 1540, Pope Paul III received them with great kindness and approved the new order, on the condition that the number of its members be restricted to sixty. Four years later, Pope Paul III removed this restriction.

From the beginning, the Jesuits had three magnificent goals. First, they would **restore Catholic education in Europe**. Second, they would **evangelize the newly discovered lands**. Third, they would **reconvert the Protestants**. In their motto, the Jesuits pledged to work *ad majorem Dei gloriam* ("to the greater glory of God"). With God's help, Ignatius and his order largely accomplished all of these goals.

Pope Paul III Approves the Society of Jesus, Domingos da Cunha

The Jesuits Take the Field

Pope Paul III soon began using the Jesuits to halt the religious revolt. Each Jesuit went through a long training period before his ordination to the priesthood. As a result, the Jesuits became renowned for their piety, virtue, and learning. Furthermore, despite being men of outstanding virtue and ability, the Jesuits refused to accept high honors in the Church. A Jesuit became a bishop or cardinal only when commanded by the pope. It pleased the laity to see such devotion to duty without expectation of reward. A new respect for the priesthood developed.

Among the goals of the Jesuits was the education of children and young people. To accomplish this goal, the Jesuits opened schools and colleges throughout Europe. Jesuit colleges became known as fortresses of the Faith.

Chapter 23: The Catholic Reformation

Jesuit schools and colleges became so famous that even many Protestants sent their sons to be educated by the Jesuits. A Jesuit education was once considered the finest in the world.

The primary goal of the Society of Jesus was to win back those parts of Europe that had been lost to Protestantism. Despite strong Protestant opposition and even the threat of death, the Jesuits began their work of preaching and teaching the truths of the Faith. They brought the Mass and the sacraments to people whom for years had been deprived of these instruments of grace. They were so successful that much of Europe that had been lost was won back to the Catholic Faith.

The Council of Trent

From the moment that he was consecrated pope, Paul III had no greater desire than to convoke an ecumenical council. The Church taught that only a pope could convoke a council. However, history had shown that the emperor's support and protection was necessary if the council ever actually met. The Council of Constance in 1418 had succeeded because it had the support and protection of Emperor Sigismund. Yet, in this time of crisis, the pope (the spiritual head of Christendom) and the emperor (its temporal head) were unable to work together. Paul, who was otherwise an excellent pope and a holy man, seemed to feel that the council could be held without Charles or his support. Charles, who spent most of the 1530s and 1540s fighting the Protestants, the French, and the Muslims, was angry that the pope failed to support him in those wars. As a result, the council was delayed.

In June 1536, Pope Paul III officially proclaimed the council, which was to meet in Mantua the following year. However, although Paul established commissions that would make reports and recommendations, it would be nine years before the council finally met. It would be 27 years before it finished its work: the true reformation of the Catholic Church.

In the meantime, wars and strife caused the council to be postponed. For example, in 1537, the duke of Mantua informed the pope that Mantua was unsafe and not a suitable site for the council. By 1541, Charles and Paul had decided that the little town of Trent, in the mountains of northern Italy, would be the best site for the conference, given all the problems facing Christendom. In 1542, the Diet of Speyer accepted Trent as the site. However, a few months later, Charles' arch-enemy, King Francis I, declared war on him, again delaying the council.

Finally, on December 13, 1545, the council convened in Trent. The **Council of Trent** met, with breaks, from 1545 to 1563. The goals of the council were straightforward. First, it would **defend the Catholic Faith and the sacraments**. Second, it intended to

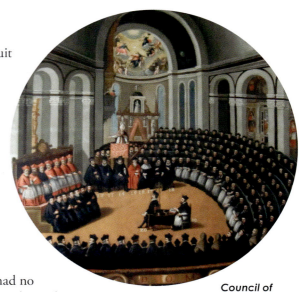

Council of Trent, Laurom

Council of Trent
Church council, held in response to the confusion, abuses, and heresies of the age; clearly explained the Church's teachings, especially those that had been attacked by Protestants.

Map of Italy Showing Trent

Witness to the Faith 355

List of Books of the Bible

Old Testament

- Genesis
- Exodus
- Leviticus
- Numbers
- Deuteronomy
- Joshua
- Judges
- Ruth
- 1 Samuel
- 2 Samuel
- 1 Kings
- 2 Kings
- 1 Chronicles
- 2 Chronicles
- Ezra
- Nehemiah
- Tobit
- Judith
- Esther
- 1 Maccabees
- 2 Maccabees
- Job
- Psalms
- Proverbs
- Ecclesiastes
- Song of Songs
- Wisdom
- Sirach
- Isaiah
- Jeremiah
- Lamentations
- Baruch
- Ezekiel
- Daniel
- Hosea
- Joel
- Amos
- Obadiah
- Jonah
- Micah
- Nahum
- Habakkuk
- Zephaniah
- Haggai
- Zechariah
- Malachi

New Testament

- Matthew
- Mark
- Luke
- John
- Acts of Apostles
- Romans
- 1 Corinthians
- 2 Corinthians
- Galatians
- Ephesians
- Philippians
- Colossians
- 1 Thessalonians
- 2 Thessalonians
- 1 Timothy
- 2 Timothy
- Titus
- Philemon
- Hebrews
- James
- 1 Peter
- 2 Peter
- 1 John
- 2 John
- 3 John
- Jude
- Revelation

---

restore charity among all Christians. Third, it aimed to **abolish the scandals** caused by greed and ambition. Fourth, it sought to **unite all Christians against their common threat, the Muslim Turks**. While all of these goals were extremely important, ***the council's primary task was to answer the false teachings of the Protestants and defend the Catholic Faith and the sacraments***.

The religious basis of the entire Protestant Revolt was the denial of certain fundamental teachings of the Catholic Church and the substitution of new *false* doctrines in their place. Therefore, it was essential that the Council of Trent clearly explain the Church's doctrines in these matters. Lutheranism contained many errors, but they may be summarized as follows: First, the Bible is the sole rule of faith (*sola Scriptura*), as interpreted by the private judgment of each person ("the priesthood of the believer"). Second, human nature is essentially corrupted by Original Sin. Third, salvation (justification) is by faith alone, independent of good works, because when a person has faith, God externally applies the merits of Christ to his soul and *declares* him just; therefore, he cannot lose this salvation no matter what he does. The results of these errors were the revolt against the authority of the Church and Tradition, the rejection of free will, and the denial of the value and necessity of the sacraments.

The Council of Trent devoted years to refuting these doctrinal errors. By the end of the council, Catholics had the answers they needed to better understand their Faith and defend it.

The Bible

When Luther translated the Bible into German, Protestants hailed it as a great accomplishment. In fact, Luther's Bible was a cornerstone of his theology. However, he selectively omitted certain parts of the Bible because they clearly refuted his new ideas. For example, Luther claimed that salvation was by faith alone and that works played no part. Yet in the Epistle of St. James, the Apostle writes, "What good is it, my brothers, if someone says he has faith but does not have works? Can that faith

356 *Chapter 23: The Catholic Reformation*

save him? If a brother or sister has nothing to wear and has no food for the day, and one of you says to them, 'Go in peace, keep warm, and eat well,' but you do not give them the necessities of the body, what good is it? So also faith of itself, if it does not have works, is dead" (James 2:14-17). The Epistle of James makes it crystal clear: **faith without works is dead**. This contradicts one of Luther's most fundamental doctrines.

One of the first tasks of the Council of Trent was to officially proclaim the official list of the books of the Bible—the same books that had been accepted and revered by the Church as Sacred Scripture for more than a thousand years. Second, the council declared that the *Vulgate* of St. Jerome was the *only* standard authorized text. The council also defined that *Sacred Scripture and Sacred Tradition* are the two sources of Divine Revelation. As for Luther's doctrine of the *priesthood of the believer* (or *private interpretation*), the council asserted that in matters of faith and morals no one may interpret the Scriptures contrary to the authoritative interpretation of the Catholic Church or the unanimous consensus of the Fathers of the Church.

St. Jerome **(Detail from an Altarpiece), Carlo Crivelli**

Original Sin

Luther had begun his revolt because he felt personally unworthy of salvation. He struggled with the idea of justification. John Calvin took this notion to its extreme and declared his doctrine of predestination. The Council of Trent needed to explain the proper understanding of justification. The council began with Baptism and Original Sin.

Babies are born with Original Sin on their souls. How is this sin removed? The Council of Trent stated that Original Sin is removed by the merit of Jesus Christ, which is applied to a person's soul by the Sacrament of Baptism. A *tendency* to evil still remains, but this tendency itself is not sin. This tendency is quite different from Luther's contention that human beings are *essentially* corrupted by Original Sin.

Justification

How is a sinner justified? Luther taught that one is saved by faith alone, so his actions (good works) have no effect on his salvation; thus, Confession and the other sacraments are not necessary. However, the Council of Trent affirmed that, while justification is freely given by God to those who are born again in Christ at Baptism, this grace of justification can be increased in them through good works and the sacraments. Moreover, it is possible for someone to fall from this state of grace, and thus lose his salvation, by committing a mortal sin, but he can be restored to a state of grace through Confession. Also, God does not merely *declare* a sinner just; He renews the person internally so that he *becomes* holy and just.

Witness to the Faith 357

Marriage, Gari Melchers

Banns of Matrimony
Public announcement of an impending marriage.

The Sacraments

The destruction of the Mass and the sacraments were the foremost goals of the religious revolutionaries. Wherever they seized control, they abolished the Mass and the sacraments. Thus, the Council of Trent took great pains to defend these fountains of grace from their enemies.

As the council did with so many other doctrines, it sought not to expand doctrine but rather to explain doctrines that had existed for fifteen hundred years. The council reaffirmed the traditional Catholic doctrine of the sacraments. The council *reaffirmed* their divine institution, as well as their nature, the appropriate minister, and their spiritual effects. The council also explained how a person needs to be disposed in order to receive the sacraments worthily and fruitfully. It dealt especially with the Holy Eucharist and the Mass, which the Protestants had not only physically attacked but also misrepresented doctrinally.

With regard to the Real Presence, the council reaffirmed that the Body, Blood, Soul, and Divinity of Jesus Christ are really and substantially contained in the Holy Eucharist. Moreover, the council declared that if anyone maintains that the words of consecration are only symbolic or figurative, let him be *anathema* (that is, formally excommunicated from the Catholic Church).

Additional Decrees

In light of Henry VIII's divorce, the council also addressed the Sacrament of Matrimony. The council affirmed the power of the Church to establish impediments to marriage. The council also defined the indissolubility of marriage and instituted **banns of matrimony** (public announcements of an impending marriage). Moreover, it stressed the life-long nature of marriage.

One of the goals of the Council of Trent was to stop the scandals in the Church that had been caused by greed and ambition. Most of those scandals were caused by unworthy priests and bishops, or priests and bishops who failed to take their vocations seriously. In order to address these issues, the council issued a number of disciplinary decrees in addition to its doctrinal statements.

The council began by reminding bishops of the duties of their vocations. Bishops were to reside personally in their dioceses and could be absent for only two or three months each year, and never during Advent or Lent. (Recall that Cardinal Wolsey had been absent from the diocese of York for more than a decade.) Bishops failing to comply with this rule could be deprived of part of their income. If a bishop stubbornly refused to reside in his diocese, his case could be referred to the pope, who could depose the bishop. Every two years, bishops were required to visit the various parts of their dioceses to reform the morals of both the clergy and the laity and to safeguard Church discipline. They were to hold diocesan synods every year and provincial councils every three years.

The council also reminded priests of their duties. It spoke of the need for priests to live by good example so as not to scandalize the laity. It also reminded them of their need to catechize their parishioners.

The council addressed monastic life as well. It reminded monks and nuns about the rules governing their vocations. To suppress abuses that had crept into the monastic life, the council fixed the minimum age of religious profession at 16 for boys and 12 for girls. It reminded monks about the rules governing poverty. For nuns, it reminded them that most orders had strict rules governing travel outside the convent.

The Council of Trent had never intended to compile a complete statement of the Catholic Faith—that is, a catechism. Its goal had been more specific: to clarify those doctrines that the Protestants were attacking. However, the council recognized that a **catechism** would be a valuable resource in its battle with the Protestants. Therefore, the council directed that a catechism summarizing Catholic doctrine be written. The Church first published this catechism in 1566. Many catechisms, based on this catechism, followed. (For example, in 1992, the *Catechism of the Catholic Church* was published, followed in 1997 by the Second Edition, which includes the official Latin text promulgated by Pope John Paul II.)

Catechism
A complete statement of the Catholic Faith.

The Catholic Reformation Realized

The doctrinal and disciplinary decrees of the Council of Trent were in place. Now the Church needed to implement the work that the council had begun. For this purpose, the Holy Spirit called forth some of the greatest champions the Faith has ever known, and raised up a line of saintly popes.

Oral Exercises

1. What were the three goals of the Jesuits?
2. Which pope finally called the Council of Trent?
3. What did the Council of Trent teach about the Bible?
4. What did the Council of Trent teach about (a) Original Sin and (b) justification?
5. What did the Council of Trent teach about the sacraments?
6. What did the Council of Trent teach about the Holy Eucharist?

Witness to the Faith

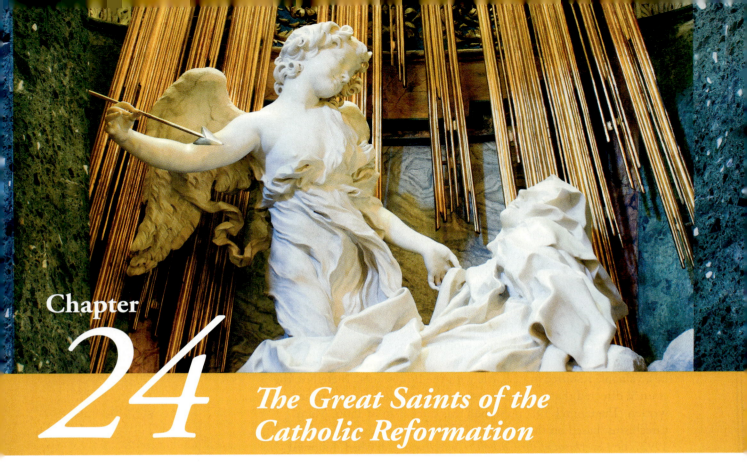

Chapter 24: The Great Saints of the Catholic Reformation

Introduction

A Catholic person living in 1534 might well have despaired. Pope Clement VII had shown that he had almost no ability to take a stand in defense of the Church. Protestants were ravaging Germany and Switzerland. Henry VIII was on the verge of taking England out of the Church. But even in those dark days, Catholics could still take comfort in the words that Our Lord spoke to St. Peter at Caesarea Philippi about the Church: "The gates of Hell shall not prevail against it" (Matthew 16:18). Catholic men and women of incredible devotion and ability were about to make themselves known. Remarkable popes were about to wear the Fisherman's Ring. Spain was about to provide some of the greatest saints in all of history. The Jesuits were about to change the face of the world. The first decades of the sixteenth century had been dark, but the Son of God had founded a Church that would shine forth against all sin and darkness.

The Popes of the Catholic Reformation

Pope Paul III

Paul III was not able to convoke the Council of Trent until 1545. However, he worked tirelessly to reform the Church in the years before

Congregation of the Holy Office (Roman Inquisition)
Set up by Pope Paul III to defend the Faith and to condemn heretical statements.

The Ecstasy of St. Teresa, Bernini

1535 A.D. – 1644 A.D.

1535 A.D.
St. Angela Merici and company become the first Ursuline Sisters and devote themselves to teaching children.

1542-1552 A.D.
St. Francis Xavier evangelizes in the Far East.

1563 A.D.
The Council of Trent holds its last meeting.

1570 A.D.
The Tridentine Mass becomes the standard form of the Mass, remaining so for the next four hundred years.

1571 A.D.
At the Battle of Lepanto, the navy of the Holy League defeats that of the Turks, saving Europe from the Muslim threat by sea.

1562-1582 A.D.
St. Teresa of Avila and her Discalced Carmelites reform the Carmelite Order.

1582 A.D.
Pope Gregory XIII issues a new calendar, one that corresponds more closely to the seasons. In Switzerland, St. Peter Canisius founds the College of Saint Michael.

1583 A.D.
Fr. Matteo Ricci becomes the first missionary to penetrate the Chinese mainland.

1597 A.D.
The crucifixion of the Twenty-Six Martyrs of Nagasaki marks the beginning of Japan's persecution of Christians.

1606-1644 A.D.
Fr. Roberto de Nobili works to spread the Gospel in India.

---

the council met and, in fact, during his entire papacy. One of his most important measures was the institution of the **Congregation of the Holy Office**, or the **Roman Inquisition** (not to be confused with the Inquisition established in the Middle Ages after the Albigensian Crusade). The main purpose of the Roman Inquisition was to defend the Catholic Faith by issuing decrees and pointing out heretical statements of doctrine that deserved condemnation.

In October 1549, Pope Paul III was 81, remarkably old for those days. During that month, he confirmed that Michelangelo would remain the architect for St. Peter's Basilica during his lifetime. He ordered that the Jesuits should be answerable only to the pope and not to any local bishops. Also, no Jesuit should be granted high positions in the Church without the approval of the head of the order. On

Witness to the Faith   361

November 9, Pope Paul III made his last Confession and publicly begged forgiveness for his nepotism. He died the following day.

Pope Julius III

The conclave to elect Pope Paul III's successor met at the end of November. Eventually, all but three of the 54 members of the College of Cardinals attended. Initially, it appeared that they might elect **Cardinal Reginald Pole**, the only English cardinal. Pole, a holy and well-educated man, had served as one of the three papal legates overseeing the Council of Trent. He would ultimately become Queen Mary Tudor's most trusted servant and advisor. Had he lived long enough, he might have returned England to the Church. On the other hand, had Pole been elected pope, he might have been one of the greatest popes ever to reign. However, God had other plans.

The conclave soon became deadlocked between the pro-French and pro-imperial cardinals. Fifty-two ballots were cast. Finally, the cardinals chose a compromise candidate, Cardinal Giovanni del Monte, who had been one of the other legates at Trent. He chose the name **Julius III** (1550-1555).

Pope Julius III immediately reconvened the Council of Trent and announced his decision to work closely with Emperor Charles V. This second session continued the council's important plans for reform. However, ongoing wars with the Protestants delayed the third meeting for eleven years.

In August 1553, when Pope Julius learned that Mary Tudor had been crowned queen of England, he wept for joy. He appointed Reginald Pole as papal legate to England, with the task of returning England to the Church. By December 1555, it seemed that Queen Mary and Cardinal Pole had made progress in their efforts to return England to the fold. News of their success reached Rome, and Julius said Mass in thanksgiving. Three months later, he was dead from illness and the treatments for it. Within three years, the work of Cardinal Pole was cut short as well, when he and Queen Mary died within hours of each other on November 17, 1558.

Pope Paul IV

The conclave to elect Julius III's successor quickly chose Marcellus II, the last pope to keep his own name. Marcellus was a true reformer, but he reigned less than three weeks before a stroke killed him. He was only 53 years old.

For the second time in two months, the Sacred College convened. This time, the cardinals elected a man quite unlike Marcellus. They elected Cardinal Gian Caraffa, who took the name Paul IV (1555-1559). Caraffa was an unusual man. Together with Saint Cajetan, he had helped found the Theatines, one of the most humble and modest religious orders. He was totally dedicated to reform, which was why he was elected. However, he was also loud with a short temper, and he was one of the worst judges of character in the history of the papacy.

Julius III
Pope from 1550 to 1555; reconvened the Council of Trent and appointed Cardinal Reginald Pole as papal legate to England.

Pope Julius III

362 *Chapter 24: The Great Saints of the Catholic Reformation*

During his pontificate, Paul IV made three of his nephews cardinals. He secretly began investigating another (innocent) cardinal for heresy. He also enacted several unjust measures against Jews living in Rome. However, he did remove Cranmer as archbishop of Canterbury and install Cardinal Pole in that office. He also worked with the Inquisition, and although he did not reconvene the council, he worked to reform the Church. But his personal intemperance and nepotism had damaged the Church. When he died on August 18, 1559, the people of Rome cut the head off a statue of him and threw it in the Tiber.

Pope Pius IV

On September 3, the conclave convened to elect a new pope. Sadly, political intrigues and national politics took precedence over religious convictions. For more than four months, the cardinals negotiated without any candidate obtaining the two-thirds majority necessary to elect a Supreme Pontiff. Finally, at the end of December, the little-known cardinal of Milan, Gian Angelo de Medici (no relation to the Medici family of Florence), was elected pope. He took the name Pius IV (1559-1564).

Pope Paul IV

In January 1562, Pope Pius IV reconvened the Council of Trent for the third and final time. Under his leadership, the council finally concluded its work and issued its various decrees and doctrinal statements. Final decrees of the council included affirmation of the existence of Purgatory, as well as praise for the invocation of saints and the veneration of images and relics—all of which the Protestants had denied. A final decree declared that the pope's authority was superior to that of any council. This decree was almost unanimously accepted.

The Council of Trent met for the final time on December 4, 1563. On that day, it authorized the granting of indulgences. However, indulgences were not to be given in exchange for money.

Two days later, in a consistory with his cardinals and several ambassadors, Pius IV declared that the Council of Trent was the most important council in the past 500 years. He was certainly correct. Pius, who was not a particularly inspiring man, had done what more talented men had failed to do. He had led the council to its successful conclusion. Unlike the Protestants, the Catholic Church had spoken with one voice.

Pope Pius IV

Despite numerous invitations and opportunities, the Protestant leaders never attended the council or showed any real interest in its work. Negotiations, Diets, and councils had failed to resolve the religious controversies. In an age when everyone agreed that there should be only one national religion, all that remained was the battlefield. The battle lines would begin to be drawn in the months following the council, as various

Witness to the Faith

nations (for example, Spain, Portugal, and Poland) accepted the decrees of the council, whereas others (such as France and Germany) ignored them.

Pope Pius IV did not live to see the Council of Trent ("Tridentine") reforms that he had helped create. He became sick in early December 1565 and died a few days later. He received the Last Rites from one of the cardinals he had appointed: his nephew, Charles Borromeo.

Pope St. Pius V

As the conclave met to elect a new pope, every cardinal knew that his vote would be the most important in his lifetime, perhaps in the history of the Church. A holy man, dedicated to reform, had to be chosen. For the first time in decades, religious convictions trumped all other considerations. On January 7, 1566, the cardinals voted openly rather than in secret. Over his protestations that he was not worthy, they unanimously chose Cardinal Antonio Ghislieri, the head of the Roman Inquisition. In the history of the papacy, there have been some popes as good as **Pope Pius V** (1566-1572), but none greater.

Before his election, Pope Pius V had been one of the leaders of the Dominican Order. He had overseen the teaching of Dominican novices and played a leading role in the Inquisition in Italy. He prayed and fasted daily. He brought his reforming zeal to the papacy. He denounced nepotism and simony. He worked to ensure that only the finest men became bishops and cardinals. Once such men were appointed, Pius insisted that they obey the council's decrees regarding the requirements that bishops actually live in their dioceses and work diligently as pastors to care for the souls of the laity. Pius also enforced these rules. He decreed that any bishop who failed to follow these policies would be removed from his diocese within a month.

Of all Pope Pius V's decrees, his most long-lasting and significant was his decision to **standardize the Mass**. In 1570, following the directives of the Council of Trent, Pius promulgated a revision of the Mass that restored the prayers and rubrics of the liturgy to a state more consistent with its original form. Pius declared that this standardized form of the Mass (often known as the **Tridentine Mass**) would be the official Mass of the Roman Rite. For the next four hundred years, Masses offered in churches of the Roman Rite were based on this standardized form of the Mass.

Pius V also played a leading role in one of the most decisive battles in the history of the world. On October 7, 1571, a naval battle took place between the Muslim Turks and the **Holy League**. The Holy League was a coalition of Catholic maritime nations, including the Papal States and Spain, that Pius V had brought together to defend Europe against Muslim aggression. On October 7, the Catholic fleet defeated the Turkish fleet at the **Battle of Lepanto**

> **Pope Pius V**
> Pope from 1566 to 1572; standardized the Tridentine Mass and worked zealously for reform.

> **Holy League**
> An alliance of Catholic seagoing nations that Pius V brought together to defend Europe against Muslim aggression.

Pope Pius V

*The Battle of Lepanto,
Antonio de Brugada*

(the Gulf of Corinth in Greece). At the moment of victory, Pius V, who was hundreds of miles away in Rome having a meeting with the papal treasurer, suddenly rose, threw open the window, and exclaimed, "This is not the moment for business; make haste to thank God, because our fleet this moment has won a victory over the Turks." In commemoration of this crucial victory, Pius V later instituted the **Feast of Our Lady of Victory** (which today is celebrated on October 7 as the Feast of the Holy Rosary in the Traditional calendar, and Our Lady of the Rosary in the Novus Ordo calendar). The Turks never again posed a naval threat to Christendom.

On May 1, 1572, Pope Pius V died after a pontificate of only six years. Both spiritually and physically, he had saved Christendom. The process of his canonization began almost immediately. Surprisingly, it would be 1712 before he was declared a saint.

Pope Gregory XIII

The conclave that elected Pope Gregory XIII (1572-1585) went quickly, smoothly, and without discord. Gregory, a 70-year-old canon lawyer, was elected on May 13, 1572. Despite his age, he reigned thirteen years.

Gregory XIII, who chose his name to honor another reformer, Pope Gregory I, continued the policies of Pius V. He insisted that bishops comply with the rules of the council. His main concerns remained the defense of the Church against Protestants and the reconversion of nations lost to Protestantism. Thus, he worked closely with the Jesuits to help Catholics in England, Ireland, and France.

Gregory's work on conversions led to what is perhaps his finest and longest-lasting contribution to the Faith: the establishment of various seminaries in Rome. In 1564, Pope Pius IV had decided to establish

Battle of Lepanto
Naval battle on October 7, 1571, in which the Catholic fleet defeated the Muslim Turks, who never again posed a naval threat to Christendom.

Feast of Our Lady of Victory
Feast instituted by Pope St. Pius V in thanksgiving for Our Lady's assistance in the Battle of Lepanto (today celebrated on October 7 as the Feast of Our Lady of the Rosary).

Pope Gregory XIII

Julian Calendar
Calendar created by Julius Caesar. By 1582, it was about ten days off.

Christopher Clavius
Jesuit astronomer and mathematician who helped Pope Gregory XIII create a new calendar.

Christopher Clavius

Gregorian Calendar
Calendar instituted by Pope Gregory XIII. It is still in use today.

a seminary in Rome, which he had placed under the direction of the Jesuits. In 1572, Gregory rebuilt this college and put it on a strong financial footing. He added a strong course of studies that would prepare men for the priesthood. Ultimately, Gregory wanted to have seminaries in Rome for every nationality where young men could be trained for the priesthood. He began with the German College, but the English College was also founded during his pontificate. The English College, which the Jesuits managed, sent young men into the most dangerous mission field in Europe: Elizabethan England. Gregory even established the Greek College in the hopes of undoing the Great Schism and the loss of Constantinople to the Turks.

The achievement for which Pope Gregory XIII is most known is his renovation of the calendar that Julius Caesar had created (the **Julian calendar**). A year under Caesar's calendar lasted 11 minutes and 14 seconds longer than the actual sun year. This amounted to three extra days in 400 years. By 1582, the date on the calendar and the actual seasons were out of sync by about ten days. Working with Jesuit astronomer and mathematician **Christopher Clavius**, Pope Gregory issued a papal decree creating a new calendar. The new calendar moved the date ahead ten days and added Leap Year. Because Pope Gregory XIII had instituted the new calendar, it was named in his honor, the **Gregorian calendar**. This calendar is so mathematically precise that it is still used today.

Amazingly, despite the fact that the Gregorian calendar merely involved a mathematical adjustment having nothing to do with religion, every Protestant European nation refused to accept it, simply because the pope had issued it. There was no rational reason to reject the calendar, and doing so caused great difficulty. (It is a sad commentary on the hatred that Protestants had for the Church.) Some Protestant nations failed to accept the new calendar until the eighteenth century! Great Britain and its American colonies remained the most obstinate. They did not change to the Gregorian calendar until 1752!

Great Saints Work to Reform the Church

The Council of Trent and the popes had laid forth the plans and decrees for the Catholic Reformation. However, it remained for bishops to implement these decrees if they were to have any effect. The bishop most responsible for carrying out the reforms enacted by the Council of Trent was **St. Charles Borromeo**, a nephew of Pope Pius IV.

St. Charles Borromeo

Although Charles Borromeo was the pope's nephew, he never sought favors or honors. Instead, he devoted himself to the service of the Church. In fact, Charles was an exceptionally holy man who deserved high Church office and simply happened to be related to the pope. During his uncle's pontificate, he acted as the pope's chief adviser. Charles Borromeo, as much as anyone, successfully implemented the reforms of the Council of Trent.

Charles Borromeo exemplified the role of bishop as envisioned by the Council of Trent. In 1565, after the death of his uncle Pius IV, Charles left Rome for his archdiocese, Milan. He remained in Milan for the rest of his life, constantly refusing to accept higher office, determined to reform his archdiocese. Milan was one of the largest archdioceses in the world, with over 1 million Catholics and more than 2,000 churches.

Charles completely reformed this archdiocese. He had the assistance of several religious orders, including the Jesuits, whom he placed in charge of his seminary in Milan. Charles also founded several other seminaries, including one for priests who had late vocations. In addition, he founded a congregation of secular priests called the **Oblates of St. Ambrose**. Their main duties included visiting churches, teaching catechism, and overseeing colleges and seminaries. Charles believed that strongly orthodox colleges and seminaries were the best ways to reform the clergy, who would then pass the Faith on to the laity. Of course, he also passionately supported catechetical instruction to young people on Sundays.

In 1576, a terrible plague ravaged Milan. Charles turned the bishop's residence into a hospital. He personally nursed the sick, heard their Confessions, and administered the Last Rites to them.

Charles Borromeo died in November 1584. He was only 46. He had accomplished as much in his short lifetime as any bishop in the history of the Church.

St. Philip Neri

As scandal and heresy plagued the Church in the early sixteenth century, devout men and women found ways to reform the Church. Many formed new religious orders. **St. Philip Neri** started a unique religious community.

Philip Neri was born in Florence in 1515 to a noble family. He received his early education from the Dominicans. When he was 18, his wealthy uncle promised to make him his heir if he would enter his business and work for him. Philip tried it for a time, but underwent a conversion experience and found he had lost all interest in worldly things. So, in 1533, he traveled to Rome, where he devoted himself to a life of study.

Philip possessed a great love for the poor. In Rome, he began to work with the poor and the sick. His work among Rome's most hopeless and helpless would one day earn him the nickname "The Third Apostle of Rome" (after Saints Peter and Paul). For the next eighteen years, he ministered as a layman to the needy.

Following the advice of his confessor, Philip became a priest in 1551. He continued to assist the people of Rome. As word of his holiness spread, hundreds of young men came to him seeking advice. He spent many hours every day hearing Confessions. His house had a large room that he turned into a chapel, or oratory, where every day a large group of men came together for prayer.

> **St. Charles Borromeo**
> Archbishop of Milan; devoted himself completely to teaching and caring for his people, especially in the formation of priests.

> **Oblates of St. Ambrose**
> Association of priests founded by St. Charles Borromeo.

St. Charles Borromeo

> **St. Philip Neri**
> Worked with the poor and sick, and founded the Congregation of the Oratory; nicknamed the "Third Apostle of Rome."

Witness to the Faith

Congregation of the Oratory (Oratorians)
Community founded by St. Philip Neri, devoted to prayer and good works but not bound by vows.

Chiesa Nuova, the Church in Rome Founded by St. Philip Neri

Company of St. Ursula (Ursulines)
An order of religious sisters founded by St. Angela Merici, devoted to teaching children.

Before long, the demands on Philip's time and energy became more than he could manage alone. He needed others to help him. In 1156, he founded a new kind of religious community, called the **Congregation of the Oratory**. It is one of the most unusual orders ever founded. Its members (which include both priests and lay brothers), the **Oratorians**, live in community while providing their food at their own expense, but they are not bound by vows, and they may quit the congregation at any time. The congregation's various houses are independent of one another, and they have no superior general. All major decisions are based on a majority vote of the assembled congregation.

Through their enthusiasm and personal holiness, the Oratorians helped reform the Church. In 1575, Pope Gregory XIII approved the Congregation of the Oratory, which soon spread into other countries. St. Philip Neri died on May 25, 1595, after spending the day as he normally did: hearing Confessions and receiving visitors.

St. Angela Merici

St. Philip Neri was not the only Italian to start a new religious order in sixteenth-century Italy. In 1535, a holy woman named Angela Merici founded an order of religious sisters known as the **Company of St. Ursula** (or the **Ursulines**). Angela was born in 1474 in Brescia, Italy. Orphaned at the age of 10 along with her younger sister, she was raised by her uncle. Young Angela was very distressed when her sister suddenly died without receiving the Last Sacraments. When Angela was old enough, she joined the Third Order of St. Francis. When she was 20 years old, her uncle died, and she returned to her family home.

Angela believed that young girls in Italy needed a better Catholic education than they were receiving. She decided to dedicate her time to teaching girls in her home, which she converted into a school. Angela's school became so successful that the leaders of a neighboring city invited her to start a school in their town. She happily accepted their offer. She spent her days teaching and doing works of charity, and she spent her nights in prayer.

In 1524, Angela suddenly lost her eyesight during a pilgrimage to the Holy Land. There, she had a vision to found a community of women who would devote themselves to the education of children. After she recovered her sight, she returned to Italy. In 1535, she chose twelve other women and founded the Ursulines. St. Angela Merici served as the first superior of the order. Though the Ursuline Sisters continued to live in their own homes, they regularly met together for prayer. They devoted their time to teaching children and caring for the sick.

The Ursulines received great encouragement from St. Charles Borromeo, who helped spread the order throughout Italy. Soon they had houses in France and Germany. They were the first sisters to come to the New World, where they were established in Canada in 1636. In 1727, they opened a convent in New Orleans, where they founded the first school taught by religious sisters within the present boundaries of the United States.

St. Angela Merici died on January 27, 1540. She was buried in Brescia, where she had lived almost her entire life. Pope Pius VII canonized her in 1807.

St. Teresa of Avila

During the years following the Council of Trent, holy men and women formed new religious orders, and several of the older religious orders underwent a reform. However, no order was more thoroughly reformed than the Carmelites. **St. Teresa of Avila**, one of the Catholic Church's greatest saints, renewed the Carmelites. She is one of only three women to be named a Doctor of the Church. (St. Catherine of Siena and St. Thérèse of Lisieux are the others.)

Saint Angela Merici

Saint Teresa of Avila, Peter Paul Rubens

Teresa was born in Avila, Spain, to noble parents in 1515. Even as a young child, she possessed a deep love of the Catholic Faith and an indomitable character. As a little girl, she and her brother left their home for Morocco, intending to die as martyrs at the hands of the Muslims, but her uncle stopped them before they had gone very far.

At the age of 20, St. Teresa entered the Carmelite *Convent of the Incarnation* in Avila and became a nun. For many years, Teresa lived in the convent, where she dedicated her life to prayer but did nothing to draw any particular attention to herself. However, like St. Ignatius, she was suddenly called by God to a higher purpose at the Church's moment of crisis.

In 1562, Teresa left her convent because the nuns had become very worldly. She founded a smaller but stricter convent elsewhere in Avila. Under her rule, the nuns spent most of their time in prayer, contemplation, and manual labor. They also strictly practiced chastity and were protected by being cloistered. Her new reformed order was known as the **Discalced Carmelites**, because the nuns did not wear shoes. Five years later, Teresa founded two more reformed Carmelite convents.

In many ways, St. Teresa of Avila resembled St. Ignatius of Loyola. Like Ignatius, Teresa was an exceptional leader who possessed a great talent for organization. She was firmly convinced that the Protestant Revolt would not have occurred if the religious orders had remained true to their ideals. Therefore, she threw herself, body and soul, into founding Carmelite convents where the nuns would strictly observe the rules.

In 1567, Teresa met **St. John of the Cross**, a recently ordained 25-year-old Spanish priest. John was considering what to do with his future priestly career. After speaking with Teresa about her reform of the Carmelites, he decided to join her on a trip to establish another convent.

St. Teresa of Avila
Carmelite nun, mystic, visionary, and Doctor of the Church; reformed the Carmelite Order.

Discalced Carmelites
St. Teresa of Avila's reformed Carmelites.

St. John of the Cross
Carmelite priest, visionary, and Doctor of the Church; assisted St. Teresa of Avila in her reform of the order.

Witness to the Faith 369

St. John of the Cross

During the next months, John discovered in Teresa a mentor and spiritual advisor. In November 1568, St. Teresa and St. John founded the first men's community of the Discalced Carmelites. Later, John began to have mystical visions of Our Lord. Throughout the remainder of his life, he worked with Teresa to govern and improve the Discalced Carmelites. John died on December 14, 1591. Pope Benedict XIII canonized him in 1726, and Pope Pius XI declared him a Doctor of the Church in 1926.

After her meeting with St. John of the Cross, St. Teresa founded several convents over the next few years. In 1571, the head of the Carmelites placed her in charge of the Convent of the Incarnation at Avila, where the nuns were personally hostile to her. However, her charm and holiness won them over, and they accepted her reforms. (The Convent of the Incarnation still exists and continues to draw young women with a vocation to the Carmelites.)

In June 1580, Pope Gregory XIII finally decreed that the Discalced Carmelites were a separate province of the Carmelite Order.

Teresa of Avila continued to found and reform convents up to the moment of her death in 1582. By that time, she had founded sixteen convents and helped reform many others. Pope Gregory XV canonized her in 1622. Pope Paul VI declared her a Doctor of the Church in 1970.

Jesuit Saints Answer the Call

In this time of crisis, the Holy Spirit blessed the Society of Jesus with some of the most magnificent saints the Church has ever known. During the sixteenth century, Jesuits followed the example of St. Ignatius of Loyola and helped reform the Church and implement the decrees of the Council of Trent. Some, such as theologians Peter Canisius and Robert Bellarmine, educated Europe. Others, such as Edmund Campion, sought to reclaim the lands lost to the Protestants. Finally, Jesuits like Francis Xavier, Matteo Ricci, and Robert de Nobili evangelized the world. Several of these brave priests died as martyrs. Many left their native lands behind for faraway places, knowing that they would never see their homes or loved ones again.

St. Peter Canisius

During its long history, the Society of Jesus has given the Church many great theologians. **Peter Canisius** ranks among the greatest Jesuit theologians of the sixteenth century. He was born in 1521 in Nijmegen (today the Netherlands), which was part of the Holy Roman Empire. When he was a teenager, his father sent him to the University of Cologne, where he earned his degree in 1540. While studying at Cologne, he met Peter Faber, one of

St. Peter Canisius Teaching

the founders of the Jesuits. In 1543, Peter Canisius joined the Jesuits, the first Dutchman to enter the order.

For the next thirty-five years, he worked to win back those areas of central Europe that had been lost to the Protestants. He won converts in Germany, Austria, Hungary, and Poland. He worked so successfully for the preservation of the Faith in Germany that Catholic historians have justly dubbed him the "*Second Apostle of Germany*." (St. Boniface was the first "Apostle of Germany.")

Peter's success was due primarily to the catechisms he wrote. Because of these catechisms and his popular defense of the Catholic Faith as a preacher, St. Peter Canisius became known as the "Hammer of Heretics" (as St. Anthony of Padua had been known several centuries earlier). Contemporaries referred to St. Peter's catechisms as "banners of war, which gleamed in the religious struggles and won the most glorious victories" (Fr. J. Laux, *Church History* [Charlotte, N.C.: TAN Books, 1989]). Peter's catechisms were translated into every European language and reprinted many times. Like the *Baltimore Catechism*, St. Peter's catechisms were written in the form of questions and answers. He stressed the points of Catholic doctrine disputed by the Protestants, giving a clear and thorough explanation of the Catholic teaching. In addition to his writings, Peter was also a brilliant preacher and teacher.

Robert Bellarmine

Peter soon became one of the leading theologians in Germany. In this capacity, he attended the Council of Trent. He also served as an adviser to Emperor Frederick I.

In 1580, under the authority of Pope Gregory XIII, Peter traveled to Fribourg, Switzerland, where he founded the Jesuit College of Saint Michael. The college trained young Catholic men, many of whom became Jesuits. (The College of Saint Michael remains the only Catholic university in Switzerland.) Peter Canisius spent the remainder of his life in Fribourg, preaching, writing, and promoting Catholic reform. He died in 1597. He is buried at the college he founded, where he spent so many years teaching. In 1925, Pope Pius XI canonized him and declared him a Doctor of the Church.

St. Robert Bellarmine

Although Jesuits did not seek high Church offices, one of the leading theologians of the Catholic Reformation was the distinguished Jesuit Cardinal **Robert Bellarmine**. Born in Italy in 1542 to a noble family, as a young man he showed the intellectual gifts that would make him almost universally known later in his life. His father hoped he would enter politics, but his mother had higher ambitions for him: the Jesuits. In 1560, he entered the order. The Jesuits immediately recognized that

> **Peter Canisius**
> One of the first Jesuits; worked successfully in countries of central Europe that had become Protestant; called the "Second Apostle of Germany" (after St. Boniface).

> **Robert Bellarmine**
> Brilliant theologian who worked as a professor and preacher and wrote important works, including a catechism.

Witness to the Faith

in Robert they had acquired a pearl of great price. They sent him to the finest colleges, where he studied theology and philosophy.

In 1569, the Jesuits sent him to the University of Leuven in Flanders to complete his studies. At Leuven, he was ordained and began teaching at the university. He quickly gained a reputation as a professor and a preacher, attracting both Catholics and Protestants to his sermons. He stayed in Leuven for seven years, until reasons of health forced him to return to Italy. In 1576, Robert traveled to Rome, where Pope Gregory XIII commissioned him to teach theology at the Roman College, which Gregory had rebuilt.

For the next eleven years, Robert Bellarmine taught theology in Rome. He also wrote his most important book, *Disputations on the Controversies of the Christian Faith*. Catholic theologians have described it as the definitive defense of papal authority. This monumental work was the earliest attempt to systematize the various controversies of the time. It dealt a tremendous blow to Protestantism throughout Europe.

Pope Clement VIII (1592-1605) also highly valued Robert Bellarmine's abilities, and he commissioned him to write a catechism. Upon its completion, Pope Clement ordered that the catechism be used throughout the papal territories and expressed his wish that it be used in every country. It was translated into many different languages and met with phenomenal success. When the First Vatican Council addressed the issue of a universal catechism, it suggested Robert Bellarmine's catechism as a model. In 1599, Pope Clement made Robert Bellarmine a cardinal, and three years later made him archbishop of Capua.

Throughout his life, Robert Bellarmine defended the Church. In his 70s, he was made the bishop of Montepulciano, his old home. He served as its bishop for four years. Then he retired to the Jesuit college of St. Andrew in Rome. During his retirement, he wrote several short books intended to help ordinary people in their spiritual life. St. Robert Bellarmine died in Rome in 1621.

The Jesuits Evangelize the Far East

One of the Jesuits' main goals was to evangelize the newly discovered and distant lands. Jesuits evangelized the native peoples of North and South America (discussed in a later chapter). They also traveled to the Far East, where they brought the Catholic Faith to the peoples of China, Japan, and India. These brave men left on a journey that, for them, took longer than it takes men now to travel to the moon. Unlike the astronauts, these men knew they would almost certainly never return home.

St. Francis Xavier

Born in Navarre (now part of Spain) in 1506, **Francis Xavier** was a descendant of the kings of

Francis Xavier
One of the first Jesuits; brought the Catholic Faith to India and Japan.

St. Francis Xavier Baptizes an Oriental Princess

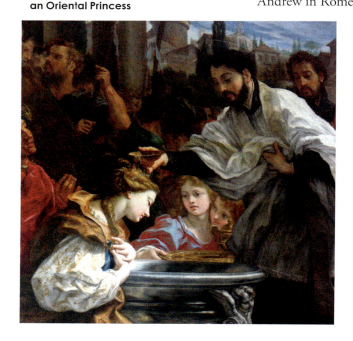

Aragon and Navarre. The greatest missionary since St. Paul, Francis became the Apostle of India and Japan. In March 1540, six months before the pope gave his final approval to the Jesuit Order, Francis Xavier (one of its seven founders) agreed on a single day's notice to depart for the Far East. On April 7, 1541, 35-year-old Francis sailed from Portugal for India. On May 6, 1542, he landed at the Portuguese stronghold of **Goa, India**, where he immediately began his missionary work.

Francis began by instructing the Portuguese themselves, who had been poorly catechized, and then the native Indians who lived outside of Goa. Over the next few years, he established a number of churches and a seminary for the education of native clergy. Wherever St. Francis went, he converted many to the Catholic Faith. This was fertile ground for the Church, as there were millions to be converted.

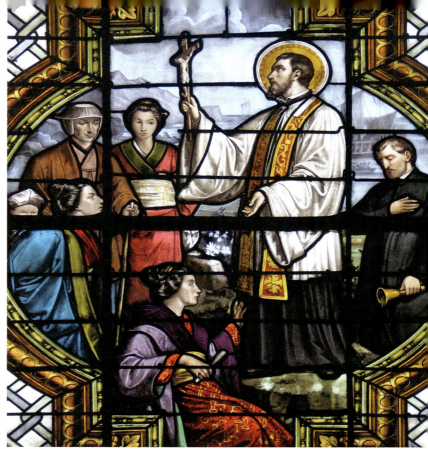

St. Francis Xavier in Japan

On August 15, 1549, Francis entered Japan, where the Portuguese had established a small presence six years earlier. There, Francis established a Jesuit province. He followed his usual practice of translating the basic prayers, the Creed, and the Ten Commandments into Japanese. However, the language barrier initially proved a great problem. For a time, he showed the Japanese people paintings of the Madonna and Child. Francis worked for two years in Japan, during which time other Jesuits joined him. They planted the seeds of the Catholic Faith. For the next forty-five years, the Jesuits were the only missionaries in Japan until the Franciscans joined them in 1631.

After working for more than two years in Japan, Francis returned to India early in 1552. However, he planned to travel to China as soon as possible. He left for China in April, but by August he had traveled only as far as **Sancian Island**, off the coast of mainland China. The Chinese prohibited the entry of foreigners into China, and he could not find anyone brave enough to take him to the Chinese mainland.

On November 13, 1552, Francis wrote his last letter stating his determination to enter China. A week later, he fell ill. On December 2, 1552, the greatest missionary the Church had known since St. Paul died.

Francis Xavier was buried, and his body was covered with lime. After a year, the body was exhumed and was found totally incorrupt. The

Goa, India
Portuguese stronghold in India, where St. Francis Xavier's missionary work in India began.

Sancian Island
An island off the coast of China, where St. Francis Xavier died.

Witness to the Faith

Matteo Ricci
Jesuit who brought the Catholic Faith to the Chinese mainland and even to its capital.

Macau
Chinese peninsula where the Portuguese had a trading post, a sort of European foothold in China.

following year, the body was returned to India, incorrupt. It was buried for five months, but in 1554, the body was brought to Goa, still incorrupt. In 1694, one hundred forty-two years after his death, his body was exhumed again, and was examined by the local bishop and a French Jesuit; it was still incorrupt. However, this evidence of sanctity was not necessary. The world and the Catholic Church already well knew that he was a saint. Francis Xavier had been canonized more than seventy years before.

The Jesuits in China

Francis Xavier had been only 46 when illness prevented him from entering China. It would be another Jesuit, **Matteo Ricci**, who would take up the great saint's work and finally bring the Gospel to China. Father Ricci was one of the most intelligent men in Europe. He had received a superb education from Robert Bellarmine, among others. In addition to his theological training, he had been trained in mathematics and astronomy.

In 1577, his superiors assigned him to India to help catechize the people there and fulfill their sacramental needs. He left immediately. By the end of Lent in 1582, Father Ricci's superiors decided that he should begin getting ready to evangelize China.

In August 1582, Ricci arrived at **Macau**, a small peninsula on China's southern coast where the emperor of China had permitted the Portuguese to establish a trading post. However, outside of Macau, few conversions had been made. Fr. Ricci decided that the best way to win the Chinese to the Faith would be to enter into their lives, learn their language, and adopt their customs. Therefore, he devoted himself to becoming Chinese. He learned classic Chinese, the most difficult major language in the world. By 1583, Ricci spoke Chinese well enough to be understood. Over time, the people began treating him as a member of the Chinese nobility.

Matteo Ricci

In 1583, the governor of Zhaoqing, who had heard of Ricci's abilities as a mathematician, invited Ricci and fellow Jesuit Michele Ruggieri to Zhaoqing, a province northwest of Macau. Now firmly on mainland China, Ricci could begin his conversion work in earnest. In the spring of 1584, Ricci baptized his first Chinese converts. In the fall, he published a translation of the Ten Commandments and the *Catechism of the Council of Trent*. He wrote a book in the Chinese language called *A True Account of God*.

Most Chinese, including their leaders and teachers, followed the doctrines of **Confucius**, who, although not a religious leader, was a philosopher of ethics. Instead of attacking the teachings of Confucius, which would have turned the Chinese against him, Father Ricci respected them and showed that in many ways they were like the teachings of Christ. In fact, Matteo Ricci was the one

374 *Chapter 24: The Great Saints of the Catholic Reformation*

who Latinized the Chinese name of *Kung Fu-tze* to "Confucius." To gain the acceptance of the Chinese philosophers, Ricci even dressed as they did.

For the next seventeen years, Matteo Ricci worked to spread the Catholic Faith throughout China. He developed an incredible reputation with the Chinese as a mathematician, astronomer, and scholar. In 1601, he was invited to the imperial court in Beijing to be an advisor to the emperor. In Beijing, Ricci met China's leaders, some of whom he converted to Catholicism.

In 1605, Matteo Ricci founded the Cathedral of the Immaculate Conception in Beijing. At the time, there were about two hundred Catholics in Beijing and more than one thousand in China overall. By 1609, with his health declining, Ricci began writing a history of the Chinese missions. Matteo Ricci died on May 11, 1610. The emperor allowed him to be buried in a cemetery where only the greatest Chinese were interred.

When Father Ricci died, German Jesuit **Johann Adam Schall von Bell** took his place. Father Schall was a learned mathematician and astronomer. He arrived in Macau in 1619 and, after learning Chinese, was sent into mainland China three years later. In 1630, Fr. Schall was sent to Beijing, where he worked not only as a missionary but also as an astronomer.

Confucius
Chinese philosopher of the sixth and fifth centuries B.C.

Johann Adam Schall von Bell
Jesuit astronomer and missionary in China; befriended the young emperor, and thus gained influence with high-ranking Chinese.

Witness to the Faith 375

Johann Adam Schall von Bell

In 1644, Schall's work as an astronomer attracted the attention of the new 12-year-old Chinese emperor. Schall showed the Chinese how to calculate the time of solar and lunar eclipses, something the Chinese scholars could not do. Consequently, the emperor made him the director of his astronomy bureau and put him in charge of mathematical studies. The emperor also allowed the Jesuits greater freedom to convert the Chinese and build churches throughout China. During the next fourteen years, several hundred thousand Chinese became Catholics.

Over the next few years, Fr. Schall established a very close relationship with the young emperor, who called him "grandpa" and even celebrated his 18th birthday at Schall's house. Schall's relationship with the emperor presented the best opportunity to convert China to the Faith. However, the emperor had several wives and, while the Church had accepted some native customs, the Church could not accept polygamy. Thus, although the emperor may have recognized the truth of Catholicism in his head, he never became a Catholic in his heart. Nevertheless, because of Schall's influence, many high-ranking Chinese officials became Catholic.

In 1661, the emperor died. The new emperor proved less friendly to Christianity. In 1664, Schall's enemies imprisoned him along with several other Jesuits. They were ultimately released, but exiled back to Macau. Father Adam Schall died on August 15, 1666. Chinese people everywhere venerated his memory.

The Jesuits in Japan

Francis Xavier had laid a solid foundation for conversions in Japan. The Jesuits were making conversions slowly but surely. By 1582, there were perhaps as many as 150,000 Christians in Japan.

Twenty-Six Martyrs of Japan
A group of Christians crucified at the beginning of Japan's long and terrible persecution.

In 1585, Toyotomi Hideyoshi became ruler of Japan. Two years later, he ordered all Christian missionaries to leave Japan. However, most missionaries ignored his order and continued working to convert the Japanese people. For a time, Hideyoshi mostly ignored the Christians, but in 1597 he decided to act. On February 5, 1597, Hideyoshi had twenty-six Christians crucified on a hill near Nagasaki in order to frighten any Japanese who may have been thinking of converting. These brave souls are known as the **Twenty-Six Martyrs of Japan**.

376 *Chapter 24: The Great Saints of the Catholic Reformation*

They included five Franciscan missionaries, three Japanese Jesuits, and seventeen Japanese laymen, including three teenage boys.

The martyrdoms at Nagasaki proved to be only the beginning of a centuries-long persecution of Christians in Japan. Almost all the Jesuits who remained in Japan suffered martyrdom. By 1632, probably no Catholic clergy remained in the country. Yet amazingly, the Faith survived despite the lack of priests. When Commodore Perry forced an entry into Japan in 1854, he discovered that Christianity was not dead. A few thousand Catholics had managed to practice their religion in secret, and mostly correctly, for two hundred years.

The Jesuits in India

Of the various nations in the Far East, none presented as many challenges to conversion as India, yet nowhere were the Jesuits more successful. India was a country of many different peoples who had no common language until the British imposed English in the nineteenth century. The country had three major religions—Islam, Hinduism, and Buddhism—and these religions are quite different from one another. Islam has many beliefs that are not common to Hinduism and Buddhism, and vice versa. Buddhism is an offshoot of Hinduism, and there are some similarities between them, but there are also some important differences—most notably that Hinduism has many false

Robert de Nobili

Map of World, Highlighting India

Witness to the Faith 377

gods, whereas traditional Buddhism does not hold to a belief in any god. Islam, for its part, vigorously maintains that there is only one God, but it rejects the truth of the Holy Trinity, and it is militantly opposed to Christianity. Thus, the missionaries who followed Francis Xavier had to deal with very different environments, depending on whether they were preaching to Muslims, Hindus, or Buddhists.

The first missionaries to India made the mistake of trying to make converts accept, not only the Catholic Faith, but also the social customs of Europe. (The first converts at Macau had adopted European customs.) However, the customs of India were very different from the customs of Europe. For example, India had a centuries-old *caste system*. No other country in the world had anything like the caste system. While European countries had social classes, they were nothing like the Indian system. In the caste system, every contact by a person of a higher caste with one of a lower caste was considered a personal defilement of the person of the higher caste. The highest caste was called the *Brahmins*. The Brahmins refused to become members of a religion that conflicted with the caste system. Consequently, the converts St. Francis Xavier made were all from lower castes, mostly laborers and fishermen.

In order to attract the Brahmins to Catholicism, an Italian Jesuit named **Robert de Nobili** decided to adopt the customs of India. When he arrived in India in 1606, he received permission from his bishop to dress as a Brahmin. He also began to live like a Brahmin and follow their dietary customs. In the summer of 1608, a well-known Brahmin visited him to learn more about this intriguing foreigner. This man explained Hinduism to Father de Nobili and taught him his language, **Sanskrit**. By 1609, Father de Nobili had made about fifty converts. Over the next thirty-five years, he worked unceasingly to convert the people of India, especially the Brahmins. In 1644, age and disability forced Father de Nobili to leave his mission work. He died in 1656 at the shrine where St. Thomas the Apostle had been martyred some fifteen hundred years earlier.

Edmund Campion

As dangerous as the Far East was, one of the most dangerous places in the world for a priest to evangelize was Elizabethan England. In England, during the reign of Queen Elizabeth I (1559-1603), any priest found in the kingdom was executed. Nevertheless, some of the English Jesuits returned to their homeland in disguise. Traveling secretly from house to house, they said Mass for a few people at a time. These brave men brought the sacraments

English Jesuit Edmund Campion Is Hanged

Robert de Nobili
Jesuit missionary to India.

Chapter 24: The Great Saints of the Catholic Reformation

to England's Catholics. Priest hunters caught and killed many, but Catholic priests continued to go to England and spread the Faith.

One of the most famous English Jesuits is **Edmund Campion**. Born in London on January 24, 1540, Edmund received an excellent education, eventually earning his master's degree from Oxford University in 1564. In 1571, he secretly traveled to **Douay** (also called "Douai"), where he entered the English College. (Douay is currently in northern France, but was then ruled by Spain.) Two years later, he received a divinity degree and became a deacon in the Church. He then traveled to Rome, where he joined the Jesuits. After studying for several years, he was ordained a priest in 1578.

In 1580, the Jesuits launched a missionary campaign to England. In late June, disguised as a jewel merchant, Edmund Campion arrived in London and immediately began preaching the Catholic Faith. From this moment forward, his life was in constant danger, and he lived like a hunted outlaw, which, technically, he was. Nevertheless, he said Mass and administered the sacraments.

As Edmund's presence became known, the priest hunters sought him out more vigorously. On July 14, 1581, he preached in Lyford, but a priest hunter captured him there and took him to London.

For many months, Edmund was imprisoned in the Tower of London, where he was questioned and tortured. However, he refused to deny his Faith. On November 20, 1581, after a very brief trial, he was convicted of treason. On December 1, Edmund Campion was hanged, along with fellow Jesuits Alexander Briant and Ralph Sherwin. In 1970, Pope Paul VI canonized all three, along with thirty-seven other men and women who had been martyred at various times during the English persecutions, as the **Forty Martyrs of England and Wales**.

> **Sanskrit**
> The classical language of India.

> **Edmund Campion**
> Jesuit missionary and martyr of Elizabethan England.

> **Douay (or Douai)**
> City where the Catholic seminary known as the English College was located, which Edmund Campion attended.

> **Forty Martyrs of England and Wales**
> A group of men and women martyred at various times during the English persecutions, who were canonized together by Pope Paul VI.

Oral Exercises

1. Which pope standardized the Mass after the Council of Trent?
2. Where was St. Charles Borromeo a bishop?
3. Name the three women who are Doctors of the Church.
4. Who is known as the "Second Apostle of Germany"?
5. Who founded the religious community called the Congregation of the Oratory?
6. Who founded the Ursulines?
7. Who was the great Jesuit missionary who became the Apostle of India and Japan in the 1500s?
8. Who was Matteo Ricci?
9. Who was Robert de Nobili?
10. Who was Edmund Campion?

Witness to the Faith 379

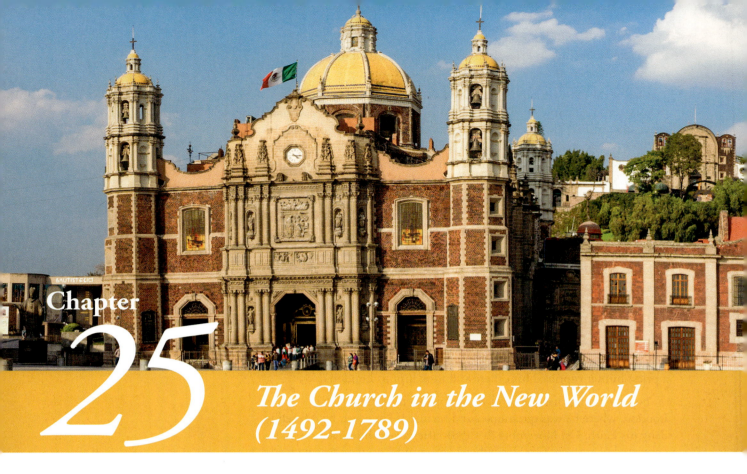

Chapter 25

The Church in the New World (1492-1789)

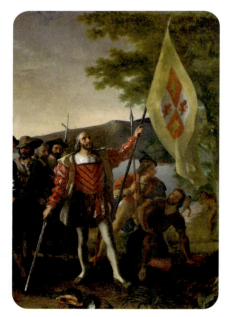

Landing of Columbus, John Vanderlyn

Introduction

With the fall of Grenada, the 770-year Reconquista ended. The Catholic kings could now turn their attention to other matters. Several months before the capture of Grenada, a red-haired Italian sailor had approached Queen Isabel with an audacious plan: *sail west* to reach the Indies in the East! The plan was incredibly bold. If successful, it would open up new trade routes as well as create the ability to outflank the Muslims. For a nation that had fought the Muslims for 770 years, it was an intriguing prospect. However, Isabel told the mariner that first Grenada had to be captured. So he waited.

After Grenada's fall, Queen Isabel decided to take a risk on the mariner. Three ships and their crews were a small investment for what might be an incredible return. Although the mariner was probably the greatest sailor ever to live, he was totally wrong about the size of the Earth, as virtually every other European maritime nation had told him. Had he not inadvertently made the greatest discovery in the history of the world, he and his men would have died of starvation. Yet, so often, fortune favors the bold.

In 1492, Christopher Columbus sailed west in search of a sea route to India. Although he did not find such a route, he did discover the Americas. He took possession of the new land in the name of the king

Basilica of Guadalupe (left) and Capuchin Church (right)

1531 A.D. – 1789 A.D.

1531 A.D.
Our Lady appears to Juan Diego; Mexico becomes overwhelmingly Catholic.

1534-1538 A.D.
Bishop Valverde works to organize the Church in Peru, and missionaries come to preach the Catholic Faith to the Incas.

1565 A.D.
The first permanent settlement and the first parish in the continental United States are founded at St. Augustine, Florida.

1608 A.D.
Many Jesuits preach the Gospel in Canada. Among them are the eight North American Martyrs.

1634 A.D.
Cecil Calvert establishes Maryland, the only one of the original thirteen English colonies to be founded as a Catholic colony.

1673 A.D.
Fr. Marquette and Louis Joliet explore the Mississippi River.

1682 A.D.
William Penn founds Philadelphia, capital of Pennsylvania, a haven for Quakers and ultimately for anyone escaping religious persecution.

1689 A.D.
After the "Glorious Revolution," a law is enacted in the New York colony which makes it illegal for any priests to be there.

1768-1785 A.D.
St. Junipero Serra establishes his missions in California.

1789 A.D.
The Constitution of the United States is established.

and queen of Spain. Other Spanish explorers followed. Ponce de Leon came to Florida, Balboa discovered the Pacific Ocean, and Cortes began the conversion of Mexico. Coronado visited what is now the southwestern United States, and Hernan de Soto explored the Mississippi River. With the explorers came Spanish missionaries: Franciscans, Dominicans, and Jesuits. They came to preach the Gospel to the people of the New World.

Catholic Spain

Following the conquest of Grenada in 1492, Spain became a unified nation for the first time in almost 800 years. In the following decades, as other nations dealt with Church scandals and Protestant upheavals, Spain did not, because in Spain the Church had been so thoroughly cleansed of corruption that the Protestant Revolt never gained the slightest foothold.

Witness to the Faith

Francisco Cisneros
Franciscan cardinal, the person most responsible for the reform of the Church in Spain.

The person most responsible for reforming the Church in Spain was Franciscan Cardinal **Francisco Cisneros**. He turned Spain into a bastion of Catholicism that not only would fight Protestantism in Europe but also would send missionaries to evangelize the world.

Francisco Cisneros became archbishop of Toledo and chancellor of Spain in 1495. When Queen Isabel, as a kindly jest, surprised him with the announcement of his new position, the humble Franciscan fled, feeling unworthy of the honor. Nevertheless, Queen Isabel and Pope Alexander VI convinced Cisneros to accept the appointment. (Despite his otherwise poor record, Alexander's interaction with Isabel in Spain was rather good. He accepted her requests and rarely interfered with the reforms in Spain.)

As archbishop of Toledo, Cisneros immediately began a reform of the Spanish Franciscans, then all the mendicant orders in Spain, and finally the Church overall. Despite opposition, Cisneros reformed the Church in Spain, with the support of Queen Isabel. Cardinal Cisneros died in 1517 as he traveled to meet the newly arrived King Charles.

Thus, it was from a thoroughly Catholic Spain that explorers, known as *conquistadors* (conquerors), set forth to discover and explore new lands. They sought treasure, but they also sought converts. Almost every Spanish expedition included priests. As a result, the places explored and settled by the Spanish (and the Portuguese) in the New World, such as Mexico and South America, became Catholic countries. For the most part, even today, they retain their Catholic identities.

Relief Sculpture of Juan Diego Gathering Flowers with Our Lady of Guadalupe

Chapter 25: The Church in the New World (1492-1789)

Mexico

In 1521, Hernan Cortes conquered Mexico for Spain. Over the next five years, twelve Franciscans arrived. They founded missions. Soon Dominicans and Augustinians joined them. Despite the efforts of these missionaries, the Gospel would not have spread so rapidly in Mexico had it not been for the appearance of **Our Lady at Guadalupe**.

On the morning of December 9, 1531, a humble Christian native of Mexico named **Juan Diego** saw a vision of the Blessed Mother on the slopes of **Tepeyac Hill**, just outside Mexico City. Speaking in the native Mexican language, she told Juan that she would like a church built on the site, and she instructed him to tell his bishop. When Juan told his bishop, Franciscan **Juan de Zumarraga**, about the vision, Bishop Zumarraga told him to return to the hill and ask the Lady for a miraculous sign to prove that she was the Blessed Mother.

His uncle's serious sickness delayed Juan, but on December 12, he returned and relayed the bishop's request to the Blessed Mother. Our Lady told Juan to gather flowers from the Tepeyac hilltop, even though it was winter, when no flowers bloomed. On the hilltop, he found a double miracle: not only were flowers blooming, but also they were Castilian (Spanish) roses, which were not native to Mexico! He gathered them up, and the Blessed Mother herself arranged them in his *tilma* (cloak).

When Juan Diego returned and presented the roses to Bishop Zumarraga, they discovered a miraculous image of Our Lady on his tilma. Juan's uncle, who had been on his deathbed, was also miraculously cured, just as Our Lady had assured Juan he would be. Juan's uncle told Bishop Zumarraga that the Blessed Mother had appeared to him as well and that she wished to be venerated as *Our Lady of Guadalupe*.

News of the appearance of Our Lady of Guadalupe quickly spread throughout Mexico. From 1532 through 1538, eight million native Mexicans converted to Catholicism! Throughout Mexico, the missions prospered. The Church built schools and colleges to educate a native clergy who went out to preach the Faith. Later, the Jesuits, who had been working in Florida, moved their missionary activity to the northwestern coast of Mexico, where they worked among the native people. For centuries, the Church in Mexico grew steadily. Schools and colleges multiplied. Eventually, the entire country became Catholic.

With the possible exception of the Shroud of Turin, Juan Diego's tilma is the most venerated relic in the Catholic Church. Since 1531, the tilma has not deteriorated despite a bomb attack and exposure to candle soot, dirt, and other natural elements. In 1709, a basilica was built to house the miraculous tilma. Today, the Basilica of Our Lady of Guadalupe is one of the most visited religious sites in the world.

In 1754, Pope Benedict XIV declared Our Lady of Guadalupe the patroness of New Spain. She is still recognized as the patron saint of all the Americas. In 2002, Pope John Paul II canonized St. Juan Diego.

Our Lady of Guadalupe
Patroness of the Americas; her appearance to St. Juan Diego in 1531 led to the conversion of Mexico practically overnight.

St. Juan Diego
Christian native of Mexico to whom Our Lady of Guadalupe appeared in December 1531.

Tepeyac Hill
Site of the appearance of Our Lady of Guadalupe.

Juan de Zumarraga

Juan de Zumarraga
Bishop to whom Juan Diego brought Our Lady of Guadalupe's message.

Francisco Pizarro
Conqueror of Peru in the 1500s.

Incas
Native people of Peru. The Incan Empire was centered in Peru until the coming of Pizarro.

Vincente Valverde
Dominican missionary to Peru; eventually, became bishop of Cuzco.

National University of San Marcos
Oldest university in the New World; founded in Lima in 1551.

St. Rose of Lima
Known for her penances and works of charity; became a Third Order Dominican and was mystically married to Christ.

St. Rose of Lima,
Bartolomé Esteban Murillo

Peru

The conversion of Peru began amidst the bloody conquest of the Incan Empire by **Francisco Pizarro** and his brothers, evil men who dishonored the legacy of Spain in the New World. In 1534, after Pizarro had pacified the **Incas**, Father **Vincente Valverde**, one of the Dominicans who had accompanied him, became bishop of Cuzco. In September 1538, Bishop Valverde began building a cathedral, a convent, and a monastery. Other missionaries began preaching the Faith to the Incas.

Unlike the cruel Pizarro brothers, the missionaries worked to help the Incas. In addition to building churches, the Dominicans built schools and colleges. The Dominicans founded the **National University of San Marcos** in Lima in 1551, making it the oldest university in the New World.

A Third Order Dominican became the New World's first saint. She is known as **St. Rose of Lima**. Rose was born to parents of Spanish descent in Lima in 1586. As a young girl, she chose to emulate St. Catherine of Siena. Although her parents wished her to marry, Rose wanted to dedicate her life to Our Lord. She tried to enter a convent, but her parents refused to allow it. In obedience to her parents, she remained at home, and she became a member of the Third Order of Saint Dominic. She dedicated her life to caring for the homeless, the sick, and the elderly. She died in 1617. Pope Clement X canonized her in 1671.

In 1567, the king of Spain, Philip II, asked the Jesuits to send missionaries to Peru. The first Jesuits arrived in Lima in April of the following year. In Peru, the Jesuits followed their normal pattern of conversions. They built schools and churches to begin educating and converting the native peoples. They founded a seminary to train native clergy as well as teach foreign priests the local languages. They also established the first printing press in the Americas.

Paraguay

From Peru, the Jesuits sent missionaries into Paraguay, beginning in 1586. In Paraguay, the Jesuits developed a new model for conversions. They established settlements called **reductions**. These were villages composed entirely of native converts and governed by a native chief, although the Jesuits oversaw the overall operation of the reduction.

In keeping with their mandate, the Jesuits' main emphasis was on the conversion and education of the local people. Thus, they placed the church at the center of the village. All reductions also had a school and a hospital. In the town square, the Jesuits erected a cross and a statue of the patron saint of the particular reduction.

In addition to preaching the Catholic Faith, the Jesuits taught the natives how to read and write as well as how to farm. The missionaries also taught the natives European trades, such as carpentry, weaving, and boat building. The reductions became economically self-sufficient, not only supporting themselves but also producing enough extra that they were able to trade their surplus.

Ultimately, the Jesuits would establish about thirty reductions in what are now Paraguay, Argentina, Bolivia, and Brazil.

Florida

The first missionaries to the territory that is now the United States were three Dominicans led by **Father Luis Cancer de Barbastro**. In 1549, Father de Barbastro and his companions attempted to found a mission near present-day Tampa Bay, Florida. The Dominicans sailed from Mexico to Florida. They brought a Native American woman, who they thought had converted to the Faith, with them to act as an interpreter. However, upon reaching the shores of Florida, she betrayed them. The priests suffered martyrdom at the hands of a local tribe. Luis de Barbastro is known as the "proto-martyr of Florida."

In 1565, the first permanent settlement **and the first parish** in the continental United States were founded at St. Augustine, Florida. Dominicans, Franciscans, and Jesuits all labored in this new mission land. St. Francis Borgia, the third superior general of the Jesuits, sent missionaries to Florida in 1566 and 1568. In preaching the Faith, they traveled as far north as the Rappahannock River in Virginia, where they suffered martyrdom at the hands of the natives.

Franciscan missionaries took up the work and were somewhat successful in converting the Native American populace. However, Governor **James Moore**, the English and violently anti-Catholic governor of the Carolinas, invaded Florida several times in 1704 and 1706. He destroyed the Spanish missions in Florida, which abruptly ended the work of the missionaries. In 1763, when Spain ceded Florida to England, the Spanish population withdrew. Almost no Catholics remained in Florida.

Canada

The French settled Canada. In 1608, King Henry IV of France asked the Jesuits to preach the Gospel in Canada. Henry had seen how Spanish missionaries had given Spain a stronghold in the New World. He hoped that the French Jesuits would have the same effect in Canada.

The Jesuits founded a school at Quebec and began converting the Native Americans. From Canada, missionaries came south into the territory that is now the United States. In 1604, they said Mass in present-day Maine. They established a permanent settlement in 1613 near Bar Harbor (Maine). Twenty years later, the Capuchins founded a mission on the Penobscot River. Shortly afterward, the Jesuits settled on the Kennebec River. These missions lasted until the beginning of the eighteenth century, when English soldiers from Massachusetts destroyed them and murdered the priests.

> **Reductions**
> Villages established by Jesuit missionaries in South America for their native converts; residents learned not only the Catholic Faith but also reading, farming, and trades.

> **Father Luis Cancer de Barbastro**
> The first missionary, along with his two companions, to the present-day United States; known as the "proto-martyr of Florida."

> **James Moore**
> Violently anti-Catholic governor of the Carolinas; repeatedly invaded Florida and destroyed the Spanish missions there in 1704 and 1706.

Map of North America, Highlighting Canada

Witness to the Faith 385

St. Isaac Jogues
French Jesuit priest and missionary in Canada; was martyred by the Iroquois tribe.

North American Martyrs
St. Isaac Jogues and seven other French Jesuit missionaries martyred by the Iroquois.

Jacques Marquette
French Jesuit priest who traveled the Wisconsin and Mississippi Rivers and preached the Gospel to the natives along the way.

Louis Joliet
French explorer whom Fr. Marquette accompanied down the Mississippi.

St. Isaac Jogues

In 1642, a gallant Jesuit priest, **St. Isaac Jogues**, suffered martyrdom at the hands of the Iroquois. The first time the Iroquois took him prisoner, they cruelly tortured him. The Satanic nature of the torture is evidenced by the fact that the Iroquois gruesomely severed the fingers that Father Jogues would use to hold the Sacred Host during Mass. Dutch Protestants finally rescued him, and he returned to France. Father Jogues traveled to Rome, where, despite the loss of his fingers, Pope Urban VIII permitted him to say Mass, saying, "It is not fitting that Christ's martyr should not drink Christ's Blood."

Despite his sufferings, Father Jogues desired to return to Canada. He loved the native people and had a deep desire to convert them. Upon his return, he visited the Iroquois village near Auriesville, close to present-day Albany. He hoped to create peace between the Iroquois and their long-time enemies, the Hurons. Although unsuccessful, he did not give up hope. He tried again, and this time the Iroquois took him prisoner. They lured him to a lodge, where they murdered him. Over the next three years, the Iroquois killed five other Jesuit missionaries. Pope Pius XI canonized these Jesuit martyrs on June 29, 1930. They are known as the **North American Martyrs**.

Father Jacques Marquette

The Jesuits counted amazing theologians, philosophers, teachers, and even astronomers among their numbers. In **Jacques Marquette**, the Jesuits had not only a holy priest but also one of history's greatest explorers. Father Marquette explored the Mississippi River and preached the Gospel to the natives living along its shores.

Father Marquette and the Indians, **Wilhelm Lamprecht**

Born in France in 1637, Jacques joined the Jesuits as a young man. In 1666, he was assigned to preach the Faith in Canada. Upon arriving at his new post, he began learning various native languages. Over the next several years, he made numerous converts. He also established missions in present-day Michigan and Wisconsin. In 1673, Father Marquette accompanied French explorer **Louis Joliet** down the Wisconsin and Mississippi Rivers as far as the Arkansas River (about 435 miles from the Gulf of Mexico). They turned back when they encountered evidence of a Spanish presence and wished to avoid a conflict. Two years later, Father Marquette returned to preach to the Illinois tribe, and he established the Immaculate Conception Mission at Kaskaskia, where he died at the age of 39.

386 Chapter 25: The Church in the New World (1492-1789)

St. Kateri Tekakwitha

Despite the danger, French Catholic missionaries continued to work among the Native American tribes. One of their greatest successes involved a young Mohawk girl named **Kateri Tekakwitha**. A French priest from Canada had baptized Kateri's mother, but another tribe, who hated Christians, had captured her and forced her to marry a non-Christian. After Kateri's birth, her mother secretly taught the Catholic Faith to Kateri and her brother. After a few years, both her parents and her brother died of smallpox. Kateri was forced to live with an uncle who hated Christians. If her uncle caught her praying, he would not give her food.

Eventually, because Kateri was slowly dying of starvation, some French Canadian priests helped her escape to a Jesuit mission in Quebec, a difficult journey of 200 miles. Upon arriving at the mission, Kateri practiced her Catholic Faith freely. However, in 1670, she died from smallpox at the age of 24. The Jesuits reported that, fifteen minutes after Kateri's death, the terrible smallpox scars on her face miraculously disappeared. In 2012, Pope Benedict XVI canonized St. Kateri Tekakwitha, "The Lily of the Mohawks."

Catholicism in the English Colonies

England's colonies in North America were founded at a time when England was bitterly persecuting the Church. Puritans or Anglicans settled almost all the English colonies, which meant that few Catholics lived in them. In colonial America, only two English colonies were friendly to Catholics. The first was Maryland, which English Catholic George Calvert planned and his son Cecil Calvert founded. The second was Pennsylvania, which was founded by William Penn, a Quaker who believed in religious toleration.

Maryland

Of the thirteen original English colonies, only Maryland was founded by a Catholic. In 1634, **Cecil Calvert**, the second Lord Baltimore, established Maryland as a Catholic colony. He named the colony in honor of **Henrietta Maria**, the queen of England.

Jesuit priests accompanied the first settlers who arrived in March 1634. In order to foster good relations with the natives, the settlers purchased the land upon which they founded the first permanent settlement, the **village of St. Mary's**. Wherever the settlers established a new settlement, they built a chapel and a school. As they had endured much persecution in England, the Catholics in Maryland tolerated all religions. The Catholic settlers also worked successfully to convert the local native tribes and to establish a relationship with them to trade goods.

Later, Protestants, at the instigation of an enemy of the Baltimore family, began to oppress the Catholics. The Protestants sent a number of Jesuit missionaries back to England in chains. They deprived many Catholics of their possessions and banished them from the colony. The

St. Kateri Tekakwitha

St. Kateri Tekakwitha
A young woman of the Mohawk tribe (a group of Iroquois); embraced the Catholic Faith despite her relatives' opposition, and practiced it with great devotion.

Cecil Calvert
The founder of Maryland; established it as a Catholic colony.

Henrietta Maria
Queen of England and namesake of Maryland.

Village of St. Mary's
First permanent settlement of Maryland.

Note on Catholic Population in Maryland

Even in Maryland, Catholics comprised probably no more than 10 percent of the population.

Witness to the Faith 387

Maryland Toleration Act
Passed to address the persecution of Catholics by Protestants in Maryland; guaranteed religious freedom to all Christians.

Ferdinand Farmer
Missionary priest in rural Pennsylvania who brought the sacraments to Catholics in remote places.

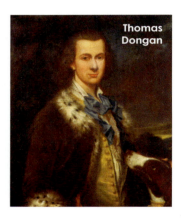

Thomas Dongan

Thomas Dongan
Catholic governor of the colony of New York; convinced the colonial assembly to grant religious liberty to everyone.

Thomas Harvey
Jesuit who accompanied Dorgan and founded a school in New York.

situation became so bad that in 1649, at the insistence of Lord Baltimore, the Assembly of Maryland passed the celebrated **Maryland Toleration Act**, which guaranteed religious freedom and toleration to all Christians.

Pennsylvania

In 1681, Charles II of England gave land in America to William Penn to settle a debt that he owed to William's father. In October 1682, William Penn arrived in Pennsylvania and founded the colony's capital, Philadelphia. Penn intended to create a colony that would provide a refuge for Quakers suffering persecution in Europe. Ultimately, Penn granted religious freedom to everyone, including Catholics.

The history of religious freedom in Pennsylvania ranks among the best of the original colonies. In 1686, Catholics erected a chapel in Philadelphia, and in 1730 the Jesuits sent Father Joseph Greaton to Philadelphia as the first resident priest. Over the years, the Faith grew, and Catholics built St. Joseph's church in 1733, St. Mary's in 1763, and Holy Trinity in 1768. However, the congregations remained small and consisted mainly of Irish and German immigrants.

Outside of Philadelphia, priests would "ride the circuit," providing Mass and the sacraments to people in rural areas who saw a priest infrequently. These "priests on horseback" included such famous missionaries as Jesuit Father **Ferdinand Farmer**. Born in Germany in 1720, Farmer entered the Jesuit novitiate in 1743. Upon becoming a priest, he was sent by the order to the English colonies in 1752. He was assigned to Saint Mary's church in Lancaster, Pennsylvania, and the surrounding area. During the next six years, he traveled on horseback, ministering to the few Catholics scattered around his district. In 1758, Father Farmer was transferred to Philadelphia and later to New York City. During his career, Father Farmer performed 3,317 Baptisms and 568 Marriage ceremonies. He died in August 1786 at the age of 65.

New York

Of the other original colonies, only New York showed any willingness to grant Catholics any religious freedom. In 1683, King James II of England, a Catholic, appointed **Thomas Dongan**, also a Catholic, to be the governor of the colony of New York. On October 14, 1683, Dongan convoked the first representative assembly in New York. He convinced the members to enact a decree granting religious liberty to all people of the colony.

Before Dongan left for America, he had consulted with Jesuit leaders. They decided to send Jesuit **Thomas Harvey** with Dongan to act as his chaplain and to found a Jesuit school in the new mission territory. Father Harvey established a school that opened in the fall of 1684. Amazingly, even Protestant leaders in New York sent their sons to the Jesuit school. In the years that followed, other Jesuits were sent to New York, ministering to Catholics there and in neighboring New Jersey.

Chapter 25: The Church in the New World (1492-1789)

The situation in New York was proceeding rather well when, in 1688, England experienced the so-called "Glorious Revolution," which replaced Catholic King James with his Protestant daughter and her husband. The new English rulers replaced Dongan as governor. In 1689, an anti-Catholic law was enacted in New York. This law decreed that any priest caught in the New York colony could be imprisoned for life. Any priest who escaped from prison and was recaptured could be hanged. Consequently, Catholicism in the New York colony began to fade. The few Catholics who continued to live in New York City were forced to go to Philadelphia to receive the sacraments. Even as late as the American War for Independence, New York Catholics wishing to receive the sacraments had to travel to Philadelphia.

Distrust of Catholics

The colonial period was marked by distrust and mockery of the Catholic Faith. By 1763, there were only about 7,000 Catholics in the English colonies. The vast majority lived in Maryland and Pennsylvania. There were perhaps thirty priests, almost all Jesuits, in the colonies. Even though there were so few Catholics and priests, Catholics in general and priests in particular were often under suspicion. For example, Protestant colonists thought that the Jesuits were working to provoke slave rebellions. Because French Jesuits were working to convert the Native Americans, English colonists were convinced that English Jesuits were conspiring with the French and the Native Americans. Protestants in the colonies held the belief, which some Americans would continue to hold even as late as the early twentieth century, that Catholics were not good Americans because they "answered to a foreign ruler"—that is, the pope.

In addition to the distrust, Catholicism was mocked relentlessly in the colonies. In 1765, Harvard University sponsored a talk on "Popish Idolatry." New York City annually held a festival in which the pope was burned in effigy.

The Church in Spanish and French Areas

Although English colonists mocked and distrusted Catholics, which meant fewer conversions, the Church thrived in areas settled by the Spanish and French.

Catholicism in the Southwest

The missionaries who accompanied Spanish explorer **Francisco Coronado** in 1514 made the first attempts to spread the Catholic Faith to the Native Americans in the future southwestern United States. In the ensuing years, Spanish missionaries made various additional attempts to establish permanent missions in these areas. Three Franciscans, who gave

Francisco Coronado

Francisco Coronado
Spanish explorer of the southwestern United States.

Witness to the Faith 389

New Mexico its name, made one such effort in 1581. Other Franciscans founded Santa Fe in 1609 and built that city's first parish church in 1622.

California

Of all the holy men who dedicated their lives to spreading the Gospel message in North America, perhaps none achieved so much as **Father Junipero Serra**, a Spanish Franciscan. Junipero Serra was born in 1713 on the Spanish island of Majorca. In 1730, Father Serra entered the Franciscan Order and, after seven years of study, prayer, and reflection, became a priest. A brilliant man, Father Serra taught philosophy at the Franciscans' Lullian University for several years.

Despite a bright future as a teacher, Junipero Serra had always longed to be a missionary. Therefore, in 1749, he left Spain for Mexico City. He landed at Vera Cruz and walked to Mexico City because, as a Franciscan, he felt that it was not necessary to ride the provided donkey. During the walk, Father Serra somehow injured his left foot so severely that he would limp for the rest of his life. Despite this painful wound, he never found it "necessary" to ride anywhere. He walked thousands of miles.

In Mexico City, Junipero was assigned to the missionary college of San Fernando de Mexico, where he learned some of the native languages. He volunteered for the Sierra Gorda Indian Missions, where he spent about nine years teaching and catechizing the native peoples. Then he was recalled to Mexico City. Over the next ten years, Father Junipero Serra became famous as an outstanding preacher and missionary.

In 1768, Father Serra received the appointment to which he would dedicate the remainder of his life. Along with fifteen other Franciscans, he traveled to California to spread the Gospel and establish missions. In 1769, he founded the mission of San Diego, and then, in quick succession, San Carlos, San Antonio de Padua, San Gabriel, San Luis Obispo, San Francisco, San Juan Capistrano, Santa Clara, and San Buenaventura. Although the main purpose of the missions was to evangelize the Native Americans, the missions also sought to organize the natives into a productive workforce, who would eventually own and manage the land that they worked.

Toward the end of his life, Father Serra received papal approval to administer the Sacrament of

Mission San Carlos Borromeo

Confirmation. During the last three years of his life, he revisited all the missions from San Diego to San Francisco to confirm those whom he had baptized. He confirmed about 5,300 people, almost all of whom were Native Americans. Father Serra died in 1785 at Mission San Carlos Borromeo, where he is buried. Pope Francis canonized Junipero Serra on September 23, 2015.

Louisiana

Catholics built the first church in Louisiana in 1717 in Robeline. The following year, Jean-Baptiste de Bienville founded the city of New Orleans, and the Capuchins erected a brick church on the site of the present cathedral. In 1727, a group of French Ursuline nuns arrived in New Orleans to take charge of the Royal Hospital and to provide an education for the colony's girls and women. They instructed black girls and Native American girls, as well as the daughters of the French settlers. Their school, the Ursuline Academy, remains the oldest continuously operating school for girls and the oldest Catholic school in the United States. They also opened the first convent for women in the United States.

In 1766, Louisiana became a Spanish colony. During this period, the Church continued to grow under Spanish rule. The Church established

Father Junipero Serra
Spanish Franciscan missionary who established nine missions in California.

Witness to the Faith

Jacques Gravier
French Jesuit missionary priest in what is now Illinois; served for about twenty years until his martyrdom.

Pierre Gibault
The "Patriot Priest of the West"; also served in the Midwest, and supported the American cause in the War for Independence.

John Barry

two new parishes in 1772 and 1787. Eventually, Louisiana was returned to France, from whom the United States purchased Louisiana in 1803.

Catholics in the Northwest Territory

In 1687, Jesuit **Jacques Gravier** became head of the Immaculate Conception mission, which Father Marquette had founded at Old Kaskaskia in 1675. He worked at the mission for ten years under incredible hardships and sufferings. In 1696, he established the Mission of the Guardian Angel on the site of present-day Chicago. Four years later, Father Gravier transferred the Immaculate Conception mission to present-day Kaskaskia. In 1706, the Peoria tribe attacked Father Gravier. He died two years later from the wounds he received.

When France lost the Northwest Territory to Great Britain in 1763 (after the French and Indian War), the British expelled the Jesuits. Jesuit Father **Pierre Gibault**, known as the "Patriot Priest of the West," left Quebec and, in 1768, came to Kaskaskia, where he served the French and Native American Catholics. He also labored at Vincennes, Mackinac, Detroit, and Peoria. In 1770, he blessed the first church in St. Louis, which stood on the site of St. Louis' Old Cathedral. His travels and dedication to the people in his district made him extremely popular and earned the respect of almost everyone.

When the American War for Independence began, Father Gibault strongly supported it. He was in Kaskaskia when an American force under George Rogers Clark arrived. Father Gibault told Clark that he backed the American cause, but that his primary concern was for the Catholics in his congregation. Clark assured him that Catholics would have religious freedom in the new country. Father Gibault's influence made it possible for George Rogers Clark to achieve military victory in the Northwest Territory and secure it for the United States.

Catholics in the War for Independence

The American War for Independence, which led to the creation of the United States, proved most favorable to religious freedom for Catholics. In 1789, the Constitution of the United States was adopted, which provides in Article VI that "no religious Test shall ever be required as a Qualification to any Office or public Trust under the United States." At the time, most colonies required religious tests for those seeking to hold public office. Protestants did not trust Catholics to govern patriotically. However, in 1791, the Congress added the Bill of Rights, which included the First Amendment to the Constitution. The First Amendment specifically mandates that the federal government cannot make laws that prohibit the free exercise of religion.

While many factors led to the enactment of the Constitution and the Bill of Rights, the memory of the heroic deeds performed by Catholics during the War of Independence certainly created a more favorable environment for Catholics in the new United States. Like Father Gibault, the great majority of Catholics favored independence from Britain. Many fought in the Continental army and navy. Catholic generals came from Europe to aid the American cause. Catholic naval officer **John Barry** won several battles and would become known as the "Father of the American Navy."

Catholics were also involved at the highest levels of government during the War for Independence and the Constitutional Convention. Among them were **Charles Carroll**, who signed the Declaration of Independence, and Thomas Fitzsimons and Daniel Carroll, who signed the Constitution. During the War, Thomas Sim Lee, another Catholic, served as governor of Maryland from 1779 to 1783. He also worked closely with many of the Founding Fathers.

Charles Carroll

Catholics in the New United States

By 1789, Catholics represented only a tiny segment of the American population. However, the new United States was a land of almost limitless opportunities. People from Europe, including many Catholics, seeing such opportunities, began flocking to these shores. In 1789, the Catholic Church in the United States was just a mustard seed. But from mustard seeds, great trees grow.

Oral Exercises

1. What event led to the rapid spread of the Catholic Faith in Mexico?
2. Who was the first native of the Americas to be canonized?
3. What were the Jesuit reductions?
4. Who was the "proto-martyr of Florida"?
5. Who is known as the "Lily of the Mohawks"?
6. What family was most influential in founding Maryland?
7. What were the only two English colonies that were friendly to Catholics in colonial America?
8. Who was the most important person in the history of the California missions?
9. Why was Father Pierre Gibault known as the "Patriot Priest of the West"?
10. Name at least three Catholics who aided America during the War for Independence.

John Barry
Irish Catholic and American naval officer who won several battles in the American War for Independence; known as the "Father of the American Navy."

Charles Carroll
Sole Catholic signer of the Declaration of Independence.

Chapter 26

The Church in England and Northern Europe in the 16th and 17th Centuries

William Cecil
Chief minister of Queen Elizabeth I, a skilled statesman but also a dedicated enemy of the Catholic Church.

Introduction

During the reign of Pope Sixtus V (1585-1590), the religious fate of two of the greatest nations on Earth would be decided. Their futures would not be decided in a court, a Diet, or a conference room. They would be decided on the battlefield. For the next fifty years, questions of religion would almost all be decided by battle.

England on the Brink

Henry VIII died in 1547. Although he was a murderer, an adulterer, and a schismatic, Henry was not a heretic. Two monarchs reigned after Henry's death. Edward VI, who was a Protestant, did not rule long enough to destroy the Catholic Church or to completely implant Protestantism in England. Mary, a devout Catholic, did not rule long enough to restore the Catholic Church in England or to completely free England from Protestantism. England's next monarch, provided that he or she reigned for more than a few years, would decide the future of Catholicism in England.

Elizabeth and Cecil Take England Out of the Church

Queen Mary I died on November 17, 1559. Her half-sister Elizabeth succeeded her as queen of England. Less than six weeks later, it became

The Return of Mary, Queen of Scots to Edinburgh, James Drummond

1560 A.D. – 1690 A.D.

1560 A.D.
The Act of Uniformity orders that the Book of Common Prayer be used throughout England.

1566-1567 A.D.
Revolts break out in Holland, ransacking churches. Philip suppresses the rebellion, reclaiming present-day Belgium.

1568 A.D.
Mary Stuart, Queen of Scots, after reclaiming and then losing her throne in Scotland, looks for help from Elizabeth, but is instead imprisoned.

1588 A.D.
The English Navy destroys the Spanish Armada sent to invade England.

1605 A.D.
The conspiracy of the "Gunpowder Plot" is uncovered, and the Catholic Faith becomes associated with the plot for centuries to come.

1642-1649 A.D.
Mounting tension between King Charles I and Parliament erupts into the English Civil Wars, which result in the defeat and execution of Charles.

1649-1651 A.D.
Oliver Cromwell attacks Ireland.

1658 A.D.
The monarchy is restored under Charles II.

1688 A.D.
Mary and William of Orange replace King James II in the so-called "Glorious Revolution."

1690 A.D.
A wave of English persecutions is launched against Irish Catholics, but fails to destroy their faith.

---

apparent that Queen Elizabeth I would not support the Catholic Church; in fact, she would oppose it. At Christmas Mass, she told the bishop of Carlisle not to elevate the Sacred Host. When he did, she left the Mass. Two days later, she issued an order that the Host was not to be elevated during Mass. The writing was on the wall.

Although Elizabeth reigned as queen, the real power behind the throne was her chief minister, **William Cecil**. He was one of the finest and most able statesmen in history, but he was also utterly devoted to the Protestant cause, which meant the destruction of the Catholic Church in England. In the words of historian Warren Carroll, "No more dedicated, brilliant, indefatigable, and deadly enemy of the Catholic Church ever lived than William Cecil" (W. Carroll, *The Cleaving of Christendom*, p. 258).

Witness to the Faith   395

Mary, Queen of Scots

Act of Uniformity
Again ordered that the Book of Common Prayer be used by all.

Church of England (Anglican Church)
The Church of England, begun under Henry VIII and Elizabeth I.

When Parliament met in January 1560, Cecil had packed it with Protestants. Parliament voted once again to take England into schism and make the ruling monarch the head of the Church. In April, Parliament passed the **Act of Uniformity**, which ordered the use of the Book of Common Prayer by all the people in England and thus restored the Protestant religion as it had existed under Edward VI.

Although the majority of the English people were not doctrinally Protestant, they were willing to follow their queen into schism. However, the Catholic bishops were not. Cardinal Pole, an excellent judge of men, had appointed the English bishops. Unlike the weak bishops of Henry VIII's reign, these men were staunch Catholics in the model of St. John Fisher, willing to give their lives for the Faith. When all but one of these men strenuously objected to the new laws, Elizabeth and Cecil immediately removed them from office. To replace the former bishops, Cecil created an entirely new hierarchy. Elizabeth herself appointed her mother's former chaplain, Matthew Parker, as archbishop of Canterbury. The bishops in the present **Church of England**, or **Anglican Church**, ecclesiastically descend directly from him. Then other bishops were **invalidly** consecrated. Additionally, Elizabeth and Cecil removed about four hundred priests, and many others resigned. In their place, other men were "ordained" to the "priesthood." However, these men were Protestants, not Catholics, and they were not truly priests.

Elizabeth then began a relentless persecution of Catholics in Great Britain and Ireland. The Catholic Faith was declared illegal, Mass was abolished, and any priest found in England was executed for treason. It seemed that the only hope for a Catholic restoration would be a change of monarchs.

Mary Stuart

One interesting fact about monarchies is that there is nearly always a descendant who might be found to replace or succeed the current monarch. Such was the case with Queen Elizabeth. In fact, she faced a claimant with a stronger claim to the throne than hers.

Upon the death of Queen Mary I, the king of France, Henry II, formally proclaimed that his daughter-in-law, **Mary Stuart** of Scotland, was the rightful queen of England. In fact, by any reasonable standard, she was. Almost all Catholics, and many non-Catholic English citizens, presumed that Elizabeth was not a legitimate heir, being the daughter of an adulterous relationship. This meant that Henry VIII's next closest relative was in line for the throne. Mary Stuart was the granddaughter of Henry VIII's oldest sister, Margaret, making Mary Henry VIII's grandniece. She was next in the line of succession.

Although Mary Stuart was born in Scotland, she had been raised in France since she was about 5 years old, and she had a great love for France. Her father, Scottish King James V, died less than a week after her birth, making her heir to the Scottish throne. Although, when she was a child, Scotland regents ruled on her behalf, she was in fact the queen of Scotland—Mary, Queen of Scots. Her mother was Marie of Guise, a member of the most powerful family in France. Moreover, Mary was married to Francis, the heir to the French throne. If her husband became king, she would be queen of France as well. However, her French sympathies caused great distress to the king of Spain.

For more than sixty years, France had been the implacable enemy of Spain. In this critical moment, King Philip II of Spain, one of the finest rulers in history and a man who probably would have preferred the priesthood to the throne, made a terrible decision. He felt that he could not support the meek, 16-year-old Catholic princess (Mary, Queen of Scots), because he believed she was too much under the control of the French king. Instead, he chose to support Elizabeth, hoping that she would uphold the Catholic Faith. It was perhaps the worst decision of his life and one that he would regret as long as lived. In fact, eventually, he would send a Spanish Armada to attempt to undo his mistake. Thus, Mary remained in France.

Mary Stuart
Better known as Mary, Queen of Scots; had a claim to the English throne, but was executed by her cousin Elizabeth.

However, when her husband died in 1560, Mary decided to return to Scotland to reclaim her throne. While Queen Mary in France was a concern, Queen Mary in Scotland was a real threat to Queen Elizabeth. Elizabeth feared that Mary, who had a viable claim to the throne of England, would seek to depose her. Elizabeth also worried that her Catholic subjects, whose lives she had made very difficult, would give their allegiance to the young Catholic princess. Finally, Elizabeth was concerned that Mary could depend on the sympathy and assistance of the French people. Thus, Elizabeth saw her three greatest enemies embodied in Mary: Scotland, France, and the Catholic Church.

The Church in Scotland

When Mary arrived in Scotland in 1561, the religious situation was desperate. Though Scotland was a small, poor nation, the Scots were determined to retain the freedom that their beloved King Robert the Bruce had won from England at

King Philip II of Spain

Witness to the Faith

Cardinal David Beaton

Cardinal David Beaton
Spiritual leader of Catholics in Scotland during the time of Henry VIII; murdered by revolutionaries.

John Knox
John Calvin's most ardent disciple, leader of Protestantism in Scotland.

the beginning of the fourteenth century. Mary's father, **King James V**, despite being a weak ruler, remained steadfast in the Catholic Faith. James was aided in his determination to keep Scotland Catholic by the remarkably effective archbishop of St. Andrews, James Beaton, who also served as the chancellor of Scotland. As archbishop, James Beaton worked energetically to suppress heresy. In 1528, he found Patrick Hamilton, a member of the royal family, guilty of heresy and turned him over to the secular authorities for execution. As chancellor, he sought to maintain the close relationship that Scotland had with France.

Following James Beaton's death in 1539, his nephew, **Cardinal David Beaton**, became archbishop of St. Andrews and chancellor of Scotland. David Beaton had been named Scotland's first cardinal the previous year. Cardinal Beaton proved to be an even more ardent and effective protector of the Catholic Faith than his uncle.

In 1542, Henry VIII invaded Scotland because King James refused to take the nation into schism. At the end of November, a battle ensued in which the English completely routed the Scots, who fled almost before the battle even began. King James was mortally wounded and died a few weeks later.

Because Mary Stuart was still a child, her mother, Marie of Guise, became regent. Archbishop David Beaton remained chancellor. He continued the policies of his uncle, both religiously and secularly. He maintained close relations with France and strengthened the laws against heresy. However, his strength and determination made him the mortal enemy of the Scottish Protestants.

On May 28, 1546, a band of fifteen Protestants broke into Cardinal Beaton's home. As he stood unarmed before them, they attacked and murdered him. In killing David Beaton, the Protestant revolutionaries had killed Catholic Scotland. Beaton had no one who could take his place as the Catholic spiritual and secular leader of the nation.

Marie of Guise sent her young daughter to France for protection, but she herself remained in Scotland. However, Marie had almost no power. Scotland was under the dominion of the Protestants. They took their orders from John Calvin in Geneva.

John Knox

The leader of the Protestant revolutionaries in Scotland was **John Knox** (1505-1572), John Calvin's "best" student. In John Knox, the Protestants had a leader who was brutally determined to destroy the Catholic Faith. In fact, as a young man, he had served as an armed bodyguard to one of the leading Protestants in Scotland.

Although John Knox did not participate in the murder of Cardinal David Beaton, in April 1547 he joined the assassins who had seized Beaton's home, the Castle of St. Andrews. During his time with the rebels, he publicly expounded his theories on the Church, calling for the abolition of the Mass and the sacraments. He also followed Luther's central theories on salvation by faith alone (*sola fide*) and Scripture alone (*sola scriptura*).

Eventually, Marie of Guise decided to storm the Castle of St. Andrews and capture the murderers. With the help of the French, the castle was taken at the end of July. Knox and his associates were taken prisoner. As punishment for his role in the conspiracy, Knox was sentenced to serve as a galley slave, a fate few men survived. However, after he had served nineteen months, the French released Knox as part of a prisoner exchange.

Statue of John Knox in Edinburgh

Upon his release, John Knox went to England, where he received protection from Thomas Cranmer. In England, Knox preached his brand of Protestantism, and his following grew. He became so popular that, in 1551, he became chaplain to King Edward VI.

Following Edward's death and the ascension of Mary Tudor to the throne, Knox fled England in 1554. He went to Geneva, where he joined John Calvin. For the next several years, he remained in Geneva, becoming John Calvin's most ardent disciple. In the summer of 1558, Knox published a vicious pamphlet stating that women should never rule a kingdom. Although the targets of his attack were Mary Tudor and Marie of Guise, he unluckily published it only a few months before Elizabeth Tudor became queen. Because of the pamphlet, she hated Knox for the rest of his life and did little to help him.

With Protestant Elizabeth now ruling England, Knox decided it was safe to return home to Scotland. In May 1559, he arrived. On August 19, 1561, Mary, Queen of Scots, returned to Scotland to rule in her own right. The week after Mary landed in Scotland, John Knox gave a violent sermon against her, declaring that he feared one Mass more than ten thousand armed enemies. In response, Mary summoned Knox to appear before her. They met in person the following week.

Mary was an 18-year-old princess—beautiful, gentle, and charming. She deeply loved the Catholic Church. Knox was a 47-year-old man who had survived nineteen

Witness to the Faith 399

months as a galley slave. He was a bitter, merciless enemy of the Catholic Church. The two could not possibly coexist.

At this point, Scotland was divided into two factions. One group, allied with the French, supported the Catholic Church. The other group, supported by England, sought to destroy the Catholic Church and replace it with something else. Scotland's Protestant nobles formed a powerful league known as the **Lords of the Congregation**. Their leader was Mary Stuart's traitorous half-brother, James Stuart, the Earl of Moray. Soon the Lords of the Congregation abolished the French garrisons in Scotland. A Protestant Parliament forbade the Mass in Scotland and established the **Presbyterian Church**.

Lords of the Congregation
League formed by Scottish Protestant nobles.

Presbyterian Church
Church established in Scotland after Catholicism became illegal.

Mary, Queen of Scots

From the moment she landed in Scotland, the life of Mary, Queen of Scots, took on a dramatic intensity that few people have ever known. Although she was the queen, enemies surrounded her. Searching for someone trustworthy and supportive, Mary chose her Catholic cousin, 18-year-old **Henry Stuart, Lord Darnley**. She married him in July 1565, after having known him for less than six months. In marrying Lord Darnley, Mary hoped not only to consolidate her power but also to restore Catholicism in Scotland. Sadly, the young queen married Darnley without really getting to know him. He was tall and strikingly handsome, but he was also disloyal, greedy, and cowardly.

Less than six months after the wedding, the ambitious Darnley demanded royal authority—that is, to be made co-ruler of Scotland.

Murder of David Rizzio, Jean Lulves

400   Chapter 26: The Church in England and Northern Europe in the 16th and 17th Centuries

When the queen refused his demands, he had her Italian secretary, David Riccio, assassinated in front of her. Mary, five months pregnant, turned on Darnley and accused him of trying to murder her and their unborn child by inducing a miscarriage so that he might be Scotland's sole ruler. Otherwise, why was the attack made right in front of her? Darnley had no answer. Evidence suggests that John Knox had consented to the murder of Riccio. Three months later, Mary gave birth to a son, whom she named James. Although James would be baptized a Catholic, he would be taken from his mother at an early age and raised as a Protestant. Meanwhile, Mary was so powerless that the week after her son's Baptism in December, she was forced to pardon the men who had murdered David Riccio.

Later, when Mary learned that Darnley was ill, she went to nurse him. By February 1567, it seemed that the two had reconciled. However, in early April, the Earl of Bothwell, determined to be king of Scotland, had agents plant a bomb that killed Darnley. Mary found herself alone in the hands of Darnley's murderers. On April 24, Bothwell, at the head of a band of 800 armed men, took her prisoner.

On May 15, Bothwell forced Mary to marry him in a Protestant ceremony. The Lords of the Congregation immediately circulated the rumor that Mary Stuart had consented to Darnley's murder in order to marry Bothwell. In June, the Lords rebelled, seized power, and captured Mary, whom they imprisoned. On July 25, they forced her to abdicate in favor of her 1-year-old son, who was proclaimed James VI. The Earl of Moray assumed the regency during James' youth. Bothwell fled to Norway, where his creditors arrested him. They took him to Denmark, where he died in prison. Eleven months later, in early May 1568, loyal followers helped Mary to escape.

In May 1568, Mary Stuart faced the most critical decision of her life. She could return to France, where her relatives could protect her, though she likely would never be queen of Scotland again. On the other hand, she could travel to England and try to gain the support of her cousin Queen Elizabeth to help her regain the Scottish throne. Though Mary must not have realized it, Queen Elizabeth was her deadliest enemy. History will probably never be able to explain why Mary chose to walk into the lioness' den. She fled to England seeking assistance and asylum from Elizabeth, who promptly cast her into prison.

The Last Days of Mary, Queen of Scots

In 1569, the leading Catholic nobles in the north of England rebelled in support of Queen Mary. The Catholic army fought its way as far south as Durham. In thanksgiving, they celebrated the last Mass

The Abdication of Mary, Queen of Scots, Joseph Severn

Henry Stuart, Lord Darnley
Mary Stuart's cousin and second husband; father of her son, who became King James I of England; tried to force her to grant him royal authority.

Mary Stuart Goes to the Gallows, Scipione Vannutelli

Francis Drake
An English pirate whom Queen Elizabeth I supported for his attacks on Spanish ports and shipping; led the force that defeated the Spanish Armada.

Spanish Armada
Spain's naval force, launched in hopes of invading England and restoring Catholicism there.

ever held in Durham's magnificent cathedral. However, in the face of a larger and stronger Protestant army, they disbanded, unable to free Queen Mary. In February 1587, after nineteen years of captivity, Mary was executed on false charges. Meanwhile, in Rome and Madrid, Pope Sixtus V and King Philip II of Spain were closely watching the developing situation in England.

The Spanish Armada

On October 24, 1585, King Philip wrote to Pope Sixtus that he was definitely committed to invading England. Philip's reasons for the invasion were simple and straightforward. **He wished to preserve the Church, restore Catholic Christendom, and aid the Catholics being persecuted in England.** Additionally, since becoming queen, Elizabeth had supported the attacks of English pirates such as **Francis Drake**, whom she knighted after a particularly profitable attack on Spanish ports and shipping. English pirates had also attacked Spanish ports in Spain and the New World. In fact, in July 1585, Elizabeth had personally commissioned Drake to attack the Spanish treasure fleet. Drake actually attacked Spain itself on October 17, 1585. Additionally, England had supported the Dutch rebels seeking to oust Philip from the Low Countries, where his father, Charles V, had been born. Philip was finally determined to end English aggression against his nation, his people, and the Catholics in England. In these goals, he had the complete support of Pope Sixtus. From the viewpoint of any honest person, his counterattack on England, after so many provocations, was completely justified.

For many years, Philip delayed the launch of the Spanish Armada. However, the execution of Mary, Queen of Scots, as well as stories of terrible martyrdoms in England, such as that of St. Margaret Clitherow in 1586, compelled Philip to act. Upon learning of the execution of Queen Mary Stuart, he went into seclusion for a week, almost certainly to pray. He then decided to launch the greatest naval fleet the world had ever seen.

The **Spanish Armada**, an invasion fleet, left Spain in late May 1588. At daybreak on July 21, the English fleet engaged the Armada off Plymouth. The Spanish were the world's greatest soldiers, but this was a naval battle, and England possessed the world's finest sailors and captains. Drake and his fellow captains destroyed the Spanish Armada.

This was arguably the most important naval battle in world history. At stake were not only the Catholics then living in England but also every future English-speaking person. Had Philip been able to invade and restore Catholicism in England, Catholics likely would have settled England's New World colonies. The United States would have been a Catholic nation, at least at its birth. The impact of a United States with such a Catholic heritage can probably never be imagined. The whole world might have been different.

The Spanish Armada off the English Coast,
Cornelis Claesz van Wieringen

The Survival of Catholicism in England

The Spanish Armada represented the last, best hope to restore Catholicism in England. Although the war with England continued until the death of Elizabeth, Philip was forced to focus his attention elsewhere. However, he never abandoned the Catholics in England. Despite the terrible persecutions, some of the worst in history, Catholicism survived in England, due mostly to the incredible bravery of missionaries like Edmund Campion.

Pope Pius V had excommunicated Queen Elizabeth I in 1570. Parliament retaliated by passing the so-called "treason laws," which declared that anyone who obeyed the pope was a criminal. Parliament also voted to confiscate the property of all English Catholics who had fled England and sought refuge in continental Europe.

Meanwhile, England's refugees began organizing in the hopes of restoring the Catholic Faith. William Allen, the former headmaster at St. Mary's College, Oxford, who was ordained a priest in 1565, believed that the English people had not voluntarily surrendered the Faith. Based on his experiences as a missionary in England, Allen felt that preaching the truths of the Faith would restore the English people to the Church. Thus, he decided to establish a Catholic seminary to educate and train English priests. On September 29, 1568, he established the English College in Douay (currently spelled "Douai"), under the protection of King Philip II. (He also helped Pope Gregory XIII establish the English College in Rome.) In March 1578, Dutch rebels forced him to temporarily move Douay College to Rheims (currently spelled "Reims"), but it returned to Douay in 1593. Douay College became the main center for training missionaries to return to Elizabethan England. Although dozens were imprisoned and executed, men like Edmund Campion continued to preach in England.

Witness to the Faith

King James I of England

Douay-Rheims Bible
Translation of the Latin Vulgate into English, completed by Douay College.

Gunpowder Plot
A plot by a group of Catholics to blow up the Houses of Parliament; its discovery disgraced Catholicism in England for three hundred years.

In addition to sending missionaries to England, Douay College also printed a number of pamphlets and other Catholic literature. One of the main projects of the college was the development, under William Allen's direction, of the **Douay-Rheims Bible**, a translation of the Latin Vulgate into English. The New Testament was published in 1582, but a lack of funds caused the Old Testament to be delayed until 1609. In 1587, Pope Sixtus made William Allen a cardinal.

King James I

When Queen Elizabeth died on March 24, 1603, she had no children. Her closest heir would have been Catholic Mary Stuart, the Queen of Scots. However, Elizabeth had ensured that Mary would never become queen of England, by having her executed. Thus, Mary's son, James Stuart, the king of Scotland, succeeded Elizabeth on the English throne.

The Gunpowder Plot

King James I (1603-1625) had been raised as a Protestant, married a Protestant, and thoroughly embraced Protestantism. He not only hated Catholicism but also feared it. In 1597, James wrote a book in which he explained his theory of monarchy, called "the divine right of kings." Under this theory, the king is subject to no earthly authority, such as the pope or the Church, and is answerable only to God. This idea ran counter to the Catholic Church's position, as established by Pope Gregory VII and his successors, that kings are answerable to the Church and the pope, and can even be deposed by the pope. Additionally, because James was kidnapped when he was 16, he lived in constant fear of assassination.

When James became king of England, English Catholics hoped that he would be tolerant of Catholicism, since his mother had been such a devout Catholic. However, James had been taken from Mary shortly after his birth and had no memory of her. Still, at the outset of his reign, it seemed that he would take a more gentle approach to the Church than Elizabeth had.

The reality, however, soon proved quite different. James had been king of England for less than a year when he decided to begin persecuting the Church. Angered by the number of conversions that priests, who had returned to England, were making, he made it clear that he would not allow Catholicism to grow in his realm. At the beginning of March 1604, he ordered all Jesuits out of the country and imposed more restrictive laws against Catholics. He encouraged his officials to kill all the Jesuits in England as well as anyone who helped them. By 1605, it was obvious to every English citizen that James would persecute the Church just as vigorously as Elizabeth had.

This was the background for the conspiracy known as the **Gunpowder Plot**. The conspirators planned to place thirty-six barrels of gunpowder in the cellar under the Houses of Parliament, and blow up the king, his son, and Parliament. Though the conspirators were dreadfully misguided, they were committed Catholics who had lived for forty-five years under terrible persecution. They had no prospect of a future in which they could openly practice the Catholic Faith. Nevertheless, it was an act of pure terrorism, which would brand English Catholics as revolutionaries and murderers. Rather than making the situation better and ending the persecutions, it would make things much worse.

The plot was discovered, and its leader, Robert Catesby, was condemned to death, along with eight other conspirators. One conspirator, Guy Fawkes, who had been assigned the task of exploding the bomb, was caught actually carrying gunpowder into the cellar. Catholicism in England was crippled for the next three hundred years. The Catholic Faith would be linked for three centuries to the plot. Every November 5, until the twentieth century, England celebrated Guy Fawkes Day with fireworks. They also hanged the pope in effigy.

King James Persecutes the Puritans

Another group hoping for more favorable treatment under King James was the **Puritans**. They called themselves "Puritans" because their goal was to "purify" Anglican worship of any trace of Catholicism. They were essentially English Calvinists. However, despite being a Protestant, James hated the Calvinists almost as much as he hated the Catholics, from his time in Scotland, where John Knox's version of Calvinism was dominant. James felt that the Calvinists tried to guide secular leaders, something he could not tolerate.

Elizabeth had dealt severely with the Puritans by enacting a law that imprisoned those who failed to attend Anglican services and exiling those who refused to make the profession accepting Anglican beliefs. James, too, persecuted the Puritans. He had about three hundred Puritan ministers exiled from the kingdom. Other Puritans left voluntarily, seeking religious freedom; among them were the American Pilgrim Fathers.

> **Puritans**
> A group of Calvinist-like English Protestants who sought to "purify" Anglican worship of any trace of Catholicism.

The Embarkation of the Pilgrims, Cornelis Robert Walter Weir

King Charles I, Queen Henrietta Maria, and Their Children

King Charles I

King James I died in March 1625. His son, **Charles I**, who ruled from 1625 to 1649, succeeded him. Charles was not pro-Catholic, but he had no strong feelings against Catholicism. In fact, his wife, French Princess **Henrietta Maria**, whom he loved very much, was a devout Catholic. However, during Charles' reign, Puritans began to gain control of Parliament. They thought that Charles was too lenient to Catholics. To eradicate Catholicism completely, the Puritans demanded that the children of Catholics be raised as Protestants. To satisfy their demands, Charles sometimes employed harsh measures against the Catholics. Nevertheless, life for Catholics improved slightly under his reign. Their taxes were reduced, and they were permitted to attend Mass in their homes.

From the beginning of his reign, Charles I and Parliament failed to work together. Parliament wanted more power, and Charles believed in the divine right of kings. The religious disagreements only added to the tensions. By the end of November 1640, Charles and Parliament completely distrusted each other. By mid-1642, both sides had begun preparing for armed conflict, the **English Civil War**.

For several years, Charles waged war against the Puritan Parliament and its allies, the Scottish Presbyterians, who also had grievances against Charles. By January 1647, Charles had been utterly defeated. In August, a Puritan army led by **Oliver Cromwell** occupied London and seized control of the government. Cromwell was now the ruler of England, and he had Charles tried and condemned to death. King Charles I was beheaded on January 30, 1649.

Oliver Cromwell

Since the summer of 1647, Puritan dictator Oliver Cromwell had ruled England. In a short period, this man had risen from an unknown country gentleman to the dictator of England, Scotland, and Ireland. A relative of Henry VIII's minister Thomas Cromwell, Oliver had become a Puritan in his thirties. He was the greatest military leader of the time and had the wealth of England supporting him. Sadly, he would use that skill and power to do great harm to Catholics, especially in Ireland.

Charles I
Conflicted with Parliament, largely because of his belief in the divine right of kings; was executed after the English Civil War.

English Civil War
A war between King Charles I and the Puritan Parliament, which ended with Oliver Cromwell seizing power and Charles being beheaded.

Oliver Cromwell
Ruler of England for ten years after the English Civil War.

In August 1649, he landed in Ireland with the express purpose of destroying the Catholic Church there. He first attacked the city of **Drogheda**, which he captured, slaughtering its 3,500 citizens, including women and children. The massacre of Drogheda set the pattern he would follow throughout the Emerald Isle. For the next two years, he swept over Ireland like a demonic plague, slaughtering the Irish people.

In 1651, he returned to England and received a hero's welcome. For the next seven years, he ruled England and defended her from various opponents, notably the Scots. In September 1658, Oliver Cromwell died. He was one of the greatest enemies the Catholic Church has ever known.

Drogheda
City in Ireland; first of many places where Oliver Cromwell attacked and slaughtered the Irish people.

Charles II

With the exception of Oliver Cromwell, there has never been a military dictatorship in England. After his death, the English people restored the monarchy under Charles II, the son of Charles I. Charles II restored Anglicanism to its original position in England. He also tried, though without much success, to suspend the penal laws against Catholics. He had sympathy for Catholics because in his youth they had helped him escape from Cromwell in September 1651. For six weeks, he had evaded Cromwell's forces before fleeing to France in disguise. Among those who had aided him was a priest named John Huddleston, who told him about the Catholic Faith. It is possible that Charles had undergone a conversion experience at the time, but never publicly acknowledged it because he knew it would prohibit him from becoming king of England. However, on his deathbed, he called for a priest, and Father Huddleston almost miraculously appeared. As Charles made his deathbed conversion, he told Father Huddleston, "You that saved my body have now come to save my soul." Charles II died in February 1685.

James II

Unlike Charles II, his brother and successor, James II, was a well-known Catholic, the last Catholic to rule England. During Charles II's reign, the Anglicans had feared that James might become king. James, for his part, probably acted too rashly in trying to create an atmosphere of tolerance for Catholics. His attempts to create religious liberty for Catholics caused tension with Parliament.

James II might have ruled until his death (1701), had two events not occurred in June 1688, which caused Parliament to depose him. The first was the birth of a son and heir, which would create a Catholic dynasty. The Anglicans had feared such an event when James II had become king. His Catholic heir would replace his daughter Mary and her husband, William of Orange, who were Protestants, in the line of succession. Charles II, not having children, expected Mary, James' oldest daughter, to succeed James. As a result, Charles had Mary and her sister Anne raised as Anglicans, so that Parliament would accept them as potential monarchs. The birth of a son to James II jeopardized this plan and upset the Anglicans.

Oliver Cromwell

Witness to the Faith

King James II

King William III

Queen Mary II

The second event was James' prosecution of seven Anglican bishops for sedition. Parliament viewed the prosecution as an attack on the Anglican Church. When James lost the trial at the end of June, anti-Catholic riots broke out in England and Scotland. Parliament invited William and Mary to replace James II, who fled to France. The reign of William III and Mary II inaugurated a period of religious tolerance between the Protestant sects, in which Catholics would eventually be included.

The Church in Ireland

Despite their best efforts, the English had failed to conquer most of Ireland. The more the Irish people were persecuted, the more loyal to the Church they became. Heroic priests, educated in seminaries abroad, cared for their spiritual needs. Under Elizabeth, six bishops and hundreds of priests suffered martyrdom. Oliver Cromwell massacred the Irish and destroyed their towns. He drove the Irish out of the northern counties and gave their land to Scottish Protestants. These northern Irish counties would be the source of religious and political conflict between England and Ireland until the twenty-first century.

The last Irish martyr was St. Oliver Plunkett (1629-1681). St. Oliver was the archbishop of Armagh and the Primate of All Ireland. He maintained his duties in the face of the English persecution but was eventually arrested. The English tried and falsely convicted him for treason. He was dragged behind a horse to Tyburn, where he was hanged, drawn, and quartered. Pope Paul VI canonized him in 1975.

In 1690, during the reign of William and Mary, the Irish revolted against their English oppressors. The English again were determined to exterminate the Irish and destroy the Faith. Catholics were deprived of all religious and civil rights. Children were offered their parents' land if they became Protestants, and were allowed to take possession of it even while their parents were living. Catholics were forbidden to buy land or build schools. The English offered a bounty to anyone revealing a priest's hiding place. They shipped twenty thousand Irish men and women to America as indentured servants.

Despite the massive persecutions, the Irish held staunchly to the Catholic Faith. The work of St. Patrick and the early monks had indeed been well done. The Faith was too deeply rooted to be torn, burned, or gouged out of the hearts of the people. Irish exiles became messengers of the Gospel in other lands. As in earlier years, when Irish missionaries had carried the Faith and learning to all the countries of Europe, so now, driven from their homes by fire and sword, Irish immigrants carried the Faith across the sea to the lands where they found peace and refuge.

> **Prince William of Orange**
> Protestant prince of Holland; replaced Catholic King James II as king of England in the "Glorious Revolution."

Calvinism in Holland

Calvinism made little progress in Holland during the life of Emperor Charles V, who had been born there. When he abdicated, he placed Holland under the rule of his son Philip II of Spain. During Philip's reign, the Calvinists spread rumors about him. Notably, they said he would introduce the Spanish Inquisition into Holland, something Philip had no intention of doing. Consequently, Philip became the object of ever-increasing fear and suspicion. As a result, the people of Holland, under **Prince William of Orange**, rebelled and declared themselves independent of Philip's lawful rule.

During the first few weeks of the Dutch revolt, Prince William of Orange gave permission for unlimited Calvinist services in Antwerp. Calvinist revolutionaries swept over Holland. Mobs roamed the land, plundering churches and persecuting the clergy, monks, and nuns. On August 20, 1566, almost all the religious images and paintings in Antwerp's forty-two churches were destroyed. In Ghent, Brussels, Utrecht, and Amsterdam, the Calvinists destroyed thousands of art treasures. Of Holland's major cities, only the churches in Bruges were defended. At Gorkum, seventeen priests and two lay brothers were cruelly mutilated and hanged for refusing to deny the supremacy of the pope.

In 1567, Philip II sent an army under the Duke of Alba to suppress the revolt. However, he was not completely successful.

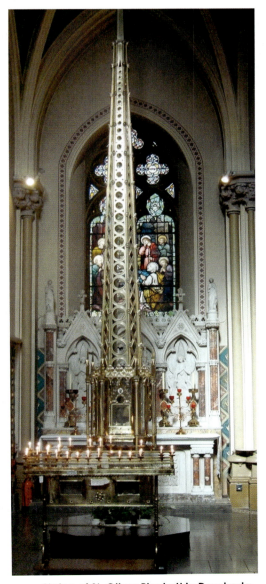

Shrine of St. Oliver Plunkett in Drogheda

Witness to the Faith

Seventeen Priests Are Martyred for the Faith at Gorkum, Holland, on July 9, 1572

Spain succeeded in regaining only the ten southern provinces (present-day **Belgium**), and these returned to the Catholic Faith. The Catholic cathedrals in Belgium are beautiful works of art, especially the cathedral in Antwerp, which is filled with paintings by the great artist Peter Paul Rubens. The Protestant cathedrals in the **Netherlands**, on the other hand, resemble nothing so much as giant whitewashed barns, lacking any art or beauty, though they were once treasure houses of Catholic art.

Queen Christina of Sweden

In all of European history, no monarch has ever given up the crown for the Faith—with one exception.

The most aggressively Protestant country in Europe at this time was Sweden, where simply being a Catholic meant death or exile. Other countries

List of Peter Paul Rubens' Works of Art in This Book

Many of Rubens' paintings have been used in this book:
- *Christ Giving the Keys to St. Peter*: p. 39
- *The Labarum*: p. 43
- *Triumphant Entry of Constantine into Rome*: p. 45
- *The Founding of Constantinople*: p. 46
- *The Death of Constantine the Great*: p. 47
- *St. Ambrose and Emperor Theodosius*: p. 66
- *St. Francis Receiving the Stigmata*: p. 234
- *Pope Nicholas V*: p. 297
- *Portrait of Pope Leo X*: p. 301
- *Saint Ignatius of Loyola*: p. 353
- *Saint Teresa of Avila*: p. 369
- *The Miracles of Saint Ignatius of Loyola*: p. 426
- *Immaculate Conception*: p. 476

imposed these penalties only on priests. Yet it was from Sweden that one of the most amazing conversions in all of history occurred: the conversion of **Queen Christina of Sweden**.

Christina ascended the throne of Sweden in 1644, at the age of 18. She was a young woman of extraordinary intellectual gifts. The more Christina considered the official Lutheranism of Sweden, the less she liked it. She knew that if she became a Catholic, she would be removed from, or forced to abdicate, her throne. She did not flinch from the prospect.

In October 1649, philosopher Rene Descartes came to Sweden to instruct her. From Descartes, she learned to value truth more than a crown. In July 1650, the Portuguese ambassador arrived in Sweden with a Jesuit priest. Queen Christina soon began talking to the priest about the Catholic Faith. By the summer of 1652, she had decided to become Catholic and abdicate. On June 9, 1654, she relinquished her throne. That night, she traveled in disguise to Antwerp in Catholic Belgium. On Christmas Eve, she professed her Catholic Faith, attended midnight Mass, and received the Holy Eucharist.

She planned to travel to Rome, where she would spend the rest of her life. One year later, on December 23, Pope Alexander VII received her in Rome. She died in 1689 and is buried in St. Peter's Basilica.

Queen Christina of Sweden

Oral Exercises

1. Who was John Knox?
2. What was the Gunpowder Plot?
3. Who was Oliver Cromwell?
4. What did Oliver Cromwell do in Drogheda?
5. Who was the last Catholic monarch of England?
6. Who led the Dutch revolt against Spain?
7. What is unique about Queen Christina of Sweden?
8. Where is the tomb of Queen Christina of Sweden?

Belgium
Southern part of Holland; was reclaimed by Spain after the Dutch rebellion, and so remained Catholic.

Netherlands
Northern part of Holland; became a Protestant country.

Queen Christina of Sweden
Became convinced that Catholicism was true, rather than Lutheranism, her country's official religion, so she gave up her throne to enter the Catholic Church.

Witness to the Faith

Chapter 27
The Fate of France (1600-1700)

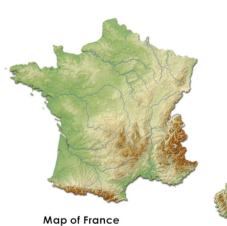

Map of France

Huguenots
A group of French Calvinists; religious wars broke out in France between them and the Catholics.

The Seventeenth Century: A Time of Choosing

In a real sense, the first half of the seventeenth century was the last chance for most European nations to choose their national religion. After 1648, no nation would change its majority religion, or even come close to doing so. It was a time of choosing.

Although in most cases, the choice of national religion would be made by national leaders, and nearly always on the battlefield, the Church continued to work to convert and evangelize individuals. As in every century, great saints affected the world.

In the seventeenth century, the Church, and the Jesuits especially, made a special effort to support great art. The artistic era known as the Baroque Age was the most magnificent period of art in world history. It developed as a direct result of the Catholic Reformation. Even Protestants recognized the magnificence of Baroque art. They too chose to create Baroque paintings.

Christendom in Crisis

At the beginning of the seventeenth century, there were great European powers. Germany was a patchwork quilt of quarreling Catholic and Protestant principalities. Spain, under Isabel and Ferdinand, Charles V, and King Philip II, had become an impregnable fortress of Catholicism

Stained-Glass Window of St. Vincent de Paul

1572 A.D. – 1673 A.D.

1572 A.D. Over two thousand Huguenots are killed in Paris in the St. Bartholomew's Day Massacre.

1590 A.D. Henry of Navarre, a Calvinist prince who has inherited the throne of France, besieges a French Catholic army inside Paris, but a Spanish army forces him to retreat.

1593 A.D. France has peace again when Henry is reconciled to the Church and crowned king. St. Francis de Sales is ordained and assigned to Geneva.

1598 A.D. The Edict of Nantes guarantees religious liberty to the Huguenots.

1618 A.D. The Thirty Years' War begins with disagreements about who should become the next Holy Roman Emperor.

1624 A.D. St. Vincent de Paul and a few companions found the first house of the Congregation of the Missions, known today as the Vincentians.

1630 A.D. The Edict of Restitution seems to have ended the war, but fighting breaks out again with the attacks of Gustavus Adolphus. Galileo publishes his *Dialogue on the Two Great World Systems*.

1648 A.D. The Peace of Westphalia finally ends the Thirty Years' War.

1673 A.D. Our Lord begins appearing to St. Margaret Mary.

where Protestantism could gain no foothold, however small. With the defeat of the Spanish Armada, England was lost to the Faith, at least for the foreseeable future. France, the *eldest daughter of the Church*, hovered on the brink. She was the greatest prize in the eyes of John Calvin. If she fell, Christendom would be irretrievably lost.

Calvinism Spreads to France

In 1559, Catherine de Medici (1519-1589), the widow of King Henry II, became the ruler of France after the accidental death of her husband. Because her son, Charles IX, was too young to reign, Catherine became regent. Catherine sought to make peace with the Calvinist revolutionaries, known as the **Huguenots**. However, it is the nature of the revolutionary never to make peace. Thus, Calvinism continued to spread throughout France, and many members

Witness to the Faith 413

Admiral Gaspard de Coligny

Admiral Gaspard de Coligny
Leader of the Huguenots, who was killed by Catherine de Medici and her son, King Charles IX, in the St. Bartholomew's Day Massacre.

St. Bartholomew's Day Massacre
A preemptive attack by the French monarchy against the Huguenot leaders, which got out of control and led to a mob killing thousands of Calvinist civilians.

of the nobility embraced Calvinism. In 1561, the Calvinists held a service in Paris, which more than 6,000 people attended. On March 1, 1562, the first of six religious wars broke out in France.

In 1572, Catherine decided that the only solution to the ongoing religious warfare was for her daughter Marguerite to marry Henry of Navarre, a Calvinist prince. On August 18, they married, despite Pope Gregory XIII's refusal to grant a dispensation for the wedding. Great crowds flocked to Paris for the ceremony—among them, about two thousand Calvinists. The Calvinist leader in France was **Admiral Gaspard de Coligny**, whom Catherine both feared and hated. On the morning of August 22, she attempted, but failed, to have him assassinated.

There were still thousands of Calvinists remaining in Paris from the wedding, and the situation was becoming increasingly dangerous for everyone. Catherine and her son, King Charles IX, believed that the Calvinists planned to kill them in retaliation for the attempt on Coligny's life. In a preemptive strike, they decided to kill Coligny and about thirty Calvinist leaders. It was August 23, the eve of St. Bartholomew's Day. Although their plan had been to kill only the Calvinist leaders, the violence soon spread. The Catholic mob, hearing that there was a plan to kill the king and thinking that the king had ordered them to attack, killed every Calvinist they could, including women and children. During the **St. Bartholomew's Day Massacre**, the mob killed more than two thousand people.

After the massacre, Catherine sent word to all the rulers of Europe, including Pope Gregory XIII, telling them that the massacre had been necessary because of a plot that had been discovered against the life of the king. Having no other information, Pope Gregory believed her. He had a solemn hymn of gratitude sung in Rome, not for the death of the Calvinists, but for the safe delivery of the royal family. Nevertheless, the massacre horrified him. Only later would he learn the truth.

William Shakespeare once wrote: "The evil that men do lives after them; the good is oft interred with their bones." King Charles IX died of tuberculosis less than two years later. His brother, Henry III, succeeded him to the throne.

Pope Sixtus V

The pontificate of Pope Gregory XIII had been turbulent, even controversial. He had reformed the calendar and had been the great benefactor of Jesuit education in Europe. Yet the St. Bartholomew's Day Massacre had occurred during his pontificate (although he personally had nothing to do with it). The conclave to choose his successor knew that the next pope would need the soul of a warrior, for the future of the Church would be decided on the field of battle. Thus, they chose a pope who would fight for the Church. He decided to be called Sixtus V (1585-1590).

Realizing what was at stake in England, Pope Sixtus V fully supported Philip II during his Spanish Armada campaign. In fact, he even offered Philip a million ducats of gold if the Armada could launch before the end of 1587. Although at times Philip and Sixtus had a tempestuous relationship, both men were dedicated to the defense of the Catholic Faith, especially in France and England.

On the morning of August 1, 1589, an insane monk mortally wounded French King Henry III. Henry had reigned for fifteen years, but had no children. As the king lay dying, he called his brother-in-law Henry of Navarre, the Calvinist prince, to his bedside. He begged Henry of Navarre to become Catholic, and he recognized him as his successor. The following day, Henry III died, and Henry of Navarre proclaimed himself King Henry IV. However, he did not become Catholic.

In fact, for the next several months, Henry IV won a number of victories over French Catholic armies who opposed him. Nevertheless, the key to France was Paris, its capital, and he was unable to capture it. By the end of April 1590, Henry was besieging Paris for a third time. Inside its walls, its starving defenders, encouraged by their priests, refused to surrender. If Paris fell, so would France.

In 1590, Spain possessed the finest soldiers in the world. Had they landed in England, they might have conquered it in a few weeks. England had defeated the Spanish because they could not access England except by sea, but they did not need their Armada to reach France. In September, a Spanish army relieved the siege of Paris and forced Henry's army to retreat. Catholicism in France had triumphed for the time being. However, Pope Sixtus V had not lived to see it, having died after a brief illness that August.

Pope Gregory XIV

The conclave to elect Sixtus V's successor recognized that Philip II had

Henry of Navarre

Witness to the Faith 415

become the de facto leader of Christendom. They elected the papal nuncio to Madrid as the next pope—a man who had worked closely with King Philip. He took the name Urban VII. Twelve days later, he was dead from malaria.

When the conclave reconvened, they once again elected a man who had Philip II's complete support as well as that of St. Philip Neri: Cardinal Paleotto. He took the name Gregory XIV (1590-1591). Pope Gregory informed Philip II that Paris must be held against Henry of Navarre. To that end, Gregory renewed the decree of excommunication against Henry which Sixtus V had issued. Gregory was as committed as Philip II and Pope Sixtus to stopping a Calvinist from becoming king of France. However, after a pontificate of less than eleven months, he died.

Pope Clement VIII

Following the death of Gregory XIV, the Sacred College elected Pope Innocent IX. During his two-month papacy, he continued the policies of his predecessor regarding King Henry IV. After his death, the College of Cardinals elected a good and holy cardinal, who took the name Clement VIII (1592-1605).

In Pope Clement VIII, the Sacred College had chosen wisely. He was a reformer and was personally devout. Even as pope, he heard Confessions for many hours during Holy Week. A canon lawyer, he was a natural diplomat. After a long negotiation, Clement reconciled Henry of Navarre to the Church on July 25, 1593. Seven months later, Henry was crowned king of France.

Although only God can know the truth of a person's heart, from the time of his conversion until his death in 1610, King Henry IV was actively and visibly Catholic. In 1598, he issued the **Edict of Nantes**, which guaranteed full liberty of conscience and toleration to the Huguenots. However, had Henry reverted to Calvinism, France might very well have been lost to the Faith. At least for the time being, France had been saved for the Church.

St. Vincent de Paul

When Henry of Navarre was finally reconciled with the Catholic Church, it ended thirty years of religious warfare in France. Moreover, despite the efforts of the Huguenots, France remained predominantly Catholic. However, the wars that had raged during the sixteenth century had negatively affected religious practices and beliefs. The situation tended to be worse in rural districts, where the people, who generally were poor, were often not as well catechized as in the larger cities. One of the wonderful saints who worked to improve the lives of the poor in France during this period was **St. Vincent de Paul**.

Vincent was born in 1581 to a family of poor shepherds. When he was young, his parents realized that he had a brilliant mind, so they sacrificed to help him become a priest. He worked his way through college and was

Edict of Nantes
Guaranteed toleration and liberty of conscience to the Huguenots.

St. Vincent de Paul
One of the first to aid the poor in an organized way; founded religious orders for this purpose.

416   *Chapter 27: The Fate of France (1600-1700)*

ordained in 1600. At first, his life as a priest was not particularly devout. However, in 1605, Vincent experienced an incredible ordeal that changed his life forever.

While he was on a sea voyage, Muslim pirates captured him. They took him to Tunis, where they sold him into slavery to an apostate Christian. Vincent converted him, and they both escaped to France in 1607. Vincent then traveled to Rome, where he continued his studies for two years. Upon his return to France, he became chaplain to Queen Margaret.

In 1613, Count Emmanuel de Gondi, a royal naval officer and the brother of the archbishop of Paris, selected Vincent to tutor his son, the future Cardinal de Retz. While working as a tutor, Vincent recognized the vocation to which he would devote the rest of his life. Perhaps because he had been raised in a poor family, he felt a special devotion to the poor. Thus, he began preaching to the poor tenant farmers working on Count de Gondi's estates.

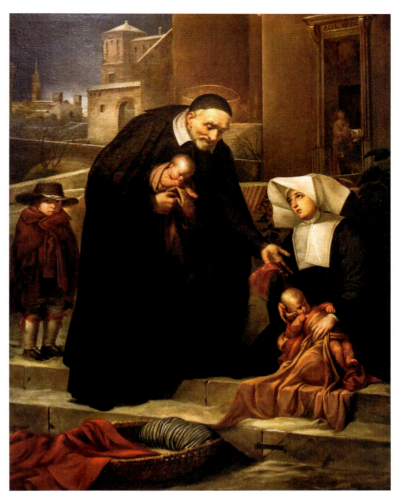

St. Vincent de Paul with a Daughter of Charity

His success in preaching to the poor convinced Vincent that he should found an order of priests dedicated to teaching and assisting the poor in rural areas. In 1624, Vincent and a few other priests founded the first house of the Congregation of the Missions, which Pope Urban VIII officially recognized in January 1633. Since the priory of St. Lazarus in Paris was their first headquarters, the members of the Congregation of the Mission are sometimes called Lazarists (or Lazarites), as well as Vincentians. During the next few years, the Vincentians established houses in other European nations as well as North Africa. Their main goal was always to provide religious instruction to the poor. Today, thousands of Vincentians help the poor all over the world.

While St. Vincent was primarily concerned with the salvation of souls, he also realized that the poor needed food, shelter, and comfort. In seventeenth-century France, charitable care of the poor was completely disorganized. St. Vincent knew that there must be some orderly system to distribute aid to the poor and the unfortunate. Otherwise, the undeserving might benefit at the expense of the truly needy.

Witness to the Faith

In 1633, St. Vincent de Paul and St. Louise de Marillac founded the Daughters of Charity in Paris. The first community was composed of twelve peasant girls dedicated to helping the poor and the sick. The Daughters of Charity were a remarkable group for the time. First, they were poor and of a low social status. Second, they were working among the needy at a time when most religious sisters tended to live in cloistered communities. Determined that the order succeed, St. Vincent personally recruited its members and supervised their training. The Daughters of Charity were indeed successful! They established soup kitchens to feed the poor, hospitals, and orphanages.

During his lifetime, the charitable work of St. Vincent's followers expanded throughout Europe. When St. Vincent de Paul died in 1660, the poor lost a true champion. However, he had made an indelible mark upon the world. The interest he created in helping the poor, the sick, and the unwanted caused many religious orders to be founded for their care.

St. Francis de Sales

The other giant of the Catholic Faith during this period was **St. Francis de Sales**. Francis was born in 1567 in southeastern France to a noble family. He attended a Jesuit high school and then studied law at the University of Padua, where he received his degree in 1592. Despite his legal studies, Francis felt called to a religious vocation. He was about to begin his career as an attorney and marry a wealthy noblewoman when he declared his intention to become a priest. Despite his family's objections, they could not sway Francis from his decision. He was ordained a priest in 1593 and assigned to Geneva.

Since 1532, when Geneva had fallen under John Calvin's control, the see of the bishop of Geneva had been located at Annecy, a town in France about 20 miles south of Geneva. At Annecy, Francis de Sales devoted himself to preaching, hearing Confessions, and ministering to the people. Risking his life, he journeyed through the entire area, which the Calvinists controlled, preaching constantly. Francis even met with Calvinist leader Theodore Beza in Geneva; however, nothing came of their meeting. Nevertheless, by his learning, kindness, and holiness, Francis converted many others.

In 1599, the bishop of Geneva made Francis his coadjutor (assistant) bishop. In 1602, when the bishop died, Francis became bishop of Geneva. Because his diocese was so engaged with the Calvinists in Geneva, Francis realized that the Catholics in his diocese needed to be well catechized so that they did not fall into heresy. As a result, he stressed catechetical

> **St. Francis de Sales**
> Holy, gentle priest who preached and ministered to the people in the diocese of Geneva and converted many from Calvinism. As bishop of Geneva, he devoted himself to ensuring that Catholics in his diocese were well catechized and to reforming the clergy and religious communities there.

St. Francis de Sales Gives the Rule for the Visitation Order to St. Jane Frances de Chantal

Chapter 27: The Fate of France (1600-1700)

instructions for all Catholics in his diocese. Francis also knew that many Catholics had fallen away from the Faith because the clergy lacked discipline or even lived sinful lives that gave bad example. Thus, he sought to reform his clergy and the religious communities by creating rules so that they would live holier lives. Francis set the standard himself by dressing, acting, and living more like a simple priest than a prince. To that end, he heard Confessions and constantly preached at Mass. To ensure that his regulations were enforced, he personally visited the various parishes scattered through the rugged Alpine mountains of his diocese.

During his lifetime, St. Francis wrote countless letters, delivered numerous sermons, and wrote two simple little books on the spiritual life. However, it was his personal life, filled with virtue and self-sacrifice, that most affected those around him. His motto was, "He who preaches with love, preaches effectively." Although only God will ever know for sure, historians estimate that St. Francis de Sales converted as many as 70,000 Calvinists to the Catholic Faith.

Map of France, Showing Annecy

Often, when a priest or bishop becomes well known for his preaching, he is invited to preach in other dioceses. Such was the case with Bishop de Sales. In 1604, he was preaching in Dijon, where he met a devout widow, Baroness Jane Frances de Chantal. He became her spiritual adviser. On June 6, 1610, St. Francis de Sales and St. Jane Frances de Chantal founded the Order of the Visitation of Holy Mary (or simply the Visitation Order) in Annecy. The Visitation Order was meant for women called to the religious life who lacked the strength or desire to accept the physical rigors of other orders. Originally, the Visitation sisters visited the poor and the sick in their homes, just as the Blessed Mother had visited her cousin Elizabeth. Later, the order changed this mission and became an order of cloistered, contemplative nuns with a special devotion to the Sacred Heart of Jesus. Jane Frances de Chantal died in 1641. Pope Clement XIII canonized her in 1767.

St. Francis de Sales died in 1622. Pope Alexander VII canonized him in 1665. In 1877, Pope Pius IX proclaimed him a Doctor of the Church.

The Conclaves of 1605

In 1605, the Sacred College met twice: the first time, to elect the successor to Pope Clement VIII; the second time, to elect the successor to Pope Leo XI, who had ruled for less than a month. The second conclave provided two great moments in Church history. The first involved Cardinal Robert Bellarmine, the remarkable Jesuit and a leading candidate for the papacy. Bellarmine declared to the Sacred College that he would do nothing to become pope and would resign from the Sacred College if they tried to elect him. The second involved the election of Cardinal Borghese, who took the name Paul V (1605-1621). He demonstrated that popes named Paul had the determination

Pope Paul V, Caravaggio

Witness to the Faith 419

of their apostolic namesake. In the case of Paul V, he would desperately need that determination, as Europe was soon to erupt in the horrifying religious world war known as the Thirty Years' War.

The Thirty Years' War (1618-1648)

The peace that the Protestant and Catholic princes had made in 1555 at Augsburg, Germany, did not last. In fact, it had never really existed at all. From the Peace of Augsburg until the outbreak of the **Thirty Years' War** in 1618, the Holy Roman Empire was continually in a state of unrest from the underlying religious conflict. Although Catholics, Lutherans, and Calvinists never formally fought a religious war, the sides were so utterly opposed to each other that a full-blown religious war was inevitable. Gradually, what began as a war in the empire developed into a conflict involving most of the other European nations.

By the beginning of the seventeenth century, the Holy Roman Empire was a fragmented collection of largely independent states. The position of Holy Roman Emperor was mainly titular, but the emperors did directly rule Austria, Bohemia, and Hungary. For years, the Hungarian nobles had chafed under Hapsburg rule. Their struggle against the Hapsburg dynasty reached its height during the last years of the reign of Emperor Rudolf II (1576-1612).

In 1607, the Hungarian nobles revolted, forcing Rudolf to transfer the rule of Hungary and Austria to his more compliant brother, Matthias. In 1608, the Calvinists in the empire banded together and formed the League of Evangelical Union. This prompted Catholics to form the Catholic League in 1609.

Thirty Years' War
Triggered by the tensions between Catholic and Protestant nations; involved most of the great European powers and ravaged Europe.

Archduke Ferdinand II of Austria, Francesco Terzi

By 1617, it was clear that Matthias, now Holy Roman Emperor and king of Bohemia, would die without an heir. To ensure an orderly transition during his lifetime, Matthias sought to have his nearest male relative, his cousin Archduke Ferdinand II of Austria, elected to the separate thrones of Bohemia and Hungary. Ferdinand was a staunch Catholic, which made him very unpopular in Protestant Bohemia. The Protestant leaders of Bohemia, fearing they might lose the religious rights that Emperor Rudolf II had granted them, desired a Protestant ruler. Nevertheless, in 1617, the Bohemian nobility duly elected Ferdinand as the crown prince and, upon the death of Matthias, the king of Bohemia.

In May 1618, Ferdinand sent two Catholic councilors as his representatives to Prague to administer the government of Bohemia in his absence. Bohemian rebels suddenly seized them and threw them out of the palace window, some 50 feet above the ground. They were miraculously saved when they landed in a pile of horse manure. This event, known as the *Defenestration of Prague*, started the Thirty Years' War. The weakness of both Emperor Ferdinand and the

420 Chapter 27: The Fate of France (1600-1700)

Cardinal Richelieu at the Siege of La Rochelle, Henri-Paul Motte

Bohemians caused the war to spread. Ferdinand was compelled to call on his nephew, King Philip IV of Spain, who sent an army to support the emperor. The Bohemians, desperate for allies against the emperor, appealed to the German Protestants.

Under the command of 60-year-old General John Tilly, a devout Catholic, the Catholic League's army pacified Upper Austria, while Ferdinand's forces pacified Lower Austria. The two armies united and moved north into Bohemia. Tilly decisively defeated the Protestants at the Battle of White Mountain, near Prague, on November 8, 1620. This victory restored the Catholic Faith in Bohemia and led to the dissolution of the League of Evangelical Union. In Rome, Pope Paul V gave thanks for the victory.

Meanwhile, in France, a sinister figure was moving onto history's stage. Louis XIII had become king of France in 1610, following the assassination of his father Henry IV (Henry of Navarre). However, the real ruler of France was **Cardinal Armand Richelieu** (1585-1642), a man with absolutely no principles but astonishing personal ambition. Consecrated a bishop in 1608, he lusted to be a cardinal. In 1622, he obtained the red hat. In August 1624, he became prime minister of France. His goal was to make France the greatest power in the world, whatever the cost. To that end, he worked time and again with the Huguenots against fellow Catholics and the Catholic Church, and he almost always succeeded.

Meanwhile, in Rome, Pope Paul V had died in 1621 and been succeeded by Pope Gregory XV (1621-1623). Despite his brief pontificate, Pope Gregory XV achieved a great deal. He supported the

| **Cardinal Armand Richelieu** Ambitious politician who devoted his life to making France the most powerful nation in Europe.

Witness to the Faith   421

Bust of Albrecht von Waldstein

Edict of Restitution
Proclamation by Emperor Ferdinand II that the property which had been taken from the Catholic Church since 1555 (involving more than 500 churches and monasteries) would be restored to the Church.

Gustavus Adolphus
King of Sweden and military genius; led the German Lutherans to many victories in the Thirty Years' War from 1630 until 1632, when he was killed at the Battle of Lutzen.

Catholic League, the emperor, and the Jesuits in France. He established the Congregation for the Propagation of the Faith, which trained missionaries for Protestant as well as non-Western nations. Finally, he canonized Teresa of Avila, Francis Xavier, Ignatius of Loyola, and Philip Neri. Already unwell at the time of his election, Pope Gregory died suddenly on July 8, 1623. He was 67 years old.

Pope Urban VIII (1623-1644), who had the support of Cardinal Richelieu, succeeded Gregory XV. Urban tried to end the Thirty Years' War. However, despite his long pontificate (he was only 55 when he was elected), he was unable to do so. Moreover, despite Cardinal Richelieu's support, Urban wrote to his nuncio in France, deploring the condition of the Church there, especially among the hierarchy. Although Richelieu rarely made a mistake, Pope Urban was no friend to the French cardinal.

Despite the victory at White Mountain, peace in the empire was short lived, as Denmark resumed the war. Danish involvement began when Lutheran King Christian IV of Denmark helped the Lutheran rulers of neighboring Lower Saxony by leading an army against the imperial forces. Denmark feared that recent Catholic successes threatened its sovereignty as a Protestant nation. France and England aided Denmark by subsidizing its war efforts.

To fight Denmark and its allies, Emperor Ferdinand II enlisted the military aid of Albrecht von Wallenstein, a Catholic Bohemian nobleman with a large army. Although a Catholic, Wallenstein was a dedicated astrologer (a practice condemned by the Church), so Ferdinand did not fully trust him. The combined forces of Wallenstein and Tilly forced King Christian to retreat. In 1626, Wallenstein and Tilly each defeated Protestant armies in battle. However, unable to invade and conquer Denmark, Wallenstein decided to make peace. The peace treaty stated that Christian IV could keep control of Denmark but must abandon his support for the Protestant German states.

Over the next two years, the Catholic powers won more victories and gained control of more territory. At this point, the Catholic League persuaded Emperor Ferdinand II to take back Catholic Church property that had been taken since 1555, which, according to the Peace of Augsburg, were rightfully the possessions of the Catholic Church. Over 500 churches and monasteries were involved. The proclamation was called the **Edict of Restitution**.

The Edict of Restitution proved remarkably effective. In 1630, the Church reestablished six Catholic dioceses in Germany, along with about two hundred monasteries and convents. The Protestants were furious but helpless. Without outside support, they could do nothing. It seemed like the Thirty Years' War was finally over. In fact, but for two men, it should have been.

At this moment in history, the greatest general of the age was a Protestant, as well as the king of Sweden, **Gustavus Adolphus**. Young, determined, and incredibly able, Adolphus had everything that was

422 *Chapter 27: The Fate of France (1600-1700)*

needed to help the German Lutherans, except one thing: money. Sweden was a small, poor country. He required somebody to pay for his war. Cardinal Richelieu was that somebody. In January 1631, Catholic France signed an alliance with Protestant Sweden to subsidize their war against Catholic Germany. For the next four years, Swedish-led armies drove back the Catholic forces, regaining much of the land the Protestants had lost.

In 1631, at the Battle of Breitenfeld, Gustavus Adolphus' forces defeated the Catholic League led by General Tilly. In December 1631, Pope Urban wrote in vain to the king and queen of France and to Cardinal Richelieu, urging them to stop aiding Adolphus and the Protestants in Germany. The following year, the now 73-year-old Tilly, who commanded his army from his deathbed, met Adolphus in battle for the final time. The Swedish king was victorious. With the steadfast Tilly dead, Ferdinand II had to call again upon the untrustworthy Wallenstein.

Wallenstein and Adolphus clashed in the Battle of Lutzen in 1632, one of the most important military turning points in the history of the world. The Swedes prevailed, but Adolphus was killed while leading a cavalry charge. In 1634, the Protestant forces, lacking his military genius, were defeated at the Battle of Nordlingen. The following year, the two sides signed a peace treaty. However, this treaty failed to satisfy the ambitious Richelieu, because it did not weaken Spain or Germany enough. France then openly entered the war. Richelieu declared war on Spain in May 1635, and on the Holy Roman Empire in August 1636.

French military efforts initially met with disaster, and the Spanish counter-attacked, invading French territory. The Hapsburg forces won several victories and even threatened Paris in 1636 before being thrown back toward the borders of France. Widespread fighting ensued, with neither side gaining an advantage. In 1642, Cardinal Richelieu died.

***Death of Gustavus Adolphus of Sweden at the Battle of Lutzen,* Carl Wahlbom**

Witness to the Faith

Peace of Westphalia
A series of treaties that finally ended the Thirty Years' War.

Galileo Galilei
One of the first to teach heliocentrism (that the Earth revolves around the sun), a theory then considered contrary to Scripture, though never officially declared heresy.

Although he lay in his grave, he had achieved his goal. France was the strongest country in Europe. It was also still Catholic, despite all he had done. (Interestingly, Cardinal Richelieu left most of his estate to St. Vincent de Paul.) A year later, Louis XIII died a holy death in the arms of St. Vincent, leaving his 5-year-old son Louis XIV on the throne. His prime minister, Cardinal Jules Mazarin, began working to end the war. When Pope Urban VIII learned of Cardinal Richelieu's death, he said, "If there is a God, Cardinal Richelieu has a lot to answer for. If there be none, he certainly has had a successful career."

A series of treaties, known as the **Peace of Westphalia**, finally ended the Thirty Years' War in 1648. It was an epic moment in the history of the Church. From this moment forward, Christendom would be permanently divided between Catholic and Protestant. All nations that were Protestant in 1624 and all nations that were Catholic in 1624 would remain so. Spain, previously the strongest country in Europe, was in decline. Germany was shattered into various small states. France was now the strongest nation in Europe and would be for nearly 170 years.

Galileo

As the Thirty Years' War raged throughout Europe, the Church dealt with an issue that her enemies still use to attack her after almost four centuries: the matter of **Galileo Galilei**. In the early seventeenth century, Galileo had revived the Copernican theory that the Earth revolved around the sun—that is, the heliocentric theory. At the time, the leading idea was that the sun revolved around the Earth, which was thought to be immovable. This was due to passages in Joshua 10 stating that "the sun stood still" and the "sun halted halfway across the heavens; not for an entire day did it press on." Thus, a theory claiming that the Earth revolved around the sun was considered contrary to Scripture and therefore heretical.

In 1615, Galileo traveled to Rome to defend his heliocentric theory before the Inquisition, which included Cardinal Robert Bellarmine. The Inquisition held that his system was scientifically false and contrary to Scripture, so he must cease teaching it as *fact*. The Inquisition did not say he could not teach it as a hypothesis. Galileo agreed. Cardinal Bellarmine, who found Galileo's ideas interesting, even wrote to him encouraging him in his work.

In 1630, Galileo wrote a book entitled *Dialogue on the Two Great World Systems*, which supported the heliocentric theory. In the book, Galileo made it clear that he considered his theory *as absolutely true, not simply a hypothesis*, and he ridiculed opposing views. His book also included some anti-Copernican comments which Pope Urban VIII had made. Naturally, this made Pope Urban unhappy.

In August 1632, after the Jesuits had publicly criticized the *Dialogue*, Urban established a commission of theologians to examine it. On June 16, 1633, the Inquisition censured Galileo for advocating the

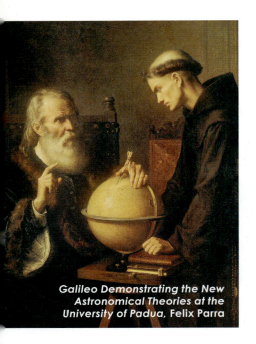

Galileo Demonstrating the New Astronomical Theories at the University of Padua, Felix Parra

424 *Chapter 27: The Fate of France (1600-1700)*

heliocentric view of the universe, which the Inquisition deemed to be contrary to Scripture. It forbade him from teaching the idea, even as a theory, and banned his *Dialogue*. However, the ruling of the committee was disciplinary, not doctrinal. He was not convicted of heresy but of disobedience to his promise of 1616. Moreover, **neither Pope Urban VIII nor any other pope ever declared or taught as a matter of Faith that Galileo's theory was heretical**, although Pope Urban VIII personally felt that it was not scientifically supported.

Catholic Reformation Art

The Protestant Revolt was fought not only on the battlefield with guns and swords, but also on canvas with oil paint and brushes. During the sixteenth and seventeenth centuries, Catholic art and architecture flourished as never before. A new style of art, called Baroque, emerged and became popular. Its greatest supporters were the Jesuits. **Baroque art was a direct response to the iconoclasm of the Protestants, especially the Calvinists, who destroyed beautiful paintings and statues.** In answer to this destruction, the Church created art so magnificent and so breathtaking that even Protestants looked upon it with awe.

As part of its effort to evangelize the people, the Church decided that the arts should communicate religious themes more directly and *create an emotional involvement* in the viewer. Baroque art had an exuberance and joy about it. Baroque churches were covered in pictures painted in bright and glorious colors. Even the ceiling had paintings on it, often showing the Ascension or the Assumption. The walls glittered with gold leaf. There were beautifully carved pillars, pulpits, and choir lofts. Everywhere people looked, they saw paintings of angels and saints. Baroque art drew people into churches. It still does. In a way, the Baroque style seemed to tell people that, in spite of her suffering, the Church had survived, and the Truth she taught had been victorious.

Among the artists credited with the creation of Baroque art is **Michelangelo Merisi da Caravaggio** (1571-1610). Caravaggio introduced intense emotion, dramatic lighting, and an amazing naturalism based on close physical observation to his art. These three elements became the key components of Baroque art. From 1600 until his death, Caravaggio was the most sought-after painter in the world. Sadly, he lived a life of personal immorality, which led to his premature death. But his artistic brilliance influenced generations of painters who followed him. Historians consider him one of the ten greatest painters in history.

The greatest painter of the Baroque Age, as well as one of the finest and most prolific painters in history, was **Peter Paul Rubens** (1577-1640). Rubens numbered the Jesuits among his best clients. For the Jesuits, he created a number of magnificent altarpieces, including *The Miracles of Saint*

> **Baroque**
> An artistic style marked by elaborate detail and dramatic glory; meant to draw the viewer in emotionally.
>
> **Michelangelo Merisi da Caravaggio**
> One of the greatest and most influential of Baroque artists, and even of all artists; introduced the intense emotion, dramatic lighting, and naturalism that became typical of Baroque art.
>
> **Peter Paul Rubens**
> Great Baroque painter of Belgium; produced a vast body of work, shown today all over the world.

The Crucifixion of St. Peter, Caravaggio

Witness to the Faith

The Miracles of Saint Ignatius of Loyola, Peter Paul Rubens

Rembrandt van Rijn
Great Dutch Baroque artist; clever with *chiaroscuro* (the use of light and shadow).

Diego Velazquez
One of the great Spanish artists; worked for King Philip IV, but also created religious images.

Bartolomé Esteban Murillo
Another great Spanish artist; his paintings are almost entirely religious.

Nicholas Poussin
Leading French artist of the seventeenth century.

Francis Xavier and *The Miracles of Saint Ignatius of Loyola*. Rubens and his workshop painted more than two thousand paintings. He was active in his native Belgium, as well as in Italy, Spain, and England. A master of large, imposing canvases, he excelled in painting figures that seem larger than life. His painting *The Last Judgment* is a gigantic canvas, reminiscent of Michelangelo's Sistine Chapel masterpiece by the same name. Because Rubens' body of work is so enormous, most large museums have at least one of his paintings in their collection. The churches in Antwerp, where he lived, possess several of his canvases. Art collectors consider his paintings among the most valuable of the "Old Masters."

Meanwhile, in Holland, another of the great Old Masters was also at work. Historians consider **Rembrandt van Rijn** (1606-1669) not only the greatest Dutch painter but also one of the ten greatest painters in the history of art. Although Rembrandt's mother was Catholic, his father was a Calvinist, and while his own religious beliefs are unclear, he had his children baptized as Calvinists. However, he filled his art with the drama and love of God typical of the Baroque Age.

The key to Rembrandt's genius was his inventive technique. He cleverly manipulated light and shadow to obtain truly remarkable effects. He could depict the serenity of Christ in the *Supper at Emmaus* with just as much ease as the surprise on the faces of Belshazzar and his party guests in *Belshazzar's Feast*.

God blessed Spain with two incredible Baroque painters, **Diego Velazquez** (1599-1669) and **Bartolomé Esteban Murillo** (1618-1682). Velazquez was the court painter for King Philip IV, which meant that he painted a number of portraits of the king and the royal family. However, he also created several religious paintings, most notably *The Coronation of Mary*, *The Adoration of the Magi*, and *The Education of the Virgin*. Velazquez is also considered one of the ten greatest painters of all time.

Bartolomé Esteban Murillo (1618-1682) was born in Seville, the youngest son in a family of fourteen. In 1642, he traveled to Madrid, where he met Diego Velazquez, himself a native of Seville. Velazquez welcomed his young compatriot and gave him access to the royal galleries, where Murillo saw the great masterpieces. Murillo remained in Madrid for three years before returning to Seville, where he spent the rest of his life. In contrast to Velazquez's art, Murillo's body of work consists almost entirely of religious paintings. With the exception of a few portraits and some paintings of street urchins and flower girls, he created very few secular pictures. He is most famous for his magnificent paintings of the Madonna and is considered the world's foremost painter of the Immaculate Conception, for which he possessed a deep devotion. (The doctrine of the Immaculate Conception had been publicly upheld by Pope Paul V in 1617.) Murillo painted this subject more than twenty times without repeating himself.

In France, **Nicholas Poussin** (1594-1665) was the leading artist of the seventeenth century. As a young man, he worked in Rome, but in 1640

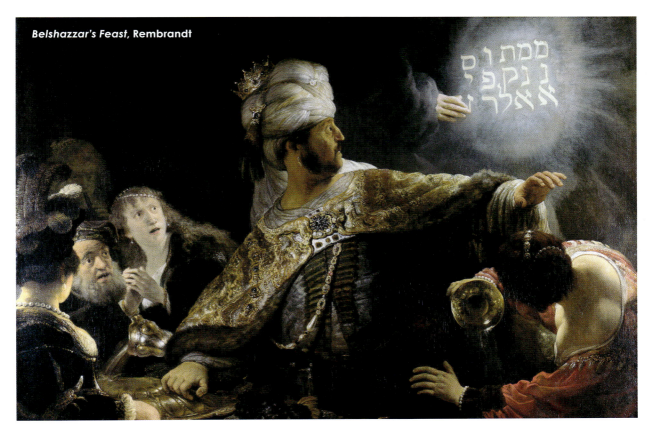
Belshazzar's Feast, Rembrandt

The Coronation of Mary, Diego Velazquez

Immaculate Conception of the Blessed Virgin Mary, Bartolomé Esteban Murillo

Witness to the Faith   427

The Holy Family Arrives in Egypt, Nicholas Poussin

King Louis XIII made him the official court painter, and he returned to Paris. After only two years, he returned to Rome, where he spent the rest of his life. He created a tremendous number of paintings, many of them religious. Among his most famous religious works are a series of paintings on the Seven Sacraments, *The Holy Family Arrives in Egypt*, and *The Adoration of the Golden Calf*.

Christian Music

Many historians consider the Baroque Age to be the golden age of music. Of the three greatest Baroque composers, only one, Mozart, was Catholic. Nevertheless, much of the music of the Baroque Age was essentially Church music, and Catholic Church music at that.

Many historians consider **Johann Sebastian Bach** (1685-1750) to be the greatest composer who ever lived. Bach, who came from a family of musicians and composers, composed more than one hundred and fifty Church cantatas, five Masses, two Passions, and two *oratorios* (large musical compositions including an orchestra, a choir, and a soloist). For the last twenty-seven years of his life, Bach worked as the musical director for the St. Thomas Lutheran Church in Leipzig, where he is buried. Bach is so beloved among Lutherans that they honor him with a feast day.

Bach's contemporary, **George Frederick Handel** (1685-1759), was born in Germany but spent most of his adult life in England. Like Bach, Handel was a prolific composer who wrote forty-two operas, twenty-nine oratorios, and hundreds of lesser works. Handel wrote incredibly beautiful religious music, much of which he based on scenes from the Bible (for example, Israel in Egypt, Samson, and Joshua). His two acclaimed masterpieces are *Judas Maccabaeus* and *Messiah*. Handel's *Messiah* is his most famous work. In *Messiah*, Christians enthusiastically sing the praises of the risen Christ in the most glorious music.

Wolfgang Amadeus Mozart (1756-1791) was born in Austria and raised Catholic. Throughout his life, he remained devoted to the Catholic Faith. Despite a short career, he managed to write six hundred compositions, including operas and symphonies. Many, such as the *Marriage of Figaro* and *The Magic Flute*, are considered some of the finest musical pieces ever composed. Many historians consider his *Requiem Mass*, which was unfinished at his death, to be the pinnacle of Church music.

Devotion to the Sacred Heart

The Baroque Age also witnessed one of the most significant spiritual events in the history of the Church. This event concerned devotion to the Sacred Heart of Jesus. Devotion to the Sacred Heart was not new. St. Bernard, St. Gertrude, and St. Bonaventure had promoted it during the Middle Ages. However, in the last decades of the seventeenth century, it

---

Johann Sebastian Bach, George Frederick Handel, and Wolfgang Amadeus Mozart
The three great composers of the Baroque period.

St. Margaret Mary Alacoque
Nun to whom Jesus Christ appeared and asked for veneration of His Sacred Heart; devotion to the Sacred Heart of Jesus took root and spread because of her visions.

428 *Chapter 27: The Fate of France (1600-1700)*

became one of the most enduring and beloved devotions in the Church because of Our Lord's appearances to a Visitation nun, **St. Margaret Mary Alacoque**.

In 1673, Our Lord began appearing to Margaret Mary Alacoque in her convent at Paray-le-Monial in France. Our Lord requested that His wounded Heart, which was "inflamed with love" for mankind, be venerated, and He promised to bless every place where its image is exposed and honored. He asked St. Margaret Mary to receive Holy Communion frequently and to observe a Holy Hour before the Blessed Sacrament every week. Moreover, He asked that reparation for ingratitude to His Sacred Heart, and for offenses against the Blessed Sacrament, be made through the reception of Holy Communion on the first Friday of each month. He also requested that the Church have a liturgical feast in honor of His Sacred Heart.

Initially, the mother superior of the convent did not believe Sister Margaret Mary. But Margaret Mary eventually received the aid of the convent's chaplain, the Jesuit priest St. Claude de la Colombiere, who declared that her visions were real. In 1683, a new nun was elected mother superior, who also believed in the authenticity of St. Margaret Mary's visions. Three years later, the convent began privately supporting the devotion. Meanwhile, because of Fr. de la Colombiere, the Jesuits also promoted the devotion. However, it would not be until the middle of the eighteenth century that the Church would officially recognize this devotion.

Sister Margaret Mary Alacoque worked her entire life to spread this beautiful devotion to the Sacred Heart of Jesus. She died in 1690 and was buried at the Visitation Monastery in Paray-le-Monial. Her body is incorrupt. In 1920, Pope Benedict XV canonized her.

Father Claude de la Colombiere also served as chaplain to the duchess of York. In November 1678, the English imprisoned him, believing he was engaged in treason. Because he was French, they expelled him from England. But his imprisonment had impaired his health. Fr. Claude died in 1682 at the age of 41. Pope St. John Paul II canonized him in 1992.

Oral Exercises

1. Who helped St. Vincent de Paul found the Daughters of Charity?
2. Where was St. Francis de Sales a bishop?
3. Who helped St. Francis de Sales found the Visitation Order?
4. What was the *Defenestration of Prague*?
5. What was the Edict of Restitution?
6. Why did the Inquisition censure Galileo?
7. Does the Galileo affair disprove papal infallibility? Why or why not?
8. Name three influential Baroque artists.
9. Who is most responsible for spreading the devotion to the Sacred Heart?

Witness to the Faith   **429**

Chapter 28
The Church in the Age of the "Enlightenment" (1700-1774)

Introduction

Following the Thirty Years' War, France became Europe's military, artistic, and intellectual leader. The people of Europe began looking to Paris, the capital of France, rather than Rome, the seat of the papacy, for leadership. As so often happens when people turn from God to men, the consequences were terrible.

The Papacy in the Second Half of the 17th Century

Following the death of Pope Urban VIII, the Sacred College elected Pope Innocent X (1644-1655), over the objections of Cardinal Richelieu's successor, Cardinal Jules Mazarin. Cardinal Mazarin felt that Pope Innocent X was too friendly with Spain, France's longtime foe. Mazarin's objections showed that France was determined to control every aspect of European society, even the Catholic Church.

Pope Innocent X proved to be a strongly orthodox pope, who condemned the French heresy known as **Jansenism**, which in some ways was similar to Calvinism. Jansenism taught that Christ died only for a few elect. It also asserted that human nature is depraved due to Original Sin, and it discouraged frequent reception of Holy Communion. Pope Innocent X also supported the Irish, both spiritually and militarily, when Cromwell invaded Ireland.

> **Jansenism**
> French heresy which taught that Christ died only for a few elect; it also asserted that human nature is depraved due to Original Sin, and it discouraged frequent reception of Holy Communion.

Stained-Glass Window of St. John Baptiste de la Salle

1672 A.D. – 1773 A.D.

1672 A.D.
The Turks attack Poland, nearly taking Ukraine, but Jan Sobieski's army drives them back. Sobieski later becomes king of Poland.

1682 A.D.
King Jan Sobieski and his Polish army defeat an attempted Turkish invasion at Vienna.

1685 A.D.
Louis XIV of France revokes the Edict of Nantes and declares Protestantism illegal.

1725 A.D.
St. John Baptiste de la Salle's Order of Christian Brothers is approved.

1732 A.D.
St. Alphonsus Liguori founds the Redemptorists.

1750-1758 A.D.
Pombal charges the Jesuits with various crimes and is eventually able to banish them from Portugal.

1763-1764 A.D.
The Jesuit schools in France are closed, and the priests themselves are ordered to renounce their vows or be banished.

1767 A.D.
The Jesuits are expelled from Spain and the Spanish territories overseas.

1773 A.D.
Pope Clement XIV issues a Brief of Suppression against the Jesuits, but it is not enforced.

Pope Innocent's successor, Pope Alexander VII (1655-1667) is notable for his support of the Jesuits and for proclaiming the doctrine of the Immaculate Conception in 1661, almost two hundred years before Pope Pius IX infallibly defined it as a dogma. Like Innocent X, Pope Alexander VII also suffered conflicts with the French.

In 1661, Cardinal Mazarin died, and 22-year-old King Louis XIV began to rule France in his own right. At times, Louis behaved like a sincere Catholic; for example, he was determined to root out heresy. On the other hand, he was an **absolute monarch**, who believed that no earthly power should control him. He even tried to exercise control over the Church and the pope. For the rest of his 72-year reign, the longest in European history, he sought to influence papal elections and control the Church.

Witness to the Faith   431

Louis IV's first chance to influence a papal election occurred in 1667, when he told the French cardinals to support the cardinal who became Pope Clement IX (1667-1669). Two years later, after the next conclave had become deadlocked, 80-year-old Clement X (1670-1676) was elected. Pope Clement surprised his fellow cardinals by living more than six years, during which time he helped missionaries in the New World. He also helped the Poles in their struggle against the Muslim Turks.

Jan Sobieski
Became king of Poland after saving Ukraine from a Turkish invasion; defeated the Turks again ater in a crucial battle at Vienna.

In June 1672, the Turks attacked Poland and demanded that the Poles surrender Ukraine to them. Facing the relentless Turkish onslaught, the Poles fell into disarray and were unable to defend Ukraine. It seemed that Ukraine was destined to fall to the Muslims, but at this critical moment, a Polish nobleman named **Jan Sobieski** (soh-byez-kee) raised an army and marched into Ukraine. Sobieski defeated the Turks in September 1672. In October, Pope Clement X proclaimed a crusade. He called for all Catholic rulers to aid Poland in its battle against the Turks. When the Polish Parliament met in January 1674 to elect a new king, Pope Clement told them to elect a man "of spirit." No one in Europe possessed the fighting spirit of Jan Sobieski. The Poles loved the pope and followed his advice. They elected Sobieski. It would prove a most significant decision.

Europe Is Saved

Following the death of Clement X, the Sacred College elected Pope Innocent XI (1676-1689). Innocent came to the throne of St. Peter at a time when Europe faced its greatest peril since the time of Pius V, and from the same enemy: the Muslim Turks.

In May 1682, the Turks launched an attack on Vienna, the capital of the Holy Roman Empire. If Vienna fell, not only would it be a crushing moral blow to Christendom, but it would also open Europe to a Turkish invasion. The very existence of Christendom was at stake. The Turks, realizing the importance of Vienna, attacked the city with an army of over 100,000 soldiers. On July 14, Turkish cannons began to bombard the city.

Sobieski Sending Message of Victory to the Pope after the Battle of Vienna, Jan Matejko

The Holy Roman Emperor called for help from the one man he knew would respond: Jan Sobieski. The Polish king immediately left his capital of Warsaw for Vienna. Along the way, he stopped at the great Polish shrine of Our Lady of Czestochowa (Chens-tah-koh-vuh), home of the Black Madonna. Sobieski would not fight the enemies of the Faith without the power of the Faith to support him.

Meanwhile, Pope Innocent XI called for Catholic rulers to aid Vienna. He called particularly on King Louis XIV of France, the strongest nation in Europe. Louis refused.

On the other hand, Jan Sobieski was marching his army to Vienna. He wrote to Pope Innocent. Sobieski could not promise to save the city, but he did make one promise: he would fight to the death! In early September, Sobieski and his army arrived outside of Vienna. On the morning of September 12, 1682, he personally led his army into battle against the Turks. He swept them from the field of battle like a raging thunderstorm sweeps away leaves. By the afternoon, Vienna and Europe had been saved. Sobieski sent Pope Innocent XI the Turkish battle flag as a trophy.

Louis XIV and the Church

Although King Louis XIV sought to control the papacy, he had limited success. In fact, most of the popes who governed during Louis' reign opposed him. However, in France itself, Louis continually exerted more control over the Church.

Cardinal Richelieu had made the king the supreme power in France, and Louis was determined to exercise that power. The Church came more and more under the control of King Louis, and bishops and priests became more like government employees than religious leaders. The effect on the Church was, of course, devastating, as unworthy men became priests and bishops. Moreover, the laity of France began to associate the Church with the government.

Louis began to exercise control over the appointment of bishops. He claimed that the pope only had the right to confirm bishops that he appointed. Louis convened a national synod and demanded that the French clergy agree that the pope was not infallible, even in matters of faith and morals, unless the universal Church agreed with him, and that a general council had greater authority than the pope. Pope Innocent XI condemned these decrees and refused to confirm the appointment of any bishop who supported them.

Louis XIV of France, Hyacinthe Rigaud

In response, Louis imprisoned the papal nuncio. Louis might even have attacked Rome, but he was engaged in so many wars with his European neighbors that he could not afford to send an army there. Eventually, he made peace with the pope.

Since the beginning of the seventeenth century, Catholic evangelists such as St. Francis de Sales had managed to reconvert large numbers of Huguenots. Over the course of the century, the number of Calvinist preachers and churches dwindled. The nobility counted few Calvinists in its numbers. Most Calvinists were merchants and farmers. Because they were no longer the leaders of society, the French government had chosen largely to leave them alone and respect the religious liberty that the Edict of Nantes had given them.

When Louis XIV came to power, he took a more dynamic attitude toward the conversion of the Huguenots. To lead this effort, Louis chose the Bishop of Meaux, Jacques-Bénigne Bossuet, the foremost orator and one of the most brilliant clerics in Europe. While Bishop Bossuet had

Witness to the Faith

success among the nobility, he made little progress with the middle class. When the Huguenots refused conversion, Louis renounced the Edict of Nantes in October 1685 and declared Protestantism illegal in France. As a result, perhaps as many as 400,000 Huguenots emigrated; many came to the French colonies in the New World.

The Rise of Rationalism

Rationalism
The belief that human reason alone is sufficient to attain truth and guide one's behavior, with no need for guidance from Divine Grace.

Among its many false doctrines, the Protestant Revolt had taught that, by using reason, each person could interpret Sacred Scripture according to his own designs: the doctrine of the "priesthood of the believer." Over time, some people came to the logical conclusion that if they could use reason to learn divine truths, then there was no need for a church to guide them. Some philosophers took this a step further and began to claim that there was no need for guidance from Divine Grace; they believed that human reason alone was sufficient to attain truth and guide one's behavior. This way of thinking is called **rationalism**.

The Enlightenment
A philosophical movement beginning in the seventeenth and eighteenth centuries which regarded only the material world and human reason as reliable, considering all religion as superstition.

During the seventeenth and eighteenth centuries, rationalism continually exerted a greater influence on the leaders of European society. These rationalist thinkers began a movement that they called the **Enlightenment**. They named their movement the "Enlightenment" because they claimed that they had *enlightened* the world from the darkness of superstition that the Catholic Church had imposed upon the world through religious faith. In other words, they falsely claimed that the truths of the Faith had kept men and women in darkness, but now their new rationalist philosophy, free from God, would "enlighten" them. Of course, the rationalists ignored the fact that the Church had started all the schools and universities in Europe since the fall of the Roman Empire.

Rationalists had no respect for the teachings of the Church, the Church Fathers, or the intellectual traditions of Christianity. They placed all their "faith" in human reason. They felt that human beings would achieve goodness and could find happiness if they could be allowed to follow their own inclinations. The Church and its rules, such as the Ten Commandments, were the obstacles that stood in the way of people's perfect happiness. The rationalists wholeheartedly embraced history's second oldest "faith": faith in man. The serpent had first preached this "faith" to Eve in the Garden. Sadly, this was a period when there was a general decline in Catholic fervor.

Deism

Deism
Belief that all knowledge of God is based on reason and nature alone, not supernatural revelation. Deists believe that God exists, but that He has little or no involvement with the world He created.

Rationalists in England called their philosophy **Deism**, which is the belief that all knowledge of God is based on reason and nature alone, not supernatural revelation. Deists believe that God exists, but that He has little or no involvement with the world He created. In other words, after He created the world, He left it to itself and does not interfere with it. According to this viewpoint, God can be compared to a watchmaker, who makes a very beautiful and intricate watch and then lets it run on its own. Thus, Deists recognize no miracles or Divine Providence.

434 *Chapter 28: The Church in the Age of the "Enlightenment" (1700-1774)*

The Enlightenment in France

It was in France that rationalism gained its greatest and most devoted adherents. France had become Europe's leader in most areas, including intellectual disciplines. Many of the most revered thinkers in Europe were French. These thinkers exerted a great deal of influence over the nobility and leaders of France, who had become very worldly during the reign of Louis XIV.

The leading French thinker of the time, who is considered the "great apostle of the Enlightenment," was a man named Francois-Marie Arouet, whom history now knows as **Voltaire** (1694-1778). Voltaire had a brilliant mind; however, he used it against the Church. He considered it his mission in life to destroy Christianity and the Catholic Church. His entire life's work can be summarized in his favorite phrase, "*Ecrasons l'Infame*" ("Let us crush the infamous thing")—that is, the Catholic Church. Voltaire ridiculed everything sacred and holy. He thought that by mocking the Church and religion, he could destroy it.

There was also in France a small group of writers called the *philosophes*. They rallied around Voltaire and wrote articles expressing their materialistic view of the world and their disdain for religion. They published these articles in the main journal of French rationalism, the *Encyclopedia*. The *philosophes* considered religion nothing more than superstition. They hated the Catholic Church because of its firm stand on matters of doctrine, especially issues pertaining to morality. The main author of the *Encyclopedia* was Denis Diderot. Diderot's most fervent desire was that "the last king might be strangled with the entrails of the last priest."

Another very influential French Enlightenment thinker was **Jean-Jacques Rousseau**. Unlike Voltaire, Rousseau did not rant against Catholicism, but he proposed many false and dangerous ideas. He explained his corrupt ideas about education, marriage, and the family in a novel he wrote, called *Emile*. Many of the erroneous ideas about education that exist today can be traced back to Rousseau. The archbishop of Paris, Christopher de Beaumont, condemned the ideas that Rousseau presented in *Emile*. He declared that this book sought to destroy the foundations of Christianity and to promote moral standards that were contrary to the Gospel.

In his book *Confessions*, Rousseau mocked morality. Because he was an exciting and influential writer, his books led many people away from the truth and lowered moral standards. In *The Social Contract*, Rousseau developed the political principle that the right to govern is derived, not from God, but *solely* from the people. As such, the people could at any time destroy the government, since they empower it.

Voltaire

> **Voltaire**
> Leading French thinker and writer who is considered "the great apostle of the Enlightenment"; sought to destroy Christianity and the Catholic Church.

> **Jean-Jacques Rousseau**
> French Enlightenment thinker who proposed false and dangerous ideas about education, marriage, the family, and government.

The Enemies of the Jesuits

Unfortunately, the Enlightenment was more than just a group of idle, well-dressed men sitting around card tables in France and chatting about their hatred for religion. It was actually an attack on the Church. The enemies of the Church knew that to destroy her, they first had to destroy her most effective defenders: the Jesuits.

Since their inception, the Jesuits had been the Church's front-line troops in the war against the Protestant Revolt. Other orders had also waged this battle, but the Jesuits had been the most visible and vocal. Moreover, the Jesuits had been incredibly effective. Through their schools and mission efforts, they had reconverted tens of thousands of Protestants and brought them back into the Church. By the beginning of the seventeenth century, the Jesuits were running seven hundred colleges and schools and more than three hundred missions around the world. Additionally, the Jesuits exerted a great deal of influence over many European kings and princes to whom they acted as personal confessors and tutors. If the enemies of the Faith were to be victorious, they needed to destroy the Jesuits. Voltaire himself declared: "Once we have destroyed the Jesuits we will have the game in our hands." Surprisingly, despite the number of enemies the Jesuits had in France, the first attack against them came, not in France, but in strongly Catholic Portugal.

Portugal

In 1640, Portugal won its independence from Spain. Over the following century, it maintained its staunchly Catholic identity. In 1750, Portugal was a loyally Catholic nation where the Protestant revolt had made no impact. Yet, even in the most Catholic nations, there are enemies of the Church, and at this moment one such man, the **Marquis de Pombal**, came into power in Portugal. He was the prime minister for Portugal's weak monarch, King Joseph I. Pombal wanted to destroy the Jesuits and the Church so that, in his mind, he could enrich and strengthen Portugal.

Pombal's opportunity occurred in 1750 when he signed a treaty with Spain. Under the treaty, Portugal exchanged land for the seven districts of Spanish-controlled Paraguay, where the Jesuit reductions were located. (Pombal may have believed that the reductions contained gold mines.) When the land exchange was complete, the Jesuits tried to relocate the natives to land that was not controlled by Portugal. However, during the harsh journey from the reductions, the natives revolted and were suppressed by Spanish and Portuguese troops. Although the Jesuits were working to help the natives, Pombal immediately blamed the Jesuits for the deaths of the locals. He had several Jesuits arrested and charged with horrendous crimes, mostly to publicly embarrass them. Knowing that only the pope had the authority to suppress the Jesuits, Pombal requested that Pope Benedict XIV investigate the charges he had leveled against them.

Marquis de Pombal

Marquis de Pombal
Prime minister for King Joseph I of Portugal; banished the Jesuits from that country.

436 Chapter 28: The Church in the Age of the "Enlightenment" (1700-1774)

In many ways, Pope Benedict XIV (1740-1758) was an excellent choice for the Jesuits. Although he had been chosen as a compromise candidate after a six-month conclave, he was a good man dedicated to defending the Church in an era of terrible anticlericalism. His efforts resolved many issues with European monarchs who were determined to usurp papal authority by appointing bishops. When he learned that Pombal wanted him to investigate the charges against the Jesuits, he was willing, but very skeptical of the charges. Nevertheless, he appointed Cardinal Saldanha to investigate. Sadly, the 83-year-old Benedict died five weeks later. Meanwhile, Pombal continued to work for the expulsion of the Jesuits from Portugal.

The conclave of 1758 faced one of the greatest challenges in the history of the Church: the possible suppression of the Jesuits. The man the Sacred College elected would need the courage and determination of St. Peter or St. Leo the Great—men who had been willing to die for the Faith. In 1758, the Sacred College elected **Pope Clement XIII** (1758-1769). Clement was a good and holy man. He would bend, but he would not break.

Meanwhile, as Clement's election was ongoing, Cardinal Saldanha had ignored Pope Benedict's instructions and, without hearing any evidence from the Jesuits, decided against them. He ordered the withdrawal of their faculties in Lisbon. In September 1758, a plot to murder the king was discovered, and, although no evidence implicated the Jesuits, they were blamed. Many Jesuits were arrested, and their schools were closed. The following September, Pombal banished the Jesuits from Portugal. He had them all arrested. Some, he exiled to the Papal States; others, he imprisoned. In one of the great ironies of history, after Pombal had fallen from power and been abandoned by his friends, he ended up dying in the arms of a Jesuit priest.

France

Meanwhile, in France, the enemies of the Jesuits were waiting for their opportunity to imitate Pombal's example. Perhaps no other nation had so many able people committed to the destruction of the Jesuits. Led by men like Voltaire, the enemies of France's Jesuits were determined to suppress the order. However, unlike in Portugal, the French Jesuits had protection from the king. Louis XIV had died in 1715, leaving his 5-year-old great-grandson to become Louis XV. The now-grown Louis XV, despite living a personally immoral life, supported the Jesuits. Thus, the enemies of the order had to proceed cautiously. They needed an excuse to suppress the Jesuits. It came in May 1761.

Pope Clement XIII
Pope from 1758 to 1769; steadfastly defended the Jesuits against their enemies all over Europe.

Pope Clement XIII

Witness to the Faith

King Louis XV of France

The Jesuits had established a mission on the French island of Martinique in the Caribbean. They employed the local population on the mission lands, and used the money the mission earned to promote both the spiritual welfare and the physical prosperity of the people. The mission was so successful that Father Antoine La Valette, the leader of the mission, borrowed money to expand it. He expected to be able to repay the money, but circumstances in 1755 that were beyond his control made it impossible.

In response, La Valette's creditors in France demanded that the Jesuits in France repay the money. The French Jesuits refused, arguing that there was no connection between the Jesuits in France and those in Martinique. Based on the organization of the Jesuit Order, their argument was sound. The different houses of the order were independent of one another. The resources of each house came from different sources and were allocated to different missions. Nevertheless, Father La Valette's creditors insisted on bringing the case to trial, and the local French court decided in their favor. Believing that the court had erred, the Jesuits appealed the decision to the French Parliament.

The appeal to Parliament was a fatal mistake. Parliament was filled with enemies of the Jesuits, who took this opportunity to launch an investigation into the entire Jesuit Order in France, not merely the La Valette matter. Beginning in April 1762, Parliament launched its attack on the Jesuits, accusing them of various criminal and immoral acts. A few months later, Parliament declared that it was illegal for the Jesuits to remain in France.

To his credit, King Louis XV objected to Parliament's declaration, and for eight months tried to protect the Jesuits. Despite his protests, Parliament's order went into effect on April 1, 1763. The government closed all the Jesuit colleges in France. In March 1764, the Jesuits were required to renounce their vows or be banished. However, the fighting spirit of St. Ignatius of Loyola was alive in the hearts of these noble priests; all but a handful of them refused to renounce their vows. In November 1764, King Louis unwillingly signed an edict dissolving the Jesuit Order throughout French territory.

Spain

In March 1766, the most Catholic nation in Europe, Spain, launched its own attack on the Jesuits. At the time, the king of Spain was Charles III. Although he was personally a decent man, he was a weak king, influenced by advisors who loathed the Jesuits. Much of the real power in Spain lay in the hands of the Count of Aranda, who hated the Jesuits. In March 1766, an angry mob stormed the royal palace to protest an unpopular law. King Charles, fearing for his life, fled. Jesuit priests appeared to quell the riot and disperse the crowd. Yet Aranda and his followers accused the Jesuits of causing the riot and fomenting rebellion in an attempt to overthrow King Charles.

Rather than ignoring these charges as clearly nonsensical, Charles appointed a commission to investigate them. Apparently unbeknownst to him, the commission was filled with men who wished to suppress the Jesuits. They informed King Charles that the charges were true. Charles ordered a commission to create a plan to expel the Jesuits from Spain. He sent secret orders to every magistrate in any town where a Jesuit lived. On the morning of April 2, 1767, the magistrates opened their orders and arrested all 6,000 Jesuits living in Spain. Despite the protests of Pope Clement XIII, Charles marched the priests to the coast and deported them to the Papal States.

King Charles III of Spain

The Jesuits were also expelled from Spain's overseas lands in Mexico, the Philippines, and elsewhere. In late June of 1767, Spanish soldiers expelled the Jesuits from their missions in Mexico. In 1769, they were forced to leave the Philippines. The natives were heartbroken at the loss of their priests, but short of open rebellion, there was nothing they could do.

In Naples, King Ferdinand IV, the son of Charles III, followed his father's example and suppressed the Jesuits there. He also arrested the Jesuits and had his soldiers deport them to the Papal States.

The Suppression of the Jesuits

At this point, the Catholic kings of Europe now joined together to destroy the Church's greatest defenders and attack the pope. Louis XIV had been a member of the **Bourbon family**. During his reign, through marriages, wars, and political maneuvers, he had placed members of his family on the thrones of many European nations. The Bourbon kings of Europe, including France and Spain, banded together in an unholy alliance, whose goal was the suppression of the Jesuits. The Bourbon rulers threatened, harassed, and insulted Pope Clement XIII to his face. Despite the threats to the Church and to his own person, Clement remained steadfast in his support for the Jesuits. In the end, the constant harassment proved too much for the elderly pontiff. Clement XIII died on February 2, 1769, after one of the most heroic pontificates in Church history. His death was no doubt hastened by the ill treatment he had received at the hands of his rebellious subjects. He was 75.

> **Bourbon family**
> The royal family of France in the seventeenth and eighteenth centuries; came to rule in other European nations, including Spain.

Witness to the Faith

Pope Clement XIV

As the conclave met to elect a successor to Pope Clement XIII, the cardinals needed to address only one question: what would the new pope do with the Jesuits? Although none of the cardinals specifically promised to suppress the Jesuits, Cardinal Lorenzo Ganganelli made it known that if he were elected, the Bourbon rulers would have a friend on the throne of St. Peter. In May 1769, he was elected pope. He chose the name **Clement XIV** (1769-1774). It was an interesting choice for a man who had hinted that he would suppress the Jesuits. The prior Pope Clement had defended them to the death! Meanwhile, the Bourbons waited.

In the history of the papacy, unworthy men have become pope. However, sitting in the Chair of St. Peter, supported by the power and guidance of the Holy Spirit, does something to the soul of a man. The story of Pope Vigilius (537-555), the only antipope to become pope, is one remarkable example of a man who underwent a complete change of heart. Clement XIV seems to have been deeply affected by the Chair of St. Peter as well. Whatever *Cardinal* Ganganelli had promised, or seemed to have promised, in order to be elected, when he became *Pope* Clement XIV, he took no action against the Jesuits. In fact, the more the kings of Europe pushed him to suppress them, the more steadfast he became in his refusal to do so. For four years, Pope Clement XIV resisted every sort of pressure that was brought to bear as he negotiated for the life of the Society of Jesus.

Clement XIV
Pope who suppressed the Jesuits in 1773, under pressure from the kings of Europe.

Finally, in 1773, King Charles III threatened to take Spain out of the Church unless Clement suppressed the Jesuits. It seems highly unlikely that he could have really done so, however. The Spain of St. Ignatius of Loyola, St. John of the Cross, and St. Teresa of Avila would never leave the Church. Spain was still the most Catholic country in Europe. The Spanish still loved the Jesuits and the pope. A strong pope might have had the courage to call the king's bluff—and over the next 230 years, the Holy Spirit would bless the Church with some of its finest pontiffs, including several saints and one called "the Great"—but Pope Clement XIV was not the measure of these men.

Chapter 28: The Church in the Age of the "Enlightenment" (1700-1774)

In 1773, Pope Clement XIV issued the Brief of Suppression against the Jesuits. To indicate that he acted unwillingly, he intentionally did not include the customary phrase *motu proprio* (of our own accord). The brief made no charges against the Jesuits. It placed no blame on the Jesuit Order as a whole or on the conduct of any individual Jesuit. It contained no condemnation of any Jesuit teachings. Pope Clement merely stated that "the Church could not enjoy true and lasting peace so long as the Society remained in existence." In other words, he suppressed the Jesuits for being divisive. Once the brief was published, the bishops communicated its contents to the Jesuits in their dioceses.

Interestingly, the Jesuits were never fully suppressed, because certain non-Catholic rulers refused to publish the suppression brief. In Russia, Empress Catherine the Great, a Russian Orthodox ruler, did not publish the suppression document, so the Jesuits in Russia continued to teach in the two colleges they had established in Russia. Catherine appreciated the quality of a Jesuit education and refused to allow the colleges to be closed, even by the pope. Her successors requested that the Jesuits be allowed to continue teaching and, in 1778, Pope Pius VI approved this arrangement. The Jesuits continued to recruit members and operate schools in Russia.

Protestant ruler Frederick the Great of Prussia also admired the Jesuits. He refused to publish the suppression order, so the Jesuits worked in Prussia for many years.

Pope Clement XIV fell ill shortly after issuing the suppression decree. On his deathbed, he stated that he had cut off his right hand. He died on September 22, 1774. Following the issuance of the suppression decree, Voltaire felt that he had won a great victory. He declared that in twenty years (1793), the Church would be no more. He was very nearly correct.

New Religious Orders

Even as the enemies of the Church were attacking its greatest defenders, holy saints were forming new religious orders. For example, in 1705, St. Louis de Montfort founded the Company of

St. Louis de Montfort

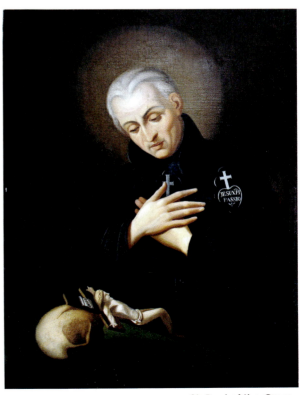

St. Paul of the Cross

Witness to the Faith 441

St. John Baptiste de la Salle
Priest who founded the Christian Brothers to educate poor boys; he is regarded as one of the founders of modern education.

St. Alphonsus Liguori
Founder of the Redemptorists, an order focused on preaching and spiritual direction; expert in moral theology and author of important theological works.

Mary, a missionary congregation. In 1725, St. Paul of the Cross founded the Passionists, a religious order with a special devotion to Our Lord's Passion. Among two of the more important orders started during this time were the Christian Brothers, founded by St. John Baptiste de la Salle, and the Redemptorists, established by St. Alphonsus Liguori.

St. John Baptiste de la Salle (1651-1714) served as a priest at the Cathedral of Reims in France. Part of his vocation was to act as the spiritual director for the Sisters of the Child Jesus. The sisters cared for and educated poor French girls.

At this time, unless members of the lower or middle classes entered the Church, they had little chance to advance socially or economically. Father La Salle realized that an education would give them the opportunity to lead better lives. Therefore, he founded a religious order of men who would provide an education to poor boys. For this purpose, he founded a religious organization composed of lay brothers. He called the members of his congregation the Institute of the Brothers of the Christian Schools. In the United States, they are more commonly known as the Christian Brothers. Pope Benedict XIII approved the order in 1725.

St. Alphonsus Liguori

442 Chapter 28: The Church in the Age of the "Enlightenment" (1700-1774)

To prepare members of his Christian Brothers for a career in teaching, St. John founded the first teacher's college. He also worked out a system whereby a number of children could be taught in a class at the same time. John Baptiste de la Salle is rightly regarded as *one of the founders of modern education.*

St. Alphonsus Liguori (1696-1787) founded the Congregation of the Most Holy Redeemer (the Redemptorists) in 1732. The mission of the Redemptorists is to preach the Gospel and provide spiritual direction to people. The order developed very rapidly. When St. Alphonsus was crippled with arthritis and no longer able to travel around the country preaching, he focused on his writing. A prolific writer and an expert in moral theology, he published a nine-volume work called *Moral Theology*. He also published his famous *The Glories of Mary* and *The Way of the Cross*. Pope Gregory XVI canonized him in 1839, and Pope Pius IX proclaimed him a Doctor of the Church in 1871.

A Light in the Darkness

The Enlightenment had resulted in the suppression of the Jesuits, the Church's greatest defenders. The next pope would face a Europe, not enlightened, but cloaked in darkness. He would do battle against one of the Church's greatest enemies and, after perhaps the most heroic pontificates in Church history, die in exile as a humble monk.

St. John Baptiste de la Salle

Oral Exercises

1. What Polish leader saved Vienna from the Turks?
2. What is rationalism?
3. What is Deism?
4. Who is considered the "great apostle of the Enlightenment"?
5. Name one French Enlightenment thinker.
6. Who was Pombal?
7. Which pope suppressed the Jesuits?
8. To what royal family did the kings who threatened Pope Clement XIII belong?
9. Who founded the Christian Brothers?
10. Who founded the Redemptorists?

Witness to the Faith 443

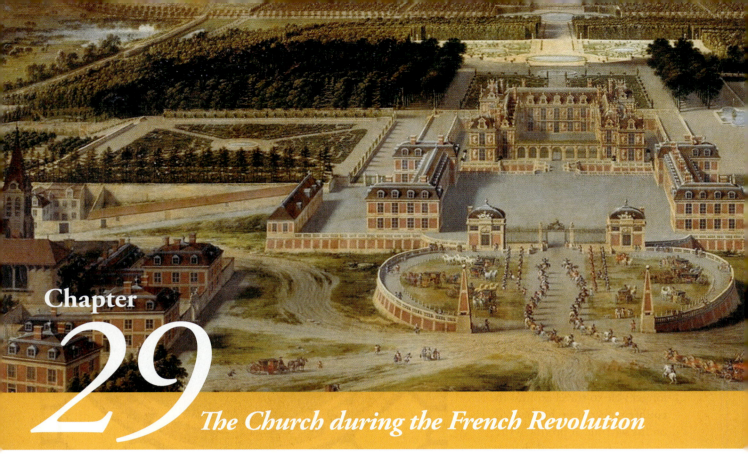

Chapter 29
The Church during the French Revolution

Introduction

A **revolution** is the overthrow of a government or social order, often through violence and other extreme measures. The *Catechism of the Catholic Church* (no. 2243) states that armed resistance to oppression by political authority is legitimate if, and only if, certain specific moral criteria are met. A revolution against one's government is a very serious matter, not to be undertaken without grave reasons and careful consideration of the consequences. As corrupt as many governments are, responding with violence, without truly considering the common good, can lead to even worse problems.

Unlike the American War for Independence, which sought to change the government, the French Revolution (as well as the Communist Revolution in Russia in 1917, which will be discussed in a later chapter) sought to change society itself. Changing the government was only part of the goal. The great enemy of the French Revolution was the Catholic Church, because this revolution put man in the place of God. As such, anything that helped the revolution to succeed was considered by the revolutionaries to be justified. Once the French Revolution began and this mindset took hold, the Reign of Terror that soon followed was inevitable.

> **Revolution**
> The overthrow of a government or social order, often through violence and other extreme measures.

The Palace of Versailles, Pierre Patel

1789 A.D. – 1794 A.D.

1789 A.D.
On May 5, the Estates General meets for the first time in 175 years. In late June, the National Assembly is formed. On July 14, a revolutionary mob storms the Bastille in Paris, murdering the garrison and the mayor of Paris.

1790 A.D.
The Civil Constitution of the Clergy becomes law. All priests and bishops are required to take an oath supporting it. The clergy in France are separated into "jurors" (those who take the oath) and "non-jurors" (those who refuse).

1791 A.D.
The new government abolishes the contemplative orders and creates a new State church to replace the Catholic Church.

1792 A.D.
The revolutionaries attack the royal palace and depose and imprison King Louis XVI and his family. Priests, religious, and other Catholics begin to be martyred in great numbers.

1793 A.D.
The king and queen are executed. France is at war with most of western Europe. Catholics of the Vendee rise up to free their country from the Reign of Terror, but are unable to take the city of Nantes.

1794 A.D.
In the spring, Robespierre has Danton killed. That July, Robespierre himself is killed by colleagues who fear that he might otherwise order their deaths.

Modern Distortions about the French Revolution

Modern secular historians teach that the uprising in France was spontaneous and driven by the overwhelming oppression of the people by the king and the nobility. They teach that the Paris prison, the *Bastille*, was filled with prisoners when the mob stormed the Bastille and released them. In reality, there were only seven prisoners. They portray Queen Marie Antoinette as an empty-headed girl. As proof, they claim that, when she was told the peasants had no bread, she said, "Then let them eat cake." However, she did not say these words. (Actually, it was the wife of Louis XIV, Marie's great-great-grandmother, who said this.) Marie was a devout Catholic and a devoted mother who oppressed no one. As in most things involving the Church and the attacks

Witness to the Faith   445

Louis XVI of France

upon her, her defenders are attacked, and her attackers are applauded. However, the actions of the French Revolutionaries were so heinous that even those who defend them admit that they went too far.

Why Did the French Revolution Happen?

France in the 1780s was a country with problems, but none so severe as to lead to a revolution. Before the revolution, France had been at peace for six years. There was no famine or pestilence. Although there was not an overabundance of food, the people had enough to eat. The ideas of the Enlightenment, while somewhat popular among the nobility, had not really touched the common people. The common people were not clamoring for a change in religion. Unlike Voltaire and his followers, the common people loved the Catholic Church. There was also no political group calling for the overthrow of the government, because there was no systematic oppression of the people. The problems with the government were mainly problems of neglect. Those in power were not doing their jobs very well. When people were oppressed, it was more from omission than commission.

Still, France had problems. The Estates General, the national representative body, had not met in almost 175 years before it met in 1789. This shows that the government had lost contact with the people. Reform was needed. But nothing in France's history can fully explain why this revolution occurred. The only other event similar to the French Revolution is the Communist Revolution in Russia in 1917. However, in Russia, there was war, famine, pestilence, and a group calling for revolution.

Moreover, the violence and hatred that so many people expressed toward the Church during the French Revolution is shocking, given the conditions of eighteenth-century France. First, the population of France was about 95 percent Catholic; the rest were Huguenots. Second, the Church provided all primary and secondary education in France. The people of France received a Catholic education. Third, the Church ran the charitable organizations, including hospitals and orphanages. It cared for the sick and the poor. In almost every aspect of daily life, the Catholic Church was the leading influence on the people of France, who loved the Church.

Furthermore, contrary to modern secular propaganda, the priests and bishops of France were not leading corrupt and decadent lives at the expense of their parishioners. Most French clerics led lives characterized by self-denial and a deep devotion to the Faith and their parishioners. The greatest evidence for this can be seen in the heroic virtue these clerics displayed when faced with mass martyrdom at the hands of the revolutionaries.

Calling of the Estates General

By 1789, the French government was running out of money. Moreover, King Louis XVI had tried every method to obtain enough money to run his government. On the advice of his finance minister, and with no other choice, Louis convoked the **Estates General**. Because of the nature of the French monarchy, as shaped by Cardinal Richelieu, the Estates General had not met since 1614.

The Estates General consisted of three groups, or Estates. In recognition of their importance and the esteem in which the people held them, the First Estate consisted of the entire clergy, both priests and bishops. The Second Estate consisted of France's nobility. The Third Estate included everyone else—that is, the common people. Of the 1200 deputies elected to the Estates General, more than half were from the Third Estate.

Each of the Estates elected its own deputies. The local assemblies that selected the deputies also drew up *cahiers*, or grievance lists, which the deputies took with them to Paris. The cahiers denounced absolute royal power, infringements on personal liberty, and unjust taxation. However, no complaint was made against the monarchy or the Church. The Estates General assembled on May 5, 1789, at the royal palace of Versailles, about 12 miles from Paris.

The National Assembly

Almost immediately, the Third Estate began demanding that fundamental changes be made to the government. They proposed to form a single assembly of the three-branch Estates General. King Louis, the nobles, and most of the clergy opposed this idea. The meetings became noisy debates, as the Third Estate lurched from crisis to crisis.

In an attempt to gain control of the situation, King Louis locked the doors to the hall where

> **Estates General**
> The three groups composing the French government: the clergy, the nobles, and deputies representing the common people.

Opening of the Estates General, May 5, 1789

Witness to the Faith 447

The National Assembly Taking the Tennis Court Oath, Jacques-Louis David

Bastille
Paris' fortress prison, stormed at the beginning of the French Revolution. Seven prisoners were freed, and the garrison and the mayor were killed.

the Estates General had been meeting. The deputies of the Third Estate, along with their supporters in the First and Second Estates, moved to a nearby tennis court, where they continued to meet. In late June 1789, they declared themselves the National Assembly. They said they represented all the people of France. They swore not to disband until France had a new and written constitution. Although Louis had the soldiers to crush the National Assembly, he hesitated. After more of the nobles and clergy joined the Third Estate in the National Assembly, he consented to its existence.

Storming the Bastille

Meanwhile, revolutionary agitators were active among the people of Paris. These agitators claimed that the **Bastille** (Paris' fortress prison) was full of innocent prisoners being held for their political beliefs. In reality, the Bastille contained only seven prisoners: four forgers, one felon, and two insane men! Nevertheless, on the morning of July 14, a mob gathered before the prison. The mob stormed the Bastille. They murdered the garrison and the mayor of Paris. This grisly event marked the "triumph" of the Parisians over the authorities. Sadly, this day is still celebrated in France as a national holiday.

Suppression of the Church

For the revolutionaries, their most critical job was to destroy "the infamous thing," the Catholic Church. In November 1789, the National Assembly seized the property of the Catholic Church, which it then sold. In return for the money received from the sale of the stolen property, the government took on the task of supporting the Church and the clergy. Priests and bishops thus became paid employees of the French government. In the spring of 1790, the monasteries, convents, and other religious houses were suppressed. The government sold the land and other possessions.

The new government's next step was to deprive the clergy of their liberty. The Assembly accomplished this by enacting the **Civil Constitution of the Clergy**. This document completely reorganized the Church in France. It granted all French citizens, regardless of their religious affiliation, the right to elect bishops and pastors. Thus, Protestants and even atheists could vote for Catholic bishops and priests. The priests of the parish were to have no say in the matter, and the pope could not intervene in any way. On August 24, 1790, the Civil Constitution of the Clergy became law.

When Pope Pius VI (1775-1799) was presented with the Civil Constitution of the Clergy, he privately rejected it. His rejection caused the National Assembly to demand that all clergy in France take an oath to support it. A substantial majority of France's clergy heroically refused. Only six of the 134 French bishops took the oath. The question of the oath split the Church in France into two factions. Those who took the oath were known as *jurors* (from the Latin *jurare*, meaning "to take an oath"). Those who refused to swear the oath were known as the *non-jurors*.

In February 1791, the revolutionaries openly moved against the Church. On February 13, the National Assembly abolished all religious orders in France except those engaged in teaching or charitable works. Thus, **all the contemplative orders were closed down**. One week later, on February 20, the Assembly created its own "church" to replace the Catholic Church. Any bishop who remained loyal to Pope Pius VI and refused to swear the oath to the Civil Constitution of the Clergy was to be replaced by a "bishop" willing to swear this oath.

In March 1791, Pope Pius VI publicly condemned the Civil Constitution of the Clergy. He prohibited priests from taking the oath. Many priests who had taken the oath retracted their promise after the pope's public condemnation.

> **Civil Constitution of the Clergy**
> A document making priests and bishops mere elected officials, chosen purely by the citizens, regardless of those people's religion.

The Storming of the Bastille, Jean-Pierre Houel

Witness to the Faith

Maximilien Robespierre
Leader of the government of the French Revolution.

Georges-Jacques Danton
Important revolutionary leader who became head of the Committee of Public Safety, but was later executed by Robespierre.

In November 1791, all the clergy in France were required to take the oath within eight days. If they declined, the government would stop paying their salaries and expel them from their parishes. King Louis XVI bravely refused to approve these and similar measures. When in the end he lost his crown and his life, it was due in part to this refusal.

Louis XVI Becomes a Prisoner

On August 10, 1792, the revolutionary mob attacked the royal palace. They massacred the king's Swiss Guard, who had laid down their weapons at King Louis' command. The enraged mob killed every man they could find in the palace who had served the king, from noblemen to cooks. The Assembly then deposed and imprisoned the king and his family, despite promises in the new constitution that he would remain untouched. The election of a new legislative body, the National Convention, was ordered. In one stroke, the revolutionaries had ended the monarchy, the constitution, and the existing Assembly.

The September Massacres

On September 5, 1792, elections were held for the National Convention. The first deputy elected was **Maximilien Robespierre**, who would become the architect of the Reign of Terror. Next elected was **Georges-Jacques Danton**. Danton emerged as a leader when he was elected as Minister of Justice in the new government.

Prior to August 10, 1792, the penalty for failing to take the oath to support the Civil Constitution of the Clergy was the loss of the priest's parish or diocese. This was a severe penalty for most priests, whose only source of income was from the parish. However, after August 10, when King Louis XVI was deposed, the penalty became even more severe: the non-jurors were treated as traitors. By August 15, 1792, the new government of France began to arrest them. What followed was one of the greatest persecutions of the Church since the days of the Roman Empire.

On September 2, 1792, the martyrdoms began. In less than 2 hours, 120 priests suffered martyrdom. That night, 76 more priests perished. For four days, the streets of Paris ran red with the blood of the martyrs, as thousands died. Many of those killed were priests and nuns, as well as other religious. Some of those killed were "guilty" only of treating those going to their deaths with kindness.

Storming of the Tuileries on August 10, 1792, Jean Duplessis-Bertaux

450   CHAPTER 29: The Church during the French Revolution

Toward the end of 1792, the clergy began to leave France. They fled to Spain, Germany, England, the United States, and especially the Papal States, where they were warmly welcomed. Despite the mortal danger, many priests remained in France. Disguised, they continued to bring the sacraments to the people of France.

The Execution of King Louis XVI

On September 21, 1792, the first regular session of the National Convention met. The Convention had three tasks before it. It needed to decide the fate of imprisoned King Louis, create a more permanent government, and decide how best to continue waging the war in which France was engaged. The Convention abolished the constitution of 1791, officially dethroned King Louis XVI, and declared France a republic. Louis was tried and executed on January 21, 1793. His execution made a profound impact not only in France but also throughout all of Europe and even in the United States. Sadly, he would be only the first member of the French royal family to die at the hands of the revolutionaries.

The Rising of Europe

Whatever the reasons and justifications of later secular historians, those who were then alive understood very well what the execution of King Louis XVI meant. When the news of Louis' execution reached London, Great Britain immediately broke off diplomatic relations with France. In Parliament, the prime minister of Great Britain, William Pitt, recognized that **the revolution would try to destroy England, Europe, and the world**. He declared that England stood resolved to fight the French with all that it had.

On February 1, 1793, the Convention declared war on England and the Netherlands. France was now at war with every western European nation except Spain. They would address that situation the following month. An alliance against France developed that included Austria, Prussia, the larger German states, Great Britain, and the Netherlands. For a time, it seemed that all of these great powers must surely prevail against the revolutionary government, no matter how powerful a nation France was. However, the anti-French allies were not sufficiently united in purpose or policy to pursue a common aim or strategy. Meanwhile, the French government instituted a draft to mobilize large conscripted armies. The French armies fought with fanatical fury and turned back their enemies.

Maximilien Robespierre

Georges-Jacques Danton

Witness to the Faith

The Persecution Continues

Despite their ongoing international wars, the revolutionaries never lost sight of their eternal foe: the Catholic Church. In France, the persecutions intensified. More "non-jurors" were arrested. Soon, laws were passed aimed at the non-jurors. New laws condemned people to death for hiding a priest in their home. Local officials vigorously enforced the laws.

The victims of the renewed persecution fell into three categories: the *recluses*, the *deported*, and the *condemned*. The *recluses* were old or infirm priests. The French authorities rounded them up and imprisoned them. In prison, their jailers subjected these old and sickly men to extreme hardships. Forced to move from one prison to another, many of them died under the brutal treatment of their captors. One revolutionary official had a particularly demonic inspiration. He suggested drowning the priests in the Loire River by loading them into boats and sinking the boats. The first time, they drowned 80 priests. The second time, the local officials drowned 137 priests.

It would seem that it would be a blessing to be deported from such a hellish place as revolutionary France. However, the "*deported*" priests suffered as much as, if not more than, the *recluses* did. Soldiers drove hundreds of priests in carts to the various French ports to be deported. Although the priests were to be exiled, this was not possible, because the British fleet was blockading all the French ports. As a result, the government confined the priests in the holds of the French ships, a much smaller and more confined space than a French prison. In the holds, these brave priests died from hunger or even suffocated. Of the 825 priests imprisoned on two ships at the port of Rochefort, 542 died.

Finally, there were the *condemned*. The revolutionary authorities simply martyred these priests. The *condemned* included priests who had secretly celebrated Mass, as well as men and women who had dared to offer them a meal or a place to sleep. It also included nuns who had refused to take the oath. The Church has beatified dozens of these martyrs.

New Forms of Revolutionary Worship

For the revolutionaries, it was not enough to kill all the priests; they sought to replace the Catholic Faith with one of their own making. Moreover, because Catholicism permeated French culture and society, the existing culture and society had to be destroyed and replaced with a new revolutionary one. Even the calendar had to be changed to reflect a new "godless" society.

Thus, the first step in creating a new revolutionary society was to replace the Gregorian calendar with one created by the revolutionaries. The new Revolutionary Era was to begin on September 22, 1792. The date the French Republic was created, which the revolutionaries deemed far more important than the birth of Our Lord, marked the beginning of this new era. The new week was to be 10 days. The tenth day took the

---

The Vendee
A region of western France in which Catholics rose up against the new government to try to free their country.

Catholic and Royal Army
The army formed by the people of the Vendee, composed mostly of peasants and farmers.

---

452 *Chapter 29: The Church during the French Revolution*

place of Sunday. On the calendar, the revolutionaries replaced the names of saints with the names of people whom the revolutionaries thought appropriate, and they changed the names of all the months.

The creation of the new calendar also marked a new period of attacks against the Church. The Convention declared that Notre Dame Cathedral in Paris, the symbol of French Catholicism for almost a thousand years, would now be known as the "Temple of the Goddess of Reason." Revolutionaries removed the religious images from the cathedral, and they replaced the Mass with a blasphemous "Festival of Reason." They even crowned this abomination by putting a dancer in Notre Dame to impersonate the new "goddess."

Notre Dame was not the only church to suffer such indignities. Throughout France, churches, especially the great French cathedrals, were subjected to similar sacrileges. Most of the churches in Paris were closed. At the end of November, the government issued orders to close all the Catholic churches in France. Anyone asking to have a church reopened would be executed.

Map of France, Highlighting the Vendee

The Rising in the Vendee

Revolutionary madness was sweeping through Paris. However, at least in the **Vendee**, the people remained devoted to the Catholic Faith. The area known as the Vendee is located in western France, halfway down the coast, around the city of Nantes. The Vendeans had a strong sense of personal freedom and responsibility. They also had a fervent love for the Catholic Church. More than three-fourths of the priests there refused to take the oath to support the Civil Constitution of the Clergy.

In order to fight its enemies, the revolutionary government had instituted a military draft. When the government's conscription decree arrived in the Vendee, the people understood it meant more than the horrors of war. It meant fighting for a government that had murdered their king and was attempting to destroy the Catholic Church. The drawing of lots for the draft was set for March 12, 1793. On that day, the Catholics of the Vendee rose up against the revolution. Composed almost entirely of peasants and farmers, these men formed the **Catholic and Royal Army**. Many wore crosses and images of the Sacred Heart.

Within a week after the uprising had started, the Catholic and Royal Army had freed most of the Vendee and parts of the neighboring areas from revolutionary control. At this point, the revolutionary government became aware that something was happening in western France. The Convention decreed

Jacques Cathelineau

Witness to the Faith 453

Marie Antoinette with Her Children Marie Therese, Louis Charles, and Louis Joseph, Elisabeth Louise Vigee Le Brun

Martyrs of Compiegne
Sixteen Carmelite nuns who died by the guillotine rather than renounce their Catholic Faith.

that any Frenchman carrying arms against the government would be executed within one day of his capture.

On April 6, the Convention created the Committee of Public Safety. The Committee worked in secret. It protected the revolution, not only from those actively fighting it, but also from those who might not be supporting it strongly enough. The head of the Committee was Georges-Jacques Danton.

Meanwhile, in the Vendee, the fighting spirit of Clovis and Clotilde (see Chapter 6) lived and thrived: "If only I had been there with my Franks!" Throughout the month of May, the Vendeans continued to be victorious. By the end of the month, they had taken almost full control of the Vendee. Only the port city of Nantes remained in revolutionary hands. On June 15, the Vendeans decided to attack Nantes. By capturing Nantes, they would gain a port from which they could receive supplies from England. On June 29, the Catholic army attacked this strongly defended city. It was a valiant effort, but it failed when their commanding general, Jacques Cathelineau, was killed. For the next two months, the Vendeans fought a defensive action to hold the land they had taken.

Robespierre and the Reign of Terror

While Danton was in the country with his family for three weeks, Robespierre took over the Committee of Public Safety. One of the most radical revolutionaries, Robespierre removed Danton from the Committee. From that moment, the Committee became the real government of France. Robespierre became a virtual dictator in a Reign of Terror. Almost two thousand people lost their lives during this time.

On October 16, 1793, following a two-day show trial, Queen Marie Antoinette was executed. The following day, the Catholic and Royal Army suffered a devastating defeat. The Vendee was lost. One hundred thousand refugees from the Vendee fled into northern France, away from the army that had defeated them.

Although Robespierre had removed him from the Committee of Public Safety, most revolutionaries still respected Danton. Thus, Robespierre could not move directly against him. Instead, he began to have Danton's supporters arrested in January 1794. That same month, the last remnants of the Catholic and Royal Army were destroyed. On March 31, Robespierre arrested Danton, who was tried and found guilty. In the end, Danton rejected the evil that he had caused. He asked for the pardon of God and men for the part he had played in the revolution.

From Danton's death on April 5 until the execution of Robespierre on July 28, 1794, thousands of people were executed throughout France. Many more were in prisons awaiting execution. One of the last groups killed before the Reign of Terror ended was a group of sixteen Carmelite nuns known as the **Martyrs of Compiegne**. When brought before the revolutionaries, these nuns chose to die rather than renounce the Catholic Faith.

The convent's novice was murdered first, and the prioress last. It took about half an hour to guillotine the sixteen nuns. During this time, the normally screaming mob remained silent. The only sound heard was the voices of the praying nuns. Each of these nuns walked willingly to the scaffold, including the two oldest nuns, who were almost 80 years old and had to be helped by the soldiers. Pope Pius X beatified these sixteen nuns in 1906.

By this point, the Reign of Terror had finally become too frightening even for the revolutionaries to endure. The members of the Convention lived in constant dread and agitation. They feared that at any moment Robespierre would order their deaths. Thus, out of fear for their own lives, Robespierre's colleagues plotted his downfall. On July 26, the conspirators denounced him as he spoke before the Convention. Amid shouts of "Down with the tyrants!" the Convention ordered the arrest of the dictator and his friends. Then they ordered his execution. The death of Robespierre on July 28, 1794, marked the end of the Reign of Terror. The worst was over for the people of France, but not for her priests.

Martyrs of Compiegne

Oral Exercises

1. What is a revolution?
2. What was the Civil Constitution of the Clergy?
3. Who were the "non-jurors"?
4. Who were the *recluses*, the *deported*, and the *condemned*?
5. Why did the Vendeans rise up against the revolutionaries?
6. Who were the Martyrs of Compiegne?

Witness to the Faith 455

Chapter 30
The Church during the Age of Napoleon

Directory
The corrupt and incompetent five-man team that took up executive power in France after the fall of Robespierre.

Napoleon Bonaparte
French general and then dictator; he was the supreme power in Europe until he was defeated and exiled.

The Directory Persecutes the Church

After the fall of Robespierre, the Committee of Public Safety lost its dictatorial powers. The National Convention (the legislative body in France at that time) then created a new constitution that placed executive power in the hands of a five-man **Directory**, which ruled from November 1795 until November 1799. The five members were all completely corrupt and incompetent. Under their leadership, the people of France began to starve. Like prior revolutionary governments, its members hated the Church. The Directory deported a number of priests to a penal colony in French Guiana, a land of jungles in South America off the coast of the Atlantic Ocean. Many other priests were tortured and imprisoned at Rochefort in southwestern France. Others were imprisoned in islands off the French coast, where most of them died of diseases.

The Rise of Napoleon Bonaparte

The Directory faced serious economic problems, arising from its wars and inflation. France needed conquests, not only to end the war, but also to obtain plunder. Therefore, in 1796, the Directory sent a great army into Italy to defeat the Austrian army and to establish French control over the Italian states. The commander of the French army was General **Napoleon Bonaparte**—possibly history's greatest

456 Chapter 30: The Church during the Age of Napoleon

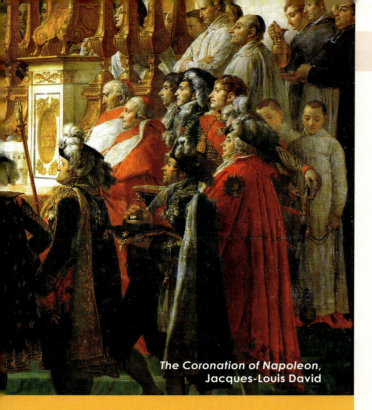

The Coronation of Napoleon, Jacques-Louis David

1798 A.D. – 1815 A.D.

1798 A.D.
A French army takes Pope Pius VI prisoner. Napoleon Bonaparte takes control of Egypt, but is defeated at the Battle of the Nile.

1799 A.D.
Pius VI is taken to France. Napoleon sets up the Consulate, with himself as the First Consul.

1800 A.D.
Napoleon takes power in Italy and forces Austria to sign a treaty with him, becoming the supreme power in Europe.

1801 A.D.
Napoleon signs a Concordat with Pope Pius VII, giving the Church some rights in France.

1804 A.D.
Napoleon is elected emperor, and has Pius VII take part in his official coronation.

1805-1807 A.D.
The British defeat Napoleon's navy at the Battle of Trafalgar. The Holy Roman Empire is officially abolished.

1809 A.D.
Napoleon makes Pius VII a prisoner at Savona, Italy.

1812 A.D.
Napoleon attempts an invasion of Russia, but fails. His army is reduced to one-sixth of what it was.

1813-1814 A.D.
Various nations of Europe rise up and defeat Napoleon, who is exiled to Elba. The French monarchy is restored, and Pius VII returns to Rome.

1815 A.D.
Napoleon attempts to take power again but is defeated at the Battle of Waterloo and exiled to the island of St. Helena.

general, but unfortunately not one of its most upright leaders.

Napoleon Bonaparte was born in Corsica in 1769. He attended the military academy at Brienne. Upon his graduation, he received a commission in the artillery corps. The French Revolution created an opportunity for the talented and ambitious young man to play a leading role in France. In February 1794, he became a brigadier general, following his capture of Toulon from Royalist forces. On October 3, 1795, he achieved national fame, and in particular gained the attention of the new government's leaders, when he fired his cannon on a Paris mob threatening the National Convention. To reward his actions, the newly created Directory gave him command of France's army in Italy. (In an interesting character note, despite typically being coldly pragmatic

Witness to the Faith   457

Napoleon Crossing the Alps, Jacques-Louis David

and unconcerned about morals, Napoleon refused to serve against the Vendeans during their uprising in 1793.)

During 1797 and 1798, Napoleon won many brilliant victories in Italy. As a result, Austria was forced to sign a peace treaty with France. The treaty made France dominant in Italy and Western Europe. Napoleon returned to France as a national hero.

Napoleon was next assigned to Egypt. He proposed to conquer Egypt, which he would use as a base for an attack on British-controlled India. In May 1798, a French expedition sailed from France with thirty-eight thousand troops. Outside Cairo, at the Battle of the Pyramids, Napoleon won control of Egypt. However, at the Battle of the Nile (August 1, 1798), the British fleet destroyed the French fleet. This defeat cut off Napoleon's communications with France and crippled his plan to conquer India. In August 1799, he left his troops and returned to France. Meanwhile, France had invaded the Papal States and taken Pope Pius VI prisoner.

The Election of Pope Pius VI

Giovanni Angelo Braschi was born in Cesena on Christmas Day in 1717. Like many Catholic children, he received a solid Jesuit education. In 1758, he was ordained to the priesthood. In 1773, after a distinguished life of service, he was made a cardinal by Pope Clement XIV. Following the death of Pope Clement in 1774, Cardinal Braschi was one of the forty-four cardinals in attendance at the conclave.

The main issue confronting the cardinals was the matter of the Jesuits. The Jesuit question divided the Sacred College into two factions. One faction consisted of those cardinals, mainly Italians, who strongly supported the Jesuits and opposed their suppression. The other faction, who favored the suppression of the Jesuits, came from the Bourbon nations which had pushed for their suppression. French Cardinal Pierre de Bernis led these so-called "crown cardinals."

Chapter 30: The Church during the Age of Napoleon

The conclave began on October 5, 1774, but because the Sacred College was divided, none of the more well-known candidates received the two-thirds majority of votes required for election. After more than two months, someone proposed Cardinal Braschi for the first time. Because he was considered moderately pro-Jesuit, the crown cardinals rejected him. Nevertheless, Cardinal de Bernis felt that Braschi might be the best choice if no better candidate could be elected.

Meanwhile, December became January, which dragged into February, with the cardinals still deadlocked. Cardinal de Bernis began to realize that Braschi was the best pope that the crown cardinals could elect. Braschi soon gained support among the other cardinals. On February 15, 1775, on the 265th ballot, Cardinal Giovanni Angelo Braschi was elected to the papacy. He chose the name **Pius VI** (1775-1799) to honor Pope St. Pius V.

Pius VI's election had been long and contentious. His papacy would be one of the longest in history. It would also be one of the most heroic.

> **Pope Pius VI**
> Opposed the French Revolution; encouraged and helped the suffering French Catholics. He was captured by an invading French army, and spent his last days in exile.

Pius VI Versus the Revolution

Almost from the beginning, Pope Pius VI had seen that the French Revolution was the mortal enemy of the papacy and the Catholic Church. The revolutionaries hated Pius VI for a number of reasons, not the least of which was the fact that he was pope. They hated him because he rejected and condemned the Civil Constitution of the Clergy, encouraged the non-jurors to stand firm in their faith, and sheltered Catholic refugees.

During his campaign in Italy, Napoleon had taken control of large parts of Italy. He demanded a large sum of money from the pope. After his victories over Austria, Napoleon forced Pius VI to sign the oppressive Treaty of Tolentino. This treaty greatly increased the amount of money that the Holy See had to pay to France. It also stated that French troops would occupy Italy until the pope paid.

On January 11, 1798, the Directory and Napoleon ordered French troops to occupy Rome. The excuse for the occupation was the murder of a French general in a riot two weeks earlier. On February 10, French troops under General Louis-Alexandre Berthier entered Rome unopposed. They disarmed the papal troops, forced their way into the Vatican, pillaged the pope's apartments, and plundered the Eternal City. General Berthier told the pope that he had three days to leave Rome. Pius replied that he would never leave Rome or desert his Church. When Berthier demanded that

Pope Pius VI, Pompeo Batoni

Witness to the Faith

Pius give him the Fisherman's Ring, Pius refused. The 80-year-old pope, who was suffering partial paralysis in both his legs, told the French general that he needed to keep the ring to pass on to his successor. Berthier replied that there would be no successor. Pius VI would be the last pope.

The Final Days of the Hero Pope

On February 20, 1798, Pope Pius VI heard Mass as dawn was breaking. Then his captors bundled him into a coach to take him to France. A cold winter rain was falling. Despite the wintry weather, countless numbers knelt on the side of the road awaiting the pope's blessing as his carriage drove past.

French troops escorted Pius VI out of Rome to Siena and then to a Carthusian monastery in Florence. Crowds filled the streets and the town squares at every place through which his carriage drove. As the sick and dying pope traveled, the people sought his blessing and asked about his health. Along the way, he constantly urged them to be strong in the Faith.

On March 25, 1799, he was ordered to leave Florence for Parma in northern Italy. No longer able even to raise his hand in blessing, he had to be lifted into his carriage. The troops finally drove him over the Alps into France. As the people in Italy had done, the French people of the various border towns came out to greet and warmly welcome him.

Pius VI spent the last months of his life in exile in the citadel of Valence. There, like Our Lord on the Cross, he prayed for the forgiveness of his enemies. He also prayed for three specific intentions: that the Catholic Faith would be restored to France, that the pope would be restored to Rome, and that peace would be restored to Europe. Pope Pius VI died at Valence on August 29, 1799, having reigned the longest of any pope since St. Peter up to that time. The revolutionaries believed they had won. However, the enemies of the Church always seem to make one mistake: they forget Christ's promise to a humble fisherman that "the gates of hell shall not prevail against it."

In 1949, another pope named Pius (Pope Pius XII) moved Pope Pius VI's remains to the Chapel of the Madonna in the grotto below St. Peter's Basilica. The remains were placed in a marble sarcophagus. The inscription on the wall above the sarcophagus reads in part, "The mortal remains of Pius VI, consumed in unjust exile … were placed fittingly here … in 1949."

The Election of Pius VII

Pope Pius VI had been concerned that Napoleon might try to take control of the papacy by forcing the College of Cardinals to elect someone chosen by him. So Pius VI had ordered that the conclave which elected his successor must meet in a location not controlled by Napoleon. On November 30, 1799, the cardinals met in the Benedictine monastery on the island of San Giorgio Maggiore in the lagoon opposite the city of Venice.

The Death of Pope Pius VI, G. Beys

Pope Pius VII
Pope during most of Napoleon's reign; tried when possible to cooperate with Napoleon, but ended up clashing with him and being imprisoned by him.

460 Chapter 30: The Church during the Age of Napoleon

Only six months earlier, the French revolutionaries had essentially martyred Pope Pius VI. Every cardinal at the conclave must have realized that to be elected pope meant martyrdom. After several months of discussion, on March 14 the Sacred College elected the humble bishop of Imola, Cardinal Luigi Chiaramonti, a Benedictine. He chose the name **Pius VII** (1800-1823). The choice of the name could not have been more telling to the cardinals, the Church, the world, and the French Revolution. He would maintain the policies of his predecessor and defend the Church—even unto death.

Napoleon Becomes Ruler of France

At this point, the conditions in France were perfect for a man of Napoleon's abilities. The Directory was corrupt and incompetent. Almost everyone was starving. The people wanted someone who could govern efficiently and provide food for their tables. Napoleon, though a revolutionary, was competent and able to feed the people. With the help of his brother Lucien and other politicians, the 30-year-old Napoleon Bonaparte seized power on November 9, 1799, thus ending the Directory. Soldiers drove out protesting members of the legislature. Napoleon's new government was called the **Consulate**. It ruled France from 1799 until 1804. Napoleon was made First Consul with a ten-year term. He was basically an absolute dictator. From the time he took power in November 1799 until his final defeat fifteen years later, France was almost constantly at war.

> **Consulate**
> The original form of Napoleon's government, in which he had a ten-year term. This term had not ended before Napoleon obtained power for life.

In a display of his military brilliance, Napoleon, to the amazement of his enemies, suddenly crossed the snow-covered Alps into Italy during the spring of 1800. On June 14, he won a decisive battle over the Austrians at the Battle of Marengo. All of Italy was now under his control. As a result of the battle, Austria was forced to sign a peace treaty with Napoleon. In 1802, Britain was compelled to sign a treaty as well. Napoleon was now the supreme power in Europe.

The Concordat of 1801

Napoleon Bonaparte accepted the French Revolution's worldview. This meant that he was no friend to the Catholic Church. Throughout his entire life, he was probably an atheist. However, he had a pragmatic view of the Church. He knew that the people of France were essentially Catholic. He realized that to gain their obedience and control them,

Pope Pius VII in 1805

Concordat of 1801
An agreement between Napoleon and the Catholic Church which provided for the free exercise of the Catholic Faith, but with some government restrictions.

he had to let them have their Faith. Nevertheless, he wanted to control the Church. Moreover, he ultimately wanted the pope to crown him emperor of Europe. Thus, five days after his victory at Marengo, Napoleon began negotiations with the Holy See, which resulted in the **Concordat of 1801**.

The Concordat did not fully restore the Church in France to its former position. It provided that the Catholic Faith could be freely exercised in France, but **public worship** had to conform to the rules that the government stipulated were necessary for public peace. Under the Concordat, Napoleon had the right to nominate bishops, but the pope had the power to confer the canonical institution. Bishops and priests were required to swear allegiance to the government. In return, the government would financially support the clergy. In an act of heroic unselfishness, the Church in France relinquished any claim to the Church property that had been seized during the revolution.

It seems that the Concordat was somewhat one-sided in favor of Napoleon. Undoubtedly, the situation was far from ideal, but the ultimate goal of the Church is the salvation of souls. Therefore, to restore the sacraments to the people of France, Pius VII accepted Napoleon's terms. Given that Pius returned the signed Concordat after only 37 days, he must have believed that it was the best deal he could make.

Interestingly, when Napoleon was finally defeated, he declared that the Concordat was his "worst mistake." When Napoleon violated the Concordat, it transformed Pope Pius VII into a symbol of righteous opposition to him. For all his military genius, Napoleon could not overcome the humble Benedictine monk.

The War Resumes against Napoleon

Among all the European powers, Great Britain best recognized Napoleon for who he truly was: the inheritor of the French Revolution. The British knew that there could be no lasting peace with him. All treaties were merely lulls in the struggle between Napoleon and Great Britain. In 1803, the war between England and Napoleon resumed. By 1805, Austria, Russia, and Sweden had joined Britain to end French domination of Europe.

Trafalgar
Naval battle in which the British defeated Napoleon, ending his ambitions at sea.

To destroy his resolute enemy, Napoleon had to invade Great Britain. A successful invasion depended on his controlling the English Channel long enough to transport his armies across it in barges. However, the combined French and Spanish navies could not control the English Channel. Therefore, in 1805, Napoleon turned to meet the Austrian and Russian armies in the east. He ordered his naval forces into the Mediterranean. In one of history's most decisive battles, the British navy caught Napoleon's naval forces. The British destroyed the combined French and Spanish fleets at **Trafalgar** off the coast of Spain. The British victory permanently destroyed Napoleon's naval power and any chance of invading England.

462   *Chapter 30: The Church during the Age of Napoleon*

The Battle of Trafalgar,
Clarkson Frederick Stanfield

Despite the failure of his forces at sea, Napoleon remained undefeatable on land. He again proved his military talents when he crushed a larger combined Austrian and Russian army at Austerlitz in December 1805. The defeat at Austerlitz spelled the end for the Holy Roman Empire. It also alarmed Prussia, which had been working with France since 1795. Prussia now declared war on Napoleon. However, the very highly regarded Prussian army received a terrible beating from Napoleon's forces at the Battle of Jena in October 1806. Napoleon next turned to the Russians. His defeat of the Russians led not only to a peace treaty but also to an alliance with Russia in 1807.

Napoleon's empire was now at its zenith. He had carved up Europe with Russia. As long as his alliance lasted, Great Britain could accomplish little. Napoleon then compelled Spain to become his ally. In 1806, he officially abolished the Holy Roman Empire. Francis II, the last Holy Roman Emperor, became known simply as the emperor of Austria. Napoleon completely dominated all of continental Europe. All that stood between him and world domination was the British navy.

Napoleon Is Crowned Emperor

In 1802, Napoleon had become First Consul for life with the powers of a king. In 1804, he told one of his ministers that the French had not had an emperor since Charlemagne, but he would become the second. Thus, in that same year, he had the French people elect him emperor. However, Napoleon wanted more than an election; he wanted to be crowned in the manner of Charlemagne. This would not only legitimize his reign but also ensure the legitimacy of his heirs. So he invited Pope Pius VII to Paris to crown him emperor. Given that

Francis II

Witness to the Faith 463

Napoleon dominated Europe, Pius felt that it would be best to comply. Pius also hoped that, in exchange for this courtesy, Napoleon might be willing to grant more concessions to the Church in France.

When Pope Pius VII arrived in Paris on November 2, 1804, Napoleon deliberately treated him disrespectfully. Napoleon wanted to show that he was the ruler of Europe and that the pope was nothing more than his personal chaplain. The actual coronation took place on December 2, 1804, in Notre Dame Cathedral. In this ceremony, Napoleon wanted to make clear that he was a new kind of king, whose authority came from his own power. Thus, the ceremony began with Pope Pius VII anointing him, but at the moment of coronation, Napoleon took the crown from the pope's hands and placed it upon his own head. It was the low point of Pius VII's papacy. Although the pope remained in Paris until the spring, he could not obtain any additional concessions from Napoleon.

Europe Rises against Napoleon

Between 1807 and 1809, the freedom-loving people of Europe rose again to try to overthrow Napoleon's yoke of tyranny. In 1807, Napoleon invaded Portugal. The following year, the people of Spain revolted against the oppression of their country. Great Britain sent an army to aid the Spanish rebels. The French army in Spain was not able to crush the rebels or dislodge the British army from the Iberian Peninsula. In 1809, Austria attacked the French in an attempt to free Germany. Great Britain sent an army to attack the French in Holland. Napoleon again completely defeated these nations. He forced a very harsh treaty on Austria.

Napoleon Imprisons Pope Pius VII

Almost from the beginning of his pontificate, Pius VII had clashed with Napoleon. Whenever possible, Pius had worked with him in order to bring peace to Europe, and the sacraments to the people. Thus, he had agreed to the Concordat of 1801 and had "officiated" at Napoleon's coronation. Yet, despite the Holy Father's best efforts, the proud dictator would continually attempt to bend the Church to his will, as he had done with the nations around him.

Jerome Bonaparte

One of the first disputes between Napoleon and Pius VII involved the marriage of Napoleon's brother Jerome. In 1803, Bishop John Carroll of Baltimore had married Jerome Bonaparte to Elizabeth Patterson of Baltimore, a wealthy American. Napoleon wanted all of his family members to marry European royalty. Therefore, he wanted Jerome's marriage annulled. However, since the marriage was sacramentally valid, Pope Pius VII refused to grant an annulment. (Napoleon himself arrogantly declared the marriage invalid on March 11, 1805.)

As this incident demonstrated, Napoleon sought to control the pope and the Church. First, he desired to control the appointment of bishops. Second, he wanted to rule all of Europe, including Rome and the Papal States. In January 1806, he told Pius VII that he might be the pope in Rome, but that he, Napoleon, was its emperor.

A much more intense confrontation between Pope Pius VII and Napoleon was soon to arise. Throughout all of Napoleon's wars, Pius had remained strictly neutral. Ironically, his very neutrality became a point of conflict. In order to defeat England, Napoleon had instituted a system that barred England from trading with Europe. Napoleon demanded that Pius exclude British and other neutral ships from docking in the Papal States. Pius told Napoleon that he was the Vicar of a God of peace, which meant that the Church would always take a position of peace. He reminded Napoleon that his predecessors departed from a policy of peace only when faced with defending themselves from aggression or defending attacks on the Church. Thus, Pius declared that he would not surrender his neutrality.

Finally, in 1808, Napoleon demanded that Pius VII abandon his neutral status and join a confederation of Italian princes who supported Napoleon. Once again, Pius defied Napoleon's demands. In June 1809, Napoleon retaliated by seizing the Papal States. In response, Pius bravely excommunicated Napoleon, branding him an enemy of the Church.

The excommunication infuriated Napoleon, who did not like being defied. He ordered his soldiers to arrest the pope. On the night of July 6, 1809, Napoleon's troops stormed into the papal residence. Pius VII was sitting behind his desk, attended by six cardinals. They arrested him and bundled him into a carriage to take him to France. As they had done with Pius VI, they hurried Pius VII through Italy and on to Grenoble. Everywhere he went, the Italian and French crowds thronged the roads, kneeling as he blessed them. Through a series of miscommunications and mistakes, the French finally returned Pius VII to Savona, Italy, near Genoa, on August 17.

Although the French housed him comfortably in Savona and permitted him to say Mass, Pius VII was not allowed to function as pope. He was closely guarded, and not allowed to have any advisors or a secretary. Because he was not allowed to act as pope,

Interior of Savona Cathedral

Witness to the Faith 465

Pius decided to offer passive resistance to his captors. He reverted to the role of a simple Benedictine monk. He would pray, meditate, and mend his cassock. He would not invest new bishops in France or any territory controlled by Napoleon. On September 8, Pope Pius VII said Mass in Savona Cathedral. The choir sang out: "You are Peter." After Mass, the pope remained with most of the congregation to say a Rosary before the Blessed Sacrament. Napoleon had armies of more than 500,000 nearly unbeatable soldiers, yet one humble Benedictine was defeating his plans.

The Invasion of Russia

From 1809 to 1812, Napoleon's empire appeared invincible. However, the forces that would defeat it were at work. The British navy steadily destroyed all of Napoleon's overseas trade. The Spanish, who had fought 770 years to expel the Muslims, continued to fight to expel Napoleon. The anger of the conquered peoples grew ever greater. More importantly,

Napoleon Watching the Fire of Moscow, Adam Albrecht

France's relationship with Russia declined. Finally, Napoleon decided to impose his will on Russia and attack it.

In June 1812, Napoleon led an army of six hundred thousand men, the largest army the world had ever known, into Russia. This time, his enemy refused to fight; the Russians simply retreated eastward. As the Russian soldiers retreated across the vastness of Russia, they burned and destroyed whatever the invaders could use. Finally, the Russians made a stand at Borodino, but were defeated. Moscow lay open to the French, but there was no triumphal entry into Moscow for Napoleon. The Russians had burned the city and deserted it.

Napoleon's Withdrawal from Russia, **Adolph Northen**

Napoleon had no choice but to retreat to Smolensk, where he hoped to find food for his troops. But there were no supplies at Smolensk. The only course was to return to France. As Napoleon's retreating troops made their long journey home, they were hounded constantly by the Russians, who fiercely and relentlessly attacked them. They were also brutalized by the pitiless Russian winter, where the temperature fell to 30 degrees below zero. Finally, the remnants of the once-proud French army staggered back to Europe with less than one hundred thousand men. It was the greatest military disaster in history. Suddenly, Napoleon did not seem so invincible. Austria declared its neutrality, which lasted only briefly, and Prussia made an alliance with Russia. It was the beginning of the end for Napoleon, but he turned his attention to the pope, whom he still held prisoner.

Napoleon Again Confronts the Pope

By June 1812, Napoleon had lost patience with the humble pope. Enraged that Pius refused to do his bidding, Napoleon ordered him moved. The French transferred Pius to Fontainebleau, just outside of Paris. The journey was made speedily, brutally, and secretly to prevent any public outcry. On the trip, Pius fell ill and even received the Last Rites. It was this exhausted pope, sick with fever, whom Napoleon again attempted to cajole.

In his weakened, feverish state, Pius VII agreed to surrender the Papal States to Napoleon. Pius also agreed that if he failed to invest a bishop within six months after Napoleon nominated one, the metropolitan bishop would be allowed to confer the investiture without declaring that he acted in the name of the Holy See. These decrees, made under duress, almost immediately filled Pius with regret. Had he known of Napoleon's defeat in Russia, perhaps he never would have agreed to them, even in his weakened state, but he was completely isolated. Nevertheless, he would soon revoke them.

Witness to the Faith

Allied Victory over Napoleon

The disaster in Russia had been a decisive defeat for Napoleon. Now was the time for the British-led coalition of nations allied against him to defeat him, finally and completely. Yet, despite the debacle in Russia, Napoleon still possessed resources. In addition to France, he controlled most of Germany and all of Italy. His armies had also chased the British out of Spain and into Portugal.

In October 1813, Napoleon gathered an army to meet the combined forces of Russia, Prussia, Austria, and Sweden at Leipzig. The French army suffered an overwhelming defeat and was forced to flee across the Rhine River, as the coalition armies hastened the downfall of the tyrant.

The next step was for the allies to invade France. They moved into eastern France, while the British liberated Spain and entered France from the south. Napoleon fought brilliantly to repulse the invasion, but the allied armies proved too much for him. As they entered Paris, the allies found that the French people were exhausted from nearly a quarter century of war and revolution. The allies were not vindictive. They brought peace rather than revenge to France.

The allies restored the Bourbon dynasty and ended all revolutionary policies. As Louis XVI's son, Louis XVII, had died in captivity, Louis XVI's brother returned to rule as King Louis XVIII. Once peace was made with France, the allied troops went home. Napoleon was exiled to the island of Elba, off the coast of Italy.

Louis XVIII

Napoleon's Return from Elba, Charles de Steuben

Not long before, with defeat looming on the horizon, Napoleon had proposed yet another treaty to Pius VII. This treaty would have acknowledged Napoleon as the ruler of Rome and of the former Papal States presently annexed to the French empire. A healthy Pius had refused.

With his defeat at hand, Napoleon released Pope Pius VII. On May 24, 1814, after five years of captivity, Pius re-entered Rome amid universal rejoicing. Ten weeks later, **he restored the Jesuits**.

The Battle of Waterloo

Although Napoleon had been exiled to Elba, he had not written "the end" to his part of history. On February 26, 1815, he escaped from Elba—less than ten months after he had arrived there. Two days later, he

The Battle of Waterloo,
William Sadler

landed on the French mainland. The troops sent to arrest him became the core of his new army. As Napoleon's army approached Paris, King Louis XVIII fled. The allies formed a new army and defeated Napoleon at the **Battle of Waterloo** on June 18, 1815. After the Allied victory, the commander of the Allied forces, the Duke of Wellington, acknowledged that the allies had barely won. He hinted that if another ten thousand troops had been at Napoleon's disposal, Napoleon would have won the decisive battle. But Napoleon had deployed those troops elsewhere. About a month before the Battle of Waterloo, the fervently Catholic people of the Vendee had risen in revolt once again, and Napoleon had sent more than ten thousand soldiers to stop them. Perhaps, unbeknownst to the Vendeans, their valiant efforts had indirectly saved France and Western civilization.

This time, the allies exiled Napoleon to the most remote place on Earth at the time, the island of St. Helena. The tiny island of St. Helena was located off the Atlantic Ocean, a thousand miles from anywhere. There, guarded by the British navy, Napoleon lived the remainder of his life. He died on May 5, 1821, almost certainly poisoned by French Royalists who feared that he would somehow return to France. Although Napoleon had been a lifelong atheist, in the last months of his life, he may have found the Catholic Faith. Before he died, he made his last Confession and received the Last Rites.

Battle of Waterloo
The battle in which Napoleon was finally defeated on June 18, 1815.

Oral Exercises

1. During the last months of his life, in addition to praying for his enemies, what three specific intentions did Pope Pius VI pray for?
2. Why did Napoleon agree to the Concordat of 1801?
3. Why did Pius VII agree to the Concordat of 1801?
4. Why did Pope Pius VII excommunicate Napoleon?
5. What did Napoleon do when Pope Pius VII excommunicated him?
6. While Pius VII was a prisoner, how did he oppose Napoleon?
7. Which pope restored the Jesuits?

Witness to the Faith

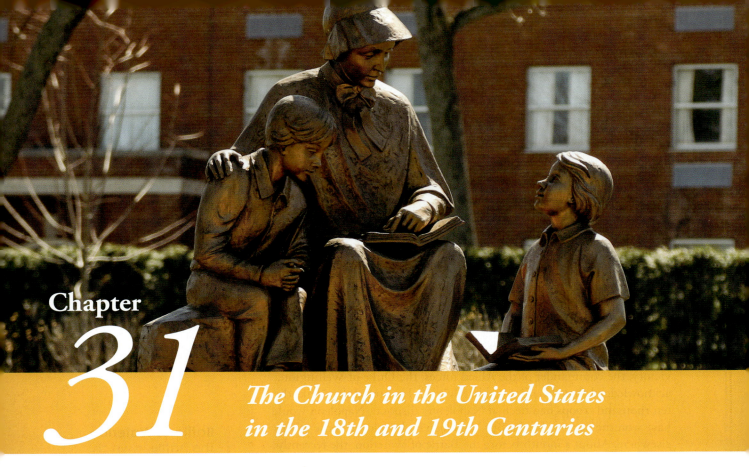

Chapter 31

The Church in the United States in the 18th and 19th Centuries

Introduction

Even as Pope Pius VII faced the Church's great enemies, he never forgot that he was the pope of all Catholics everywhere, nor did they forget him. In December 1811, while Pius VII was Napoleon's prisoner, Catholics in Korea wrote to Pius seeking his blessing. In North America, a tiny group of English-speaking Catholics also sought the pope's blessing and advice. They belonged to a young nation that had recently won its independence. It was called the United States of America.

Establishment of the American Hierarchy

Prior to America's War for Independence, the Church had not organized England's American colonies into a diocese. The bishop who oversaw the Catholic Church in England administered to them. However, with the establishment of a new nation, the Catholics in the United States wanted their own hierarchy.

In 1784, at the request of America's Catholics, Pope Pius VI appointed **Father John Carroll** as *prefect* of the United States, thus making him responsible for all the Catholics in the entire nation. In 1789, Pope Pius made Baltimore the first diocese in the United States, and John Carroll its bishop. Thus, John Carroll was the **first bishop in the United States**.

Father John Carroll
First bishop in the United States. As the bishop of Baltimore, the first diocese in the U.S., he did much for the growth of the Church in America, especially in forming a native clergy.

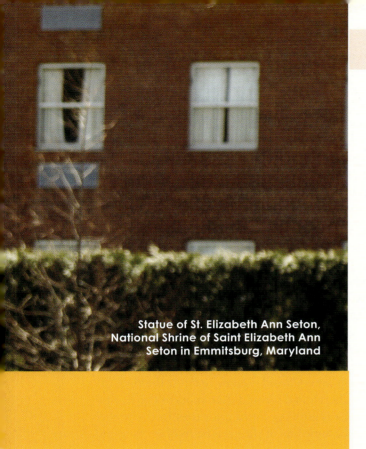

Statue of St. Elizabeth Ann Seton, National Shrine of Saint Elizabeth Ann Seton in Emmitsburg, Maryland

1789 A.D. – 1889 A.D.

1789 A.D. Father John Carroll becomes the bishop of Baltimore, effectively the bishop of the entire United States.

1791-1806 A.D. The Sulpicians found the first seminaries in the United States.

1845-1850 A.D. A great number of Irish emigrate to the United States, increasing the country's Catholic population.

1809 A.D. St. Elizabeth Ann Seton and her companions found the Sisters of Charity in America.

1829 A.D. The First Provincial Council of Baltimore discusses issues of importance to the Church in America.

1834-1854 A.D. Some notable instances of anti-Catholic violence break out.

1852 A.D. The bishops of the U.S. hold their first Plenary Council in Baltimore.

1861-1865 A.D. During the Civil War, priests and nuns give heroic service to the wounded on both sides, helping to diminish anti-Catholic prejudice in the U.S.

1884 A.D. The Third Plenary Council is held, and the *Baltimore Catechism* is created. Catholic University of America is constructed four years later.

1889 A.D. Mother Cabrini and her sisters arrive in New York City.

At that time, the diocese of Baltimore was *the only diocese* in the United States. Bishop Carroll's diocese extended from Georgia to Maine, and west to the Mississippi River. Vast as this territory was, it probably included only about 35,000 Catholics. Most of them lived in Maryland, Pennsylvania, and New York.

The Mustard Seed Grows

In 1789, the United States was a *mission territory*. Bishop Carroll realized that in order for the Church to grow in this new nation, it would need a native clergy. Thus, developing a native clergy became a primary goal for him. In 1789, Bishop Carroll founded a college for young men at Georgetown, on the banks of the Potomac River. When Pius VII restored the Jesuits, Bishop Carroll placed them in charge of Georgetown College. In 1815, Georgetown was given the rank of a university.

Witness to the Faith   471

Bishop Carroll also relied heavily on religious orders to spread the Gospel message in his mission diocese. Dominicans, Augustinians, and Carmelites all worked in the United States. The most important order to assist Bishop Carroll was the Sulpicians. During the French Revolution, many Sulpician priests fled to the United States from France. In 1791, the Sulpicians founded St. Mary's Seminary in Baltimore. It was the first seminary founded in the new United States. In 1806, the Sulpicians founded Mount St. Mary's Seminary in Emmitsburg, near Baltimore. Both seminaries still exist today and have provided the Church with many wonderful priests.

By 1807, there were about 50,000 Catholics in the United States. The handful of parishes had expanded to seventy, and there were about eighty Catholic churches. In 1808, Pius VII elevated the see of Baltimore to an archdiocese and made Bishop Carroll an archbishop. That year, dioceses were also created in New York City, Philadelphia, Boston, and Bardstown (Kentucky). Bardstown later became the Diocese of Louisville. Another diocese was added to the United States after the Louisiana Purchase in 1803 when the Diocese of New Orleans, which had been formed in 1793, became a diocese in the United States. Archbishop John Carroll died in 1815. At the time of his death, the Catholic Church had planted deep roots in the United States. The mustard seed was growing into a great tree. In the next two hundred years, it would become one of the greatest trees in the world.

The Church Grows Rapidly in the 19th Century

In 1800, there were probably less than 50,000 Catholics living in the United States. This represented an insignificant percentage of the overall population of more than 5 million. Fifty years later, the number of Catholics exceeded 1 million and might possibly have been as high as 1.6 million, making Catholicism America's single largest denomination. By the end of the century, there were more than 10 million Catholics in the United States.

During the nineteenth century, the Church grew quickly in the United States. Four factors accounted for this increase. First, the Church grew naturally, as Catholic parents had children. Second, hundreds of thousands were converted to the Catholic Faith, while few left the Church for other religions. Third, more Catholics became American citizens as new states joined the United States, which increased the overall population. Finally, the leading reason for growth was the large number of immigrants from Catholic countries, especially Ireland.

During the early nineteenth century, the Holy Spirit blessed the Catholic Church in the United States with many great priests and bishops, such as John Carroll. One of the most remarkable men to serve the Church during this early period was **Demetrius Augustine Gallitzin**. Demetrius Gallitzin was born in 1770 into a royal family in Russia. In 1792, he journeyed to Baltimore, intending only to do some

Demetrius Augustine Gallitzin

A Russian prince who became a priest in the United States and spent his life ministering to the people of western Pennsylvania.

traveling and learn about the newly formed United States. But he quickly discerned a call to the priesthood.

On November 5, 1792, within a week of arriving in Baltimore, Demetrius entered the Sulpician seminary there, becoming one of its first students. In 1795, Bishop Carroll ordained him. Demetrius was the second priest to be ordained in the United States. (Stephen Theodore Badin was the first.) Following his ordination, Father Gallitzin made his way westward and settled in the Allegheny Mountains. For forty-one years, he ministered to the people of western Pennsylvania. For his efforts in spreading the Faith, Father Gallitzin is known as the "Apostle of the Alleghenies." He died on May 6, 1840.

The first bishop of the diocese of Bardstown, Kentucky, was Benedict Joseph Flaget, a Sulpician. When he arrived in Bardstown in 1811, one of his first acts was to found a seminary. Bishop Flaget lived in one little log cabin, and his seminarians lived in another. Later, they built a church, a proper seminary building, and the Cathedral of St. Joseph.

Benedict Joseph Flaget

In 1821, Bishop Flaget advised Pope Pius VII that his diocese was large enough that it should be divided into two dioceses. In June, Pope Pius created the Diocese of Cincinnati out of the Bardstown diocese. Father Edward Fenwick, a Dominican, became the first bishop of Cincinnati in 1822.

In 1817, the Vincentians built two log cabins in St. Louis, Missouri. These simple cabins would become the Kenrick Theological Seminary of St. Louis.

In 1841, Father Edward Sorin and six lay brothers from the Congregation of the Holy Cross came to northern Indiana at the invitation of Bishop Celestine de la Hailandiere, the bishop of Vincennes. They founded the University of Notre Dame the following year.

Unlike in the French-controlled lands in North America, like Quebec and New Orleans, there had been no Catholic schools for girls in England's colonies during the colonial era. Catholic parents in those colonies would have to send their daughters to France or Belgium for a more formal education than they could receive at home. However, with the establishment of the United States and the outbreak of the French Revolution, more educational opportunities for girls became available in America.

Edward Sorin

In 1792, a number of Poor Clare nuns fled revolutionary France and came to the United States. They opened a convent in Frederick, Maryland. In 1799, they opened a school for girls at Georgetown. The school quickly grew, as did the convent associated with it. In 1804, when the Poor Clares were able to return to France, Visitation nuns took over the school's operation. Both the school (Georgetown Visitation Preparatory

Witness to the Faith

School) and the monastery (Georgetown Visitation Monastery) are still functioning. In fact, the school is one of the oldest continuously operating schools for girls in the United States, as well as the oldest Catholic school for girls in the original thirteen colonies.

Anti-Catholic Resentment

The growth of the Church in the United States inflamed the hatred of religious bigots, who feared that Catholicism was becoming too powerful and influential. They began to persecute Catholics, often through violence.

Because of immigration, the number of Catholics in the United States increased dramatically during the first half of the nineteenth century. Many of these immigrants came from Ireland. From 1845 to 1850, Ireland suffered a terrible famine. People had to either leave Ireland or starve to death. Because they spoke English, the vast majority came to the United States. Most of these immigrants were Catholic.

The growing number of Catholic immigrants aroused the resentment of many Americans. Some American Protestants did not like Catholics or Catholicism. Other Americans did not like immigrants. These Americans tended to be more prosperous people who thought that because immigrants were poor and foreign—which they were—they were also filthy, lazy, and criminals, which they were not. Poorer Americans believed that the new immigrants would take jobs away from them. Some of these anti-Catholic extremists started what was known as the **Nativist movement** (or "Native Americanism"). They considered Catholics to be a national menace. The Nativist movement grew into a political party called the Know-Nothing Party. Later in the century, the Know-Nothing Party became involved with a racist, anti-Catholic group known as the Ku Klux Klan.

Nativist Movement
Political anti-Catholic, anti-immigration movement, which gave rise to violence and grew into the Know-Nothing Party.

The Nuns of the Battlefield Monument in Washington, D.C.

Chapter 31: The Church in the United States in the 18th and 19th Centuries

In 1834, anti-Catholic mobs burned a convent and murdered a nun in Massachusetts. In 1844, mobs destroyed two Catholic churches and a convent in Philadelphia. The next year, anti-Catholic leaders threatened to riot in Boston and New York City. (These three cities had very large Irish Catholic populations.) Mobs destroyed two churches in New England in 1854. Also that year, a mob tarred and feathered, and nearly killed, Father John Bapst, a Swiss Jesuit teaching Native American tribes and Irish immigrants in Maine.

Following Our Lord's injunction to "turn the other cheek," the Church responded to the threats and violence through peaceful means. The American bishops called councils, which strengthened the organization of the Church and helped promote conversions in the new American territories in the West and Southwest.

Anti-Catholic bigotry was suspended during the American Civil War (1861-1865), when priests and especially nuns aided the wounded of both sides. Over six hundred nuns from twelve religious communities served as nurses during the Civil War. Not only did the nuns serve in hospitals behind the lines; they also served on the actual battlefields, where they put into practice the corporal works of mercy. Their heroism and self-sacrifice greatly increased the prestige of the Catholic Church and did much to diminish, though not eliminate, the anti-Catholic sentiment in the United States. After the war, these nuns established hundreds of hospitals across the United States.

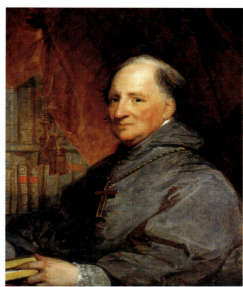

Bishop John Carroll

Provincial and Plenary Councils

Bishops call diocesan synods, as well as provincial and plenary councils, to create rules and address issues confronting the Church. A **provincial council** involves the bishops of a specific, limited area, such as a group of dioceses. A **plenary council** involves all the bishops of an entire nation. The rules established by these synods and councils help bishops govern the Church in a particular area or country, and provide guidance for priests and the laity. The first diocesan synod in the United States met in 1791 at Bishop Carroll's house in Baltimore.

In 1829, Archbishop James Whitfield, the fourth archbishop of Baltimore, convoked the First Provincial Council of Baltimore. At this council, Archbishop Whitfield and his four fellow bishops addressed sacramental matters, such as issues of Baptism and Matrimony. They dealt with disciplinary issues, such as working on holy days of obligation. The council also dealt with legal issues regarding the rights of the Church to own property. Finally, the bishops discussed an issue that they considered among the most important in the life of the Church: the education of Catholic children. They declared that Catholic schools should be built.

In 1833, the archbishop and nine bishops held the Second Provincial Council of Baltimore. Over the next sixteen years, councils met about every three years.

Provincial Council
Involves the bishops of a specific, limited area, such as a group of dioceses.

Plenary Council
Involves all the bishops of an entire nation.

Immaculate Conception,
Peter Paul Rubens

The Seventh Provincial Council convened in 1849, attended by two archbishops and twenty-three bishops. This extremely important council issued several decrees. Among the most important, the council fathers urged the Holy Father to define as a dogma the Immaculate Conception of the Blessed Mother. Second, they asked for permission to hold a plenary council in Baltimore in 1850 to establish national policies, especially concerning the education of children. In 1851, Pope Pius IX granted permission for the Catholic bishops in the United States to hold their plenary council.

The First Plenary Council was convened in Baltimore in 1852. Six archbishops and twenty-six bishops attended. Archbishop Francis Kenrick of Baltimore presided as the Apostolic Delegate. The assembled bishops approved the acts of all the previous seven provincial councils of Baltimore and issued several decrees concerning the Catholic Faith. They professed their allegiance to the Holy Father as the divinely appointed visible head of the Church. They also declared their belief in the entire Catholic Faith as taught by the popes and the Church councils.

The council's main concern was the creation of a Catholic school system. The bishops saw that Protestant teachers in the public (government) schools were working to convert Catholic students to Protestantism. The bishops saw this as a threat to the Church, as well as to the parents and family stability of those children. The council exhorted bishops to establish a Catholic school in every parish and to pay the teachers from the parish funds. Bishops were encouraged to begin these schools as soon as possible, since Catholic boys and girls were in spiritual danger in schools not directed by Catholic motives. Thus, America's parochial school system was born.

Between 1852 and 1866, the Church received several blessings. The huge increase in immigration during the 1850s doubled the Catholic population in the United States. The number of parishes multiplied from 1,411 in 1852 to 3,366 in 1866. Because of the massive increase in the Catholic population, as well as the serious social and educational issues facing the Church after the Civil War, the bishops appealed to Rome for permission to convene a second plenary council. With the permission of the Holy See, the Second Plenary Council of Baltimore met in 1866. Seven archbishops, thirty-eight bishops, and more than 120 priests attended the council.

As with the first council, this second council focused strongly on education. Among its mandates, the council issued the following decrees. First, Catholic teachers working in public schools should be hired to work in Catholic schools when possible. Second, every parish should build a parochial school. Third, parents who could not afford to send their children to a parochial school should send them to Sunday catechism classes at their local church for sacramental preparation, especially for First Confession and First Holy Communion, as well as Confirmation. The council fathers also recommended that a Catholic university be built in the United States.

The priests and bishops at the council also recognized that, with the end of slavery, the Church had a duty to do more to aid freed slaves. Among its decrees, the council passed a resolution asking priests to dedicate as much time as possible to helping educate black Americans, especially black children.

The attempts to create a Catholic school system and raise children as Catholics stirred up anti-Catholic prejudice and anger in the United States. Nevertheless, the drive of the priests and bishops to build Catholic schools could not be stopped. Determined to raise a generation of children taught in Catholic schools, these leaders began to build!

In 1866, about 2.5 million Catholics lived in the United States. By 1884, that number had more than doubled. Immigration continued to be a major reason for the rapid growth in the Catholic population. Once again, the bishops feared that children not attending Catholic schools would fall prey to the evangelization efforts of teachers in the public schools. In 1875, some bishops, concerned with low parochial-school attendance, wrote to the Vatican office responsible for spreading the Catholic Faith. They sought advice on increasing Catholic school enrollment. Rome responded by directing the bishops to build schools where there were none, and to improve existing schools so that they were as good as the public schools. The United States bishops began taking steps to carry out these directives.

In 1883, Pope Leo XIII summoned a number of American archbishops to Rome to discuss the status of Catholic education in the United States. After meeting with the archbishops, Pope Leo XIII approved the Third Plenary Council.

The Third Plenary Council was held in Baltimore in November 1884, with James Cardinal Gibbons presiding. In addition to Cardinal Gibbons, eleven archbishops and fifty-eight bishops attended. This council, too, focused on education, but this time the council fathers took much stronger positions on this issue. For example, they *mandated*, rather than requested, that priests establish Catholic schools in their parishes within two years of the close of the council. They also expressed the desire that the parochial schools be free. In order to be excused from sending their children to a Catholic school, parents had to obtain permission from their local bishop! Believing that Catholic schools needed to be more competitive with the public schools, the bishops decided to implement a nationally standardized curriculum. The Third Plenary Council also appointed a commission to prepare a catechism for use in Catholic schools throughout the United States. It became the famous **Baltimore Catechism**.

Baltimore Catechism
Catholic catechism produced after the Third Plenary Council, for use in Catholic schools throughout the United States.

James Cardinal Gibbons

Witness to the Faith 477

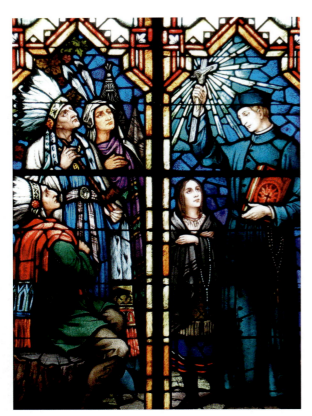

Kateri Tekakwitha Learns about the Faith

The council also addressed the need for Catholic higher education. Over the next fifteen years, the Church would build 100 Catholic high schools in the United States. By 1920, there would be 1,500!

Moreover, the bishops felt that it was time to found a Catholic university, and the council created a commission to begin planning its construction. In 1888, the cornerstone for the first building of the **Catholic University of America** was laid in Washington, D.C.

The Third Plenary Council also stressed the education of the clergy and the importance of founding seminaries, and the council addressed the curriculum to be taught at seminaries. In addition, the council decreed that there should be six holy days of obligation in the United States, and asked the Vatican to begin the beatification process for Isaac Jogues, Rene Goupil, and Kateri Tekakwitha.

Finally, the Third Plenary Council took a giant step forward by removing the mission territory status of the United States. This prepared the Church in the United States for the move from a missionary nation to a country ready to provide for its own support. In fact, the United States would become the Catholic Church's largest financial supporter in the following century.

Under the influence of the Third Plenary Council, Catholic education was reorganized in the United States. The amazingly successful national system of Catholic parish schools began because of the strong support of the bishops throughout the country.

The Catholic School System in the United States

Early in our nation's history, American leaders decided that having educated citizens was the best way to secure the blessings of liberty. As early as 1642, the Colony of Massachusetts required that parents ensure their children's ability to read. For the Puritans in Massachusetts, reading and salvation went hand in hand. In the Puritan's doctrine of the "priesthood of the believer," each person had to interpret Scripture for himself. Therefore, people had to know how to read and interpret the Bible so that they could attain eternal salvation.

Five years later, Massachusetts passed another law, which required towns to pay teachers to teach children to read, making education free to the parents. Other colonies soon followed the example of Massachusetts. Thus, the American free public school system was born.

To ensure that people were educated, the various states established free government-run schools for all children. Soon, every state had a public school system. Not all who worked to establish these schools did so out of zeal for children's salvation; many of those who were most active in creating the public school system were influenced by

Catholic University of America
The first Catholic university founded in the United States.

the false ideas of the Enlightenment. As a result, they tried to prevent Christianity from having any influence in public schools. This attitude was entirely contrary to the spirit of the American settlers and colonists. The colonists, whether Catholic or Protestant, did everything they could to provide a religious education for their children.

During the nineteenth century, America's public schools were generally Christian schools, but the Christianity they taught was Protestant. The Church has always taught that Catholicism must **permeate** all parts of education. She could not allow her children in schools that were teaching Protestantism.

In 1852, Massachusetts passed a compulsory education law. It required students between the ages of 8 and 14 to attend public school or an approved private school for at least twelve weeks per year. At first glance, this law might seem fair, but in reality the "approved" private schools were too expensive for most immigrants—that is, Catholics—to attend. So, effectively, this law forced them to attend public schools.

Three years later, Massachusetts required that students read the Bible in school. This meant the Protestant, *King James*, version of the Bible. Other states had similar requirements for Bible study. In 1852, the First Plenary Council had specifically called for priests to oppose the use of the King James Bible in the public schools.

Because of the actions of Massachusetts and other states, Catholics rallied to support their bishops and pastors. They built schools of their own. In a sense, it was a task that surpassed the creation of the great cathedrals of the Middle Ages. Most Catholics were poor, and the Catholic schools received no aid from the government. In addition, Catholics paid taxes that supported the government-run public schools.

While the construction of the school buildings was an immense accomplishment, Catholic education existed only because of the self-sacrifice of the religious orders. Young men joined teaching orders such as those founded by St. John Baptiste de la Salle, and taught Catholic boys. Orders of nuns, like the Sisters of Charity, flourished and taught young girls. When immigrants came to America, nuns and brothers of their own nationality came as well. Since these religious spoke the immigrants' languages, the children of immigrants could enter into the life of their new nation without losing the Faith of their old nation. Moreover, since these brothers and nuns had taken a vow of poverty, they worked in the classroom for only what they needed to live. They lived in a religious community, so their living expenses (food, housing, etc.) were very small. The self-sacrifice of these priests, brothers, and nuns, who dedicated their lives to teaching Catholic children, made the growth of Catholic education in the United States possible.

Exceptional American Bishops of the 19th Century

During the nineteenth century, the Holy Spirit blessed the Catholic Church in America with some of its finest bishops. Most of these men

St. Isaac Jogues

served as the first bishops of the dioceses in which they were installed. They also toiled in a nation that generally did not like Catholics. Despite the challenges, these outstanding bishops led the Church in the United States from a small handful of churches and parishes to become the largest denomination in the country. Moreover, because of the great zeal these men possessed in adhering to the truths of the Faith, the Catholic Church in America during the nineteenth century never suffered any significant heresy.

Besides Bishops Carroll, Flaget, and Fenwick, among the more outstanding bishops in a group of exceptional men, the following deserve special recognition: Jean-Louis Lefebvre de Cheverus, who was made the first bishop of Boston, Massachusetts, in 1810; John England, first bishop of Charleston, South Carolina (1820); Simon Bruté, first bishop of Vincennes, Indiana, now the Archdiocese of Indianapolis (1834); and Jean-Baptiste Lamy, first bishop of Santa Fe, New Mexico (1850). In addition to these outstanding prelates, four additional bishops merit individual distinction.

Archbishop John Hughes

John Hughes (1797-1864) was the fourth bishop of the diocese of New York and its first archbishop. Born in Ireland, he immigrated with his family to America in 1817. Discerning his call to the priesthood as a young man, he went to Mount Saint Mary's College at Emmitsburg and worked there for a year as a gardener before being admitted as a student. In 1826, he was ordained. He was assigned to the Philadelphia diocese, where his abilities attracted widespread attention.

In 1837, Pope Gregory XVI named Father John Hughes coadjutor bishop of the diocese of New York. In this role, he served as the assistant bishop to New York's 73-year-old Bishop John Dubois. In 1842, following the death of Bishop Dubois, John Hughes became bishop of New York. In 1851, while on a papal visit, Pope Pius IX personally chose him to be the first archbishop of New York.

During his years as a priest, Father Hughes had earned a reputation as a vigorous defender of the Church and the laity. His great zeal for Catholic education inspired him to fight for public support of Catholic schools. He soon realized that he could not make non-Catholics understand that Catholics were being treated unfairly. The government was depriving Catholics of the right to share in the educational benefits for which they were being taxed. Therefore, Bishop Hughes began building Catholic schools in every parish in his diocese.

Bishop Hughes also vigorously defended the Church against bigotry and intolerance. Many American Protestants

John Hughes
Fourth bishop and first archbishop of New York; vigorously defended his flock and showed generous patriotism, especially during the Civil War.

John Hughes

believed that a person could not be both a good American and a good Catholic. The Nativist movement was the leading source of this intolerance. As previously noted, in 1844 members of this anti-Catholic movement burned two Catholic churches and a convent in Philadelphia. They planned to have a meeting the following year in New York City. Bishop Hughes urged the mayor not to allow the meeting, lest violence break out, but he also made plans of his own to protect Church property. His fearless attitude prevented the Nativists from holding their meeting. Over the years, his great love of the people and his self-sacrificing patriotism won the support of fair-minded Americans. For a while at least, the power of anti-Catholic bigotry was broken.

During the Civil War, Archbishop Hughes provided a wonderful example of patriotism. He inspired priests and nuns to go onto the battlefields and into hospitals to care for the sick and wounded. He also traveled to France and obtained support for the Union. When Archbishop John Hughes died, President Lincoln honored his service to America.

Among his other notable achievements, Archbishop Hughes founded Fordham University. Deeply distressed by the condition of the poor in New York, he established the Society of St. Vincent de Paul there. He also laid the cornerstone for St. Patrick's Cathedral on the Feast of the Assumption in 1858. John Hughes died on January 3, 1864. After St. Patrick's Cathedral was completed, his remains were moved and reburied under the sanctuary. This magnificent Gothic cathedral stands as a fitting monument to this great Catholic bishop.

Bishop St. John Neumann

Of the many outstanding leaders who guided the fledgling Church in the United States through the rough times of the nineteenth century, only one U.S. bishop achieved the highest of all honors: being canonized a *saint*. That man was **St. John Neumann** (1811-1860). John Nepomucene Neumann was born in Bohemia in 1811. He received his education for the priesthood in his native land. However, in 1835, after completing his clerical studies, he was unable to find a parish in Bohemia where he could serve as a priest. Therefore, John came to America. In 1836, he was ordained a priest in New York City by Bishop John Dubois. For four years, Father Neumann worked as a missionary in the western part of New York State. In 1840, he joined the Redemptorist Order. Over the next years, his intelligence and hard work garnered great admiration and attention. In March 1852, he was consecrated Philadelphia's fourth bishop. He administered his diocese with great zeal, love, and wisdom for the rest of his life.

Bishop John Neumann was one of the leading theologians at the First Plenary Council of Baltimore. Following the recommendations of the council, he took the few existing Philadelphia Catholic schools and organized them into the first diocesan school system. He increased the

St. Patrick's Cathedral, New York City

> **St. John Neumann**
> Fourth bishop of Philadelphia; organized the first diocesan school system.

St. John Neumann Helping an Immigrant Family

John McCloskey
First bishop of Albany, then the second archbishop of New York, and the first cardinal in the United States.

number of parochial schools in his diocese from a handful to 200. For this reason, he is sometimes called the "Father of the Parochial School System."

Bishop Neumann had a great personal devotion to the Blessed Mother. Pope Pius IX invited him to Rome when the Holy Father defined the dogma of the Immaculate Conception. Bishop Neumann also had a great devotion to the Blessed Sacrament. He established the Forty Hours' Devotion in his diocese. He used every means to inflame the people with love for their Eucharistic Savior.

John Neumann died in 1860. Pope Paul VI canonized him in 1977. After his canonization, the National Shrine of St. John Neumann was constructed in Philadelphia to house his remains.

Cardinal John McCloskey

The first cardinal in the United States, **John McCloskey** (1810-1885), was born in New York City to Irish immigrant parents. He attended Catholic elementary school and Mount St. Mary's College, from which he graduated in 1826. The following year, a tragic accident seriously injured him. During his recovery, McCloskey discerned that he had a vocation and returned to Mount St. Mary's, where he began studying for the priesthood. On January 12, 1834, Bishop John Dubois ordained John McCloskey as a priest for the diocese of New York.

Over the next years, McCloskey served as a priest while continuing his studies at Catholic colleges and universities in Europe. In 1843, Pope Gregory XVI appointed McCloskey as coadjutor bishop of New York. Bishop John Hughes presided at his consecration as bishop.

On May 21, 1847, Pope Pius IX named John McCloskey the bishop of the newly created Diocese of Albany, New York. As bishop, McCloskey built a cathedral and more than quadrupled the number of parishes. He also built a seminary, and the number of priests in his diocese almost tripled. Additionally, he attended the First Plenary Council of Baltimore. Following the council's exhortation that every parish have a school, Bishop McCloskey built fifteen parochial schools.

> **James Gibbons**
> Bishop and apostolic vicar of North Carolina; brought the sacraments to the scattered Catholics in his large diocese and evangelized the Protestants there.

After Archbishop John Hughes died in 1864, Pope Pius IX named John McCloskey New York's second archbishop. He resumed construction of the new St. Patrick's Cathedral, which Bishop Hughes had started. He dedicated the magnificent cathedral in May 1879. In 1866, he attended the Second Plenary Council of Baltimore. Three years later, he attended the First Vatican Council, where he voted for the doctrine of papal infallibility.

During his twenty-one years as archbishop of New York, John McCloskey increased the number of parishes by eighty-eight, and he specifically created a parish for black Catholics. During this time, the number of priests in his diocese more than doubled to four hundred. The number of children attending New York's parochial schools increased as well.

In March 1875, while Archbishop McCloskey was attending a consistory in Rome, Pope Pius IX elevated him to the Sacred College, making him the United States' first cardinal. Although he was eligible to vote in the election of Pius IX's successor, Cardinal McCloskey arrived in Rome too late to participate in the conclave, which elected Pope Leo XIII.

After a lengthy illness, John McCloskey died on October 10, 1885. He was buried in St. Patrick's Cathedral. The man who delivered the eulogy at Cardinal McCloskey's funeral was his good friend, Bishop James Gibbons, America's second cardinal.

Cardinal John McCloskey

Cardinal James Gibbons

James Gibbons (1834-1921) was born in Baltimore on July 23, 1834, to Irish immigrants. In 1839, his father moved the family back to Ireland for health reasons. However, his father's health failed to improve, and he died in 1847. In 1853, James' mother returned to the United States, settling the family in New Orleans.

Witness to the Faith

Cardinal James Gibbons

Martin John Spalding

In 1855, believing that he had a vocation, James entered St. Charles College in Maryland, before entering St. Mary's Seminary in Baltimore two years later. During his time in the seminary, his health diminished so severely that it appeared he would not be ordained. Yet, by the grace of God and the strength of his own will, he completed seminary. On June 30, 1861, he was ordained a priest by Archbishop Francis Kenrick in Baltimore Cathedral.

Over the years, Father Gibbons served at various parishes, eventually becoming secretary to Baltimore's archbishop, Martin John Spalding, in 1865. As secretary, he helped Archbishop Spalding prepare for the Second Plenary Council of Baltimore. During the council, the archbishop recommended that the state of North Carolina be made an apostolic vicariate (a type of mission diocese) and that Father Gibbons be placed in charge. The council agreed. In March 1868, Pope Pius IX made Father Gibbons the apostolic vicar of North Carolina, as well as a bishop. At the age of 34, James Gibbons was one of the youngest bishops in the world.

North Carolina, while geographically large, is located in what is known as the "Bible Belt"—a predominantly Protestant section of the South. Bishop Gibbons' diocese probably contained fewer than seven hundred Catholics. His main mission, besides ensuring that Catholics had access to the sacraments, was to evangelize the Protestants in his diocese.

As Bishop Gibbons engaged in his conversion efforts, he discovered that none of the existing apologetics books met his needs. Undeterred, he wrote his own book, *Faith of Our Fathers*. Published in 1876, it would become one of the best-selling religion books in history. By 1917, it had sold over 1.4 million copies, an incredible number for those times, ranking it with the Bible and *Uncle Tom's Cabin* as among the best-selling books of the nineteenth century. *Faith of Our Fathers* made Bishop James Gibbons a celebrity. His sermons even began attracting non-Catholics who appreciated his perspective on Christianity.

In 1869, Bishop Gibbons attended the First Vatican Council in Rome, where he voted in favor of papal infallibility. In July 1872, Pope Pius IX named James Gibbons the bishop of Richmond, Virginia, where he served until the pope named him the bishop of Baltimore in May 1877. In 1886, Pope Leo XIII elevated James Gibbons to the rank of cardinal. In 1903, Cardinal Gibbons had the honor of participating in the papal conclave that elected Pope Pius X, thus becoming the first American ever to vote in an election of a pope.

Cardinal Gibbons' influence extended well beyond the Church. Almost every American president from Rutherford B. Hayes to Woodrow Wilson sought his counsel and advice. Some became his close friends. In 1917, former President Theodore Roosevelt said to Cardinal Gibbons: "Taking your life as a whole, I think you are the most respected, venerated, and useful citizen of our country." Cardinal James Gibbons died on March 24, 1921. He was buried in Baltimore Cathedral, where he had been baptized more than eighty-six years earlier.

American Saints of the Nineteenth Century

The Holy Spirit also blessed the Church in America during the nineteenth century with several saints. In addition to Bishop Neumann, the Church has canonized Elizabeth Ann Seton, Rose Duchesne, Mother Theodore Guerin, and Frances Xavier Cabrini. Moreover, Pope Benedict XVI canonized two saints who worked with the lepers in Hawaii: Marianne Cope (1838-1918), a Franciscan nun; and Father Damien (1840-1889), a priest of the Sacred Hearts of Jesus and Mary.

St. Elizabeth Ann Seton

Elizabeth Ann Bayley (1774-1821) was born in New York City and raised in the Episcopal Church. When she was 19, she married William Seton. God blessed them with five children. After William became ill, his doctor advised the family to move to Italy because its warmer climate would improve his health. Despite this move, William died in 1803, leaving Elizabeth to care for their five children. While staying with Catholic friends in Italy, she learned about the Catholic Faith and decided to convert. In 1805, after she returned to the United States, Bishop Carroll received **Elizabeth Ann Seton** and her children into the Church, despite the opposition of her family and friends, who then abandoned her.

In 1806, St. Elizabeth Ann Seton and three other women opened a Catholic school for girls in Baltimore—the first free Catholic school in the United States. Since the women wished to devote themselves more completely to God, they formed a religious community, which they called the Sisters of Charity. Although she was still raising her children, Elizabeth Ann Seton was elected the order's first superior. She spent the rest of her life leading and developing the new order. Dedicating themselves to educating and caring for the poor, the Sisters of Charity grew and established new convents around the country.

Elizabeth Ann Seton died in 1821. Pope Paul VI canonized her in 1975. She is the first native-born American citizen to be canonized. She is considered the founder of the Catholic school system in the United States. Several Catholic churches and schools, including one home study school, are named in her honor.

St. Elizabeth Ann Seton
Converted to Catholicism from the Episcopal Church; established a Catholic school for girls, the first free Catholic school in the United States; founded the Sisters of Charity, who dedicated themselves to educating and caring for the poor.

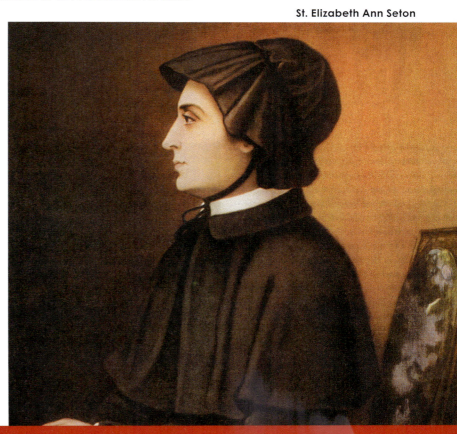

St. Elizabeth Ann Seton

Witness to the Faith 485

St. Rose Philippine Duchesne

St. Rose Duchesne

Rose Philippine Duchesne (1769-1852) was born in Grenoble, France. When she was 18, she entered the Visitation Order. However, when that order was suppressed during the French Revolution, she joined St. Madeleine Sophie Barat to found the Society of the Sacred Heart. In 1818, Rose came to New Orleans to work in the American missions. She founded her main mission in St. Charles, Missouri (the site of her shrine). Six additional missions followed, which included schools and orphanages. She had a special concern for Native Americans, and she devoted much of her work to their care and education. During her lifetime, Pope Leo XII noted her accomplishments and blessed her work. Pope St. John Paul II canonized her in 1988.

Mother Theodore Guerin

Anne-Therese Guerin (1798-1856) was born in France in 1798. At the time of her birth, the French Revolution was trying to destroy the Catholic Church in France. Because the government was closing Catholic schools, Anne-Therese's mother homeschooled her. At the age of 10, Anne-Therese felt called to be a religious sister. She wanted to enter a religious community when she was 15, but could not because she had to care for her sister and sick mother. In 1825, she was able to join the Sisters of Providence and took the name **Sister St. Theodore**. She spent the next years teaching and caring for the poor.

In 1839, Simon Bruté, the bishop of Vincennes, Indiana, sent his coadjutor bishop, Celestine de la Hailandiere, to France to find a religious order that could come to his

486 Chapter 31: The Church in the United States in the 18th and 19th Centuries

diocese to teach and assist with the poor. Bishop Bruté knew the value of such an order, having worked with St. Elizabeth Ann Seton and her Sisters of Charity. Although Bishop Bruté died in June, his successor, Bishop Celestine de la Hailandiere, continued his work with the Sisters of Providence. In October 1840, Sister St. Theodore and five other sisters from the order arrived in Vincennes. The head of the new mission would be Sister St. Theodore.

Mother Theodore and her fellow Sisters of Providence immediately began their missionary activities. From 1840 to 1855, they opened several parish schools in Indiana. In late 1840, they established a boarding school for girls. This school later became St. Mary of the Woods College, the oldest Catholic college in Indiana. Mother Theodore also established two orphanages in Vincennes. She was canonized a saint by Pope Benedict XVI in 2006.

> **Rose Philippine Duchesne**
> French missionary sister in the American frontier; founded schools in the wild new territory and had a special love for Native Americans.

> **Anne-Therese Guerin (Sister St. Theodore)**
> French missionary sister who opened schools and orphanages in Indiana, including the oldest Catholic college there.

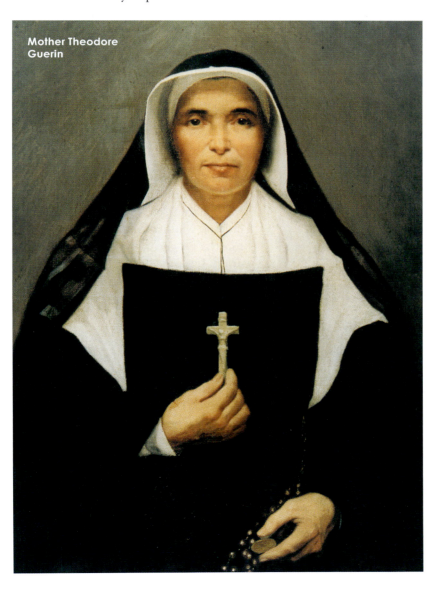

Mother Theodore Guerin

Witness to the Faith

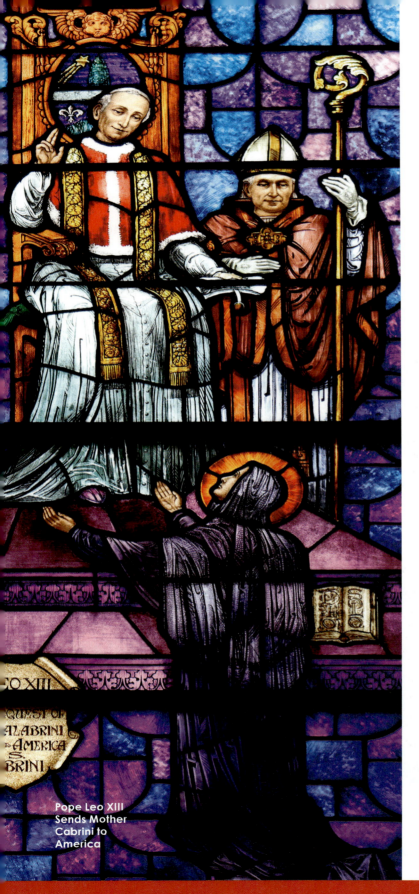

Pope Leo XIII Sends Mother Cabrini to America

Frances Xavier Cabrini

Frances Cabrini (1850-1917) was born in a small town in Italy in 1850, the youngest of thirteen children. She was born two months prematurely, and her health was delicate her entire life. Despite her health issues, this incredibly energetic woman accomplished more than most people would in two lifetimes.

When Frances was 13, her parents sent her to study with the Daughters of the Sacred Heart. At the age of 18, she became a teacher. However, when she tried to become a member of the order, the sisters refused her because of her frail health. So she continued to support her parents until they died. In 1877, Frances was finally allowed to take religious vows. She added "Xavier" to her name to honor the great Jesuit missionary, St. Francis Xavier.

Frances then became the mother superior of an orphanage. When the orphanage was closed in 1880, she and seven other sisters founded the Missionary Sisters of the Sacred Heart of Jesus. Mother Cabrini acted as the superior general of the order until her death. Over the next seven years, Mother Cabrini's order worked with the poor and orphans. The order's success brought her to the attention of Pope Leo XIII.

Mother's Cabrini's dream was to be a missionary to China, like her namesake. In September 1877, she asked Pope Leo for permission to start a mission there. However, Pope Leo recommended that, rather than going east, she go west to the United States to help the Catholic immigrants there.

In 1889, Pope Leo XIII sent Mother Cabrini with six other sisters to New York City. There, with the permission of Archbishop Michael Corrigan, she founded an orphanage. It was the first of sixty-seven charitable institutions she founded across the United States, South America, and Europe. In 1909, Mother Cabrini became an American citizen. She died on December 22, 1917. Pope Pius XII canonized her in 1946. St. Frances Xavier Cabrini is the patron saint of immigrants.

The Catholic Church at the Turn of the Century

By 1900, more than 10 million Catholics lived in the United States. Catholics compromised about 14 percent of the entire population. Most lived in the industrial Northeast. Following the decrees of the three plenary councils of Baltimore, America's Catholic bishops had dedicated themselves to creating a robust parochial school system that rivaled the government-run public school system. By 1900, about 3,500 parochial schools operated in the United States. The bishops could say, "Mission accomplished."

The United States no longer held the status of "mission territory." The nation had two cardinals, over 90 bishops, and more than 12,000 priests. The Catholic Church in the U.S. was not merely financially independent; it was becoming wealthy. In the next century, the United States would become the leading financial supporter of nearly all Catholic projects worldwide. Meanwhile, Catholic social service organizations sought to help America's needy through a variety of programs.

Although Catholics still faced prejudice, Americans more readily accepted Catholics into American society. In the new century, Catholic lay men and women became leaders in all parts of society, from entertainment to politics. Both major political parties sought the "Catholic vote," and Catholics would run for the nation's highest office.

As the twentieth century began, the Catholic Church in the United States faced the same challenges it had in the previous century, but it was now larger, better funded, and better prepared for the challenges. To paraphrase St. Matthew (13:31-32): In 1800, the Church in this nation was like a mustard seed that a person took and sowed in a field. It was the smallest of seeds. However, when full grown, it was the largest of plants, and the birds of the sky could come and dwell in its branches. By 1900, the Catholic Church in the United States of America had grown quite large. In the next century, it would grow even larger.

Frances Cabrini
Italian foundress of the Missionary Sisters of the Sacred Heart; served Catholic immigrants in the United States.

Oral Exercises

1. Who was the first bishop in the United States?
2. Name four reasons the Church grew so rapidly in the United States during the nineteenth century.
3. Why did the bishops start the Catholic school system in the United States?
4. Who was the only U.S. bishop to be canonized?
5. Who was the first cardinal in the United States?
6. What is the name of Cardinal Gibbons' best-selling book?
7. Where did Elizabeth Ann Seton learn about the Catholic Faith?
8. What religious order did St. Elizabeth Ann Seton found?
9. In what state did Mother Theodore mostly work?
10. Who is the patron saint of immigrants?

Witness to the Faith   489

Chapter 32
The Church in the Nineteenth Century (1815-1878)

The Catholic Revival

Because of Pope Pius VII's heroic defiance of Napoleon, the Catholic Church became more respected throughout Europe. In particular, the British began to soften their anti-Catholic policies. As a result, the Church experienced a great revival throughout much of Christendom. In fact, for the next two hundred years, as the Holy Spirit blessed the Church with some of its finest popes, the Church really enjoyed a golden age.

Almost immediately upon his return to Rome from his captivity, Pius VII began to undo the damage that the Enlightenment, the French Revolution, and Napoleon had done to the Church and to Christendom. One of his first acts was to restore the Jesuits. Once more, these loyal priests worked to spread the Faith around the world. Pius also began making concordats with various European governments to protect the rights of the Church.

France

After Napoleon's defeat, the Church in France experienced an amazing rebirth over the next several decades. A number of Catholic laymen, led by Count Francois-René de Chateaubriand, sought to restore the Church to its rightful place as the leading influence of French culture and society. Chateaubriand, because of the quality and extent

> **Romanticism (Romantic Movement)**
> An artistic and literary movement that tended to emphasize emotion and the beauty of nature, and was often inspired by medieval culture.

490 Chapter 32: The Church in the Nineteenth Century (1815-1878)

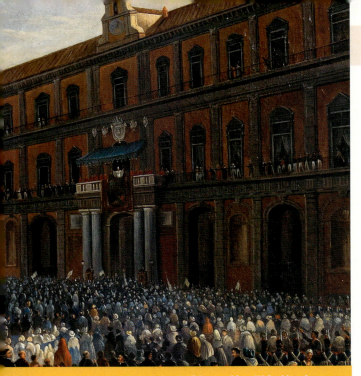

The Arrival of Pope Pius IX in Naples, **Salvatore Fergola**

1829 A.D. – 1870 A.D.

1829 A.D.
In England, The Act of Catholic Emancipation is passed.

1832 A.D.
The Miraculous Medal begins to be distributed.

1837-1839 A.D.
Archbishop Clemens of Cologne is imprisoned for upholding the Church's teaching on mixed marriages; he is eventually released because of the Catholic outcry in Germany.

1848 A.D.
Revolutions break out in various parts of Europe, including Italy. Pope Pius IX is forced to flee to Naples.

1850 A.D.
Pope Pius IX restores the Catholic diocesan hierarchy in England.

1858 A.D.
Our Lady appears to St. Bernadette at Lourdes.

1862-1877 A.D.
Otto von Bismarck attacks the Church in Germany through the *Kulturkampf*.

1869 A.D.
The First Vatican Council meets at St. Peter's Basilica.

1870 A.D.
King Victor Emmanuel invades the Papal States and Rome. Pope Pius IX surrenders to avoid any bloodshed.

of his writings, is credited with founding the movement known as **Romanticism** (or the **Romantic Movement**) in French literature and is considered the most important French author of the first half of the nineteenth century. Chateaubriand directly attacked the anti-Catholicism of the Enlightenment with a strong defense of the Catholic Faith in *The Genius of Christianity*, which he wrote in the 1790s. Although forced to live in exile in America and England during the French Revolution, he eventually served in the government of restored Kings Louis XVIII and Charles X. However, his primary loyalty remained to the Catholic Church, which he, along with other like-minded Catholics, defended against intrusions by the government. Because of this, he fell out of favor with the government and died a recluse, but a devoted Catholic, on July 4, 1848.

Witness to the Faith

Another leader of France's Catholic rebirth was the brilliant writer **Henri Lacordaire**. In some ways, the life of Henri Lacordaire recalls that of St. Augustine. Born in 1802, Henri was raised by his widowed mother after his father died when he was a young child. Although raised Catholic, he lost his faith when he went away to school. While studying to become a lawyer, he had a conversion experience and, in 1824, decided to become a priest. Three years later, he was ordained. Over the next several years, he began working with radical Catholics who supported revolutionary movements, which erupted in 1830. In October 1830, he founded a newspaper along with three other priests.

In 1832, when Pope Gregory XVI condemned some of the ideas in this newspaper, Lacordaire declared that he only sought to be obedient to the Church, and he resigned as editor. He abandoned his career as a journalist and, in 1839, became a Dominican in Rome (because the order was illegal in France at the time). Despite the law, Lacordaire returned to France as a Dominican. He began publicly preaching and came to be regarded as the finest preacher in France. He also began establishing monasteries. In 1850, the Dominican Order was officially re-established in France, under his direction. Father Henri Lacordaire died in 1861.

Henri Lacordaire

Another prominent French author who fought for the Church in France was Joseph de Maistre. Born in 1753, he was blessed to receive a Jesuit education and remained a staunch defender of the Jesuits his entire life. In his 1819 book *On the Pope*, he showed that throughout history the pope was the foremost champion of Christianity against all its enemies. Throughout his life, de Maistre wrote against the anti-Catholic doctrines of the Enlightenment. He died two years after publishing *On the Pope*.

Other influential French authors who defended the Church during this period include the priest Robert Lamennais, the historian René Montalembert, and the poet Alphonse Lamartine. These men zealously fought for the Catholic Faith with the best of intentions, but made some mistakes. Lamennais and Montalembert joined with Henri Lacordaire to found their newspaper. The paper began propounding views that the Church deemed too radical and too favorable toward the French Revolution. Pope Gregory XVI declared that some of the ideas they held regarding the role of the Church and government did not agree with the teachings of the Church. Lacordaire and Montalembert submitted to the judgment of Pope Gregory, but Lamennais remained obstinate, and he renounced his faith in 1833. The following year, Pope Gregory condemned some of his writings. Lamennais became even more radical as he grew older. He died in 1854, still unreconciled to the Church.

Of all the leaders of the Catholic renaissance in France, arguably none has had the lasting impact of **Blessed Frederic Ozanam** (1813-1853). As a young man, he became involved in the Catholic literary movement and became friends with Count Chateaubriand, Henri Lacordaire, and René Montalembert. While his friends had a great interest in politics,

Henri Lacordaire
A writer and leader of the Catholic revival in France; worked as a journalist, then entered the Dominicans and re-established the Dominican Order in France.

Frederic's concern lay in aiding the poor. In May 1833, Frederic and a group of other young men founded the Society of Saint Vincent de Paul. Its main purpose was to visit the poor in their own homes.

Ozanam and the founders of the Vincent de Paul Society based their mission on the work of the Daughters of Charity of Saint Vincent de Paul, a religious congregation that worked with the poor in the slums of Paris. Frederic's first act of charity was to take winter firewood to a poor widow. Because the Vincent de Paul Society was a lay society, Frederic continued to work as a lawyer, teacher, and author. He married and had a daughter. Unfortunately, he had always been a sickly person, and he died in 1853 at the age of 40. Pope St. John Paul II beatified him in 1997.

Blessed Frederic Ozanam
A layman who founded the Society of St. Vincent de Paul to serve the poor in their own homes.

Germany

In Germany, the Catholic revival was tied to the Romantic Movement (Romanticism)—the same movement that Chateaubriand had started in French literature. As was the case elsewhere in Europe, in Germany, Romanticism affected not only literature, but also art, music, and architecture. Essentially, Romanticism was a reaction against *classicism* (that is, the imitation of classical Greek and Roman culture) and against the rationalism and materialism of the Enlightenment. It tended to emphasize emotion and the beauty of nature, and was often inspired by medieval culture.

The greatest writers of the German Classic Period (1748-1805), such as Johann Wolfgang von Goethe and Frederick Schiller, were heavily influenced by and supported the Enlightenment and its revolutionary ideals. Their works, while not always overtly anti-Christian, often contained images and scenes that were contrary to Catholic morality and fundamental Christian teachings. For example, in an early work by Goethe, his hero commits suicide.

On the other hand, Goethe's dramatic play *Faust* (1832), which many historians consider the greatest work in German literature, contains a number of Catholic images. After the hero, Faust, falls into temptation and commits sin, he atones for his sins, and in the end his soul is saved. The final scene depicts Gretchen, who loves Faust, praying to the Blessed Mother to intercede for him. Because of her love and prayers, angels carry Faust's soul to Heaven.

Faust reflects the themes that prevailed in much of Germany's Romantic literature. Germany's classic writers had modeled their books after the ancient pagan cultures of Greece and Rome. However, many of the authors of the Romantic Movement found inspiration for their work in the history of Germany during the Middle Ages. These authors, reacting to the paganism of the Enlightenment, returned to a time that honored Catholicism. They showed how the Catholic Church had enriched the lives of the people, not led them into darkness. *Faust* is based on a German folk tale about a man, Johann Faust, who lived at the end of the Middle Ages.

Count Francois-René de Chateaubriand

Witness to the Faith

The Alte Pinakothek in Munich, Germany

Joseph van Gorres
A writer and leader of Germany's Catholic revival.

Nazarene Movement
Catholic subdivision of German Romantic art; the members lived in Rome as artist-monks.

One of the key leaders of Germany's Catholic revival was a reformed revolutionary, **Joseph van Gorres** (1776-1848). Gorres initially supported the French Revolution, but changed his opinion after visiting revolutionary France. He became even more opposed when Napoleon conquered Germany. Following Napoleon's final defeat, Gorres began to identify with Romanticism and became outspoken in his defense of the Church and his declaration of her greatness. He became a regular contributor to the magazine *Der Katholik (The Catholic)*, which would become the leading Catholic magazine in Germany. Eventually, Gorres became recognized as a leading defender of the Catholic Faith.

In 1827, King Ludwig I of Bavaria, who strongly supported the Catholic revival in Bavaria, assisted Gorres in obtaining a professorship at the prestigious University of Munich. During his time at the university, through his lectures and voluminous writings, Gorres defended the Church and the rights of Catholics from government intrusion. His scholarly works influenced not only Germany but also the entire Catholic world. As a result, he met with religious leaders from many Catholic nations, including French leaders Lacordaire, Lamennais, and Montalembert. When Joseph van Gorres died in 1848, the Church in Germany lost its strongest and most able defender.

As noted, Romanticism in Germany was not limited to literature. In fact, one of the greatest Catholic art movements in history occurred during this period. Known as the **Nazarene Movement**, it was the Catholic subdivision of German Romantic art. In 1809, six students from Vienna's Academy of Art formed the Brotherhood of St. Luke, named to honor the patron saint of painters. Led by Johann Friedrich Overbeck (1789-1869) and Franz Pforr (1788-1812), the young painters banded together to create a renewal of Catholic art, which they saw as an instrument for moral education and a way to revive the Catholic Church after the attacks of the Enlightenment. In 1810, four of these young men moved to Rome, not simply to study the great masters,

but because the Eternal City was the center of the Catholic Church. In Rome, they adopted a monastic lifestyle that included living in the abandoned monastery of Sant'Isidoro. They essentially became the artistic and spiritual successors of Beato Angelico. As humble artist-monks, they wandered the streets of Rome, whose citizens dubbed them "Nazarenes" because of their long hair and beards. By 1830, the group had disbanded, as the members had died or returned to Germany.

Although largely ignored by modern art historians because of their determination to create sacred art in conformity with Catholic doctrine, the Nazarenes had a far-reaching influence on the history of art. In Italy, their presence led to the formation of a group known as the Purists, Italian artists who sought to create religious art modeled after Renaissance art, especially that of Raphael. In England, they influenced another young group of artists known as the Pre-Raphaelite Brotherhood. The Nazarenes' influence was greatest in Germany. With the exception of Johann Friedrich Overbeck, who remained in Rome, all the surviving Nazarenes became directors of important German art academies and galleries.

During this period, through the efforts of two Catholic brothers, **Sulpiz and Melchior Boisseree**, one of Germany's greatest art museums was established. In 1804, alarmed by the destruction of Church art and its acquisition by anti-Christian governments, the Boisseree brothers began purchasing Catholic medieval art, mostly to protect it. In time, the brothers started a museum to show the art, but it closed after a few years. In 1827, they sold their magnificent collection to King Ludwig I of Bavaria. King Ludwig added their paintings to the Bavarian royal collection, and the combined collections became the foundation for the *Alte Pinakothek* (Old Picture Gallery). Located in Munich, the Alte Pinakothek is among the finest art museums in the world. The Boisseree collection still forms a key segment of this museum's medieval and early Renaissance collection.

Sulpiz and Melchior Boisseree

Two brothers who purchased Catholic medieval art to protect it, eventually selling the art to King Ludwig I of Bavaria. The collection can still be seen in the Alte Pinakothek museum.

Witness to the Faith

Clemens August von Droste-Vischering

Archbishop of Cologne, imprisoned for his defense of the Church's teaching on mixed marriages.

In addition to their work as art historians, the Boisserees also played a key role in the construction of Germany's greatest nineteenth-century architectural achievement. Among the great centers of the Catholic revival in Germany were Munich, Munster, Landshut, and Cologne.

The people of Cologne had begun construction of their cathedral in 1248, the apex of the Gothic period. Cologne Cathedral was planned to be the greatest church in Germany, as it was to be the home church for the Holy Roman Emperor. For the first eighty years, work proceeded well, but it slowed down after 1322, and it stopped completely in 1473. At that point, the south tower was complete only to the belfry level. (Expecting to complete the work, the builders left the crane on the tower—for 400 years!) Some work was done inside, but even this stopped during the sixteenth century. With the advent of Romanticism and the discovery of the cathedral's original plans, a new effort was made to complete the cathedral. In 1842, with the help of the Boisserees and other Catholics, work on Cologne Cathedral resumed. Builders finished the nave and added the towers. Germany's largest cathedral was completed on August 14, 1880—632 years after Cologne's Archbishop Konrad von Hochstaden (1198-1261) laid the foundation stone.

Although the Catholic revival in Germany had many wonderful moments, the Church also experienced struggles. While Bavaria was a Catholic region, Protestants ruled Prussia, the location of Cologne Cathedral. Prussia was the site of one of the more serious matters that German Catholics faced in the first half of the nineteenth century. The issue that caused the confrontation concerned mixed marriages (that is, Catholics marrying non-Catholics).

In 1830, Pope Pius VIII (1829-1830) issued a decree forbidding priests from performing a mixed marriage unless the future husband and wife agreed that their children would be raised Catholic. The Prussian government objected to this decree, insisting that in a mixed marriage, sons should follow the religion of their fathers, and daughters should follow the religion of their mothers.

Archbishop Clemens

In 1835, **Clemens August von Droste-Vischering** became archbishop of Cologne. He would spend most of his ten-year episcopate fighting with the Prussian government over the rights of the Church. Archbishop Clemens insisted that his priests follow the papal order regarding mixed marriages, regardless of the Prussian government's demands to the contrary. For defying the government, the 64-year-old Archbishop Clemens was arrested on November 20, 1837, by order of Prussia's king, Frederick William III, and imprisoned.

The imprisonment of Archbishop Clemens for defending the Church galvanized Catholics throughout Germany. Other bishops defended Clemens and the pope's

Chapter 32: The Church in the Nineteenth Century (1815-1878)

decree, and they too were imprisoned. In December, Pope Gregory XVI praised Archbishop Clemens and condemned his arrest. The Prussian government claimed that the archbishop had committed treason. In response, in 1838 Joseph Gorres published his most important work, *Athanasius*, an indictment of the policies of the Prussian government and a stirring defense of the Catholic Church. Gorres' book and the courage of Archbishop Clemens had a profound impact on the people of Germany. This sad incident actually marked the height of the Catholic revival in Germany, as so many Catholics rallied to the defense of a clearly innocent man. The Catholic outcry finally compelled the government to release Archbishop Clemens in April 1839. Gorres and Clemens had won a great victory for the Catholic Church in Germany.

Edmund Burke

Great Britain

Unlike France and Germany, Great Britain had been openly hostile to the Catholic Church since the late sixteenth century. Yet, in the span of only a few decades, during the first half of the nineteenth century, the situation in Britain improved dramatically. As with all such great events, the blessings of the Holy Spirit and the courage and devotion of Catholic men and women altered the course of history.

The first major change involved Catholics being granted the rights of citizens, a process also known as **Catholic Emancipation**. Daniel O'Connell led this movement. The second event was the Oxford Movement, led by notable English clerics such as St. John Henry Newman. The final development was the restoration of the Catholic hierarchy in Great Britain, an effort also involving Newman.

Catholic Emancipation

In the late eighteenth century, Edmund Burke, England's leading political thinker and a member of Parliament, began to argue that Britain's government should treat Catholics better. Although Burke was not Catholic himself, his mother was Catholic. As Burke became more well known and admired for his opposition to the French Revolution, his views on the Church began to receive a more receptive audience, especially in Parliament.

For example, in 1774, Parliament enacted the Quebec Act, which gave Catholics in Canada more freedom. Parliament subsequently passed other laws, which allowed Catholics to own and inherit land. In 1782, the Church was allowed to establish Catholic schools in Great Britain. In 1791, the British Roman Catholic Relief Act granted even more rights to Catholics, including the right to freely practice their Catholic Faith, although with some minor restrictions.

Catholic Emancipation
A process in which British Catholics were granted the rights of citizens.

Witness to the Faith

Bolstered by these new pro-Catholic laws, Irish Catholics met together in early December of 1792 at a large Catholic convention in Dublin, Ireland. They agreed to petition King George III for full emancipation.

Based on the political activism of the Irish Catholics, the Irish Parliament adopted the Roman Catholic Relief Act in 1793. This act gave Irish Catholics the right to vote, to serve on juries, and to hold certain civil and military offices. It also permitted them to attend Trinity College in Dublin, Ireland's preeminent university. On the other hand, Catholics were still not allowed to serve in the Houses of the Irish Parliament or to hold positions in the higher offices of the British Empire.

In 1801, political concerns caused the Kingdom of Great Britain (England and Scotland) to merge with the Kingdom of Ireland. This union created the United Kingdom of Great Britain and Ireland. (Even today, Great Britain is officially known as the United Kingdom.) There was now one Parliament for England and Ireland: the Parliament of Great Britain. Representatives of the Irish people *could* become members of the British Parliament, but there was an obstacle for Catholics: Members of Parliament were required to take the Oath of Supremacy, which Henry VIII had enacted and Elizabeth I had restored. Those who took the Oath acknowledged the king or queen of England as the Head of the Church. Of course, Catholics could not take this oath. Under the leadership of the eminent Irish patriot **Daniel O'Connell** (1775-1847), Irish Catholics resolved to fight this injustice. O'Connell opposed any violent insurrection. He and his followers would battle for change only through peaceful, legal means.

Daniel O'Connell started his campaign for emancipation in 1810. As an experienced attorney, he understood the British legal system. In 1823, he founded the Catholic Association. Its goal was to gain the full rights of citizenship for the Catholics of England and Ireland. Over the next few years, the Catholic Association grew quite large and politically powerful. In 1826, Irish Catholics agreed to oppose any candidate for Parliament who did not favor emancipation. Two years later, Daniel O'Connell was elected to Parliament by a large majority.

Daniel O'Connell
Irish patriot and leader of the Catholic Emancipation movement in Ireland.

Trinity College in Dublin, Ireland

O'Connell's election presented a serious problem to the British government. They knew that he would not take the Oath of Supremacy. In fact, he had been elected purposely to challenge the Act of Supremacy. Yet, if they failed to allow him to take his seat in Parliament, Ireland (which was about 85 percent Catholic) might very well break into armed insurrection, despite O'Connell's objection to violence.

For the next few years, England's leaders worked to eliminate the anti-Catholic requirement. After a period of negotiation, the Act of Catholic Emancipation was enacted in 1829. Catholics could now hold public office or become members of Parliament without having to renounce their Faith or swear an oath contrary to it. In 1830, Daniel O'Connell took his seat as a member of Parliament. He served until 1847. In 1841, he became the mayor of Dublin, the first Catholic to hold that office in more than 150 years.

For the remainder of his life, Daniel O'Connell fought for the rights of Catholics as well as Ireland's independence from Great Britain. He insisted that the Irish people had the right to govern themselves and not be subject to England, especially since England was Protestant. Although he did not live to see Ireland obtain her independence, he kept the dream of freedom alive in the hearts of Irish men and women everywhere. Daniel O'Connell died while on a pilgrimage to Rome in 1847.

Contemporary Poster Showing Daniel O'Connell Refusing to Take the Anti-Catholic Oath

The Oxford Movement

The **Oxford Movement**, which would have a monumental impact on the Catholic Church in England during the first half of the nineteenth century, actually had its origins in the Church of England, the Anglican Church. By the beginning of the nineteenth century, the Church of England had fallen into disarray. State control had paralyzed its spiritual growth. A large number of Anglican theologians questioned many of its beliefs. They felt that Anglicanism, if it were to survive, needed to broaden its appeal to the general public. They believed that the Church of England needed to become more open-minded (liberal) in its theology and be willing to accept anyone as a member who professed the most basic dogmas of Christianity. Because they favored a broad range of beliefs, these theologians came to be known as the "Broad Church." To Anglican theologians who held more traditional views, these notions threatened the very existence of the Church of England.

The dispute between these liberal and traditional factions caused a split in the Anglican Church. Those who favored the older traditions came to be known as the **High Church**. Those who believed in a more broad approach were called the **Low Church**.

In the beginning, most members of the High Church movement were professors at Oxford University, or were associated with the university. For

Oxford Movement
A movement that began at Oxford University and gradually led to the conversion of John Henry Newman and others from the Anglican Church to the Catholic Church.

High Church
Anglicans who favored maintaining traditional doctrine.

Low Church
Anglicans who wanted to allow a broad range of beliefs.

Witness to the Faith   499

example, Richard Froude, a leading Anglican priest, had graduated from Oxford and returned to teach as a professor. It was at Oxford that Froude met and became close friends with **John Henry Newman** (1801-1890), another professor at Oxford. Newman was a brilliant academic as well as an Anglican priest serving at Christ Church Cathedral in Oxford, a highly prestigious position in the Anglican Church. Froude convinced Newman of the value of tradition. He talked to Newman about the importance of a Church being free from State control and possessing a strong and independent hierarchy, in contrast to the current Anglican situation.

Newman studied the Church Fathers and began to move from his "Low Church" leanings toward a more "High Church" position. Together with Froude, he began to advocate a return to the early Christianity of the Fathers and a revival of early dogma and theology. However, neither Newman nor Froude was ready to leave the Church of England. They felt that a *via media* (middle way), a position between Catholicism and the Low Church—that is, the High Church—was viable.

In the summer of 1833, Newman wrote the first in a series of pamphlets called *Tracts for the Times*, which explained the beliefs of the High Church. The goal of these tracts was to refute the Low Church by declaring that the Church of England needed specific rules and doctrines, not some broad-based, ill-defined notion of "Christianity." Those supporting these tracts came to be known as **Tractarians**.

In the ninety tracts written between 1833 and 1841, Newman and other members of the Oxford Movement addressed various topics, including Apostolic succession, the liturgy, and the constitution of the Anglican Church. Newman also began preaching the "middle way" in his sermons. The tracts and his sermons created enthusiasm among clergymen and students. However, members of the Low Church accused the Tractarians of favoring Catholicism over Anglicanism. While Newman conceded that the Catholic Church was correct on some points, he was still far from becoming a Catholic.

In September 1839, Newman began to read St. Augustine. Newman would later write that Augustine "pulverized" the *via media*. In 1841, in an attempt to prevent some of the Tractarians from becoming Catholic, Newman published the 90th and final tract. He attempted a Catholic interpretation of the doctrines of the Anglican Church. He argued that the Anglican Church did not deny the fundamental truths of the Catholic Church but had only sought to correct some of the abuses that had crept into the Church during the sixteenth century. The tract caused a firestorm in the Church of England. The heads of Oxford University and the bishop of Oxford condemned the work. They demanded that Newman cease publishing the tracts, which he did, and that he retract his statements, which he did not.

Even the High Church Anglicans had good reasons to be alarmed by Newman's tract. Many Anglicans, disillusioned at

St. John Henry Newman
Brilliant Oxford professor and Anglican priest who was a leader of the Oxford Movement. After converting to the Catholic Church, he was ordained a Catholic priest, and eventually appointed as a cardinal.

Cardinal Newman

the perceived failings of the Church of England, were converting to Catholicism. Newman now believed that the Church of England was not the true Church, but he was still not ready to convert.

Newman left Oxford in 1842. Along with a small group of friends, he moved to the country to live quietly away from public scrutiny. (Richard Froude almost certainly would have joined Newman, but he had died in 1836 at the age of 36.) The men began a deep inquiry into the nature of their religious beliefs. The following February, Newman published a formal retraction of his most violent attacks on the Catholic Church.

In 1844, William George Ward, an Anglican priest and one of the Tractarians, published his *Ideal of a Christian Church*. In this work, he identified the Roman Catholic Church as that ideal. He argued that the only hope for the Church of England was to submit to the authority of the Catholic Church. Oxford University condemned the book. In September 1845, Ward entered the Catholic Church.

Interior of Brompton Oratory

One month later, John Henry Newman entered the Catholic Church as well. Late in the evening of October 8, an Italian priest, Father Dominic Barberi, heard Newman's first Confession. The next day, Newman was received into the Catholic Church. He left behind his family, his friends, and a promising career at Oxford and in the Anglican Church. Perhaps he might have become archbishop of Canterbury, but Our Lord had a greater future planned for him.

On the advice of Monsignor Nicholas Wiseman, the apostolic vicar for England, Newman journeyed to Rome. After studying for the priesthood, Newman was ordained a Catholic priest and joined the Oratorians, the order that St. Philip Neri had founded. At the end of 1847, Newman returned to England. Upon his return, he founded an English Congregation of the Oratory in Birmingham, in February 1848. The following year, he sent another Anglican convert, Father Wilfrid Faber, to establish the Brompton Oratory in London.

The Oxford Movement caused many Anglicans to rethink their most fundamental beliefs about the Catholic Church. Many leading Anglicans became Catholic. Anti-Catholicism was still a major force in England. However, because of men like St. John Henry Newman and the work of the Oratorians, there was hope for change. The Catholic Church had an opportunity not present since the time of Henry VIII. Pope Pius IX decided to act!

Tractarians
Those who supported *Tracts for the Times*, in which John Henry Newman and other members of the Oxford Movement argued for a High Church form of Anglicanism.

Witness to the Faith 501

Restoration of the English Hierarchy

Since the ascension of Queen Elizabeth I to the throne in late 1558, there had been no Catholic hierarchy in England. Although Britain had seen a number of conversions and passed laws legalizing Catholicism (such as the Catholic Relief Act of 1829), the English Catholic hierarchy remained vacant. In 1840, eight apostolic vicars administered to the Church in Britain, which the Church considered mission territory. During the 1840s, millions of Irish Catholics immigrated to England because of Ireland's potato famine. Suddenly, the Catholic population in Britain became quite large. British Catholics asked the pope to return England to normal status and restore the hierarchy. In 1846, Pius IX became pope. He decided to restore the Catholic hierarchy in England.

On September 29, 1850, Pope Pius IX issued the bull *Universalis Ecclesiae*, which restored the Roman Catholic diocesan hierarchy in England. Because the Church of England was using the names of the old Catholic dioceses, new dioceses had to be created with different names. Pius made Nicholas Wiseman a cardinal and the first archbishop of Westminster, rather than archbishop of Canterbury. Westminster, in London, became the main Catholic diocese, and Westminster Cathedral became the mother Catholic church for Britain. In addition to Westminster, Pius divided England into twelve other dioceses.

Over the past three centuries, anti-Catholicism had become so integrated into English society that the sudden restoration of the hierarchy aroused a storm of anti-Catholic bigotry in Great Britain. Windows were broken in Catholic churches, and anti-Catholic demonstrations were held throughout London. During this great hurricane of religious bigotry, Cardinal Wiseman remained calm. He appealed to the English people's sense of fair play. He gently chided the Protestants, seeking to dispel their prejudices. Thanks to Cardinal Wiseman's gentle and loving response, the violence and furor were quelled, and the grievances forgotten.

More Anglicans joined the Church, including such notable clerics as Gerard Manley Hopkins, who became a Jesuit priest and an English poet, and Henry Edward Manning. Manning became a cardinal and the second archbishop of Westminster. In 1879, Pope Leo XIII made John Henry Newman a cardinal, although he had never been a bishop. Newman, Wiseman, and Manning were three outstanding cardinals who guided the Catholic Church in England during much of the nineteenth century.

John Henry Cardinal Newman died on August 11, 1890, after one of the most illustrious careers of any English cleric. Pope Francis canonized him on October 13, 2019.

Gerard Manley Hopkins

Trouble in Italy

One of the most serious problems that the popes of the nineteenth century faced had little to do with religion or morality. It involved the temporal authority of the pope and the Papal States. After Napoleon's defeat, the allies had returned the Papal States to the pope. The threat to the pope's temporal authority came from various groups who sought to unify Italy by capturing the Papal States. This dispute regarding the temporal authority of the pope in Rome and the rest of the Papal States is called the *Roman Question*.

In 1814, one of the leading statesmen in Europe declared that Italy was "only a geographical expression." This was because there was no real nation of Italy. There were only groups of principalities occupying the land on the Italian peninsula. One of these principalities was the Papal States. Different groups, such as the Carbonari, a secret revolutionary society, wanted to unite Italy. The Carbonari also wanted to rid Italy of any Catholic influence. Led by **Giuseppe Mazzini**, a fallen-away Catholic and lifelong revolutionary, the Carbonari sought to undermine the Church. Other groups seeking to unify Italy, although they may have wanted to oust the pope from ruling the Papal States, did not hate the Church. Nevertheless, the pope had to deal with these various nationalist groups.

Giuseppe Mazzini
An Italian revolutionary leader who took power in Italy by force.

Pope Leo XII

Pope Pius VII died on August 20, 1823, after a pontificate of more than 23 years. He had faced down Napoleon and restored the Jesuits. He has been declared a Servant of God.

The conclave of 1823 elected Cardinal della Genga, despite his insistence that his fellow cardinals not elect him. In very bad health, he even went so far as to tell them that they were "electing a corpse." Cardinal della Genga chose the name Leo XII (1823-1829). Despite a pontificate affected by constant sickness, Leo surprised everyone by ruling for five and a half years.

During his pontificate, Leo XII took strong action against the Carbonari in the Papal States. He ordered a few of the worst members executed, and others either imprisoned or exiled. Several hundred were placed on probation with the police. Leo may have been physically ill, but he was strong enough to act against the Church's enemies. Leo XII died on February 10, 1829.

Pope Gregory XVI

Pope Pius VIII (1829-1830) succeeded Leo XII. His twenty-month pontificate is best remembered for his decree on mixed marriages. He died as Europe exploded into revolution.

Pius VIII died on December 1, 1830. For fifty days, the cardinals were unable to choose a successor. Finally, on February 2, 1831, with revolution about to break out in the Papal States, the Sacred College elected Cardinal Mauro Cappellari,

Statue of Giuseppe Mazzini

Witness to the Faith **503**

Pope Gregory XVI

who chose the name Gregory XVI (1831-1846). The next day, revolutionaries seized Bologna in the Papal States. Gregory, like his predecessors, never wavered in the face of the revolution. He called upon the Austrians for aid. They managed to suppress the revolution temporarily. Mazzini was forced into exile. For the remainder of his pontificate, Gregory faced uprisings in the Papal States.

In July 1831, Mazzini, while in exile in France, founded the "Young Italy" movement. The goal was to create a united Italy by means of a general insurrection. Mazzini believed that a violent revolution would unite Italy. In 1833, Giuseppe Garibaldi, a talented soldier, joined Young Italy. Mazzini also started similar revolutionary movements in other European nations.

During his pontificate, Gregory XVI issued two remarkable encyclicals. In the first, *Mirari Vos* (Encyclical on Liberalism and Religious Indifferentism), which he wrote in 1832, he condemned religious indifferentism (the idea that any religion can be a means of bringing about one's eternal salvation). He also denounced the Carbonari and other secret societies seeking to overthrow the governments in Italy, and he defended marriage and clerical celibacy.

In 1839, Pope Gregory condemned "the inhuman slave trade in Negroes and all other men" in his encyclical *In Supremo Apostolatus*. In condemning slavery, he reviewed the history of the Church's position on slavery, including several condemnations by earlier popes. Pope Gregory not only condemned this heinous practice but also went so far as to "prohibit and strictly forbid any Ecclesiastic or lay person from presuming to defend as permissible this traffic."

Blessed Pope Pius IX

For some reason, most popes who choose the name *Pius* seem to have pontificates of special importance (for example, Pius I, V, VI, and VII). Two weeks after Pope Gregory XVI's death on June 1, 1846, the Sacred College convened. The main issue was the governance of the Papal States. Although it seemed that a long conclave might ensue, on the second day the Sacred College elected Cardinal Mastai-Ferretti. He chose the name Pius IX (1846-1878). **His nearly 32-year pontificate would be the second longest in Church history.** Only St. Peter had reigned longer.

Pius IX was only 54 years old when he was elected—young for a pope—and in very good health. He was known to be a man with a kindly and loving disposition who got along well with people, a good quality in a pope.

Initially, Pius IX took a moderate view of the *Risorgimento*, the Italian unification movement. At that time, there were eight separate provincial governments on the Italian peninsula. The people of Italy wanted a united country. When Pius was elected, they called him the "Patriot Pope," thinking he also wanted a united Italy. Whether or not this was true, he was a peacemaker willing to work with the people he governed. Thus, he appointed laymen to important positions in the government of the Papal States. He announced that there would be a parliament in Rome so that the people would have more of a voice in the conduct of government affairs. However, in 1848, nearly all of Europe broke into revolution.

In March 1848, five days of rioting began in Milan. The people built barricades, and revolutionary violence swept over Italy. The Austrians entered Milan and quelled the violence in that city and throughout Italy.

While Pius IX might have continued supporting Italian unification, he would not support it under revolutionary violence. In the middle of September 1848, he appointed Count Pelegrino Rossi as his prime minister. Rossi was determined to preserve the Papal States; the Italian revolutionaries hated him. On November 15, one of Mazzini's henchmen murdered Count Rossi in broad daylight, *in front of Pope Pius IX*, as they walked to attend a meeting. The revolutionaries disarmed the Swiss guards and imprisoned the pope in the Quirinale Palace. With the help of the Bavarian ambassador, on November 24 Pius fled in disguise to the Kingdom of Naples. Rome was left to the revolutionaries. Pius now resolved to resist any attempt to remove the Papal States from his authority. He quickly announced that the revolutionaries had forced him to leave Rome but that he was continuing to perform his duties as pope.

In February 1849, an assembly proclaimed the Roman Republic under a government headed by Mazzini. From exile, Pope Pius IX excommunicated all active members of this revolutionary government.

Mazzini's followers plundered the churches and killed many priests. On Easter Sunday, they desecrated St. Peter's Basilica by having a secular ceremony instead of the Mass.

Meanwhile, on April 29, Pius IX condemned both Mazzini and the *Risorgimento*. His condemnation of the *Risorgimento* turned most of the Italian people against him, even into the twentieth century. It was an act of heroic courage, worthy of Pius VI and Pius VII.

In the face of revolutionary violence, Pope Pius IX called upon the rulers of Europe for help. In answer to his plea, France, Spain, and Austria sent troops. In late June, French troops began besieging Rome. Realizing that he was outmatched, Garibaldi and his soldiers abandoned the city. On July 3, French troops marched into Rome and dissolved the Roman Republic. From exile, Pope Pius gave thanks. Meanwhile, throughout 1849, Austrian troops regained much of the Papal States that had been lost.

In April 1850, Pius IX returned to Rome. He took up residence in the Vatican because his guards could defend it more easily than the Quirinale Palace. French troops remained in the city to maintain order

Pope Pius IX

Witness to the Faith

and ensure the pope's safety. A week after returning to Rome, Pope Pius IX issued a statement condemning the Church's treatment by the Roman (Italian) Republic.

The End of the Papal States

For the next decade, Mazzini, Garibaldi, and the new prime minister of Piedmont-Sardinia, Camille Cavour, worked to implement the *Risorgimento*. As part of the unification process, Cavour needed to drive the Austrians from northern Italy. Austria had always considered northern Italy, especially Milan, to be part of its empire. In 1859, after a brief war, Sardinia won most of northern Italy, including Milan, from Austria. The following year, Garibaldi conquered the Kingdom of the Two Sicilies. This southern kingdom was the largest of the Italian states.

Meanwhile, almost two-thirds of the Papal States had fallen to Sardinia. On September 18, 1860, while attempting to stop additional losses to Sardinia, a papal army fought a decisive battle at Castelfidardo against the Sardinians. The heavily outnumbered papal army was defeated, reducing the Papal States to the area around Rome. Only the presence of French troops in Rome stood in Cavour's way of creating a united Italy with Rome as its capital.

In March 1861, the Kingdom of Italy was officially proclaimed. King Victor Emmanuel II, the king of Sardinia, was declared king of Italy. Rome was regarded as the real capital of the new nation. But the pope still governed Rome, and French soldiers defended it. The Italians did not have the power to oust the French troops.

King Victor Emmanuel II

However, in 1870, France and Prussia went to war. Since France needed all of its soldiers, French Emperor Napoleon III recalled his soldiers from Rome. Immediately, Victor Emmanuel invaded what remained of the Papal States. His army, led by Garibaldi, besieged Rome. On September 20, 1870, Pope Pius IX, rather than have any bloodshed, surrendered the city and the Papal States. The Italians allowed the pope to retain St. Peter's Basilica and the Vatican Palace, but when they offered Pius IX a treaty, he refused to accept its terms. Until his death, he remained a "voluntary prisoner" in the Vatican. Strained relations between the papacy and Italy's new leaders continued for decades. It was not until 1929 that the Italian government and Pope Pius XI signed a peace treaty.

Firstly a Shepherd

Despite all his troubles, Pope Pius IX never forget that he was firstly a shepherd. Thus, in September 1850, he restored the Catholic hierarchy in England. On December 8, 1854, he defined the dogma of the **Immaculate Conception**, which infallibly proclaims that "the most Blessed Virgin Mary, in the first instance of her conception, by a singular grace and privilege granted by Almighty God, in view of the merits of Jesus Christ, the Savior of the human race, was preserved free from all stain of original sin."

Immaculate Conception
The doctrine that the Blessed Virgin Mary was conceived without Original Sin.

506 Chapter 32: The Church in the Nineteenth Century (1815-1878)

In December 1864, he issued the encyclical **Quanta Cura**, which condemned the idea that society could function without reference to God or religion. Along with this encyclical, he issued *The Syllabus of Errors,* a list of eighty previously condemned errors, such as rationalism, pantheism, indifferentism, and liberalism.

The First Vatican Council

On December 6, 1864, Pope Pius IX suggested to his cardinals that the Church hold an ecumenical council; they agreed. The **First Vatican Council** (also known as Vatican I) opened on December 8, 1869 (the Feast of the Immaculate Conception) in St. Peter's Basilica.

In its first sessions, the Vatican Council defined the Church's teachings on God the Creator and Divine Revelation. The council also taught that there can be no real contradiction between faith and reason, because both are from God. Faith does not destroy reason but enhances it. In addition, the council condemned several heresies, including rationalism, materialism, and atheism. Finally, the council addressed the topic of **papal infallibility**.

Although the Church had never officially defined papal infallibility as a dogma, such noted theologians as Robert Bellarmine had defended this doctrine. Moreover, Pope Pius IX had recently employed the doctrine in December 1854 when he infallibly proclaimed the dogma of the Immaculate Conception. Furthermore, almost every Catholic accepted the doctrine of papal infallibility. While almost no bishop doubted the truth of this doctrine, they wondered whether it was prudent to define the dogma *at that time*. The issue confronting the council was *whether to proclaim the dogma publicly*. The question divided the bishops into two camps.

A substantial majority of the bishops favored the declaration, as did Pope Pius IX, but a large minority believed it was not the appropriate time to make such a declaration. Those bishops came from countries with large Protestant populations like France, Germany, and the United States. They argued that a public declaration would create a barrier to reunion with the Protestants and the Eastern Orthodox Church. They asserted that it would antagonize the governments of Europe, which it did. Finally, they thought it was unnecessary, because nearly every Catholic already accepted this teaching without an official statement. Despite

> **First Vatican Council**
> Defined the Church's teachings on God the Creator and Divine Revelation; affirmed that both faith and reason are from God; condemned several heresies, including rationalism, materialism, and atheism; and defined the dogma of papal infallibility.

> **Papal Infallibility**
> The dogma declaring that the pope cannot err when he speaks *ex cathedra* ("from the chair" of St. Peter)—that is, when, as the Supreme Shepherd and Teacher of all Christians, he defines a doctrine of faith or morals for the entire Church.

Engraving of the First Vatican Council, Karl Benzinger

Witness to the Faith 507

Otto von Bismarck
Prime minister of Prussia who sought to unify Germany; attacked the Catholic Church through various laws and policies.

Kulturkampf
"Culture war"; Otto von Bismarck's campaign against the Catholic Church.

The Battle of Koniggratz, Georg Bleibtreu

the opposition, the council voted overwhelmingly in favor of the dogma (451 to 88). Two-thirds of the 48 American bishops voted "no," believing it imprudent because of its anticipated effect on American Protestants.

The Council declared that the pope is infallible when he speaks *ex cathedra* (Latin, meaning "from the chair" of St. Peter)—that is, "when in the exercise of his office as pastor and teacher of all Christians he defines, by virtue of his supreme Apostolic authority, a doctrine of faith or morals to be held by the whole Church." The pope's decision must be permanent and settle the question at hand. It must be binding on the entire Church. The pope is the rock upon which the Lord Jesus Christ built His Church, and He promised that the gates of Hell would not prevail against it. Defining the dogma of papal infallibility was the most significant accomplishment of the First Vatican Council.

Bismarck and the *Kulturkampf*

In 1862, **Otto von Bismarck** became prime minister of Prussia. Bismarck was a man completely without morals, willing to do anything to achieve his goals. His goals were to unify Germany and make Prussia the leader of the new Germany. Austria, the leader of the old Germany, stood in his way, as did the Catholic Church. He resolved to break both. In July 1866, he destroyed the Austrian army at the Battle of Koniggratz. By 1871, a united Germany, dominated by Prussia, had been created, with Bismarck as its first chancellor. Bismarck turned next to the eternal enemy of all tyrants: the Catholic Church.

The bishops of Germany had warned that declaring papal infallibility would have political consequences in Germany, especially in Protestant Prussia. Their prediction would soon be proven right. The decree on papal infallibility provided an excuse for the Prussian government to persecute Catholics in Germany. This persecution evolved into a larger attempt to change German society. It became

Chapter 32: The Church in the Nineteenth Century (1815-1878)

known as the **Kulturkampf** (the culture war). It more correctly should have been called the "Prussian War against the Catholic Church." Bismarck saw the Catholic revival in Germany, the independence of the Catholic Church in Germany, and the Church's support for Austria (a thoroughly Catholic nation) as absolutely intolerable.

Bismarck launched his attack against the Church through a group known as the "Old Catholics." These "Catholics" denied papal infallibility. Some of them were professors of theology in the state colleges and universities. Germany's Catholic bishops, as the protectors of orthodoxy, forbade these "Old Catholics" to teach. When they refused to comply, the bishops rightly excommunicated them.

These excommunicated professors should not have been allowed to teach theology at any college or university in the country. However, because they were teaching in state-run institutions, they appealed to the German government. The head of the government was Bismarck, who, seeing an opportunity to injure the Church, objected to the bishops' decision and allowed the teachers to continue in their jobs. The bishops then unsuccessfully appealed to the German king.

When priests began to speak in support of their bishops, Bismarck had the pretense he needed to begin suppressing the Church. In 1871, Prussia passed the Pulpit Law, which made it a crime for any cleric to make a public statement that was critical of the German government. The war was on!

In January 1872, Adalbert Falk became the Prussian minister for education and worship. He sought to abolish any religious education in the German schools. In March 1872, the government took control of the Prussian primary school system. Under the new law—the crown jewel of the Kulturkampf—neither Catholic nor Protestant churches would have any say over the education of Germany's children.

In July, Bismarck passed a law that expelled the Jesuits. The next year, any religious orders that supported them, including the Vincentians and the Redemptorists, were also expelled from the German Empire. Teaching orders were banished as well. In December, Pope Pius IX denounced these anti-Catholic laws.

In 1873, Bismarck intensified his persecution of the Church. In May, the government passed the first of the **Falk Laws** (also called the **May Laws**). These infamous regulations, enacted over the next three years, sought to subject the priests and bishops of Germany to the authority of the government, not only in civil cases but also in religious matters. Priests could be appointed only with government approval. Catholic seminaries were now under the control of the German government, which had to approve the curriculum. Any bishop who opposed the Falk laws would be deposed. Despite the threat, the German bishops heroically opposed the Falk laws, and the clergy followed the example of their bishops.

The conflict between Bismarck and the Catholic Church became even more bitter. In the following year, the government imprisoned

Adalbert Falk

Falk Laws (May Laws)
Laws that were part of the *Kulturkampf*; a set of laws aimed at enabling the government to manipulate the clergy in Germany.

St. John Vianney, the Curé of Ars

Jean Marie Vianney (Curé of Ars)
Pastor of the little village of Ars, France, who became famous as a confessor; he is the patron saint of parish priests.

three bishops. Catholic schools were closed. In February 1875, Pope Pius IX issued an encyclical declaring the Falk Laws invalid. In May, another law closed all the monasteries in Prussia and expelled all religious orders except those who cared for the sick. The bishop of Munster and the archbishop of Cologne were exiled. In 1877, the bishop of Limburg was imprisoned. Exiled bishops administered their dioceses through delegates. In parishes where Catholic worship had been forbidden because the priests had been exiled, priests secretly said Mass and administered the sacraments.

Bismarck had hoped that the Falk Laws would unify and strengthen Germany, but by 1877 it was clear that they had created discord and weakened the government. The Catholic political party in Germany had actually become stronger. Catholics had become more determined to support the Church. Even staunch Protestants were upset at the attacks on religion. Consequently, Bismarck gradually had to abandon the fight. The government slowly abolished the Falk Laws. By 1886, the government had repealed most of the anti-Catholic laws. The last remnants of the Kulturkampf disappeared when all the laws against the Jesuits were abolished during World War I.

Pope Pius IX did not live to see the end of the persecution in Germany. He died in 1878, having guided the Church longer than any pope since St. Peter. Pope John Paul II beatified him in 2000.

Three Great Saints of the Nineteenth Century

The Curé of Ars

Evening had fallen in the little French village of Dardilly. As they ate dinner, the family of Matthew Vianney heard a knock on the front door. Matthew went to open it. A man, looking cautiously around to ensure that no one saw him, quickly entered the house. He had traveled from a nearby town to tell the Vianneys that the next night a priest would say Mass in the barn at the edge of the village. The following evening, after darkness had fallen, the Vianney family quietly left their home. In the barn, they found their neighbors gathered around a stranger. The unfamiliar man was the priest who, after hearing their Confessions, said Mass. Such were the childhood memories of **Jean Marie Vianney**, who grew up in revolutionary France.

Jean Marie Vianney was born in 1786. His father was a farmer and, even as a child, Jean helped on the family farm. Every day on his way to work in the fields, he stopped in the church to pray. As a young boy, Jean felt called to the priesthood. In 1806, he entered the seminary. Though he struggled with his studies, he had a strong vocation and persevered. With the help of his fellow seminarians, he completed his education. On August 13, 1815, the bishop of Grenoble ordained him a priest.

In 1818, Father Vianney became the parish priest of Ars, a poor village near Lyons, France. Directing souls in his confessional, this simple parish priest, the **Curé of Ars**, (French, meaning "priest of Ars"), became known throughout France and the entire Christian world. Father Vianney had not been at Ars long when people began coming to him from other parishes, then from all over France, and finally from other countries, to have him hear their Confessions. During the last ten years of his life, he spent 16 to 18 hours a day in the confessional. Common sense, remarkable insight, and supernatural knowledge characterized his spiritual direction. He would sometimes be able to perceive sins withheld in an imperfect Confession.

Our Lord bestowed a special blessing on Father Vianney which allowed him to spend so many hours in the confessional. For the last forty years of his life, he neither ate nor slept enough to sustain human life. Yet he worked incessantly with unfailing kindness, patience, and cheerfulness until he was more than 73 years old. He died on August 4, 1859. Pius XI canonized him in 1925. Jean Vianney is the patron saint of parish priests.

> **St. Catherine Labouré**
> Sister who spread devotion to the Miraculous Medal after Our Lady appeared to her.

St. Catherine of Labouré

In 1830, Our Blessed Mother appeared three times to a member of the Daughters of Charity of St. Vincent de Paul. The sister's name was **Catherine Labouré**. During the second visit, the Blessed Mother appeared inside an oval frame, standing on a globe. Dazzling rays of light emanated from rings on her fingers over the globe. She told Sister Catherine that the rays symbolized the graces that would be bestowed on all who ask for them. Some of the rings did not shed light, representing the graces for which people forget to ask. Around the edges of the oval frame, in golden letters, appeared these words in French: "O Mary, conceived without sin, pray for us who have recourse to thee." The frame then rotated, showing Sister Catherine its back. Catherine saw a circle of twelve stars and a large letter "M" surmounted by a cross. Underneath the cross and the "M" was the Sacred Heart of Jesus crowned with thorns, and the Immaculate Heart of Mary pierced by a sword.

Our Lady told Catherine to take these images to her confessor and tell him that they should be engraved on medals. Our Lady promised abundant graces to those who would wear the

St. Catherine of Labouré

Witness to the Faith 511

St. Bernadette and
Our Lady of Lourdes

medals. Catherine did as Our Lady asked. After an investigation of two years, her spiritual director obtained approval from the archbishop of Paris to produce the medal. The first medals were created on June 30, 1832. With their distribution, the devotion spread rapidly throughout the world. Those who wore the medal reported receiving enormous blessings. Soon the medal came to be called the Miraculous Medal. Pope Pius XII canonized Catherine Labouré in 1947.

St. Bernadette

On February 11, 1858, a 14-year-old French girl named **Bernadette Soubirous** was gathering firewood with her sister on the banks of a little stream near Lourdes, France. She happened to glance up at a nearby grotto. A beautiful woman surrounded by a heavenly light was standing in the grotto. She wore a dazzling white dress and a white veil. Around her waist, she wore a blue sash. Her hands were folded in prayer, and she held a rosary. Startled, Bernadette fell to her knees, pulled out her own rosary and began to pray. When she finished the last "Glory Be," the Lady disappeared.

Bernadette told her parents and neighbors about the incident. The next Sunday, she returned to the same place and again saw the Lady. She waited until Thursday before she returned, and again the same events occurred. This time, the woman told Bernadette to come to the grotto every day for fifteen days. As a reward, she promised to make Bernadette happy, not in this world, but in the next.

Soon a large group of people began following Bernadette on her daily journey. Some came because they were curious, but others came because they believed that they were witnessing a miracle. They could not see the Lady, but they could tell from the look on Bernadette's face and the way in which she knelt and prayed that the Lady was there.

During Bernadette's ninth visit, the Lady told her to drink and wash from a nearby spring. Bernadette could see no spring, but she still tried to do as the Lady asked. She dug in the dirt with her bare hands and then tried to drink some muddy drops. When she turned to the crowd, she had smeared mud on her face but had not revealed a

512   *Chapter 32: The Church in the Nineteenth Century (1815-1878)*

spring. However, over the next few days, a spring began to flow from Bernadette's muddy patch. Some devout people followed her example by drinking and washing in the water, which was soon reported to have healing properties.

During the thirteenth apparition, Bernadette told her family that the Lady said to ask the priests to build a chapel at the grotto. Accompanied by two of her aunts, Bernadette went to her parish priest with the request. The priest told Bernadette that the Lady must identify herself. On her next visit, Bernadette asked the Lady her name. The Lady smiled but said nothing. On March 25, 1858, the Feast of the Annunciation, the Lady answered the question. She said, *"I am the Immaculate Conception."* Four years earlier, Pope Pius IX had defined the dogma of the Immaculate Conception. However, Bernadette's parents, teachers, and priests all later testified that Bernadette had never heard the words "Immaculate Conception" from them.

For a time, the bishop hesitated to build the requested chapel. He wanted to be certain that the vision was real. The proof was not long in coming; already, miracles were happening. People who drank from the spring and washed with its water were cured of various sicknesses. These miracles convinced the bishop that the Blessed Mother had appeared to Bernadette. He began construction of the chapel. Eventually, a magnificent basilica, hospital, and shrine were built there. Every year, millions of pilgrims travel to Lourdes seeking physical and spiritual healing.

Disliking the attention she was receiving, Bernadette went to a boarding school run by the Sisters of Charity. The sisters taught her to read and write. In 1866, at the age of 22, she entered the order and moved to the sisters' motherhouse at Nevers. She spent the rest of her brief life there, working in the infirmary and as a sacristan, and creating beautiful embroidery for altar cloths and vestments. On April 16, 1870, she died of tuberculosis at the age of 35. Pope Pius XI canonized her on December 8, 1933. Our Lady had kept her promise. Bernadette's happiness did not come in this world but in the next. St. Bernadette is the patron saint of the sick and the family.

St. Bernadette Soubirous
Young French girl who, at the age of 14, saw visions of Our Lady of Lourdes; later, she entered the Sisters of Charity.

Oral Exercises

1. Who were some of the leaders of the Catholic revival in France?

2. Where were the great centers of the Catholic revival in Germany?

3. Who led the Catholic Emancipation movement in the nineteenth century in Great Britain?

4. Who was the leader of the Oxford Movement?

5. Name three English cardinals during the nineteenth century.

6. Which pope restored the Catholic hierarchy in England?

7. What was the most significant (and controversial) accomplishment of the First Vatican Council?

8. What were the Falk Laws?

9. With what sacrament is the Curé of Ars (St. Jean Vianney) most closely associated?

10. What does the dogma of the Immaculate Conception infallibly proclaim?

Witness to the Faith   513

Chapter 33

The Church Faces Modernism and World War I (1878-1919)

Pope Leo XIII
Reigned from 1878 to 1903. Wrote several important encyclicals; condemned communism, socialism, and other evils; and took various measures to improve life for Catholics around the world.

Introduction

As the Church passed through the last decades of the nineteenth century and entered the first years of the twentieth century, it faced great threats. Pope Pius IX had warned against rationalism, materialism, and atheism. These terrible philosophical errors became even greater dangers in the years after his death. As has happened all too often in history, the pope's warning was ignored by many.

Yet, as rationalism, materialism, atheism, and other great heresies afflicted the world, the Holy Spirit blessed the Church with some fine popes. Between 1878 and 1922, only three men reigned. They guided the Church during times of peace and during one of history's most terrible wars. Surprisingly, despite the holy lives that these popes led, only one has been canonized thus far.

The Election of Pope Leo XIII

As often happens after a long pontificate, the Sacred College elected an elderly man whom they expected to have a rather short pontificate. Such was the case in 1878, when the Sacred College elected the long-time archbishop of Perugia, Vincenzo Pecci. Born in March 1810, Archbishop Pecci was almost exactly 68 years old when, as **Pope Leo XIII** (1878-1903), he began one of the longest pontificates

The Apotheosis of St. Pius X, Biagio Biagetti

1871 A.D. – 1920 A.D.

1871 A.D. France loses the Franco-Prussian War and forms a new government, the Third Republic.

1891 A.D. Pope Leo XIII issues *Rerum Novarum*.

1905 A.D. Pope Pius X issues a decree urging frequent reception of Holy Communion. In France, the Third Republic repeals Napoleon's Concordat, denying government support to any Church activity and confiscating Church property.

1907 A.D. Pope Pius X issues two encyclicals condemning modernism.

1910 A.D. Pope Pius X lowers the age for receiving First Holy Communion.

1914-1918 A.D. World War I ravages Europe. Pope Benedict XV pleads for peace and tries to assist the victims.

1919 A.D. The Treaty of Versailles is signed, establishing the terms of peace between the Allies and Germany after World War I. Germany is treated harshly, prompting Pope Benedict XV to later warn that "the seeds of former enmities remain." The situation in France begins to improve, as Catholics in Parliament restore some rights to the Church.

1920 A.D. Pope Benedict XV canonizes Joan of Arc.

in history on February 20, 1878. He would reign until he was 93 years old.

In choosing Leo XIII, the College of Cardinals had elected an extraordinary man. Leo was not only a remarkable theologian, philosopher, and intellectual but also a brilliant diplomat and economist. He was also a prophet, as we will see.

Leo the Diplomat

As Popes Pius VI and VII had demonstrated, one of the main functions of the Holy Father is ensuring that the people can receive the sacraments. In 1878, as Leo XIII ascended to the Chair of St. Peter, nations throughout the world were threatening the free access of Catholics to the sacraments. Leo immediately acted to remedy the situation.

In Germany, he worked with the Catholic political party to help abolish the

Witness to the Faith   515

May Laws and counteract the Kulturkampf. Leo's diplomacy and support helped German Catholics to rid themselves of these terrible laws. Later, Leo formed a strong relationship with Germany's king, Kaiser Wilhelm II.

In 1870, after France's humiliating defeat in the Franco-Prussian War, France formed a new government, the Third Republic. This new government was largely anti-Catholic and enacted several anti-clerical laws. In 1884, Leo XIII issued an encyclical addressed to the people of France. While he recognized the State's right to rule, he condemned any philosophy that desired to "eradicate the foundations of Christian truth," because these errors would cause the "certain ruin of the State." He believed that the teachings of the Church were "very effective for the maintenance of order and the salvation of the republic." He concluded by urging the bishops and the clergy to defend the freedom of the Church, and asked the laity to work for the common good.

The deteriorating relations with Italy caused by the *Roman Question* (the dispute regarding the temporal authority of the pope in Rome and the rest of the Papal States) must have saddened Leo. Nevertheless, he remained firm and continued following the policies of Pope Pius IX. Most notably, he continued Pius IX's prohibition against Italian Catholics voting in elections. Although a ban on voting seems appalling to Americans, the Italian government had forcibly seized the Papal States and continued to enact anti-Catholic legislation. From Leo's perspective, participating in elections would legitimize these unjust acts. Nevertheless, Leo still attempted to negotiate with the Italian government to resolve the differences between the Church and the State, although to no avail.

In Great Britain, Leo restored the Scottish hierarchy, which had been vacant since 1603, but Scottish Catholics remained a tiny minority. John Knox and his followers had dealt the Church in Scotland a near-death blow. Even today, Scotland is predominantly Protestant.

Leo XIII also addressed issues in the Americas. In 1886, he named Archbishop James Gibbons the second cardinal in the United States. Two years later, he wrote an encyclical to the bishops of Brazil, congratulating them on the abolition of slavery in Brazil. In 1897, he sent an apostolic letter to all the bishops of Latin America, explaining their rights and responsibilities.

Leo the Scholar

Throughout his life, Pope Leo XIII had always valued education. He had received an excellent Jesuit education and earned doctorates in theology and canon law. In 1879, Leo published *Aeterni Patris* (Encyclical on the Restoration of Christian Philosophy). In the face of rampant secularism in colleges and universities, he called for a return to the philosophy of St. Thomas Aquinas. Leo also declared St. Thomas Aquinas the patron saint of colleges and universities. Moreover, Leo took direct action. He appointed professors who accepted the philosophy of St. Thomas Aquinas to Church-controlled colleges in Rome.

Pope Leo XIII

516 Chapter 33: The Church Faces Modernism and World War I (1878-1919)

In order to advance knowledge and research, Leo opened the Vatican Archives to scholars in 1883. Leo explained that he chose to do this because the Church had nothing to fear from the truths of history. Among the noted scholars to study in the Vatican Archives was Ludwig von Pastor, who wrote one of the greatest histories of the papacy—upon which this history is based—and used the Archives extensively for his research. Leo also refounded the Vatican Observatory, which Pope Gregory XIII, creator of the Gregorian calendar, had originally founded.

Pope Leo and the Rosary

Leo XIII had such a great devotion to Our Blessed Lady and the Rosary that he is often called the "Rosary Pope." The declaration of the dogma of the Immaculate Conception and the veneration of the Miraculous Medal had renewed devotions to the Blessed Mother. Pope Leo XIII inflamed these fires by issuing eleven encyclicals promoting the Rosary! In September 1883, he issued his first, *Supremi Apostolatus Officio* (Encyclical on Devotion of the Rosary), in which he encourages Catholics to pray the Rosary because it is such an effective spiritual weapon. In addition, Leo declared October to be the month of Mary as "Our Lady of the Rosary."

Pope Leo XIII also supported Marian shrines, especially Lourdes, and encouraged pilgrimages to them. To support the Miraculous Medal, he declared the Feast of the Miraculous Medal in 1894. He likewise encouraged Catholics to wear the scapular.

Finally, more than any previous pope, Leo XIII spoke plainly of Our Lady as the "mediatrix of all graces." In *Dei Matris* (Encyclical on the Rosary, 1892), Leo notes that Mary "dispenses grace with a generous hand from that treasure with which from the beginning she was divinely endowed in fullest abundance that she might be worthy to be the Mother of God." In *Fidentum Piumque Animum* (Encyclical on the Rosary, 1896), Leo wrote that because Mary is truly Our Lord's Mother, she is "a worthy and acceptable 'Mediatrix to the Mediator.'" Two years later, in another Rosary encyclical, Leo wrote, "From her, as from an abundant spring, are derived the streams of heavenly graces." The theme of Mary as mediatrix would be embraced by all future popes, especially Pope St. John Paul II, who had a very special devotion to the Blessed Mother.

The Blessed Mother Presents the Rosary to St. Dominic with Pope Leo XIII

Witness to the Faith 517

Rerum Novarum

In 1848, German philosopher **Karl Marx** had written the *Communist Manifesto*. According to Marx, no one should own private property, capitalism was evil, and workers could use violence to obtain "justice." From his writings came the twin evils of socialism and communism. Over the next fifty years, these evils caused unspeakable suffering. In 1891, Pope Leo XIII answered Karl Marx in one of the most important encyclicals in Church history.

Issued on May 15, 1891, **Rerum Novarum** (Encyclical on Capital and Labor) addresses the rights and duties of workers and employers. Leo begins by assessing the evils of communism and socialism, and declares that they are not the solution. He defends the right to own private property. He writes that while capitalism itself is not evil, it cannot be unrestrained. Workers have rights, such as the right to organize and the right to be paid a "living wage," but they do not have the right to use violence to obtain their goals. Leo urges workers and owners to work together for the mutual benefit of both. In an age of child labor, he asserts that workers must never be assigned tasks that are unsuited to their age or sex. He also insists that owners provide workers time off to attend to their spiritual needs. Finally, as several other popes have done, Leo stresses that the family is the fundamental element of society and must be protected.

Rerum Novarum is such a critical encyclical that in 1931, on the fortieth anniversary of its promulgation, Pope Pius XI issued *Quadragesimo Anno* (Encyclical on Reconstruction of the Social Order). Pius XI echoed most of Leo's points but went further regarding socialism. He declared that "no one can be at the same time a sincere Catholic and a true socialist." In 1991, Pope St. John Paul II issued *Centesimus Annus* (Encyclical on the Hundredth Anniversary of *Rerum Novarum*). Like his predecessors, John Paul II condemned socialism. He affirmed the right to own private property, the importance of human dignity, and the need for owners to pay their workers a living wage.

Pope Leo XIII and his successors provided a framework for a just social economic system based on Christian principles. Unfortunately, too few have listened.

Leo the Prophet

At important times throughout history, usually in moments of crisis, Our Lord has granted the pope a vision. The revelation of the outcome of the Battle of Lepanto to Pius V is perhaps the most famous. Our Lord also granted Leo XIII a prophetic vision.

On October 13, 1884, as Pope Leo XIII finished saying Mass, he collapsed to the floor. His attendants feared that the 74-year-old pontiff had suffered a heart attack or stroke, but the truth was far worse. For several minutes, Leo lay motionless. When he revived, he exclaimed: "Oh, what a terrible picture I was permitted to see!"

Karl Marx
German political philosopher who wrote the *Communist Manifesto*. From his writings came the twin evils of communism and socialism.

Karl Marx

Rerum Novarum
Encyclical of Pope Leo XIII which addresses the rights and duties of workers and employers; rejects communism and socialism, and defends the right to own private property.

He later explained that Our Lord had granted him a vision of the twentieth century, during which the power of Satan would reach its utmost. In response to this terrible prophecy, Leo composed the Prayer to St. Michael, and he asked that it be recited at every Mass. Until about 1970, it was. Recently, many priests have renewed this tradition by leading the faithful in this prayer after Mass: "St. Michael the Archangel, defend us in battle; be our protection against the wickedness and snares of the devil. May God rebuke him, we humbly pray; and do thou, O Prince of the Heavenly Host, by the Power of God, cast into hell Satan and all the evil spirits who prowl about the world seeking the ruin of souls. Amen."

Leo and the Missions

During the second half of the nineteenth century, the major European powers (including France, Germany, and Italy) became involved in what was known as the Great Race. This was a race to acquire colonies in Africa and Asia. The Europeans needed colonies for raw materials that were scarce in Europe. Colonies could also provide food for Europe. Additionally, overseas colonies granted European nations a degree of prestige. Unfortunately, despite being Christians, the Europeans treated the natives of the colonies very badly. Leo XIII took several steps to aid these indigenous peoples.

First, Leo wrote a number of encyclicals defending indigenous peoples. In 1890, he wrote *Catholicae Ecclesiae* (Encyclical on Slavery in the Missions), which specifically condemns the African slave trade. He noted that "the Church from the beginning sought to completely eliminate slavery, whose wretched yoke has oppressed many people."

St. Michael the Archangel, Luca Giordano

In addition, Leo authorized missionaries to evangelize indigenous peoples. For example, he strongly supported the efforts of the **White Fathers**, a missionary society founded in 1868 by Cardinal Charles Lavigerie, the archbishop of Algiers. Lavigerie had to overcome the resistance of the French colonial governor of Algeria, who despised the local population. Cardinal Lavigerie was determined to build schools, hospitals, and orphanages to help them. He also wanted his priests to evangelize the native Muslim population. The White Fathers made substantial gains, and the Church in Africa continues to grow rapidly. The White Fathers, who still exist today, work almost exclusively in Africa, educating and evangelizing its people.

White Fathers
A missionary society that has served the people of Africa since the mid-1800s.

The Death of Leo XIII

Pope Leo XIII died on July 20, 1903. He was 93 years old, the oldest pope in Church history. At the time of his death, only Pius IX and St. Peter had reigned longer. Leo had guided the Barque of Peter through perilous shoals, and had foreseen that even greater dangers lay ahead. In the future, those chosen to walk in the Shoes of the Fisherman would need to be exceptional men. The next pope certainly qualified.

The Election of Pope St. Pius X

Two weeks after the death of Leo XIII, the Sacred College elected the cardinal of Venice, Joseph Sarto. The newly elected pope chose the illustrious papal name "Pius." **Pope St. Pius X** (1903-1914) would bring even greater glory to that name.

On October 4, 1903, Pope St. Pius X issued his first encyclical, *E Supremi* (Encyclical on the Restoration of All Things in Christ), which set the tone for his entire pontificate. He declared his intention "**to restore all things in Christ**" ("*instaurare omnia in Christo*"), which became his motto. Four months later, on the fiftieth anniversary of the dogma of the Immaculate Conception, in a second encyclical he expressed his belief that the best way to restore all things in Christ was through the intercession of the Blessed Mother. Pius asked, "Can anyone fail to see that there is no surer or more direct road than by Mary … that we may be holy and immaculate in the sight of God?"

Cardinal Charles Lavigerie

The Pope of the Holy Eucharist

In many ways, Pius X remained a simple parish priest, even when he became a bishop, a cardinal, and then the pope. Born into a family of ten children, he had a great love of children. He often carried candy in his pockets to give to children as he walked the streets. Even as bishop, he continued to personally teach catechism to children. As a priest, he understood the importance of frequent Confession and Holy Communion, especially in the troubled times in which the Church found itself in the twentieth century.

Pope St. Pius X
Reigned from 1903 to 1914; promoted frequent reception of Holy Communion, lowered the age for First Holy Communion, and condemned modernism.

In 1905, Pope Pius X issued a decree advising Catholics to receive Holy Communion frequently, and even daily if possible.

520 CHAPTER 33: *The Church Faces Modernism and World War I (1878-1919)*

"Holy Communion is the shortest and safest way to Heaven," he wrote. Many Catholics had come to believe that the Eucharist was to be received infrequently. Others felt that they were not worthy or holy enough to receive often. Pope Pius reminded them that Our Lord desired frequent reception of His Holy Body and Blood. Pius also advocated regular Confession. Five years later, Pope Pius X issued another decree, recommending that children receive their First Confession and First Holy Communion when they attain the "age of reason" (around 7 years old) and are able to understand that Our Lord is truly present in the Holy Eucharist. Prior to this decree, children waited until they were 12 or 13 before receiving First Holy Communion. These two decrees earned Pius X the title "Pope of the Holy Eucharist."

Church Music

Since the Baroque period, sacred music at Mass had become more *flamboyant*. Although the music being used was not inappropriate for Mass and was quite reverent by today's standards, Pope Pius X, in accord with his desire for simplicity in all things, insisted upon a return to Gregorian Chant. He felt that Gregorian Chant would focus people's minds on the Mass, rather than distract them as classical and Baroque compositions were doing.

The Code of Canon Law

When Pius became pope, the **Code of Canon Law**, the system of laws governing the Church, had not been rewritten in more than 800 years. By the nineteenth century, the Code had become large and unwieldy. Worse, some sections in the Code actually appeared to contradict other sections. At the Vatican Council, several bishops had asked that a new, more easily understood Code be written. However, the council never took up this task. Thus, it fell to Pius X to attempt to create a *single volume* of clearly defined laws. Pius called together the best legal minds in the Church to reorganize and rewrite the Code of Canon Law in order to update it and make it more simple and coherent. Although the new Code would not be published until after his death, it would have a major impact on the Church for nearly 100 years.

Code of Canon Law
The system of laws governing the Church.

Modernism

As the Catholic Church entered the twentieth century, many theologians and philosophers claimed that the Church had to embrace

Witness to the Faith 521

Denis-Auguste Affre

new, "modern" ideas. For example, they rejected much of the Bible, because they said it was not based on scientific fact. These theologians preached a heresy known as "modernism." Modernists rejected practically all the teachings of the Catholic Church. Thus, Pope Pius X called modernism the "synthesis of all heresies." Like his namesake, Pius IX, Pope Pius X would become the sword and shield of the Church, and he would do battle with the modernists.

In 1907, Pope Pius X issued two encyclicals condemning modernism. The first, *Lamentabili Sane*, served as an updated *Syllabus of Errors*, restating the errors of modernism. On September 8, 1907, he issued his landmark encyclical, *Pascendi Dominici Gregis* (Encyclical on the Doctrines of the Modernists). In this encyclical, the Holy Father systematically explained modernism and the threat it posed to the Church. In fact, he declared that modernism "means the destruction not of the Catholic religion alone but of all religion."

To counteract the modernists, Pope Pius X urged the following: First, study and teach scholastic philosophy, especially St. Thomas Aquinas. Second, choose directors and professors who are not modernists for seminaries and Catholic universities. (Three years later, Pius mandated that all clergy and teachers in Catholic seminaries take an "Oath against Modernism." This requirement lasted until 1967.) Third, require an *imprimatur* on religious books. Although modernists continued to attack the Church—and likely will do so until the end of time—these policies slowed them down.

The Church in France

Since at least the eighteenth century, there had been a strongly anti-Catholic sentiment in France. Although most of the population of France was Catholic, and many were devout, the leaders of France tended to be hostile toward the Church. They saw the Church as an adversary that sought to weaken their power. At times, this hostility led to violent persecution and even martyrdom.

After the French Revolution, Napoleon came to power. He signed the "Concordat of 1801" with Pope Pius VII. Following Napoleon's ouster, the Bourbon dynasty was restored, and the Church in France experienced a rebirth. Nevertheless, several more bloody, anti-clerical revolutions occurred in France. In 1848, revolutionaries killed the archbishop of Paris, Denis-Auguste Affre. In 1871, following France's defeat in the Franco-Prussian War, revolutionaries again seized Paris. They murdered several hostages, including the archbishop of Paris, Georges Darboy.

After the Franco-Prussian War, France formed a new government, the **Third Republic**. Although there were some in the Third Republic who supported the Church, this new government also contained members who hated the Church. The entire history of the Third Republic, which lasted until 1940, was one of constant strife between the French government and the Church.

Almost immediately, the Third Republic began passing laws directed against the Church. Fearing Church control of education, in 1882 the government passed a law requiring children to attend public schools, where no religion was taught. Later, other laws were passed that further weakened the Church. Catholic universities were not permitted to grant degrees. Divorce was legalized, and civil marriage was mandated. Chaplains were removed from the army, and priests were forced to serve as soldiers. Despite these assaults, Pope Leo XIII tried to work with the Third Republic. In fact, he wrote two encyclicals to the bishops and people of France, encouraging them to try to cooperate with the government. For a time, Catholics in France managed to slow down the anti-Catholicism.

Third Republic
The government formed in France after the Franco-Prussian War; was significantly hostile to the Catholic Church.

However, at the turn of the century, the French government renewed its vigorous attack on the Church. The government closed all the parochial schools. Between 1902 and 1903, almost 6,000 parochial schools were forced to close. The government then passed its infamous "Associations Law," which disbanded all religious orders in France. All members of religious orders were forced to leave France.

Finally, in 1905, the Third Republic took the ultimate step: it repealed Napoleon's 1801 Concordat! The Catholic Church and the French government were officially separated. In the future, there would be no State support for any Church activity, such as paying the salaries of priests. The government confiscated all Church property and evicted bishops from their residences. Seminaries became the property of the Republic. Pope Pius X protested the violation of the Concordat and condemned the actions of the Republic, but the damage had been done.

That the government of France, a Catholic nation, the "Eldest Daughter of the Church," should turn away from the Church after more than 1,400 years is beyond tragic. The suppression of the religious orders and the abolishment of the parochial schools

Georges Darboy

Witness to the Faith 523

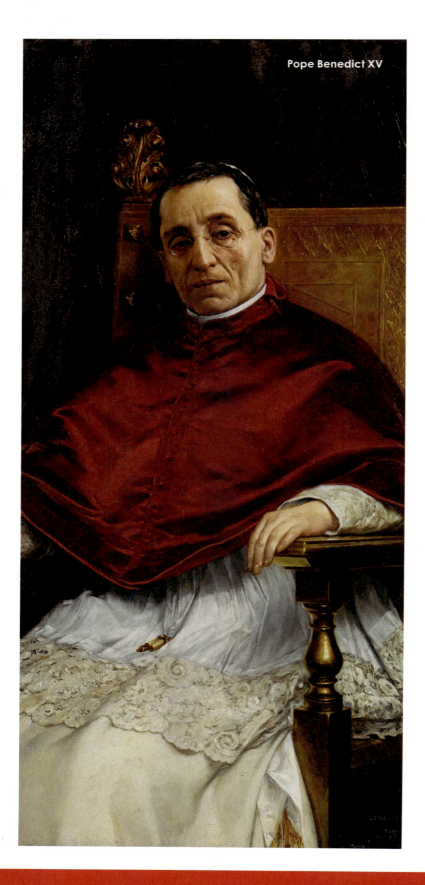
Pope Benedict XV

fulfilled the wildest dreams of the French revolutionaries. Yet, as happens time and again, the enemies of the Church failed to destroy the Church, even in France. In fact, from this unspeakable adversity, some good arose.

First, because the government no longer paid priests' salaries, parishioners began to support their priests directly. As a result, the priests and people grew closer together. Both developed a deeper love and appreciation for each other and the Church. Second, the government could no longer interfere in the appointment of bishops. This had been a constant source of friction between Church and State since Napoleon's time. Now bishops were appointed by the pope, to whom they gave their full allegiance. Thus, even from such a great evil, some small triumphs emerged.

The Death of Pius X

Leo XIII had been a clever diplomat. Pius X had been a quiet warrior. Both defended the Church in their own way. However, in 1913, Pius suffered a heart attack, from which he never fully recovered. In August 1914, his condition worsened as the world fell into its darkest period. On August 20, as the guns of August sounded the outbreak of World War I, Pius X died. Recognized immediately as a saint, Pius X was canonized in 1954 by Pius XII.

The Election of Benedict XV

As the Sacred College met to elect a successor to Pius X, the world was engaged in perhaps the most terrible war in its history. When the conclave opened on August 31, 1914, the world had already been at war for over a month. Germany, following the ruthless philosophy of Otto von Bismarck, had invaded neutral Belgium, violating various treaties as well as all international rules of war. Clearly, the war would be the main issue facing the new pope. The cardinals realized they needed a diplomat. On September 3, they chose Cardinal Giovanni Battista della Chiesa, the archbishop of Bologna, who had spent many decades in the Vatican diplomatic service.

Packages from Benedict XV Delivered to Italian POWs

Cardinal della Chiesa, who was only 59 years old, chose to be called **Benedict XV** (1914-1922) after Benedict XIV, who had also served as archbishop of Bologna.

The Pope Begs for Peace

Of all the world's leaders, no one dedicated himself more to ending the war than Pope Benedict XV. On September 8, in his first statement as pope, he begged the warring nations to stop fighting. Less than two months after his election, he wrote his first encyclical, *Ad Beatissimi Apostolorum*, in which he appealed for peace. On December 7, 1914, Benedict called for a Christmas Truce, asking that "the guns may fall silent at least upon the night the angels sang." Benedict's "Peace Note" of August 1917, written to the leaders of the warring nations, called the war the "suicide of civilized Europe."

At the beginning of the war, Benedict declared the Vatican to be neutral. From his position of neutrality, he begged for peace and offered to help mediate a peace, but both sides rebuffed his overtures. Germany's leaders were mostly Protestant, and France's prime minister hated the Church. Other leaders felt that he was acting on behalf of their enemies. Had these leaders listened, the lives of millions of soldiers might have been spared.

The Church during the War

During the war, the Church did its utmost to alleviate the suffering of soldiers and civilians. Pope Benedict created an agency to facilitate communication for prisoners of war (POWs) and assist in helping

Pope Benedict XV
Reigned from 1914 to 1922; worked for peace and the relief of soldiers and civilians during World War I.

Witness to the Faith

The Signing of Peace in the Hall of Mirrors, Versailles, 28th June 1919, William Orpen

British Newspaper Announcing the Signing of the Peace Treaty in 1919

families locate missing prisoners and soldiers. He helped in the exchange of tens of thousands of POWs, especially those suffering serious illnesses. He condemned the blocking of supplies to the starving people of Central Europe. In May 1915, Benedict denounced the Muslim Ottoman Empire's genocidal attack on Armenian Christians in Anatolia (modern-day Turkey).

Benedict had a special concern for the children victimized by the war. In 1916, he appealed to the people of the United States on behalf of the starving children of Belgium. In November 1919, he wrote an encyclical in which he appealed to the entire Church to help the starving children in Central Europe.

Benedict the Diplomat

During the pontificate of Pius X, relations with many European countries, such as France, Germany, and Italy, had declined. Pope Benedict XV's peace efforts, as well as his charitable work, created more positive relationships with many nations. As a result, during and immediately after the war, the interactions between these nations and the Vatican improved.

In 1919, Catholics won enough seats in the French Parliament to restore certain rights to the Church and the people. The following year, Pope Benedict canonized St. Joan of Arc, the most beloved of French saints.

In Germany, following the death of Otto von Bismarck, the Catholic political party increased its influence. Catholics demanded that the laws suppressing the Jesuits be abolished. Finally, in 1917, the German government rescinded those terrible anti-Jesuit laws.

The relationship between the Vatican and the government of Italy had been cold for some time. Leo XIII had allowed Italian Catholics to vote in local elections but not national elections. Benedict XV extended Leo's policy to allow Catholics to vote in national elections. This improved the relations between Church and State, while also creating a pro-Church political party. Soon this party began to win seats in the Italian Parliament, replacing anti-Catholic politicians with good Catholics.

The Treaty of Versailles

Although no one had worked harder for peace than Pope Benedict XV, the leaders of the world declined to invite him to the post-war peace conference at Versailles. Benedict deeply desired to participate. However, the Italian government, still angry with the pope over the Roman Question, had orchestrated a secret agreement that banned the pope from participating. In June 1919, the Treaty of Versailles was signed, establishing the terms of peace between the Allies and Germany after World War I. Germany was treated harshly.

Pope Benedict XV realized almost immediately that the Treaty of Versailles contained serious flaws. In May 1920, he issued his encyclical *Pacem, Dei Munus Pulcherrimum* (Encyclical on Peace and Christian Reconciliation). He wrote that, although treaties had been signed, "the germs of former enmities remain." He also said that "there can be no stable peace or lasting treaties … unless there be a return of mutual charity to appease hate and banish enmity."

The Prophecy Fulfilled

Pope Benedict XV was correct. The Treaty of Versailles, which treated Germany so unfairly, had planted the seeds of hate that would help spawn the rise of Nazism in Germany. In Russia, another great evil was about to spread its malevolence across the world. The prophecy of Pope Leo XIII was about to be fulfilled.

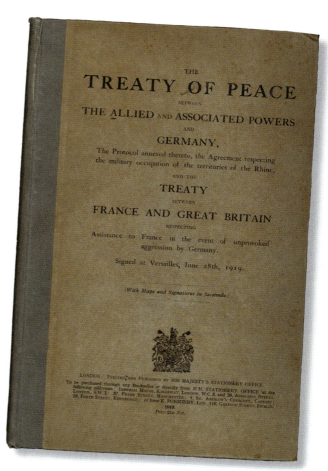

Cover of the Treaty of Versailles in English

Oral Exercises

1. What was the subject of *Rerum Novarum*?
2. What did Pope Leo XIII write about private property?
3. Which pope wrote the Prayer to St. Michael?
4. What was the motto of Pope Pius X?
5. What two decrees regarding Holy Communion earned Pius X the title "Pope of the Holy Eucharist"?
6. What heresy did Pope Pius X call the "synthesis of all heresies"?
7. Which pope dedicated his pontificate to ending World War I?
8. Name at least three things the Church did during World War I to alleviate the suffering of soldiers and civilians.

Witness to the Faith

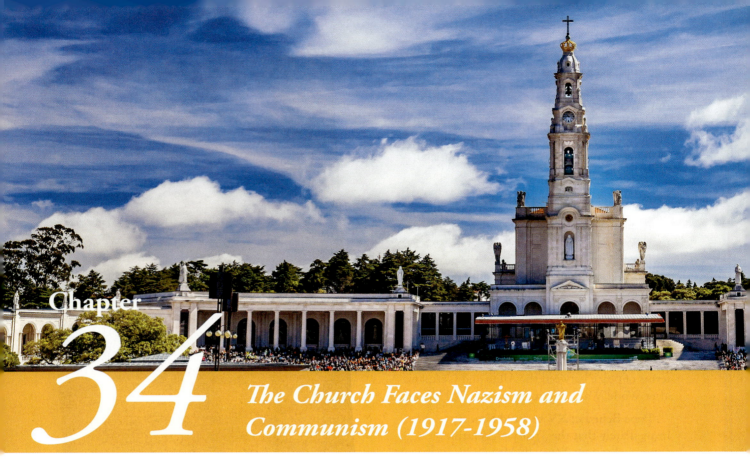

Chapter 34

The Church Faces Nazism and Communism (1917-1958)

Vladimir Lenin
Russian revolutionary who took over the government of Russia and established it as a communist state.

October Revolution
The communist revolution in 1917 which brought Vladimir Lenin to power in Russia.

Introduction

Pope Leo XIII had prophesied that the devil would run rampant during the twentieth century, and history shows all too clearly that this prophesy was true. The twentieth century would be the bloodiest in human history. History's three most brutal tyrants would come to power: Adolf Hitler, Joseph Stalin, and Mao Zedong. Together, they would murder more than 100 million people. At Fatima, Our Blessed Mother would warn the world one more time. Too few people have listened.

The Rise of Communism

In 1917, the inhuman soul-crushing system of atheistic communism seized control of an entire nation. For more than eighty years, this barbaric ideology, the greatest danger the Church has ever faced, would murder hundreds of millions of people in its relentless onslaught on the Church, faith, and humanity. If a single man could claim responsibility for the spread of international revolution and communism, that man would be **Vladimir Lenin**.

Although Lenin was Russian, nationality meant little to him. He desired a *world-wide revolution*. In 1917, he was in Switzerland. The German government, determined to win the war at all costs, put him on a locked armored train and sent him like a biological weapon to Russia.

Shrine of Our Lady of Fatima, Fatima, Portugal

1917 A.D. – 1950 A.D.

1917 A.D.
Our Lady appears in Fatima, Portugal. Vladimir Lenin seizes power in Russia. In Mexico, the Constitution of Queretaro is established.

1922 A.D.
The Union of Soviet Socialist Republics (USSR) officially comes into existence.

1927 A.D.
The Cristero Rebellion breaks out in Mexico.

1929 A.D.
Pope Pius XI and Benito Mussolini sign the Lateran Treaty.

1931 A.D.
A communist government comes to power in Spain and begins persecuting the Church. By the end of the decade, thousands of Catholic priests and religious have been murdered.

1933-1937 A.D.
Adolf Hitler signs a concordat with the Vatican, but quickly violates it. Pope Pius XI issues *Mit Brennender Sorge*.

1936-1939 A.D.
The Spanish Civil War is fought between the communist Republicans and General Francisco Franco's Nationalists. The communists are ousted from power.

1939-1945 A.D.
World War II rages in Europe. The Vatican remains officially neutral, but Pope Pius XII opposes the Nazis' atrocities and gives assistance to many refugees.

1949 A.D.
A communist government under Mao Zedong takes control of China.

1950 A.D.
Pope Pius XII defines the dogma of the Assumption.

Lenin promised the Germans that he would seize power in Russia, make peace with Germany, and take Russia out of the war.

Under other circumstances, Lenin likely could not have taken power. However, the war had affected Russia far more than it had affected the Western powers. First, Russia was a poor nation, completely unprepared for war. Thus, hundreds of thousands of Russian soldiers died needlessly in battle, not only through poor leadership but often because they did not have guns or even boots! Moreover, nearly the entire population was starving to death. Under these circumstances, the Russians would be willing to follow anyone if he promised to end the war. In October 1917, they did exactly that.

At the end of October, Lenin launched his **October Revolution**, which eventually led to his takeover of Russia.

Witness to the Faith

In March 1918, he signed a peace treaty with Germany, which ended the war for Russia. Although Lenin ceded more than 25 percent of Russia to Germany under the treaty, he did not care. He had ended Russia's participation in the war. Also, communists never kept treaties anyway.

Over the next several years, Lenin consolidated his power. He murdered his enemies. He suppressed the Russian Orthodox Church. In 1922, Russia ceased to exist and was replaced with the **Union of Soviet Socialist Republics** (USSR), also known as the **Soviet Union**, a communist empire which would eventually expand to include fifteen socialist republics.

Lenin almost immediately began his attempt to spread communism across the world. In 1919, he ordered his armies to attack Poland to spread communism into Europe. The Poles defeated Lenin's armies and saved Europe from communism for more than 25 years. A heroic Polish priest led the Poles during a critical battle and drove back the communists. When the Soviet communists met their final defeat many years later, it would also be at the hands of a brave Polish priest.

Our Lady of Fatima

As Europe engaged in its "suicidal" war, and Russia raced into the sinister horror of communism, three children in a small town in Portugal were sent a message of peace and hope for the world. On May 13, 1917, "a woman all in white, more brilliant than the sun" appeared to 10-year-old Lucia dos Santos and her cousins Francisco and Jacinta Marto (who were 9 and 7, respectively). The three children were tending their sheep outside the small town of Fatima. When Lucia asked where the beautiful woman had come from, she responded, "I come from Heaven." The woman held a rosary in her hand and asked the children to "say the Rosary every day, to bring peace to the world and an end to the war."

The Blessed Mother appeared to the three children six times over the next six months. She encouraged them to pray the Rosary. She warned that if people did not stop offending God, another massive war would follow World War I, and Russia would spread its errors throughout the world, doing unspeakable harm to millions. Both of these warnings came to pass. But she also promised that Russia would be converted if it was consecrated to her Immaculate Heart, and then there would be peace in the world.

The final apparition of **Our Lady of Fatima** occurred on October 13, 1917, when Our Lady performed the Miracle of the Sun to demonstrate the truth of the children's statements to the public. Although not well documented outside of Portugal at the time, the event was witnessed by as many as 100,000 people, who had come to Fatima in expectation of a miracle. Numerous eyewitnesses testified that after a rain shower, the dark clouds broke and the sun appeared as an opaque, spinning disc in the sky. It seemed paler than normal, so people could look at it without hurting their eyes. It began to spin like a pinwheel and cast multicolored lights across the sky. The sun then zigzagged toward the Earth before returning to the sky. People's wet clothes, as well as the wet ground, were suddenly dry.

Union of Soviet Socialist Republics (Soviet Union)
Communist empire which began in Russia and would eventually expand to include fifteen socialist republics.

Our Lady of Fatima
Appeared to three young children in Portugal in 1917. She asked them to pray the Rosary for peace, and warned that people must stop offending God. She also warned about Russia, but promised that it would be converted if it was consecrated to her Immaculate Heart.

---

530 *Chapter 34: The Church Faces Nazism and Communism (1917-1958)*

Although secular historians dislike acknowledging the hand of God in history, the timing of Our Lady's final apparition cannot be a coincidence. Her appearance at Fatima on October 13, 1917, occurred *twelve days* before Lenin seized power in Russia. Pope Leo XIII and Our Lady of Fatima had delivered the message of Heaven. But there are none so deaf as those who refuse to hear.

Pope Benedict XV and Russia

Once Lenin took power, he quickly attacked Christianity. On February 5, 1918, he decreed that the government would no longer support the Russian Orthodox Church. The Church could no longer own property. Religion could not be taught in any school that taught non-religious subjects.

The communists then began a systematic persecution of religious. Most of those persecuted were members of the Russian Orthodox Church. Catholics were persecuted as well. From 1918 through 1920, the Communist Party in Russia murdered hundreds of thousands of Russians, including numerous bishops and thousands of priests and other religious. Despite this terrible persecution, the promise of Our Lady of Fatima gave Benedict XV hope that Russia could be converted.

Our Lady of Fatima

In 1920, Benedict reached out to the Russians. His major goal was to end the Great Schism that had existed since 1054. To that end, the pope sent a greeting to Patriarch Tikhon of Moscow, who had declared that the communists were the "monsters of the human race" and the "enemies of the truth of Christ." While they may have had some doctrinal disagreements, both the pope and the patriarch knew their true enemy. Of course, the communists saw the overture as anti-communist.

The following year, Pope Benedict XV tried to deal directly with the communist government. After the war, Russia had suffered from famine and disease, which were killing millions. In 1921, the United States began sending relief, mostly food, to the Russian people. Benedict believed that the Vatican could create its own relief effort. He hoped that a Catholic relief effort would demonstrate to the Russian people the Church's good will and love for them. Moreover, Benedict hoped that providing food to Russia would move the communists to modify their anti-religious policies. Unfortunately, Benedict died in January 1922, before he could implement his plan. The task of trying to help suffering Russia would fall to his successor.

Witness to the Faith

Pope Pius XI

Catholic Action
A movement that sought to involve the laity in apostolic work, to promote Catholic values in all aspects of society.

The Election of Pius XI

On January 5, 1922, Pope Benedict XV caught a cold, which quickly turned into pneumonia. In an age before modern medicine, the pneumonia grew worse. On January 22, 1922, Benedict died. He had been elected mainly for his diplomatic prowess. By the time he died, the Vatican had established diplomatic relations with all of the world's great powers except the United States and Russia.

On February 6, the conclave elected Achille Ratti, the archbishop of Milan. He chose to be called Pius XI (1922-1939) because of his warm childhood memories of Pius IX and Pius X, who had given him a job in the Vatican Library. Like other popes named Pius, he would staunchly defend the Church and the Deposit of Faith.

Pius XI Seeks Peace

To anyone who had survived the horrors of the "Great War" (World War I), the desire for peace was paramount. Thus, it came as no surprise that Pope Pius XI called for peace and charity in his first encyclical, *Ubi Arcano Dei Consilio* (Encyclical on the Peace of Christ in the Kingdom of Christ), which he issued on December 23, 1922. "Since the close of the Great War," Pius states, "individuals, the different classes of society, [and] the nations of the earth have not as yet found true peace." Pius goes on to enumerate the problems plaguing the world. He acknowledges that times are difficult and require work and sacrifice from both the clergy and the laity if conditions are to improve. But doing this work is vital and part of the life of a Christian. Pius concludes that this work is "indissolubly bound up with the restoration of the Kingdom of Christ and the re-establishment of that true peace which can be found only in His Kingdom – 'the peace of Christ in the Kingdom of Christ.'"

The Social Teachings of Pius XI

In his first encyclical, Pope Pius XI had called upon Catholics to take an active part in changing society. He wanted Catholics to help Christianize a world that was becoming more and more secular. Since the nineteenth century, the **Catholic Action** movement had worked to revive Catholicism and oppose anti-clerical movements in Europe. The publication of *Ubi Arcano Dei Consilio* revitalized the Catholic Action movement.

The idea behind Catholic Action was to involve the laity in an organization supervised by the bishops which would actively spread Catholic values and political ideas. Catholic Action was not a political party, although it worked with political parties. The ideal of this movement was to promote Catholic values in all aspects of society, such as the media, youth groups, and unions.

To promote his vision of the Kingdom of Christ, Pope Pius XI also approved associations of young Catholic industrial workers who wanted to Christianize the work force. These groups would provide a Catholic alternative to communist and socialist trade unions. Pius would take up the issue of unions again in his encyclical *Quadragesimo Anno*.

In 1930, Pope Pius XI issued another crucial, long-reaching encyclical, *Casti Connubii* (Encyclical on Christian Marriage). Since its earliest days, the Church has always been the greatest defender of women, children, marriage, and the family. England had been lost to the Church because of the pope's defense of Catherine of Aragon's marriage. Writing in response to certain evil laws that attacked the family, Pius clearly sets forth the Church's long-established doctrines. He shows how Christian marriage and the family are the foundation for any good society. He teaches that **parents have the power and the right to educate their children**. This power comes from the sacramental graces of Matrimony. *Casti Connubii* would serve as a foundation stone for future encyclicals from Pope Paul VI and Pope St. John Paul II.

On May 15, 1931, the fortieth anniversary of *Rerum Novarum*, Pope Pius XI promulgated *Quadragesimo Anno* (Encyclical on Reconstruction of the Social Order), one of his most significant encyclicals. In addressing the issues of modern society, Pius XI argues for the reconstruction of economic and political life based on religious values. He restates many of the propositions found in *Rerum Novarum*, including Pope Leo XIII's warnings against socialism and unrestrained capitalism. Pius pictures an economy based on cooperation and unity between workers and employers.

As the world entered a new age in communications, so did the Church. In this same year, Pius XI established the Vatican Radio. He was the first pope to broadcast on radio.

Pope Pius XI and His Successor, Pacelli, with Marconi at the Start of the Vatican Radio – 1931

Pius XI and the Soviet Union

Prior to his death, Pope Benedict XV had begun negotiations to send aid to Russia. Pius XI had served as papal nuncio to Poland during the communist invasion. He had been in Warsaw during the fighting. He knew how evil the communists were. But he also wanted to help ease the suffering of the starving people of Russia. Therefore, he continued the negotiations.

Although later historians would criticize him for working with the communists, Pope Pius XI could not be certain that the planned mission would fail. In 1922, he believed that he could help starving people and evangelize them. Moreover, the Church had often been forced to work with evil governments. In 1801, Pius VII had signed an accord with Napoleon, an evil dictator. Pius XI was trying to work with Lenin, another evil dictator. The negotiations succeeded, and the communists agreed to allow the Church to distribute food. By the end of September 1922, the relief effort was successfully underway. The following year, the Catholic relief effort was feeding more than 150,000 Russians per day.

In December 1922, the communists launched an attack on the Catholic Church in Russia. They closed all the Catholic churches in Petrograd (St. Petersburg) and three churches in Moscow. The following

> **Note on the USSR Abolishing Religion**
>
> In 1922, the year that the Soviets decided to abolish religion in the USSR, they murdered almost 30 bishops and more than 1,200 priests.

Benito Mussolini
Prime minister and then dictator of Italy.

Jan Cieplak

Lateran Treaty
Treaty that recognized the independence of the Holy See, and granted other benefits to the Church, in exchange for the pope's recognition of the unified Kingdom of Italy with Rome as its capital.

March, soldiers arrested Jan Cieplak, the Catholic archbishop of Mogilev, as well as fourteen other Catholic priests. After a "show trial," the Soviets sentenced Cieplak to death. The Vatican influenced the international community to pressure the Soviets, not yet a world power, to commute Cieplak's sentence to ten years in prison. Additional international pressure caused the communists to release Cieplak in 1924. He died of natural causes in Passaic, New Jersey, in February 1926.

The communist attack nearly destroyed the Catholic Church in Russia. By the end of the 1930s, there were only two functioning Catholic churches in the entire country: one in Moscow, and one in St. Petersburg. The Vatican relief mission appeared to have failed. It had achieved none of its goals. The Vatican had asked that confiscated Church property be returned, but it remained in the hands of the communists. The religious persecution had intensified, not diminished. More priests were imprisoned, not fewer. The Vatican had not reckoned with the bad faith of the communists. Nevertheless, for the twenty months that the relief mission functioned, it fed hundreds of thousands of Russians. For that reason alone, it was not a total failure.

Settling the Roman Question

Since his election, Pope Pius XI had been determined to settle the "Roman Question" and develop more friendly relations with the Italian government. Once again, he would have to deal with an evil man in order to accomplish good. In October 1922, the prime minister of Italy was **Benito Mussolini**.

In 1860, the forces of King Victor Emmanuel had seized most of the Papal States when the modern unified nation of Italy had been founded. Ten years later, the remainder of the Papal States, including Rome, had also been taken. Since 1860, relations between the Italian government and the papacy had been strained. The popes had refused to recognize the confiscation of Rome and the Papal States, thus creating the so-called "Roman Question." Pope Pius IX and his successors had chosen to live as voluntary "prisoners" in the Vatican to protest the government's seizure. For its part, the Italian government, despite overseeing the most Catholic nation on Earth, enacted numerous anti-Catholic laws.

Since Leo XIII, various popes had worked with the Italian government to come closer to an agreement. For example, they had relaxed the ban on voting in elections. Pope Pius XI decided the time had come to sign a treaty ending the long breach between the papacy and the government of Italy. He hoped that the sovereign independence of the Holy See would be recognized once more. He also wished to see Catholicism restored to its rightful place in Italy. In 1929, Pope Pius XI accomplished his goals when he signed the **Lateran Treaty** with the government of Italy.

Under the terms of the Lateran Treaty, the pope recognized the unified Kingdom of Italy, with Rome as its capital. In exchange for this recognition, the pope received many valuable considerations.

534 *Chapter 34: The Church Faces Nazism and Communism (1917-1958)*

First, Catholicism became the official religion of Italy. Second, the government agreed to pay the salaries of priests and bishops. Third, Church marriages would be legally recognized. Previously, couples had to have a civil ceremony in addition to their sacramental marriage. Fourth, the treaty required that the Catholic Faith be taught in all primary and secondary public schools. Fifth, Catholic organizations received full government recognition. Finally, all clerics and religious were removed from the jurisdiction of the civil courts. Thus, they could not be subjected to "show trials," such as were occurring in the Soviet Union.

The Signing of the Lateran Treaty (with Benito Mussolini Seated in the Middle)

In addition to these critical religious provisions, the Lateran Treaty also granted secular benefits to the Church. First, the Italian government recognized that the pope was an independent secular ruler with supreme authority over Vatican City. Pius XI thus became the first pope to be acknowledged as a temporal ruler since Pius IX. Second, the Italian government provided financial compensation for the land it had seized from the Church since 1860.

It seemed that conditions between the Vatican and Italy had finally become friendly. However, the relationship between Pius XI and Benito Mussolini deteriorated badly over the next years. Mussolini had been willing to sign the Lateran Treaty to help consolidate his authority. Once he felt secure in power, his tyrannical ambitions began to impinge on the freedom of the Church. In 1931, he disbanded the Catholic youth groups in Italy. He wanted only youth groups sponsored by his political party, the **Fascists**, to exist. (**Fascism** is a dictatorial, militaristic form of government which places the good of the State above the rights of individual persons.)

Because of Mussolini's policies, Pius XI wrote *Non Abbiamo Bisogno* (Encyclical on Catholic Action in Italy) to the bishops of Italy on June 29, 1931. This encyclical condemned the Fascists' conception of a totalitarian State and their unjust treatment of the Church. The pope protested against Mussolini's closing of Catholic Action and the Catholic Youth Association earlier in the year. Pius was especially concerned about the attempts of the Fascists "to monopolize completely the young" from their earliest years up to adulthood "for the exclusive advantage of a party and of a regime based on an ideology which clearly resolves itself into a true, a real pagan worship

Fascists
Mussolini's political party; those advocating the dictatorial form of government known as fascism.

Fascism
A dictatorial, militaristic form of government which places the good of the State above the rights of individual persons.

Witness to the Faith 535

of the State." Because of Mussolini's desire to usurp the rights of parents and the Church, relations with the Fascist government of Italy continued to worsen throughout the remainder of Pope Pius XI's pontificate.

The Persecutions

Pius XI had dedicated his pontificate to peace and the restoration of the Kingdom of Christ on Earth. It seemed that if any nation would protect the Catholic Faith and restore the Kingdom of Christ, it would be Mexico (the home of Our Lady of Guadalupe) or Spain (land of the Reconquista). Surely, in these two nations so devoted to the Church, the Faith would be protected, and Our Lord would be exalted! Yet, during the reign of Pope Pius XI, these two countries experienced some of the worst persecutions in the history of the Church.

Mexico and the Cristero Rebellion

Following the apparition of Our Lady of Guadalupe in 1531, Mexico had undergone one of the most miraculous conversion experiences in history. Almost overnight, the entire nation had become Catholic. However, in the nineteenth century, a series of incompetent, greedy, and increasingly anti-Catholic rulers began to change Mexico.

General Antonio Santa Anna, who ruled Mexico on and off during much of the first half of the nineteenth century, typified the incompetent and greedy leaders. Santa Anna lost the province of Texas and other Mexican land to the United States. He fell from power for the final time in 1854.

General Antonio Santa Anna

The revolt that removed Santa Anna eventually replaced him with Benito Juarez, who became president of Mexico in 1858. Unlike Santa Anna, Juarez was competent, but he was committed to destroying the Catholic Church in Mexico. Juarez enacted several anti-Catholic laws, and he abolished religious orders in Mexico.

In an attempt to protect the Church, Catholics invited Austrian Archduke Maximilian to rule Mexico in 1864. Although Maximilian was initially successful, in 1867 Juarez overthrew his government. Juarez served as president until he died in 1872.

Following Juarez's death, Porfirio Diaz become president of Mexico. Diaz governed from 1876 until 1911. Diaz was a strong leader, who ruled Mexico with an iron fist. Although he brought order and security to Mexico, he did so by force. On the other hand, unlike Juarez, he did not hate the Church. In fact, during his time as president, the Church in Mexico grew stronger.

In 1910, Diaz was elected president for the eighth time, but it was clear to everyone that he had cheated. Mexico fell into civil war, and Diaz fled. Eventually, two men came to power in Mexico: Venustiano Carranza and Alvaro Obregon. Since the destruction of the Aztec Empire, the Catholic Faith in Mexico has never had two such great enemies as these men. They dedicated their lives to eradicating the Catholic Faith in Mexico.

Venustiano Carranza, who served as president of Mexico from 1914 to 1920, and Alvaro Obregon, who served from 1920 until 1924, were both communists. Both viciously persecuted the Church. During these persecutions, more than 5,000 priests, bishops, and religious were killed. Carranza exiled the Mexican bishops.

In 1917, Carranza and Obregon helped create Mexico's constitution, the **Constitution of Queretaro**. It contained numerous provisions specially intended to harm the Church and diminish her authority. For example, one section *required* that children receive a *secular* education. Under the constitution, the Church could not own land or run any schools. The government could limit the number of priests in a Mexican state. There could be no Catholic political parties.

This anti-Catholic document almost destroyed the Church in Mexico. Although it remains Mexico's constitution, in 1992 some of the worst provisions were removed. For example, the Church can now own property, and the restrictions on the number of priests have been eliminated.

Obregon's successor, Elias Calles, was a communist and a bitter atheist who hated the Church. He ruled Mexico from 1924 to 1935. Like his predecessors, he was determined to destroy the Church. He began his presidency by launching a vigorous assault on the Church. His first step was to expel all foreign-born priests. Next, he enforced the constitutional provision limiting the number of priests in each Mexican state. The governors of the states enacted Calles' orders with brutal efficiency. In one state, where 523 priests had formerly served the people, the government allowed only fifty. In another state, only thirty priests were allowed to remain. In yet another state, the government permitted only five priests and tried to force those five to marry. In 1926, Calles issued a decree forbidding priests from teaching in the schools. Also, schools were prohibited from possessing chapels. Calles threatened, with exile or death, anyone who spoke against his policies and actions.

In the face of Calles' persecution, Mexico's bishops suspended all Church services. However, the bishops believed that a country that had been saved from the darkness of the Aztecs would not fall to the communists. They boldly put their faith in God, Our Lady of Guadalupe, and the Catholic people of Mexico.

On July 31, 1926, all forms of public worship were suspended throughout Mexico. Catholics could still visit their parish churches to pray, but no priests administered the sacraments. Then the bishops and many priests voluntarily went into exile. A few priests remained and worked among the faithful at the risk of their lives. During this period, Pope Pius XI enacted some extraordinary regulations for the people of Mexico. For example, couples were permitted to marry without a priest, simply in the presence of witnesses such as their parents.

During this terrible persecution, the Catholics of Mexico displayed great courage. Often town leaders would gather the members of the parish in the local church. They would recite the prayers of the Mass

Constitution of Queretaro
The constitution created in 1917 for Mexico, which contained many anti-Catholic provisions.

Elias Calles

Witness to the Faith 537

Cristero Rebellion
An uprising of Catholic guerrilla fighters against the communist government of Mexico.

Note on the Cristero Rebellion

In one of the most disappointing episodes of American history, the United States government supported the Calles government later in the rebellion.

Manuel Avila Camacho

and teach catechism to the children. Thus, even without priests, they kept the Catholic Faith alive in Mexico.

Catholics also resisted the persecution in more active ways. The Catholic political party, which had been divided, set aside its differences and organized a political response. Catholics began an economic boycott. For example, they stopped attending movies and using public transportation. However, Calles treated any opposition to his regime as treason. He increased his persecution of Catholics, and it soon became bloody. Calles ordered the murder of men and women from every rank of society.

In August 1926, as the persecution reached its height, the Catholics of Mexico began to fight back. Following some small-scale attacks, formal war broke out on January 1, 1927. The Catholic rebels called themselves *Cristeros*, invoking the name of Jesus Christ under His title "Cristo Rey," or "Christ the King"—the title that Pope Pius XI had used for Our Lord in his first encyclical. In November 1926, Pius had written an encyclical decrying the persecution of the Church in Mexico.

At first, Calles disregarded the **Cristero Rebellion**, because the rebels were so poorly equipped. They fought using guerrilla tactics, and, like all successful guerrilla fighters, they equipped themselves with the weapons of their defeated enemies. With the battle cry of "Viva Cristo Rey! Viva la Virgen de Guadalupe!" (Long live Christ the King! Long live the Virgin of Guadalupe!), the Cristeros began to win battles.

Meanwhile, although most of the world ignored the plight of the Cristeros, Pius XI did not. He praised the Catholics of Mexico for their courage and heroism. On December 12, 1926, America's Catholic bishops had published its *Pastoral Letter on Mexico*, in which they condemned the "war against religion in Mexico" and offered their support to the bishops, priests, and people there. The Knights of Columbus, a Catholic charitable organization, printed millions of pamphlets supporting the Cristeros, as well as two million copies of the bishops' pastoral letter.

By 1929, the Cristeros seemed to have gained a slight edge in the war, but at a great price; thirty thousand Cristeros had been killed. At this point, to end the bloodshed, the United States intervened. In June 1929, the Mexican bishops, the Cristeros, and the Calles government agreed to a peace treaty. The Church recovered the use of its property, and religious instruction was allowed in the churches but not in the schools. The bishops resumed Catholic sacramental life in Mexico.

However, communists only honor a treaty as long as it suits their own purposes, and Calles was a communist and a totally dishonorable man. He did not abide by the terms of the treaty for long. Within two years, he had resumed the persecutions. Over the next years, he murdered about 6,000 Cristeros. On September 29, 1932, Pope Pius XI once again condemned the government of Mexico for its persecution of the Church. The pope also condemned the government for breaking its treaty promise not to apply the anti-clerical provisions of the Mexican constitution. Despite the encyclical, the government continued its persecution until 1940, when Manuel Avila Camacho, a Catholic, became president of Mexico. He finally returned Mexico to the Catholic Church.

The damage that Carranza, Obregon, Calles, and their minions did to the Church in Mexico was devastating. In 1926, there had been about 4,500 Catholic priests serving the Mexican people. By 1934, over 90 percent of them had suffered some form of persecution. More than 4,100 had voluntarily left Mexico, had been forced into exile, or had been murdered. The government licensed only 334 priests to serve 15 million Catholics. By 1935, seventeen of Mexico's thirty-one states had no priests at all.

In 1925, 95 percent of the population of Mexico was Catholic. As of 2010, that number had decreased to 83 percent. While the majority of the remaining 17 percent are Christians, 5 percent say they belong to no religion at all. "And Jesus wept" (John 11:35).

The Catholic Church has rightly recognized more than two dozen of those murdered during Calles' persecution as martyrs, because they died for the Faith. One of the more notable martyrs is Jesuit priest **Blessed Miguel Pro**. By the express orders of President Calles, a firing squad shot Father Miguel Pro on November 23, 1927. Typical of the communists, Calles felt a trial was unnecessary, since Father Pro was a Catholic priest. Father Pro would have admitted his "guilt" to that charge! Declining a blindfold, he faced the firing squad, with a crucifix in one hand and a rosary in the other. As the soldiers prepared to shoot, he held his arms out like Our Crucified Lord and exclaimed, "Viva Cristo Rey!" Pope John Paul II beatified him in 1988.

The Spanish Civil War (1936-1939)

The second great persecution of the Catholic Church during the pontificate of Pius XI occurred in Spain. A new government came to power in Spain in 1931. This government called itself "Republican," but it was communist to its core. Like all communist governments, it was extremely anti-Catholic. The government secularized education and prohibited the teaching of the Catholic Faith in schools. Many Catholic schools were closed, and some were even destroyed. The communists expelled the Jesuits from Spain.

In May 1931, Archbishop Pedro Segura of Toledo, the leader of the Church in Spain, wrote a pastoral letter. He urged Spanish Catholics to obey and respect the new government, but he also wrote that he thought the establishment of a republic was not good for Spain. This letter served as the government's excuse to burn and loot churches and convents throughout the country. In June, after Archbishop Segura returned to Spain from a meeting in Rome with Pope Pius XI, the government had him arrested and deported.

Blessed Miguel Pro

Blessed Miguel Pro
Jesuit priest martyred in Mexico during the persecution of the Catholic Church, under Elias Calles.

General Francisco Franco
Leader of the Nationalist forces in Spain which ousted the communist government after the Spanish Civil War.

General Francisco Franco

In 1932, Pius XI protested the actions of the Spanish government. He urged Catholics in Spain to fight against these injustices with all legal means. In June 1933 (eight months after his encyclical condemning the Mexican government), Pius issued an encyclical denouncing the persecution of the Church in Spain. He condemned the government's seizure of Church buildings, seminaries, and monasteries, and of the homes of priests and bishops. They were now treated as the property of the Spanish government, and the Church had to pay rent and taxes to use them. Pius also condemned the government's seizure of religious vestments, liturgical instruments, statues, pictures, and other items necessary for worship.

Throughout the spring of 1936, the persecution in Spain grew even worse. On May 1, thousands of communists paraded down Madrid's main street carrying pictures of Lenin and reigning Soviet leader Josef Stalin. Three days later, a number of churches in Madrid were attacked, as were several religious. A communist mob killed three nuns. From May until July, there were more murders and attacks on priests and nuns. Churches were regularly bombed and destroyed.

On July 18, 1936, civil war broke out between the Republicans (the communists) and the Nationalists, who were led by **General Francisco Franco**. That morning, Franco sent out a radio broadcast explaining his reasons for taking up arms against the Spanish government. Catholics supported Franco and his Nationalist forces. During the three-year war, the communists destroyed thousands of churches and murdered thousands of Spain's clergy.

About 1,200 years earlier, Pelayo had stood in his mountain cave surrounded by Muslims. He refused to surrender or leave. Now that same spirit galvanized Spain's priests and bishops. Aware of the dangers, *all of Spain's bishops decided to remain in their dioceses.* The bishop of Cuenca summarized the feelings of his fellow bishops: "I cannot go; here alone is my responsibility, whatever may happen."

By August 1936, the Nationalist forces had mobilized and begun to reclaim Spain from the communists. For the next three years, the Spanish Civil War raged on. In communist-controlled areas, priests and religious continued to suffer martyrdom. Slowly, the Catholic forces led by Franco began to conquer Spain. Most of Spain fell quickly to Franco, with the exception of Madrid, which held out for two and a half years.

At the end of December 1936, General Franco, now recognized as the head of the Nationalist government, signed a concordat with the Church. He promised full freedom for Catholics. He pledged to work closely with the Church and bring Spanish laws into conformity with Catholic doctrine. During the thirty-six years that he governed Spain after the Civil War, he strove to keep his agreement.

The total number of Catholic priests and other religious martyred in Republican-held territories during the Spanish Civil War was 6,832. It is the greatest number of religious martyred in a single country in the history of the Catholic Church, exceeding the number of religious martyred by the French Revolution and the 1917 Communist Revolution in Russia combined. Almost 12 percent of the religious in Spain were martyred. Most of the martyrdoms occurred during the first six months of the war. In a 1937 letter, the Spanish bishops estimated that of the 42,000 churches and chapels in Spain, 20,000 had been destroyed. In Barcelona, a communist stronghold, only ten churches in the entire diocese escaped undamaged.

In 1939, the Nationalists won the civil war against the Republicans. Many secular historians believe that the wrong side won. These historians point out that Francisco Franco, the leader of the Nationalist forces, received aid from Nazi Germany during the war. Yet they almost never mention that thousands of Catholic priests and nuns were brutally murdered by the communist Republicans. Furthermore, the Republicans also received foreign aid during the war, and most of this aid came from the Soviet Union.

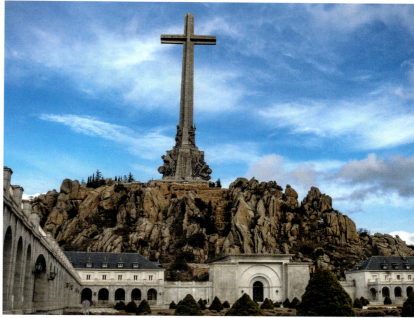

The Valley of the Fallen (Memorial Dedicated to the Spaniards Who Died during the Spanish Civil War) and the Basilica of the Holy Cross in El Escorial, Spain

Although Franco accepted German military aid to defeat the Republicans, Spain did not join Germany in World War II. In 1940, the year of Nazi leader Adolf Hitler's greatest power, Franco refused Hitler's demands that Spain assist him. Spain officially remained neutral during World War II.

Germany

In January 1933, Nazi leader Adolf Hitler became the chancellor of Germany. Germany's Catholic bishops did not trust Hitler, although he publicly promised that Christianity would be part of his rebuilding of Germany.

Soon after Hitler became chancellor, he asked the Vatican for a concordat. Because Pius XI believed that written treaties provided the best protection of the Church's rights, he agreed. The treaty with Germany guaranteed freedom for the Church, for Catholic organizations, and for Catholic youth groups. It also promised the Church the right to teach religion in German schools.

In reality, however, Hitler seems to have signed the concordat to lend credibility to his government rather than for any honest motive. Almost before the ink was dry, he began to violate the treaty. The Nazis seized control of education, abolished the Catholic political party, and

Witness to the Faith

Mit Brennender Sorge
Encyclical in which Pope Pius XI condemned the evils committed by the Nazis; the first official denunciation of Nazism by any major organization.

Mit Brennender Sorge
(Written in German)

Es ist der bestimmte Wille des Heiligen Vaters, daß das vorstehende Apostolische Sendschreiben „allen etwaigen Schwierigkeiten zum Trotz in wirksamer Weise zur Kenntnis der Gläubigen" gebracht wird.

Daher ordne ich an, daß dieses Päpstliche Rundschreiben in 3 Teilen und zwar der erste Teil am Palmsonntag, wie in anderen Diözesen beim vormittägigen Gottesdienst, der Rest am Nachmittag sowie bei einem Gottesdienst des Karfreitags in vollständigem Wortlaut verlesen wird.

Es ist zu wünschen, daß das Rundschreiben des Heiligen Vaters möglichst unter den Pfarrangehörigen verbreitet wird.

Speyer, den 17. März 1937.

✝ **Ludwig**
Bischof von Speyer.

An die ehrwürdigen Brüder Erzbischöfe
und Bischöfe Deutschlands
und die anderen Oberhirten
die in Frieden und Gemeinschaft
mit dem Apostolischen Stuhle leben

über die Lage der Katholischen Kirche
im Deutschen Reich

Papst Pius XI.

Ehrwürdige Brüder
Gruß und Apostolischen Segen!

Mit brennender Sorge und steigendem Befremden beobachten Wir seit geraumer Zeit den Leidensweg der Kirche, die wachsende Bedrängnis der ihr in Gesinnung und Tat treubleibenden Bekenner und Bekennerinnen inmitten des Landes und des Volkes, dem St. Bonifatius einst die Licht- und Frohbotschaft von Christus und dem Reiche Gottes gebracht hat.

Diese Unsere Sorge ist nicht vermindert worden durch das, was die Uns an Unserem Krankenlager besuchenden Vertreter des hochwürdigsten Episkopats wahrheits- und pflichtgemäß berichtet haben. Neben viel Tröstlichem und Erhebendem aus dem Bekennerkampf ihrer Gläu-

began arresting priests and nuns. The Catholic bishops of Germany protested these violations of the concordat, mostly to little avail. Between 1933 and 1936, the Vatican sent dozens of letters to the Nazi government, protesting the treatment of the Church and the violations of the concordat. Most of these letters went unanswered.

In 1937, Pius issued the encyclical ***Mit Brennender Sorge*** (Encyclical on the Church and the German Reich). Unlike most encyclicals, which are written in Latin, this one was written in German. Pius wrote specifically in response to the Nazis' attacks on the Church and Christianity. He condemned the Nazi ideology of racism and totalitarianism. He also condemned Germany's violations of the 1933 concordat. Since no anti-Nazi material was allowed into Germany, copies of the encyclical had to be smuggled into the country and secretly printed. A group of brave motorcyclists covertly distributed them. On Palm Sunday, it was read from the pulpit of every Catholic church in Germany. The encyclical was the first official denunciation of Nazism by any major organization.

Mit Brennender Sorge enraged Hitler and the Nazis. Many German Catholics who participated in the secret printing and distribution were discovered and sent to prison or concentration camps. Other priests and monks were arrested to humiliate the Church. Sadly, for the most part, the Western democracies remained silent.

The Last Days of Pius XI

For the remainder of his pontificate, Pius XI continued to denounce the Nazis and Hitler's anti-Semitic policies. In 1938, Mussolini attempted to pass anti-Jewish laws in imitation of Hitler's anti-Semitic ideas. Pius condemned them as well.

Pope Pius XI died on February 10, 1939. The world was on the brink of another world war. The next pontiff would need to be a great diplomat if he was to survive. The conclave of 1939 would choose such a man.

The Election of Pius XII

Pius XI was succeeded by his secretary of state, **Cardinal Eugenio Pacelli**. Upon his election, Cardinal Pacelli chose to be called **Pius XII** (1939-1958) to honor his friend Pius XI. An accomplished diplomat, Pope Pius XII would continue

542   *Chapter 34: The Church Faces Nazism and Communism (1917-1958)*

Pope Pius XI's struggle against the Nazis. He would do so as a virtual prisoner in the Vatican during World War II. After the war, he fought against the evil of communism as well.

Before becoming pope, Eugenio Pacelli had one of the most illustrious careers of any man to wear the Fisherman's Ring. Born in 1876 to a noble Italian family, Eugenio decided as a young boy that he wished to be a priest. After he was ordained in 1899, his first assignment was to *Santa Maria in Vallicella* (a church in Rome also known as *Chiesa Nuova*), where he had served as an altar boy. An extremely bright and able priest, he advanced rapidly in the Church. He worked on the new Code of Canon Law and, in 1901, he joined the Vatican's diplomatic service, an area in which he excelled.

During World War I, Father Pacelli maintained the Vatican's registry of prisoners of war (POWs). In 1915, he traveled to Vienna to assist the apostolic nuncio in negotiations with Austria. Two years later, Pope Benedict XV made Father Pacelli an archbishop and sent him as papal nuncio to Germany. In Munich, Archbishop Pacelli conveyed the pope's peace plan to the German government. The plan was rejected, and the war continued for another year.

Pope Pius XII

After the war, Archbishop Pacelli remained in Germany, working to improve relations between the government and the Church. He also worked on diplomatic arrangements between the Vatican and the Soviet Union. Pacelli played a leading role in negotiating Pope Pius XI's effort to send food to the starving people in Russia. He also met with the Soviet communists in the hopes of reducing the persecutions. Not surprisingly, the communists refused.

In December 1929, Pius XI elevated Archbishop Pacelli to the Sacred College. Two months later, Pius appointed him Vatican Secretary of State. In this role, Cardinal Pacelli signed concordats with a number of countries. He also made many diplomatic visits throughout Europe, as well as North and South America. In 1936, he visited the United States and met with President Franklin Roosevelt. In December 1939, President Roosevelt appointed an envoy to the Vatican. The appointment re-established diplomatic relations, which had been broken since 1870 following Italy's confiscation of the Papal States. The 1933 concordat with Germany was the most important of

Cardinal Eugenio Pacelli (Pope Pius XII)
Reigned from 1939 to 1958; denounced the crimes of the Nazis and Soviets, and helped save many Jews during World War II.

Witness to the Faith 543

Cardinal Pacelli's treaties. Like Pius XI, he hoped that the concordat would strengthen the Church's legal position. Following the Nazis' continual violation of the treaty, Cardinal Pacelli, along with the archbishop of Munich, helped write *Mit Brennender Sorge*.

Pius XII and World War II

Pius XII's pontificate began on the eve of World War II. Like Benedict XV, Pius sought to be a "Pope of Peace," but on September 1, 1939, Germany invaded Poland, thus initiating the war. During the war, Pius adopted a policy of impartiality, much as Benedict XV had done during World War I. He also took many of the same actions that Benedict had taken. For example, in 1939, Pius turned the Vatican into a distribution center to help the people seeking aid who came there from around the world. He also created an information office for POWs and refugees, which operated from 1939 until 1947.

Despite being surrounded by his enemies, Pope Pius XII spoke out against atrocities. In his first encyclical in October 1939, he condemned the invasion of Poland by the Nazis and the Soviet Communists. He denounced the totalitarian state as a threat to the family and the education of children. He also condemned the anti-Jewish policies of the Nazis. In a December 1939 speech at the Vatican, Pius denounced the Soviet Union's attack on Finland. In January 1940, in a radio broadcast, he condemned the murder of more than 15,000 Polish civilians. For these stands against the Nazis and the Soviets, even the secular media praised his courage. *Time* magazine credited Pius XII and the Catholic Church for "fighting totalitarianism more knowingly, devoutly, and authoritatively, and for a longer time, than any other organized power." *The New York Times* newspaper also praised him for opposing Nazi anti-Semitism and aggression.

Israel Zolli
The chief rabbi of Rome, to whom Pope Pius XII gave refuge in the Vatican during the Nazi occupation; was later baptized a Catholic, choosing the name Eugenio in gratitude to the pope.

In 1943, after the Nazis occupied Rome, Hitler apparently planned to arrest Pope Pius XII and several cardinals. Pius told the leading bishops that if the Nazis seized him, his resignation would take effect immediately. The Holy See would move to neutral Portugal, where the College of Cardinals would elect a new pope. Hitler's scheme never materialized.

In 1945, as the war approached its conclusion, Pius urged the Allies to treat the defeated nations mercifully. He hoped to avoid the animosities that the 1919 Treaty of Versailles had caused. In April, he published an encyclical in which he called for all people, especially young children, to pray for peace in the coming month. The war in Europe ended on May 8, 1945.

Pius XII and the Jews

Throughout the war, the Church worked to help the Jews, who were the victims of violent Nazi persecution. Under Pope Pius XII's leadership, the Church saved hundreds of thousands of Jews—perhaps as many as 860,000—from the Nazis. After the war, many Jews publicly thanked the pope for his help. In September 1945, the general secretary of the World Jewish Council presented Pius XII with an award "in recognition of the work of the Holy See in rescuing Jews from Fascist and Nazi persecutions." In 1945, the chief rabbi of Palestine, Yitzhak Herzog, declared: "The people of Israel will never forget what His Holiness and his illustrious delegates are doing for our unfortunate brothers and sisters in the most tragic hour of our history…."

Most revealing of the assistance that Pope Pius XII provided is the conversion of the chief rabbi of Rome, **Israel Zolli**, to whom Pius granted refuge in the Vatican after the Nazis occupied Rome in 1943. On February 13, 1945, Rabbi Zolli was baptized a Catholic. He chose "Eugenio" as his Christian name in gratitude to the pope who had done so much for the Jews and his family during the war. His wife was baptized with him. One year later, his daughter also became Catholic.

Pius XII and China

Since the end of the seventeenth century, the people of China had struggled to become Catholic. Their struggle resulted from the Church's objection to the Chinese custom of honoring dead relatives, the so-called "Chinese Rites." For the Chinese, honoring the dead was an ancient ritual. In fact, the seventeenth-century Jesuit missionaries to China had said that the practice was a secular ritual compatible with Catholicism. However, in 1704, Pope Clement XI determined that the Chinese Rites were a superstition which conflicted with Church teachings. He prohibited them for Catholics. As a result, very few Chinese converted.

Within a month of becoming pope, Pius XII reviewed the practices of the Chinese Rites and declared that these ceremonies, which were part of the Chinese culture, were not superstition and did not violate Church teachings. Within a few years, the Church in China began to flourish like never before.

In 1943, the government of China established diplomatic relations with the Vatican. Three years later, Pope Pius created the first Chinese cardinal and established a local hierarchy. The Church seemed to be well on her way to making significant conversions in China. However, in 1949, after years of civil war, the Communist Party of China, led by **Mao Zedong**, came into power.

As all communists have done, Mao Zedong persecuted the Church. During the early 1950s, the communists worked to eliminate the Catholic Church in China. By 1953, many bishops and priests, both native Chinese and foreign, had been arrested and thrown into prison, where many died. In 1957, the government established the **Chinese Patriotic Catholic Association**, the State-run "church." By 1958,

> **Mao Zedong**
> The leader of the communist takeover of China.

Mao Zedong

> **Chinese Patriotic Catholic Association**
> The State "church" established in China by Mao Zedong's communist government.

Assumption of Mary,
Andres de Rubira

when all the Catholic bishops had been arrested, killed, or exiled, the communists installed "bishops" from the Patriotic Catholic Association in their sees.

Starting in 1951, Pope Pius XII responded to these attacks on the Church by issuing a number of encyclicals. In June 1958, in one of his final encyclicals, he specifically addressed the Church in China. He described and protested the systematic persecution of bishops, priests, and religious and the creation of the Patriotic "church." He concluded by blessing and comforting those who remained faithful to the true Church, assuring them that their sufferings would one day bring about calmer, happier days.

Pius XII and the Soviet Union

Since the 1917 revolution in Russia, the communist government had been overtly hostile to the Catholic Church. The communists had stolen Church property, arrested priests, and dissolved Catholic institutions. Benedict XV and Pius XI had protested these actions and denounced communism. Despite the protests, the communists were determined to destroy religion in Russia and in every other nation conquered by the Soviet Union.

In 1953, Soviet leader Josef Stalin died. Pope Pius XII tried to open negotiations with the new government, hoping that the Church might again evangelize the people of the Soviet Union. For the remainder of his papacy, Pius continued working for persecuted Catholics in the USSR.

546 Chapter 34: The Church Faces Nazism and Communism (1917-1958)

The Dogma of the Assumption

Throughout his life, Eugenio Pacelli had a great devotion to the Blessed Mother. In 1946, Pope Pius XII issued the encyclical *Deiparae Virginis Mariae*, (Encyclical on the Possibility of Defining the Assumption of the Blessed Virgin Mary as a Dogma of Faith). In this encyclical, the pope asked the world's bishops for information concerning the devotion that the clergy and the people had regarding the Assumption of the Blessed Mother into Heaven. Like the doctrine of the Immaculate Conception, the Assumption had been accepted and celebrated for centuries but never officially defined. Pope Pius was considering declaring the Assumption an official dogma, but before he did, he wanted feedback from the bishops.

On November 1, 1950, Pope Pius XII, speaking *ex cathedra* ("from the chair" of St. Peter), defined the dogma of the Assumption of Mary. He infallibly declared that "the Immaculate Mother of God, the ever Virgin Mary, having completed the course of her earthly life, was assumed body and soul into heavenly glory." In this dogmatic statement, the phrase "having completed the course of her earthly life" leaves open the question of whether or not Our Blessed Mother died before her Assumption; either is possible. What is certain, however, is that Mary's Assumption was a divine gift to her as the Mother of God.

Pope Pius XII

Pius XII and His Eternal Reward

Pope Pius XII fell ill in 1953, and considered resigning because he felt he could not properly fulfill his duties. However, other than a lighter workload, he continued as pope despite the illness. He died on October 9, 1958.

Pope Paul VI opened the cause of Pius XII's canonization in 1965. In December 2009, Pope Benedict XVI declared him *Venerable*, the penultimate step before canonization. As of 2020, he has yet to be canonized.

Oral Exercises

1. What did Our Lady of Fatima ask the children to do?
2. What great miracle did Our Lady of Fatima perform?
3. Who wrote *Casti Connubii*?
4. Name two things the pope taught in *Casti Connubii*.
5. Why did Pope Pius XI sign concordats?
6. What were some important gains the Church made as a result of the Lateran Treaty?
7. What was the name of the Jesuit priest martyred by the communists in Mexico, by the express orders of Elias Calles?
8. What was the name of the side that Catholics supported during the Spanish Civil War?
9. What is some of the evidence that Pope Pius XII helped the Jews during WWII?
10. What is the Chinese Patriotic Catholic Association?
11. What is the dogma of the Assumption?

Witness to the Faith   547

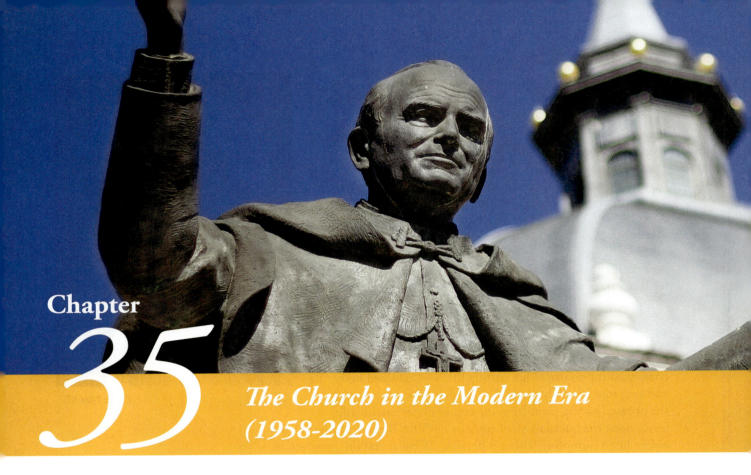

Chapter 35
The Church in the Modern Era (1958-2020)

Pope John XXIII
Reigned from 1958 to 1963; convoked the Second Vatican Council and was known for his humility and kindness.

Introduction

When speaking of the "modern era," most historians simply mean the period after World War II until the present. The term "modern" has no implications either positively or negatively. It serves merely as an adjective, such as "information" age or "space" age. Even the Church historian does not necessarily imply a negative connotation, and, in fact, none should be implied. The period following War World II *is* the modern era—that is, contemporary times.

Yet the Church historian cannot deny that during these years, the heresy known as *modernism* has become an even greater threat to the Church. Modernists deny that eternal truths exist. They claim that truth depends on the times in which one lives. Modernists have proclaimed that in modern times the Church should abandon its old views of the Bible, morality, and doctrine, and adopt modern ideas that conform to new scientific discoveries and ways of thinking.

Fortunately, in the past seventy years, the Holy Spirit has blessed the Church with excellent popes. They have led the Church in times of calm and crisis. They have proclaimed the splendor of the Church and warned the world of the necessity of peace. They have confronted modernism and its proponents, and have strived to stop them from advancing.

Statue of Pope St. John Paul II

The Election of John XXIII

The conclave of 1958, which met to elect Pope Pius XII's successor, did not face any imminent threats. Nor was there a clear choice for pope, as there had been in 1939 when Pius XII, the secretary of state, was elected. Because there was no obvious favorite, the Sacred College appears to have settled on a compromise candidate. They elected Angelo Roncalli, the 76-year-old cardinal archbishop of Venice. He chose to be called **John XXIII** (1958-1963).

At first glance, it looked like the Sacred College could not have elected anyone *less like* his predecessor than John XXIII. Pope Pius XII had been born into a family of nobility and looked like a prince. He was tall, athletic, and handsome. His wire-rimmed glasses made him look wise and scholarly. Pope

1962 A.D. – 2013 A.D.

1962-1965 A.D.
The Church holds the Second Vatican Council.

1968 A.D.
Pope Paul VI issues *Humanae Vitae*.

1969 A.D.
Pope Paul VI approves the *Novus Ordo* form of the Mass.

1973 A.D.
Pope Paul VI meets with the Coptic patriarch of Alexandria, and they issue a joint declaration and creed.

1979 A.D.
John Paul II makes his first visit as pope to his homeland, Poland, and inspires the creation of the Solidarity movement.

1984 A.D.
John Paul II holds the first World Youth Day.

1989 A.D.
The Soviet Union's grip on Eastern Europe slips away.

1999 A.D.
Pope John Paul II visits Romania, the first time since the Great Schism that a pope has visited a country with an Eastern Orthodox majority.

2005 A.D.
Pope John Paul II dies and is succeeded by Pope Benedict XVI.

2013 A.D.
Pope Benedict XVI resigns, and is succeeded by Pope Francis.

Witness to the Faith 549

John XXIII had been born into a family of poor sharecroppers. He was short (5 feet 2 inches) and stout (200 pounds), and he had a great sense of humor, which he often aimed at himself. On one occasion, as he walked about Rome, a woman commented on his size. He replied that the Sacred Conclave was not a beauty contest. Nevertheless, despite their physical dissimilarities and family backgrounds, Pius XII and John XXIII had much in common.

Angelo Roncalli was born in Italy on November 25, 1881. He was one of thirteen children. Like Eugenio Pacelli (Pius XII), Roncalli felt called to the priesthood. After he was ordained in 1904, Roncalli worked with the missions in Italy. In 1925, Pope Pius XI consecrated him as a bishop and made him an ambassador to Bulgaria, thus beginning Roncalli's long diplomatic career. Ten years later, Pius XI named him an ambassador to Turkey and Greece. During World War II, Bishop Roncalli worked to save thousands of Jews from the Nazis. He worked especially in Greece, Turkey, and Bulgaria, where he had many contacts from his time as an ambassador. He personally intervened with King Boris III of Bulgaria not to deport Jews from his nation.

In 1944, after the Allies liberated France, Pope Pius XII sent Bishop Roncalli to France as apostolic nuncio. In 1953, Pius XII elevated him to the Sacred College, naming him cardinal archbishop of Venice, a post once held by Pope Pius X. Cardinal Roncalli remained in this position until the death of Pius XII, when he was elected pope.

Pope John XXIII

A Name Chosen in Humility

Roncalli's choice of papal name surprised his fellow cardinals. When they asked by what name he would be called, he said, "I will be called John." Because the Pisan antipope had been called "John XXIII" during the Western Schism, popes had avoided the name "John" since the schism ended in 1415. However, Cardinal Roncalli chose the name out of humility. As he explained to his fellow cardinals, he chose "John" because it was his father's name, the name of the parish church where he was baptized, and the name of innumerable cathedrals around the world. He continued: "Twenty-two Johns of indisputable legitimacy have [been pope], and almost all had a brief pontificate. We have preferred to hide the smallness of our name behind this magnificent succession of Roman popes."

John XXIII Calls the Second Vatican Council

In addition to their backgrounds in diplomacy, Pius XII and John XXIII shared another goal. They were both utterly determined to defend the Church against modernism. By 1958, despite encyclicals from Pius IX and Pius X, modernism seemed to be making great strides in the Church. Pope John XXIII realized that something more was needed. Historically, when the Church has faced a great crisis, such as the Arian heresy or the Protestant Revolt, the pope has convoked an ecumenical council. Pope John XIII convoked the Second Vatican Council (or Vatican II).

550   *Chapter 35: The Church in the Modern Era (1958-2020)*

The First Vatican Council had convened as the modernists were launching their first attacks. In the face of a heresy that denied truth, the council declared papal infallibility, the ultimate declaration of truth. Vatican II would reaffirm the Church's teachings.

Social Teachings of John XXIII

Pope John XIII wrote two important encyclicals during his pontificate. In *Mater et Magistra* (Encyclical on Christianity and Social Progress), issued on May 15, 1961, the seventieth anniversary of *Rerum Novarum*, he reaffirms Leo XIII's teachings, especially on the right to own private property and the importance of the family. Interestingly, probably because of his own background, John writes of the values of agriculture and the family farm. John concludes with several practical suggestions for improving the current social order. Finally, he reminds his readers that his main "concern is with the doctrine of the Catholic and Apostolic Church. She is the Mother and Teacher of all nations … She is ever powerful to offer suitable, effective remedies for the increasing needs of men, and the sorrows and anxieties of this present life."

On April 11, 1963, shortly before he died, he issued *Pacem in Terris* (Encyclical on Establishing Universal Peace in Truth, Justice, Charity, and Liberty). In this encyclical, Pope John XIII teaches that conflicts should be settled by negotiations, not war and violence. Such advice holds a special significance in an age of nuclear weapons. John XXIII stresses that all governments must respect individual human rights. These rights include freedom of worship, political freedom, and the right to emigrate from one nation to another.

A Brief Pontificate

Upon his election, John XXIII had said that almost all popes named John had brief pontificates. His pontificate lasted only four years and seven months. He died on June 3, 1963. He did not live to see Vatican II complete its work. That would fall to his successor.

John XXIII was canonized by Pope Francis on April 27, 2014. Throughout his life, he had practiced humility and kindness. As pope, he had visited prisoners in Rome's jails, and children in the local hospital. In Pope St. John XXIII, people saw God's goodness. For that reason, they called him "the good pope."

The Election of Paul VI

The main issue facing the cardinals in the 1963 conclave was the election of a pope who supported Vatican II. One of the leading candidates in 1958 had been the archbishop of Milan, **Giovanni Battista Montini**. Although he was not a cardinal, as archbishop of Milan, he held one of the

> **Giovanni Battista Montini (Pope Paul VI)**
> Reigned from 1963 to 1978; completed Vatican II, approved the *Novus Ordo* form of the Mass, engaged in a worldwide missionary effort to spread the Catholic Faith, and worked to confirm and clarify Church teachings.

Pope Paul VI

Witness to the Faith

most prominent positions in the Church. Milan had been the archdiocese of St. Ambrose and St. Charles Borromeo. After a two-day conclave, the Sacred College elected Montini, now a cardinal, on June 21, 1963. He chose to be called **Paul VI** (1963-1978).

Paul's Path to the Throne of Peter

In Paul VI, the Sacred College elected a man of high character and exceptional qualifications. Giovanni Battista Montini was born in Italy on September 26, 1897. Educated in primary and secondary school by the Jesuits, he entered the seminary in 1916. In May 1920, he was ordained a priest. From 1922 until 1954, Father Montini worked in the Vatican's State Department. In 1937, he began working for Cardinal Pacelli, eventually becoming one of his closest and most influential advisors. Their relationship continued when Pacelli became Pope Pius XII.

During World War II, Montini worked closely with Pius XII. He helped the pope answer the thousands of letters he received asking for spiritual and material assistance. Montini aided in the creation of the office that provided information on prisoners of war (POWs) and refugees. He also assisted in starting the Pontifical Assistance Commission. This agency helped the people of Rome and other refugees with food and shelter.

Father Montini acted as a sort of "secret agent" during World War II, especially after the Nazis occupied Rome. Montini helped Allied POWs who had escaped from prison camps. He also helped save innumerable Jews. Pius XII tasked the young priest with delivering secret messages. He carried out his work in the face of deadly danger. Montini, and all those who helped to hide Jews, risked their lives, and they knew it.

In 1954, Pius XII made Father Montini the archbishop of Milan, the largest archdiocese in Italy and one of the largest in the world. As archbishop, he used new approaches and technology to reach the people of his archdiocese. He sought to reintroduce the Catholic Faith in a place where many had lost their faith. Archbishop Montini recognized that Western Europe had effectively become mission territory. In 1958, Pope John XXIII made him a cardinal.

When Cardinal Montini was elected pope on June 21, 1963, he chose the name "Paul" in honor of St. Paul, the Church's greatest missionary. The name reflected Pope Paul VI's determination to engage in a worldwide missionary effort to spread the Catholic Faith. Pope Paul took his name seriously. During his pontificate, he visited every continent but Antarctica. One of his first acts as pope was to reopen the Second Vatican Council, which had closed with the death of Pope John XXIII.

The Second Vatican Council

Six days after his election, Pope Paul VI announced that he would continue the **Second Vatican Council**. He reopened the council on September 29, 1963. In doing so, he said that he wanted the council

Cardinal Montini Walking in St. Peter's Square, 1962

Opening of Second Session of Vatican II

to work to better explain the Catholic Faith. He asked the council fathers not to repeat or create new dogmatic definitions, but to explain the Church's teachings in simple terms. He also wanted the council to address Church reforms. Furthermore, he wished the council to explore the possibility of unifying with other Christians, *but only on Catholic terms*. The council also discussed the Mass.

On September 14, 1964, Pope Paul VI opened the council's third session. He told the council fathers that the *Dogmatic Constitution on the Church* (*Lumen Gentium*) was the most important document they had produced. Issued in November 1964, *Lumen Gentium* dealt with almost every aspect of the Church. It called upon all Christians to strive to become holier. Its final section formally declared that the Blessed Mother "is acknowledged and honored as being truly the Mother of God and Mother of the Redeemer." As the Mother of Our Lord, she is also Mother of the Church. The council concluded on December 8, 1965, the Feast of the Immaculate Conception.

Marian Devotion

Pope Paul VI's decision to declare Mary the Mother of the Church did not surprise those who knew him. Throughout his life, he had a strong devotion to the Blessed Mother. He often spoke at Marian congresses and loved to visit Marian shrines. As pope, he attempted to travel to Poland on a Marian pilgrimage, but the communist government would not allow it. During his papacy, he often wrote of Mary in his encyclicals.

For example, in his first encyclical, *Ecclesiam Suam* (Encyclical on the Church), issued in August 1964, Pope Paul VI calls Mary "a most loving teacher" and the "ideal of Christian perfection." He regards devotion to the Blessed Mother as "of paramount importance in living the life of the Gospel." His second encyclical, *Mense Maio* (Encyclical on Prayers

Second Vatican Council (Vatican II) Strove to better explain Church teachings and address issues that needed reform.

Witness to the Faith   553

Madonna of the People,
Federico Barocci

during May), focuses specifically on the Blessed Mother, to whom the month of May is traditionally dedicated as the Mother of God. "Since Mary is rightly to be regarded as the way by which we are led to Christ," Pope Paul writes, "the person who encounters Mary cannot help but encounter Christ likewise." He goes on to write that God "has appointed Mary most holy as the generous steward of His merciful gifts." In another encyclical, Paul encourages devotion to the Rosary.

The New Form of the Mass

Since 1570, with a few exceptions, the Mass had been said in Latin everywhere in the world. During Pope Pius XII's reign, the Vatican relaxed the rules on the use of Latin in the Mass. The Church allowed local languages (the vernacular) to be used during Baptisms, funerals, and other events. In his 1947 encyclical *Mediator Dei*, Pius XII wrote that using a nation's "mother tongue" would "be of much advantage to the people." The belief was that using the vernacular would encourage greater participation in the Mass by the congregation.

One of the first topics that Vatican II addressed was revising the Mass. The council's stated goal was to revise the Mass "in such a way that the intrinsic nature and purpose of its several parts … may be more clearly manifested, and that devout and active participation by the faithful may be more easily achieved." In April 1969, Pope Paul VI approved the **Novus Ordo** ("New Order") form of the Mass.

The Novus Ordo form of the Mass included many significant changes to the traditional form of the Mass (the Tridentine Mass). Some prayers were removed, and some new prayers were added. The pope's approval also included permission to use local languages instead of Latin.

Novus Ordo ("New Order")
The current ordinary form of the Mass, approved by Pope Paul VI in 1969.

Not everyone welcomed these changes. Some were unhappy with what appeared to be the sudden ban on the centuries-old form of the Mass to which they were accustomed and which they had grown up attending. Also, many modernists began "experimenting" with the newly approved Novus Ordo form of the Mass. Some churches replaced Gregorian Chant with pop and folk music. Guitars replaced organs. Some churches made changes to their sanctuaries, which some Catholics viewed as sacrilegious. These issues remain to this day, but with hope for improvement, as many devout Catholics strive for reverent participation in the Mass, as envisioned by Pope Pius XII and Pope Paul VI.

Humanae Vitae

In 1968, the world was closer to global revolution than ever before. Terrorist organizations sprang up around the world. All over the world, there were revolts against established governments. From Berkeley, California, to Paris, France, students revolted in the name of "freedom." It was the same so-called "freedom" that the revolutionaries had promised in France in 1789 and in Spain in 1936. It was the same "freedom" that the serpent had promised Eve in the Garden. It was freedom from the Church and morality, and this so-called "freedom" ultimately leads to slavery. On July 25, 1968, as the world tottered on the brink, Pope Paul VI issued the most controversial encyclical of the twentieth century: **Humanae Vitae** (Encyclical on the Regulation of Birth), which condemned artificial birth control.

Promulgating *Humanae Vitae* was an act of great courage. Paul VI knew that much of the world would denounce him. He was right. He would spend the remaining ten years of his papacy on the Cross, as the secular media and even a large number of Catholics decried his decision and howled with rage at him. However, for those "who have ears to hear," Pope Paul VI had spoken the truth.

In this monumental encyclical, Pope Paul VI explicitly reaffirmed the Catholic Church's teachings regarding marriage and birth control. **The policies of Pope Paul VI reflected the teachings of all his predecessors**, especially Pope Pius XI in *Casti Connubii* and Pope John XXIII in *Mater et Magistra*. Despite enormous pressure, especially from many Western European nations and the United States, Paul VI never altered his, or the Church's, position.

In *Humanae Vitae*, Pope Paul VI explains the nature of marriage and marital love as designed by God. **Marriage is the union of one man and one woman, joined together by a loving God**. Children are a gift from God, resulting from the love of the husband and wife. Pope Paul VI affirms this profound truth about marriage and family in the first two lines of his encyclical: "The transmission of human life is a most serious role in which married people collaborate freely and responsibly with God the Creator. It has always been a source of great joy to them, even though it sometimes entails many difficulties and hardships." Paul VI goes on to explain that a husband and wife have a duty to always remain open to receiving children lovingly, and to not seek to frustrate the design and plan of the Author of life.

Humanae Vitae affirms the Church's teachings on the **two main purposes of marriage: the procreation and upbringing of children and the good of the husband and wife**. Through the mutual gift of themselves in their loving union, a husband and wife cooperate with God's loving design for marriage: "Marriage, then, is … the wise and provident institution of God the Creator, whose purpose was to effect in man His loving design. As a consequence, husband and wife, through their mutual gift of themselves,

> **Humanae Vitae**
> Monumental encyclical by Pope Paul VI which reaffirms the Church's teachings on marriage and family, and condemns artificial birth control.

Karol Jozef Wojtyla (Pope John Paul II) Reigned from 1978 to 2005; focused on the "universal call to holiness" and the dignity of human life, and helped bring about an end to communism in Poland and in the rest of Eastern Europe.

which is specific and exclusive to them alone, develop that union of two persons in which they perfect one another, cooperating with God in the generation and rearing of new lives."

Reaction to *Humanae Vitae* was mixed and immediate. Many Catholics and theologians in the United States and most of Western Europe, with the exception of Italy, Spain, Portugal, and Poland, openly dissented and even contradicted the pope. The people of South America, on the other hand, supported him. For the rest of his papacy, Pope Paul suffered constant verbal attacks for *Humanae Vitae*, but he was a man of great courage. On its tenth anniversary, he reconfirmed its teachings. Pope John Paul II, in the face of even greater opposition, later endorsed and expanded upon *Humanae Vitae* in his 1995 encyclical *Evangelium Vitae* ("The Gospel of Life").

Orthodox Churches

Reunification with the Orthodox Churches had been a goal of the popes for hundreds of years. During his pontificate, Paul VI continued working toward this goal, as he met several times with the leaders of the Eastern Orthodox Churches. He was the first pope in centuries to meet personally with these leaders. His meeting with the patriarch of Constantinople led to the withdrawal of the excommunications of the Great Schism of 1054. This was a major step toward restoring communion between Rome and Constantinople. In December 1965, the two prelates issued a joint declaration, which, while not ending the schism, showed a desire for a closer relationship between the two Churches.

In May 1973, Paul VI met several times with the Coptic patriarch of Alexandria. Following the meetings, the two leaders issued a joint declaration and creed. The joint creed showed that there are now few theological differences between the Coptic Church and the Catholic Church.

Pope Paul VI's Final Months

On August 6, 1978, less than two weeks after he reaffirmed the teachings of *Humanae Vitae*, Pope Paul VI died. His confessor, a Jesuit priest who had heard the pope's weekly Confession, said: "If Paul VI was not a saint, when he was elected Pope, he became one during his pontificate. I was able to witness not only with what energy and dedication he toiled for Christ and the Church but also and above all, how much he suffered for Christ and the Church."

Pope John Paul I

Chapter 35: The Church in the Modern Era (1958-2020)

On October 14, 2018, the Catholic Church officially recognized what Pope Paul VI's confessor had already believed: he is a saint. On that day, Pope Francis canonized Pope St. Paul VI.

Pope John Paul I

Following Paul VI's death, Cardinal Albino Luciani was elected pope on August 26, 1978. He chose the name John Paul I to honor his two immediate predecessors. Pope John XXIII had made him a bishop, and Pope Paul VI had made him a cardinal. Pope John Paul I died on September 28, 1978, after reigning as pope for only thirty-three days.

The Election of Pope John Paul II

On October 16, 1978, after a three-day conclave, the Sacred College elected a pope whom many Catholics consider to be one of the finest in Church history—perhaps even the most outstanding pope since St. Peter. His name was Cardinal **Karol Jozef Wojtyla** (Karr-ol Yoo-zef voy-Tih-wah), better known as **Pope John Paul II** (1978-2005).

Pope John Paul II's accomplishments certainly merit his inclusion on the list of the most exceptional popes in history. Only 58 years old at the time of his election, John Paul was one of the youngest popes ever elected. Moreover, he was an athlete in excellent health. As pope, he maintained his exercise regimen of swimming and jogging. His nearly 27-year pontificate would be the third longest, surpassed only by St. Peter and Blessed Pius IX. His pontificate was not only lengthy but also filled with innumerable significant events. His dynamic, charismatic personality made him one of the world's most influential leaders during his pontificate. He focused on "the universal call to holiness" and the dignity of human life. His will and determination helped bring about an end to communism, first in his native Poland and then in the rest of Eastern Europe. He also nearly doubled the number of people who had been canonized or beatified by the Church. During his pontificate, John Paul II canonized 483 people and beatified 1,340 others.

The Path to the Priesthood

Karol Jozef Wojtyla was born on May 18, 1920, in Wadowice, Poland. In his youth, he served as an altar boy and enjoyed playing sports, especially soccer. He remained physically active throughout his entire life.

Pope John Paul II

Witness to the Faith

Karol grew up during a unique period in Polish history. The period from 1920, following the defeat of the Soviet invasion, until 1939, when the Nazis invaded, was the first time since 1772 that Poland was a free country. (Poland would not be free again until 1989.) Thus, Karol grew up in a free country, but with an understanding of how fragile and precious freedom was. Though Karol would visit almost 130 nations during his lifetime, his heart never left Poland.

In the summer of 1938, after graduating at the top of his high school class, Karol moved to Krakow. He enrolled in the Jagiellonian University, where he studied philosophy. His education came to a sudden, unexpected end, however, when the Nazis invaded Poland on September 1, 1939, and closed the university. To escape the Nazis, who were murdering Poles or sending them to concentration camps, Karol fled east along with thousands of other Poles. However, the Soviet Communists had invaded eastern Poland, and they were just as evil and murderous as the Nazis. Karol was forced to return to Krakow. From 1940 to 1944, to avoid deportation by the Nazis, Karol took on a variety of jobs, including working in a chemical plant. He also secretly resumed his studies.

In early 1941, Karol began to discern that he had a priestly vocation. In October 1942, increasingly aware of his calling to the priesthood, he went to the cardinal archbishop of Krakow, Adam Stefan Sapieha. He told Archbishop Sapieha that he wanted to study for the priesthood. For the next two years, Karol secretly attended seminary classes conducted by the archbishop.

On August 6, 1944, the Nazis rounded up all the able-bodied men and boys in Krakow, in order to avoid an uprising there like the one that had occurred in Warsaw. Karol narrowly escaped the Nazis by hiding in his uncle's basement. The Nazis arrested more than eight thousand men and boys, but Karol escaped to the archbishop's palace. He spent the rest of the war there, disguised as a priest.

Hitler Watching German Soldiers Marching into Poland

On January 17, 1945, in the face of the advancing Soviet army, the Nazis fled Krakow. In 1945, the Poles exchanged one group of evil oppressors for another. Communists from the Soviet Union replaced Nazis from Germany as the occupiers of Poland.

On November 1, 1946, Archbishop Sapieha ordained Karol Wojtyla a priest. Father Wojtyla chose to say his first Mass in Wawel Cathedral's crypt church, where Poland's monarchs and national heroes are buried. The site of the Mass was deeply symbolic, uniting Father Wojtyla's two great loves: the Catholic Church and Poland.

Archbishop Sapieha then sent Father Wojtyla to Rome, where he studied theology and philosophy for two years. In the summer of 1948, he returned to Poland. The archbishop assigned him as the parish priest to the village of Niegowic, about 15 miles from Krakow. The following March, he was assigned to St. Florian's Church in Krakow.

Over the next ten years, Father Wojtyla became one of the most active and well-known priests in the Krakow Archdiocese. He taught theology and ethics at the Jagiellonian University and then at the Catholic University of Lublin. He wrote a series of articles in Krakow's Catholic newspaper dealing with contemporary Church issues. He also wrote original literary works. In addition, he became spiritual director to a group of young adults. Besides praying and performing the corporal works of mercy, the youth group went camping and kayaking. Father Wojtyla and his group also celebrated Mass outdoors, despite the communist prohibition against it.

Bishop and Cardinal

Father's Wojtyla's actions brought him to the attention not only of Poland's bishops but also of Pope Pius XII. On July 4, 1958, Pius named him auxiliary bishop of Krakow. At the age of 38, Karol Wojtyla was the youngest bishop in Poland and one of the youngest bishops in the world.

Beginning in October 1962, Bishop Wojtyla participated in Vatican II, where he worked on several important documents. During the council, the archbishop of Krakow died. On January 13, 1964, Wojtyla was chosen to replace him. In June 1967, Pope Paul VI elevated him to the Sacred College. The following year, Cardinal Wojtyla assisted Pope Paul VI in writing *Humanae Vitae*.

As archbishop of Krakow, Wojtyla worked closely with **Cardinal Stefan Wyszynski** (Vi-shin-skee). Cardinal Wyszynski was the archbishop of Warsaw and the leader of the Church in Poland from 1946 until his death in 1981. He was a national Polish hero and, after John Paul II, probably the most beloved Pole of the twentieth century. A staunch anti-communist, he is quite rightly credited with saving the Catholic Church in Poland. For his defiance of them, the communists arrested and imprisoned Cardinal Wyszynski from 1953 until 1956.

Cardinal Wojtyla deeply loved and respected Cardinal Wyszynski. After Wojtyla's election as pope, the cardinals came in procession to kneel before him, to make their vows and kiss his ring. As the elderly Cardinal Wyszynski began to kneel, Pope John Paul II stood up, stopped him from kneeling, and hugged him.

John Paul II, Fearless Foe of Communism

In August 1920, Ignacy Skorupka, a Polish priest, had died defending Warsaw from the Soviet invasion. His sacrifice, and those of thousands of other Poles, had saved Europe from communism for

> **Cardinal Stefan Wyszynski** Archbishop of Warsaw and leader of the Church in Poland from 1946 to 1981; he was a national Polish hero, who saved the Catholic Church in Poland.

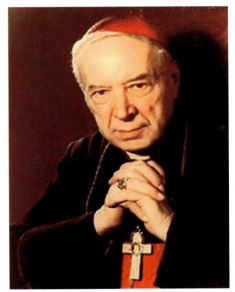

Cardinal Stefan Wyszynski

Witness to the Faith

almost 25 years. Now another Polish priest would write the final chapter on the communist horror story in Europe.

John Paul II's second trip as pope was to Poland in June 1979. Wherever he went, ecstatic crowds constantly surrounded him. On June 2, 1979, he offered Mass in Victory Square in Warsaw. In his homily, he called for a free and independent Poland. He called for it as "a Son of the land of Poland and … also Pope John Paul II." His nine-day visit uplifted the spirit of the entire nation, and sparked the formation of the Solidarity movement in 1980. **Solidarity** was the first independent labor union in Poland since the communist takeover. On future trips to Poland, Pope John Paul II gave support to Solidarity. This movement eventually brought freedom to Poland. **Lech Walesa**, the founder of the Solidarity movement, credited John Paul II with giving the Poles the courage to rise up against the communists, saying the pope started a chain of events that led to the fall of communism. Walesa explained that before John Paul II's pontificate, no one knew how to get rid of communism.

Over the next ten years, Pope John Paul II traveled to dozens of nations, many ruled by communists or other dictators. Wherever he went, he preached his message of religious freedom, national independence, and human rights. He made lasting positive impacts in every country he visited. None remained the same after he departed. The process that he began in Poland would finally lead to the end of the Soviet Union's domination of Eastern Europe in 1989. John Paul II was the spiritual inspiration behind the Soviet Union's downfall. He was the catalyst for peaceful change in Poland, which spread like wildfire through Soviet-controlled Europe. However, the communists did not give up without a fight. Some believe the Soviets were responsible for Pope John Paul II's nearest brush with death.

On May 13, 1981, as John Paul II entered St. Peter's Square to address an audience, a Turkish gunman shot and nearly killed him as part of an assassination plot involving three other men. The pope was rushed to the hospital. He underwent surgery for 5 hours to treat his wounds. Before the operation began, he told his doctors not to remove his Brown Scapular.

Although the shooter's motives remain unclear, some believe that the leaders of the Soviet Union ordered the assassination. Two of the other conspirators were Bulgarians; one was the Bulgarian military attaché, possibly working for the Soviet secret police. Seeing their grip on Eastern Europe slipping away, the frightened Soviets may have decided to murder the man they felt was the cause of their problem. Only God, and those behind this assassination attempt, truly know who was responsible for it.

Solidarity
The first independent labor union in Poland since the communist takeover. It began in 1980, after Pope John Paul II's visit.

Lech Walesa
Founder of the Solidarity movement in Poland.

Pope John Paul II at Mass in Victory Square

560 *Chapter 35: The Church in the Modern Era (1958-2020)*

But, thanks to the intervention of Our Blessed Mother, the attempt failed.

That the attack took place on May 13, the anniversary of the first apparition of Our Lady of Fatima, cannot be a coincidence. John Paul II, who had a lifelong devotion to the Blessed Mother, always attributed his survival to her intercession. He said, "One hand fired the gun, and another guided the bullet." A year after the assassination attempt, John Paul II visited Fatima to give thanks to Our Lady for saving his life.

John Paul's Moral Teachings

Pope John Paul II's theology mirrored that of his predecessors. He had been involved in writing *Humanae Vitae*, and as pope he continued to defend the right to life. In his encyclical *Evangelium Vitae*, he explicitly affirmed Catholic moral teachings condemning abortion, euthanasia, and other grave injustices against the sanctity of human life. He also taught about the dignity of women and the importance of the family for the future of mankind.

Pope John Paul II Visiting Ukraine in 2001

John Paul and Young People

Throughout his priesthood, Karol Wojtyla had always had a special relationship with Catholic young people. He had served as spiritual director to Krakow university students and would take them camping, hiking, and kayaking. They became his friends. As pope, he realized that if he could do this with a small group of young people, he could do it with the world's young people. Thus, he developed the idea of **World Youth Day**, which he established in 1984.

His goal was to bring together young Catholics from all over the world to celebrate the Catholic Faith. During his pontificate, John Paul organized nine World Youth Days, including one in the United States (Denver, 1993). Tens of millions of young Catholics, filled with love for their Faith and the pope, attended the World Youth Days during John Paul II's pontificate.

The Eastern Orthodox Churches

Healing the divisions between the Catholic and Eastern Orthodox Churches was one of Pope John Paul II's major goals, as it had been for his immediate predecessors. He worked diligently to end the break caused by the Great Schism of 1054. On January 25, 1988, John Paul issued an apostolic letter commemorating the thousandth anniversary of the Baptism of Kievan Rus' (the mass Baptism of the people of Kiev, during which they accepted Orthodox Christianity). The pope stated: "The two forms of the great tradition of the Church, the Eastern and the

> **World Youth Day**
> A gathering of young Catholics from all over the world with the pope, held every few years, to celebrate the Catholic Faith; started by Pope John Paul II in 1984.

Statue of Pope St. John Paul II at Jasna Gora Monastery in Czestochowa, Poland

Pope Benedict XVI
Reigned from 2005 to 2013; called for spiritual renewal in the face of the Western world's loss of faith, and addressed moral issues, with a special emphasis on respect for human life.

Western, the two forms of culture, complement each other like the two 'lungs' of a single body." In his 1995 encyclical *Ut Unum Sint* (Encyclical on Commitment to Ecumenism), he returned to this theme, exclaiming "The Church must breathe with her two lungs!" In other words, **the Holy Catholic Church, both East and West, must breathe as one**. This expression demonstrates the pope's profound understanding of the importance of, not only the Roman Rite of the Catholic Church, but also all the Eastern Rite Catholic Churches, which are in full communion with the pope and are part of the Holy Catholic Church. At the same time, the encyclical shows the pope's clear commitment to unity and reconciliation with the Eastern Orthodox Churches, which share many of the cultural aspects of the Eastern Rite Catholic Churches but are not yet in full communion with the Catholic Church.

To further this process of unity, in May 1999 Pope John Paul II visited Romania at the invitation of the patriarch of the Romanian Orthodox Church. This historic event marked the first time since the Great Schism that a pope had visited a country with a majority Eastern Orthodox population. In June 2001, the pope visited Ukraine, another country with a large Orthodox population. In a show of unity, the bishops of the Ukrainian Greek Catholic Church and the Roman Catholic bishops of the Ukraine had jointly invited the pope to Ukraine. John Paul II said in Ukraine that his "most fervent wish" was to end the Great Schism.

In 2001, Pope John Paul II also traveled to Greece, where he met with the head of the Greek Orthodox Church and publicly apologized for the 1204 sacking of Constantinople. This terrible act had remained a source of strife even after almost 800 years. Later, the two prelates prayed the Our Father together. This broke an Orthodox rule against praying with Catholics.

Throughout his pontificate, John Paul II sought to visit Russia. About half of all the Orthodox Christians in the world live there and belong to the Russian Orthodox Church. Yet, unlike so many other patriarchs, the Russian Orthodox leaders showed no interest in a papal visit or in reunion.

Pope St. John Paul the Great

Beginning in the early 1990s, the always-healthy and physically active John Paul II was slowed down by various health issues. In 2001, he was diagnosed with Parkinson's disease. Nevertheless, he continued to travel and speak to huge crowds. He said that his visible suffering formed part of his ministry. On April 2, 2005, Pope John Paul II spoke his final words to his aides in Polish: "Let me go to the house of the Father." He died a few hours later.

Almost immediately after his death, much of the laity began referring to him as "John Paul the Great" and began calling for his canonization. There is no canonical process for declaring a pope "Great." The title is bestowed through popular and continued use. In his first address after becoming pope, Benedict XVI spoke of his predecessor as "the great Pope John Paul II," and several more times during his pontificate, he referred to John Paul II as "the Great." Since Pope John Paul II's death, Catholics have routinely referred to him as "John Paul the Great," thus making him one of only four popes so honored.

At John Paul II's funeral, the 1.5 million attendees in St. Peter's Square began shouting to make him a saint immediately. In response to this outpouring of love, Pope Benedict XVI decided to waive the normal five-year waiting period that is normally required before the beatification process may begin. Pope Benedict beatified John Paul II on May 1, 2011. On April 27, 2014, a little over nine years after his death, Pope St. John Paul the Great was canonized by Pope Francis.

The Election of Benedict XVI

On April 19, 2005, after a two-day conclave, the Sacred College elected 78-year-old Cardinal Joseph Ratzinger as pope. He chose to be called **Benedict XVI** (2005-2013) to honor Pope Benedict XV, whom he called "that courageous prophet of peace," as well as St. Benedict, the co-patron of Europe. Even before John Paul II's death, Cardinal Ratzinger had been seen as his likely successor.

Born in Bavaria, Germany, in 1927, Joseph Ratzinger grew up during the Nazi regime. Despite his family's opposition to the Nazis, they managed to survive. Benedict would later write that he felt "an angel seemed to be guarding" the family. Following the war, Joseph entered the seminary, and in June 1951 was ordained a priest.

Pope Benedict XVI

Witness to the Faith 563

Pope Francis

Starting in 1957, Father Ratzinger began a long and distinguished career teaching doctrine and theology at several German universities. He also wrote a number of best-selling books about theology. His work attracted the attention of Pope Paul VI, who made him archbishop of Munich in March 1977, and a cardinal three months later.

In 1981, Pope John Paul II made Cardinal Ratzinger head of the Congregation for the Doctrine of the Faith, which is responsible for promoting and safeguarding Catholic doctrine around the world. Cardinal Ratzinger sought to ensure that no one in the Church was teaching heresy. Pope John Paul II and Cardinal Ratzinger had been friends since 1977. They shared similar backgrounds. Both had lived under oppressive regimes. Both were blessed with a deep understanding and appreciation of the Catholic Faith. Cardinal Ratzinger would be the pope's closest advisor until John Paul II's death. Thus, in electing Joseph Ratzinger, the College of Cardinals, almost all of whom had been appointed by John Paul II, sought to continue the policies of his pontificate. Cardinal Ratzinger might well have chosen to be called "John Paul III."

The Pontificate of Benedict XVI

During his pontificate, Benedict continued the policies of his friend and predecessor. He emphasized the need for the West to return to its fundamental Christian values, the values imparted to it by St. Benedict. He spoke of how the people of the West had lost their way. Many believed that they had no need for God and could succeed in life on the basis of their own merits. Thus, he called for a spiritual renewal. In his first encyclical, *Deus Caritas Est* (Encyclical on Christian Love), he stressed the urgent need for prayer "in the face of the activism and the growing secularism of many Christians."

In *Caritas in Veritate* (Encyclical on Integral Human Development in Charity and Truth), Pope Benedict VI continued the pro-life message of John Paul II. He addressed the moral issues of the twenty-first century, with a special emphasis on respect for human life. He declared that respect for life must be the foundation for all social and economic programs.

The Resignation of Benedict XVI

On February 11, 2013, Pope Benedict XVI announced that, because of his advanced age (almost 86 years old) and deteriorating health, he would resign at the end of the month. The announcement was both sudden and surprising. Only a handful of popes have ever resigned. In fact, in the past

800 years, only two other popes have done so: Celestine V, who resigned in 1294 because he felt overwhelmed by the office, and Gregory XII (1406-1415), who resigned to end the Great Western Schism. Pius XII and John Paul II, despite serious illnesses, continued to serve until their deaths.

The Election of Francis

Following the resignation of Benedict XVI, the Sacred College met to elect a new pope. On March 13, 2013, after a two-day conclave, Argentinian Cardinal **Jorge Mario Bergoglio** was elected.

Born in Buenos Aires, Argentina, Jorge Mario Bergoglio was ordained in 1969. Pope John Paul II made him the archbishop of Buenos Aires in 1998, and a cardinal in 2001. Upon his election to the papacy, Cardinal Bergoglio chose to be called **Pope Francis**, in honor of Saint Francis of Assisi.

The election of Cardinal Bergoglio was in many ways not surprising. First, he had been "runner-up" to Cardinal Ratzinger in the 2005 conclave. Second, most observers realized that the time had come to elect a non-European pope. Some thought that the new pope might be an African, since the Church in Africa was growing rapidly. Others thought he might be an American. In electing Cardinal Bergoglio, the conclave elected the first pope from the Americas, as well as the first Jesuit pope.

Jorge Mario Bergoglio (Pope Francis)
Elected in 2013; the current reigning pope, as of this writing in 2020.

The Pontificate of Pope Francis

As Francis has been pope for only about seven years at this writing, it is difficult to judge his pontificate from a historical perspective. Highlights include being the first pope ever to meet with the patriarch of the Russian Orthodox Church since the Great Schism of 1054; and canonizing three recent popes (John XXIII, Paul VI, and John Paul II), as well as Junipero Serra. Like Pope John Paul II, he has spoken against abortion many times, and has also focused on missionary outreach, emphasizing the need to evangelize and re-engage souls, both Catholics and non-Catholics, whose views of the Church have soured.

On December 17, 2019, Pope Francis turned 83. Let us always remember to pray for the Holy Father and for the Church.

Oral Exercises

1. Who called the Second Vatican Council?
2. As Pope Paul VI affirmed in *Humanae Vitae*, what is marriage?
3. What does the Church teach are the two main purposes of marriage?
4. Which three popes have reigned the longest?
5. Which pope canonized the most saints?
6. What was the Solidarity movement?
7. Who was Cardinal Stefan Wyszynski?
8. Why did Pope John Paul II establish World Youth Day?
9. What did Pope John Paul II mean when he said, "The Church must breathe with her two lungs"?
10. What does the Congregation for the Doctrine of the Faith do?

Witness to the Faith   565

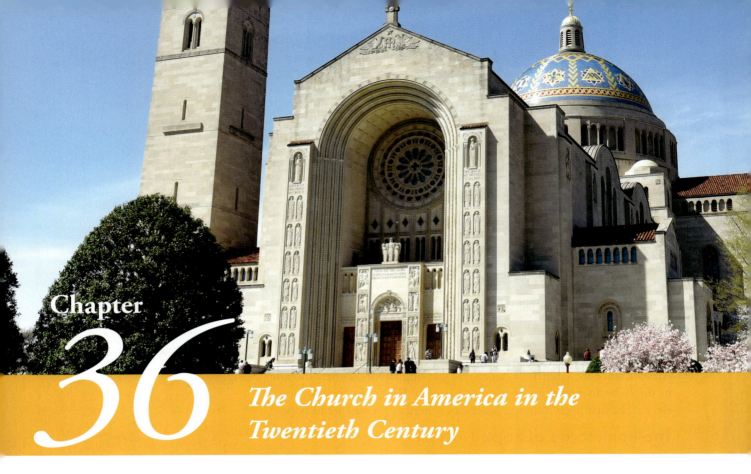

Chapter 36
The Church in America in the Twentieth Century

St. Stanislaus Kostka Church, Chicago, Illinois

Introduction

The history of the Catholic Church in the United States during the twentieth century covers a wide range of persons, movements, trials, and triumphs. The century began with a time of growth. During the 1920s, Catholics became a significant political force. In fact, for the first time, one of America's two major political parties nominated a Catholic for president. Following World War II, the Catholic Church in the United States became a leading force against communism. By the middle of the century, the growth of the Church in this country culminated in a period of prosperity.

In the 1960s and 1970s, the Church in America faced serious challenges, both internally and externally. These challenges became more serious in the 1980s and 1990s, as young Catholics fell away from the Faith. Nevertheless, in those last two decades before the end of the twentieth century, signs of new growth and a fresh strength emerged. As the Church entered the first decades of the twenty-first century, a new generation of vigorous young priests and bishops, burning with the zeal of the first Apostles, answered the call.

The Beginning of the Century: Immigration

During the mid to late 1800s, the Irish, and to a lesser extent the Germans, dominated Catholic immigration, but the turn of the

Basilica of the National Shrine of the Immaculate Conception, Washington, D.C.

1908 A.D. – 1993 A.D.

1908 A.D.
Pope Pius X declares that the United States is no longer mission territory.

1914-1918 A.D.
During World War I, Catholics prove their patriotism, as they support the war effort and enlist in great numbers.

1925 A.D.
Pierce v. Society of Sisters overturns a law that had required children to attend public schools. The Ku Klux Klan begins to decline.

1926 A.D.
Chicago hosts the International Eucharist Congress.

1928 A.D.
Al Smith is the first Catholic to run for president of the United States as the candidate of a major political party, sparking much anti-Catholic prejudice.

1955 A.D.
The Church has a significant influence over American culture, and 75 percent of Catholics regularly attend Sunday Mass.

1960 A.D.
John F. Kennedy is the first Catholic to be elected president of the United States.

1975 A.D.
Sunday Mass attendance has decreased to 54 percent.

1991 A.D.
Archbishop John O'Connor founds the Sisters of Life.

1993 A.D.
Pope John Paul II visits Denver for World Youth Day.

century saw a shift. The greatest numbers of Catholic immigrants began coming from Italy and Poland. The Poles were particularly loyal to their national heritage and established separate parish churches. Many Poles settled in Chicago. Even today, people can attend Mass in Polish inside one of the beautiful Polish churches, such as St. Stanislaus Kostka or the Basilica of St. Hyacinth, that fill Chicago's Polish district.

At the beginning of the twentieth century, most American Catholics lived in the Northeast and the Midwest. New York, Philadelphia, and Chicago were all Catholic strongholds. A steady stream of immigrants contributed significantly to the Church's ongoing growth. There were more than 10 million Catholics in the United States in 1900, making Catholicism the largest religious denomination in the country. By the

Witness to the Faith

Father Francis Duffy
Irish-American priest and chaplain of the "Fighting 69th" regiment in World War I; the most decorated military chaplain in American history.

Statue of Father Francis Duffy in Times Square, New York City

1920s, there were almost 20 million, and Catholics accounted for close to 20 percent of the population.

The Church in the United States had grown so much by the early 1900s that it received official recognition from Rome. In 1908, Pope Pius X removed the United States from the jurisdiction of the Congregation for the Propagation of the Faith, meaning the country was no longer considered "mission territory." The pope officially recognized that Catholicism was well established in the United States.

Catholics in World War I

While American Catholics rejoiced in their newfound recognition, other Americans viewed the large numbers of Catholic immigrants with growing suspicion. They questioned whether those immigrants, with their religious allegiance to the pope in Italy, were wholeheartedly committed to their new country. When the United States entered World War I, American Catholics proved their patriotism. The bishops organized a National Catholic War Council, which led Catholic support of the war effort. The archbishops delivered a statement to President Woodrow Wilson, promising that America's Catholics would work for an American victory in the war. The laity demonstrated the truth of this statement by enlisting in the military in large numbers. In fact, Catholics enlisted in disproportionately high numbers, comprising 25 percent of the army and 50 percent of the navy.

In New York City's Times Square stands the larger-than-life statue of a stern-looking man in military attire. In his hands, he holds not a gun, but a Bible. Behind him towers a Celtic cross. The inscription on the cross reads: *Lieutenant Colonel Francis P. Duffy, May 2 1871 – June 26 1932, Catholic Priest … A Life of Service for God and Country.* **Father Francis Duffy** was one of the most beloved Catholics to serve in the U.S. military during the Great War. An Irish-American parish priest in New York, Father Duffy traveled to Europe to act as chaplain for the "Fighting 69th," an Irish regiment with many Catholic soldiers. In the grim trenches of World War I, Father Duffy inspired and comforted the soldiers. He spent his days offering Mass and hearing Confessions on the front lines. He repeatedly endangered his life to bring the sacraments to the dying, and often appeared in the heat of battle. He frequently accompanied litter-bearers as they searched for wounded.

Father Duffy's success, of course, cannot be measured in numbers, but it is likely that there is more than one soul that is in Heaven today thanks to his ministry. His effect on the soldiers' morale did not go unnoticed by his military superiors. His courage won him the Distinguished Service Cross and the Distinguished Service Medal, making him the most decorated military chaplain in American history. After the war, Father Duffy returned to his parish in New York. He published his memories of the war in the bestselling *Father Duffy's Story*. His book improved the opinion that many Americans had of Catholics. Yet anti-Catholic prejudice remained a challenge for the growing Church.

The Ku Klux Klan Attacks the Church

On Saturday, May 17, 1924, thousands of men in trains and cars descended on the small city of South Bend, Indiana. Many carried white robes under their arms. Seemingly helpful young men offered directions to the visitors as they arrived. Upon following the directions, the visitors found themselves in narrow alleys from which they emerged without their white bundles and sometimes with a few bruises. The visitors were members of the **Ku Klux Klan (KKK)**, one of the most vicious anti-Catholic groups in American history. The KKK, which still exists today, has violently targeted black Americans, as well as Catholics and Jews. The young men were the "Fighting Irish" students of Notre Dame University, a Catholic stronghold. Hearing that hooded Klansmen were on every street corner of South Bend, 500 students had run the 2 miles into town to show that they would not be intimidated. The KKK had planned a rally. They were met with resistance.

The clash between the Notre Dame students and the KKK was only one event in the larger conflict that occurred throughout the United States in the 1920s. American Catholics had proven their loyalty during World War I, but many of their countrymen still distrusted them. The KKK was at the forefront of American anti-Catholicism.

While today nearly every American views the Klan unfavorably because of its promotion of racism, in the 1920s the KKK enjoyed more popularity. The 1915 film *Birth of a Nation* depicted the Ku Klux Klan as patriots working to improve American morality. In addition to the violence for which they are now notorious, the Klan organized social events, such as picnics and parades. They also promoted Protestant values such as Bible reading in schools and the prohibition of alcohol. This benevolent facade helped the Klan gain popularity. From 1922 to 1925, their membership grew from 1.2 million to 5 million. Their large membership enabled the Klan to win elections and gain political power.

In 1922, the KKK launched a political attack against Catholics in Oregon. Klan members sponsored a bill *mandating* that school-aged children attend public school. Although the law meant that children could not attend other private schools, the Klan's main goal was to prohibit children from attending Catholic schools. Anti-Catholic governor Walter M. Pierce signed the bill into law. A group of Catholic nuns challenged the law in court. The case eventually came before the United States Supreme Court, which unanimously declared the law unconstitutional in the landmark decision *Pierce v. Society of Sisters* (1925). Christian and Catholic schools would later argue that because of the *Pierce* decision, religious schools should be subjected only to minimal state regulation.

In 1925, the KKK began to decline. People started to speak out and tell the truth about the Klan. Actions such as the attempt to close Catholic schools angered many fair-minded Americans. As people realized the truth about the KKK, membership in the organization plummeted.

Walter M. Pierce

> **Ku Klux Klan (KKK)**
> Vicious anti-Catholic group, which has violently targeted black Americans, as well as Catholics and Jews.

Witness to the Faith

The Rise of a Catholic Society in America

While the KKK rose and fell, Catholics in the United States had been quietly growing in strength. Their numbers had grown so much that they were able to develop a network that enabled them to live much of their lives in a Catholic setting. Their Catholic Faith set them apart; it was central to their identity, and it marked every part of their lives, generally more so than religion did for their Protestant countrymen. Thus, in the first decades of the twentieth century, they formed what almost amounted to a separate Catholic culture within American society. They could receive their education in Catholic schools and colleges, join Catholic workers' associations, socialize with and marry other Catholics, and finally die in a Catholic hospital. Many of these separate Catholic organizations had existed for much of the history of the United States, but they saw great growth in the early twentieth century. For example, in 1900, there were only 100 Catholic high schools in the country. By 1920, there were more than 1,500.

In 1926, Chicago hosted the **International Eucharistic Congress** in honor of the Real Presence of the Lord Jesus Christ in the Holy Eucharist. This massive event caught the attention of Catholics and non-Catholics alike and showed the strength and influence of the Catholic Church in America. At the time, it was the largest Catholic gathering ever in the United States. Catholics flocked to Chicago, not only from other parts of the country, but also from around the world. Both Catholics and non-Catholics in Chicago worked together to ensure the success of the congress. A special train, painted red for the occasion, carried the papal delegation of cardinals from New York to Chicago. On the first day of the congress, 62,000 Catholic schoolchildren formed the choir for the outdoor Mass, attended by 400,000 at Soldier Field, Chicago's football stadium. For the five days of the congress, the people of Chicago saw their streets fill with pilgrims from all over the world.

Two years later, in 1928, Catholicism became a heated political issue when Democrat **Al Smith** became the first Catholic to run for president of the United States as the candidate of one of America's two major political parties. Smith's candidacy brought anti-Catholic prejudice to the surface. Propaganda emerged against Catholics, as Smith's opponents preyed upon the American people's fear and ignorance. They spread rumors that if Smith became president, the pope

> **International Eucharistic Congress**
> A gathering in Chicago, in 1926, of Catholics from around the world, in honor of the Real Presence of Jesus Christ in the Holy Eucharist. At the time, it was the largest Catholic gathering ever in the United States.

Twenty-Eighth International Eucharistic Congress in Chicago, Illinois, 1926

would rule America through him and deny citizenship to Protestants. Smith lost the election in a landslide. (On the other hand, for many Catholic women, it was the first time they had voted in a national election.)

The level of prejudice that the election revealed shocked American Catholics. It increased their motivation to develop their own counterculture. During the 1930s, many Catholics began to invest more in their own organizations than in American society as a whole.

The "Triumphal Era" of American Catholicism

As Catholics focused on developing their parishes, schools, and societies, Catholicism in America blossomed into its "triumphal era" during the 1930s, 1940s, and 1950s. The Church flourished. Funds were plentiful. The Church in the United States became the largest contributor to the Vatican—a status it still retains. Large numbers of men and women generously gave their lives to religious vocations. By the 1950s, Catholics formed close to 40 percent of the population of the Northeast, where Catholicism was strongest, and 23 percent of the entire country's population, and they practiced the Faith devoutly. In Philadelphia, for example, 90 percent of Catholic families attended Mass every Sunday. In addition to these interior strengths, the Church began to exert an unprecedented influence over American culture.

The scene of a First Holy Communion in the 1940s or 1950s provides a snapshot of the Church's strength at the time. Every spring, large groups of children filled the front pews of the parish church. The little girls wore white dresses and veils, while the boys dressed in their best (usually, first) suits. Nuns wearing full habits shepherded the children into place. The youngsters would don their First Holy Communion attire again for the Feast of Corpus Christi, when they would process through the streets while the priest carried the Blessed Sacrament in a monstrance. The girls would scatter flower petals along the way.

The rituals and traditions of triumphal-era Catholicism were the familiar rhythm of daily life. Mass was celebrated with solemn reverence in every parish. Catholic homes were filled with sacred pictures and statues. Children received a patron saint at Baptism and celebrated the yearly feast day of this saint. Catholics lit candles, wore scapulars, prayed the Rosary, walked in procession, and abstained from meat every Friday. Homes, cars, and even pets all received special blessings. It was common for people to attend the parish church during the week for daily Mass, special devotions such as adoration and novenas, or social gatherings. While these practices continue today, in the 1940s and 1950s they were widespread.

Al Smith Giving a Speech

> **Al Smith**
> The first Catholic to run for president of the United States as the candidate of a major political party.

Witness to the Faith   571

The large numbers of religious contributed significantly to the flourishing of the Church, especially through their work in Catholic schools. Since nuns and brothers took vows of poverty and did not have families to support, many dioceses could offer an affordable, or even free, Catholic education to children. The *Baltimore Catechism* was the text from which children studied their Catholic Faith. Catholic schools also kept families close to the parish community.

Priests were plentiful and greatly respected. Most of them lived in community with other priests. Most parishes had several priests; in fact, there were so many priests that a priest would normally not become a head pastor until he was in his fifties. Seminaries could afford to be selective and often had waiting lists. Studying for the priesthood was one of the best opportunities for young men to obtain an education. Since priests were usually among the nation's best-educated people, they often gave advice on a variety of matters, not just spiritual concerns. Sometimes parishioners would even turn over their personal finances to priests to manage.

Catholics Use Mass Media

The development of communication technologies, particularly radio in the 1930s and 1940s, and then television in the 1950s, provided the Church with new opportunities to spread the Faith. Now a priest could speak with, not only several hundred people in the pews, but also millions of radio listeners and television viewers. Two exceptional priests took to the airwaves to bring the Catholic Faith to as many Americans as possible: **Fulton J. Sheen** and **Patrick Peyton**.

Of the two, Fulton Sheen (1895-1979) is more well known today. In the 1930s and 1940s, he gave weekly talks on the radio show *The Catholic Hour*. His second broadcasting enterprise, and that for which he is most famous, was his weekly television show, *Life Is Worth Living*. Consecrated as a bishop in 1951, Fulton Sheen began the program the same year. He always appeared dressed in his episcopal regalia, complete with pectoral cross and scarlet cape. He discussed a variety of topics, ranging from parenting teenagers, to communism, to reflections on the Gospel. Bishop Sheen's combination of wit, stage presence, and unabashed proclamation of the truth proved irresistible to the American public. At its peak, his show had 30 million weekly viewers, including non-Catholics, while still others listened on the radio. Bishop Sheen remained humble in the face of his outstanding success, attributing it more to the Catholic Faith he preached than to his own talents.

Fulton Sheen died on December 9, 1979. During his lengthy career, he presented

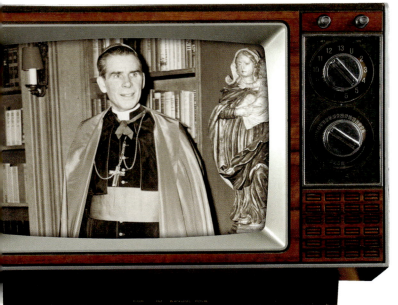

Bishop Fulton Sheen on His Famous TV Show, *Life Is Worth Living*

hundreds of hours of radio and television shows. He wrote more than seventy books, as well as many magazine and newspaper articles. From 1952 to 1957, during the run of his television program, he may have been the most popular television personality in America. The Church has opened the case for Bishop Sheen's canonization.

Fulton J. Sheen
Influential archbishop and host of the television show *Life is Worth Living*, watched by millions of Americans every week.

Father Patrick Peyton (1909-1992) was an Irish farm boy whose family prayed the Rosary together every night. As a teenager, he considered a religious vocation, but he needed to earn money to help his family when his father became too sick to work the farm. His sisters, who had gone to America, sent word that there was work there for strong young men. Patrick and his brother Thomas decided that they could be more help to the family if they went to the United States. In May 1928, Patrick and Thomas came to America.

Eventually, both boys discerned priestly vocations and entered the seminary in 1929. Struck with tuberculosis during his years of formation, Patrick miraculously recovered after praying the Rosary. This event instilled in him a deep devotion to the Blessed Virgin Mary. He dedicated his priesthood to her and always referred to himself as "Mary's donkey."

Patrick Peyton
A priest who promoted family prayer, especially the Rosary, through his radio show and rallies.

As Father Peyton began his priestly work, he realized the importance of helping Catholics build strong and loving families. He promoted daily family prayer, particularly the Rosary, as a keystone of family unity. Wanting to bring the Rosary into the homes of as many people as possible, Father Peyton eventually went to Hollywood.

In 1947, he began a weekly radio show called *Family Theater of the Air*. Every week, some of Hollywood's biggest stars participated in his programs. He coined the famous phrase, "The family that prays together stays together." Father Peyton's zeal for promoting the Rosary made him tireless in his efforts. In 1948, he began to hold Rosary rallies, which led him to travel around the world, attracting crowds of millions. Father Peyton realized that through the Rosary, communism would be overcome, and Russia would be converted.

Father Peyton died on June 3, 1992, about two and a half years after the fall of the Berlin Wall. He lived to see the power of the Rosary overcome communism. Like Bishop Fulton Sheen, Father Patrick Peyton is being considered for canonization. On December 18, 2017, Pope Francis declared him Venerable.

Positive Portrayal of Catholics in Film and Television

The positive image of Catholics in mid-century America was evident, not only in the wide audiences that Father Peyton and Bishop Sheen garnered, but also in Hollywood's consistently affirmative depictions of Catholics. Bing Crosby famously starred as Father Charles O'Malley in the hit movies *Going My Way* (the

Bing Crosby in *Going My Way*

Witness to the Faith 573

Legion of Decency
An office established by the U.S. bishops in the 1930s which rated Hollywood films based on their moral content.

Cardinal Francis Spellman

highest-grossing movie of 1944) and its sequel *The Bells of St. Mary's* (the highest-grossing movie of 1945). There were many other popular movies in which priests and nuns were portrayed as heroes, outstanding citizens with moral authority, and great influences for good. The movies were immensely successful, not only drawing crowds but also receiving no fewer than 34 Oscar nominations from 1943 to 1945. One reason for this success was probably the large number of Catholics in the U.S. However, the success of these movies also indicates that Catholic values were attractive to the average American.

Catholic influence on Hollywood was not limited to movies with strictly Catholic content; it also extended to the moral content of many other movies. The large number of Catholics, the obedience of Catholics to their religious authorities, and Hollywood's fear of boycotts combined to give Catholic bishops considerable influence over movie makers. In the 1930s, the U.S. bishops established the **Legion of Decency**, an office that rated Hollywood films based on their moral content. Church bulletins and Catholic newspapers publicized the Legion's ratings so that Catholics were aware of any movie that had objectionable content. Many Protestant leaders supported the Legion and encouraged their congregations to follow the Legion's ratings.

Catholics Lead the Fight against Communism

For much of the twentieth century, with the exception of a few so-called "intellectuals," most Americans strongly opposed communism. No group of Americans was more fervently anti-communist than Catholics. Even before the century began, the American bishops joined the Vatican in condemning Marxism for its atheism. The bishops subsequently condemned the Communist Revolution of 1917 that brought Lenin to power in Russia. In the 1920s, during the communist persecution of the Church in Mexico, America's bishops and the Knights of Columbus led the fight to help Mexico's Catholics and bring communist atrocities to the attention of the American public. In the 1930s, the bishops condemned American communists for supporting the revolutionary policies of the Soviet Union. They also condemned those American communists who supported the anti-Catholic Republicans during the Spanish Civil War.

During World War II, when circumstances forced America to ally itself with Stalin's Soviet Union, Catholics warned against trusting the Soviets or expecting them to change. After the war, the Church noted that Stalin had gained more power and influence from World War II. At the height of the Cold War, from 1945 to 1970, Catholic anti-communism reached its peak.

In the twenty-five years after World War II, bishops, priests, and ordinary Catholics joined with America's leaders to fight communism. Priests frequently delivered anti-communist sermons. The bishops wrote pastoral letters reminding Catholics of the implacable evil facing them.

Among the leading anti-communist voices was New York's sixth archbishop, Cardinal Francis Spellman (1889-1967). Another leader in the fight was Bishop Fulton Sheen. In his radio and television programs, Bishop Sheen reached millions with his anti-communist message. In one broadcast, he declared: "Communism is to the social body what leprosy is to the physical body; in fact, it is more serious, for communism affects personality directly, while disease affects the mind and soul only indirectly.... **Communism is intrinsically evil.**"

The Catholic anti-communist movement began to slow down after American involvement in the Vietnam War in the early 1960s, the death of Cardinal Spellman in 1967, and the cancellation of Bishop Sheen's second television show (*The Fulton Sheen Program*) the following year. Over the next years, liberal Catholics began to suggest that the Church needed to focus on "social justice" rather than communism. During the 1970s, the Catholic fight against communism became less obvious.

In 1978, with the election of Pope John Paul II, followed two years later by the election of President Ronald Reagan, American anti-communists rejoiced. Both men were committed to ending what Reagan called the "evil empire"—the Soviet Union. Catholics once again became vocal and active in their support for their pope and their president. With the eventual fall of the Soviet Union in 1991, their prayers were answered.

The Catholic President

Although the Church in the United States would experience a decline during the 1960s, many Catholics began the decade in a spirit of hope. For the first time in America's history, a Catholic was elected president of the United States. However, in his campaign to win the election, he minimized the importance of his Catholic Faith.

As in 1928, Catholicism became an issue during the 1960 presidential campaign. Catholic presidential candidate **John F. Kennedy** faced widespread prejudice. Even then, some Protestants believed that, if he were elected president, he would take orders from the pope. To address these

Ronald Reagan

John F. Kennedy
The first Catholic to be elected president of the United States.

Witness to the Faith 575

John F. Kennedy

fears, Kennedy told a convention of Baptist ministers in Houston that he was "not the Catholic candidate for president"; he was "the Democratic Party's candidate for president who also happens to be a Catholic." He went on to say, "I do not speak for my Church on public matters, and the Church does not speak for me."

When John F. Kennedy won the presidential election in 1960, the "national popular vote" was one of the closest in history. In a time before precise exit polling, it is hard to discern the effect that his Catholicism or his speech had on voters. Some historians believe that he won some of the heavily Catholic northeastern states because the attacks on his religion prompted Catholics in those states to support him.

Hint of Trouble

In many ways, the 1940s and 1950s were the Golden Age of the Catholic Church in America. The Church had more influence on American culture and society than ever before, or since. On the other hand, there are temptations associated with such great influence. Some began to see the priesthood and religious life as paths to power and respect, rather than as positions of service to the people of God. Also, with large numbers of children to educate, the memorized formulas of the *Baltimore Catechism* were efficient, but many children did not receive the deeper formation that they needed. During the next twenty years, the Church experienced a decline for which it seemed ill prepared.

The Decline of American Catholicism

In 1969, Pope Paul VI approved the Novus Ordo form of the Mass. As a result, many of the external rituals of Catholic worship were altered. For example, the prayers and hymns of the Mass were no longer in Latin but in English. The priest faced the people instead of facing the altar.

In introducing these changes, the Holy Father and the bishops were striving to serve the needs of people in the twentieth century, to express the same faith and devotion through forms that people could better understand. Yet some misunderstood this endeavor, and confused adjusting to the needs of the modern world with conforming to the secularism of modern culture. For example, some parishes removed parts of their beautiful art and architecture, and discarded their sacred music for less reverent, more popular styles.

These *external* changes marked a deep upheaval that took place in the Catholic Church in the United States. Many Catholics began to miss Mass on Sunday. Many religious left their orders. In place of the *Baltimore Catechism*, children received a religious formation that emphasized emotions and failed to convey the fullness of Catholic teaching. At the same time, the Church lost much of its influence on the culture.

A primary reason for the decline of authentic Catholicism during the 1960s and 1970s was the rise of modernism. The modernists found an opportunity for mischief after the Second Vatican Council. The documents that the council released *did not teach modernism*. However, most Catholics never read the documents. Instead, they depended on the clergy and, foolishly, on the media to let them know what the council said. Modernists taught that the council had called for radical changes and sweeping innovations in the Church. For example, they claimed that the council had suggested that monks and nuns abandon their habits. Of course, the council had never said that.

When people pointed out that the modernists were not telling the truth, the modernists justified themselves by invoking the so-called "spirit of Vatican II." They claimed that this "spirit" embodied what the council fathers had *intended*. But this was just an excuse to promote their ideology, which ran contrary to Catholic teaching.

Over the next decades, the modernists devastated the Church in the United States. As they attempted to make Catholicism "relevant" to modern culture, they discarded many of its beautiful traditions and distorted or downplayed its teachings. Modernist teachers and pastors led the flock astray. The results were shocking.

Many religious abandoned their vows. The stream of new vocations dwindled to a trickle, and in some cases dried up completely. Catholic Mass attendance fell dramatically. In 1955, 75 percent of U.S. Catholics regularly attended Sunday Mass. By 1975, the number had fallen to 54 percent. Some left because of the dramatic changes in the liturgy. Others grew lukewarm because the teachings of the modernists undermined their faith. The modernists' version of "Catholicism" was not truly Catholic; it was no better than Protestantism. If the Holy Eucharist is not truly the Body and Blood of Christ, and if Jesus did not actually rise from the dead, there is no compelling reason for people to center their lives on the Catholic Faith. Instead, going to Mass becomes little more than a cultural event that one celebrates at Christmas and Easter when the choir is especially good.

Christ with the Eucharist, Juan de Juanes

Modernism had particularly negative effects in Catholic higher education. The Church teaches that both faith and science lead to truth, because God has created everything that science discovers, just as He has revealed all that faith believes. However, modernists believe that faith and science contradict each other, and that faith is mere superstition, whereas science is rational; therefore, faith must give way to science. As the modern approach to science moved further away from Church teachings,

Witness to the Faith

Catholic colleges in the United States faced an identity crisis. At the time, the Jesuits ran most of these colleges. Rather than defending the Catholic Faith as they had since the time of St. Ignatius of Loyola, the Jesuits began conforming their institutions to *worldly* standards. They hired lay teachers, and their curriculum became increasingly secular. Some teachers even challenged official Church teachings in the name of "academic freedom." With higher education in a state of disarray, the future looked bleak.

Yet modernism cannot be blamed for all of the problems the Church experienced in America. American culture in general was in a state of upheaval in the 1960s and 1970s. In 1973, the Supreme Court decision in *Roe v. Wade* made abortion legal in all 50 states. Although the Church has strongly protested, then and ever since, she has been "a voice crying in the wilderness." Furthermore, too many so-called "Catholic" politicians have dissented from the Church's position, claiming a "personal" opposition to abortion but voting time and again to support it.

The 1970s saw the influence of the Legion of Decency wane. Movies and television shows became increasingly immoral. At the same time, riots in opposition to the Vietnam War damaged property and showed a lack of respect for legal authority. As the nation became wealthier, many people turned away from God and religion, and instead embraced materialism. Catholics were harmed not only by problems within the Church but also by the collapse of the Judeo-Christian society itself, which had existed in America for more than 350 years. Catholics could not live within this secularized society and not be at least somewhat influenced by it.

A Renaissance in America

The history of the Catholic Church is one of resurrection. Following the death of Our Lord Jesus Christ on the Cross, He rose from the dead. After the Roman persecutions, the Church rose up from the catacombs. Time and again, the Church will rise because Our Lord has promised that "the gates of hell shall not prevail against it" (Matthew 16:18).

Following the turbulent decades of the 1960s and 1970s, the Church in America began to rise again. **John O'Connor**, the archbishop of New York from 1984 to 2000, led the way in addressing the widespread problems in the Church and in secular culture. Before being consecrated as a

Prisoners' Barracks at the Dachau Concentration Camp, 1945

578 Chapter 36: The Church in America in the Twentieth Century

bishop, he visited the site of the Nazi concentration camp at Dachau. This visit moved him to dedicate his life to protecting human life, which was under serious threat in the United States. He became a leader of America's pro-life movement.

In 1990, Archbishop O'Connor wrote a newspaper column in which he explored the idea of a religious community dedicated to the pro-life cause. The response was so enthusiastic that in 1991 he founded a new religious order, the **Sisters of Life**. The Sisters of Life dedicate themselves to upholding the dignity of every human life, especially those at risk from abortion. In addition to the normal vows of poverty, chastity, and obedience, they take a fourth vow: "to protect and defend the sacredness of human life."

In founding the Sisters of Life, Archbishop O'Connor incorporated the authentic teachings of the Catholic Church, as he did throughout his ministry. He emphasized the traditional monastic life with the *requirement* of religious habits for the sisters. While many religious orders, which had lost their Catholic identity, struggled for vocations, the Sisters of Life flourished.

Other religious communities that promoted authentic Catholic teaching and a traditional religious way of life also grew and thrived. Young Catholics eagerly answered Our Lord's call, and each year these faithful religious orders would see an intake of new postulants. This new generation of dedicated religious men and women gave hope to the entire Church. Similarly, dioceses that remained faithful to true Catholicism attracted men to the priesthood in large numbers. These trends have continued to this day.

World Youth Day and EWTN

In August 1993, Pope John Paul II visited Denver, Colorado, for World Youth Day and sowed the seeds to foster a further renewal and rebirth for American Catholics, especially young Catholics. At the time, Denver was an unlikely venue for a religious event. Crime had been a serious issue for the past few months. But the Holy Father chose Denver deliberately. He wanted to bring the Gospel to the secular world. Local authorities were apprehensive as thousands of young people descended on the city. Miraculously, crime came to a standstill. During the event, the police did not make a single felony arrest. The pope's visit continues to bear fruit today, as various influential Catholic organizations credit their inspiration to World Youth Day in Denver. In fact, Denver itself is slowly becoming a home to more and more Catholic organizations.

Perhaps the most important organization to benefit from World Youth Day was the **Eternal Word Television Network (EWTN)**, founded by a devout Poor Clare nun known as Mother Angelica. Although the network had begun broadcasting in 1981, its live coverage of World Youth Day marked a turning point in its popularity. The

John O'Connor
Archbishop of New York from 1984 to 2000 who dedicated his life to protecting human life and was a leader of America's pro-life movement.

Sisters of Life
Religious order established in 1991 by Archbishop John O'Connor, which is dedicated to upholding the dignity of every human life.

Eternal Word Television Network (EWTN)
Catholic television network, started in 1981 by a devout nun known as Mother Angelica, which became more influential in 1993, after its live coverage of World Youth Day.

Witness to the Faith   **579**

network, which broadcast World Youth Day into homes throughout the nation, became the national leader of authentically Catholic programming. Devout Catholics, poorly educated Catholics, and even non-Catholics began to tune in. Many Catholics developed a deeper knowledge of their Faith, supplementing what had been lacking in their religious education during the upheaval of the 1960s and 1970s. Others returned to the Faith. Still others became Catholic. Mother Angelica died on Easter Sunday, March 27, 2016, but her legacy of faith and devotion still lives on in the millions of hearts she touched, especially through her untiring work at EWTN.

Catholic Education

The 1980s also saw new efforts emerge in the area of Catholic education. Many parents, disappointed by what they considered an insufficient religious education in Catholic schools, took matters into their own hands. They started private, parent-run Catholic schools. Other parents decided to take a more direct approach and teach their children themselves. Thus, the Catholic homeschooling movement was born. Courageous laymen founded new Catholic colleges as alternatives to the secularized Jesuit universities. One of the most prominent of these is Christendom College in Front Royal, Virginia. These institutions, and others like them, provide authentically Catholic academic life, where faith and reason work together.

In 1999, Pope John Paul II returned to the United States, this time to St. Louis. The 78-year-old pope was frail and clearly ill. Yet, as he stood before the youth of America, they gave him strength. The aged pontiff told 20,000 young people at a youth rally that "tonight the pope belongs to you." He went on to tell them that Jesus Christ wants them "to be light to the world, as only young people can be light. It is time to let your light shine!" Later in his homily, he emphasized the importance of the family, Christian marriage, and the culture of life.

Chapel at Christendom College

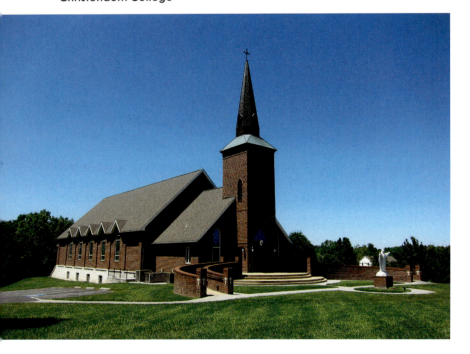

New Catholic Leaders

In 1984, Ronald Reagan declared that it was "morning in America." He said that it was a time of optimism. It was a time to look forward, because the new day would bring hope and prosperity. The 1980s and 1990s were also morning in America for the Church. The ideas of

580 *Chapter 36: The Church in America in the Twentieth Century*

modernism had caused problems, and many still remained, but the future looked brighter. As the new millennium dawned, the next decades for the Church in America were a time of hope and optimism, as new young leaders embraced authentic Catholic teaching and tradition.

Nowhere was this more apparent than in America's seminaries. The "old guard," who had embraced modernism, was dying out. New, young priests, appalled by the failures of modernism, and filled with the Holy Spirit, eagerly awaited the chance to re-evangelize Catholics. Many of these bright, young priests were graduates of Catholic colleges like Christendom.

The Church of Faith Will Remain

In 1969, Joseph Ratzinger, the future Pope Benedict XVI, commented on the problems in the Church: "It seems certain to me that the Church is facing very hard times. The real crisis has scarcely begun. We will have to count on terrific upheavals. But I am equally certain about what will remain at the end: not the Church of the political cult, which is dead already, but the Church of faith. She may well no longer be the dominant social power to the extent that she was until recently; but she will enjoy a fresh blossoming and be seen as man's home, where he will find life and hope beyond death."

The story of the Church in America during the twentieth century contains both triumph and tragedy. The losses of the 1960s and 1970s are great tragedies. The Church no longer has the dominant influence on American culture that she once held. Nevertheless, God continues to be with His people, and the beauty of authentic Catholicism generates an irresistible attraction on the human heart. We may be nostalgic about the past, but we can also look to the future with new hope.

Pope Benedict XVI

Oral Exercises

1. During the mid to late 1800s, what groups dominated Catholic immigration?
2. Who is the most decorated military chaplain in American history?
3. What was the name of the first Catholic to run for president of the United States as the candidate of a major political party?
4. Name two priests who, from the 1940s to the 1960s, used radio and television to spread the Faith.
5. What was the name of the Catholic organization that rated Hollywood films based on their moral content?
6. Name two American bishops who led the fight against communism during the 1950s and 1960s.
7. Who was the first Catholic elected president of the United States?
8. What heresy devastated the Church in the United States during the 1960s and 1970s?
9. Name the archbishop of New York from 1984 to 2000, who was a leader of America's pro-life movement.
10. Who founded the Eternal Word Television Network (EWTN)?

582

LIST OF POPES

A note on the number of popes: One of the most consistent attacks on the Faith is that Catholics do not know how many popes there have been. Our Protestant brethren usually launch this attack. Have there been 265 popes or 266, or some other number entirely? The Church has an official list of the popes. However, due to death and politics, there have been issues regarding the numbering of the popes. Let us look at two examples.

In 752, Pope Stephen II died after his election but before his consecration as pope. This has resulted in a problem with the numbering of popes named Stephen. His successor, not thinking about Protestants a thousand years later, also decided to be called Stephen. Thus, some lists of popes include the elected but not consecrated Stephen, while others do not. As explained in the text of this history, we have decided to include him in the list. The following list from the *Annuario Pontificio*, the Vatican's official list, does not include him. In the sixteenth century, the Vatican added him to the official list but, because of a change in canon law, removed him in 1961. Officially, he is no longer considered a pope.

In the first half of the eleventh century, Benedict IX was pope on three separate occasions. Thus, he is listed three times, although one of his pontificates was very brief, and at the end of the previous one. For this reason, some lists do not acknowledge the "break" in his papacy and only count him twice. As of 2020, according to the *Annuario Pontificio*, the current pope, Francis, is the 266th pope.

While the Church's official list of popes does not include antipopes, for historical purposes they are included in the following list (italicized).

1. Peter	33-67	
2. Linus	67-76	
3. Cletus	76-88	
4. Clement I	88-97	
5. Evaristus	97-105	
6. Alexander I	105-115	
7. Sixtus I	115-125	
8. Telesphorus	125-136	
9. Hyginus	136-140	
10. Pius I	140-155	
11. Anicetus	155-166	
12. Soter	166-175	
13. Eleutherius	175-189	
14. Victor I	189-199	
15. Zephyrinus	199-217	
16. Callistus I	217-222	
Hippolytus	217-235	
17. Urban I	222-230	
18. Pontian	230-235	
19. Anterus	235-236	
20. Fabian	236-250	
21. Cornelius	251-253	
Novatian	251-258	
22. Lucius I	253-254	
23. Stephen I	254-257	
24. Sixtus II	257-258	
25. Dionysius	259-268	
26. Felix I	269-274	
27. Eutychian	275-283	
28. Caius	283-296	
29. Marcellinus	296-304	
30. Marcellus	307-309	
31. Eusebius	310	
32. Miltiades	311-314	
33. Sylvester I	314-335	
34. Marcus	336	
35. Julius I	337-352	
36. Liberius	352-366	
Felix II	355-357	
37. Damasus I	366-384	
Ursinus	366-367	
38. Siricius	384-399	
39. Anastasius I	399-401	
40. Innocent I	402-417	
41. Zosimus	417-418	
42. Boniface I	418-422	
Eulalius	418-419	
43. Celestine I	422-432	
44. Sixtus III	432-440	
45. Leo I (the Great)	440-461	
46. Hilary	461-468	
47. Simplicius	468-483	
48. Felix II (III)	483-492	
49. Gelasius I	492-496	
50. Anastasius II	496-498	
51. Symmachus	498-514	
Lawrence	498-507	
52. Hormisdas	514-523	
53. John I	523-526	
54. Felix III (IV)	526-530	
55. Boniface II	530-532	
Dioscorus	530	
56. John II	533-535	

57.	Agapetus I	535-536	98.	Paschal I	817-824	139.	Sylvester II	999-1003
58.	Silverius	536-538	99.	Eugene II	824-827	140.	John XVII	1003
	Vigilius	537-538	100.	Valentine	827	141.	John XVIII	1003-1009
59.	Vigilius	538-555	101.	Gregory IV	827-844	142.	Sergius IV	1009-1012
60.	Pelagius I	556-561		*John*	844	143.	Benedict VIII	1012-1024
61.	John III	561-574	102.	Sergius II	844-847		*Gregory*	1012
62.	Benedict I	575-579	103.	Leo IV	847-855	144.	John XIX	1024-1032
63.	Pelagius II	579-590	104.	Benedict III	855-858	145.	Benedict IX	1032-1045
64.	Gregory I (the Great)	590-604		*Anastasius*	855			
65.	Sabinian	604-606	105.	Nicholas I (the Great)	858-867			
66.	Boniface III	607	106.	Adrian II	867-872			

(Benedict appears three times
as pope because he was twice
deposed and restored.)

67.	Boniface IV	608-615	107.	John VIII	872-882	146.	Sylvester III	1045
68.	Adeodatus I	615-618	108.	Marinus I	882-884	147.	Benedict IX	1045
69.	Boniface V	619-625	109.	Adrian III	884-885	148.	Gregory VI	1045-1046
70.	Honorius I	625-638	110.	Stephen V	885-891	149.	Clement II	1046-1047
71.	Severinus	640	111.	Formosus	891-896	150.	Benedict IX	1047-1048
72.	John IV	640-642	112.	Boniface VI	896	151.	Damasus II	1048
73.	Theodore I	642-649	113.	Stephen VI	896-897	152.	Leo IX	1049-1054
74.	Martin I	649-655	114.	Romanus	897	153.	Victor II	1055-1057
75.	Eugenius I	655-657	115.	Theodore II	897	154.	Stephen IX	1057-1058
76.	Vitalian	657-672	116.	John IX	898-900		*Benedict X*	1058
77.	Adeodatus II	672-676	117.	Benedict IV	900-903	155.	Nicholas II	1059-1061
78.	Donus	676-678	118.	Leo V	903	156.	Alexander II	1061-1073
79.	Agatho	678-681		*Christopher*	903-904		*Honorius II*	1061-1072
80.	Leo II	682-683	119.	Sergius III	904-911	157.	Gregory VII	1073-1085
81.	Benedict II	684-685	120.	Anastasius III	911-913		*Clement III*	1084-1100
82.	John V	685-686	121.	Lando	913-914	158.	Victor III	1086-1087
83.	Conon	686-687	122.	John X	914-928	159.	Urban II	1088-1099
	Theodore	687	123.	Leo VI	928	160.	Paschal II	1099-1118
	Paschal	687-692	124.	Stephen VII	929-931		*Theodoric*	1100-1102
84.	Sergius	687-701	125.	John XI	931-935		*Albert*	1102
85.	John VI	701-705	126.	Leo VII	936-939		*Sylvester IV*	1105-1111
86.	John VII	705-707	127.	Stephen VIII	939-942	161.	Gelasius II	1118-1119
87.	Sisinnius	708	128.	Marinus II	942-946		*Gregory VIII*	1118-1121
88.	Constantine	708-715	129.	Agapitus II	946-955	162.	Callistus II	1119-1124
89.	Gregory II	715-731	130.	John XII	955-964	163.	Honorius II	1124-1130
90.	Gregory III	731-741	131.	Benedict V	964		*Celestine II*	1124
91.	Zachary	741-752	132.	Leo VIII	964-965	164.	Innocent II	1130-1143
92.	Stephen II	752-757	133.	John XIII	965-972		*Anacletus II*	1130-1138
93.	Paul I	757-767	134.	Benedict VI	973-974		*Victor IV*	1138
	Constantine II	767-768		*Boniface VII*	974; 984-985	165.	Celestine II	1143-1144
	Philip	768	135.	Benedict VII	974-983	166.	Lucius II	1144-1145
94.	Stephen III	768-772	136.	John XIV	983-984	167.	Eugene III	1145-1153
95.	Adrian I	772-795	137.	John XV	985-996	168.	Anastasius IV	1153-1154
96.	Leo III	795-816	138.	Gregory V	996-999	169.	Adrian IV	1154-1159
97.	Stephen IV	816-817		*John XVI*	997-998			

170. Alexander III	1159-1181	206. Martin V	1417-1431	249. Clement XIV	1769-1774
Victor IV	1159-1164	*Clement VIII*	1424-1429	250. Pius VI	1775-1799
Paschal III	1164-1168	*Benedict XIV*	1424	251. Pius VII	1800-1823
Callistus III	1168-1175	207. Eugene IV	1431-1447	252. Leo XII	1823-1829
Innocent III	1179-1181	*Felix V*	1439-1449	253. Pius VIII	1829-1830
171. Lucius III	1181-1185	208. Nicholas V	1447-1455	254. Gregory XVI	1831-1846
172. Urban III	1185-1187	209. Callistus III	1455-1458	255. Pius IX	1846-1878
173. Gregory VIII	1187	210. Pius II	1458-1464	256. Leo XIII	1878-1903
174. Clement III	1187-1191	211. Paul II	1464-1471	257. Pius X	1903-1914
175. Celestine III	1191-1198	212. Sixtus IV	1471-1484	258. Benedict XV	1914-1922
176. Innocent III	1198-1216	213. Innocent VIII	1484-1492	259. Pius XI	1922-1939
177. Honorius III	1216-1227	214. Alexander VI	1492-1503	260. Pius XII	1939-1958
178. Gregory IX	1227-1241	215. Pius III	1503	261. John XXIII	1958-1963
179. Celestine IV	1241	216. Julius II	1503-1513	262. Paul VI	1963-1978
180. Innocent IV	1243-1254	217. Leo X	1513-1521	263. John Paul I	1978
181. Alexander IV	1254-1261	218. Adrian VI	1522-1523	264. John Paul II	1978-2005
182. Urban IV	1261-1264	219. Clement VII	1523-1534	265. Benedict XVI	2005-2013
183. Clement IV	1265-1268	220. Paul III	1534-1549	266. Francis	2013-
184. Gregory X	1271-1276	221. Julius III	1550-1555		
185. Innocent V	1276	222. Marcellus	1555		
186. Adrian V	1276	223. Paul IV	1555-1559		
187. John XXI	1276-1277	224. Pius IV	1559-1565		
188. Nicholas III	1277-1280	225. Pius V	1566-1572		
189. Martin IV	1281-1285	226. Gregory XIII	1572-1585		
190. Honorius IV	1285-1287	227. Sixtus V	1585-1590		
191. Nicholas IV	1288-1292	228. Urban VII	1590		
192. Celestine V	1294	229. Gregory XIV	1590-1591		
193. Boniface VIII	1294-1303	230. Innocent IX	1591		
194. Benedict XI	1303-1304	231. Clement VIII	1592-1605		
195. Clement V	1305-1314	232. Leo XI	1605		
196. John XXII	1316-1334	233. Paul V	1605-1621		
Nicholas V	1328-1330	234. Gregory XV	1621-1623		
197. Benedict XII	1334-1342	235. Urban VIII	1623-1644		
198. Clement VI	1342-1352	236. Innocent X	1644-1655		
199. Innocent VI	1352-1362	237. Alexander VII	1655-1667		
200. Urban V	1362-1370	238. Clement IX	1667-1669		
201. Gregory XI	1370-1378	239. Clement X	1670-1676		
202. Urban VI	1378-1389	240. Innocent XI	1676-1689		
Clement VII	1378-1394	241. Alexander VIII	1689-1691		
203. Boniface IX	1389-1404	242. Innocent XII	1691-1700		
Benedict XIII	1394-1424	243. Clement XI	1700-1721		
204. Innocent VII	1404-1406	244. Innocent XIII	1721-1724		
205. Gregory XII	1406-1415	245. Benedict XIII	1724-1730		
Alexander V	1409-1410	246. Clement XII	1730-1740		
John XXIII	1410-1415	247. Benedict XIV	1740-1758		
		248. Clement XIII	1758-1769		

586

IMAGE ATTRIBUTIONS

Chapter 1

Christ Giving the Keys to St. Peter: Public Domain: Wikimedia, Perugino

Map of Palestine: Nathan Puray, Seton Home Study School

Stained Glass Window of the Resurrection: Photo taken by Seton staff

Pentecost: Public Domain: Wikimedia, Restout

Peter and John Healing Lame Man: Public Domain: Wikimedia, Nicolas Poussin

Martyrdom of St Stephen: Public Domain: Annibale Carraci

The Angel Appearing to the Centurion Cornelius: Public Domain: Jacob Backer

The Conversion of St. Paul: Public Domain: Murillo

Paul is Arrested, basilica of Saint Paul Outside the Walls, Rome, Italy: Copyright: zatletic, Adobe Stock

St. Paul's Missionary Journeys: Nathan Puray, Seton Home Study School

Statue of St. Paul: Copyright: Lucian Milasan, Adobe Stock

St. Timothy: Public Domain: Wikimedia

Icon of St. Luke the Evangelist from the royal gates of the central iconostasis of the Kazan Cathedral in St. Petersburgh: Public Domain: Wikimedia

Paul in Athens: Public Domain: Raphael

Paul is Arrested, basilica of Saint Paul Outside the Walls, Rome, Italy: Copyright: zatletic, Adobe Stock

Papal Basilica of St. Paul outside the Walls. Rome, Italy: Copyright: dbrnjhrj, Adobe Stock

St. John Miraculously Escapes Martyrdom: Public Domain: Daniel Halle

Chapter 2

The Christian Martyrs' Last Prayer: Public Domain: Jean-Léon Gérôme

The Crucifixion of Saint Peter: Public Domain: Caravaggio

Portrait of roman emperor Nero Claudius Caesar Augustus Germanicus isolated on white background: Copyright: Ruslan Gilmanshin, Adobe Stock

Saint Peter: Public Domain: Wikimedia, Marco Zoppo

Portrait of Saint Linus: Public Domain: Basilica of St. Paul Outside the Walls

Portrait of Saint Cletus: Public Domain: Basilica of St. Paul Outside the Walls

Portrait of Saint Clement: Public Domain: Basilica of St. Paul Outside the Walls

Siege and Destruction of Jerusalem by Romans Under Titus: Copyright: Corbis, David Roberts

Saint Ignatius of Antioch: Public Domain: Wikimedia

Saint Ignatius and Saint Polycarp, stained glass window in the Saint Augustine church in Paris, France on January 10, 2018: Copyright: Adobe Stock

Saint Pothin: Public Domain: Wikimedia, Lucien Bégule

Saint Blandina: Public Domain: Wikimedia, Lucien Bégule

The Basilica of Saint Cecilia: Copyright: e55evu, Adobe Stock

Marble Bas-relief of the Saint Cecilia of Rome: Public Domain: Wikimedia, Balthasar Schmitt

Sacra Conversazione Mary with the Child, St Felicity of Carthage and St Perpetua: Public Domain, Wikimedia

Saint Irenaeus of Lyon: Public Domain: Wikimedia, Lucien Bégule

Statue of Saint Denis: Copyright: Adobe Stock, Jose Ignacio Soto

Lawrence before Valerianus: Public Domain: Wikimedia, Fra Angelico

Bust of Emperor Gallienus: CC BY-SA 3.0: Wikimedia, Sailko

Bust of Diocletian: CC BY-SA 2.0: Carole Raddato

Bust of Maximian: CC BY-SA 3.0: Wikimedia, Pierre Selim

Bust of Galerius: CC BY-SA 3.0: Wikimedia, Shinjirod

Bust of Constantius Chlorus: CC BY-SA 2.0, Carole Raddato

Tetrarchy Map: CC BY-SA 3.0: Coppermine Photo Gallery

The 20,000 Martyrs of Nicomedia: Public Domain: Wikimedia

Head of Maxentius from Dresden Colosseum: CC BY-SA 1.0: Wikimedia, Jebulon

Bronze statue of Constantine I in York, England, near the spot where he was proclaimed Augustus in 306: Copyright: Adobe Stock, Natalia Paklina

Painting of *Burial of Saint Cecilia*: Public Domain: Luis de Madrazo y Kuntz

Photo of Catacomb of St. Callixtus: Photo by Seton Staff.

Fresco of Good Shepherd: Public Domain: from ceiling of catacombs of St. Callixtus

Chapter 3

Baptism of Constantine: Public Domain: Wikimedia, Gianfrancesco Penni

16th Century Portugese Painting of Pentecost: Public Domain

The Fire of Rome, 18 July 64 AD: Public Domain: Wikimedia, Hubert Robert

Antique roman coins: Copyright: Adobe Stock, Patricia Hofmeester

Baptism of the Neophytes: Public Domain: Wikimedia, Masaccio

Saint Augustine: Public Domain: Wikimedia, Philippe de Champaigne

Christ giving the Keys of Heaven to St. Peter: Public Domain: Wikimedia, Peter Paul Rubens

Saint Irenaeus of Lyon: Public Domain: Wikimedia, Lucien Bégule

Stained glass depiction of Justin Martyr. Great St Mary's church in Cambridge: Public Domain: Wikimedia

Origen, Church Father: Public Domain: Wikimedia

Quintus Florens Tertullian, 160-220, church father and theologian: Public Domain: Wikimedia

Saint Cyprien évêque de Carthage: Public Domain: Wikimedia

Constantine Receives the Standard with the Monogram of Christ as the Imperial Sign (the Labarum): Public Domain: Wikimedia, Peter Paul Rubens

The Battle of the Milvian Bridge: Public Domain: Wikimedia, Giulio Romano

Arch of Constantine and The Colosseum, Rome: Copyright: Adobe Stock, Marco Rubino

Licinius Augustus: Public Domain: Wikimedia, Hubert Goltzius

Triumphant Entry of Constantine into Rome: Public Domain: Wikimedia, Peter Paul Rubens

The Founding of Constantinople: Public Domain: Wikimedia, Peter Paul Rubens

The Death of Constantine the Great: Public Domain: Wikimedia, Peter Paul Rubens

Chapter 4

Council of Nicea: Public Domain, Wikimedia

Altar of St. Peter and Paul in Zagreb cathedral dedicated to the Assumption of Mary and to kings Saint Stephen and Saint Ladislaus: Copyright: Adobe Stock

Map of Roman Roads in 125 AD: Seton Home Study School

Christ of the Cross: Public Domain: Wikimedia, Carl Bloch

The Burial of St. Lawrence: Public Domain: Wikimedia, Alejo Vera

The Holy Spirit: Copyright: Paolo Gallo, Adobe Stock

587

Arius: Public Domain: Wikimedia

Detail from painting of Pope Sylvester: Public Domain

The fresco of scene as Emperor Constantine speak on the council in Nicaea (325) in church Hospital de los Venerables Sacerdotes by: Copyright: Adobe Stock, Juan de Valdes Leal

Stained glass of Saint Athanasius: Public domain

Athanasius Sent Into Exile by Otto Bitschnau: Copyright: Adobe Stock

Constantine II: CC BY-SA 3.0: Wikimedia, TcfkaPanairjdde

Bust of Constans: Public Domain: Wikimedia, Marie-Lan Nguyen

Presumed bust of emperor Constantius II (317 - 361), son and successor of Constantine the Great. Temporary exhibition in Colosseum: CC BY-SA 1.0: Wikimedia, Jebulon

The Persecution of Athanasius: Public Domain: Wikimedia, Otto Bitschnau

Pope Liberius: Public Domain: Wikimedia

Coin of Julian the Apostate: Wikicommons, Classical Numismatic Group: CC BY-SA 2.5

Cornelius_Hazart_-_1667_-_Kerckelijke_Historie_-_Emperor_Jovinian.jpg

Drawing of the Emperor Jovian: Public Domain: Cornelius Hazart

Valens, emperor with ensigns, Trier, 364-378 AD: CC BY-SA 1.0: Wikimedia, Daderot

Coin depicting Valentinian: Wikicommons, International Numismatic Club: CC BY-SA 4.0

Icon of the Three Cappadocians: Public Domain

The Mass of St. Basil: Public Domain: Wikimedia, Pierre Subleyras

Statue of Theodosius I: CC BY-SA 4.0: Wikimedia, Benjamin Nunez Gonzalez

Illustration of the Council of Constantinople: Public Domain

Western Roman emperor Gratian: Public Domain: Wikimedia, Cornelius Hazart

Bust of Roman Emperor Magnus Maximus in the Capitoline Museums: Public Domain: Wikimedia

A Statue of emperor Valentinian II - Marble - Aphrodisias Geyre - Aydin - 387 – 390 Ad: Public Domain: Wikimedia

St. Ambrose Absolving Theodosius, Pierre Subleyras: Public Domain

Chapter 5

Saint Augustine: Public Domain: Wikimedia, Philippe de Champaigne

Portrait of Saint John Chrysostom of Antioch (Hagios Ioannis Chrysostomos): Public Domain: Wikimedia

Saint John Chrysostom and Empress Eudoxia: Public Domain: Wikimedia, Jean Paul Laurens

Stained Glass of Saint Ambrose, Germany: Public Domain

St. Ambrose and Emperor Theodosius: Public Domain: Wikimedia, Peter Paul Rubens

St. Jerome: Public Domain: Wikimedia, Hans Memling

Saint Jerome in his study: Public Domain: Wikimedia, Caravaggio

Saints Augustine and Monica: Public Domain: Wikimedia, Ary Scheffer

St. Augustine Disputing with the Heretics: Public Domain: Google Art Project, Pablo Vergos

14th century manuscript of Augustine's *City of God*: Public Domain: NYPL Digital Collections

Stained glass image of Saint Augustine, Public Domain

Portret van Nestorius: Public Domain: Wikimedia, Romeyn de Hooghe

San Cirilo de Alejandría en el Concilio de Éfeso: Public Domain: Wikimedia, Francisco Meneses Osorio

Madonna mit Kind: Public Domain: Wikimedia, Franz Ittenbach

The Saints Anthony and Paul in the Desert: Public Domain: Wikimedia, David Teniers

St. Martin and the Beggar: Public Domain: Wikimedia, Alfred Rethel

Statue of St. Peter in Saint John Lateran, Rome: CC BY-SA 4.0: Wikimedia, Biso

Illustration for Papal Infallibility with Triple Tiara on Bible: Public Domain: Wikimedia

Saint Athanasius of Alexandria, fresco on the ceiling of the Saint John the Baptist church in Zagreb, Croatia: Copyright: Adobe Stock

St. Augustine Ordained a Bishop: Copyright: Flickr, Fr. Lawrence Lew, OP

Detail of St. Lawrence on stained glass window in St. Stephen the Martyr Daily Mass Chapel in Omaha: Public Domain: Wikimedia

Chapter 6

Baptême de Clovis: CC BY-SA 4.0: Wikimedia, G. Garitan

Map of Invasions of the Roman Empire 1: CC BY-SA 2.5: Wikimedia, MapMaster

Bishop Wulfila explains the Gospels to the Goths: Public Domain: Wikimedia

The Sack of Rome: Public Domain: Wikimedia, Évariste Vital Luminais

Châlons - église Saint-Loup: CC BY-SA 3.0: Wikimedia, Fab5669

Portion of a stained glass window in Truro Cathedral: Public Domain: Wikimedia

St. Patrick stained glass window: CC BY-SA 4.0: Wikimedia, Adreas F. Borchert

Gold St. Patrick's Cross: Copyright: Adobe Stock

Stained glass window of Saint Patrick preaching to Laoghaire: Public Domain

St. Patrick's Catholic Cathedral in Armagh: Copyright: Nagalski, iStockPhoto

Detail from *Attila and his Hordes Overrun Italy and the Arts*: Public Domain: Wikimedia, Eugene Delacroix

Pope St. Leo the Great: Public Domain: Wikimedia, Francisco Herrera the Younger

Meeting Between Leo the Great and Attila: Public Domain: Wikimedia, Raphael

Clovis et Clotilde: Public Domain: Wikimedia, Antoine-Jean Gros

Battle of Tolbiac, Public Domain: Wikimedia, Ary Scheffer

Detail from *Baptism of Clovis*: Public Domain: Wikimedia, Master of St. Giles

Romulus Augustulus resigns the Roman crown to Odoacer: Public Domain: Wikimedia

16th century statue of Theoderic the Great: Public Domain: Wikimedia, Peter Vischer the Elder

Mosaic of Justinian I: Public Domain: Wikimedia, Meister von San Vitale

Mosaic of Pope Felix IV (III): Public Domain: Wikimedia

Pope Agapetus I: Public Domain: Wikimedia

Pope Silverius: Public Domain: Wikimedia

Mosaic of empress Theodora: Public Domain: Wikimedia

Pope Vigilius: Public Domain: Wikimedia

Mosaic Icon of Virgin and Child in Hagia Sophia: Public Domain: Wikimedia

Hagia Sophia in summer, Istanbul, Turkey: Copyright: Adobe Stock

San Benito de Nursia: Public Domain: Wikimedia, El Greco

Portinari Triptych (left wing): Public Domain: Wikimedia, Hans Memling

Page from Book of Kells: Copyright: Adobe Stock, Warren Rosenberg

Interior of Monte Cassino: Copyright: Adobe Stock, Mssimo Santi

Exterior of Monte Cassino: Public Domain: Pixabay, krystainwin

Jubilee Saint Benedict Medal: Public Domain: Wikimedia, Desiderius Lenz

St Finian and His Pupils: CC BY-SA 4.0: Wikimedia, Andreas F. Borchert

Saint Columban Stained Glass Window: Public Domain: Wikimedia

Saint Columba stained glass window: Copyright: Flickr, Fr. Lawrence Lew, OP

Picture of Basilica of Saint Peter in Luxeuil-les-Bains, France: Photo taken by Seton staff

Icon of Emperor Tiberius: Public Domain: Wikimedia

Stained Glass of Pope St. Gregory the Great: Public Domain

Theodelinda married Agilulf (detail): Public Domain: Wikimedia, Fratelli Zavattari

Egbert of Wessex map: Public Domain: Wikimedia, Mike Christie

St Augustine of Canterbury and Pope Gregory the Great: Copyright: Flickr, Br. Lawrence Lew, OP

Statue of King Ethelbert of Kent: Copyright: Adobe Stock

Canterbury Cathedral: Public Domain: Pixabay, Waylin

Chapter 7

Willibrord Preaching to the Frisians: Public Domain: Wikimedia, George Sturm

St. Paulinus of York: Copyright: Flickr, Br. Lawrence Lew, OP

St. Felix of Burgundy: Public Domain: Wikimedia

Oswald of Northumbria: Public Domain: Wikimedia

Whitby Abbey: Public Domain: Pixabay, DarkWorkX

St. Theodore of Tarsus: Copyright: Flickr, Br. Lawrence Lew, OP

The Venerable Bede translates John: Public Domain: Wikimedia, James Doyle Penrose

St. Rupert Baptizes the Bavarian Duke Theodo II: Public Domain: Wikimedia, Francis de Neve

Saint Kilian: Public Domain: Wikimedia

St Willibrord Preaches the Gospel: Pieter Dierckx: Public Domain

Basilica in Echternach: Public Domain: Wikimedia

Map of Mecca and Saudi Arabia: CC BY-SA 3.0: Wikimedia, Norman Einstein

Rub al Khali Sand Dunes: CC BY-SA 3.0: Wikimedia, Nepenthes

Abu Bekr: Public Domain: Wikimedia

Map of expansion of Caliphate: Public Domain: Wikimedia, DieBuche

Fariz: Public Domain: Wikimedia, January Suchodolski

Roderic, King of the Visigoths: Public Domain, Wikimedia

Clotilde at the Tomb of her Grandchildren: Public Domain: Lawrence Alma-Tadema

Tomb of Clovis in Basilica of St. Denis: Public Domain: Wikimedia

Map of Merovingian dynasty: CC BY-SA 3.0: Wikimwsi, Rudric

Don Pelayo: Public Domain: Wikimedia, Luis de Madrazo

Pelayo in the Battle of Covadonga: Public Domain: Wikimedia, Luis de Madrazo

Chapter 8

The Coronation of Charlemagne - King of the Lombards: CC BY-SA 4.0: Wikimedia, Claudius Jacquand

Fulda Cathedral: CC BY-SA 4.0: Wikimedia, Sfintu1

Statue of Charles Martel: CC BY-SA 4.0: Wikimedia, J.B.Debay-Giogo

Battle of Tours: Public Domain: Wikimedia, Charles de Steuben

Abbot Fulrad Giving Pepin's Written Guarantee to Pope: Public Domain: Wikimedia

Charlemagne: Public Domain, Jean-Louis-Ernest Meissonier

The Destruction of Irminsul by Charlemagne: Public Domain: Wikimedia, Heinrich Leutemann

Paderborn Cathedral: Copyright: Adobe Stock, karlo54

Charlemagne Recieves the Submission of Widukind at Paderborn: Public Domain: Wikimedia, Ary Scheffer

William of Toulouse: Public Domain: Wikimedia, Antonio de Pereda

Roland at Roncevaux: Public Domain: Wikimedia, Gustave Doré

Detail from Stainglass of Coronation of Charlemagne: CC BY-SA: Wikimedia, Wolfgang Sauber

Leonine Triclinium Mosaic of St Peter, Leo III, and Charlemagne: Copyright: Flickr, Br. Lawrence Lew, OP

The Coronation of Charlemagne: Public Domain: Wikimedia, Friedrich Kaulbach

German cathedral in Aachen during fall with yellow leafs at trees with blue sky: Copyright: Adobe Stock, Andreas Basler

Charlemagne recieves manuscripts from Alcuin by Jules Laure: Public Domain

Casket of Charlemagne: Public Domain: Wikimedia

Chapter 9

Photo of Hagia Sophia: Copyright: Adobe Stock

Jasna Gora: Public Domain: Wikimedia, January Suchodolski

John of Damascus: Public Domain: Wikimedia, Francesco Bartolozzi

Coin of Constantine VI and Irene: CC BY-SA 3.0: Wikimedia, PHGCOM

Tarasius, Patriarch of Constantinople: Public Domain, Wikimedia

Coronation of Charlemagne: Public Domain, Wikimedia, Raphael

Painting of the Blessed Trinity, Philippe de Champagne: Public Domain

St Ignatius of Constantinople: CC VY-SA 3.0: Wikimedia, Gmihail

Stained Glass of Pope St. Nicholas: Photo by Seton staff

Coin of Basil the Macedonian: CC BY-SA 4.0: Wikimedia

Portrait of John VIII in Basilica of St. Paul Outside the Walls, Rome: Public Domain

Bust of Leo VI: CC BY-SA 3.0: Wikimedia, Xenophon

Statue of Pope Paul VI and Patriarch Atenogoras I: Copyright: Adobe Stock

Chapter 10

Fresco of baptism of Czech prince Bořivoj: Copyright: Adobe Stock

Map of Scandinavia: Copyright: Adobe Stock, Duncan de Young

Statue of St. Ansgar: Copyright: Adobe Stock

Arrival of King Olaf I of Norway: Public Domain: Wikimedia, Peter Nicolai Arbo

Statue of Saints Cyril and Methodius: Copyright: Adobe Stock

Slavic Tribes in the 7th to 9th century: CC BY-SA 4.0: Wikimedia, Jirka.h23

Sts. Cyril and Methodius in Rastislav: Public Domain: Wikimedia, Anselm Wisiak

Example of Early Cyrillic Manuscripts: Public Domain: Wikimedia, Prince Miroslav

Map of Croatia: Copyright: Adobe Stock

Demetrius Zvonimire: Public Domain: Wikimedia

King Boris of Bulgaria: CC BY-SA 4.0: Wikimedia, Ζαρκαδάκης

Map of Europe: Copyright: Adobe Stock

Portrait of Boleslaus I the Brave: Public Domain: Wikimedia, Marcello Bacciarelli

Stained Glass Window of the Murder of Stanislaus of Krakow: Photo taken by Seton staff.

The Baptism of St. Stephen: Public Domain: Wikimedia, Gyula Benczur

The Baptism of Vladimir: Public Domain: Wikimedia, Viktor Vasnetsov

Chapter 11

The Battle of Ostia: Public Domain: Wikimedia, Raphael

Map of Italy: Copyright: Adobe Stock

Lothair I: Public Domain: Wikimedia

Stained Glass of Louis the Pious: Photo taken by Seton staff.

Charles the Bald: Public Domain: Wikimedia, François Séraphin Delpech

Portrait of Louis the German: Public Domain: Wikimedia

Woodcut of medieval king investing a bishop: Public Domain: Wikimedia, Philip Van Ness Myers

Photo of Santiago de Compostela Cathedral: Copyright: Adobe Stock, Jose Ignacio Soto

Pope John VIII: Public Domain: Wikimedia

Pope Martin II: Public Domain: Wikimedia

Pope Adrian III: Public Domain: Wikimedia

Pope Stephen V: Public Domain: Wikimedia

Pope Formosus: Public Domain: Wikimedia

Arnulf of Carinthia: Public Domain: Wikimedia

Pope Stephen VII: Public Domain: Wikimedia

Pope Romanus: Public Domain: Wikimedia

Pope Theodore II: Public Domain: Wikimedia

Pope Formosus and Stephen VI: Public Domain: Wikimedia, Jean-Paul Laurens

Pope John IX: Public Domain: Wikimedia

Pope Benedict IV: Public Domain: Wikimedia

Pope Leo V: Public Domain: Wikimedia

Pope Sergius III: Public Domain: Wikimedia

St. John Lateran Basilica and Palace: CC BY-SA 3.0: Wikimedia, Peter Clarke

Interior of Lateran Basilica: CC BY-SA 4.0: Wikimedia, tango7174

Apse of Lateran Basilica: CC BY-SA 4.0: Wikimedia, tango7174

King Hugh of Italy: Public Domain: Wikimedia

Portrait of Marozia: Public Domain: Wikimedia

Mosaic of Otto the Great: Public Domain, Wikimedia, Axel Mauruszat

Throne of Charlemagne: CC0: Wikimedia, Jebulon

Adalbert, King of Italy: Public Domain: Wikimedia

589

Photo of Castel Sant'Angelo: Public Domain: Pixabay, Walkerssk

Otto II: Public Domain: Wikimedia, Meister des Registrum Gregorii

Holy Roman Emperor Theophano: CC BY-SA 3.0: Wikimedia, Gunther Falchner

Detail from *The Baptism of Vajk*: Public Domain: Wikimedia, Gyula Benczúr

St. Henry II: Copyright: Flickr

St Wolfgang von Regensburg: Public Domain: Wikimedia, Matthaus Schiestl

Pope Benedict VIII: CC BY-SA 3.0: Wikimedia, Diana

Miniature of Conrad II: Public Domain: Wikimedia

Henry III: Public Domain: Wikimedia

Photo of Imperial Crown: Public Domain: Wikimedia

Pope Leo IX: CC BY-SA 1.0: Wikimedia, BartBassist

Chapter 12

Detail of fresco in baroque sanctuary (Sancta Sanctorum) in church Monasterio de la Cartuja with St. Bruno and glory of Eucharist by Palomino: Copyright: Adobe Stock

Photo of Abbey of Cluny: Public Domain: Wikimedia

Statue of St. Dunstan: Copyright: Flickr

Pope St. Leo IX: CC BY-SA 3.0: Wikimedia, Gfreihalter

St. Peter Damian: Public Domain: Wikimedia, Andrea Barbiani

Roger I of Sicily at the Battle of Cerami in 1063: Public Domain: Wikimedia, Prosper Lafaya

Maria Del Priorato: CC BY-SA 3.0: Wikimedia, Lalupa

Pope Gregory VII: CC BY-SA 3.0: Wikimedia, Gfreihalter

Stained Glass of Pope Gregory VII: CC BY-SA 4.0: Wikimedia: GFreihalter

Portrait of Henry IV, Holy Roman Emperor: Public Domain: Wikimedia, Jan van Bijlert

Henry at Canossa: Public Domain: Wikimedia, Eduard Schwoiser

Rudolph of Swabia: Public Domain: Flickr, Library of the University of Sevilla

Portrait of Robert Guiscard: Public Domain: Wikimedia, Merry-Joseph Blondel

Henry V: CC BY-SA 3.0: Wikimedia, Acoma

King Henry II: Public Domain: Wikimedia

Archbishop Thomas Becket, Benjamin West: Public Domain

St. Bruno: Public Domain: Wikimedia, Nicolas Mignard

St. Robert of Molesme: CC BY-SA 3.0: Wikimedia, Gunter Seggebaing

Bust of St. Bernard of Clairvaux: CC BY-SA 1.0: Wikimedia, Zarateman

Clairvaux Abbey: CC BY-SA 3.0: Wikimedia, Prosopee

St. Norbert of Xantem: Public Domain: Wikimedia, Jan de Hoey

Chapter 13

Statue of El Cid in Burgos, Spain: Copyright: Adobe Stock

Alfonso the Chaste of Asturias: Public Domain: Wikimedia, Mariano de la Roca y Delgado

Ramiro I of Asurias: Public Domain: Wikimedia, Isidoro Lozano

Statue of Alfonso III: Public Domain: Wikimedia, Luis Garcia

Cathedral of Santiago de Compostela: Copyright: Adobe Stock

St. James the Apostle: Public Domain: Wikimedia, Bartolome Esteban Murillo

Ramiro II: Public Domain: Wikimedia, Rufino Casado

Bust of Almanzor: CC BY-SA 4.0: Wikimedia, Discasto

Ruins of the Monastery of Sahagun: Copyright: Adobe Stock, KarSol

Chapter 14

Pope Urban II Calls the First Crusade: CC BY-SA 3.0: Wikimedia, Artgate Fondazione Cariplo

Pope Urban II: Public Domain: Wikimedia, Francisco de Zurbarán

Council of Clermont: Public Domain: Wikimedia, Jean Colombe

Peter the Hermit Preaching the First Crusade: Public Domain: Wikimedia

Map of Early Crusades: CC BY-SA 2.0: Wikimedia, Norman B. Leventhal Map Center

Detail from *Godfrey of Bouillon is Proclaimed King of Jerusalem*: Public Domain: Wikimedia, Federico de Madrazo y Kuntz

Siege of Antioch: Public Domain: Wikimedia, Jean Colombe

King Louis VII of France: Public Domain: Wikimedia

Emperor Conrad III: Public Domain: Wikimedia

Surrender to Saladin after the Battle of Hattin, Said Tahseen: Public Domain

King Richard the Lionheart: Public Domain: Wikimedia, Merry-Joseph Blondel

Fresco of Pope Innocent III: Public Domain: Wikimedia

The Crusaders Conquering the City of Zara in 1202: Public Domain: Wikimedia, Andrea Vicentino

Conquest Of Constantinople By The Crusaders In 1204: Public Domain: Wikimedia, David Aubert

Detail from *Baldwin I of Constantinople with His Wife and Daughter*: Public Domain: Wikimedia, Jan Swerts

Detail from *Honorius III Approving the Rule of St. Dominic*: Public Domain: Wikimedia, Leandro Bassano

Louis IV of Thuringia on Crusade With Emperor Frederick II: CC BY-SA 4.0: Wikimedia, Wolfgang Sauber

St. Louis of France: Copyright: Flickr

St. Louis French King Going On a Crusade: Public Domain: Wikimedia, Jan Matejko

The Dedication: Public Domain: Wikimedia, Edmund Blair Leighton

Jerusalem: Public Domain: Pixabay: Walkerssk

Crusader on Horseback: Copyright: Adobe Stock

Knights Hospitaller Insignia: Public Domain

Knights Templar Insignia: Public Domain

Teutonic Knights Insignia : Public Domain

Chapter 15

The Tomb of Pope Innocent III: CC BY-SA 2.5: Wikimedia, Marie-Lan Nguyen

Louis VII and Conrad III on the Second Crusade: Public Domain: Wikimedia

Emperor Frederick Barbarossa: Public Domain: Wikimedia, Bernardo Cane

Pope Adrian IV: Public Domain: Wikimedia, G Francisi

Pope Alexander III Monument: CC BY-SA 3.0: Wikimedia, Sailko

Sens Cathedral: Copyright: Adobe Stock, Claudio Colombo

Battle of Legnano, Massimo d'Azeglio: Public Domain

Reconciliation of Pope Alexander III and Frederick Barbarossa: CC BY-SA 3.0: Wikimedia, Sailko

St. Mark's Basilica: Public Domain: Wikimedia

Tomb of Pope Alexander III: CC BY-SA: 3.0: Wikimedia, Domenico Guidi

Emperor Henry VI: Public Domain: Wikimedia

Pope Celestine III: CC BY-SA 3.0: Wikimedia, Sailko

Innocent III: Public Domain: Flickr, USCapitol

The Royal Destiny of the Infant Frederick II: Public Domain: Wikimedia, Pelagio Palagi

King Philip Augustus: Public Domain: Wikimedia

Our Lady of the Rosary: Copyright: Flickr

Stained Glass from St. Dominic Church in Washington, D.C.: Pope Honorius Approves the Dominican Order: Photo taken by Seton staff.

Approval of the Franciscan rule by Pope Innocent III: Public Domain: Wikimedia, Antonio Carnicero

St. Francis Receiving the Stigmata: Public Domain: Wikimedia, Peter Paul Rubens

St. Dominic Blesses Simon de Montfort: Pope Honorius Approves the Dominican Order: Photo taken by Seton staff.

The Pope and the Inquisitor: Public Domain: Wikimedia, Jean-Paul Laurens

Frederick II: CC BY-SA 4.0: Wikimedia, Geak

Pope Honorius III: CC BY-SA 4.0: Wikimedia, Jose Luiz Bernardes Ribeiro

Pope Gregory IX: Public Domain: Wikimedia, Alvesgaspar

The Court of Emperor Frederick II in Palermo: Public Domain: Wikimedia, Arthur von Ramberg

Relic of the True Cross: Copyright: Flickr

Council of Lyons: Public Domain: Wikimedia

Pope Innocent IV: Public Domain: Wikimedia

Rudolph I of Germany: CC BY-SA 3.0, Michael Manas

Chapter 16

Our Lady Queen of Heaven Stained Glass: Copyright: Flickr

Madonna with Child: Public Domain: Wikimedia, Duccio di Buoninsegna

Stained Glass of Christ Holding the Eucharist: Copyright: Flickr

Our Lady of the Rosary: Copyright: Flickr

Brown Scapular: CC BY-SA 4.0: Wikimedia, Wellcome Images

Stained Glass of St. Bonaventure: Photo taken by Seton Staff

Stained Glass of St. Albert the Great: Photo taken by Seton Staff

Sorbonne Square in Paris: Copyright: Adobe Stock, VV Voennyy

Stained Glass of St. Thomas Aquinas: Photo taken by Seton Staff

Dante Alighieri: Public Domain: Wikimedia, Sandro Botticelli

Engraving of Geoffrey Chaucer: Public Domain: Wikimedia, Charles Cowden Clarke

Mainz Cathedral: Copyright: Adobe Stock, citylights

Abbot Suger: CC BY-SA 4.0: Wikimedia, Giogo

Interior of the Basilica of Saint-Denis in Paris: CC BY-SA 3.0: Wikimedia, Bordeled

Notre Dame de Paris Cathedral: Copyright: Adobe Stock, Edush Vitaly

Konrad von Hochstaden: CC BY-SA 4.0: Wikimedia, Raimond Spekking

Cologne Cathedral, Germany: Copyright: Adobe Stock

Milan Cathedral: Copyright: Adobe Stock

Immaculate Conception Stained-Glass Window from the Cathedral of Mdina in Malta: Copyright: Flickr

Rose Window of Chartes Cathedral: Copyright: Flickr: Br. Lawrence Lew, OP

West Portal of Chartres Cathedral: Copyright: Adobe Commons, Vakery Egorov

Royal Portal of Chartres Cathedral Statues: CC BY-SA 4.0: Wikimedia, Andreas F. Borchert

The Sacrifice of Isaac: CC BY-SA 2.5: Wikimedia, Filippo Brunelleschi

The Sacrifice of Isaac: CC BY-SA 3.0: Wikimedia, Lorenzo Ghiberti

North doors of the Baptistry (Florence): CC BY-SA 4.0: Wikimedia, Yair Haklai

The Madonna Enthroned with Angels and Prophets: Public Domain: Wikimedia, Cimabue

Front of Maesta: Public Domain: Wikimedia, Duccio

Chapter 17

Relief of Saint Catherine of Siena near Sant Angelo Castle: Copyright: Adobe Stock

Map of Viterbo, Italy: Copyright: Adobe Stock

Gregory X: Public Domain: Wikimedia, Artaud de Montor

Innocent V: CC BY-SA 4.0: Wikimedia, Wolfgang Sauber

Adrian IV: CC BY-SA 4.0: Wikimedia, PHGCOM

John XXI: Public Domain: Wikimedia, Roque Gamerio

Nicholas III: Public Domain: Wikimedia, PHGCOM

Martin IV: Public Domain: Wikimedia, Artaud de Montor

Honorius IV: CC BY-SA 4.0: Wikimedia, PHGCOM

Nicholas IV:Public Domain: Wikimedia

Celestine V: Public Domain: Wikimedia, Bartolome Roman

Boniface VIII: Public Domain: Wikimedia, Artaud de Montor

Philip the Fair, Jean Louis Bezard: Public Domain

Colonna Strikes Pope Boniface, Alphonse-Marie-Adolphe de Neuville: Public Domain

Map of Avignon, France: Copyright: Adobe Stock

The Final Day of Jacques de Molay, the Last of the Knights Templar: Public Domain: Wikimedia, Fleury-Francois Richard

The Coronation of Louis Bavaria in Rome: Public Domain: Wikimedia, August von Kreling

Charles IV: Public Domain: Wikimedia, Jan Vilimek

Palace of the Popes: CC BY-SA 3.0: Wikimedia, Jean-Marc Rosier

Bridget of Sweden, Maso da San Friano: Public Domain

The Mystic Marriage of Saint Catherine of Siena: Public Domain: Wikimedia, Christopher Unterberger

Saint Catherine of Siena Leads Pope Gregory XI Back to Rome, Giorgio Vasari: Public Domain

Delivery of the Keys of San Angel Castle to Pope Urban VI: Public Domain: Wikimedia, Alessandro Casolani

Map of Great Western Schism: CC-BY-SA-3.0: Wikicommons: lankazame / mipmapped / willtron

Antipope Clement VII: CC BY-SA 4.0: Wikimedia, Henri Auguste Cesar Serrur

Gregory XII: Public Domain: Wikimedia, Justus van Gent

Antipope Benedict XIII: CC BY-SA 3.0: Wikimedia, Valdavia

Antipope Alexander V: Public Domain: Wikimedia

Cathedral of Pisa: Copyright: Adobe Stock

Statue of John Wyclif: Public Domain: Wikimedia, Orf3us

Hus at the Council of Constance, Karl Friedrich Lessing: Public Domain.

Martin V: Public Domain: Wikimedia, Pisanello

Chapter 18

The Surrender of Granada: Public Domain: Wikimedia, Francisco Pradilla y Ortiz

Alfonso I of Aragon: Public Domain: Wikimedia, Francisco Pradilla y Ortiz

Urraca of Leon: Public Domain: Wikimedia, Carlos Mugica y Perez

Alfonso VII of Leon: Jose Maria Rodreguez de Losada

Las Navas de Tolosa: Public Domain: Wikimedia, Francisco de Paula Van Halen

Ferdinand III of Castile: Public Domain: Wikimedia, Carlos Mugica y Perez

Cathedral of Burgos: CC BY-SA 4.0: Wikimedia, Eduardo Elua

King Alfonso X of Castile: Public Domain: Wikimedia, Joaquin Dominguez Becquer

Sancho IV of Castile: Public Domain: Wikimedia, Luis Ferrant y Llausas

King Pedro of Castile: Public Domain: Wikimedia, Joaquin Dominguez Becquer

Antipope Benedictus XIII: Public Domain: Wikimedia, Pedro de Luna

Ferdinand II of Aragon: Public Domain: Wikimedia, Bernardino Montanes

Isabel of Castile: Public Domain: Wikimedia, Luis de Madrazo

The Surrender of Granada: Public Domain: Wikimedia, Vicente Barneto y Vazquez

Chapter 19

Sistine Chapel Ceiling: Public Domain: Wikimedia, Michelangelo

Appearance of Sts. Catherine and Michael to Joan of Arc: Public Domain: Wikimedia, Hermann Stilke

Joan of Arc in Battle: Public Domain: Wikimedia, Hermann Stilke

Joan of Arc's Death at the Stake: Public Domain: Wikimedia, Hermann Stilke

Pope Eugene IV: Wikimedia: CC BY 3.0, Sailko

Pope Nicholas V: Public Domain: Wikimedia, Peter Paul Rubens

Pope Pius II: Public Domain: Wikimedia, Pinturicchio

Pope Alexander VI: Public Domain: Wikimedia, Cristofano dell'Altissimo

Savoarola Preaching Against Prodigality: Public Domain: Wikimedia, Ludwig von Langenmantel

Pope Julius II: Public Domain: Wikimedia, Raphael

Pope Leo X: Public Domain: Wikimedia, Peter Paul Rubens

The School of Athens: Public Domain: Wikimedia, Raphael

Fresco of *The Last Judgment*, Giotto de Bondone: Copyright: Stefano Piazza, Adobe Stock

The Virgin of the Annunciation: Wikimedia: CC BY 2.0, Fra Angelico

Merode Altarpiece: Public Domain: Robert Campin, Metropolitan Museum of Art

591

The Descent from the Cross: Public Domain: Wikimedia, Rogier van der Weyden

The Adoration of the Mystic Lamb (Part of the Ghent Altarpiece): Public Domain: Wikimedia, Jan van Eyck

The Annunciation: Public Domain: Hans Memling: Metropolitan Museum of Art

The Mona Lisa: Public Domain: Wikimedia, Leonardo da Vinci

The Last Supper: Public Domain: Wikimedia, Leonardo da Vinci

Moses: Michelangelo: Wikimedia: CC BY 3.0, Jorg Bittner Unna

Sistine Madonna: Public Domain: Wikimedia, Raphael

The Disputation of the Holy Sacrament: Public Domain: Wikimedia, Raphael

The Transfiguration: Public Domain: Wikimedia, Raphael

Gutenberg Inventing Printing Press: Public Domain: Wikimedia, Jean-Antione Laurent

Portrait of Leo X: Public Domain: Wikimedia, Raphael

Chapter 20

Luther Hammers 95 Theses to Door: Public Domain: Wikimedia, Ferdinand Pauwels

Erfurt Cathedral: Copyright: Adobe Stock, pixelliebe

Martin Luther: Wikimedia: CC BY-SA 4.0, Jorg Blobelt

John Tetzel: Public Domain: Wikimedia

Luther Nailing 95 Theses: Public Domain: Wikimedia, Julius Hubner

Pope Leo X: Public Domain: Wikimedia, Peter Paul Rubens

Cardinal Thomas Cajetan and Martin Luther: Public Domain: Wikimedia, Ferdinand Pauwels

Luther and Eck Dispute in Leipzig, Carl Friedrich Lessing: Public Domain

Holy Roman Emperor Charles V: Public Domain: Wikimedia, Alfred Rethel

Luther at the Diet of Worms: Public Domain: Wikimedia, Anton von Werner

St. Katharine's Church in Zwichau: Wikimedia: CC BY-SA 2.5, Andre Karwath

Battle of Frankenhausen: Public Domain: Wikimedia, Mechanical Curator Collection

Pope Adrian VI: Public Domain: Wikimedia, Jan van Scorel

Pope Clement VII: Public Domain: Wikimedia, Sebastiano del Piombo

Philip Melanchthon: Public Domain: Wikimecia, Lucas Cranach the Elder

Council of Trent: Wikimedia: CC BY-SA 3.0, Laurom

Charles V at Muhlberg: Public Domain: Wikimedia, Titian

Abdication of Charles V: Public Domain: Wikimedia, Louis Gallait

Chapter 21

The Marburg Colloquy: Public Domain: Wikimedia, Christian Karl August Noack

Interior of Abbey of St. Gall: Wikimedia: CC BY-SA 3.0, 3s

John Calvin, Unknown Artist: Public Domain

Michael Servetus: Public Domain: Wikimedia, Christian Fritzsch

Theodore Beza: Public Domain: Wikimedia

Chapter 22

An Allegory of the Tudor Succession, The Family of Henry VIII: Public Domain: Wikimedia, Yale Center for British Art

Catherine of Aragon: Public Domain: Wikimedia, Michael Sittow

Anne Boleyn and Henry VIII: Public Domain: Wikimedia, Daniel Maclise

Cardinal Thomas Wolsey: Public Domain: Wikimedia

Thomas Cromwell: Public Domain: Wikimedia, Hans Holbein

Henry VIII Condemns St. John Fisher to Death for Refusing to Sign the Oath of Supremacy and Divorce: Lawrence OP: CC BY-NC-ND 2.0, Flickr

Thomas More: Public Domain: Wikimedia, Hans Holbein

Jane Seymour: Public Domain: Wikimedia, Hans Holbein

Anne of Cleves: Public Domain: Wikimedia, Hans Holbein

Catherine Howard: Public Domain: Wikimedia, Ans Holbein

Catherine Parr, Unknown Artist: Public Domain

Edward VI: Public Domain: Wikimedia, William Scrots

Cardinal Reginald Pole: Public Domain: Wikimedia, Sebastiano del Poimbo

Mary Tudor: Public Domain: Wikimedia, Antonis Mor

Philip II of Spain: Public Domain: Wikimedia, Alonso Sanchez Coello

Coronation of Elizabeth I of England: Public Domain: Wikimedia

Chapter 23

The Altar of St. Ignatius of Loyola, Church of the Gesu in Rome: Photo taken by Seton Staff

Pope Clement VII: Public Domain: Wikimedia, Sebastiano del Piombo

Pope Paul III: Public Domain: Wikimedia, Titian

St. Ignatius of Loyola: Public Domain: Wikimedia, Peter Paul Rubens

Pope Paul III Approves the Society of Jesus: Public Domain: Wikimedia, Dominigos da Cunha

Council of Trent: Wikimedia: CC BY-SA 3.0, Laurom

Map of Italy: Copyright: schwabenblitz, Adobe Stock

St. Jerome: Lawrence OP: CC BY-NC-ND 2.0, Flickr

Marriage: Public Domain: Wikimedia, Gari Melchers

Chapter 24

The Ecstasy of St. Teresa: Wikimedia: CC BY-SA 4.0, Livioandronico2013

Pope Julius III: Public Domain: Wikimedia, Girolamo Sicciolante

Medal of Pope Paul IV: Wikimedia: CC BY 3.0, Sailko

Pope Pius IV: Public Domain: Wikimedia, Cerchia di Tiziano

Pope Pius V: Public Domain: Wikimedia, Follower of Bartolomeo Passarotti

The Battle of Lepanto: Public Domain: Wikimedia, Antonio de Brugada

Pope Gregory XIII: Public Domain: Wikimedia, Andraes Praefcke

Christopher Clavius: Public Domain: Wikimedia, Francesco Villamena

St. Charles Borromeo: Public Domain: Wikimedia, Guercino

Chiesa Nuova (Santa Maria in Vallicella): Copyright: Adobe Stock, ArTo

St. Angela Merici: Wikimedia: CC BY-SA 3.0, Benoit Lhoest

Teresa of Avila: Public Domain: Wikimedia, Peter Paul Rubens

John of the Cross: Lawrence OP: CC BY-NC-ND 2.0, Flickr

Peter Canisius: Wikimedia: CC BY-SA 3.0, GFreihalter

Robert Bellarmine: Public Domain: Wikimedia

St Francis Xavier Baptizes An Oriental Princess: Public Domain

Stained Glass of St. Francis Xavier in Japan: Photo taken by Seton staff

Matteo Ricci: Wikimedia: CC BY-SA 4.0, Paolobon 140

Map of China: Copyright: Peter Hermes Furian, Adobe Stock

Johann Adam Schall von Bell: Public Domain: Wikimedia

Map of Japan: Copyright: Alex Yeung, Adobe Stock

Robert de Nobili: Public Domain: Wikimedia

Map of World Highlighting India: Copyright: corben_dallas, Adobe Stock

Edmund Campion is Hanged, Stained glass: Photo taken by Seton staff

Chapter 25

Basilica of Guadalupe and Capuchin Church (Basilica Square): Copyright: Adobe Stock, Byelikova Oksana

Landing of Columbus: Public Domain: Wikimedia, John Vanderlyn

Gathering Flowers with Our Lady of Guadalupe: Lawrence OP: CC BY-NC-ND 2.0, Flickr

Juan de Zumarraga: Public Domain: Wikimedia

Rose of Lima: Public Domain: Wikimedia, Bartolome Esteban Murillo

Map of North America: Copyright: ad_hominem, Adobe Stock

Father Marquette and the Indians: Public Domain: Wikimedia, Wilhelm Lamprecht

Stained Glass of St Kateri Tekakwitha: Photo taken by Seton staff

Thomas Dongan: Wikimedia: CC BY-SA 4.0, DiggingSpace

Francisco Coronado: Wikimedia: CC BY-SA 3.0, Billy Hathorn

Statue of Junipero Serra: Lawrence OP: CC BY-NC-ND 2.0, Flickr

Mission San Carlos Borromeo: Copyright: Melastmohican, Adobe Stock

John Barry: Wikimedia: CC0, Smallbones

Charles Carroll: Public Domain: Wikimedia, Michael Laty

Chapter 26

The Return of Mary, Queen of Scots to Edinburgh: Public Domain: Wikimedia, James Drummond

William Cecil: Copyright: Morphart, Adobe Stock

Mary, Queen of Scots: Public Domain: Wikimedia, Jacob de Wet II

King Philip II of Spain: Public Domain: Wikimedia, Titian

Cardinal David Beaton: Pubic Domain: Wikimedia, Quicumque

Statue of John Knox: Wikimedia: CC BY-SA 4.0, CPClegg

Murder of David Rizzio: Public Domain: Wikimedia, Jean Lulves

The Abdication of Mary Queen of Scots: Public Domain: Wikimedia, Joseph Severn

Mary Stuart Goes to the Gallows: Public Domain: Wikimedia, Scipione Vannutelli

The Spanish Armada Off the English Coast: Public Domain: Wikimedia, Cornelis Claesz van Wieringen

King James I of England: Public Domain: Wikimedia, John de Critz

The Embarkation of the Pilgrims: Public Domain: Wikimedia, Robert Walter Weir

King Charles I, Queen Henrietta Maria, and Their Children: 23 Henrietta Maria and Charles I

Statue of Oliver Cromwell in his home town St Ives in Cambridgeshire, England: Copyright: Adobe Stock

James II of England: Public Domain: Wikimedia, Peter Lely

William III: Public Domain: Wikimedia, Godfrey Kneller

Mary II: Public Domain: Wikimedia, Godfrey Kneller

Shrine of St. Oliver Plunkett in Drogheda: Photo taken by Seton staff

Stained Glass, Seventeen Priests are Martyred for the Faith at Gorkum: Photo taken by Seton staff

Self Portrait of Peter Paul Rubens: Public Domain: Wikimedia, Peter Paul Rubens

Queen Christina of Sweden: Public Domain: Wikimedia, Jacob Heinrich Elbfas

Chapter 27

St. Vincent de Paul: Wikimedia: CC BY-SA 4.0, Giogo

Map of France: Copyright: schwabenblitz, Adobe Stock

Admiral Gaspard de Coligny: Public Domain: Wikimedia, Francois Clouet

Henry of Navarre: Public Domain: Wikimedia, Jacques Boulbene

St. Vincent de Paul with a Daughter of Charity: Lawrence OP: CC BY-NC-ND 2.0, Flickr

St. Francis de Sales Gives the Rule for the Visitation Order to St. Jane Frances de Chantal: Public Domain: Wikimedia, Valentin Metzinger

Map of France: Copyright: schwabenblitz, Adobe Stock

Pope Paul V: Public Domain: Wikimedia, Caravaggio

Archduke Ferdinand II of Austria: Public Domain: Wikimedia, Francesco Terzi

Cardinal Richelieu at the Siege of La Rochelle: Public Domain: Wikimedia, Henri-Paul Motte

Bust of Albrecht von Wallenstein: Wikimedia: CC BY-SA 4.0, Kwerdenker

Death of Gustavus Adolphus of Sweden at the Battle of Lutzen: Public Domain: Wikimedia, Carl Wahlborn

Galileo Demonstrating the New Astronomical Theories at the University of Padua: Public Domain: Wikimedia, Felix Parra

The Crucifixion of St. Peter: Public Domain: Wikimedia, Caravaggio

The Miracles of St Ignatius of Loyola: Public Domain: Wikimedia, Peter Paul Rubens

Belshazzar's Feast: Public Domain: Wikimedia, Rembrandt

The Coronation of Mary: Public Domain: Wikimedia, Diego Velazquez

Immaculate Conception of the Blessed Virgin Mary: Public Domain: Wikimedia, Bartolomé Esteban Murillo

The Holy Family in Egypt: Public Domain: Wikimedia, Nicolas Poussin

Stain Glass of the Sacred Heart: Public Domain: Wikimedia, Wilfredor

Chapter 28

St. John Baptiste de la Salle: Lawrence OP: CC BY-NC-ND 2.0, Flickr

Sobieski Sending Message of Victory to the Pope After the Battle of Vienna: Public Domain: Wikimedia, Jan Matejko

Louis XIV of France: Public Domain: Wikimedia, Hyacinthe Rigaud

Voltaire: Public Domain: Wikimedia, Nicolas de Largilière

Marquis de Pombal: Public Domain: Wikimedia, Antonio Joaquim de Santa Barbara

Pope Clement XIII, Pompeo Girolamo Batoni: Public Domain

King Louis XV of France: Public Domain: Wikimedia, Maurice Quentin de La Tour

Charles III of Spain: Public Domain: Wikimedia, Anton Raphael Mengs

Pope Clement XIV: Public Domain: Wikimedia

St Louis de Montfort: Public Domain: Wikimedia

St Paul of the Cross: Wikimedia: CC BY-SA 4.0, Miguel Palafox

St Alphonsus Liguori: Wikimedia: CC BY-SA 3.0, Andreas F. Borchert

St. John Baptiste de la Salle: Public Domain: Wikimedia, Oxxo

Chapter 29

Palace of Versailles: Public Domain: Wikimedia, Pierre Patel

Louis XVI of France: Public Domain: Wikimedia, Antoine-Francois Callet

Opening of the Estates General: Public Domain: Wikimedia, Auguste Couder

The National Assembly Taking the Tennis Court Oath: Public Domain: Wikimedia, Jacques-Louis David

The Storming of the Bastille: Public Domain: Wikimedia, Jean-Pierre Houel

Storming of the Tuileries: Public Domain: Wikimedia, Jean Duplessis-Bertaux

Maximilien Robespierre: Public Domain: Wikimedia, Pierre Roch Vigneron

Georges-Jacques Danton: Public Domain: Wikimedia, Musee Carnavalet

Map of Vendee in France: Wikimedia, CC BY-SA 2.5, Marmelad

Jacques Cathelineau: Public Domain: Wikimedia, Anne-Louis Girodet de Roussy-Trioson

Marie Antoinette with Her Children: Public Domain: Wikimedia, Elisabeth Louise Vigee Le Brun

Martyrs of Compiegne: Wikimedia, CC BY-SA 3.0, GFreihalter

Chapter 30

The Coronation of Napoleon: Public Domain: Wikimedia, Jacques-Louis David

Napoleon Crossing the Alps: Public Domain: Wikimedia, Jacques-Louis David

Pope Pius VI: Public Domain: Wikimedia, Pompeo Batoni

The Death of Pope Pius VI: Public Domain: Wikimedia, G.Beys

Pope Pius VII: Public Domain: Wikimedia, Jacques-Louis David

The Battle of Trafalgar: Public Domain: Wikimedia, Clarkson Frederick Stanfield

Francis II: Public Domain: Wikimedia

Jerome Bonaparte: Public Domain: Wikimedia, Sebastian Weygandt

Interior of Savona Cathedral: Wikimedia, CC BY-SA 3.0, Wkight94

Napoleon Watching the Fire of Moscow: Public Domain: Wikimedia, Adam Albrecht

Napoleon's Withdrawal from Russia: Public Domain: Wikimedia, Adolph Northen

Louis XVIII of France: Public Domain: Wikimedia, Francois Gerard

593

Napoleon's Return from Elba: Public Domain: Wikimedia, Charles de Steuben

Battle of Waterloo: Public Domain: Wikimedia, William Sadler

Chapter 31

Statue of Elizabeth Ann Seton: Lawrence OP: CC BY-NC-ND 2.0, Flickr

Benedict Joseph Flaget: Public Domain: Wikimedia

Edward Sorin: Public Domain: Wikimedia

The Nuns of the Battlefield Monument in Washington D.C.: Public Domain: Wikimedia

Bishop John Carroll: Public Domain: Wikimedia, Gilbert Stuart

Immaculate Conception: Public Domain: Wikimedia, Peter Paul Rubens

James Cardinal Gibbons: National Portrait Gallery: Public Domain

Stained Glass, Kateri Tekakwitha Learns about the Faith: Photo taken by Seton staff

St. Isaac Jogues: Lawrence OP: CC BY-NC-ND 2.0, Flickr

John Hughes: Public Domain: Wikimedia, Mathew Brady

St. Patrick's Cathedral NYC: Wikimedia, CC BY-SA 4.0, Agasadej

Stained glass, St. John Neumann Helping an Immigrant Family: Photo taken by Seton staff

Cardinal John McCloskey: Public Domain: Wikimedia, George Peter Alexander Healy

Cardinal James Gibbons: Public Domain: Wikimedia

Martin John Spalding: Public Domain: Wikimedia

St. Elizabeth Ann Seton Portrait: Public Domain

St. Rose Philippine Duchesne: Fr, Lawrence Lew OP: CC BY-NC-ND 2.0, Flickr

Mother Theodore Guerin: Public Domain: Wikimedia

Frances Cabrini Sent to USA: Fr. Lawrence Lew OP: CC BY-NC-ND 2.0, Flickr

Chapter 32

The Arrival of Pope Pius IX in Naples: Public Domain: Wikimedia, Salvatore Fergola

Cardinal James Gibbons: Public Domain: Wikimedia, Théodore Chassériau

Count Francois-René de Chateaubriand: Public Domain: Wikimedia, Anne-Louis Girodet de Roussy-Trioson

Alte Pinokothek: Wikimedia: CC BY 3.0, Guido Radig

Archbishop Clemens: Public Domain: Wikimedia, Charles Baugniet

Edmund Burke: Public Domain: Wikimedia, Steven Christe

Trinity College in Dublin Ireland: Copyright: Kit Leong, Adobe Stock

Daniel O'Connell refusing to take the oath of supremacy / S.S. Frizzell ; J.H. Bufford's Sons, Lith. Boston: Public Domain

Cardinal Newman: Public Domain: Wikimedia, John Everett Millais

Interior of Brompton Oratory: Wikimedia: CC BY-SA 3.0, Diliff

Henry Edward Manning: Public Domain: Wikimedia

Gerard Manley Hopkins: Public Domain: Wikimedia

Statue of Giuseppe Mazzini: Wikimedia: CC BY-SA 3.0, Abraham Sobkowski OFM

Pope Gregory XVI: Public Domain: Wikimedia, Paul Delaroche

Pope Pius IX: Public Domain: Wikimedia

Victor Emmanuel II: Public Domain: Wikimedia, Giuseppe Camino

Engraving of the First Vatican Council: Public Domain: Wikimedia, Karl Benzinger

The Battle of Koniggratz: Public Domain: Wikimedia, Georg Bleibtreu

Adalbert Falk: Public Domain: Wikimedia

St. John Vianney: 29 cure of ars

St. Catherine of Laboure: Fr. Lawrence Lew OP: CC BY-NC-ND 2.0, Flickr

St. Bernadette and Our Lady of Lourdes: Lawrence OP: CC BY-NC-ND 2.0, Flickr

Chapter 33

The Apotheosis of St. Pius X: Wikimedia: CC BY-SA 4.0, Didier Descouens

Pope Leo XIII: Public Domain: Wikimedia

The Blessed Mother Presents the Rosary to St. Dominic with Pope Leo XIII: Public Domain: Wikimedia, Mefusbren69

Karl Marx: Public Domain: Wikimedia, John Jabez Edwin Mayal

St. Michael the Archangel: Public Domain: Wikimedia, Luca Giordano

Cardinal Charles Lavigerie: Public Domain: Wikimedia, Ludovic Baschet

Pope Pius X: Lawrence OP: CC BY-NC-ND 2.0, Flickr

Denis-Auguste Affre: Wikimedia: CC BY-SA 4.0, G)69

Georges Darboy: Public Domain: Wikimedia, Robert Jefferson Bingham

Pope Benedict XV: Public Domain: Wikimedia, Antonio Fabres

Packages from Benedict XV Delivered to Italian POWs: Public Domain: Wikimedia, Feuerreiter-Pascalina Lehnert

The Signing of Peace in the Hall of Mirrors, Versailles: Public Domain: Wikimedia, William Orpen

British Newspaper Announcing the Signing of the Peace Treaty 1919: Public Domain: Wikimedia

Cover of the Treaty of Versailles in England: Public Domain: Wikimedia

Chapter 34

Shrine of Our Lady of Fatima: Copyright: Bill Perry, Adobe Stock

Our Lady of Fatima: Photo taken by Seton staff

Pope Pius XI: Public Domain: Wikimedia, Alberto Felici

Pope Pius XI and His Successor, Pacelli and Marconi at the Start of the Vatican Radio: Public Domain: Wikimedia

Jan Cieplak: Public Domain: Wikimedia

The Signing of the Lateran Treaty: Public Domain

General Antonio Santa Anna: Public Domain: Wikimedia, Carlos Paris

Elias Calles: Public Domain: Wikimedia, Library of Congress

Manuel Avila Camacho: CC BY 4.0: Wikimedia

Miguel Pro: Public Domain

Francisco Franco: Public Domain

The Valley of the Fallen: Copyright: Adobe Stock, JUAN ANTONIO

Mit Brennender Sorge: Public Domain: Wikimedia, Joachim Specht

Pope Pius XII: Public Domain: Wikimedia, Michael Pitcairn

Mao Zedong: Public Domain: Wikimedia

Assumption of the Virgin: Public Domain: Wikimedia, Andres de Rubira

Pope Pius XII: Wikicommons: Public Domain

Chapter 35

Statue of Pope St. John Paul II: Copyright: Manuel: Adobe Stock

Pope John XXIII: Public Domain

Pope Paul VI: Public Domain: Wikimedia, Vatican City

Cardinal Montini Walking in St. Peter's Square: Wikimedia: CC BY-SA 3.0, Constantino Pasquale

Opening of Second Session of Vatican II: Public Domain: Wikimedia, Peter Geymayer

Madonna of the People: Public Domain: Wikimedia, Federico Barocci

Autumn Baby: PublicDomainPictures: CC0 Public Domain, pixabay

Pope John Paul I: Public Domain: Wikimedia, Anefo

Pope John Paul II: Wikimedia: CC BY-SA 3.0, Jolanta Dyr

Hitler Watching German Soldiers Marching into Poland: Wikimedia: CC BY-SA 3.0, Bundesarchiv

Stefan Wyszynski: Public Domain: Wikimedia, Janusz Trocha

John Paul II at Mass in Victory Square: Public Domain: Wikimedia

Pope John Paul II Visiting Ukraine in 2001: Wikimedia: CC BY-SA 3.0, Pig1995z

Statue of Pope St. John Paul II at Jasna Gora Monastery: Copyright: chris, Adobe Stock

Pope Benedict XVI: Wikimedia: CC BY-SA 2.0, Dennis Jarvis

Pope Francis: Wikimedia: CC BY-SA 2.0, Jeffrey Bruno

Chapter 36

Basilica of the National Shrine of the Immaculate Conception D.C.: Copyright: demerzel21, Adobe Stock

St. Stanislaus Kostka Church: David Wilson: CC BY 2.0, Flickr

Statue of Father Francis Duffy: Public Domain: Wikimedia, Daderot

Walter M. Pierce: Public Domain: Wikimedia, Library of Congress

28th International Eucharistic Congress in Chicago: Public Domain: Wikimedia, Kaufmann and Fabry Co.

All Smith Giving Speech: Public Domain: Wikimedia, Bain News Service

Bishop Fulton Sheen on His Famous TV, Life is Worth Living: Public Domain / Vintage TV: Copyright: Adobe Stock

Bing Crosby in Going My Way: Public Domain: Wikimedia

Cardinal Francis Spellman: Public Domain: Wikimedia: Anefo

Ronald Reagan: Public Domain: Wikimedia

John F. Kennedy: Public Domain: Wikimedia, Cecil Stoughton

Christ with the Eucharist: Public Domain: Wikimedia, Juan de Juanes

Prisoners' Barracks at the Dachau Concentration Camp: Public Domain: Wikimedia, Sidney Blau

Chapel of Christendom College: Wikimedia: CC BY-SA 4.0, AgnosticPreachersKid

Pope Benedict XVI: Wikimedia: CC BY 2.0, Sergey Gabdurakhmanov

Every attempt has been made to provide proper credit and attribution for all sources used within the text and images. If any source was inadvertantly omitted or cited incompletely, corrections will be made in the next printing.

License information:
CC BY-NC-ND 2.0: https://creativecommons.org/licenses/by-nc-nd/2.0/
CC BY-NC-ND 3.0: https://creativecommons.org/licenses/by-nc-nd/3.0/
CC BY-NC-ND 4.0: https://creativecommons.org/licenses/by-nc-nd/4.0/
CC BY-SA 1.0: https://creativecommons.org/licenses/by-sa/1.0/
CC BY-SA 2.0: https://creativecommons.org/licenses/by-sa/2.0/
CC BY SA 2.5: https://creativecommons.org/licenses/by-sa/2.5/
CC-BY-SA 3.0: https://creativecommons.org/licenses/by-sa/3.0/
CC-BY-SA 4.0: https://creativecommons.org/licenses/by-sa/4.0/
CC-BY 2.0: https://creativecommons.org/licenses/by/2.0/
CC BY 3.0: https://creativecommons.org/licenses/by/3.0/
CC0: https://creativecommons.org/choose/zero/

596

INDEX

Aachen, 127-133

Act of Supremacy, 341-342

Adalbert, St., 147, 155-156

Adolphus, Gustavus, 422-423

Ageltrude, 167-169

Alberic, 171

Albert the Great, St., 232, 246-248

Albigensian heresy (See also Cathari), 234-236

Alcuin, 132-133

Alfonso the Chaste (King), 200

Alfonso III (the Great), 201-202

Alfonso VI (king), 204

Almanzor, 203

Almohads, 283

Almoravids, 204-205

Alphonsus Liguori, St., 442-443

Ambrose, St., 60-69

America (See United States), 380-393, 470-489, 566-581.

Angela Merici, St., 368-369

Anglicans and Anglicanism, 396, 405-408, 499-502

Anglo-Saxons, 101-102

Anselm, St. (archbishop of Canterbury), 192

Ansgar, St., 148

Anthony of Egypt, St., 72

Apostles, The, 5-20

Apostolic Fathers, 37-39

Arabia, 10, 72, 110-113

Arius and Arian Heresy, 53-60

Armagh, 83-84

Assumption, Dogma of the, 547

Asturias, Kingdom of, 198

Athanasius, St., 49, 54-58

Attila the Hun, 84-85

Augsburg, Diet of, 326

Augsburg Confession, 326-327

Augustine of Canterbury, St., 101-104

Augustine of Hippo, St., 68-70

Avignon, 266-279

"Babylonian Captivity," 266

Baltimore, Lord, 387-388

Barbarians, 78

Barbarossa (See Frederick Barbarossa)

Bardas, 141-142

Barnabas, St., 10-12

Basil of Caesarea, 58-59

Beato Angelico (Fra Angelico), 297, 302-303

Belgium (See Netherlands)

Bellarmine, St. Robert, 371-372

Benedict of Nursia, St., 93-95

Benedict XVI, Pope, 145, 387, 485, 547, 562-565, 581

Bernadette, St., 512-513

Bernard, St., 195-196

Bismarck, Otto von (German chancellor), 508-510

Bonaventure, St., 246-248

Boniface, St., 118-123

Boris, King of Bulgaria, 153-154

Bruno, St., 194

Cajetan, Cardinal, 318, 349-350

Cabrini, Frances Xavier, 488-489

Calvert, Cecil, 387

Calvin, John, 331-335

Calvinism, 331-335

Canisius, St. Peter, 370-371

Cappadocians, The Three, 58-61

Capuchins, 348-349

Caravaggio, 425

Carlstadt, Andreas, 322

Carmelites, 369-370

Carroll, Bishop John, 470-472

Carthusians, 194

Catacombs, 32-33

Catechumens, 38-39

Cathari (heretics), 235

Catherine of Aragon, 336-338

Catherine de Medici, 413-414

Catherine Labouré, St., 511

Catherine of Siena, St., 271-275

Catholic Emancipation in England, 497-499

Catholic Reformation, 348-379

Cecilia, St., 24-25

Charlemagne, 119, 125-133, 139

Charles V (emperor), 320-321

Charles I (king of England), 406

Charles Borromeo, St., 366-377

Charles Martel, 121-122

Chateaubriand, 490-492

Christ (Life of), 3-5

Christina of Sweden (queen), 410-411

Cistercians, 283

Civil Constitution of the Clergy, 449-450

Clotilde (queen), 86

Clovis (king), 86-87, 115

Cluny (abbey), 180-181

Columba, St., 97, 106

Communion:
  Of children, 521
  Frequent reception of, 430, 520

Communism, 518, 528-547

Concordat:

France (1801), 461-462
Of Worms, 192
With Germany (1933), 541-542

Constantine the Great, 43-47

Constantinople:
Fall of, 297
Latin Empire of, 216

Cornelius, 8-9

Council of:
Baltimore, 475-476
Clermont (1095), 209
Constance (1414), 278-279
Constantinople (381), 59-60
Ephesus (431), 71
Jerusalem, 7
Lateran (769), 124, 138
Lyons (1245), 240
Milan (355), 56
Nicaea (325), 53-54
Trent, 355-359
Vatican I (1870), 507-508
Vatican II (1962), 552-554

Cranmer, Thomas, 341, 344-346

Cristero Rebellion, 538-539

Cromwell, Oliver, 406-407

Cromwell, Thomas, 340

Crusades:
First, 208-212
Second, 212
Third, 212-214
Fourth, 214-216
Fifth, 216-217
Sixth, 217
Of St. Louis, 217-219

Curé of Ars, 510-511

Cyprian of Carthage, St., 43

Cyril of Alexandria, St., 71

Cyril and Methodius, SS., 150-152

Dante, 249

Danton, Georges-Jacques, 454-455

Daughters of Charity, 418

de Marillac, St. Louise, 418

Deism, 434

Desiderius, 124-125

Diet:
Of Augsburg, 326
Of Nuremberg, 321
Of Worms, 321

Diocletian, 28-30

Dominic, St., 231-232

Dominicans, 232

Dongan, Thomas, 388

Duffy, Fr. Francis, 568

Duchesne, Rose St., 486

Eck, John, 318

Edict:
Of Milan, 44-45
Of Nantes, 416
Of Worms, 321

Edward VI (king of England), 344-345

El Cid, 205

Elizabeth I (queen of England), 378, 395-397, 401-404

England:
Catholic revival in, 497-501
Conversion of, 101-102
Interdicted, 230
Protestantism in, 336-347
Puritans in, 405-406

Enlightenment, 430-443

Estates General, 446-448

Eternal Word Television Network (EWTN), 579-580

Falk Laws (in Germany), 509-510

Fatima, Our Lady of, 530-531

Fawkes, Guy, 405

Ferdinand III, King St., 285-287

Feudalism, 162-165

Filioque Controversy, 140

Finian, St., 96

Fisher, St. John, 342

France:
Interdicted, 231

Revolution in (See Revolution, French)

Francis of Assisi, St., 232-234

Francis de Sales, St., 418-419

Francis Xavier, St., 372-374

Franciscans, 246

Franco, Francisco, 540-541

Frederick Barbarossa (emperor), 213, 224-228

Fulda (abbey), 120

Galileo, 424

Gallitzin, Father Demetrius, 472

Garibaldi, Guiseppe, 506

Gaul:
Monasticism in, 73-74

Germain of Auxerre, St. 81

Germany:
Catholic revival in, 493-497
Religious Orders banished, 509
Nazis, 541-544
Pius XII and, 542-544
St. Boniface in, 118-121
St. Peter Canisius in, 370-371

Ghibellines, 222-224,

Gibault, Father, 392

Gibbons, James (cardinal), 477, 483-484

Giotto, 302-303

Gorres, Joseph von, 494, 497

Gratian (emperor), 60

Great Britain (See England)

Gregory of Nazianzus, St., 59-60

Gregory of Nyssa, St. 58-59

Guelphs, 222-224

Guerin, Mother Theodore, 486-487

Guiscard, Robert, 184

Gunpowder Plot, 404

Gustavus Adolphus (king of Sweden), 422-423

Hapsburgs, 241

Hegira, The, 111

Henriques, Alfonso, 284

Henry II, St. (emperor), 176-178

Henry III (emperor), 178-179

Henry IV (emperor), 184

Henry V (emperor), 192

Henry II (king of England), 192-193

Henry VIII (king of England), 336-344

Henry of Navarre (Henry IV of France), 415

Henry Stuart (Lord Darnley), 400-401

Hitler, Adolf, 541-542

Hohenstaufen (family), 223-225

Holland (See Netherlands)

Holy Roman Empire, Origin of, 118

Hughes, Bishop John, 480-481

Humanae Vitae (encyclical), 554-556

Huns, 79

Iconoclasm, 135-139

Ignatius, St. (patriarch of Constantinople), 140-143

Ignatius Loyola, St., 352-354

Ignatius of Antioch St. (martyr), 22-23

Indulgences, 244-245

Infallibility, Papal, 507-508

Inquisition, The, 236-237

Interdict:
England, 230
Florence, 272
France, 231

Ireland:
Beginning of Christianity in, 82-84
Catholic emancipation in, 498-499
Monasticism in, 96-97
St. Patrick in, 82-84
"Twelve Apostles of," 97

Irenaeus, St. 26, 41

Isaac Jogues, St., 386

Islam, 110-113

James I (king of England), 404

Jerome, St., 67-68

Jerusalem:
Apostolic Council of, 7
Council of (767), 138
Fall of, 212-213
First Crusade, 208-212

Jesuits:
Founding of, 352-354
Suppression of, 439-441

Jesus Christ (See Christ), 4-5

Jews:
History of the, 2-5
Nazis and, 544-545

Joan of Arc, St., 294-295

John XXIII, Pope, 548-551

John Chrysostom, St., 42-44

John (king of England), 230

John Paul II, Pope, 518, 557-564

John Vianney, St., 510-511

Julian the Apostate, 57-58

Junipero Serra, Father, 390-391

Justification, Doctrine of, 316

Justin, St., 41

Justin (emperor), 88

Justinian, 88-89

Kaaba, The, 110-111

Kateri Tekakwitha, St., 387

Kennedy, John F. (president), 575-576

Knights:
Hospitallers, 220-221
Of St. John, 220-221
Templars, 220-221, 268
Teutonic, 220-221

Knox, John, 398-399

Ku Klux Klan, 569

Quran, The, 111-112

Kulturkampf, The, 509

La Salle, St. John Baptist de, 442-443

Lacordaire, Henri, 492

Lateran Basilica, 170

Lateran Treaty, 534-535

Lawrence, St., 28

Lay investiture, 187-188

Legion of Decency, 574

Leipzig, Disputation of, 318

Leonardo da Vinci, 306-307

Lepanto (battle), 365

Lindisfarne (island), 106

Louis VII (king of France), 193, 212,

Louis IX, St. (king of France), 217-218

Louis XIV (king of France), 433-444

Louis XV (king of France), 437-438

Louis XVI (king of France), 450-451

Louis of Bavaria, 268-270

Lourdes, 512-513

Luther, Martin, 313-325, 329-333

McCloskey (cardinal), 482-483

Maistre, Joseph de, 492

Marcus Aurelius (emperor), 23-24

Margaret Mary Alacoque, St., 428-429

Marie Antoinette, 445, 454

Marozia, 170-171

Marquette, Jacques, 386

Martel, Charles, 121-122

Martin of Tours, St., 73-74

Mary Stuart (Queen of Scotland), 396-397, 401-402

Mary Tudor (Queen of England), 342-347

Maryland (colony), 387-388

Masaccio, 302-303

Massacre of St. Bartholomew's

599

Day, 414

Mecca, 110-111

Melanchthon, Philip, 326

Mendicant Orders, 232

Merovingian dynasty, 115

Methodius, St. (See also Cyril), 150-152

Michael III (emperor), 141

Michael Cerularius, 144-145

Michelangelo, 306-307

Mieszko, Conversion of, 154-155

Miraculous Medal, 511-512

Mit Brennender Sorge (encyclical), 542

Modernism, 521-522

Mohammed, 110-113

Monasticism:
  Beginning of, 72-73
  Benedictines, 93-95
  Carthusians, 194
  Cistercians, 194-196
  Early hermits, 72-73
  In Ireland, 96-98
  Mendicant Orders, 232
  Reform of, 180-182

Monica, St., 68

Monte Cassino, 93-95

More, St. Thomas, 340-342

Muslims (See Islam)

Muhlberg (battle), 328

Muhldorf (battle), 269

Murillo, Bartolome, 426

Mussolini, 534-536

Mystery plays, 244

Nantes, Edict of, 416

Napoleon Bonaparte, 456-469

Nazism, 541-545

Nepotism, 298-299

Nero, 15

Nestorius and Nestorian Heresy, 70-71

Netherlands, 109, 118, 121, 126, 162, 209, 303, 310, 410-411, 451

Neumann, St. John (bishop of Philadelphia), 481-482

Newman, John Henry (Cardinal), 500-501

Nicene Creed, 54

Nobili, Father Robert de, 378

Norbert, St., 196-197

Normans:
  Pope Nicholas and, 184
  Rome pillaged by, 191

O'Connell, Daniel, 497-499

Origen, 42

Ostrogoths, 78-79

Otto I, the Great (German emperor), 154, 172

Otto II (German emperor), 175

Otto III (German emperor), 175-176

Oxford movement, 499-501

Palladius (bishop), 81-83

Papal States, 128

Parishes:
  In fourth century, 74
  Origin of rural, 116
  Growth of in the United States, 476

Patrick, St., 82-84

Paul, St. (Apostle), 9-15

Paul of the Cross, St., 442

Paul VI, Pope, 551-556

Pelagian heresy, 70,

Pentecost, 5-6

Pepin, 122-125

Persecutions:
  By French Revolution, 448-455
  By Genseric, 81
  By Huneric, 81
  By James I of England, 404-405
  By Queen Elizabeth I, 408-409

By Roman emperors, 18-33

Peter, St. (Apostle), 8-9

Peter Canisius, St., 370-371

Peyton, Fr. Patrick, 572-573

Pharisees, 4

Philip (deacon), 7-8

Philip Augustus, 230-231

Philip the Fair (king of France), 265-267

Philip II (king of Spain), 346-347

Philip Neri, St., 367-368

Photius (patriarch of Constantinople),, 140-144

Poland:
  Conversion of, 154-156
  Solidarity in, 560

Pole, Reginald (cardinal), 345, 362

Polycarp, St., 23

Pombal, 436-437

Poor Clares, 233

Pope
  Adrian I, 125
  Adrian II, 143
  Adrian IV, 225
  Agapetus II, 171
  Alexander III, 225-227
  Alexander VI, 299-301
  Benedict V, 173
  Benedict VIII, 177-178
  Benedict XIV, 436-437
  Benedict XV, 524-527
  Benedict XVI, 145, 387, 485, 547, 562-565, 581
  Boniface VIII, 265-267
  Celestine I, 71
  Clement I, St., 22
  Clement II, 179, 183
  Clement V, 221, 267-268
  Clement VII, 324-325
  Clement VIII, 416

Clement XIII, 437

Clement XIV, 440-441

Formosus, 166-169

Francis, 565

Gregory I, St., 98-102

Gregory II, 108, 118

Gregory III, 120

Gregory VII, 186-191

Gregory IX, 236-240

Gregory X, 241

Gregory XI, 270-273

Gregory XII, 276-277

Gregory XIII, 365-366

Honorius III, 216-217, 232, 238-239

Innocent I, 64

Innocent III, 214-216

Innocent IV, 240

John I, 88

John VIII, 143-144

John X, 169-170

John XII, 171-172

John XXII, 268-269

John XXIII, 548-551

John Paul I, 557

John Paul II, 557-563

Julius I, 55

Julius II, 301

Leo III, 129-130

Leo VIII, 173

Leo IX, 144

Leo X, 301-302

Leo XIII, 514-520

Liberius, 56

Martin V, 294

Nicholas I, 141-143

Nicholas II, 184-185

Nicholas V, 297

Paul III, 343, 352-355, 360-362

Paul IV, 362-363

Paul VI, 551-556

Peter, 8-9

Pius IV, 363-364

Pius V, 364-365

Pius VI, 449, 458-461

Pius VII, 461-462

Pius IX, 504-510

Pius X, 520-524

Pius XI, 532-536, 542

Pius XII, 542-547

Sergius III, 169

Sixtus V, 414-415

Stephen III, 123-124

Sylvester I, St., 53

Urban II, 208-212

Urban V, 271-272

Urban VI, 274-275

Urban VIII, 422, 424-425

Zachary, 120, 123

Popes:
    Election of, 74, 184
    Primacy of, 41

Predestination, Calvin's doctrine of, 332-333

Private judgment, Doctrine of, 356

Pro, Miguel, 539

Protestant Revolt, Causes of, 313-315

Protestantism:
    Beginning of, 312-318
    The Bible and, 356
    Justification and, 357
    Original sin and, 356-357

Puritans:
    In America, 387
    In England, 405-406

Quadragesimo Anno (encyclical), 518, 533

Quakers, 388

Rationalism, 434

Raphael, 301,308

"Reductions," Jesuit, 384-385

Reform, Monastic, 180-182

Reformation, Catholic, 348-359

Rembrandt, 426

Renaissance, 292-311

Rerum Novarum (encyclical), 518

Revolution, French, 444-455

Ricci, Matteo Fr., 374-375

Richelieu (cardinal), 421-424

Robert Bellarmine, St., 371-372, 424

Robespierre, Maximilien, 450

Roman Empire, 18-47

Rome:
    Bourbons' sack of, 351
    Normans pillage, 191
    Taking of (1860), 506

Rose of Lima, St., 384

Rousseau, Jean Jacques, 435

Rubens (painter), 410, 425-426

Sacred Heart, Devotion to, 428-249

Sadducees, 4

St. Bartholomew's Day Massacre, 414

St. Gall (Abbey), 332

St. Peter's Basilica, 92, 301, 307

Saracens, 160

Savonarola, 299-300

Schall, Father Adam, 375-376

Schism:
    Western, 262-279
    Greek, 134-145

Scholasticism, 246

September massacres, 450-451

Serra, Father Junipero, 390-391

Seton, Elizabeth Ann, 485

Sheen, Fulton (bishop), 572-573

Simon de Montfort, 235-236

Simony, 8

Sistine Chapel, 307

Slavery, The Church and, 504

Slavic liturgy, 151

601

Slavs, Conversion of the, 150-153

Soviet Union, 530, 533-534

Smith, Al, 570-571

Spanish Civil War, 539-541

Spanish Inquisition, 236-237

Stanislaus, St., 156

Stephen, St. (king of Hungary), 157

Stephen, St. (proto-martyr), 6-7

Storch, Nicholas, 322

Sulpicians, 472

Sweden:
    Protestantism in, 410-411
    St. Ansgar in, 148

Temple, Jewish, 3, 6

Teresa of Avila, St., 369-370

Tertullian, 42-43

Teutonic Knights, 221

Theodoric, 87-88

Theodosius, 59-61, 66

Theodosius II (emperor), 61, 71

Theophylact (family), 169-170

Third Republic, 523-524

Thirty Years War, 420-424

Thomas Aquinas, St., 246-248

Thomas a Becket, St., 192-194

Thomas a Kempis, 310

Tours, Battle of, 122

Unam Sanctam (bull), 266

United States:
    Church in, 470-489, 566- 581
    Growth of Catholic population, 476
    Catholic schools in, 477-481

University of Paris, 246

Ursulines, 368

Valens (emperor), 58-59

Vatican City, 535

Vatican Council I, 507-508

Vatican Council II, 552-554

Velazquez, Diego, 283

Vendee, Rising in the, 454-454

Vincent de Paul, St., 416-418

Vikings, 148

Visigoths, 78-81

Visitation Order (nuns), 418-419

Vladimir (Russian King), 158-159

Voltaire, 435-436

Vulgate Bible, 67-68

Walesa, Lech, 560

Western Schism, 262-279

Wilfrid, St., 109

William of Orange, 407-409

Willibrord, St., 109

Wiseman (cardinal), 502

Wolsey (cardinal), 338-340

World War I , 524-527

World War II, 541, 544

Worms:
    Concordat of, 192
    Diet of, 321
    Edict of, 321

Wyclif, John, 277-278

Zolli, Israel, 545

Zwingli, Ulrich, 330-333